**Partisan Voting Patterns**

...tes won by Republicans in 2008 Presidential election, Republican governor 2010

...tes won by Republicans in 2008 Presidential election, Democratic governor 2010

...tes won by Democrats in 2008 Presidential election, Republican governor 2010

...tes won by Democrats in 2008 Presidential election, Democratic governor 2010

# State and Local Government

## EIGHTH EDITION

Ann O'M. Bowman
*Texas A&M University*

Richard C. Kearney
*North Carolina State University*

WADSWORTH
CENGAGE Learning

Australia • Brazil • Japan • Korea • Mexico • Singapore • Spain • United Kingdom • United States

**State and Local Government,**
**Eighth Edition**
**Bowman, Kearney**

Senior Publisher: Suzanne Jeans

Executive Editor: Carolyn Merrill

Development Editor: Thomas Finn

Assistant Editor: Katherine Hayes

Editorial Assistant: Angela Hodge

Senior Marketing Manager: Amy Whitaker

Marketing Coordinator: Josh Hendrick

Marketing Communications Manager:
  Heather Baxley

Content Project Manager: Jessica Rasile

Art Director: Linda Helcher

Print Buyer: Linda Hsu

Senior Rights Acquisition Account Manager,
  Text: Katie Huha

Production Service/Compositor: Integra

Senior Photo Editor: Jennifer Meyer Dare

Cover/Text Designer: Rokusek Design

Cover Image: © Andy Z

For product information and technology assistance, contact us at
**Cengage Learning Customer & Sales Support, 1-800-354-9706**
For permission to use material from this text or product, submit all requests online at **www.cengage.com/permissions.**
Further permissions questions can be emailed to
**permissionrequest@cengage.com.**

Library of Congress Control Number: 2009943180

ISBN-13: 978-0-495-80265-5

ISBN-10: 0-495-80265-4

**Wadsworth**
20 Channel Center Street
Boston, MA 02210
USA

Cengage Learning is a leading provider of customized learning solutions with office locations around the globe, including Singapore, the United Kingdom, Australia, Mexico, Brazil, and Japan. Locate your local office at **international.cengage.com/region.**

Cengage Learning products are represented in Canada by Nelson Education, Ltd.

For your course and learning solutions, visit **www.cengage.com**

Purchase any of our products at your local college store or at our preferred online store **www.CengageBrain.com**

The eighth edition of *State and Local Government* is dedicated to the tens of thousands of students and instructors who have read our earlier editions, and to those who will follow.

Printed in the United States of America
1 2 3 4 5 6 7 14 13 12 11 10

# Brief Contents

# Contents

SOURCE: GEORGE SKENE/
MCT/Landov

SOURCE: AP Photo/
Wilfredo Lee

SOURCE: AP Photo/Kelley
McCall

SOURCE: MIKE THEILER/
epa/Corbis

SOURCE: STAN HONDA/
AFP/Getty Images

SOURCE: AP Photo/Jim
Cole

SOURCE: MARVIN FONG/
The Plain Dealer/Landov

SOURCE: AP Photo/
Bob Child

SOURCE: AP Photo/
Tim Mueller

SOURCE: MARK RALSTON/
AFP/GETTY IMAGES

SOURCE: Ronald Martinez/
Getty Images Sport/Getty
Images

SOURCE: Glyn Jones/Corbis/
Jupiter Images

SOURCE: ktsimage/
iStockphoto.com

SOURCE: Tony Freeman/
Photo Edit

SOURCE: Justin Sullivan/
Getty Images News/Getty
Images

# Preface

If someone had told us in 1990 that the first edition of *State and Local Government* would become what is now widely recognized as "the market leader" and followed eventually by an eighth edition, we would have been doubtful. That first edition broke the mold of traditional state and local texts by offering a positive, thematic approach to introducing government at the grass roots. We were gratified and delighted when the book quickly built up adoptions in research universities, four-year colleges, and community colleges across the United States. There are quite a few rival texts today, but we like to think that the competition makes ours better. We heartily thank our colleagues in the State Politics and Policy section and the Urban Politics section of the American Political Science Association for their ideas and comments on various editions of this book. And we thank as well researchers, too numerous to mention individually, for their insightful analyses that are published in scholarly journals and inform our latest edition.

The eighth edition of this book was written in the context of the most profound national economic recession since the Great Depression. In 2008–2009, housing markets collapsed, unemployment soared, and state and local revenues nosedived by as much as 20–25 percent, even as citizen cries for government assistance rang out across the country. In many respects, it was not a happy time for state and local governments.

Yet the states and their cities, counties, and towns are resilient. Many have been forced to cut critical services such as education and transportation to the bone, but they have done so proactively while ferreting out waste, furloughing and laying off thousands of workers, and conducting triage on the "extras" such as libraries, cultural affairs, and parks and recreation. Painful as the "Great Recession" has been, it has presented opportunities to use the crisis to make improvements in the way the business of government is done.

Despite the drumbeat of criticism of government and public officials in the mass media and by anti-government talk show people, we like politics and public service, particularly at the state and local levels. We believe that government can be—and often is—a force for good in society. We do acknowledge some of the concerns voiced by critics of government. Yes, there continue to be inefficiencies, and sure, there are some politicians who, once elected, seem to forget the interests of the people back home, not to mention what their parents taught them. But by and large, state and local governments work well. On a daily basis, they tackle some of the toughest issues imaginable, designing and implementing creative and successful solutions to problems ranging from crime and corrections to education and the environment.

In the eighth edition of our text, we again seek to capture the immediacy and vitality of state and local governments as they address the challenges facing the American people. A major goal is to foster continuing student interest and involvement in state and local politics, policy, and public service. Many of the students who read this text will work in state and local government. Some will run successfully for public office. All will deal with state and local governments throughout their lives. We want our readers to know that state and local governments are places where one person can still "do good," make a difference, and serve a cause. For students who go on to graduate study in political science, public administration, public policy, or related fields, states and localities are fertile fields for research. And for students taking this course because they "have to" and who purport to dislike politics and government, we invite them to keep an open mind as they explore the fascinating world of politics at the grass roots.

## The Theme of State and Local Government

This book revolves around a central theme: The growing capacity and responsiveness of state and local government. Our theme was tested in 2008–2009, but not found to be wanting. It has been decades since subnational governments were routinely dismissed as outmoded and ineffective. But despite their many challenges, state and local governments continue to be proactive, expanding their capacity to address effectively the myriad problems confronting their citizens. From Alabama to Wyoming, they are increasingly more responsive to their rapidly changing environment and to the demands of the citizens.

Our confidence in these governments does not blind us, however, to the varying capabilities of the fifty states and more than 88,000 units of local government. Some are better equipped to operate effectively than others. Many state and local governments benefit from talented leadership, a problem-solving focus, and an engaged citizenry. Others do not fare so well, and their performance disappoints. Still, as a group, states and localities are the driving forces—the prime movers—in the U.S. federal system. Even those jurisdictions perennially clustered at the lower end of various ratings scales have made quantum leaps in their capability and responsiveness.

## Features of the Text

The themes of *State and Local Government* are supplemented by boxed features that provide compelling examples of nonnational governments in action. The boxes labeled "Engaging State and Local Government" identify states and localities poised on the leading edge of problem solving. Boxes, titled "Debating Politics," raise questions for which the answers are more equivocal. Nearly all of the boxes are new to the eighth edition. Other boxes called "Breaking New Ground," describe innovative efforts in problem solving.

The **Engaging State and Local Government** boxes showcase some of the ways state and local governments are reaching out to address some of the challenges of our times. These boxes touch on key topics of interest to students to spark classroom discussion and foster engagement with state and local politics. The issues include the use of Twitter and other social networking sites, Wiki World and Second Life, settling water wars, the special interests and characteristics of Gen Y legislators, new initiatives for fighting crime, thoughtful approaches and programs for helping the poor and needy among us, state greenhouse gas auctions, and mobile Americans. The **Breaking New Ground** boxes reflect the innovative and different courses of action states and localities have taken in tackling problems and policy issues. The Debating Politics boxes present factual situations to the student and ask for their reactions. For example, the box in Chapter 2 considers legalization of medical marijuana in the context of federalism, and the box in Chapter 8 asks the reader to identify sexual harassment situations. The box in Chapter 5 reviews the efforts in some states to make it easier for third parties to get on the ballot, while another box in Chapter 6 focuses on redesigning the California legislature. Other new boxes highlight the emergence of a couple of former NBA stars as big-city mayors (Chapter 11) and the spillover growth of suburbs into adjacent states (Chapter 12). The feature in Chapter 16 addresses the controversial issue of prisons for profit, and the box in Chapter 18 contemplates the impact that states can have in reducing global warming and conserving energy by promoting "driving green."

Sincere effort has been invested in making this book accessible to the student. Each chapter opens with an outline and closes with a **Chapter Recap** to help structure student learning. The Chapter Recap sections are newly revised in this edition to better revisit important concepts and facts, providing a valuable study aid. We have included more photographs to provide visual images that bring the world of state and local government to life for the reader. Maps, tables, and figures offer an engaging format to assist in the identification of patterns and trends in the data. Many of these graphics are new to the eighth edition. As noted, boxes throughout the chapters showcase the innovative, the unusual, and the insightful in state and local politics. Lists of states appear in each chapter and facilitate comparisons across the states. The eighth edition adds more **key terms**, all of which are boldfaced, defined in the margins, and listed at the end of each chapter. References to websites in the expanded end-of-chapter list of **Internet Resources** encourage student curiosity, engagement, and individual research.

## The Content of the Eighth Edition

As in the first seven editions, this book provides thorough and completely updated coverage of state and local institutions, processes, and policies. The chapters blend the findings from the latest political science and public policy research with issues and events from the real world. It is intended to be a core text.

In Chapter 1, we introduce the functions of nonnational governments and explore the theme of capacity and responsiveness. The growing diversity in the United States and the contemporary controversy dubbed "culture wars" are featured in the chapter. Federalism's central importance is highlighted in Chapter 2, which traces the twists and turns of the federal system, from the scribblings of the Framers to the Supreme Court's latest pronouncements on the Tenth and Eleventh amendments. The fundamental legal underpinnings of state governments—their constitutions—are discussed in Chapter 3. Chapter 4 explores citizen participation and elections (including the 2009 elections), focusing on the increased access of citizens and the demands they are making on government. Chapter 5, "Political Parties, Interest Groups, and Campaigns," gets at subnational politics—the fascinating real world of candidates, lobbyists, organizations, and money.

Coverage of the three branches of government—legislative, executive, and judicial—is updated and reflects the institutional changes each branch has undergone recently. The intent of Chapter 6 is to show how legislatures actually work. In addition, responses of state legislatures to the institutional challenge posed by term limits are explored. Governors are featured in Chapter 7, including those who have misbehaved in various ways, and the issue of gubernatorial power is emphasized. Chapter 8, "Public Administration: Budgeting and Service Delivery," offers updated coverage of privatization as a strategy for improving government and the delivery of public services, as well as new material on e-government and budget transparency. In Chapter 9, the policy-making role of judges, judicial federalism, judicial accountability, and judicial selection mechanisms are emphasized.

Local governments are not treated as afterthoughts in this book. Two chapters focus solely on localities: Chapter 10 is devoted to the multiple types and structures of local government and Chapter 11 to leadership and governance, including new leadership approaches of mayors and city councils. Subsequent chapters consider localities within the context of the states: Chapter 12 focuses on the political and practical issues linking the two levels and Chapter 13 emphasizes the growing interdependence of state and local financial systems. Chapter 12 specifically tackles the issue of land use and urban sprawl, including New Urbanism approaches. Chapter 13 offers a comprehensive synthesis of the principles and political economy of taxation and spending and an overview of the strategies used by state and local governments to cope with the aforementioned economic crash.

Five policy chapters illustrate the proactive posture of state and local governments in responding to change and citizen demands. The roles of states and localities is different in each policy area. Chapter 14 examines economic development initiatives in the context of interstate and interregional competition for jobs and business. Chapter 15 focuses on the ever-important topic of public education; it includes examples of many of the most recent education reform efforts, including school choice plans, and provides up-to-date information on outcomes-based or performance-based education, No Child Left Behind, homeschooling, and charter schools. Criminal justice policy is the subject of Chapter 16. Crime statistics have been updated, as have some of the newest initiatives for community policing and criminal data applications. Social welfare and health care policy are featured in Chapter 17. The sincere efforts of state and local governments to lessen the impacts of national recession on their citizens are discussed, welfare traps are identified, and state programs aimed at plugging the gaping holes in the national health system are examined. Finally, Chapter 18 covers a wide range of environmental topics such as sustainability, ecoterrorism, and environmental justice. Of special interest are some of the success stories in "greening" states and localities.

## Teaching and Learning Aids

The PowerLecture® with ExamView® is free to adopters of the text. Its features include interactive **PowerPoint® lectures**, a one-stop lecture and class preparation tool that makes it easy for you to assemble, edit, publish, and present custom lectures for your course. You will have access to a set of PowerPoints with outlines specific to each chapter of *State and Local Government* as well as photos, figures, and tables found in the book. You will also have access to a **test bank,** written by David Floreen of Northeastern University, in Microsoft® Word and ExamView® computerized testing. It offers a large array of well-crafted multiple-choice and essay questions, along with their answers and page references. The **Instructor's Manual**, also written by David Floreen, features learning objectives, chapter summaries, suggested lecture topics, cooperative learning activities, and additional resources. The **Companion Website** for *State and Local Government*, Eighth Edition, located at www.cengage.com/politicalscience/bowman/stateandlocalgov8e, gives students access to tutorial quizzes, learning objectives, chapter glossaries, flash cards, crossword puzzles, and Internet links. Instructors also have access to the PowerPoint® slides and Instructor's Manual.

## Acknowledgments

First, we thank the reviewers of the eighth edition, who provided us with many thoughtful observations and examples:

> David Floreen, Senior Lecturer, College of Professional Studies,
>     Northeastern University, Boston
> Mohamed Yamba, California University of Pennsylvania
> Erik Root, West Liberty University
> T.M. Sell, Highline Community College
> Beth Fickling, Coastal Carolina Community College
> Steve Modlin, East Carolina University

We have incorporated their suggestions into this edition whenever possible.

We also extend our appreciation to our new partners at Cengage. Mary Beth Gaard and Edgar Garcia provided indispensable research assistance at Texas A&M University; Danielle Fuller and Jodi E. Swicegood contributed valuable research assistance at North Carolina State University. Finally, Carson, Blease, Kathy, and Joel contributed in many special ways to the final product, as usual.

A. O'M. B.

R. C. K.

SOURCE: Photo courtesy of
Ann O'M. Bowman

Ann O'M. Bowman (Ph.D. University of Florida) is professor and holder of the Hazel Davis and Robert Kennedy Endowed Chair in the Bush School of Government and Public Service at Texas A&M University. She teaches courses in state and local politics and policy, intergovernmental relations, environmental policy and management, and public policy process. Her research interests revolve around questions of institutional change, policy adoption and implementation, and intergovernmental dynamics. She has published numerous books and articles on these topics over the years.

SOURCE: Photo courtesy of
Richard C. Kearney

Richard C. Kearney (Ph.D. University of Oklahoma) is professor and director of the School of Public and International Affairs at North Carolina State University. He teaches courses in state and local politics and policy, public policy, public administration, and leadership. His research interests include comparative state politics and policy, labor relations, and human resource management policy. He has published prolifically on these and related topics.

# New Directions for State and Local Governments

1

With appropriate oratorical flourishes, the governor of Kentucky, Steven Beshear, delivered his 2009 State of the Commonwealth message to the people of the Bluegrass State. Although parts of the speech were specific to Kentucky—references to Fort Knox and to the University of Louisville, for example—many of the themes resonated beyond the state's borders. Budget shortfalls, job losses, and educational reform were topics in countless gubernatorial addresses throughout the country. In light of the fiscal challenges facing his state, Governor Beshear's tone was determined: "We need courageous leadership and visionary ideas to make transformational improvements to life in this state. Our resources may be limited but our vision doesn't have to be...These are tough times, but we cannot afford to stand still. State government can and should be a beacon of hope and a tool for progress."[1] Spirited exhortations such as these were echoed in one state capitol after another in 2009 and 2010. In Kentucky and elsewhere, state and local governments are indeed tackling difficult problems and seeking innovative solutions to contemporary problems.

- Studying state and local governments in the twenty-first century
- The capacity of states and localities
- The people: designers and consumers of government
- Linking capacity to results

# STUDYING STATE AND LOCAL GOVERNMENTS IN THE TWENTY-FIRST CENTURY

The study of state and local governments has typically received short shrift in the survey of U.S. politics.[2] Scholars and journalists tend to focus on glamorous imperial presidents, a rancorous and gridlocked Congress, and an independent and powerful Supreme Court. National and international issues capture the lion's share of media attention. Yet, state and local politics are fascinating, precisely because they are up close and personal. True, a governor seldom gets involved in an international peace conference, and state legislatures rarely debate the global narcotics trade. But the actors and institutions of states and localities are directly involved in our day-to-day lives. Education, welfare, health care, and crime are among the many concerns of state and local governments. And these issues affect all of us. Table 1.1 provides a sample of new state laws taking effect in 2010, state laws that touch our daily lives.

## From Sewers to Science: The Functions of State and Local Governments

State and local governments are busy. They exist, in large measure, to make policy for and provide services to the public. This is no easy task. Nonnational governments must perform efficiently, effectively, and equitably, and they must do so with limited financial resources. An efficient government is one

**TABLE 1.1    A Sample of New State Laws Taking Effect in 2010**

| STATE | DESCRIPTION OF THE LAW |
| --- | --- |
| California | Requires restaurants to prepare food with oils that are low in trans fats. |
| Illinois | Prohibits drivers from texting while operating motor vehicles. |
| Kentucky | Tightens state regulation of payday lenders. |
| Louisiana | Warns residents of the risks of eating certain Chinese seafood products. |
| Minnesota | Imposes a fee on non-residents who ride all-terrain vehicles on state trails. |
| Montana | Mandates that insurance companies provide coverage for autism spectrum disorders. |
| New Hampshire | Allows same-sex couples to marry. |
| New Mexico | Provides tuition waivers for medical residents who practice primary care in underserved areas of the state. |
| Texas | Requires teenagers frequenting tanning facilities to be accompanied by an adult. |
| Washington | Regulates dog breeders by limiting the number of dogs and imposing standards of care. |

SOURCE: National Conference of State Legislatures, "A Host of New Laws Ring in the New Year," www.ncsl.org (January 3, 2010).

that maximizes the output (services) from a given input (resources). A government operates effectively if it accomplishes what it sets out to do. Another expectation is that government function fairly—that its services be delivered in an equitable manner. It is no wonder, then, that state and local governments constantly experiment with new programs and new systems for producing services, all the while seeking efficiency, effectiveness, and equity. For instance, the massive restructuring of Wyoming's state government several years ago was intended, according to the governor, to produce "a better method of delivering services from the state government to the citizens."[3]

Each year, the Ford Foundation sponsors Innovations in American Government awards to recognize the creativity that abounds in governments throughout the nation. Between six and ten jurisdictions are selected for the prestigious and lucrative prize. The criteria for the awards are that the government's innovation be original, successful, and easily replicated by other jurisdictions. Among the contenders for the innovation award in 2009 were the following:

- Sacramento's Municipal Utility District's Greenergy program, which offers its customers renewable energy in the form of wind, biomass, and captured methane at affordable prices.
- Cuyahoga County, Ohio's Credit Crisis Relief program, which provides comprehensive foreclosure prevention services to homeowners.
- Return to Roots, a Virginia Web-based marketing campaign aimed at attracting former residents back to the southwestern part of the state by extolling the quality of life and job opportunities there.
- The Citywide Performance Reporting Online System, New York City's user-friendly website that gives the public access to government performance data.
- Idaho's program, Mapping Evapotranspiration from Satellites, which by producing detailed images of the water cycle enhances understanding of local and regional water-demand issues.[4]

Although some of the innovative projects are internal to government operations and carry the promise of increased efficiency, many others have a policy goal, such as energy conservation or consumer protection. The unifying characteristic is governmental willingness to try something new in an effort to improve its performance.

## Our Approach

The argument of this book is that states and localities have the capacity to play central roles in the U.S. federal system. **Capacity** refers to a government's ability to respond effectively to change, make decisions efficiently and responsibly, and manage conflict.[5] Thus, capacity is tied to governmental capability and performance. In short, states and communities with more capacity work better than those with less capacity.

But what factors make one government more capable than another? Governmental institutions such as the bureaucracy matter. The fiscal resources of

**capacity**
The ability of government to respond effectively to change, make decisions efficiently and responsibly, and manage conflict.

**jurisdiction**

The territorial range of government authority; "jurisdiction" is sometimes used as a synonym for "city" or "town."

a **jurisdiction** and the quality of its leadership make a difference. Much of the research on capacity has focused on the administrative dimension of government operations, evaluating items such as financial management, information technology, human resources, and infrastructure planning. In a 2008 study of state government performance, the highest overall scores went to Utah, Virginia, and Washington (each state received an A–) and Delaware, Georgia, Michigan, Missouri, and Texas (with grades of B+).[6] (Chapter 8 provides a list of all fifty states and their grades.) Earlier evaluations of forty large counties showed that Fairfax, Virginia, and Maricopa, Arizona, had the best grades. Among thirty-five cities examined, Austin, Texas, and Phoenix, Arizona, were at the top of the list. Other factors being equal, we would expect high-scoring states, counties, and cities to produce "better" government than low-scoring jurisdictions.

A survey in Iowa showed another side to governance. When asked about the characteristics of good government, Iowans selected trustworthiness, ethics, financial responsibility, and accountability.[7] Residents of the Hawkeye State are not unusual; all of us want our institutions and leaders to govern honestly and wisely. As political scientist David Hedge reminds us, better government is found in jurisdictions that are responsible and democratic.[8] But states and localities face significant challenges as they govern. Complex, often contradictory forces test the most capable of governments. Trends in the national economy play out at the subnational level. Problems in one jurisdiction can spill over into nearby communities. State and local governments need all the capacity they can muster and maybe even a little bit of luck to meet those challenges.

**federalism**

A system of government in which powers are divided between a central (national) government and regional (state) governments.

**Federalism**, with its overlapping spheres of authority, provides the context for state and local action. (This topic is explored in depth in Chapter 2.) Intervention by the national government in the affairs of a state or local government is defensible, even desirable in some cases. For example, the environmental problems of the 1960s and 1970s exceeded state and local governments' ability to handle them (see Chapter 18), so corrective action by the national government was generally welcomed. However, some federal actions are greeted less enthusiastically. For instance, No Child Left Behind (NCLB), the education law promoted by President George W. Bush and enacted by the U.S. Congress in 2002, is considered too intrusive by many state leaders and school districts. Since its passage, state legislators throughout the country have debated resolutions challenging the authority of this federal act; and by the time Congress began the reauthorization process in 2007, hundreds of bills had been introduced to give school districts additional flexibility to implement the law's provisions.[9]

Our approach takes into account intergovernmental relations (i.e., the relationships among the three levels of government)—particularly, the possibilities for cooperation and conflict. Jurisdictions (national, state, or local) possess policy-making authority over specific, but sometimes overlapping, territory. They confront innumerable situations in which boundaries blur and they must work together to accomplish an objective. However, cooperation in some cases is countered by conflict in other instances. Each level of government tends to see problems from its own perspective and design solutions accordingly. In sum, both cooperation and conflict define the U.S. federal system.

# THE CAPACITY OF STATES AND LOCALITIES

With notable exceptions, states and their local governments in the 1950s and 1960s were havens of traditionalism and inactivity. Many states were characterized by unrepresentative legislatures, glad-handing governors, and a hodge-podge court system. Public policy tended to reflect the interests of the elite; delivery of services was frequently inefficient and ineffective. According to former North Carolina governor Terry Sanford, the states "had lost their confidence, and people their faith in the states."[10] No wonder that, by comparison, the federal government appeared to be the answer, regardless of the question. In fact, political scientist Luther Gulick proclaimed, "It is a matter of brutal record. The American State is finished. I do not predict that the states will go, but affirm that they have gone."[11]

Those days are as outmoded as a black-and-white television. States and their local governments have proved themselves capable of designing and implementing "an explosion of innovations and initiatives."[12] As a result, even many national leaders have embraced the roles of states and localities as laboratories for policy experimentation. A *New York Times* story with the headline "As Congress Stalls, States Pursue Cloning Debate" is indicative of states pushing the policy envelope.[13] Public confidence in American ingenuity—a fundamental spirit of optimism—may shift over time, as Figure 1.1 shows, but it has maintained fairly high levels over the past two decades.

The blossoming of state governments in the 1980s—their transformation from weak links in the federal chain to viable and progressive political units—resulted from several actions and circumstances, as discussed in the next section.[14] In turn, the resurgence of state governments has generated a host of positive outcomes. During the 1990s, states and localities honed their capacity and became **proactive** rather than reactive. They faced hard choices and creatively crafted new directions. A word of caution is necessary, however. The challenges of governance can be great, and not all states enjoy the same level of capacity. Furthermore, fiscal stresses such as those endured by state governments as the first decade of the twenty-first century drew to a close sorely test the ability of even the most capable states to function effectively.

**proactive**
An anticipatory condition, as opposed to a reactive one.

## ɑ How States and Localities Increased Their Capacity

Several factors contributed to the resurgence of the states. U.S. Supreme Court decisions in the 1960s on legislative apportionment made for more equitable representation; the extension of two-party competition in the 1970s to states formerly dominated by one party gave voters more choices. At the same time, states and localities expanded their lobbying presence in

**FIGURE 1.1**

**Changes in Public Opinion about American Ingenuity**

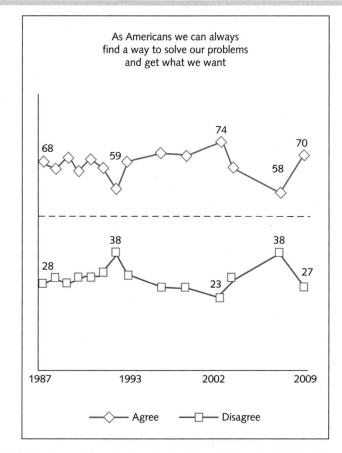

As Americans we can always find a way to solve our problems and get what we want

SOURCE: The Pew Research Center for People and the Press, "Independents Take Center Stage in Obama Era: Trends in Political Values and Core Attitudes: 1987–2009" (May 21, 2009), p. 69, http://people-press.org/reports/pdf/517.pdf.

the nation's capital, exerting influence on the design and funding of inter-governmental programs.

Most important, state governments quietly and methodically reformed themselves by modernizing their constitutions and restructuring their institutions. During the past three decades, more than three-quarters of the states have ratified new constitutions or substantially amended existing ones. Formerly thought of as the "drag anchors of state programs" and as "protectors of special interests,"[15] these documents have been streamlined and made more workable. Even in states without wide-ranging constitutional reform, tinkering with constitutions is almost endless thanks to the amendment process. Nearly every state general election finds constitutional issues on the ballot. (State constitutions are discussed in Chapter 3.)

States have also undertaken various internal adjustments intended to improve the operations of state governments.[16] Modernized constitutions and statutory changes have strengthened the powers of governors by increasing appointment and removal powers and by allowing longer terms, consecutive succession, larger staffs, enhanced budget authority, and the ability to reorganize the executive branch. Throughout the country, state agencies are staffed by skilled administrators. The bureaucracy itself is more and more demographically representative of the public. Annual rather than biennial sessions, more efficient rules and procedures, additional staff, and higher salaries have helped make reapportioned state legislatures more professional, capable, and effective. State judicial systems have also been the targets of reform; examples include the establishment of unified court systems, the hiring of court administrators, and the creation of additional layers of courts. (State institutions—legislatures, governors, state agencies, and courts—are addressed in Chapters 6–9.)

## Increased Capacity and Improved Performance

The enhanced capacity enjoyed by state and local governments has generated a range of mostly positive results. The five factors discussed below reinforce the performance of states and localities.

**Improved Revenue Systems** Economic downturns and limits on taxation and expenditures have caused states to implement new revenue-raising strategies to maintain acceptable service levels. For instance, Colorado's TABOR law (it stands for "Taxpayers' Bill of Rights"), enacted in 1992, decreased government spending to such a degree that Coloradoans voted in 2005 to suspend TABOR provisions for a five-year period. States also granted local governments more flexibility in their revenue systems. South Carolina, for example, now allows counties the option of providing property-tax relief to residents while increasing the local sales tax.

As a rule, state governments prefer to increase user charges, gasoline taxes, and so-called sin taxes on alcohol and tobacco, and only reluctantly do they raise sales and income taxes. Over time, revenue structures have been redesigned to make them more diversified and more equitable. State **rainy day funds**, legalized gambling through state-run lotteries and pari-mutuels, and extension of the sales tax to services are examples of diversification strategies. Exemptions of food and medicine from consumer sales taxes and the enactment of property-tax breaks for poor and elderly people characterize efforts at tax equity. These redesigned revenue structures helped states respond to the budget crises they confronted in the early 2000s.

States continue to tinker with their revenue-raising schemes. One successful foray into creative revenue raising has been the specialty license plate. Maryland, for example, has raised hundreds of thousands of dollars with its "Treasure the Chesapeake" plate. Monies generated by the plates are earmarked for special programs—in this case, water quality monitoring and erosion control

**rainy day funds**
Money set aside when a state's finances are healthy, for use when state revenues decline. Formally called "budget stabilization funds."

in the Chesapeake Bay. Nearly all states now offer specialty plates. In New York, for instance, owners can equip their cars, for an extra fee, with license plates honoring their favorite professional sports team or NASCAR driver. A brand new approach to generating cash for states comes from the world of retail stores: the marketing of official gift cards. For example, both Kentucky and Ohio sell gift cards that can be used at state park locations for various park services and merchandise.

Another effort of enterprising localities is to sell merchandise. Los Angeles County has marketed coroner toe tags as key chains; Portland and Tampa are among the cities that rent the entire outside surfaces of their buses to advertisers. New York City, which loses thousands of street signs (Wall Street is especially popular) to souvenir-stealing tourists, now sells replicas. But the revenue generated by those actions is dwarfed by Chicago, which has sold (actually, leased for ninety-nine years) four city-owned parking garages to an investment bank for a tidy $563 million. As these examples show, states and localities are willing to experiment when it comes to revenue enhancement.

**Expanding the Scope of State Operations** State governments have taken on new roles and added new functions. In some instances, states are filling in the gap left by the national government's de-emphasis of an activity; in other cases, states are venturing into uncharted terrain. It was states that designed the first family leave legislation, to give workers time off to care for newborn babies and ailing relatives, and the first Amber Alert systems, to broadcast information about abducted children. The federal government eventually followed suit with a national family leave act and a national Amber Alert system. In addition, states have taken the initiative in ongoing intergovernmental programs by creatively utilizing program authority and resources. Prior to federal welfare reform in the mid-1990s, several states had established workfare programs and imposed time limits on the receipt of welfare benefits, provisions that were at the center of the subsequent federal legislation.

The innovative behavior continues. For example, Illinois and Wisconsin launched I-SaveRx, the first state-sponsored program to help residents buy cheaper prescription drugs in Ireland and Canada. States persist in expanding their scope of operations, whether it is California's venture into stem-cell research or Florida's strides into bioterror readiness. New York has initiated a new program to fight childhood obesity, Active-8 Kids; Hawaii has begun construction of an extensive network of plug-in spots where electric cars can be recharged. In short, states are embracing their role as policy innovators and experimenters in the U.S. federal system.

**Faster Diffusion of Innovations** Among states, there have always been leaders and followers. The same is true for local governments. Now that states and localities have expanded their scope and are doing more policy making, they are looking more frequently to their neighbors and to similar places for advice, information, and models.[17] As a result, successful solutions spread from one jurisdiction to another. For example, Florida was the first state to create a way for consumers to stop telephone solicitations. By 1999, five more states had passed laws letting residents put their names on a "do-not-call" list for telemarketers. Seven additional states adopted similar legislation over the next two years before Congress enacted a national statute.[18] Another fast-moving innovation was a 2004 New York law that required cigarettes sold in the state to be self-extinguishing. Concerned over fire safety, California followed suit and by 2007, nineteen other states had adopted the law.[19]

Local-level innovations spread rapidly, too. Education and environmental protection offer many examples of this phenomenon. When Dade County, Florida, hired a private company to run a public elementary school, other school districts hoping to improve quality and cut costs quickly did the same. Initial experiments with privatization spawned other innovations such as charter schools. The issue of global warming was addressed at the local level in 2005, when the mayor of Seattle became the first local official to commit his city to a plan to reduce the emission of greenhouse gases. By 2009, more than 950 mayors of other U.S. cities had joined the anti-global warming bandwagon.[20]

Obviously, state and local governments learn from one another. Communication links are increasingly varied and frequently used. A state might turn to nearby states when searching for policy solutions. Regional consultation and emulation are logical: Similar problems often beset jurisdictions in the same region, a program used in a neighboring state may be politically more acceptable than one from a distant state, and organizational affiliations bring state and local administrators together with their colleagues from nearby areas. However, research has shown that states also borrow ideas from peer states, that is, states that are like them in important ways such as ideological leaning or economic base. In the search for solutions, states and localities are increasingly inclusive.[21]

**Interjurisdictional Cooperation** Accompanying the quickening flow of innovations has been an increase in interjurisdictional cooperation. States are choosing to confront and resolve their immediate problems jointly. A similar phenomenon has occurred at the local level with the creation of regional organizations to tackle area-wide problems collectively.

Interjurisdictional collaboration takes many forms, including informal consultations and agreements, interstate committees, legal contracts, reciprocal legislation, and interstate compacts. For example, all fifty states plus the District of Columbia, Puerto Rico, and the U.S. Virgin Islands have a mutual agreement to aid one another when natural disasters such as hurricanes, earthquakes, and forest fires strike. Five states—Mississippi, Minnesota, West Virginia, Florida, and Massachusetts—were among the first to band together to share information and design tactics in their lawsuits against tobacco companies in the mid-1990s; by 1998, thirty-seven other states had joined in the successful effort to recover the Medicaid costs of treating tobacco-related diseases.[22] In the same year, twenty states filed an antitrust lawsuit against Microsoft Corporation, claiming that the firm illegally stifled competition, harmed consumers, and undercut innovation in the computer software industry.

In another instance, nine eastern states decided that the best way to compel large power plants to reduce their carbon emissions was to band together in a regional effort.[23] By 2009, forty-four states and Washington, D.C. had signed on to the Streamlined Sales Tax Project, an ongoing effort to craft an interstate agreement on the simplification of sales and use taxes. The intent is to make it easier for states to collect taxes on items purchased on the Internet. In each of these instances, the states worked together because they could see some benefit from cooperation.

Increased jurisdictional cooperation fosters a healthy climate for joint problem solving. In addition, when state and local governments solve their own problems, they protect their power and authority within the federal system. It appears that states are becoming more comfortable working with one another. The beginning of the twenty-first century was indeed historic: States were engaged in more cooperative interactions than ever before.[24]

**Increased National–State Conflict** An inevitable by-product of more capable state and local governments is intensified conflict with the national government. One source of this trouble has been federal laws and grant requirements that supersede state policy; another is the movement of states onto the national government's turf. National–state conflict is primarily a cyclical phenomenon, but contention has increased in recent years. The issue of unfunded mandates—the costly requirements that federal legislation imposes on states and localities—has been particularly troublesome. In an effort to increase the visibility of the mandates issue, several national organizations of state and local officials sponsored a National Unfunded Mandate Day in the mid-1990s. Making a strong case against mandates, then governor George Voinovich of Ohio stated, "Unfunded mandates devastate our budgets, inhibit flexibility and innovation in implementing new programs, pre-empt important state initiatives, and deprive states of their responsibility to set priorities."[25] Congress responded in 1995 by passing a mandate relief bill that requires cost–benefit analyses of proposed mandates; however, the law contains some loopholes that have weakened its impact.

Some of the disputes pit a single state against the national government, as in Nevada's fight to block the U.S. Energy Department's plan to build a nuclear fuel waste storage facility at Yucca Mountain, 100 miles northwest of Las Vegas. In other conflicts, the national government finds itself besieged by a coordinated, multistate effort, for example, when ten states successfully sued the U.S. Environmental Protection Agency in 2003 over the regulation of greenhouse gases.[26]

National–state conflicts are resolved (and sometimes intensified) by the federal judicial system. Cases dealing with alleged violations of the U.S. Constitution by state and local governments are heard in federal courts and decided by federal judges. Sometimes the rulings take the federal government into spheres long considered the purview of state and local governments. For example, within the space of two days in 2009, Arizona both won and lost cases before the U.S. Supreme Court. The state was successful in its argument that state spending on language training for non-English-speaking students should not be subject to federal supervision, but it was unsuccessful in defending the actions of school officials who conducted a strip search of a middle-school student suspected of drug possession.

## Challenges Facing State and Local Governments

Increased capacity does not mean that all state and local problems have been solved. Nonnational governments face three tough challenges today: fiscal stress, interjurisdictional conflict, and political corruption.

**Fiscal Stress** The most intractable problem for states and localities involves money. State and local finances are vulnerable to cyclical peaks and troughs in the national economy as well as occasional changes in public finance. So, in 2003 and 2004, when states faced fiscal stress—insufficient revenues to cover budgeted expenditures—they responded by drawing on their rainy day funds and seeking special financing mechanisms. But these actions only went so far, and states were eventually forced to increase taxes (especially on tobacco products and alcohol), impose new fees on services, and cut spending.[27]

The national economic recession of 2008–2009 hit states and localities hard—very hard—and the impact on governmental budgets was significant. Connecticut governor Jodi Rell did not mince words when she said, "These are the worst financial times any of us can remember...let's face it, it's scary."[28] According to the National Association of State Budget Officers, forty-two states were forced to cut their enacted budgets in fiscal 2009 by a total $31.6 billion.[29] In an effort to save money, some prisons were closed in Colorado, Kansas, Michigan, North Carolina, and Washington; in some states, funding for education was reduced and cash assistance for low-income families was cut; in others, state agencies were **downsized** and employee wages were frozen. State leaders sought new revenues also: Income tax rates were increased in California, Hawaii, and New York; sales tax increases were enacted in Arizona, California, and Massachusetts, among other states. Facing the largest deficit of any state, the governor of California battled with the legislature over several money-saving proposals including "selling the Los Angeles Memorial Coliseum, San Quentin State Prison and other state property, eliminating welfare benefits for 500,000 families, terminating health coverage for nearly 1 million low-income children and closing 220 of the states' parks."[30]

Local governments felt the heat as well; Dallas, one of the country's largest cities, provides an example. To close a $190.2 million deficit in its budget, the city of Dallas made cuts in numerous city services including street repairs, arts funding, library hours, and park maintenance; in addition, nearly 800 city employees lost their jobs.[31] The story was much the same in many other localities: reduce costs as painlessly as possible, and if necessary, increase fees. Some relief was forthcoming when Congress passed the $787 billion American

**downsize**
To reduce the size and cost of something, especially government.

Recovery and Reinvestment Act, informally known as the federal stimulus plan, but many states and communities felt the fiscal pinch well into 2010.

**Increased Interjurisdictional Conflict** Tension is inherent in a federal system because each of the governmental entities has its own set of interests as well as a share of the national interest. When one state's pursuit of its interests negatively affects another state, conflict occurs. Such conflict can become destructive, threatening the continuation of state resurgence. In essence, states end up wasting their energies and resources on counterproductive battles among themselves.

Interjurisdictional conflict is particularly common in two policy areas very dear to state and local governments: natural resources and economic development. States rich in natural resources want to use these resources in a manner that will yield the greatest return. Oil-producing states, for instance, levy severance taxes that raise the price of oil. And states with abundant water supplies resist efforts by arid states to tap into these supplies. The most serious disputes often occur among neighboring states. One illustration is the protracted dispute between California and six other western states over water allocations from the Colorado River. In short, the essential question revolves around a state's right to control a resource that occurs naturally and is highly desired by other states. Resource-poor states argue that resources are in fact national and should rightfully be shared among states.

In the area of economic development, conflict is extensive because all jurisdictions want healthy economies. Toward this end, states try to make themselves attractive to business and industry through tax breaks, regulatory relaxation, and even image creation. (The Breaking New Ground box on the next page explores how states work to reverse negative images and to promote positive ones.) Conflict arises when states get involved in bidding wars—that is, when an enterprise is so highly valued that actions taken by one state are matched and exceeded by another. Suppose, for example, that an automobile manufacturer is considering shutting down an existing facility and relocating. States hungry for manufacturing activity will assemble packages of incentives such as below-cost land, tax concessions, and subsidized job training in their efforts to attract the manufacturer. The state that wants to keep the manufacturer will try to match these inducements. In the long run, economic activity is simply relocated from one state to another. The big winner is the manufacturer. (Chapter 14 explores economic development issues much more extensively.)

A particularly fascinating interjurisdictional contest involves the recurring rounds of U.S. military base closures and consolidations. Military bases are economic plums that no jurisdiction wants to lose. Thus, states mount public relations efforts to protect local bases and to grab jobs that will be lost in other states. Politics and lobbying are supposed to play no role in the Pentagon's decisions about which bases will remain open and which ones will close, but states prefer to hedge their bets. In the 2005 round, Texas devoted $250 million to defending its bases, and Massachusetts allocated $410 million for its own bases. As one observer put it, "It is a war of all against all."[32]

## BREAKING NEW GROUND

### Creating an Image

What image best captures a state's essential being? Ohio, for example, calls itself the Buckeye State, but most Americans don't know what a buckeye is (it's a shrub or tree of the horse chestnut family). Consider New Hampshire, which stamps the motto "Live Free or Die" on its license plates. A few years ago, some legislators advocated replacing the uncompromising phrase with the word *scenic*, arguing that the state needed to project a more caring image. The North Dakota legislature took the image issue to new heights when it seriously entertained a resolution that would have dropped the word *North* from the state's name. The name *North Dakota* was said to summon images of "snowstorms, howling winds, and frigid temperatures." Simply going with *Dakota*, a word that means "friend" or "ally" in the Sioux language, would project a warmer image of the state, supporters claimed. (The state senate ultimately defeated the name-changing resolution.) And when a computer graphics software firm used the icon of an outhouse to designate West Virginia, complaints from state officials led the company to change the icon to a more positive symbol: a mountain. Image and reputation are serious business: In 2004, West Virginia protested an Abercrombie & Fitch T-shirt that featured a map of the state and the phrase "It's all relative in West Virginia."

Images are not trivial. They matter because they project and reflect public perceptions, which can be both accurate and inaccurate. They offer a shorthand understanding of a place, a slice of the whole. States and communities have become much more conscious of their images in recent years, and many have launched promotional campaigns to foster positive images. Consequently, when Congress passed legislation to mint new varieties of quarters to commemorate states, it gave each state an opportunity to celebrate its uniqueness. States used the quarter design and selection process to generate reflection about the state and its image. Most states set up advisory committees to guide the process of identifying concepts that were emblematic of the state's history, physical features, and culture. For example, for its 2008 coin, Alaska considered several concepts, including a polar bear, a dog-sled musher, and a miner panning for gold. The winning design featured the inscription "The Great Land," underneath the North Star, and a grizzly bear catching a salmon. Alaska indeed.

SOURCES: "Hey! It's 'the Mountain State,'" *Newsweek* (June 21, 1993), p. 24; Dale Wetzel, "Dakotans Consider Dropping 'North' to Thaw State's Image," *The Missoulian* (June 25, 2001), p. B4; Tony Dokoupil, "Hillbilly No More," *Newsweek*, www.newsweek.com/ (March 10, 2009).

**Political Corruption** Corruption exists in government, which is no great surprise. Most political systems can tolerate the occasional corrupt official, but if corruption becomes commonplace, it undermines governmental capacity and destroys public trust. Public reaction ranges from cynicism and alienation (corruption as "politics as usual") to anger and action (corruption as a spur to reform). A survey found that the more extreme the corrupt act (a city clerk embezzling $100,000 versus a police officer accepting free food at a restaurant), the more harsh the public's judgment.[33] Even so, mitigating motives or circumstances tend to reduce the public's outrage (e.g., a public official taking a bribe but using the money to pay his sick child's hospital bills). But governmental scandals have been linked tentatively to another negative effect—a slowdown in economic growth. Research on states found that federal corruption convictions are associated with declines in job growth primarily because, from a business perspective, corruption creates uncertainty and inflates costs.[34]

States and localities have taken great precautions to reduce the amount of wrongdoing occurring in their midst. Government has much more **transparency** than it ever has before, with more openness and more rules. But the statutes and policies are only as good as the people whose behavior they regulate. Examples of corrupt behavior are not hard to find. For instance, in 2007, federal agents charged eleven public officials—mayors, city council members, and school board members—in New Jersey with taking bribes in exchange for help securing public contracts.[35] Several of the accused were later convicted on corruption charges and sentenced to jail. And the nation was captivated in 2008 when flamboyant Illinois governor Rod Blagojevich was led away in handcuffs after federal officials arrested him in a "pay to play" scandal that involved his plan to sell a vacant U.S. Senate seat. He was later impeached and removed from office by the state legislature.

A pair of economists researching corruption in the states asked statehouse reporters—folks who are familiar with the goings-on in the capitol—to assess the overall level of corruption in their state compared with other states.[36] At the top of the list was Rhode Island, followed by Louisiana and New Mexico. States at the bottom of the comparative corruption list included the Dakotas, Colorado, and Maine. Although states and localities are not corruption-free, the amount of corruption is relatively low, given the vast number of public officials serving in nonnational levels of government. Still, even a whiff of scandal can undermine public confidence in government and sap governmental capacity.

**transparency**
A characteristic of a government that is open and understandable, one in which officials are accountable to the public.

# THE PEOPLE: DESIGNERS AND CONSUMERS OF GOVERNMENT

A book on state and local governments is not only about places and governments, it is also about people—the public and assorted officeholders—and the institutions they create, the processes in which they engage, and the policies they adopt. Thus, this volume contains chapters on institutions, such as legislatures, and on processes, such as elections; it also discusses policies, such as those pertaining to education. But in each case, *people* are the ultimate focus: A legislature is composed of lawmakers and staff members who deal with constituents; elections involve candidates, campaign workers, and voters (as well as nonvoters); and education essentially involves students, teachers, administrators, parents, and taxpayers. In short, the word *people* encompasses an array of individuals and roles in the political system.

## Ethnic-Racial Composition

More than 300 million people live in the United States. Some can trace their heritage back to the *Mayflower*, whereas others look back only as far as a recent naturalization ceremony. Very few can claim indigenous (native) American ancestry. Instead, most Americans owe their nationality to some forebear who came here in search of a better life or—in the case of a significant minority, the descendants of slaves—to ancestors who made the journey to this country not out of choice but because of physical coercion. The appeal of the United States to economic and political refugees from other countries continues, with Mexicans, Central Americans, and eastern Africans among the most recent arrivals.

The United States is a nation of immigrants, and therefore ethnic richness and cultural diversity abound. Official U.S. Census estimates for 2008 put the white population at 74 percent, the African American population at 13 percent, the Latino population at 15 percent, and the Asian population at 4 percent.[37] (The numbers total more than 100 percent because of double-counting.) Approximately 34 million, or 12 percent, of the nation's population was foreign born, with 53 percent of the foreign born from Latin America, and another 25 percent from Asia.[38]

One aspect of immigration—illegal immigration—is putting the words from the sonnet inscribed on the Statue of Liberty ("Give me your tired, your poor, your huddled masses") to a severe test. Although accurate numbers are hard to come by, one 2008 estimate by the U.S. Department of Homeland Security placed the number of illegal immigrants at approximately 12 million, approximately 60 percent from Mexico.[39] Both Florida and Texas are estimated to have between 1 million and 1.5 million residents who are in the country illegally; in California, the figure is 2.7 million. In Nevada, undocumented immigrants are estimated to comprise 11 percent of the state's population; 9 percent in Arizona. Controversy has arisen over the costs of providing public services such as health care, education, and welfare to illegal immigrants. In 2009, state legislatures considered bills to clamp down on illegal immigration by requiring verification of workers' legal status and restricting the issuance of drivers' licenses to U.S. citizens and legal immigrants. But clamping down on illegal immigration is complicated by the fact that 73 percent of the children of these undocumented immigrants were born in the United States and are, therefore, U.S. citizens.[40]

Clearly, ethnicity and culture still matter, despite the image of America as a melting pot. Researchers have found that a state's racial and ethnic diversity goes a long way in explaining its politics and policies.[41] Looking toward the future, census projections for the year 2050 estimate a nation of approximately 420 million people, with the Anglo population dropping to 50 percent of the total, the African American population increasing slightly to 15 percent, the Latino population reaching 25 percent, and an Asian population of 8 percent.[42] If the predicted trends hold, state policy in the mid-twenty-first century will be affected.

## Population Growth and Migration

As a whole, the United States grew by approximately 8 percent during the period 2000–2008. Disaggregating the data by state reveals several trends. Reflecting the pattern of the previous decade, high rates of growth occurred in the western states; substantially slower growth rates characterized the Northeast and Midwest. (The map in Figure 1.2 displays the estimated percentage change in each state's population from 2000 to 2008.) Nevada and Arizona continued

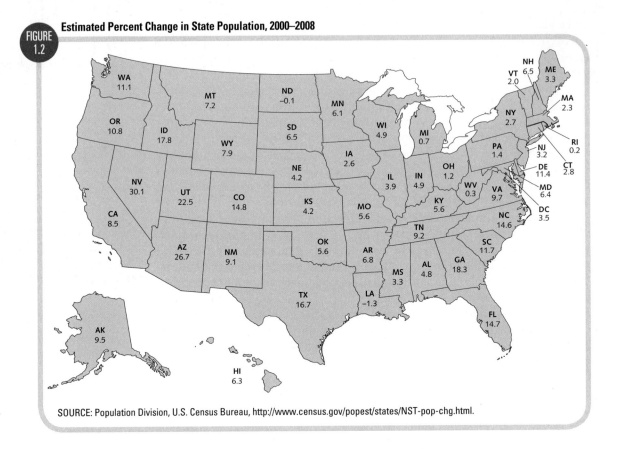

FIGURE 1.2

**Estimated Percent Change in State Population, 2000–2008**

SOURCE: Population Division, U.S. Census Bureau, http://www.census.gov/popest/states/NST-pop-chg.html.

**Sunbelt**

An unofficial region of the United States, generally consisting of the South and the West.

**Frostbelt**

An unofficial region of the United States, generally comprising the Northeast and the Midwest. The label *Rustbelt* is sometimes used as a synonym.

to outpace the growth in other states, with rates of 30.1 percent and 26.7 percent, respectively. A strong labor market and an attractive, inexpensive lifestyle are among those states' features. Only two states (Louisiana and North Dakota) were projected to have lost population during the period.[43] In percentage terms, Georgia replaced Florida as the South's growth leader (18.3 percent), with the Sunshine State (14.7 percent) close behind. California grew by an estimated 8.5 percent, which meant an increase of 2.9 million people in the Golden State. Although the pace of growth slowed in 2009, the Census Bureau's projections for the year 2025 show Nevada, California, Arizona, and New Mexico with the largest population gains, much of the growth attributed to international immigration.

For cities, the population trends are equally compelling. Higher rates of growth are much more prevalent in cities in the **Sunbelt** region than in cities of the **Frostbelt**. The growth leaders among large cities (defined as cities of 100,000 population or more) between 2000 and 2007 included many places that are suburbs such as McKinney (outside Dallas), North Las Vegas (a suburb of Las Vegas), and Gilbert (near Phoenix). Each of these Sunbelt suburbs grew by 80 percent or more during the seven-year period. At the other end of the spectrum are large, older industrialized cities of the Frostbelt that lost more than 7 percent of their population during the same time frame: Cleveland, Ohio, Flint, Michigan, and Pittsburgh, Pennsylvania.[44] (New Orleans, Louisiana, is a special case having lost a substantial portion of its population in the aftermath of Hurricane Katrina, but by 2007, many former residents had begun returning to the city.) The Engaging New Directions box pursues the impact of population change on local governments.

Population changes carry economic and political consequences for state and local governments. As a general rule, power and influence follow population. A state's representation in the U.S. Congress and its votes in the Electoral College are at stake. Speculation about the impact of the 2010 Census on state influence in the U.S. House of Representatives in 2012 has already begun. The smart money is on Texas to pick up four seats, Arizona and

Residential development in a fast-growing suburb in the Sunbelt.
*SOURCE: Charles O'Rear/Corbis*

Florida each to add two seats, and five states to gain one seat each. At the other end of the spectrum, both New York and Ohio are projected to lose two seats, while nine other states will likely lose one each.[45] Population projections suggest that the electoral influence of Sunbelt states will continue to grow into the foreseeable future. The stakes are high for local governments, too. As a central city's population size is eclipsed by its suburban population, a loss in the city's political clout results. Aware of the importance of "the count," many cities spent thousands of dollars on media advertisements, text messages, and social networking websites encouraging their residents to mail in their 2010 Census forms.

## ᘔ Political Culture

One of the phrases that a new arrival in town may hear from long-time residents is "We don't do things that way here." **Political culture**—the attitudes, values, and beliefs that people hold toward government—is the conceptual equivalent of simply saying "It's *our* thing."[46] As developed by political scientist Daniel Elazar in the 1960s, the term refers to the way people think about their government and how the political system operates. Political culture is a soft concept—one that is difficult to measure—yet it has remained quite useful in explaining state politics and policy.

According to Elazar, the United States is an amalgam of three major political cultures, each of which has distinctive characteristics. In an *individualistic political culture*, politics is a kind of open marketplace in which people

**political culture**

The attitudes, values, and beliefs that people hold toward government.

## Engaging New Directions

## People and Governments

Generally, Americans are considered a mobile people, willing to pack up and move in pursuit of new opportunities. Some destinations are more popular than others, of course. Participants in the Pew Research Center's Social and Demographic Trends project were given lists of large U.S. cities and asked to select those in which they would like to live. Denver led the list (43 percent indicated that they'd like to live in the city or the surrounding area), followed by San Diego (40 percent), Seattle (38 percent), Orlando, Tampa, and San Francisco (34 percent each). Substantially less popular as a place to live were Detroit (8 percent), Cleveland (10 percent), Cincinnati (13 percent), and Kansas City (15 percent).

Preferences for particular places are often shaped by demographics and political views. For example, the nation's largest cities, New York and Los Angeles, are magnets for young adults more so than aging baby boomers. The Pew survey also found that Las Vegas and San Antonio seem to appeal more to men than to women. Boston is a place where wealthier adults want to live; their less affluent counterparts prefer Los Angeles, Las Vegas, or Orlando. Republicans think Denver and Phoenix would be great places to call home, whereas Democrats consider San Diego or San Francisco more to their liking.

This wanderlust presents both an opportunity and a dilemma to local governments. On the surface, population growth appears to be a good thing: New residents contribute to the local economy and to the governmental tax base. But new residents also bring demands for services, such as new schools and parks, and they require additional police and firefighters. Cities and counties float bonds (i.e., borrow money) to pay for long-term capital projects such as the new roads and sewer systems needed to accommodate the growing population. Communities often worry that the features that attracted new residents to the city may disappear in the face of high growth. Such a concern led fast-growing Austin, Texas, to adopt a policy to "nurture, preserve, and promote the city's arts and creative industries in order to strengthen and sustain Austin's dynamic cultural vitality," or as it is expressed on the city's streets, "Keep Austin weird."

In jurisdictions that are losing people, the dilemmas are more acute. Population loss means less revenue, but it does not necessarily translate into fewer service obligations. Remaining residents want their bus systems to operate even if there are fewer riders and their public libraries to remain open even if there are fewer patrons. (In 2009, Philadelphia's mayor, Michael Nutter, became embroiled in major controversy when he proposed closing several of the city's branch libraries in an effort to save money.) Streets have to be maintained, garbage has to be picked up, crimes need to be investigated, and public health clinics must offer care. The dilemma for these localities is to decide where cuts in services can be made, where improvements in productivity can be gained, and where additional revenues can be found.

New directions on the part of the public, relocating from one jurisdiction to another, can send local governments in new directions as well as they seek to balance service demands with available resources.

SOURCES: Pew Research Center, "For Nearly Half of America, Grass is Greener Somewhere Else," http://pewsocialtrends.org/assets/pdf/Community-Satisfaction.pdf (January 29, 2009); Penelope Lemov, "Find Me the Money," *Governing* (May 2009), pp. 55–56; City of Austin, Economic Growth and Redevelopment Services Office, www.ci.austin.tx.us/redevelopment/ (June 10, 2009).

participate because of essentially private motivations. In a *moralistic political culture,* politics is an effort to establish a good and just society. Citizens are expected to be active in public affairs. In a *traditionalistic political culture,* politics functions to maintain the existing order, and political participation is confined to social elites. These differing conceptions about the purpose of government and the role of politics lead to different behaviors. Confronted with similar conditions, officials in an individualistic community would resist initiating a program unless public opinion demanded it; leaders in moralistic areas would adopt the new program, even without pressure, if they believed it to be in the public interest; and traditionalistic rulers would initiate the program only if they thought it would serve the interests of the governing elite.

Political culture is a factor in the differences (and similarities) in state policy. Research has found that moralistic states demonstrate the greatest tendency toward policy innovation, whereas traditionalistic states exhibit the least.[47] In economic development policy, for example, political culture has been shown to influence a state's willingness to offer tax breaks to businesses.[48] Other research has linked political culture to state environmental policy and state expenditures on AIDS programs.[49]

Today, few states are characterized by pure forms of these cultures. The mass media have had a homogenizing effect on cultural differences; migration has diversified cultural enclaves. This process of cultural erosion and synthesis has produced hybrid political cultures. For example, Florida, once considered a traditionalistic state, now has many areas in which an individualistic culture prevails and even has a moralistic community or two. In an effort to extend Elazar's pioneering work, researcher Joel Lieske has used race, ethnicity, and religion to identify contemporary subcultures.[50] With counties as the building blocks and statistical analysis as the method, he identified ten distinctive regional subcultures. A state like Pennsylvania, which Elazar characterized as individualistic, becomes a mix of "heartland," Germanic, ethnic, and rural/urban counties in Lieske's formulation. Very few states are dominated by a single subculture, except perhaps Utah, by a Mormon subculture, and New Hampshire and Vermont, by an Anglo-French subculture.

The variation among states makes for a nation that is highly diverse. However, one recent exercise in identifying the most typical state in the country proved interesting. Based on twelve key statistics—four measuring race and ethnicity, four looking at income and education, and four describing the typical neighborhood in each state—Wisconsin was found to be the microcosm of the nation.[51] Rounding out the top five were Missouri, Kansas, Indiana, and Ohio. The states least like the country as a whole were: Mississippi, West Virginia, and New York. Table 1.2 lists the states from most typical to least. The numbers refer to a standardized score with a potential range of zero to fifty.

## ⊖ Culture Wars

In 2004, when San Francisco's mayor ordered city clerks to remove all references to gender on local marriage license applications, it opened the door for same-sex marriages to take place in the city. As gay activists and supporters celebrated, many politically conservative groups denounced the action and promised legal challenges and political repercussions for the mayor. This type of social conflict over morality issues is known informally as **culture wars**, or "morality politics." And these culture wars are defining the politics of many

**culture wars**
Political conflicts that emerge from deeply held moral values.

| TABLE 1.2 | How Typical Is Your State? | | | |
|---|---|---|---|---|
| 1. Wisconsin | 36.4 | | 26. Iowa | 19.6 |
| 2. Missouri | 35.2 | | 27. Texas | 19.6 |
| 3. Kansas | 34.4 | | 28. Illinois | 19.5 |
| 4. Indiana | 30.8 | | 29. Rhode Island | 19.0 |
| 5. Ohio | 30.1 | | 30. Maryland | 18.9 |
| 6. Oklahoma | 29.9 | | 31. Colorado | 18.8 |
| 7. Oregon | 29.3 | | 32. Louisiana | 18.3 |
| 8. Nebraska | 29.0 | | 33. Idaho | 18.1 |
| 9. Georgia | 27.3 | | 34. Vermont | 17.9 |
| 10. Minnesota | 26.9 | | 35. Maine | 17.4 |
| 11. Michigan | 26.8 | | 36. New Hampshire | 17.4 |
| 12. Washington | 26.3 | | 37. Utah | 17.0 |
| 13. Wyoming | 25.9 | | 38. Hawaii | 16.3 |
| 14. North Carolina | 25.8 | | 39. South Carolina | 15.8 |
| 15. Florida | 25.6 | | 40. California | 15.3 |
| 16. Montana | 25.3 | | 41. Arkansas | 15.0 |
| 17. Virginia | 25.3 | | 42. Alabama | 14.6 |
| 18. Alaska | 25.1 | | 43. North Dakota | 13.8 |
| 19. Pennsylvania | 25.0 | | 44. Nevada | 13.5 |
| 20. Arizona | 24.8 | | 45. Connecticut | 13.1 |
| 21. Delaware | 24.1 | | 46. Massachusetts | 11.6 |
| 22. Tennessee | 22.3 | | 47. New Jersey | 11.4 |
| 23. South Dakota | 21.4 | | 48. New York | 6.5 |
| 24. Kentucky | 20.3 | | 49. West Virginia | 4.8 |
| 25. New Mexico | 20.3 | | 50. Mississippi | 2.8 |

SOURCE: Mark Preston, "The 'Most' Representative State: Wisconsin," *CNN*, www.cnn.com/2006/POLITICS/07/27/mg.thu/index.html (July 27, 2006).

communities and states. Besides gay rights, battlegrounds in the culture wars include abortion, pornography, and prayer in schools.

Morality politics tend to involve deeply held values, sometimes connected to religion, and they are less about economics than are many political issues. According to political scientist Elaine Sharp, culture wars have several distinctive features.[52] The issues are highly salient to people, eliciting passionate reactions; they mobilize people across different neighborhoods and racial and ethnic groups; and the ensuing political activism often takes unconventional forms, such as demonstrations. Throughout the country, battle lines have been drawn over issues such as more restrictive abortion laws and displaying the Ten Commandments in public buildings. But the most volatile culture war of the mid-2000s involved same-sex marriage.

The Massachusetts Supreme Court ruled in 2003 that, under the state's constitution, same-sex couples were entitled to enter into marriages, a decision that angered the governor and many Bay State lawmakers. Generally, states bar gay and lesbian couples from marrying: Forty-one states have enacted Defense of Marriage Acts (DOMAs), which define marriage as between a man and a woman; thirty of these states took it one step further and put a definition of marriage in the state constitution. In California, San Francisco's precipitous action led to a 2008 state Supreme Court ruling that same-sex couples had the right to marry in the state. However, a ballot initiative, Proposition 8, which limited marriage to one man and one woman, was passed by the voters later that year. This halted any new same-sex marriages, but those performed prior to the passage of Proposition 8 remained valid. As of 2009, four states had joined Massachusetts in allowing gay marriage: Connecticut, Iowa, New Hampshire, and Vermont. Rhode Island, New York, and Washington, D.C. recognize same-sex marriages from other states, while New Jersey allows civil unions.[53] But no matter what decision a state makes, it leaves in its wake people who are extremely dissatisfied.

One particularly interesting skirmish with culture war overtones broke out in Hamtramck, Michigan, a suburb of Detroit, over the issue of Muslim prayer calls. The city, once dominated by people of Polish ancestry, has a growing Islamic population because immigrants from Bangladesh, Yemen, and Pakistan have settled there. Muslim leaders sought an amendment to the city's noise ordinance to allow the Muslim call to prayer to be broadcast over mosque loudspeakers five times a day. They contended it was a matter of religious freedom and tolerance. The city council voted unanimously to allow the call to prayer. Opponents to the council's action argued that it would be noise pollution; they circulated petitions to put the issue on the ballot. After months of heated rhetoric, Hamtramck voters affirmed the council's action by a margin of 55 percent to 45 percent.[54] As this example shows, these hot-button issues can erupt into full-fledged culture wars, carrying the potential to divide states and localities.

# LINKING CAPACITY TO RESULTS

State and local governments have strengthened their position in the American federal system. On a regular basis, they tackle some of the most pressing problems facing the country. The interaction of three unique characteristics of our fifty-state system—diversity, competitiveness, and resiliency—makes it easier.[55] Consider the *diversity* of the United States. States and their communities have different fiscal capacities and different voter preferences for public services and taxes. As a result, citizens and businesses are offered real choices in taxation and expenditure policies across different jurisdictions.

Diversity is tempered, however, by the natural *competitiveness* of a federal system. No state can afford to be too far out of line with the prevailing thinking on appropriate levels of taxes and expenditures because citizens and businesses may opt to relocate. In essence, each jurisdiction is competing with every other jurisdiction. Such competition over the price and performance of government stabilizes the federal system.

The third characteristic, *resiliency*, captures the ability of state governments to recover from adversity. This feature was certainly put to the test during the economic downturn of 2008–2009. The stresses of that period compelled states to retrench and rethink; the fresh policy ideas that resulted were successful in some instances, unsuccessful in others. But the larger point is that state governments squared their shoulders to meet the challenges head on. Resiliency is a key component.

As one astute observer of the U.S. governmental scene has commented, "Over the past decade, without ever quite admitting it, we have ceased to rely on Congress (or the federal government, for that matter) to deal with our most serious public problems.... [T]he states have been accepting the challenge of dealing with problems that no other level of government is handling."[56] Return to the first page of this chapter and reread Governor Beshear's inspirational words. The twenty-first century began full of challenges, but states and their local governments are taking charge. In the final analysis, that is what increased capacity is all about: results.

## CHAPTER RECAP

- State and local governments are directly involved in our daily lives.

- The story of states and localities over the past two decades has been one of transformation. They have shed their backward ways, reformed their institutions, and emerged as capable and proactive.

- State resurgence is exemplified in improved revenue systems, the expanded scope of state operations, faster diffusion of innovations, more interjurisdictional cooperation, and increased national–state conflict.

- Several persistent challenges dog states and localities: fiscal stress, interjurisdictional competition, and political corruption.

- The United States is becoming more racially and ethnically diverse. The increase in population in Sunbelt states such as Nevada and Arizona outpaces the rest of the nation. Meanwhile, negative growth characterized North Dakota and Louisiana from 2000 to 2008.

- An outbreak of culture wars is redefining the politics of some communities and states.

- As a whole, the states are diverse, competitive, and resilient. Their increased capacity to govern effectively has been sorely tested in the first decade of the twenty-first century.

## Key Terms

| | | |
|---|---|---|
| capacity *(p. 3)* | rainy day funds *(p. 7)* | Frostbelt *(p. 16)* |
| jurisdiction *(p. 4)* | downsize *(p. 11)* | political culture *(p. 17)* |
| federalism *(p. 4)* | transparency *(p. 14)* | culture wars *(p. 19)* |
| proactive *(p. 5)* | Sunbelt *(p. 16)* | |

## Internet Resources

Originally, states were assigned the same (except for the two-letter state abbreviation) type of URL: **www.state.ak.us**. The suffix *gov* was reserved for the federal government. Some states such as Alaska still use this Web address. Beginning in 2003, states were authorized to use *gov* and many states have switched to it. Alabama is an example: **www.alabama.gov**. Other states have opted to do something different, such as Florida's portal at **www.myflorida.com**. The simplest might be Montana's straightforward **mt.gov**.

A website that offers a wealth of policy information about the states, along with links to multistate organizations, national organizations of state officials, and state-based think tanks is **www.stateline.org**, established by the Pew Center on the States.

Since 1933, the Council of State Governments has collected and disseminated information about state institutions, policies, and trends. Its website is **www.csg.org**.

The website of *Governing* magazine, **www.governing.com**, contains up-to-date, in-depth discussions of issues in states and localities.

At **www.census.gov**, the website of the U.S. Bureau of the Census, you can find historical, demographic data on states and localities.

A comprehensive website that will take you to the official websites of states and local governments is **www.usa.gov**.

The website for *State Politics and Policy Quarterly*, a scholarly journal that publishes research on important state-level questions, is **sppq.press. illinois.edu/**.

SOURCE: AP Photo/Ric Feld, File

# Federalism and the States

**2**

A single broad and enduring issue in American federalism transcends all others: What is the proper balance of power and responsibility between the national government and the states? The debate over this profound question was first joined by the Founders in pre-constitutional days and argued between the Federalists and Anti-Federalists. It continues today in the halls of Congress, the federal courts, and the state and local governments, over issues ranging from the mundane to the profound. For instance, which level or branch of government should have the power to determine the right to die? And what should the respective responsibilities of federal, state, and local governments be in the event of an epic natural disaster?

The first question is addressed in the case of Oregon's Death with Dignity Act of 1994, which provides that a terminally ill person, upon receiving the written agreement of two physicians, may ingest prescribed drugs to end his life. In a 1996 referendum, Oregon voters affirmed the controversial law by a 60 percent majority. In November 2001, U.S. Attorney General John Ashcroft authorized the U.S. Drug Enforcement Administration to revoke the license of any physician who prescribed the suicide drugs. Oregon quickly obtained a stay of Ashcroft's order in federal court and sued Ashcroft, a social and religious conservative. The critical issue: Did Ashcroft brazenly usurp state sovereignty and trample on states' rights? Or did the national government properly override the Oregon-established legal right of a terminally ill person to choose the time and means of her own death? U.S. district and federal appeals courts upheld Oregon's law, ruling that Ashcroft had overstepped his authority. The U.S. Supreme Court had the final word on this troubling case in 2006: The Bush administration had acted improperly in seeking to punish Oregon doctors.[1] By then, more than 200 Oregonians had chosen death with dignity.

Natural and man-made disasters such as terrorist attacks, hurricanes, fires, floods, and earthquakes bring to the forefront intergovernmental complexity. The arrival of Hurricane Katrina in New Orleans and adjoining portions of the Louisiana and Mississippi Gulf Coast in 2005 was a terrible event for local residents and a bad time for federalism. Approximately 1,330 lives were lost and $96 billion in property damages were incurred. Reactions to the disaster by all levels of government were disjointed, uncoordinated, and altogether inept. The response by the Bush White House and leaders of the Department of Homeland Security (including the Federal Emergency Management Agency—FEMA) was late and confused. Governor Kathleen Blanco and New Orleans Mayor Ray Nagin were very late in ordering a mandatory evacuation before the storm. What resulted were mass fear, chaos, and loss of life. Katrina spawned a critical analysis of American federalism that carried deep implications for all levels of government.[2]

These are the types of conflicts that define U.S. federalism. As a system for organizing government, federalism has important consequences that often, in ways both direct and hidden, affect our political and personal lives.

# THE CONCEPT OF FEDERALISM

In a nation—a large group of people organized under a single, sovereign government and sharing historical, cultural, and other values—powers and responsibilities can be divided among different levels of government in three ways: through a unitary government, a confederacy, or a federal system. To understand our federal system, we must know how it differs from the other forms of government.

## Unitary, Confederate, and Federal Systems

The large majority of countries (more than 90 percent) have a **unitary system**, in which most if not all legal power rests in the central government. The central government may create or abolish regional or local governments as it sees fit. These subgovernments can exercise only those powers and responsibilities granted to them by the central government. In France, the United Kingdom, Chile, Egypt, and the many other countries with unitary systems, the central government is strong and the regional or local jurisdictions are weak. In the United States, the states themselves function as unitary systems.

A **confederacy** is the opposite of a unitary system. In a confederacy, the central government is weak and the regional governments are powerful. The regional jurisdictions establish a central government to deal with areas of mutual concern, such as national defense and a common currency, but they severely restrict the central government's authority in other areas. If they see fit, they may change or even abolish the central government. The United States

**unitary system**
One in which all government authority is derived from a central government.

**confederacy**
A league of sovereign states in which a limited central government exercises few independent powers.

began as a confederacy, and the southern states formed a new confederacy following secession in 1861.

**federal system**

A means of dividing the power and functions of government between a central government and a specified number of geographically defined regional jurisdictions.

A **federal system** falls somewhere between the unitary and confederate forms in the method by which it divides powers among levels of government. It has a minimum of two governmental levels, each of which derives its powers directly from the people and each of which can act directly on the people within its jurisdiction without permission from any other authority. Each level of government is supreme in the powers assigned to it, and each is protected by a constitution from being destroyed by the other. Thus, federalism is a means of dividing the power and functions of government between a central government and a specified number of geographically defined regional jurisdictions. In effect, people hold dual citizenship, in the national government and in their regional government.

In the U.S. federal system, the regional governments are called states. In others, such as Canada, they are known as provinces. Altogether, there are approximately twenty federal systems in the world.

## The Advantages and Disadvantages of Federalism

As it has evolved in the United States, federalism is a reasonably effective system of government. But it is not perfect, nor is it well suited to the circumstances of most other nations. Ironically, federalism's weaknesses are closely related to its strengths.

1. *A federal system helps manage social and political conflict.* It broadly disperses political power within and among governments, enabling national as well as regional and local concerns to reach the central government. Many venues, or "democratic safety valves," exist for resolving conflicts before they reach the crisis stage. If such conflicts are not addressed satisfactorily, however, they can eventually lead to regional or ethnic conflict on a fearsome scale.

2. *Federalism promotes administrative efficiency.* The wide variety of services demanded by citizens are delivered more efficiently without a large central bureaucracy. From public elementary education to garbage collection, the government closest to the problem seems to work best in adapting public programs to local needs. Yet federalism presents problems in coordinating action across governments and boundaries. Picture trying to get 88,000 squawking and flapping chickens to move in the same direction at once. The confusion and deadly delays in responding to the victims of Hurricane Katrina illustrate this point.

3. *Federalism encourages innovation.* States and localities can customize their policies to accommodate diverse demands and needs—and, indeed, such heterogeneity flourishes. New policies are constantly being tested by the more than 88,000 government "laboratories" that exist throughout the country, thus further encouraging experimentation and flexibility. (The term *laboratory* has become literal in California, Wisconsin, and other states that decided to invest state resources in stem-cell research, in stark contrast to the federal government's funding restrictions during the Bush years). Yet

federalism's many points of involvement can encourage obstruction and delay and result in ineffective national government programs and priorities. Duplication and confusion can be the result. Fifty sets of laws on banking and lending practices can make doing business across state lines tough for an interstate firm.

4. *A federal system maximizes political participation in government.* Citizens have opportunities to participate at all three levels of government through elections, public hearings, and other means. The local and state governments fill almost 1 million offices in regular elections, serving as valuable political training camps for aspiring public leaders. The great majority of presidents and congressional representatives first wet their feet in state or local politics. But such broad participation encourages local biases inimical to national interests. Problems in locating nuclear and hazardous waste disposal facilities readily illustrate this dilemma.

# THE HISTORY OF U.S. FEDERALISM

The men who met in Philadelphia during the hot summer of 1787 to draw up the U.S. Constitution were not wild-eyed optimists, nor were they revolutionaries. In fact, as we'll see in this section, they were consummate pragmatists whose beliefs shaped the new republic and created both the strengths and the weaknesses of our federal system.

## Early History

The Framers of the Constitution held to the belief of English political philosopher Thomas Hobbes that human beings are contentious and selfish. Some of them openly disdained the masses. For example, Gouverneur Morris of New York declared of the American people, "The mob begin to think and reason. Poor reptiles! . . . They bask in the sun, and ere noon they will bite, depend upon it."[3] Most of the Framers agreed that their goal in Philadelphia was to find a means of controlling lower forms of human behavior while still allowing citizens to have a voice in making the laws they were compelled to obey. The "philosopher of the Constitution," James Madison, formulated the problem in terms of factions, groups that pursue their own interests without concern for the interests of society as a whole. Political differences and self-interest, Madison felt, led to the formation of factions, and the Framers' duty was to identify "constitutional devices that would force various interests to check and control one another."[4]

Three practical devices to control factions were placed in the U.S. Constitution. The first was a system of representative government in which citizens would elect individuals who would filter and refine the views of the masses. The second was the division of government into three branches (executive, legislative, and judicial). The legislative body was divided into two houses, each with a check on the activities of the other. Equal in power would be a strong chief executive, with the authority to veto legislative acts, and an independent judiciary. Third, the government was structured as a federal system, in which the most dangerous faction of all—a majority—would be controlled by the sovereign states. Insurrection in one state would be put down by the others, acting through the national government. Madison's ultimate hope was that the new Constitution would "check interest with interest, class with class, faction with faction, and one branch of government with another in a harmonious system of mutual frustration."[5]

Sometimes today there appears to be more frustration than harmony, but Madison's dream did come true. The U.S. federal system is the longest-lived constitutional government on earth. Its dimensions and activities are vastly different from what the Framers envisioned, but it remains a dynamic, adaptable, responsive, and usually effective system for conducting the affairs of government.

## The Move Toward Federalism

The drive for independence from the British crown by the thirteen American colonies was in large measure a reaction to "a history of repeated injuries and usurpations" and "absolute tyranny" (according to the Declaration of Independence) under a British unitary system of government.

The immediate struggle for independence left little time to develop a consensus on the form of government best suited to the future needs of American society. Hence, the move toward federalism was gradual. The first independent government established in America was a confederacy; thus Americans tested two types of government—unitary and confederate—before deciding permanently on the third, federalism.

**The Articles of Confederation**  During the War for Independence, the colonies, now called states, agreed to establish a confederation. A unicameral (one-house) Congress was created to exercise the authority of the new national government. Its powers were limited to the authority to wage war, make peace, enter into treaties and alliances, appoint and receive ambassadors, regulate Indian affairs, and create a postal system. The states held all powers not expressly granted to the Congress. The governing document was the Articles of Confederation (effective from 1776 to 1787).

The inherent weaknesses of the confederacy quickly became apparent. The states had significant authority within their own borders, but the federal government was unable to carry out its basic responsibilities or honor its financial obligations because it did not have the power to force the states to pay their share of the bill. The lack of national authority to regulate either domestic or international commerce led to discriminatory trade practices by the states. Anarchy and even warfare between the fractious states were a very real concern.[6] Indeed, the key event that brought together representatives of the states to draft a constitution for a new type of government was Shays' Rebellion. Daniel Shays, a Revolutionary War officer, led an armed revolt of New England farmers who were fighting mad about debt and taxes. The weak central government had difficulty putting down the rebellion.

**The Constitutional Convention** How did the Framers create a long-lasting and successful system of government that seems to have the best features of both unitary and confederate forms? We could say, somewhat naively, that they carefully integrated the best theories of various political philosophers into a grand plan for government. And, indeed, they were familiar with the early developments in political and theological federalism in Europe and the ancient world. They were aware of tribal confederations among the Native Americans and, most important, the Framers were well informed by their own colonial experience.[7] Truly the Framers were learned men, well schooled in the theories of politics, and most of them did believe in designing a government that would serve the people and ensure justice. But above all they were pragmatists; they developed a practical compromise on the key issues of the day, including the proper role of the national government and the states. The reconciliation of the interests and powers of the states with the need for a strong national government, what Madison called a "middle ground," was purely an American invention. Today, the United States stands as the prototypical federal system. It is our most distinctive political contribution.

Delegates representing each of the states assembled at the constitutional convention. Here, the self-interests of the large states and the small states diverged. The large states supported the Virginia Plan, which proposed a strong central government spearheaded by a powerful bicameral Congress. Because representation in both chambers was to be based on population, larger states would be favored. The smaller states countered with the New Jersey Plan, which put forward a one-house legislature composed of an equal number of representatives from each state. There were other differences between the two plans (e.g., the Virginia Plan had a single chief executive, whereas the New Jersey Plan had a multimember executive), but the issue of state representation was paramount.

The New Jersey Plan was defeated by a vote of 7 to 3, but the smaller states refused to give in. Finally, Connecticut moved that the lower house (the House of Representatives) be based on the population of each state and the upper house (the Senate) be based on equal state membership. This Great Compromise was approved, ensuring that a faction of large states would not dominate the small ones.

The Framers reached another important set of compromises by specifying the powers of the new central government and the powers to be granted (and denied) to the states. The **enumerated (delegated) powers** were listed in the Constitution along with state government powers and **concurrent powers** to be exercised by both the national and state governments. Figure 2.1 illustrates the constitutional distribution of powers.

## State-Centered Federalism

The first decades under the new Constitution witnessed a clash between profoundly different views on governing. George Washington, John Adams,

**enumerated (delegated) powers**
Those expressly given to the national government, primarily in Article I, Section 8, of the Constitution.

**concurrent powers**
Those granted by the Constitution to both the national and the state governments.

**Constitutional Distribution of Powers**

**National Government Powers:**
- Coin money
- Regulate interstate and foreign commerce
- Tax imports and exports
- Make treaties
- Make all laws "necessary and proper" to fulfill responsibilities
- Make war
- Regulate postal system

**Powers Denied:**
- Tax state exports
- Change state boundaries
- Impose religious tests
- Pass laws that conflict with the Bill of Rights

**Concurrent Powers:**
- Tax
- Borrow money
- Charter banks and corporations
- Seize property (eminent domain)
- Make and enforce laws Administer a judiciary

**State Government Powers:**
- Conduct elections
- Regulate intrastate commerce
- Establish republican forms of state and local government
- Protect public health, safety, and morals
- All powers not delegated to the national government or denied to the state by the Constitution

**Powers Denied:**
- Tax imports and exports
- Coin money
- Enter into treaties
- Impair a legal contract
- Enter compacts with other states without congressional consent

**nation-centered federalism**

Theory holding that the national government is dominant over the states.

**state-centered federalism**

Theory holding that the national government represents a voluntary compact or agreement between the states, which retain a dominant position.

Alexander Hamilton, and their fellow Federalists favored national supremacy, or **nation-centered federalism.** Opposed to is idea were Thomas Jefferson and the Republicans, who preferred **state-centered federalism.** Much of the debate then, as today, concerned the meaning of the **reserved powers** clause of the **Tenth Amendment** to the Constitution. Ratified in 1791, the Tenth Amendment gave support to the states by openly acknowledging that "the powers not delegated to the United States by the Constitution, nor prohibited by it to the States, are reserved to the states respectively, or to the people." But in fact, the Tenth Amendment was an early omen of the eventual triumph of nation-centered federalism. As pointed out by constitutional scholar Walter Berns, if the states were intended to be the dominant federal actors, they would not have needed the Tenth Amendment to remind them.[8]

Those who defended the power of the states under the Constitution—that is, state-centered federalism—saw the Constitution as a *compact*, an agreement, among the sovereign states, which maintained their sovereignty, or the right of self-governance. The powers of the national government enumerated in the Constitution were to be interpreted narrowly, and the states were obliged to resist any unconstitutional efforts by the national government to extend its authority.[9]

This **compact theory** of federalism became the foundation for states' rights arguments. In particular, it became central to the fight of the southern states against what they considered discrimination by the North. During the 1820s, a national tariff seriously damaged the economy of the southern states. The slave-based agricultural economy of the South had already begun a protracted period of decline while the North prospered. The tariff, which placed high taxes on imported manufactured goods from Europe, hit the South hard because it produced few manufactured goods. Rightly or wrongly, the southerners blamed the "tariff of abominations" for many of their economic problems. They also, of course, staunchly resisted calls for the abolition of slavery.

In 1828, Vice President John C. Calhoun of South Carolina asserted that the United States was composed of sovereign states united in a national government through a compact. The powers of the national government had been entrusted to it by the states, not permanently handed over. Calhoun claimed that a state thus had complete authority to reinterpret or even nullify (reject) the law or the compact, making it invalid within that state's borders. Most important, Calhoun declared that if a large majority of the states sided with the national government, the nullifying state had the right to *secede*, or withdraw from the Union. (Indeed, until the Civil War, when Americans referred to "my country," they usually meant their state—not the United States).

In 1832, after an additional tariff was enacted by the national government, South Carolina nullified it. President Andrew Jackson and the Congress threatened military action to force the state to comply with the law, and Jackson even threatened to hang Calhoun, who by this time had resigned from the vice presidency.[10]

Ultimately, eleven southern states (led by South Carolina) did secede from the Union, at which point they formed the Confederate States of America. The long conflict between state sovereignty and national supremacy, and the question of slavery as well, was definitively resolved by five years of carnage in such places as Antietam, Shiloh, and Gettysburg, followed by the eventual readmittance of the renegade states to the Union. The Civil War, often referred to in the South as The War Between the States, remains the single most violent episode in American history, resulting in more than 620,000 deaths (more than in all our other wars combined) and countless civilian tragedies.

## The Growth of National Power Through the Constitution and the Judiciary

After the Civil War, a *nation-centered* concept of federalism evolved. For the most part, the national government has become the primary governing force, with the states and localities generally following its lead. Recently, the states have been inclined to act more independently, but their power vis-à-vis the national government has been eroded by the Supreme Court's interpretations of key sections of the Constitution.

**The National Supremacy Clause** Article III of the Constitution established the U.S. Supreme Court. The supremacy of national law and the

**reserved powers**
Those powers residing with the states by virtue of the Tenth Amendment.

**Tenth Amendment**
The amendment to the Constitution, ratified in 1791, reserving powers to the states.

**compact theory**
A theory of federalism that became the foundation for states' rights arguments.

**national supremacy clause**

Article VI of the Constitution, which makes national laws superior to state laws.

**necessary and proper clause**

Portion of Article I, Section 8, of the Constitution that authorizes Congress to enact all laws "necessary and proper" to carry out its responsibilities.

**implied powers**

Those that are not expressly granted by the Constitution but that are inferred from the enumerated powers.

**commerce clause**

Part of Article I, Section 8, of the U.S. Constitution, which gives vests Congress the power to regulate trade with foreign countries and among the states.

Constitution is constitutionally grounded in the **national supremacy clause** (Article VI), which provides that the national laws and the Constitution are the supreme laws of the land. Later decisions of the Supreme Court established its role as arbiter of any legal disputes between the national government and the states.

**The Necessary and Proper Clause** The fourth chief justice of the United States, John Marshall, was the architect of the federal judiciary during his thirty-four years on the bench. Almost single-handedly, he made the judiciary a co-equal branch of government. Several of his rulings laid the groundwork for the expansion of national governmental power. In the case of *McCulloch v. Maryland* (1819), two issues were before the bench: the right of the national government to establish a national bank and the right of the state of Maryland to tax that bank, once it was established.[11] The secretary of the treasury, Alexander Hamilton, had proposed a bill that would allow Congress to charter such a bank for depositing national revenues and facilitating the borrowing of funds. Those who wanted to limit the power of the national government, such as James Madison and Thomas Jefferson, argued that the Constitution did not provide the government with the specific authority to charter and operate a national bank.

The crux of the issue was how to interpret the **necessary and proper clause**. The final power delegated to Congress under Article I, Section 8, is the power "to make all laws which shall be *necessary and proper* for carrying into execution the foregoing powers, and all other powers vested by this Constitution in the Government of the United States" (emphasis added). Jefferson argued that *necessary* meant "indispensable," whereas Hamilton asserted that it merely meant "convenient." Hamilton argued that in addition to the enumerated powers, Congress possessed **implied powers**. In the case of the national bank, valid congressional action was implied through the powers of taxation, borrowing, and making currency found in Article I, Section 8.

Meanwhile, the state of Maryland had levied a tax on the new national bank, which was located within its borders, and the bank had refused to pay. The bank dispute was eventually heard by Chief Justice Marshall. Marshall was persuaded by the Hamiltonian point of view. Marshall pointed out that nowhere in the Constitution does it stipulate that the only powers that may be carried out are those expressly described in Article I, Section 8. Thus, he ruled that Congress had the implied power to establish the bank and that Maryland had no right to tax it. Significantly, *McCulloch v. Maryland* meant that the national government had an almost unlimited right to decide how to exercise its delegated powers. Over the years, Congress has enacted a great many laws that are only vaguely, if at all, associated with the enumerated powers and that stretch the phrase *necessary and proper* beyond its logical limits.

**The Commerce Clause** Another important ruling of the Marshall Court extended national power through an expansive interpretation of the **commerce clause** (often referred to as the interstate commerce clause) of Article I, Section 8. The commerce clause gives Congress the power "to regulate commerce with foreign nations, and among the several states, and with the Indian tribes." In *Gibbons v. Ogden* (1824),[12] two important questions were addressed by Marshall: What *is* commerce? And how broadly should Congress' power to regulate commerce be interpreted?

The United States was just developing a national economy as the Industrial Revolution expanded. National oversight was needed, along with regulation of emerging transportation networks and of state activities related to the passage of goods across state lines (interstate commerce). The immediate question was whether New York could grant a monopoly to run a steamship service between New York and New Jersey. What was Marshall's answer? No, it could not. He defined commerce broadly and held that Congress' power to regulate commerce applied not only to traffic across state boundaries but, in some cases, also to traffic of goods, merchandise, and people *within* a state. The Court further expanded the meaning of "commerce" in various rulings during the twentieth century.

**The General Welfare Clause** The **general welfare clause** of Article I, Section 8, states that "the Congress shall have power to lay and collect taxes, duties, imposts, and excises to pay the debts and provide for the common defense and *general welfare* of the United States" (emphasis added). Before the Great Depression of the 1930s, it was believed that poor people were responsible for their own plight and that it was up to private charity and state and local governments to provide limited assistance. The Great Depression brought massive unemployment and poverty throughout the country and made necessary a major change in the national government's attitude. Despite their best efforts, the states and localities were staggered by the tremendous loss of tax revenues and the pleas to help poor and displaced persons obtain food and shelter. Franklin D. Roosevelt, who won the presidency in 1932, set in motion numerous New Deal programs that completely redefined federal responsibility for the general welfare. These programs, such as Social Security, propelled the national government into a position of dominance within the federal system and extended into fields previously within the province of the states, the localities, and the private sector.

> **general welfare clause**
> The portion of Article I, Section 8, of the Constitution that provides for the general welfare of the United States.

**The Fourteenth Amendment** Ratified by the states in 1868, the **Fourteenth Amendment** had the effect of giving former slaves official status as citizens of the United States and of the state in which they lived. It included two other important principles as well: *due process* and *equal protection* under the laws. The federal courts have used the Fourteenth Amendment to increase national power over the states in several critical fields, especially with regard to civil rights, criminal law, and election practices.

The judiciary's application of the Fourteenth Amendment to state and local governments is illustrated by many contemporary cases that have, for example, ordered local officials to hike property taxes to pay for school desegregation (*Missouri v. Jenkins*), and required formal hearings for welfare recipients before benefits are terminated (*Goldberg v. Kelly*).

> **Fourteenth Amendment**
> Enacted in 1868, this amendment contains citizenship rights, due process, and equal protection provisions that states must apply to all citizens.

## The Growth of National Power Through Congress

The U.S. Supreme Court has not been the only force behind nation-centered federalism; Congress has worked hand in hand with the judiciary. The commerce clause represents a good example. Given the simple authority to control or eliminate state barriers to trade across state lines, Congress now regulates commercial activities within a state's boundaries as well, as long as these activities purportedly have substantial national consequences (examples include banking, insurance, and corporate fraud). Congress has also used the authority of the commerce clause to expand national power into fields only vaguely related to commerce, such as protecting endangered species. The states have made literally hundreds of legal challenges to such exercise of the commerce power. Until recently, almost all of these were resolved by the U.S. Supreme Court in favor of the national government.

**Taxing and Spending Power** Probably, the most controversial source of the rise in national power in recent years has been the use of the *taxing and spending power* by Congress to extend its influence over the state and local governments. Under Article I, Section 8, Congress holds the power to tax and spend to provide for the common defense and general welfare. But the **Sixteenth Amendment**, which grants Congress the power to tax the income of individuals and corporations, moved the center of financial power from the states to Washington, D.C. Through the income tax, the national government raises huge amounts of money. A portion of this money is sent to the states and localities. Because Congress insists on some sort of accountability in the way state and local governments spend these funds, attached to federal grants are various conditions to which the recipients must adhere if they are to receive the money. These conditions include requirements for recipient governments to match national dollars with some portion of state contributions. (The interstate highway program requires one state dollar for every ten federal dollars, for example). Congress also imposes mandates and regulations directly related to the purposes of the individual grant, such as forcing the states to adopt national policies on seat belts, speed limits, and driver's licenses (noncomplying states face the loss of federal transportation dollars).

**Sixteenth Amendment**

Enacted in 1913, this amendment grants the national government the power to levy income taxes.

**Federal Pre-emption** The national government has also seized power through the process known as **federal pre-emption**. The legal basis for pre-emption is Article VI of the Constitution, the national supremacy clause. Whenever a state law conflicts with a national law, the national law is dominant.

Congressional passage of a national law that supersedes existing state legislation is directly pre-emptive. An example is the Real ID Act of 2006, which imposed national requirements on how states must validate personal identification when issuing driver's licenses. Designed to fight terrorism by imposing more strenuous requirements for obtaining a driver's license, Real ID was so unpopular that Washington, Montana, and nine other states refused to cooperate with the law. A game of intergovernmental "chicken" ensued when the

**federal pre-emption**

The principle that national laws take precedence over state laws.

Department of Homeland Security (DHS) threatened to refuse to accept those states' driver's licenses to board airplanes or enter federal buildings. For their part, states pointed out this unfunded mandate posed a threat to personal privacy and would require states to issue new, more costly licenses to all drivers to the tune of some $14.6 billion.[13] Finally, DHS blinked and granted all fifty states a five-year extension to 2014 for compliance. Meanwhile, state officials sought and gained approval to adopt their own "Enhanced Driver's License" program at significantly lower cost.[14] A series of pre-emptive actions during the early 2000s by the Bush administration drove more than thirty states to draft "sovereignty resolutions" instructing the federal government to "back off."[15]

**Smothering (Then Resuscitating) the Tenth Amendment** Actions by the Congress and the federal courts have gradually undermined the Tenth Amendment, which reserves to the states all powers not specifically granted to the national government or prohibited to the states. In fact, it is very difficult to identify any field of state activity today not intruded on by the national government today. Although the Tenth Amendment is a declaration of the original division of powers between nation and states under the Constitution, the configuration is hardly descriptive of American federalism today because Congress has forced the states to surrender more and more of their erstwhile rights and privileges.[16]

The Supreme Court has sent mixed signals on the relevance of the Tenth Amendment. A good example of the Court's fickle federalism involves the Fair Labor Standards Act (FLSA). Following forty years of case law that essentially relegated the Tenth Amendment to the basement of federalism, the Court surprisingly ruled in favor of state and local governments in the 1976 case of *National League of Cities v. Usery*. At issue was the constitutionality under the commerce clause of the 1974 amendments to the FLSA, which extended federal minimum wage and maximum hour requirements to state and local employees. In this case, the Court said that Congress did not have the constitutional right to impose wage and hour requirements on employees carrying out basic—or integral—functions, such as law enforcement or firefighting.[17]

But just nine years later, the Court reversed that decision in *Garcia v. San Antonio Metropolitan Transit Authority*. A spate of litigation had not been able to resolve the issue of just which state and local activities ertr "integral." So the Court overturned its findings in *Usery* and once again applied federal wage and hour laws to nonnational governments—in this specific instance, to a mass transit system run by the city of San Antonio.[18] What really offended the states was the written opinion of the Court, in which it excused itself from such future controversies involving state claims against congressional and executive branch power exercised under the commerce clause. Now Congress alone, with little or no judicial oversight, would be allowed to determine, through the political process, how extensively it would intrude on what had previously been state and local prerogatives. One dissenting Supreme Court justice wrote that "all that stands between the remaining essentials of state sovereignty and Congress is the latter's underdeveloped capacity for self-restraint."[19] In the view of some critics, the states were relegated to the status of any other special-interest group and the Tenth Amendment was irrelevant. Other critics more optimistically observed that the narrow 5-to-4 decision could be revisited by a more conservative Supreme Court at a later date.[20]

Sure enough, in 1995, the Court reaffirmed the Tenth Amendment in *U.S. v. Lopez* by recognizing a limit to Congress's power over interstate commerce. Ironically, this case also involved San Antonio, where a high-school student, Alfonso Lopez, was arrested for bringing a handgun to school. He was charged with violating the Gun Free School Zones Act of 1990, which banned the possession of a firearm within 1,000 feet of a school. Here, the Court ruled that in this instance Congress had unconstitutionally extended its power to regulate commerce because there was no connection between the gun law and interstate commerce.[21]

The Court continued to recalibrate the scales of power in favor of the states in a series of rulings beginning in 1997. First, the Court upheld states' authority to incarcerate sexual predators in mental institutions after their criminal sentences had been served.[22] Next, the Court ruled that Congress offended "the very principle of separate state sovereignty" by requiring local police to conduct background checks on people who want to purchase handguns.[23] More recently, the court affirmed the right of state and local governments to seize private land for commercial development[24] and the authority of states to grant tax breaks and other financial inducements to attract and keep businesses.[25]

Recent rulings based on the Eleventh Amendment have revived the notion of the sovereign immunity of the states. According to this doctrine, which dates back to the Middle Ages, a king (the state) cannot be sued without his (its) consent (the Eleventh Amendment protects states from lawsuits by citizens of other states or foreign nations). Supreme Court decisions have upheld the sovereign immunity of the states from being sued in federal courts in cases involving lawsuits by Indian tribes,[26] patent infringement when a state ventures into commercial activities,[27] and discrimination against older and disabled employees[28] workers. The Court also protected the states against private complaints taken before federal agencies.[29] But in another case, the Court restricted the states' Eleventh Amendment immunity under the Americans with Disabilities Act.[30]

**A New Era of State Resurgence?** The Supreme Court under Chief Justice William Rehnquist (1986–2005) clearly and undeniably positioned itself on the side of the states in most conflicts with the national government. However, the Supreme Court does not decide unilaterally in favor of the states in all cases, notwithstanding one justice's complaint that the majority has become "[a] mindless dragon that indiscriminately chews gaping holes in federal statutes." For example, the Court limited the authority of the states to regulate tobacco advertising[31] and ruled against state prohibitions on direct consumer purchases of wines from out-of-state vendors. As shown by the Court's willingness to overturn the Florida Supreme Court in issues concerning the ballot counting in the 2000 presidential race,[32] ideology and partisanship sometimes trump federalism. Court watchers are still studying with interest the direction that Chief Justice John Roberts will take on federalism issues.

During the Rehnquist Court, a large majority of the Court's decisions in federalism cases were by a fragile 5-to-4 margin. Two pro-state justices, William

Rehnquist and Sandra Day O'Connor, left the bench in 2005. The federalism feelings of new Chief Justice John Roberts and Justice Samuel Alito are not yet known. But the narrow pro-state balance shows early signs of tilting in the opposite direction. For instance, on grounds of interference with Interstate Commerce, a 2008 ruling struck down state laws requiring FedEx, UPS, and other firms delivering interstate tobacco shipments to ensure that recipients are of legal age.[33]

American federalism, by its nature, is ambiguous: It "was born in ambiguity, it institutionalizes ambiguity in our form of government, and changes in it tend to be ambiguous, too."[34] Judicial intervention in the affairs of state and local governments has not rendered them mere administrative appendages or relics of the past. But federal intrusions into the affairs of state and local governments continue to be burdensome and unwelcome. The Tenth and Eleventh Amendments have been useful weapons for fending off federal encroachments on the power of state and local officials, but those weapons can be shattered by a single justices' change of heart or a new appointment to the bench.

# MODELS OF FEDERALISM

Perceptions of the role of the states in the federal system have shifted from time to time throughout our history. Those who study the federal system have generally described these perceptions through various models or metaphors, which attempt to present federalism's complexity in a form that is readily understandable. Such models have been used both to enhance understanding and, when opportunities arise, to pursue ideological and partisan objectives. One complete inventory uncovered 326 models of federalism,[35] but only the best-known ones are reviewed here to demonstrate that the U.S. federal system and people's perceptions of it change over time.

## Dual Federalism (1787–1932)

The model of **dual federalism** holds that the national and state governments are sovereign and equal within their respective spheres of authority as set forth in the Constitution. The national government exercises those powers specifically designated to it, and the remainder are reserved for the states. The nation and the states are viewed as primarily competitive, not cooperative, in their relationships with one another. The metaphor is that of a layer cake, with two separate colored layers, one on top of the other.

**dual federalism**
Model in which the responsibilities and activities of the national and state governments are separate and distinct.

Dual federalism, which has its roots in the compact theory, was dominant for the first 145 years of U.S. federalism, although the Civil War and other events led to substantial modifications of the model.[36] Until 1860, the functions of the national government remained largely restricted to the delegated powers. Federal financial assistance to the states was extremely limited. The states had the dominant influence on the everyday lives of their citizens, acting almost unilaterally in areas such as elections, education, economic development, labor relations, and criminal and family law.[37] After the Civil War shattered secession and dealt the compact theory of state-centered federalism a death blow, the nation-centered view became paramount.

## Cooperative Federalism (1933–1964)

The selection of a specific date for the demise of dual federalism is rather subjective, but 1933, when Franklin D. Roosevelt became president, is a reasonable estimate. Roosevelt's New Deal buried dual federalism by expanding national authority over commerce, taxation, and the economy.

**cooperative federalism**

A model of federalism that stresses the linkages and joint arrangements among the three levels of government.

**Cooperative federalism** recognizes the sharing of responsibilities and financing by all levels of government. Beginning with the Great Depression, the national government increasingly cooperated with states and localities to provide jobs and social welfare, develop the nation's infrastructure, and promote economic development.

The cooperative aspects of this era were measured in governmental finances. The national government spent huge amounts of money to alleviate the ravages of the Depression and to get the U.S. economic machinery back into gear. (Comparisons are made with federal approaches to combating the sharp national economic recession that began in 2008). Total federal expenditures rose from 2.5 percent of the gross national product (GNP) in 1929 to 18.7 percent just thirty years later, far surpassing the growth in state and local spending during the same period. The number of federal grants-in-aid rose from twelve in 1932, with a value of $193 million, to twenty-six in 1937, with a value of $2.66 billion. A substantial amount of the federal aid was sent directly to local governments, particularly counties and school districts. The variety of grant programs also exploded, with grants for maternal and child health, old-age assistance, fire control, treatment of venereal disease, public housing, road and bridge construction, and wildlife conservation.

## Contemporary Variations on Cooperative Federalism (Since 1964)

The broad theme of cooperative federalism has many variations. All of them stress intergovernmental sharing. Among these variations are creative federalism and new federalism.

**creative federalism**

A model of cooperative federalism in which many new grants-in-aid, including direct national-local financial arrangements, were made.

**Creative federalism** was devised by President Lyndon B. Johnson to promote his dream of a Great Society. Johnson sought to build the Great Society through a massive national government attack on the most serious problems facing the nation: poverty, crime, poor health care, and inadequate education, among others. The vehicle for the attack was the federal grant-in-aid. More than 200 new grants were put into place during the five years of Johnson's presidency. Johnson's policy of vast government spending bypassed the states in distributing funds directly to cities and counties for many of the new programs, a major change. Understandably, the states did not appreciate losing influence over how localities could spend their national dollars.

**New federalism** is a model that has been employed with separate but related meanings during different presidencies. The new federalism initiated by President Richard Nixon was intended to restore power to the states and localities and to improve intergovernmental arrangements for delivering services. Among the major policy changes brought about by the Nixon administration were the establishment of ten regional councils to coordinate national program administration across the country and the granting to states and localities greater flexibility in program spending and decision making.

Ronald Reagan's brand of new federalism, like Nixon's version, sought to give more power and program authority to states and localities, at least in theory. However, Reagan's main goal—to shrink the size of the national government—soon became obvious. Reagan's new federalism initiative won congressional approval to merge fifty-seven categorical grants into nine new block grants and to eliminate another sixty categorical grants. The states got more authority, but the funding for the new block grants decreased almost 25 percent from the previous year's allocation for the separate categorical grants.[38]

The president and his congressional allies chipped away steadily at other grant programs in an effort to shrink the size of government and also terminated revenue sharing. Called *general revenue sharing* (GRS) when enacted during the Nixon administration, this program provided funds, with no strings attached, to state and general-purpose local governments (cities, counties, towns, and townships). It was discontinued largely because of the mounting national budget deficit and Congress's desire to exert greater control over, and take more credit for, the way federal monies were spent. A new form of GRS, popularly known as the "stimulus plan," was adopted by Congress in 2009 to help bail out the states from their sinking economic ships.

The Reagan legacy lived on with George H. W. Bush (senior) in the White House. Although the style was different—in the view of many state and local officials, the first Bush administration was more sympathetic—the substance remained the same.[39] The Bush administration continued emphasizing the sorting out of national, state, and local responsibilities in areas such as transportation and education.

By 1994, with the election of Republican majorities in the U.S. House and Senate and also the election of many new Republican governors, new federalism came back in style with impressive force. The new federalists, whose ranks included many Democrats as well, sought once again to sort out intergovernmental responsibilities. For the first time in recent memory, the states and localities were basically united and

> **new federalism**
> A model that represents a return of powers and responsibilities to the states.

Obama signing stimulus 2009 or American Recovery and Reinvestment Act.
*SOURCE: Jim Watson/AFP/Getty Images*

working together through a coalition of government interest groups, including the National Governors' Association and the National League of Cities, to design smaller, more efficient government with greater program and policy flexibility for the states and localities.

**devolution**

The delegating of power and programs from the federal government to state and local governments.

This planned delegating of power from the federal to state and local governments is termed **devolution**. The constellation of supporters for devolution is impressive. The governors, acting as individuals and through the National Governors' Association, found a sympathetic President Clinton and congressional majority, and a Supreme Court increasingly likely to rule in favor of state authority. Public opinion is consistently in favor of greater state and local government authority. Public opinion polls consistently show that citizens believe the state and local governments do a better job than the national government in spending money and delivering services.[40] Together, these powerful forces for devolution reversed more than a century of centralizing tendencies in U.S. federalism. This trend was so striking that it earned the moniker "devolution revolution."

The views of the second president (George W.) Bush were poorly articulated, but actions of his administration and of Republican supporters in Congress pre-empted state authority over school testing systems, driver's license procedures, and right-to-die decisions; obstructed state laws that permit the medical use of marijuana; and imposed burdensome new homeland security requirements on the states; among other pre-emptive acts. The predominance of business interests in Washington, D.C., appeared to have deterred devolution through what one writer calls "the law of political physics—that for every flurry of state and local business regulations, there is an equal and opposite" effort by business to counter it in the nation's capital.[41] The centralizing tendencies of the "War on Terror" has served as a convenient justification for other centralizing actions by President Bush and congressional supporters,[42] including citizen surveillance, nationalization of the state national guards, and various mandates that pulled power into the White House. By 2008, state dissatisfaction had reached such a peak that governors from both political parties denounced the "coercive federalism" of Washington, D.C., and increasingly pushed back by roundly criticizing some actions, ignoring others, and litigating still others.[43]

# INTERGOVERNMENTAL RELATIONS

Cooperative federalism demands positive interactions among governments at all levels. Whatever the short-term trend of federal-state-local relations, cooperative activities are constantly increasing. For that matter, so are relationships between the states and the Indian American tribes.

## Tribal Governments

With the arrival of the Europeans, the estimated 7–10 million people who lived in what is now the United States soon were severely depleted by warfare, disease, and famine. Hundreds of treaties, statutes, and other agreements notwithstanding, the

Native Americans were eventually deprived of their traditional lands and isolated on reservations. Today, some 2.5 million people identify themselves as Native American, belonging to 557 recognized tribes. About one-third of them continue to live on tribal reservations, mostly in the western portion of the United States. The Navajo Nation, for instance, has a population of more than 250,000 and covers some 17 million acres extending from northwest New Mexico to northeast Arizona and southeast Utah. At the other extreme of the tribal spectrum are the Mashantucket Pequots. Registering just thirty-five to forty members with "only the barest trace of Indian descent"[44] when officially recognized by the federal government in the 1990s, the Pequots today occupy several hundred acres in Connecticut, where they operate Foxwoods Resort Casino—the largest and most profitable such establishment in North America. On average, however, Native Americans are the poorest and least healthy group in the United States.

Tribes are semisovereign nations exercising self-government on their reservations. They are under the general authority and supervision of Congress and are subject to the federal courts and the U.S. Bill of Rights, but their legal relationship with the states is complex. Tribal governments are permitted to regulate their internal affairs, hold elections, and enforce their own laws, codes, and constitutions under congressional supervision. States are generally prevented from taxing or regulating tribes or extending judicial power over them. Off the reservation, however, Native Americans are, with some exceptions such as local hunting and fishing rights, subject to the same laws as any other state residents. They have the right to vote in tribal, federal, and state elections.

Recently, the tribes and the states have adopted a more consultative relationship[45] to pursue certain interests, such as fishing and hunting rights and regulation of reservation gaming. The highly lucrative gaming enterprises of some tribes have advanced tribal political interests and clout by providing financial resources to politicians and others.[46]

Occasionally, however, interactions among tribal governments, the state, and nearby local governments are testy. Actions concerning land use may conflict with local zoning or state environmental policy. The tax-free sale of gasoline, alcohol, and tobacco products on the reservation diminishes state sales tax revenues. Tribes seek to recover ancestral lands from present occupants. And tribal casinos sometimes offer games that are prohibited under state law. When conflicts arise, states and tribal governments may sort out their differences through compacts. Otherwise, Congress may be asked to enter the fray.

## Interstate Cooperation

**Cooperation Under the Constitution** Four formal provisions exist for cooperation among the states:

1. *The full faith and credit clause* of the Constitution binds every citizen of every state to the laws and policies of other states. This means, among many other things, that a person who has a legitimate debt in North Dakota will be made to pay even if he moves to Montana. Crossing a state boundary does not alter a legal obligation. The courts have interpreted full faith and credit to apply to contracts, wills, divorces, and many other legalities. The

clause does not, however, extend to criminal judgments. Interesting tests of the full faith and credit clause are arising from civil union and gay marriage laws enacted in a growing number of states, including Vermont, Massachusetts, New Hampshire, and California. What should happen when a same-sex married couple from one of these states seeks to have their status recognized in Alabama or one of the other states that have enacted laws denying recognition to same-sex marriages? Can a gay couple obtain a divorce in another state? Early test cases, along with laws in forty-one states abolishing marriage except between a man and a woman, indicated that for nonresidents, the answer to both questions is no.[47] But in 2008, New York, which had not yet legalized gay marriage, opted to recognize same-sex marriages performed in other jurisdictions, including Canada.[48]

2. *The interstate rendition clause* begins where full faith and credit leave off, covering persons convicted of criminal violations. Governors are required to extradite (return) fugitives to the state in which they were found guilty or are under indictment (although in certain cases they refuse).

3. *The privileges and immunities clause* states that "the citizens of each state shall be entitled to all privileges and immunities of citizens in the several states." This clause was intended by the Framers to prevent any state from discriminating against citizens of another state who happen to be traveling or temporarily dwelling outside their own state's borders. Of course, states do discriminate against nonresidents in matters such as out-of-state tuition, hunting and fishing license fees, and residency requirements for voting. The Supreme Court has upheld these and other minor discrepancies, as long as the "fundamental rights" of nonresidents are not violated.

4. Finally, the *interstate compact clause* authorizes the states to negotiate compacts, which are binding agreements between two or more states that address important cross-boundary issues. Early interstate compacts were used to settle boundary disputes. About 175 of them are in effect today in various areas, including pest control, riverboat gambling, and education.[49] Twenty-six compacts govern rights over interstate waters. Engaging Federalism: *Water Wars* describes recent water rights efforts.

**Informal Cooperation Among the States** Interstate cooperation can be facilitated through several informal methods. One example is the establishment of regional interstate commissions such as the Appalachian Regional Commission (ARC), which was created by federal law in 1965 to attack poverty in the states of Appalachia. Another example is found in the Mississippi Delta region, where several states adopted a ten-year economic development plan to help pull the area out of its own cycle of poverty.

In addition, states have developed uniform laws to help manage common problems ranging from child support to Medicaid cheating. Interstate cooperation also occurs through information sharing among elected and appointed officials and the organizations to which they belong, such as the National Governors' Association and the National Conference of State Legislatures. It may take place in legal actions, as demonstrated by state attorneys general who

## Engaging Federalism

## Water Wars

Vital for human and farm animal consumption, fishing and shell fishing, industry, electric power generation, transportation, and many other critical uses, water has elicited interstate disputes since the earliest days of the Republic. Such conflicts have been settled in a variety of ways including memoranda of understanding, enactment of identical or similar laws, voluntary associations, and litigation before the U.S. Supreme Court.

But water wars continue to rage as population increases and drought appears more frequently and persistently in some parts of the United States. Usually, states can resolve their concerns and differences rather informally. In more complex cases involving more than two disputants, the interstate compact is the method of choice. Twenty-seven interstate compacts have been ratified by states and Congress to address water issues. Recent examples include the Great Lakes Compact (eight states and two Canadian provinces) and the Colorado River Compact (seven states). But what if the states cannot reach an acceptable solution to water problems?

When the states cannot settle their own differences, the federal government becomes final and binding arbitrator. Although Congress has the power to act through statute, the most likely venue is the federal courts. After a seventeen-year fight over three shared rivers could not be resolved, Alabama, Florida, and Georgia went to court with a case both contentious and convoluted. The U.S. Army Corps of Engineers signed a 2003 agreement to boost Georgia's portion of Lake Lanier, a large reservoir that provides drinking water to northern Georgia, including megacity Atlanta. But Alabama and Florida depend on Lake Lanier water for industry, fishing, and power generation, among other uses, so they took the Corps to court, claiming that the Apalachicola, Flint, and Chattahoochee rivers were drying up (a severe and prolonged drought had exacerbated the problem). A federal appellate court ruled against the Corps and Georgia in 2008. Appeal was a possibility.

Interestingly, Georgia is also at loggerheads with Tennessee over a separate water-related issue. The Georgia–Tennessee border was originally drawn in 1818 using primitive measuring devices later found to have drawn the border 1.1 miles northward from where it should have been. The border should have been delineated up to the middle of the Tennessee River, thereby permitting the thirsty Peach State to extract water supplies from the river. Tennessee asserted that the "law of adverse possession" meant that the original boundary should remain the de facto border. Georgia disagreed. The issue remained unresolved in 2009 as it proceeded through the federal courts.

Water wars are illustrative of intergovernmental conflict that ignites local passions, but more importantly, they demonstrate that federalism "lives" and indeed will always be a work in progress—a journey, not a destination.

SOURCES: Brenda Goodman, "Georgia Loses Federal Case in a Dispute About Water," *NYTimes.com* (February 6, 2008); Craig Pittman, "States Reach Water Deal," *tampabay.com* (December 18, 2007); Dan Chapman, "Mapmaker's Border Error Raises New Water War Front," *ajc.com* (February 11, 2008).

united to sue tobacco companies and other corporate malefactors for driving up health care costs. Or one state may contract with another for a service, as Hawaii does with Arizona for a health care management information system.

## Intergovernmental Financial Relations

Revenues are the funds that governments have at their disposal. They are derived from taxes, fees and charges, and transfers from other levels of government. Expenditures are the ways in which the governmental revenues are

**grant-in-aid**

An intergovernmental transfer of funds or other assets, subject to conditions.

disbursed. Governments spend money to operate programs, build public facilities, and pay off debts.

The **grant-in-aid** is the primary mechanism for transferring money from the national to the state and local governments. The national government makes grants available for several reasons: to redistribute wealth, to establish minimum policy standards, and to achieve national goals. But grants are primarily designed to help meet the needs of state and local governments, including environmental protection, transportation, education, health care, and security. Federal grant outlays totaled about $767 billion in 2008.

**categorical grants**

A form of financial aid from one level of government to another to be used for a narrowly defined purpose.

**Discretion of Recipients** There are two major variations in grants: the amount of discretion (independence) the recipient has in determining how to spend the money, and the conditions under which the grant is awarded. A **categorical grant** can be used by the recipient government only for a narrowly defined purpose, such as removing asbestos from school buildings or acquiring land for public use.

**Block grants** are *broad-based grants*; that is, they can be used anywhere within a functional area such as transportation or health care. The difference between categorical and block grants is that the recipient government decides how block grants will be spent. For instance, a local school system can decide whether the purchase of distance education technology is more important than buying microscopes for the science laboratory. Today there are some 625 grants in existence, including 17 block grants. Block grants give nonnational governments considerable flexibility in responding to pressing needs and preferred goals. The grant mechanisms assume that state and local governments can make fair and rational choices among competing claims.

**block grants**

A form of financial aid from one level of government to another for use in a broad, functional area.

**formula grant**

A funding mechanism that automatically allocates monies based on conditions in the recipient government.

**Conditions for Grants** Grants also vary in the manner in which they are allocated. A **formula grant** makes funding available automatically, based on state and local conditions such as poverty level or unemployment rate. A **project grant** is awarded to selected applicants based on the granting agency's assessment of the strength of competing proposals. Block grants are distributed on a formula basis; categorical grants can be either formula or project based.

Another factor also affects intergovernmental financial relations: the existence of *matching requirements*. Most federal grants require that the recipient government use its own resources to pay a certain percentage of program costs. This arrangement is designed to stimulate state and local spending on programs deemed to be in the national interest and to discourage participation in a program simply because money is available. For example, if a state government wants funding through the Boating Safety Financial Assistance program administered by the U.S. Department of Transportation, it must contribute 50 percent itself. And for a local government to participate in the U.S. Interior Department's Urban Parks program, it must provide from 15 percent to 50 percent of the costs. In each case, the recipient government's commitment to boating safety or urban parks is likely to be higher because of the joint funding.

**project grant**

A funding mechanism that awards monies based on the strength of an applicant government's proposal.

# FEDERAL PURSE STRINGS

Federalism today turns less on theory and more on money. The distribution of intergovernmental monies and the conditions attached to them define the distribution of governmental power and authority. Federalism is a matter not only of which level of government will do what, but also of which level will pay for it. Some have called this "fend-for-yourself" federalism, with each jurisdiction essentially on its own in a Darwinian struggle for financial survival.

## The Importance of Federal Funds

Figure 2.2 provides a historical look at national grant-in-aid expenditures. It is important to remember that the data in the bar chart on the left side have not

**Historical Trends in Federal Grant-in-Aid Outlays**

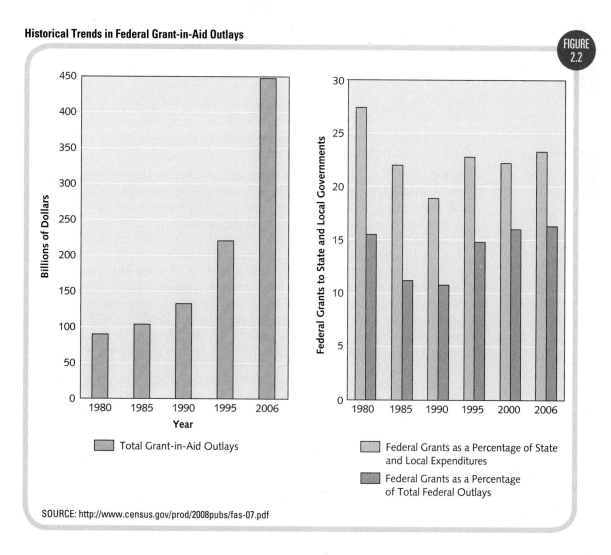

FIGURE 2.2

SOURCE: http://www.census.gov/prod/2008pubs/fas-07.pdf

**Pie Chart of Federal Aid to State and Local Governments, Amounts and Percentages by Major Agency: Fiscal Year, 2007**

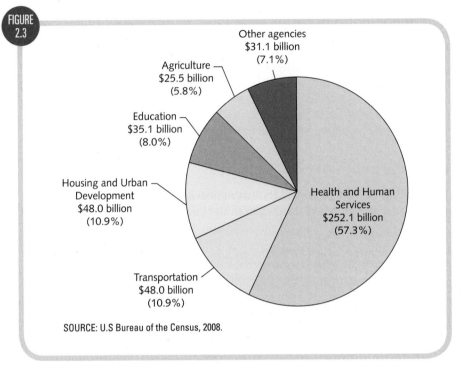

FIGURE 2.3

Other agencies
$31.1 billion
(7.1%)

Agriculture
$25.5 billion
(5.8%)

Education
$35.1 billion
(8.0%)

Housing and Urban
Development
$48.0 billion
(10.9%)

Health and Human
Services
$252.1 billion
(57.3%)

Transportation
$48.0 billion
(10.9%)

SOURCE: U.S Bureau of the Census, 2008.

been adjusted for inflation; the $91.4 billion spent in 1980 was worth vastly more than it would be today. The amounts also do not take into account the increase in population since 1980. The growing proportion of national dollars in the expenditures of states and localities should be placed in the context of the fact that aid to states and localities consumes a relatively small share of the federal government's budget (only 3 percent of GDP).

Although the Washington-funded portion of state and local government revenues is only around 23 percent, it represents an important source of resources for nonnational governments. Grants to state and local governments averaged approximately $1,514 per person in fiscal year 2006. However, the funds were not spread evenly across the country (see Table 2.1). Federal grants poured into Wyoming at the rate of $3,988 per person, whereas Virginia received only $934 per capita. These amounts shot up in 2009 as the federal stimulus package injected an additional $787 billion into state and local coffers for quick pass through for job creation.

States battle in Congress over their share of grant allocations, which are affected by factors such as military installations in the state. The states attempt to influence competitive project grant awards, and they lobby Congress to adjust the weighting of certain factors in formula grants in their favor. State and local influence is wielded by their representatives sitting in Congress and through various actions by elected state and local officials and their Washington lobbyists.

National expenditures in nongrant forms also affect state and local economies substantially. In the nongrant category are payments to individuals

| **Federal Grants to State and Local Governments in 2006** | | | TABLE 2.1 |
|---|---|---|---|
| **STATE** | **GRANTS PER CAPITA** | **STATE** | **GRANTS PER CAPITA** |
| Wyoming | $3,988 | North Carolina | $1,493 |
| District of Columbia | $3,588 | Nebraska | $1,484 |
| Alaska | $3,552 | Missouri | $1,476 |
| Mississippi | $2,545 | Oregon | $1,468 |
| Louisiana | $2,366 | Pennsylvania | $1,460 |
| New York | $2,277 | Arizona | $1,430 |
| Vermont | $2,183 | Tennessee | $1,426 |
| Montana | $2,145 | Maryland | $1,407 |
| Delaware | $2,120 | Minnesota | $1,399 |
| New Mexico | $2,106 | Michigan | $1,383 |
| Rhode Island | $2,052 | Washington | $1,378 |
| Maine | $2,047 | Utah | $1,364 |
| North Dakota | $2,038 | New Jersey | $1,355 |
| West Virginia | $1,874 | Idaho | $1,341 |
| South Dakota | $1,754 | Texas | $1,328 |
| Alabama | $1,676 | Connecticut | $1,315 |
| Arkansas | $1,612 | Florida | $1,311 |
| Kentucky | $1,604 | Wisconsin | $1,279 |
| Ohio | $1,575 | Kansas | $1,264 |
| Hawaii | $1,572 | New Hampshire | $1,259 |
| South Carolina | $1,563 | Illinois | $1,248 |
| California | $1,556 | Georgia | $1,221 |
| Iowa | $1,518 | Indiana | $1,189 |
| Massachusetts | $1,514 | Colorado | $1,119 |
| United States | $1,514 | Nevada | $960 |
| Oklahoma | $1,512 | Virginia | $934 |

SOURCE: U.S. Census Bureau (State Fact Finder).

(representing 65 percent of total federal grants today, up from 36 percent in 1980), notably through the Social Security system; Medicaid payments; purchases by the national government; and wages and salaries of federal employees, most of whom work outside of Washington, D.C. In this sense, federal expenditures emphasize people more than places.

## Here's the Check and Here's What to Do with It: Mandates, Pre-emptions, Set-Asides, and Cost Ceilings

Although many voices are crying, "Let the states and localities do it," Congress continues to impose mandates and pre-empt the states. In addition, Congress includes set-asides and cost ceilings in block grants. Old habits die hard, and one of Congress' oldest habits is to place requirements and conditions on the states. Washington-based politicians may claim to support state power in principle, but when it conflicts with other priorities, devolution takes a back seat. States, of course, have the option to turn down a federal grant. Iowa, Idaho, California, Colorado, and Pennsylvania did just by refusing to accept federal money for sex-education programs because that money could only be used for promoting abstinence.[50] These states cited research that has established that abstinence education is ineffective in preventing teen sexual activity.[51]

**federal mandate**

A requirement that a state or local government undertake a specific activity or provide a particular service as a condition of funding.

**Federal mandates** are especially burdensome when they are entirely or partially unfunded—that is, when the national government requires the states and localities to take action but does not fully pay for it, and the states and localities must foot the bill. Recent federal mandates require the states to establish elaborate and costly school testing programs, staff homeland security operations, standardize driver's licenses, and act as "immigration police" when issuing driver's licenses.

The total cost of these mandate millstones hanging round the necks of states and localities totals $34 billion today.[52] Mounting opposition to mandates without money finally convinced Congress to enact the Unfunded Mandate Reform Act of 1995 (UMRA), which provides that any bill imposing a mandate of more than $50 million (adjusted in 2008 to $68 million) on a state or local government must include a cost estimate. If passed, the legislation is supposed to include sufficient funds to pay for the mandate. Indications are that proposed laws containing unfunded mandates are facing tougher scrutiny in Congress than before and that Congress is taking a more consultative approach with state and local elected officials. However, UMRA is riddled with loopholes[53] and members of Congress still seize opportunities to revert to their mandating ways.

As noted earlier, *pre-emption* represents another intrusion of the national government into the state sphere. It takes two forms: *total* pre-emption, whereby the national government seizes all regulatory authority for a given function from states and localities; and *partial* pre-emption, whereby the national government establishes minimum national standards for state-implemented programs. Both forms prevent states from doing what they want. One example of a totally pre-emptive action is the Americans with Disabilities Act, which requires states and localities to make physical and occupational accommodation for disabled persons. Many partial pre-emptions involve environmental protection, whereby states may regulate pollution emissions as long as state standards are at least as stringent as those of the federal government. A serious concern of global pre-emption was raised by the terms of the 1994 General Agreement on Tariffs and Trade (GATT), which permits foreign corporations to challenge state laws that unfairly discriminate against them in the World Trade Organization (WTO).

Thus, when mandates and pre-emptions are taken into consideration, a less optimistic picture of intergovernmental relations emerges. To the states and localities, it seems that the country has shifted from cooperative federalism to coercive federalism or, in the words of former Governor Ben Nelson of Nebraska, demoted states from significant policy makers to branch managers "of a behemoth central government."[54]

**Set-asides** offer an alternative mechanism through which policy makers in Washington, D.C., can influence the behavior of distant governments. Set-asides are provisions in block grants that designate a certain minimum percentage expenditure on a particular activity. For example, the Alcohol, Drug Abuse, and Mental Health Block Grant contains requirements that states spend at least 50 percent of the funds on services to intravenous (IV) drug users. Congress reasoned that the sharing of hypodermic needles among addicts was contributing to the spread of the AIDS virus and that states were not doing enough to address the problem. But state leaders, although they admitted AIDS was a national priority, argued that the problem was not uniformly spread around the country. Why should Montana spend the same proportion of its funds on IV drug users as New York? Perhaps Montana should spend its drug abuse funds on alcohol abusers or meth heads. In any case, the issue is clear: Who should decide how federal funds are to be spent—the government allocating the funds or the government implementing the program?

> **set-asides**
> Requirements in block grants that assign a certain percentage of an expenditure for a particular activity.

# THE FUTURE OF FEDERALISM

For the states and localities, national political gridlock has meant a golden opportunity to reverse more than a century of centralizing forces. They have taken up the slack in the federal system, busily innovating, developing, and implementing policies in a great variety of fields, from social welfare and health care to carbon emissions and economic development. Public opinion polls consistently show that there is greater trust in state and local governments than in the federal government. As laboratories of democracy, state and local governments have designed and experimented with numerous policies that later have served as models for other states and for Congress. For instance, states have recently pioneered policy initiatives on prescription drug costs, immigration, stem-cell research, nanotechnology, and global climate change, among many other fields. Lobbyists who once focused their attentions on Washington, D.C., are now spending hundreds of millions of dollars to woo state legislators. Hordes of lobbyists representing the health care and insurance industries and other special interests have been attracted to state capitals like fleas to a dog.

Journalists and many citizens have routinely referred "to 'the government' as if there were only one—the Big One."[55] But the United States is a nation of many governments, and Washington is not the best location for addressing all the nation's complex policy problems. Whereas centrally designing and implementing policies and programs is sometimes believed to be the best approach, it can also imply wasteful and ineffective one-size-fits-all government. The trend in government, as well as in business, is to decentralize decision making to the lowest feasible level of the organization. For the U.S. federal system, that means sending decision making to the states and localities and even, in some instances, to nonprofit organizations and citizens' groups.

At the very time that the state and local governments are most needed as policy leaders and problem solvers, powerful social and economic forces seriously threaten state and local governments' capability. The collapse of financial markets and the ensuing freefall in the U. S. economy in 2009 produced frightening revenue declines in nearly all the states, putting at risk children, the poor, and the infirm. Ranks of Medicaid recipients climbed along with the homeless as crime soared. Record budget deficits in 2004–2005 constricted federal funding for state and local grants-in-aid; millions of children exist in poverty. Illegal drugs and gang activity, homelessness, and a flood of immigrants present seemingly impossible challenges for the cities. Finally, the growing disparity of wealth and income threatens our great reservoir of political and social stability: the middle class.

For its part, the federal government provokes criticism for tying the hands of the states and localities with mandates, pre-emptions, set-asides, and confused and conflicting policy directives. Most state and local governments *want* to become more creative, but they are also being *forced* to, so that they can figure out how to implement and pay for federally mandated requirements. This conflicted, ambiguous federalism is something less than empowerment.[56] When the president or Congress takes actions to squash innovative programs such as stem-cell research, the legalization of medical marijuana (see the Debating Politics box on the next page), or assisted suicide, they profess to do so for purposes of the national interest or high moral principles. But the issue is also about money and power and, perhaps at the most basic level, the need for Congress to justify its existence in an increasingly state and local policy world.

Even homeland security, usually considered to be primarily a national government responsibility, actually calls for more—not less—intergovernmental cooperation.[57] State and local governments play critical roles in all four key functions of homeland security: prevention, preparedness, response, and recovery. Local governments are first responders to any sort of domestic disaster, natural or human-caused, whereas states provide crisis management and emergency services while coordinating and steering recovery efforts.

In homeland security, disaster response, and almost all other fields, what the states and localities are demanding is cooperative, consultative relationships and flexible or facilitative federalism, in which the national government helps them through selective funding for technical assistance—a federalism in which they are treated as partners in governance, not as just another self-absorbed interest group. What they want, in a word, is empowerment.

State policy activism has flourished in the past several years. Of course, some states, including California, Massachusetts, Oregon, and Wisconsin, con-

## DEBATING POLITICS
# Decriminalizing Medical Marijuana

Thirteen states (Alaska, California, Colorado, Hawaii, Maine, Michigan Montana, Nevada, New Mexico, Oregon, Rhode Island, Vermont, Washington) have enacted laws permitting the legal purchase of marijuana for medicinal purposes. These actions directly contradict federal drug policy and regulations, which forbid any possession and use of the herb and assess a fine of up to $10,000 and up to one year in prison for mere possession of one reefer.

These state actions reflected widespread public dissatisfaction with a flawed and failed federal drug enforcement policy. Decriminalization recognized increasing evidence of the medical uses of marijuana for treating several conditions, including glaucoma (an eye disease) and neurological diseases such as multiple sclerosis. Marijuana also has been found to stimulate the appetite and suppress nausea for AIDS sufferers and for cancer patients on chemotherapy and radiation treatment.

Predictably, the new laws encountered vehement opposition from political and social conservatives and from the U.S. Food and Drug Administration (FDA), which is responsible for enforcing federal drug laws. For example, the California medical marijuana initiative was initially blocked by a federal district court judge who applied a federal law prohibiting the use of marijuana since 1937. The U.S. Supreme Court ruled in 2001 that the "medical necessity" exception is not allowed under the federal law. Both the Clinton and Bush administrations threatened doctors who recommended marijuana to their patients with criminal prosecution and the loss of their right to prescribe all prescription drugs for Medicare and Medicaid patients. In 2005, the Supreme Court concluded that state laws do not shield marijuana smokers from federal law.

When the Obama administration took over the reins of the federal government, however, the smoke began blowing in a different direction. President Obama's new attorney general stated no interest in prosecuting persons for possession of small amounts of weed or the production of medical marijuana. And his Drug Enforcement Agency

halted raids on marijuana dispensaries in decriminalized states.

Although other states are certain to consider the issue, a majority continue to outlaw all use of marijuana. Tremendous variability exists in state laws for possession, cultivation, and sale. Eleven states may impose maximum penalties of thirty years or more of incarceration. In ten states, the maximum penalty is five years or less. In many states and localities, marijuana violations are routinely overlooked by law enforcement personnel.

The marijuana issue had important economic dimensions as well. In addition to enormous criminal justice expenditures for enforcing marijuana laws and the loss of productivity from incarcerating tens of thousands of people, the economic benefits of growing marijuana are substantial. It represents a vast, untaxed black market crop in West Virginia, Kentucky, North Carolina, California, Vermont, Hawaii, and many other states. Legalization could significantly boost tax revenues. Moreover, there is a large and growing commercial market for industrial hemp (essentially the same plant but with minuscule levels of the psychoactive ingredient tetrahydrocannabinol—THC). Legally grown in much of the world for thousands of years, industrial hemp is used to manufacture rope, textiles, paper, cosmetics, animal feed, and thousands of other products. California's legislature passed a bill legalizing the farming of industrial hemp in late 2006, only to see it vetoed by Governor Schwarzenegger.

Marijuana presents a multifaceted issue that raises numerous legal, ethical, and economic questions. From the perspective of federalism, consider the following: Does the federal government have the statutory, regulatory, and constitutional powers to overrule public opinion and law in the states? If a majority of Californians or Alaskans want doctors to be able to prescribe marijuana for medical purposes, should the federal government stand in their way? What about the responsibilities of the states to respond to citizen demands, even if their preferences are out of favor with the president, and a majority in Congress, and contrary to federal law?

Is medicinal marijuana an issue properly resolved by the states, or should there be a more uniform national policy? What about recreational use and the lessons of legalization for America's youth?

SOURCES: Bob Egelko, "U.S. to Yield Marijuana Jurisdiction to States," *SFGATE.com* (February 27, 2009). *Gonzales v. Raich* No. 03-1451 (June 6, 2005); Patricia Leigh Brown, "California Seeks to Clear Hemp of a Bad Name," *New York Times* (www.nytimes.com/2006/08/28/us/28hemp.html) (August 28, 2006): 1–4; "Marijuana as Medicine: How Strong is the Science?" *Consumer Reports* 62 (May 1997): 62–63; *United States v. Oakland Cannabis Buyer's Cooperation*, No. 000151, 2001; and various articles of the *New York Times*, 1997–2005.

sistently rank high as policy initiators. But others predictably bring up the rear. Counting as policy laggards are Alabama, Mississippi, and South Carolina.[57] Why are some states more innovative than others? A host of factors come into play, including political culture, the presence of policy entrepreneurs, levels of population and population growth, urbanization, and state wealth. And whereas all states achieve policy breakthroughs at one time or another, most are also guilty of occasional boneheaded decisions. But policy diversity flourishes. Take immigration policy, for example. While Congress flailed about to no useful effect in 2007–2008, thirty-three states enacted immigration reform laws. Some, such as Arizona, Colorado, and Georgia, passed tough, anti-immigrant measures. Others, including Nebraska, gave illegals in-state college tuition rates and other resident benefits.

In fairness to the national government, remember that much federal intervention has been in response to state failures to govern effectively and fairly. Corruption, racial prejudice and exclusion, and rampant parochialism, among other shortcomings, have prompted presidential, congressional, and judicial interventions that have, on the whole, helped the states move to the much higher plane they inhabit today.

The question of the balance of power and responsibility in U.S. federalism is no less important now than it was when the representatives of the colonies met in Philadelphia's Independence Hall, first to draft the Articles of Confederation and later to design the Constitution. The focus of the debate has shifted, however, to a pragmatic interest in how the responsibility of governing should be sorted out among the three levels of government. As pointed out by an insightful observer of U.S. government, "[the] American federal system has never been static. It has changed radically over the years, as tides of centralization and decentralization have altered the balance of power and the allocation of functions among the different levels of government."[58]

With Barack Obama's accession to the White House in 2009, the state and local governments' hopes for greater respect and recognition in the nation's capital were elevated. As Andrew Romanoff, Colorado's speaker of the house, put it, "We want the federal government to recognize that there are problems that are best solved at the state level. Either give us the tools or remove the barriers so we can solve the problem. The worst thing the feds can do is say it's your problem and we're going to make it harder for you to solve it."[59]

Nothing short of a revival of state and local power and authority and responsibility is sought. Federal mandates and other encroachments on traditional state authority were legion in 2000–2008, as described above. State and local governments were treated as annoying supplicants by Congress and the administration, no better than any other greedy special interest. A much more productive relationship would be one of a partnership recognizing the governance and policy-making responsibilities of all levels of government and the superior capability of states and localities to experiment and innovate on policies of national significance.

Centripetal forces pull things to the federal center. The mortgage, credit, and banking crises in 2008–2009, continuing fears of terrorist attacks, and foreign wars, among other issues, encourage a centralizing direction, yet for many years Congress has been deadlocked along partisan and ideological lines. American federalism tends to oscillate with national government policy activism—when Washington, D.C., wanes, the states wax. When national government policy activism is at a low level, the states step in to fill the gap.[60]

An encouraging early sign that renewed respect for state and local governments was in the offing came with massive federal aid to fund state and local infrastructure projects, schools, and other needs. Another was President Obama's reversal of several pre-emptive policies of the Bush administration, including stem-cell research and medical marijuana, and instructions to federal agency heads to review and amend all regulations issued over the past ten years that unjustifiably preempt state laws. The hope, then, is for a new era of cooperative federalism to supplant the coercive federalism of previous years, as the pendulum of federalism swings once more in the direction of states and localities.

## CHAPTER RECAP

- U.S. federalism is an ongoing experiment in governance.

- A fundamental question is, what is the proper balance of power and responsibility between the national government and the states?

- Actions of the courts, Congress, and the executive branch have expanded powers of the national government.

- Over time, the trend has generally been in the direction of a stronger national government. Beginning in the early 1980s, however, there was a resurgence of the state and local governments as political and policy actors.

- The power relationships among the three levels of government are described by various models, including dual and cooperative federalism. The operative model is cooperative federalism, under the variant known as new federalism.

- A key concept in federalism is intergovernmental relations, particularly financial relationships among the three levels of government.

- The national government imposes certain controversial requirements on grants-in-aid, including mandates and pre-emptions.

## Key Terms

unitary system *(p. 25)*
confederacy *(p. 25)*
federal system *(p. 26)*
enumerated (delegated) powers *(p. 29)*
concurrent powers *(p. 29)*
nation-centered federalism *(p. 30)*
state-centered federalism *(p. 30)*
reserved powers *(p. 30)*
Tenth Amendment *(p. 30)*
compact theory *(p. 31)*

national supremacy clause *(p. 32)*
necessary and proper clause *(p. 32)*
implied powers *(p. 32)*
commerce clause *(p. 32)*
general welfare clause *(p. 33)*
Fourteenth Amendment *(p. 33)*
Sixteenth Amendment *(p. 34)*
federal pre-emption *(p. 34)*
dual federalism *(p. 37)*
cooperative federalism *(p. 38)*

creative federalism *(p. 38)*
new federalism *(p. 39)*
devolution *(p. 40)*
grant-in-aid *(p. 44)*
categorical grants *(p. 44)*
block grants *(p. 44)*
formula grant *(p. 44)*
project grant *(p. 44)*
federal mandate *(p. 48)*
set-asides *(p. 49)*

## Internet Resources

Examples of unfunded mandates are found on a Heritage Foundation webpage at **www.regulation.org/states.html**. Costs of unfunded mandates are tracked by the NCSL in their "mandate monitor" at **www.ncsl.org/standcomm/scbudg/mammon.htm**.

Federalism decisions by the U.S. Supreme Court may be reviewed at the Council of State Governments' website at **www.statenews.org** or **www.csg.org**. For other sites with federalism content, see **www.governing.com** and **www.stateline.org**.

For current information on relationships among the three levels of government, see **www.governing.com**.

The website **www.census.gov** has comparative data on the states and localities, particularly state and local finances. It is not particularly user-friendly—you'll have to dig around for what you seek.

Information on tribal governments and politics may be acquired at **www.tribal-institute.org** and **www.narf.org**.

SOURCE: Justin Sullivan/Getty Images News/Getty Images

# State Constitutions

**3**

State constitutions are alike in many important respects, but they are decidedly different in others. Consider recent public votes on state constitutional changes. In 2008, Florida voters refused to strike language from their state's constitution denying Asian immigrants the right to own land. California voters banned gay marriage, and Washington became the second state to allow assisted suicide for the terminally ill. Michigan became the thirteenth state to allow medical use of marijuana. These actions demonstrate that constitutions are, in their essence, *political* documents—products of state history, culture, events, economics, and above all, the clash of interests.

All state constitutions both distribute and constrain political power among groups and regions. They set forth the basic framework and operating rules for government, allocate power to the three branches, establish the scope of state and local governmental authority, and protect individual rights.[1] Constitutions represent the **fundamental law** of a state, superior to statutory law. They provide a set of rules for running state government, and those who master the regulations and procedures have a distinct advantage over novices. Everything that a state government does and represents is rooted in its constitution. Constitutions do not describe the full reality of a political system, but they do provide a window through which to perceive its reality. Only the federal Constitution and federal statutes take priority over state constitutions, which is why the constitution is called the fundamental law.

To most people, however, constitutional law still means the federal document. State constitutions are often neglected in secondary school and college history and political science courses. Astonishingly, one national survey discovered that 51 percent of Americans were not aware that their state had its own constitution.[2]

In the U.S. system of *dual constitutionalism*, in which there are both national and state constitutions, the national government is supreme within the

**fundamental law**

The basic legal and political document of a state; it prescribes the rules through which government operates.

spheres of authority specifically delegated to it in the U.S. Constitution. Powers granted exclusively to the national government are denied to the states. But the national Constitution is incomplete. It leaves many key constitutional issues to the states, including local finance, public education, and the organization of state and local governments.[3] In theory, state constitutions are supreme for all matters not expressly within the national government's jurisdiction or preempted by federal constitutional or statutory law. In practice, however, congressional actions and federal court interpretations have expanded the powers of the national government and, in some cases, eroded the powers of the states. And in reality many concurrent powers, such as taxing, spending, and protecting citizens' health and safety, are shared by all levels of government.

The earliest state constitutions were simple documents reflecting an agrarian economy, single-owner businesses, and horse-and-buggy transportation. As American society and the economy changed, the rules of state government also required transformation. Constitutional reform has been a regular theme throughout the U.S. experiment in federalism.

Some reforms have reflected changing political fortunes. Newly powerful groups have pressed to revise the state constitution to reflect their interests, or one or another political party has gained control of state government and sought to solidify its power. Constitutional reforms have promoted different views of politics and the public interest, as when Progressive reformers rallied for honest and efficient government in the late nineteenth and early twentieth centuries.[4] In more recent years, constitutional revisions have generally sought to make state government more efficient, effective, and responsive to shifting social and economic forces. The fact that constitutions are subject to change also recognizes that human judgment is fallible and human understanding imperfect.[5] Through constitutional reform, states can elevate their role as democratic laboratories and respond to the changing needs and opinions of citizens. This capacity for change is in sharp contrast to the seldom-amended federal Constitution.

## THE EVOLUTION OF STATE CONSTITUTIONS

When the states won their independence from Great Britain some 230 years ago, there was no precedent for writing constitutions. A constitution for the Five Nations of the Iroquois called the Great Binding Law existed, but it was oral and not particularly appropriate for consideration by the people in the colonies.[6] The thirteen colonial charters provided the foundation for the new state constitutions. These were brief documents (around five pages each) that the British Crown had granted to trading companies and individuals to govern settlements in the new territories. As the settlements became full colonies, the charters were expanded to incorporate the "rights of Englishmen"—political and civil rights first enumerated by the Magna Carta in 1215. For territories too remote from their native country to be governed by its laws, these charters also laid down some basic principles of colonial government.[7]

In a sense, the existence of these documents helped fuel the fires of independence. In what was to become Connecticut, early settlers escaping the oppressive rule of the Massachusetts Bay Colony took matters of governance into their own hands. Under the leadership of Thomas Hooker, these ambitious farmers established an independent government free from references to the Crown. The Fundamental Orders of 1639 contended that "the choice of the public magistrates belongs unto the people by God's own allowance. The privilege of election belongs to the people…it is in their power, also, to set and limit the bounds and limitations of the power [of elected officials]."[8] Years later, a representative of King James II was sent to take possession of the Fundamental Orders and unite the New England colonies under the Crown. In a night meeting, as the Orders were laid out on a table before the king's men, the candles suddenly were extinguished. When they were relighted, the document had disappeared. According to legend, a patriot had hidden the Orders in a nearby hollow tree, later to be known as the Charter Oak. Infuriated, the king's men dissolved the colony's government and imposed autocratic rule that lasted many years. But they never found the Fundamental Orders, which essentially governed Connecticut until the Constitution of 1818 was adopted.[9]

## The First State Constitutions

In a May 1776 resolution, the Continental Congress instructed the thirteen colonies "to reorganize their governments solely on the basis of 'the authority of the people.'" This task, of critical importance, had never been achieved in human history. How would "the people" write the laws of their states?[10] Following the War of Independence, the former colonies turned their attention to this task, drafting their first constitutions in special revolutionary conventions or in legislative assemblies. With the exception of Massachusetts, the new states put their constitutions into effect immediately, without popular ratification.

The making of the first state constitutions was not a simple affair. Issues of political philosophy were debated. How would citizens' "natural rights" be defined and protected? How would the principle of popular sovereignty be addressed in words and in practice? Many practical questions had to be answered in constitutional conventions, including the structure of the new government, how and when elections would be held, and how land once owned by the Crown would be distributed.

Territorial integrity was not well defined. For example, in what is now known as Kentucky, people frustrated with Virginia's rule met in 1784 and petitioned the Congress for statehood. It took six years and nine constitutional conventions before Kentucky became a state. Complicating factors causing delay involved the "necessity of communicating across the mountains, the change from the Articles of Confederation to the Constitution of the United States, Indian attacks, [and] the revelation of a plot to have Kentucky secure independence and join Spain."[11]

Other Western territories were constituted as states under terms of the Northwest Ordinance of 1787, which established the principle that the United States would expand westward by drawing boundaries for and admitting new states, rather than simply extending the boundaries of existing states to the West. Each new state, such as Ohio and Illinois, had to write its own constitution.

In content, most of these documents simply extended the colonial charters, removing references to the king and inserting a bill of rights. All the documents incorporated the principles of limited government: a weak executive branch, the separation of powers, checks and balances, a bill of rights to protect the people and their property from arbitrary government actions, and (except for Pennsylvania) a bicameral legislature.[12] The earliest constitutions were not truly democratic. Essentially, they called for government by an aristocracy. Office holding and voting, for instance, were restricted to white males of wealth and property.[13]

Only one of the thirteen original state constitutions, that of Massachusetts, survives (although it has been amended 120 times). It is the oldest functioning constitution in the world. Its longevity can be attributed in large part to the foresight of its drafter, John Adams, who grounded the document in extensive research of governments that took him all the way back to the ancients and the Magna Carta. Even after many amendments, the Massachusetts constitution reflects a composite of the wisdom of the foremost political philosophers of the eighteenth century: John Locke, Jean-Jacques Rousseau, and the Baron de Montesquieu.[14] In this enduring document, Massachusetts establishes itself as a commonwealth (from the words *common weal*, meaning "general well-being"), on the principle that its citizens have a right to protect and manage their collective interests. (Kentucky, Pennsylvania, and Virginia are also commonwealths).[15]

## Legislative Supremacy

The first state constitutions reflected the Framers' fear and distrust of the executive—a result of their experiences with the colonial governors. The governors were not all tyrants, but because they represented the British Crown and Parliament, they became a symbol of oppression to the colonists. As a result, the guiding principle of the new constitutional governments was **legislative supremacy**, and the legislatures were given overwhelming power at the expense of governors. Most governors were to be elected by the legislature, not the people, and were restricted to a single term of office. State judiciaries also were limited in authorized powers; judges, like governors, were to be elected by the legislature. The preeminence of legislative power was so great that an English observer, Lord James Bryce, was moved to remark: "The legislature...is so much the strongest force in the several states that we may almost call it the government and ignore all other authorities."[16]

**legislative supremacy**
The legislature's dominance of the other two branches of government.

## The Growth of Executive Power

Disillusionment with the legislatures soon developed, spreading rapidly through the states during the early 1800s. There were many reasons for disenchantment, including the legislatures' failure to address problems caused by rapid population growth and the Industrial Revolution; the growing amount of legislation that favored private interests; and a mounting load of state indebtedness, which led nine states to default on their bonds in a single two-year period.

Gradually the executive branch began to accumulate more power and stature through constitutional amendments that provided for popular election of governors, who were also given longer terms and the authority to veto legislative bills. The constitutions of those states admitted to the Union during the early 1800s established stronger executive powers at the outset. This trend toward centralization of power in the executive branch continued during the 1830s and 1840s, the so-called Jacksonian era; however, the Jacksonian principle of popular elections to fill most government offices resulted in a fragmented state executive branch. The governor now had to share authority with a lieutenant governor, an attorney general, a treasurer, and other popularly elected officials, as well as with numerous agency heads appointed by the legislature.

As executive power grew, public confidence in state legislatures continued to erode. This trend was reflected in the process of constitutional revision. One delegate at Kentucky's 1890 constitutional convention proclaimed that "the principal, if not the sole purpose of this constitution which we are here to frame, is to restrain the legislature's will and restrict its authority."[17] Also affecting constitutional change were broader social and economic forces in the United States, such as the extension of suffrage and popular participation in government, the rise of a corporate economy, the Civil War and Reconstruction, the growth of industry and commerce, the process of urbanization, and a growing movement for government reform. States rapidly replaced and amended their constitutions from the early 1800s to 1920s in response to these forces and others. The decade immediately after the Civil War saw the highest level of constitutional activity in U.S. history, much of it in the southern states; between 1860 and 1870, twenty-seven constitutions were replaced or thoroughly revised as Confederate states ratified new documents after secession, then redrew the documents after Union victory to incorporate certain conditions of readmission to the United States.

Constitutional change after Reconstruction was driven by the Populist and Progressive reform movements. During the late 1800s, the Populists championed the causes of the "little man," including farmers and laborers. They sought to open the political process to the people through constitutional devices such as the initiative, the referendum, and the recall (see Chapter 4). The Progressives, who made their mark during 1890–1920, were kindred spirits whose favorite targets were concentrated wealth, inefficiencies in government, machine politics, corruption, and boss rule in the cities. Reformers in both groups successfully promoted constitutional reforms such as regulation of campaign spending and party activities, replacement of party conventions with direct primary elections, and selection of judges through nonpartisan elections.

# WEAKNESSES OF CONSTITUTIONS

Despite the numerous constitutional amendments and replacements enacted during the nineteenth and twentieth centuries, by 1950, the states were buffeted by a rising chorus criticizing their fundamental laws. Ironically, many states were victims of past constitutional change, which left them with documents that were extravagantly long, frustratingly inflexible, and distressingly detailed. In general, state constitutions still provided for a feeble executive branch because they granted limited administrative authority to the governor, permitted the popular election of numerous other executive branch officials, and organized the executive into a hodgepodge of semiautonomous agencies, boards, and commissions. State judiciaries remained uncoordinated and overly complex, whereas legislatures suffered from archaic structures and procedures. Statutory detail, outdated language, local amendments (those that apply only to designated local governments), and other problems contaminated the documents and strait-jacketed state government.

## Excessive Length

From the first constitutions, which averaged 5,000 words, state documents had expanded into enormous tracts averaging 27,000 words by 1967. (The U.S. Constitution contains 8,700 words). Some of this increase resulted from growing social and economic complexity, and from a perceived need to be extremely specific about what the legislatures could and could not do. The states did have to delineate their residual powers (those powers not delegated to the national government), identify the scope of their responsibility, and specify the powers of local governments.

State constitutions are much easier to amend than the federal Constitution. But some constitutions went too far. Louisiana's exceeded 253,000 words. Georgia's contained around 583,500 words, surpassing Tolstoy's *War and Peace* in length. (The Peach State's constitution was replaced with a much briefer version in 1982). Even today the constitution of South Carolina limits local government indebtedness but lists seventeen pages of exceptions. Maryland's constitution devotes an article to off-street parking in Baltimore. Oklahoma's sets the flash point for kerosene at 115 degrees for purposes of illumination,[18] and California's addresses a compelling issue of our time—the length of wrestling matches. A constitutional initiativ in Florida prohibits "cruel and unusual confinement of pigs during pregnancy." The dubious prize for the most verbose constitution today goes to Alabama. An estimated 70 percent of the amendments to its 350,000-word document apply to only one county.[19] Table 3.1 provides an overview of the fifty state constitutions, including each one's length.

Not surprisingly, lengthy state constitutions tend to be plagued by contradictions and meaningless clauses, legal jargon, and redundancy. Some address problems that are no longer with us, such as the regulation of steamboats[20] or the need to teach livestock feeding in Oklahoma public schools.

Verbose constitutions, such as those of Alabama, Oklahoma, and Colorado, fail to distinguish between the fundamental law and particularistic issues that properly should be decided by the state legislature.[21] Excessive detail invites litigation and then the courts must rule on conflicting provisions and challenges to constitutionality; hence, the courts are often burdened unnecessarily with decisions that should be made by the legislature. Colorado's constitutional contradictions, for instance, led the speaker of the Colorado House

| TABLE 3.1 | State Constitutions, 2008 | | | | |
|---|---|---|---|---|---|
| **STATE** | **NUMBER OF CONSTITUTIONS** | **EFFECTIVE DATE** | **NUMBER OF WORDS** | **SUBMITTED TO VOTERS** | **ADOPTED** |
| Alabama | 6 | Nov. 28, 1901 | 350,000 | 1,093 | 799 |
| Alaska | 1 | Jan. 3, 1959 | 15,988 | 41 | 29 |
| Arizona | 1 | Feb. 14, 1912 | 45,793 | 254 | 141 |
| Arkansas | 5 | Oct. 30, 1874 | 59,500 | 190 | 92 |
| California | 2 | July 4, 1879 | 54,645 | 870 | 514 |
| Colorado | 1 | Aug. 1, 1876 | 74,522 | 315 | 150 |
| Connecticut | 4 | Dec. 30, 1965 | 17,256 | 30 | 29 |
| Delaware | 4 | June 10, 1897 | 19,000 | not submitted to voters | 140 |
| Florida | 6 | Jan. 7, 1969 | 51,456 | 141 | 110 |
| Georgia | 10 | July 1, 1983 | 39,526 | 86 | 66 |
| Hawaii | 1 | Aug. 21, 1959 | 20,774 | 128 | 108 |
| Idaho | 1 | July 3, 1890 | 24,232 | 206 | 119 |
| Illinois | 4 | July 1, 1971 | 16,510 | 17 | 11 |
| Indiana | 2 | Nov. 1, 1851 | 10,379 | 78 | 46 |
| Iowa | 2 | Sept. 3, 1957 | 11,500 | 57 | 52 |
| Kansas | 1 | Jan. 29, 1861 | 12,296 | 123 | 93 |
| Kentucky | 4 | Sept. 28, 1891 | 23,911 | 75 | 41 |
| Louisiana | 11 | Jan. 1, 1975 | 54,112 | 214 | 151 |
| Maine | 1 | March 15, 1820 | 16,276 | 203 | 171 |
| Maryland | 4 | Oct. 5, 1867 | 44,000 | 257 | 221 |
| Massachusetts | 1 | Oct. 25, 1780 | 36,700 | 148 | 120 |
| Michigan | 4 | Jan. 1, 1964 | 34,659 | 66 | 28 |
| Minnesota | 1 | May 11, 1858 | 11,547 | 214 | 119 |
| Mississippi | 4 | Nov. 1, 1890 | 24,323 | 158 | 123 |
| Missouri | 4 | March 30, 1945 | 42,600 | 170 | 109 |
| Montana | 2 | July 1, 1973 | 13,145 | 54 | 30 |
| Nebraska | 2 | Oct. 12, 1875 | 34,220 | 344 | 224 |
| Nevada | 1 | Oct. 31, 1864 | 31,377 | 226 | 134 |
| New Hampshire | 2 | June 2, 1784 | 9,200 | 287 | 145 |
| New Jersey | 3 | Jan. 1, 1948 | 22,956 | 76 | 42 |
| New Mexico | 1 | Jan. 6, 1912 | 27,200 | 284 | 155 |

| TABLE 3.1 (continued) | | | | | |
|---|---|---|---|---|---|
| STATE | NUMBER OF CONSTITUTIONS | EFFECTIVE DATE | NUMBER OF WORDS | SUBMITTED TO VOTERS | ADOPTED |
| New York | 4 | Jan. 1, 1895 | 51,700 | 292 | 217 |
| North Carolina | 3 | July 1, 1971 | 16,532 | 42 | 34 |
| North Dakota | 1 | Nov. 2, 1889 | 19,130 | 262 | 149 |
| Ohio | 2 | Sept. 1, 1851 | 48,521 | 275 | 163 |
| Oklahoma | 1 | Nov. 16, 1907 | 74,075 | 340 | 175 |
| Oregon | 1 | Feb. 14, 1859 | 54,083 | 478 | 238 |
| Pennsylvania | 5 | April 23, 1968 | 27,711 | 36 | 30 |
| Rhode Island | 3 | Dec. 4, 1896 | 10,908 | 11 | 10 |
| South Carolina | 7 | Jan. 1, 1896 | 32,541 | 679 | 492 |
| South Dakota | 1 | Nov. 2, 1889 | 27,675 | 223 | 213 |
| Tennessee | 3 | Feb. 23, 1870 | 13,300 | 61 | 38 |
| Texas | 5 | Feb. 15, 1876 | 90,000 | 613 | 456 |
| Utah | 1 | Jan. 4, 1896 | 18,037 | 158 | 107 |
| Vermont | 3 | July 9, 1793 | 10,286 | 211 | 53 |
| Virginia | 5 | July 1, 1971 | 21,601 | 51 | 43 |
| Washington | 1 | Nov. 11, 1889 | 33,564 | 174 | 101 |
| West Virginia | 3 | April 9, 1872 | 26,000 | 121 | 71 |
| Wisconsin | 6 | May 29, 1848 | 14,749 | 193 | 144 |
| Wyoming | 1 | July 10, 1890 | 31,800 | 123 | 97 |

SOURCE: Book of the States 2009, page 10.

to observe in 2008 that "We're one of the only states where the constitution requires simultaneous revenue reductions and spending increases."[22]

Once incorporated into a constitution, a decision becomes as close to permanent as anything can be in politics. In contrast to a statute, which can be changed by a simple legislative majority, constitutional change requires an extraordinary majority, usually two-thirds or three-fourths of the legislature. This requirement hampers the legislature's ability to confront problems quickly and makes policy change more difficult. Too many amendments may also deprive local governments of needed flexibility to cope with their own problems. Indeed, excessive detail generates confusion, not only for legislatures and court, but also for the general public. It encourages political subterfuge to get around archaic or irrelevant provisions and breeds disrespect or even contempt for government.

State constitutions are political documents and, contrary to the admonitions of reformers, may sometimes be used to address some of the most controversial issues in politics, such as abortion rights, gay marriage, sex education, affirmative action, and even smokers' rights. Many detailed provisions favor or protect special interests, including public utilities, farmers, timber companies, religious fundamentalists, and many others.

There is enormous variance in the length of state constitutions (see Table 3.1). What accounts for such disparity? Studies by political scientists find, not surprisingly, that interest groups play an important role. In states with only one strong political party, where legislative outcomes tend to be unpredictable because of dissension among members of the majority party, interest groups try to insulate their favorite agencies and programs from uncertainty by seeking protective provisions for them in the constitution.[23] Also, research indicates that long, detailed documents tend to become even longer because their very complexity encourages further amendment, until they finally become so cumbersome that political support develops for a simpler version. Finally, the easier it is to amend a constitution, the higher the amendment rate.[24]

## Problems of Substance

In addition to the contradictions, anachronisms, wordiness, and grants of special privilege found in state constitutions, their *substance* has drawn criticism. Specific concerns voiced by reformers include the following:

- *The long ballot.* Because elected executive branch officials are not accountable to the governor for their jobs, the governor has little or no formal influence on their decisions and activities. Reformers who seek to maximize the governor's powers would restrict the executive branch ballot to only two elected leaders: the governor and the lieutenant governor.
- *A glut of executive boards and commissions.* This reform of the Jacksonian period was intended to expand opportunities for public participation in state government and to limit the powers of the governor. Today, it leads to fragmentation and a lack of policy coordination in the executive branch.
- *A swamp of local governments.* There are some 88,000 municipalities, counties, and special-purpose districts in the states. Sometimes they work at cross-purposes, and nearly always they suffer from overlapping responsibilities and an absence of coordination.
- *Restrictions on local government authority.* Localities in some states have to obtain explicit permission from the state legislature before providing a new service, tapping a new source of revenue, or exercising any other authority not specifically granted to them by the state.
- *Unequal treatment of racial minorities and women.* Constitutional language sometimes discriminates against African Americans, Latinos, and women by denying them certain rights guaranteed to white males. (Although a few holdouts remain, most states have now adopted race- and gender-neutral language).

# CONSTITUTIONAL REFORM

Shortly after World War II, problems of constitutional substance began to generate increasing commentary on the sorry condition of state constitutions. One of the most influential voices came in 1955 from the U.S. Advisory Commission on Intergovernmental Relations, popularly known as the Kestnbaum Commission. In its final report to the president, the commission stated that

> the Constitution prepared by the Founding Fathers, with its broad grants of authority and avoidance of legislative detail, has withstood the test of time far better than the constitutions later adopted by the States...The Commission believes that most states would benefit from a fundamental review of their constitutions to make sure that they provide for vigorous and responsible government, not forbid it.[25]

**Model State Constitution**

An ideal of the structure and contents of a state constitution that emphasizes brevity and broad functions and responsibilities of government.

Another important voice for constitutional reform was the National Municipal League, which developed a **Model State Constitution** in 1921, which is now in its sixth version.[26]

Thomas Jefferson believed that each generation has the right to choose for itself its own form of government. He suggested that a new constitution every nineteen or twenty years would be appropriate. Between 1960 and 1980, it seems that the states took his remarks to heart. Every state altered its fundamental law in some respect during this period, and new or substantially revised constitutions were put into operation in more than half the states. During the 1970s alone, ten states held conventions to consider changing or replacing their constitution. One such state was Louisiana, which set a record by adopting its eleventh constitution; Georgia is in second place with ten.

**positive-law tradition**

A state constitutional tradition based on detailed provisions and procedure.

Two state constitutional traditions are evident today.[27] The newer **positive-law tradition** is represented by the detailed and lengthy documents of states such as Alabama, New York, and Texas. Detailed provisions tend to usurp the law-making powers of state legislatures by locking in rigid procedures and policies that typically favor strong political or economic interests. The original **higher-law tradition** is represented by the U.S. Constitution and the National Municipal League's Model State Constitution. It is embodied in brief documents that put forward basic and enduring framework principles and processes of government and recognizes that public policy choices are the proper responsibility of legislatures. Of course, no constitutional formula can be suitable for all the states because they differ too much in history, society, economics, and political culture. The best constitutions strike a balance between the need for stability and the requirement for enough flexibility to deal with emerging problems. Today the higher-law tradition is once again in favor in those states whose constitutions have become briefer, more readable, and simple enough for the average citizen to understand. In others, however, conflicts between special interests are often resolved through constitutional change, particularly through citizen initiatives (see pages 74–76).

**higher-law tradition**

A state constitutional tradition based on basic and enduring principles that reach beyond statutory law.

## The Essential State Constitution

The Model State Constitution has twelve basic articles, which are embodied to a greater or lesser extent in the various state constitutions today. The following subsections provide brief descriptions of each article and the ways in which its contents are changing.

**Bill of Rights** Individual rights and liberties were first protected in state constitutions. They closely resemble, and in some cases are identical to, those later delineated in the first eight amendments to the U.S. Constitution. Originally, the national Bill of Rights protected citizens only from actions by the U.S. government. State constitutions and courts were the principal guardians of civil liberties until the Supreme Court's interpretation of the Fourteenth Amendment extended the protective umbrella of the national courts over the states in 1925.[28] U.S. Supreme Court rulings also applied the U.S. Bill of Rights to the states, especially during the Warren Court beginning in 1953. Some states had failed to uphold their trust, particularly those that perpetuated the unequal treatment of women and minorities.

In the 1980s, however, activist states began to reassert guarantees of individual rights under state constitutions. At a minimum, all state constitutions must protect and guarantee those rights found in the U.S. Bill of Rights. But state constitutional provisions may guarantee additional or more extensive rights to citizens. Twenty-two states now have equal rights amendments that guarantee sexual equality and prohibit sex-based discrimination. (But more than half the states have banned same-sex marriages). The U.S. Constitution does not guarantee a right of privacy, but ten states do guarantee it. And thirteen states give constitutional rights to crime victims. Some constitutional provisions border on the exotic. Residents of New Hampshire hold the right to revolution, and all Massachusetts citizens enjoy freedom from excessive noise. To deter animal rights activists, Louisiana, Montana, North Dakota, and six other states have inserted the rights to hunt and fish into their constitutions. As observed above, constitutions are political documents reflecting state interests and culture; they bear the marks of the state's people, embodied in the fundamental law in response to a serious concern or issue of the time. (See Table 3.2 for other rights provisions).

The major reason for the rebirth of state activism in protecting civil liberties and rights has been the conservatism of the U.S. Supreme Court since the 1970s. One commentator accused the Supreme Court of having abdicated its role as "keeper of the nation's conscience."[29] The states' power to write and interpret their constitutions differently from the U.S. Constitution's provisions in the area of protecting civil rights and liberties has been upheld by the Supreme Court, as long as the state provisions have "adequate and independent" grounds.[30] Increasingly, civil rights and liberties cases are being filed by plaintiffs in state rather than federal courts, based on state bill of rights protections. As we observed above, constitutions are "living" documents that evolve over time and bear the temporal marks of the people of a state. Table 3.2 illustrates this point with a selection of constitutional quirks and oddities, many of them anachronisms. (See Table 3.2 for selected excerpts from state bills of rights).

| TABLE 3.2 | Excerpts from State Bills of Rights |
|---|---|

Alabama: "The legislature may hereafter, by general law, provide for an indemnification program to peanut farmers for losses incurred as a result of Aspergillus flavus and freeze damage in peanuts."

Alaska: "Public schooling shall always be conducted in English."

Illinois: "The equal protection of the laws shall not be denied or abridged on account of sex by the State or its units of local government."

Montana: "Human dignity is inviolable."

New York: "Every citizen may freely speak, write, and publish his sentiments on all subjects…."

North Carolina: "Secret political societies shall not be tolerated."

Pennsylvania: "The people have a right to clean air, pure water, and to the preservation of the natural, scenic, historic and esthetic values of the environment. Pennsylvania's public natural resources are the common history of all the people, including generations yet to come…."

Rhode Island: "The power of the state and its municipalities to regulate and control the use of land and waters in the furtherance of the preservation, regeneration, and restoration of the natural environment, and…of the rights of the people to enjoy and freely exercise the rights of fishery and the privileges of the shore…shall be liberally construed, and shall not be deemed a public use of private property."

**Power of the State** This very brief article states simply that the powers enumerated in the constitution are not the only ones held by the state—that, indeed, the state has all powers not denied to it by the state or national constitutions.

**Suffrage and Elections** The legal registration of voters and election procedures are provided for here. Recent extensions of voting rights and alterations in election procedures have been made in response to U.S. Supreme Court decisions and to federal law. Generally, states have improved election administration; liberalized registration, voting, and office-holding requirements; shortened residency requirements; and enhanced election technology and security. Some states have amended this article to provide for partial public financing of election campaigns; others have adopted provisions designed to count ballots more accurately.

**The Legislative Branch** This article sets forth the powers, procedures, and organizing principles of the legislature, including apportionment of state legislatures on the basis of one person, one vote. District lines must be redrawn every ten years (next in 2012), after the national census has revealed population changes. Nineteen states have placed term limits on their elected officials in this article.

On the basis of this article, states have taken numerous actions to approach greater conformity with the Model State Constitution, including increasing the length and frequency of legislative sessions and streamlining rules and procedures. Instead of stipulating specific dollar amounts for legislators' pay and fringe benefits (which are soon rendered inadequate by inflation), most state constitutions now establish a procedure to determine and occasionally adjust the compensation of legislators.

Interestingly, the Model State Constitution originally recommended a unicameral legislature as a means to overcome complexity, delay, and confusion. In its most recent revision, the National Municipal League tacitly recognized the refusal of the states to follow this suggestion by providing recommendations appropriate only for a bicameral body (only Nebraska has a single-house general assembly, as discussed in the Debating Politics box below).

## DEBATING POLITICS

### Is Unicam for You?

Forty-nine states have bicameral legislatures, with upper and lower houses and election of representatives through ballots that identify the candidates' political party. But a bold—even radical—constitutional amendment was adopted by the voters of Nebraska in 1934. Nebraska's unicameral, nonpartisan legislature stands alone among the states' ongoing experiments in democracy. First recommended by a legislative joint committee in 1915, the unicameral design was adopted in a popular initiative to amend the state constitution. It is allowable under the U.S. Constitution, Article IV, which permits each state to determine its own government structure.

Why Nebraska? Apparently several events were at least partly responsible for what Nebraskans have come to call "Unicam." For one thing, it was on the same statewide ballot with two other popular initiatives: repeal of Prohibition and approval of parimutuel horse racing. In addition, the bicameral

Nebraska's senators get under way on the first day of the new legislative session.
SOURCE: AP Photos/Staci E. McKey

body had been suffering increasing criticism for its apparent inability to conduct the state's business efficiently and effectively. But the key factor was the unrelenting preaching of the evils of bicameralism and the virtues of unicameralism by influential and popular U.S. Senator George W. Norris. Norris "wore out two sets of tires and two windshields" driving around on Nebraska's dusty back roads to make the case for Unicam.

Norris and other supporters argued that unicameralism has several virtues. It would eliminate conference committees, which Norris considered not only too secretive and inefficient but also apt to develop laws that nobody really wanted. By facilitating compromise between the house and the senate, Norris explained, these committees encourage the two houses to pass the buck to one another, each hoping the other would deal with the tough or complicated issues. In short, Unicam would be more efficient because legislation could be enacted more quickly and less expensively. Unicam would be small (it numbers forty-nine representatives, the smallest legislature among the states). And because Unicam is nonpartisan, representatives would be likely to focus more on the important business of the state than on national issues of partisan significance.

Critics, including the press, called the proposal dangerous and "un-American." They contended it would be an embarrassing failure. Supporters were confident that Unicam would serve as a model for the other states to follow. Both were wrong. From most reports, Unicam gets high marks for efficiency, simplicity, and effectiveness. And it remains popular except for its nonpartisan feature. The major complaint is that nonpartisanship depresses voter interest and turnout in elections because voters do not have party identification as a voting cue.

As for other states that have entertained the notion of a unicameral legislature, bills have been introduced, amended, and then pigeonholed. Predictably, legislators are loath to vote themselves out of a job. If the unicameral model is to be adopted outside Nebraska, a constitutional initiative that bypasses the legislature is the best procedural bet.

Should your state [or, if you are a Cornhusker (a Nebraskan), other states] adopt a unicameral legislature? Why or why not? What groups would you expect to favor change? Obviously, the present legislature is likely to be opposed to this change. What other groups might be expected to oppose it?

SOURCES: Pat Wunnicke, "Fifty Years Without a Conference Committee: Nebraska's Unicameral Legislature," State Legislatures 13 (October 1987): 20–23; Jack Rodgers, Robert Sittig, and Susan Welch, "The Legislature," in Robert Miewald, ed., Nebraska Government and Politics (Lincoln: University of Nebraska Press, 1984), pp. 57–86; www.nebraskalegislature.gov.

**The Executive Branch** The powers and organization of the executive branch, which are outlined in this article, have seen many notable modifications. Essentially, executive power continues to be centralized in the office of the governor. Governors have won longer terms and the right to run for reelection. Line item vetoes, shorter ballots, the authority to make appointments within the executive branch, and the ability to reorganize the state bureaucracy have also increased gubernatorial powers (see Chapter 8). A number of states have opted for team election of the governor and lieutenant governor.

**The Judicial Branch** All states have substantially revised not only their courts' organization and procedures but also the election of judges. A large majority of the states have also unified their court systems under a single authority, usually the state supreme court. Many states now select judges through a merit plan rather than by gubernatorial appointment, legislative election, or popular election (see Chapter 10). The states have also established means to investigate charges against judges and to recommend discipline or removal from the bench when necessary.

**Finance** This article consists of provisions relating to taxation, debt, and expenditures for state and local governments. In many states, tax relief has been granted to senior citizens, veterans, and disabled people. In others, taxation and expenditure limitations have been added (see Chapter 13).

**Local Government** Here, the authority of municipalities, counties, and other local governments is recognized. Most states have increased local authority through home-rule provisions, which give localities more discretion in providing services. Local taxing authority has been extended. In addition, mechanisms for improved intergovernmental cooperation, such as consolidated city and county governments and regional districts to provide services, have been created.

**Public Education** On the basis of this article, the states establish and maintain free public schools for all children. Higher education institutions, including technical schools, colleges, and universities, are commonly established in this section.

**Civil Service** The Model State Constitution sets forth a *merit system* of personnel administration for state government, under which civil servants are to be hired, promoted, paid, evaluated, and retained on the basis of competence, fitness, and performance instead of political party affiliation or other such criteria.

**Intergovernmental Relations** As recommended by the Model State Constitution, some states stipulate specific devices for cooperation among various state entities, among local jurisdictions, or between a state and its localities. They may detail methods for sharing in the provision of certain services, or they may list cost-sharing mechanisms such as local option sales taxes.

**Constitutional Revision** In this article, the methods for revising, amending, and replacing the constitution are described. Generally, the trend has been to make it easier for the voters, the legislature, or both to change the constitution.

**Constitutions Today** In general, state constitutions today conform more closely to the higher-law tradition and the Model State Constitution than did those of the past. They are shorter, more concise, and simpler, and they contain fewer errors, anachronisms, and contradictions. The latest states to enter the Union, Alaska and Hawaii, have constitutional documents that follow the Model State Constitution quite closely.

However, much work remains to be done. Some state constitutions are still riddled with unnecessary details because new amendments have continually been added to the old documents, and obsolete provisions and other relics can still be found. But more important deficiencies demand the attention of legislators and citizens in states whose constitutions inhibit the administrative and financial operations of state government and obstruct the ability to adapt to change. In some jurisdictions, the governor's formal powers remain weak; a plethora of boards and commissions makes any thought of executive management and coordination a pipe dream; local governments chafe under the tight leash of state authority; and many other problems persist. Constitutional revision must be an ongoing process if the states are to cope with the changing contours of American society and stay in the vanguard of innovation and change.

# METHODS FOR CONSTITUTIONAL CHANGE

There are only two methods for altering the U.S. Constitution. The first is the constitutional convention, wherein delegates representing the states assemble to consider modifying or replacing the Constitution. Despite periodic calls for a national constitutional convention, only one has taken place—in Philadelphia, more than two and a quarter centuries ago. Two-thirds of the states must agree to call a convention; three-fourths are required to ratify any changes in the Constitution.

The second means of amending the U.S. Constitution is through congressional initiative, wherein Congress, by a two-thirds vote of both houses, agrees to send one or more proposed changes to the states. Again, three-fourths of the states must ratify the proposals.

Since 1787, more than 1,000 amendments have been submitted to the states by Congress. Only twenty-seven have been approved (the most recent one, in 1992, limits the ability of members of Congress to increase their pay), and the first ten of these were appended to the Constitution as a condition by several states for ratification. Note that neither method for amending the U.S. Constitution requires popular participation by voters, in sharp contrast to the citizen participation requirements for state constitutional change, as we shall see in the next section.

## Informal Constitutional Change

**interpretation**
An informal means of revising constitutions whereby members of the executive, legislative, or judicial branch apply constitutional principles and law to the everyday affairs of governing.

One informal and four formal methods for amending state constitutions exist. The informal route is **interpretation** of constitutional meaning by the state legislature, executive branch, courts, or attorneys general, or through usage and custom.[31] Governors issue executive orders; courts and attorneys general produce advisory opinions on meanings of specific provisions; state agencies make decisions and implement policy. The force of habit can be a powerful influence, specific constitutional provisions notwithstanding. It is a good bet that one or more antiquated or unrealistic constitutional provisions are ignored in every state. A common example is the requirement that all bills be read, in their entirety, three times in each house for enactment. Another is the list of requirements for holding political office, such as a belief in God.

## Engaging the Constitution

### The District of Columbia: Fifty-First State?

The 588,292 residents of the District of Columbia (D.C.) demand the right to a vote in Congress. And by the way, they would also like for the District to become the fifty-first state. They make some compelling points. D.C. residents pay some $7 billion annually in taxes to the federal government; they serve on juries and in the armed forces. The District has its own license plates, prison system, and income tax. It even has its own 25 cent piece. But D.C. has no U.S. Senator and only a single, nonvoting member of the U.S. House of Representatives. Though it granted the District some authority under a home-rule charter in 1974, Congress has full veto power over the District's legislative and financial affairs. Residents say they are treated like second-class citizens who are taxed without meaningful representation—and they're not afraid to express their discontent either. The motto on their license plates is "Taxation Without Representation."

The U.S. Constitution (Article I, section 8) designates D.C. as the seat of the national government. The Framers believed that a separate district would not only prevent the state, whose territory included the national capital, from exerting powerful pressures on Congress but also prevent the national government from being dependent on any one state for services and security. It did not help that Congress, concerned about a near mutiny of General Washington's army in 1783, had to flee the early capital of Philadelphia after Pennsylvania refused to protect it.

Congress holds exclusive authority over the sixty-eight-square-mile District. Several attempts have been made to achieve D.C. statehood, including a proposed constitutional amendment that only received approval by sixteen of the necessary thirty-eight states. During the administration of President Bill Clinton, Democrats proposed establishing the state of "New Columbia" out

SOURCE: Wiskerke/Alamy

## Engaging the Constitution (*continued*)

of land that would be "donated" by Maryland, but the measure died in the U.S. House.

Constitutional problems notwithstanding, the political objections to statehood have been overwhelming. The District has no meaningful agriculture or industry (except government), so it would still require a large annual subsidy from the national government to pay for operations. It has 55 percent African American and 68 percent minority population. D.C. residents are predominantly liberal and Democratic in their political persuasion. And the capital has been rocked by numerous high-level corruption scandals during recent decades, tarnishing the reputation of the District's public officials.

The political dynamics changed significantly in 2008. D.C. voters marked their ballots for President Obama by a 93 percent margin and large Democratic majorities were elected to the House and Senate. Statehood still does not seem to be in the present hand of cards. Instead, as a step toward eventual statehood, District supporters are arguing for Congress to give the District a U.S. House vote for its representative.

Oddly, the proposal is tied to an additional House seat for Utah, which barely missed gaining another House seat in redistricting following the 2000 Census. In the potential deal, the liberal, Democratic District and conservative, Republican Utah would each receive a new House seat.

However, a serious constitutional impediment might derail the compromise. The Constitution states that the House must be "composed of members chosen...by the people of the several states." Obviously, District residents are not also residents of Maryland or Virginia, so under this language they could not elect their representative. The D.C. voting rights bill languished in 2009 and did not pass. If such a bill is enacted in the future, it is certain to be challenged on constitutional grounds.

SOURCES: Tim Craig and Paul Kane, "D.C. Vote Supporters Defer Fight in Congress," The Washington Post (June 10, 2009); Daniel C. Vock, "Obama's Rise Gives Hope to '51st State' " (January 20, 2009); www.stateline.org. Eric Pianin, "Tiny and Crowded, New Columbia Would be a Unique State," The Washington Post (June 23, 1987), pp. B1, B5.

**judicial review**

The power of the U.S. Supreme Court or state supreme courts to declare unconstitutional actions of the executive and legislative branches as well as decisions of lower courts.

State supreme courts play the most direct role in changing constitutions through interpretation. In large measure, a constitution is what the judges say it is in their decisions from the bench. Judicial interpretation of constitutions may be based on various standards, including strict attention to the express language of the document and to the original intent of the Framers or authors of amendments, deference to legislative enactments or executive actions, precedent, policy considerations, and individual rights. The power of the state supreme courts to review executive actions, legislative actions, and decisions of lower courts is known as **judicial review**. This power evolved in the states much as it did on the national level—through the courts' own insistence that they hold this authority. During recent years, as the U.S. Supreme Court has become more conservative and less activist in its interpretations of the law, some state courts have moved in the opposite direction and earned reputations as judicial activists. By ruling in 2008 that gay couples have full marriage rights under the constitution, California's Supreme Court took an activist stance, contrary to a statutory ban on such marriages.

We have already noted that state supreme courts have the authority to interpret and apply state guarantees of civil rights and liberties more broadly than the U.S. Supreme Court's interpretation of the Bill of Rights in the U.S. Constitution. For instance, the New Hampshire Supreme Court extended the right to privacy to household garbage, even when it is placed at the curb for collection. The U.S. Supreme Court does not review state court decisions that are clearly and properly based on state constitutional provisions.[32] In practice, however, state supreme courts are often guided by constitutional rulings of the U.S. Supreme Court and high courts in other states. Because courts apply similar constitutional language to many common issues, it is natural for them to share their experiences in legal problem solving.[33] Of course, the national courts are supreme under the U.S. Constitution and will strike down any serious constitutional contradictions between the nation and the states, but for about two decades now, the U.S. Supreme Court has shown "a studied deference to the work of the state judiciaries."[34]

## Formal Constitutional Change

The four formal procedures for constitutional change are legislative proposal, initiative, constitutional convention, and constitutional commission. All involve two basic steps: initiation and **ratification**. The state legislature, or in some cases the voters, propose (initiate) a constitutional change. Then the proposed amendment is submitted to the voters for approval (ratification).

**Legislative Proposal** Historically, **legislative proposal** is the most common road to revision. More than 90 percent of all changes in state constitutions have come through this method, which is permitted in all fifty states.

The specifics of legislative proposal techniques vary, but most states require either two-thirds or three-fifths of the members of each house to approve a proposal before it is sent to the voters for ratification. Twelve states require two consecutive legislative sessions to consider and pass a proposed amendment. The procedure can become quite complicated. For instance, South Carolina's legislative proposal must be passed by two-thirds of the members of each house; then it is sent to the people during the next general election. If a majority of voters approve, the proposal returns to the next legislative session, in which a majority of legislators have to concur.

Almost all states accept a simple majority for voter ratification of a proposed revision. In New Hampshire, however, two-thirds of the voters must approve the proposal. And Tennessee requires approval by a majority of the number of citizens who cast a vote for governor.

Legislative proposal is probably best suited to revisions that are relatively narrow in scope. However, some legislatures, such as South Carolina's, have presented a series of proposals to the voters over the years and thereby have significantly revised the constitution. The disadvantage to such a strategy is that it tends to result in a patchwork of amendments that can conflict with or overlap other constitutional provisions. This circumstance spawns additional revisions, which in turn lead to increased litigation in the state supreme court.

**ratification**
The formal approval of a constitution or constitutional amendment by a majority of the voters of a state.

**legislative proposal**
The most common means of amending a state constitution, wherein the legislature proposes a revision, usually by a two-thirds majority.

**initiative**

A proposed law or constitutional amendment that is placed on the ballot by citizen petition.

**Initiative** Eighteen states permit their citizens to initiate and ratify changes in the constitution and thus bypass the legislature (see Table 3.3). Only five of these initiative states are east of the Mississippi River, thus reflecting the fact that the initiative was a product of the Progressive reform movement of the early 1900s. Most of the territories admitted as states during this period chose to permit the **initiative** (known as constitutional initiative in some states). Twenty-three states also authorize the initiative for enacting statutory change (see Chapter 4).

**TABLE 3.3**    **States Authorizing Constitutional Amendment by Citizen Initiative**

| STATE | YEAR ADOPTED | NUMBER OF SIGNATURES REQUIRED ON INITIATIVE PETITION |
|---|---|---|
| Arizona | 1910 | 15 percent of total votes cast for all candidates for governor at last election. |
| Arkansas | 1909 | 10 percent of voters for governor at last election. |
| California | 1911 | 8 percent of total voters for all candidates for governor at last election. |
| Colorado | 1910 | 5 percent of total legal votes for all candidates for secretary of state at last general election. |
| Florida | 1972 | 8 percent of total votes cast in the state in the last presential election. |
| Illinois* | 1970 | 8 percent of total votes cast for candidates for governor at last election. |
| Massachusetts† | 1918 | 3 percent of total votes cast in the last gubernatorial election. |
| Michigan | 1908 | 10 percent of total votes for all candidates at the gubernatorial election. |
| Mississippi | 1992 | 12 percent of total votes for all candidates for governor at last election. |
| Missouri | 1906 | 8 percent of legal voters for all candidates for governor at last election. |
| Montana | 1904 | 10 percent of qualified electors, the number of qualified electors to be determined by the number of votes cast for governor in the preceding general election. |
| Nebraska | 1912 | 10 percent of total votes for governor at last election. |
| Nevada | 1904 | 10 percent of voters who voted in entire state in last general election. |
| North Dakota | 1914 | 4 percent of population of the state. |
| Ohio | 1912 | 10 percent of total number of electors who voted for governor in last election. |
| Oklahoma | 1907 | 15 percent of legal voters for state office receiving the highest number of voters at last general state election. |
| Oregon | 1902 | 8 percent of total votes for all candidates for governor in last election, when the governor was elected for a four-year term. |
| South Dakota | 1898 | 10 percent of total votes for governor in last election. |

*Only Article IV, the Legislature, may be amended by initiative petition.
†Before being submitted to the electorate for ratification, initiative measures must be approved at two sessions of a successively elected legislature by not less than one-fourth of all members elected, sitting in joint session.

SOURCE: Copyright 2008 The Council of State Governments. Reprinted with permission from The Book of the States. Reprinted by permission of The Council of State Governments.

The initiative is used much less often than legislative proposal in amending constitutions, although it has been attempted more frequently during the past two decades. It is also less successful in terms of the percentage of amendments that are adopted by the voters. On average, about 38 percent of all initiatives have been written into state constitutions in recent years.

The number of signatures needed for the initiative petition to be valid varies widely: Arizona requires 15 percent of total votes cast in the last gubernatorial election, whereas Massachusetts requires 3 percent (see Table 3.3). Eight states specify that the petition signatures must be collected widely throughout the state as a means of ensuring that an initiative that favors one region does not become embodied in the constitution.

In general, a petition for constitutional amendment is sent to the office of the secretary of state for verification that the required number of registered voters have signed their names. Then the question is placed on a statewide ballot in the next general election. Ratification requires a majority vote of the people in most states.

It is usually easy enough to collect the required number of signatures to place a proposed amendment on statewide ballot (for a fee, a firm will be happy to perform this service). But actual passage of the initiative is much more difficult, once it receives a close public examination and opposing interests proclaim their objections. If the legislature is circumvented altogether and propositions are placed directly on the general-election ballot by citizens, the procedure is called a **direct initiative**. If a legislature participates by voting on the citizen proposal, as in Massachusetts and Mississippi, the procedure is known as an **indirect initiative**.

The initiative is useful in making limited changes to the state constitution and, in recent years, has addressed some controversial issues that state legislatures are hesitant to confront. Voters in several states have recently addressed abortion rights, legalized gambling, school vouchers, medical marijuana, and employers who hire illegal immigrants. A California initiative authorized and promoted stem-cell research.

A major advantage of the initiative is that it permits the people's will to counter a despotic or inertia-ridden legislature. For instance, Illinois voters in 1978 reduced the size of the House of Representatives from 177 to 118 after the legislature voted itself a huge pay raise during a period of economic hardship. Another advantage is that this method appears to enhance citizen interest and participation in government.

However, the initiative can also be abused through signature fraud or by special interests with selfish motives or social agendas who seek to gain privileges, including out-of-state actors, and under crisis conditions it can result in ill-conceived, radical changes to the constitution. Indeed, the initiative can result in just the kind of excessive detail and poorly drafted verbiage that is so widely condemned by constitutional scholars and reformers. It can also make doing routine business extremely difficult. In California, for example, an initiative prevents local governments from hiking taxes without two-thirds approval of the electorate.

**direct initiative**
A procedure by which the voters of a jurisdiction propose the passage of constitutional amendments, state laws, or local ordinances, bypassing the legislative body.

**indirect initiative**
Similar to the direct initiative, except that the voter-initiated proposal must be submitted to the legislature before going on the ballot for voter approval.

The perceived excesses of the initiative have recently spawned efforts to raise the threshold for voter approval. Ironically, in a constitutional referendum, Florida voters agreed to raise the bar for initiative approval from a simple majority to 60 percent. Montana banned paid signature gatherers and restricted the time for signature acquisition to one year.[35]

**Constitutional Convention** Legislative proposals and initiatives are quite specific about the type of constitutional change that is sought. Only those questions that actually appear on the ballot are considered. By contrast, a **constitutional convention** assembles delegates who suggest revisions or even an entirely new document, then submit the proposed changes to the voters for ratification. The convention is especially well suited to consider far-reaching constitutional changes or a new fundamental law.

> **constitutional convention**
>
> An assembly of delegates chosen by popular election or appointed by the legislature or the governor to revise an existing constitution or to create a new one.

The convention is the oldest method for constitutional change in the states and is available in all fifty of them. The process begins when the electorate or the legislature decides to call for a constitutional convention. In fourteen states, the question of calling a convention must be regularly voted on by the electorate, but most convention calls are routinely rejected, most recently in Hawaii and Illinois. Alaskans and Iowans hold an automatic convention call every ten years; in New York, Maryland, and Montana the convention issue is submitted to the voters every twenty years. Except in Delaware, where the legislature can take direct action, proposals emerging from the convention must be ratified by the voters before they become part of the constitution.

Delegates to a convention are usually elected on a nonpartisan ballot by the voters from state house or senate districts. Conventions are usually dominated by professionals, such as lawyers, educators, and businesspeople. This delegate composition is not surprising because convention calls are strongly supported by higher socioeconomic groups in urban areas.

The characteristics of a delegate pool are important for several reasons. First, the delegates need knowledge of and experience in state government and politics if they are to contribute meaningfully to the debate and drafting of proposed amendments. It is usually not too difficult to attract qualified people for service; the experience is important, unique, and a privilege. Second, the delegates should represent a cross section of the state's population as much as possible. If the delegate pool does not reflect gender, racial, regional, ethnic, and other salient characteristics of the population, the fruit of its labor may lack legitimacy in the eyes of substantial numbers of voters. Finally, partisanship should be avoided when possible. Partisan differences can wreck consensus on major issues and destroy the prospects for voter ratification of amendments suggested by the convention.

Voter approval of convention proposals is problematic. If partisan, racial, regional, or other disagreements dominate media reports on the convention, voter approval is difficult to obtain. People naturally tend to be skeptical of suggestions for sweeping changes in the basic structures and procedures of government. Furthermore, if they have not been regularly involved with and informed of the progress of the convention, they may be reluctant to give their approval to the recommendations.

Delegates usually understand these dynamics and are sensitive to how their proposed changes may affect the general public. They must, for example, carefully consider how to present the proposed amendments for ratification. There are two choices: the all-or-nothing strategy of consolidating all changes in a single vote, and the piecemeal strategy, which presents each proposal as a separate ballot decision. In recent years, voters have tended to reject inclusive packages. Each suggested change is certain to offend some minority, and when all the offended minorities coalesce, they may well constitute a majority of voters.

**Constitutional Commission**  Often called a *study commission*, the **constitutional commission** is usually established to study the existing document and to recommend changes to the legislature or to the voters. Depending on the mandate, the constitutional commission may examine the entire constitution with a view toward replacement or change, focus on one or more specific articles or provisions, or be given the freedom to decide its own scope of activity. Commission recommendations to the legislature and/or governor are only advisory, thus helping to account for this method's popularity with elected officials, who sometimes prefer to study a problem to death rather than engage it head on. Some or all of the recommendations may be submitted to the voters; others may be completely ignored. Only in Florida can a commission send its proposals directly to the voters.

A constitutional commission operated in 2007 in Florida, and Utah's revision commission functions permanently. Service on a constitutional commission can be a thankless task because legislators sometimes ignore the commission's recommendations or employ them as a symbolic device for relieving political pressure. For example, Kentucky's 1987–1988 Revision Commission recommended seventy-seven changes to the constitution, but only one was referred by the legislature to the voters as a proposed amendment.[36] When used properly, however, commissions can furnish high-quality research both inexpensively and relatively quickly.

# STATE RESPONSIVENESS AND CONSTITUTIONAL REFORM

Each state's constitution is designed specifically to meet the needs of that state. The rich political culture, history, economics, values, and ideals of the state's community are reflected in its constitutional language. Through their constitutions, the states experiment with different governmental institutions and processes. As passionate patriot Thomas Paine observed more than 200 years ago, "It is in the interest of all the states, that the constitution of each should be somewhat diversified from each other. We are a people founded upon experiments, and…have the happy opportunity of trying variety in order to discover the best."[37]

State constitutions were the original guardians of individual rights and liberties, with their own bills of rights preceding those of the U.S. Constitution by many years. They have reassumed their rightful position in American government as independent state constitutional law develops further. Yet, few tasks in government are more difficult than modernizing a constitution. The process requires "sustained, dedicated, organized effort; vigorous, aggressive and imaginative leadership; bipartisan political support; education of the electorate on the issues; judicious selection of the means; and seemingly endless patience." In the words of constitutional scholar W. Brooke Graves, "The advocate of constitutional reform in an American state should be endowed with the patience of Job and the sense of time of a geologist."[38] The solemn duty of framing the original state constitutions, which was so effectively discharged by our predecessors, should be matched by the continuous oversight of present and future generations. Changes are necessary to adjust state governments to the vagaries of the future.

The constitutional changes enacted in the states since the Kestnbaum Commission report have generally resulted in documents in the higher-law tradition, documents that "are shorter, more clearly written, modernized, less encumbered with restrictions, more basic in content and have more reasonable amending processes. They also establish improved governmental structures and contain substantive provisions assuring greater openness, accountability, and equity."[39] The states have made a great deal of progress in modernizing their governments. As state constitutional scholar Richard Leach has put it, "There are not many constitutional horrors left."[40] Still, as noted above, the initiative process is cluttering constitutions and hamstringing legislators' policy-making authority in some states.

Old-style constitutions were "the drag anchors of state programs, and permanent cloaks for the protection of special interests and points of view."[41] These constitutions held back progress and delayed the states' resurgence as lead players in the drama of U.S. federalism. Recent constitutional amendments have responded to, and indeed caused, profound changes in state government and politics. Since the genesis of modern reform in the mid-1960s, some forty states have adopted new constitutions or substantially amended existing ones. Problems persist, and future constitutional tinkering and replacements will be necessary. But in most states, the constitutional landscape is much cleaner and more functional than it was a generation ago.

## CHAPTER RECAP

- The constitution is the fundamental law of a state, superior to statutory law.

- State constitutions evolved from the original colonial charters. Shifting from an original basis of legislative supremacy, they have gradually increased executive power.

- Some constitutions continue to suffer from excessive length and substantive problems.

- Constitutional reform has modernized the documents and made them conform more closely to present challenges of governance.

- Methods for changing constitutions include interpretation and judicial review, legislative proposal, initiative, constitutional convention, and constitutional commission.

## Key Terms

fundamental law *(p. 56)*
legislative supremacy *(p. 58)*
Model State Constitution
*(p. 64)*
positive-law tradition *(p. 64)*
higher-law tradition *(p. 64)*

interpretation *(p. 70)*
judicial review *(p. 72)*
ratification *(p. 73)*
legislative proposal *(p. 73)*
initiative *(p. 74)*
direct initiative *(p. 75)*

indirect initiative *(p. 75)*
constitutional convention
*(p. 76)*
constitutional commission
*(p. 77)*

## Internet Resources

For full texts of state statutes and constitutions, see individual state websites (e.g., **www.state.fl.us**).

State constitutions can also be accessed through Findlaw at **www.findlaw.com/11stategov/indexconst.html** or **www.constitution.org/cons/usstcons.htm**

The Alaska constitution draws heavily on the Model State Constitution. It is located in the State of Alaska Documents Library at **www.law.state.ak.us**

For everything you want to know about Nebraska's Unicam, go to **www.nebraskalegislature.gov**. Live webcasts of Unicam may be viewed at **www.netnebraska.org/publicmedia/capitol.html**

Another helpful site is the Center for State Constitutional Studies at **www.camlaw.rutgers.edu/statecon/**

SOURCE: GEORGE SKENE/MCT/Landov

# Citizen Participation and Elections

## 4

- Participation
- Elections
- Direct Democracy
- Citizen Access to Government
- The Effects of Citizen Participation

Tired of low-voter turnout in elections in his home state, an Arizonan came up with a clever idea: offer voters a chance to win $1 million. From that idea came a 2006 ballot proposal—the Arizona Voter Reward Act. Supporters argued that providing a financial incentive would motivate more people to vote. After all, the odds of winning the election lottery would be far better than the Powerball jackpot. Opponents contended that the million dollar prize was, in effect, bribing people to vote and furthermore, higher turnout would not necessarily mean a better outcome.[1] One thing the proposal did was to focus attention on a serious issue: the relatively low rates of voter turnout in the United States. But is a voter lottery a credible way to address the issue? Arizonans thought not and defeated the ballot measure by a 2-to-1 margin. And the turnout rate among the voting-age population in the 2006 election in the Grand Canyon state was 46 percent.

## PARTICIPATION

**participation**

Actions through which ordinary members of a political system attempt to influence decisions.

Democracy assumes citizen **participation**—acting to influence government. In contemporary America, there is persistent evidence that citizens are not much interested in participation. We have grown accustomed to reports of low-voter turnout and public hearings that few attend. In his influential book *Bowling Alone*, political scientist Robert Putnam documented this gradual disengagement of people from all sorts of community activities and organizations.[2]

On the surface, government works just fine with limited participation: The interests of the active become translated into public policy, and those who are inactive can be safely ignored because they do not vote.[3] If, however, some traditional nonvoters such as low-income, less-educated citizens went to the polls, then vote-seeking candidates would be forced to pay more attention to their interests, and public policy might be nudged in a different direction. In this light, it is important to understand both why many people do participate and why others do not. This chapter addresses individual citizen involvement in government; Chapter 5 takes up collective participation (i.e., participation by political parties and interest groups).

## Why and How People Participate

In a representative democracy, voting is the most common form of participation. For many citizens, it is a matter of civic responsibility. It is a fundamental facet of citizenship—after all, it is called "the right to vote." Citizens go to the polls to elect the officials who will govern them. But there are other methods of participation. Consider the citizen who is unhappy because the property taxes on her home have increased substantially from one year to the next. What options are available to her besides voting against incumbent officeholders at the next election? As shown in Figure 4.1, she can be

**Possible Responses to Dissatisfaction in the Community**

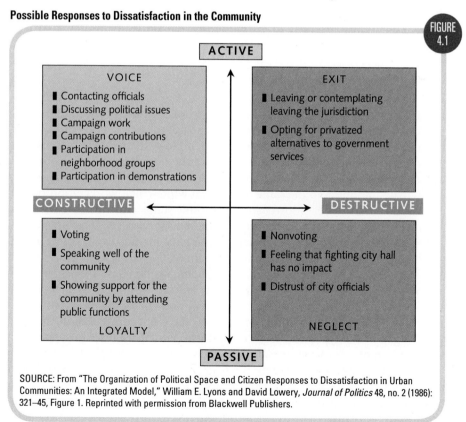

FIGURE 4.1

SOURCE: From "The Organization of Political Space and Citizen Responses to Dissatisfaction in Urban Communities: An Integrated Model," William E. Lyons and David Lowery, *Journal of Politics* 48, no. 2 (1986): 321–45, Figure 1. Reprinted with permission from Blackwell Publishers.

either active or passive; her actions can be either constructive or destructive. Basically, she has four potential responses: loyalty, voice, exit, and neglect.[4]

According to this formulation, voting is an example of *loyalty*, a passive but constructive response to government action. Specifically, this response reflects the irate taxpayer's underlying support for her community despite her displeasure with specific tax policies. An active constructive response is *voice*: The aggrieved property owner could contact officials, work in the campaign of a candidate who promises to lower tax assessments, or, assuming that others in the community share her sentiments, participate in anti-tax groups and organize demonstrations.

Destructive responses (those that undermine the citizen–government relationship) are similarly passive or active. If the citizen simply shrugs and concludes that she can't fight city hall, she is exhibiting a response termed *neglect*. She has nearly given up on the community and does not participate. A more active version of giving up is to *exit*—that is, to leave the community altogether (a response often referred to as voting with your feet). The unhappy citizen will relocate to a community that is more in line with her tax preferences. Each of these participatory options affects public policy decisions in a community. Citizens who choose the voice option frequently find themselves in the thick of things.

Every citizen confronts these participatory options. It is much healthier for the political system if citizens engage in the constructive responses, but some individuals are likely to conclude that constructive participation is of little value to them and opt for neglect or, in more extreme cases, exit.

## Nonparticipation

What motivates the citizens who choose neglect as their best option? One explanation for nonparticipation in politics is socioeconomic status. Individuals with lower levels of income and education tend to participate less than wealthier, more educated individuals do.[5] Tied closely to income and education levels is occupational status. Unskilled workers and hourly wage earners do not participate in politics to the same degree that white-collar workers and professionals do. Individuals of lower socioeconomic status may not have the time, resources, or civic skills required to become actively involved in politics.

Other explanations for nonparticipation have included age (younger people have participated less than middle-aged individuals have), race (blacks have participated less than whites have), and gender (women have participated less than men have). Of these factors, however, only age continues to affect political activity levels. African American political participation actually surpasses that of whites when socioeconomic status is taken into consideration,[6] and the gender gap in the types and levels of political participation has disappeared.[7] America's youth, however, remain less likely to vote, although the upsurge in voting among eighteen- to twenty-nine-year-olds in the 2008 presidential election may signal a new trend in youthful participation. Groups such as Kids Voting USA have developed programs to socialize children about political affairs, surmising that children who get into the habit of citizen participation at an

## BREAKING NEW GROUND

### Voting: It's Not Just for Old People

The company Urban Outfitters got itself into hot water with some folks when it started selling a T-shirt with the statement "Voting is for old people" printed on it. In fact, the Institute of Politics at Harvard contacted the retailer and asked its representatives to reconsider selling the T-shirt, arguing that it sent the wrong message. Actually, the voter turnout rate among eighteen- to twenty-nine-year-olds has increased in presidential elections since 2000. Still, it tends to lag the turnout rate of older voters. Some contend this gap occurs because political parties have failed to energize young voters; others argue that candidates and their messages have not had a youthful focus. Many believe that a step in the right direction would be to utilize youth-oriented media more effectively, such as MTV's Rock the Vote. Barack Obama's successful 2008 presidential campaign skillfully used cyberspace to rally a cadre of youthful supporters, raise money, and get out the vote.

Perhaps the most controversial suggestion came from California, where four legislators proposed giving fourteen- to seventeen-year-olds the right to vote. Not a whole vote, but a partial one. Fourteen- and fifteen-year-olds would be given one-quarter of a vote; their sixteen- and seventeen-year-old counterparts would be allowed one-half of a vote. The idea is that if young people had a sort of electoral apprenticeship, it would raise their consciousness about the importance of voting. Before dismissing this as just another wacky idea, consider that parts of Germany and Austria already allow sixteen-year-olds to vote, and Great Britain is considering a similar proposal. The California proposal would have amended the state's constitution and required a two-thirds majority of both houses before it could be put on the ballot for voters to decide.

Some embraced the idea as sensible, arguing that American youths are far more sophisticated than they used to be, with access to much more information. They would take their enfranchisement seriously and exercise a thoughtful vote. Youth rights groups are supportive of the concept, claiming that lowering the voting age would reduce some of the alienation felt by teens. After all, young people are affected by government's actions, why not let them have some say via the voting booth? However, not all supporters of the measure like the idea of fractional votes. They contend that if the vote is extended to younger people, it ought to be a full vote, not a partial one. Nine states, including Maryland and Virginia, already allow seventeen-year-olds to vote in primary elections if they will turn eighteen by Election Day. Many folks are just plain opposed to the whole idea, seeing it as conferring a measure of adulthood on children who should be enjoying childhood. They say that it burdens children too soon with adult responsibilities and opens the door for other actions such as redefining criminal statutes that differentiate between youthful and adult offenders. It was concerns such as these that have stalled the California proposal...at least for now.

SOURCES: "Voting Is for Old People," *Christian Science Monitor* (March 8, 2004), p. 8; Daniel B. Wood, "Should 14 Year Olds Vote? OK, How About a Quarter of a Vote?" *Christian Science Monitor* (March 12, 2004), pp. 1–2; Daniel deVise, "One Teen's Campaign to Restore Voting Rights," *Washington Post* (January 21, 2008); Pew Research Center, "Dissecting the 2008 Electorate: Most Diverse in U.S. History," http://pewresearch.org/assets/pdf/dissecting-2008-electorate.pdf (April 30, 2009).

early age will be more politically active as adults.[8] (The Breaking New Ground box takes up the issue of age and voting.) Another factor that exerts an independent effect on participation is where one lives. Big-city dwellers (those who live in places with a population of 1 million or more) are less likely than people in small communities (less than 5,000 inhabitants) to participate in various civic activities, including contacting local officials, attending community meetings, and voting in local elections.[9]

The explanation for nonparticipation does not rest solely with the individual. Institutional features—the way the political system is designed—may suppress participation. For example, local governments that have instituted nonpartisan elections, in which candidates run without party affiliation, have removed an important mobilizing factor for voters. Voter turnout tends to be lower in these elections than in partisan contests. City council meetings scheduled at 10 a.m. put a tremendous strain on workers who must take time off from their jobs if they want to attend; consequently, attendance is low. And local governments in which it is difficult for citizens to contact the appropriate official with a service request or complaint are not doing much to facilitate participation. Features like these play an often unrecognized role in dampening participation. Although participation in politics and government is often considered a civic duty, it is not a costless act, a point that economist Anthony Downs argued fifty years ago.[10] It is no wonder that some folks who are reasonably content with the actions of government decide that nonparticipation is a rational use of their time. These **free riders** receive the benefits of government, although they do not participate.

When nonvoters are asked why they failed to participate in an election, the responses show that a lack of enthusiasm for the candidates themselves or events in the potential voter's own life often play a role. Table 4.1 provides data from a survey conducted by Michael Alvarez and his colleagues into the reasons why people don't vote.

**free rider**

A person who enjoys the benefit of a public good without bearing the cost.

**TABLE 4.1    Reasons for Not Voting in 2008 Election**

| PERCENTAGE SAYING IT WAS A: | MAJOR FACTOR | MINOR FACTOR | NOT A FACTOR |
|---|---|---|---|
| Didn't Like Choices | 31.2 | 12.3 | 56.5 |
| Too Busy | 22.8 | 9.6 | 67.6 |
| Illness | 16.0 | 5.0 | 79.0 |
| Transportation Problems | 14.4 | 5.2 | 80.4 |
| Out of Town on Election Day | 13.8 | 3.8 | 82.4 |
| Registration Problems | 13.0 | 6.9 | 80.2 |
| Did Not Receive Ballot/Received Ballot Too Late | 12.2 | 3.6 | 84.2 |
| Line Too Long at Polling Place | 11.1 | 8.9 | 80.0 |
| Bad Time/Location | 10.1 | 9.5 | 80.4 |
| Didn't Know Where to Go to Vote | 9.2 | 10.4 | 80.4 |
| Did Not Receive Absentee Ballot | 7.8 | 3.9 | 88.4 |
| Had Wrong Identification | 7.0 | 3.4 | 89.5 |
| Forgot about the Election | 4.8 | 4.2 | 91.0 |
| Weather Issues | 2.5 | 5.4 | 92.2 |

SOURCE: Alvarez, Michael R., et al., "2008 Survey of the Performance of American Elections" http://www.pewcenteronthestates.org/uploadedFiles/Final%20report20090218.pdf (June 17, 2009).

Nonparticipants typically have lower levels of interest in politics and tend to be weakly connected to their communities.[11] In many communities, the media have launched efforts to boost participation in civic life. Television stations convene forums and town meetings on the issues of the day, and local newspapers report the views of ordinary citizens on current events. Called public or civic journalism, the idea is to reconnect people with the democratic process and, in doing so, to make them active participants in public life. This is just one effort at restoring some of the **social capital** that Putnam found lacking in contemporary communities. In the language of Figure 4.1, greater social capital leads to more constructive forms of citizen participation.

**social capital**
A dense network of reciprocal social relations that promotes greater civic engagement.

## The Struggle for the Right to Vote

State constitutions in the eighteenth and early nineteenth centuries entrusted only propertied white males with the vote. They did not encourage public involvement in government, and the eventual softening of restrictions on suffrage did not occur without a struggle. Restrictions based on property ownership and wealth were eventually dropped, but women, blacks, and Native Americans were still denied the right to vote.

In an effort to attract women to its rugged territory, Wyoming enfranchised women in 1869. The suffragists—women who were actively fighting for the right to vote—scored a victory when Colorado extended the vote to women in 1893. Gradually, other states began enfranchising women, and in 1920 the Nineteenth Amendment to the U.S. Constitution, forbidding states to deny the right to vote "on account of sex," was ratified.

Even after the Fifteenth Amendment (1870) extended the vote to blacks, some southern states clung defiantly to traditional ways that denied blacks and poor people their rights. Poll taxes, literacy tests, and white primaries were among the barriers erected by the segregationists. U.S. Supreme Court decisions such as *Smith v. Allwright* (1944), which outlawed white primaries, and federal actions such as the Civil Rights Act of 1964 and the Twenty-Fourth Amendment (1964), which made poll taxes unconstitutional, helped blacks gain access to the polls. But in some jurisdictions, informal methods designed to discourage participation by African Americans continued.

The **Voting Rights Act of 1965** finally broke the back of the segregationists' efforts. Under its provisions, federal poll watchers and registrars were dispatched to particular counties to investigate voter discrimination. To this day, counties covered under the Voting Rights Act (all of nine southern states and parts of seven other states) must submit to the U.S. Department of Justice any changes in election laws, such as new precinct lines or new polling places. Over time, judicial interpretations, congressional actions, and Justice Department rules have modified the Voting Rights Act. One of the most important modifications has been to substitute an effects test for the original intent test. In other words, if a governmental action has the effect of discouraging minority voting, whether intentionally or not, the action must be rejected. Civil rights activists welcomed this change because proving the intent of an action is much more difficult than simply demonstrating its effect.

**Voting Rights Act of 1965**
The law that effectively enfranchised racial minorities by giving the national government the power to decide whether individuals are qualified to vote and to intercede in state and local electoral operations when necessary.

## Voting Patterns

Voter turnout is affected by several factors. First, it varies according to the type of election. A presidential race usually attracts a higher proportion of eligible voters than a state or local election does; therefore, turnout is higher when a presidential contest is on the ballot than it is in off-years, when many state races occur. In 2008, with a presidential race under way, turnout was approximately 61 percent of the voting-age population; in 2006 when there was no presidential election on the ballot—but many governors' races—turnout was only 40 percent. Second, popular candidates running a close race seem to increase voter interest. When each candidate has a chance to win, voters sense that their vote will matter more than in a race with a sure winner. Third, not only partisan competition but party ideology affects voter turnout.[12] When parties take distinctive ideological stances in competitive elections, the incentive for party-identifiers to vote increases.

Nationally, voter registration stands at approximately 76 percent of the **voting-age population**. Not everyone who is of voting age is actually eligible to vote, however. Noncitizens cannot vote (although they can in school board elections in a few localities), and most states have laws barring convicted felons and the mentally incompetent from participating. When you remove the non-eligible population from consideration, registration among the **voting-eligible population** stood at approximately 88 percent in 2008. Registration matters because people who are registered tend to vote, and votes translate into political power. Thus, groups anxious to increase their electoral clout will launch registration drives among their membership.

States can also be differentiated according to voter turnout rates (see Figure 4.2 for voter turnout levels in 2008). In 2008, the highest turnout rates were recorded in Minnesota, where 78.2 percent of the voting-eligible population voted, and Wisconsin, where 72.6 percent voted. Hawaii, with 50.5 percent voting, and West Virginia, where 50.6 percent of the eligible voters participated, garnered the dubious distinctions of being the states with the lowest voter turnout in 2008.[13] States with moralistic political cultures typically experience higher voter turnout than do states with traditionalistic political cultures. States with competitive political parties (as opposed to states where one party dominates) tend to have elections with a higher proportion of voters participating; each party needs to mobilize individuals who identify with it in order to win. Finally, the states can affect turnout by the way in which they administer the registration and election processes. Is voting a convenient exercise, or is it an arduous task marked by long lines at the polling places, a requirement to show a government-issued photo ID card, and confusing ballots inside the voting booth?

Registering to vote is getting easier. Passage of the National Voter Registration Act in 1993 means that individuals can register to vote when they apply for a driver's license, welfare benefits, or unemployment compensation or when they register their automobile. States allow voters to register by mail and some states, such as Florida, have taken another step by allowing online voter registration; any computer terminal with an Internet connection can be a

**voting-age population**

Adults eighteen years of age and older.

**voting-eligible population**

The voting-age population excluding those who are noncitizens, convicted felons, or mentally incompetent, depending on state law.

**State Voter Turnout, 2008**

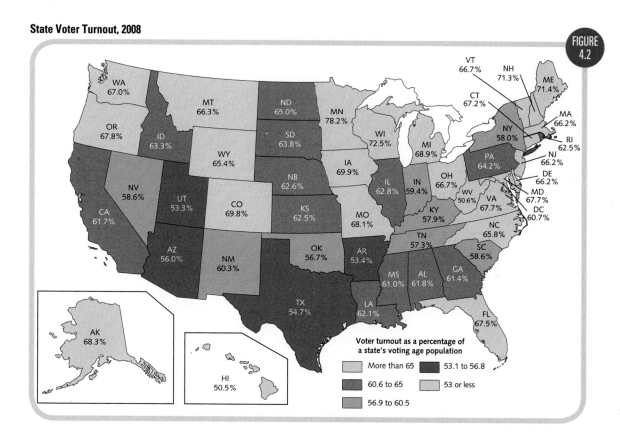

FIGURE 4.2

Voter turnout as a percentage of a state's voting age population

| | |
|---|---|
| More than 65 | 53.1 to 56.8 |
| 60.6 to 65 | 53 or less |
| 56.9 to 60.5 | |

registration site. And some states have moved the closing date for registration nearer to the actual date of the election, giving potential voters more time to register. This factor is important because campaigns tend to heighten the public's interest in the election. Most states now close their registration books fewer than thirty days before an election, and Maine, Minnesota, New Hampshire, Wisconsin, and Wyoming allow registration on election day.[14] North Dakota is the only state in the nation that does not require voter registration.

The voting experience is changing too, with many states giving their citizens the choice to cast their votes before the day of the election. The list below outlines the options:

- thirty-two states allow "no-excuse" in-person early voting, either on a voting machine or with an absentee ballot (e.g., California and Texas)
- fourteen states require an excuse (e.g., out of town on election day, disabled) for early in-person absentee voting (e.g., Kentucky and Missouri)
- four states do not allow early or in person absentee voting, but two of them have set up a vote-by-mail system for the entire state (Oregon) or specific counties (Washington).
- All states have procedures for regular absentee voting by mail, twenty-eight states do not require an excuse, twenty-two do.[15]

Does making voting easier matter? Analysis of Oregon's vote-by-mail system showed that the turnout rate increased, especially among groups such as homemakers, the disabled, and people in the twenty-six- to thirty-eight-year-old range.[16] In 2008, approximately 30 percent of voters cast their ballots before election day, up from 20 percent in the previous election cycle. In Colorado, Nevada, and Washington, votes cast prior to election day comprised more than 65 percent of the total.[17] As more states loosen the restrictions on early voting, the notion of election *day* is gradually giving way.

# ELECTIONS

Elections are central to a representative democracy. Voters choose governors and legislators, and in most states, lieutenant governors, attorneys general, secretaries of state, and state treasurers; in some, they also choose the heads of the agriculture and education departments, judges, and the public utility commissioners. At the local level, the list of elected officials includes mayors and council members, county commissioners, county judges, sheriffs, tax assessors, and school board members. If state and local governments are to function effectively, elections must provide talented, capable leaders. But elections are not just about outcomes; they are also about the process itself. Florida's troubles with ballot design, voting machines, and recount rules in the 2000 presidential election underscored the need for elections to be administered fairly and transparently.

Significant changes in election management and especially in voting technology have occurred during the past few years. Figure 4.3 shows the different kinds of voting equipment available and the percentage of the electorate using each of them. Although electronic voting machines (akin to automatic teller machines) are becoming more popular, concerns over their accuracy and security remain. At issue is whether these systems should provide a VVPAT, or voter-verified paper audit trail, to supplement the record of the count in the electronic machine's memory.

## Primaries

For a party to choose a nominee for the general-election ballot, potential candidates must be winnowed. In the pre-Jacksonian era, party nominees were chosen by a legislative caucus—that is, a conference of the party's legislators. Caucuses gave way to the mechanism of state party conventions, which were similar to national presidential nomination conventions but without most of the spectacle; popularly elected delegates from across a state convened to select the party's nominees. Then the Progressive movement made an effort to open up the nomination process and make it more democratic. Political parties adopted the **primary system**, whereby voters directly choose from among several candidates to select the party's nominees for the general election. The use of primaries has effectively diminished the organizational power of political parties.

**primary system**
The electoral mechanism for selecting party nominees to compete in the general election.

**Voting Equipment in Use**

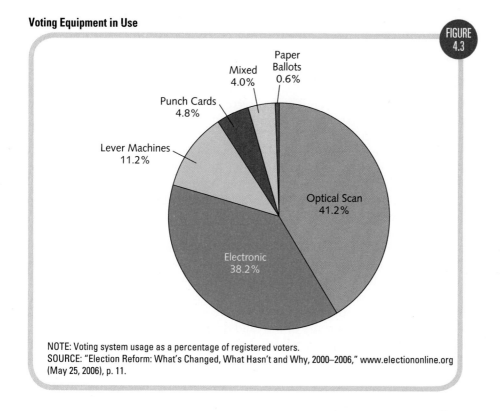

Mixed 4.0%
Paper Ballots 0.6%
Punch Cards 4.8%
Lever Machines 11.2%
Optical Scan 41.2%
Electronic 38.2%

NOTE: Voting system usage as a percentage of registered voters.
SOURCE: "Election Reform: What's Changed, What Hasn't and Why, 2000–2006," www.electiononline.org (May 25, 2006), p. 11.

FIGURE 4.3

Thirteen states still allow for party conventions in particular instances, such as nominations for lieutenant governor and attorney general (Michigan) and selection of a slate of nominees by third parties (Kansas). Connecticut, the last state to adopt primaries, operates a unique challenge system whereby party nominees for various state offices are selected at a convention; but if a contest develops at the convention and a second candidate receives as much as 15 percent of the votes, the convention's nominee and the challenger square off in a primary.[18]

**Primary Types** Primaries can be divided into two types: closed and open. The only voters who can participate in a **closed primary** for a particular party are those who are registered in that party; an **open primary** does not require party membership. However, even this basic distinction lends itself to some variation. States differ, for example, in terms of the ease with which voters can change party affiliation and participate in the closed primary of the other party. In eleven states, a voter is an enrolled member of one party (or is an Independent and may or may not be eligible to vote in either party's primary) and can change that affiliation only well in advance of the primary election.[19] New Mexico and Pennsylvania are two of the states that conduct completely closed primaries. Fifteen other closed primary states (Iowa and Wyoming are examples) allow voters to change their party registration on election day, thus accommodating shifts in voters' loyalties.

**closed primary**
A primary in which only voters registered in the party are allowed to participate.

**open primary**
Voters decide which party's primary they will participate in.

Open primaries account for (and perhaps contribute to) fleeting partisan loyalties among the public. The key difference among states with open primaries is whether a voter is required to claim publicly which party's primary he is participating in. Ten states, including Alabama and Indiana, require voters to request a specific party's ballot at the polling place. Eleven other open-primary states make no such demand; voters secretly select the ballot of the party in which they wish to participate. Idaho and Wisconsin are examples of states in which primaries are truly open.

For many years, California and Washington operated a **blanket primary**, which allowed voters to cross over from one party's primary ballot to the other's primary ballot in a single election. A voter could select from among Democratic candidates for governor and among Republican candidates for the legislature, in effect participating in both primaries. Federal court rulings in 2000 (California) and 2003 (Washington) put an end to blanket primaries and now California uses a modified closed primary system, allowing each party to decide whether unaffiliated voters can participate in its primary. Washington opted for a modified open primary approach.

Louisiana does something completely different: The Pelican State uses a single nonpartisan primary for its statewide and congressional races. Voters can choose from among any of the candidates, regardless of party affiliation. If a candidate receives a majority of votes in the first round of voting, she is elected to office; if she does not, the top two vote-getters face each other in a **runoff election**. The nonpartisan, or "unitary," primary is particularly disruptive to political party power. In New York City, Mayor Michael Bloomberg, arguing that local party machines had "a chokehold on ballot access," fought unsuccessfully to change the city's charter to allow nonpartisan primaries.[20] Not surprisingly, the chief opposition to his proposal came from the Big Apple's Democratic and Republican parties.

**blanket primary**

A primary in which a voter is allowed to vote for candidates of both parties in a single election.

**runoff election**

A second election pitting the top two vote-getters from a first election in which no candidate received a majority of the votes cast.

**Primary Runoff Elections** A runoff election is held in some states if none of the candidates for an office receives a majority of votes in the primary. Primary runoff elections are used by parties in eight states: Alabama, Arkansas, Georgia, Mississippi, North Carolina, Oklahoma, South Carolina, and Texas. (Kentucky and South Dakota use primary runoffs but only in certain instances.) In the past, these eight states were one-party (Democratic) states, so the greatest amount of competition for an office occurred in the Democratic Party's primaries, in which as many as ten candidates might enter the race. When many candidates compete, it is quite probable that no one will receive a majority of the votes, so the top two vote-getters face each other in a runoff election. This process ensures that the party's nominee is preferred by a majority of the primary voters.

Theoretically, the rationale for the runoff primary is majority rule. But political circumstances have changed since several southern states adopted the runoff primary system in the 1920s, and the Democratic Party no longer dominates the region. In fact, in many southern states, the Republican Party has overtaken the Democrats, a subject we will cover in Chapter 5. This raises an important question: Has the runoff primary outlived its usefulness? It is often difficult for a party to mobilize its voters for the second election, and voter participation in the runoff drops, on average, by one-third.[21] And they are costly to operate: Kentucky estimated the administrative cost of holding a statewide gubernatorial runoff primary to be approximately $5.4 million.[22] One solution to this problem for parties might be the "ranked choice" or "**instant runoff**" that San Francisco, California, Memphis, Tennessee, and Burlington, Vermont, and a few other cities have begun using in their municipal elections. In an instant runoff, voters rank the primary candidates in their order of preference. If no candidate receives a majority of first choices, the candidate with the fewest of them is eliminated and voters who ranked the eliminated candidate first now have their ballots counted for their second choice. The process continues until one candidate has a majority; a runoff primary election is avoided.

**instant runoff**

Voters use preference rankings to select candidates at a single election.

## General Elections

Primaries culminate in the general election, through which winning candidates become officeholders. When the general election pits candidates of the two major parties against one another, the winner is the candidate who receives more votes, that is, a majority of the votes cast. In a race in which more than two candidates compete (which occurs when an Independent or a third-party candidate enters a race), the winner may not receive a majority but instead receives a **plurality**. A few states allow candidates to run under the label of more than one party, which is called **fusion**. In New York, in 2006, for instance, Eliot Spitzer was the candidate for governor of the Democratic, Independence, and Working Families parties.

**plurality**

The number of votes (though not necessarily a majority) cast for the winning candidate in an election with more than two candidates.

Political parties have traditionally been active in general elections, mobilizing voters in support of their candidates. Their role has decreased over time, however, because general-election campaigns have become more candidate centered and geared to the candidate's own organization.[23] One new twist in the past two decades has been the emergence of legislative party caucuses as major factors in general elections. In large states with professionalized legislatures, the funds distributed to their party's nominees by legislative party caucuses run into the millions of dollars. In addition to funding, legislative party caucuses provide other types of election assistance, such as seminars on issues and campaign management, making these organizations powerful players in state politics.

**fusion**

A state election provision that allows candidates to run on more than one party ticket.

Most states schedule their statewide elections in off-years, that is, in years in which no presidential election is held. Only eleven states elected governors during the presidential election year of 2008; forty-one held their statewide races in other years. (The number sums to fifty-two because New Hampshire and Vermont limit their governors to two-year terms, thereby holding gubernatorial elections in both off- and on-years.) Among those forty-one off-year states, five—Kentucky, Louisiana, Mississippi, New Jersey, and Virginia— have elections that take place in odd-numbered years. Off-year elections prevent the presidential race from diverting attention from state races and also minimize the possible **coattail effect**, by which a presidential candidate can

**coattail effect**

The tendency of a winning (or losing) presidential candidate to carry state candidates of the same party into (or out of) office.

affect the fortunes of state candidates of the same party. By holding elections in off-years, races for governor may serve instead as referenda on the sitting president's performance in office. Generally, however, the health of a state's economy tends to be a critical issue in gubernatorial elections.[24]

## Recent State Elections

When the dust settled after the 2006 elections, it was Democrats who were smiling. For the first time since 1994, Democrats could claim a majority of the nation's governorships. By picking up open seats in five states (Arkansas, Colorado, Massachusetts, New York, and Ohio) and ousting one Republican incumbent (Maryland), Democrats increased their gubernatorial numbers to twenty-eight. Twenty-two seats were in Republican hands, including California and Texas, where GOP incumbents were reelected, and Florida. In legislative races, Democrats experienced a net gain of more than 300 seats, which was sufficient to shift partisan control of the lawmaking branch in several states. The year 2007 was quiet by comparison, only three states—Kentucky, Louisiana, and Mississippi—held gubernatorial elections and the outcome did not change the partisan balance. In the legislative elections held in these states and Virginia, the result was a net gain of one seat for the Democrats.

In 2008, gubernatorial and legislative elections were conducted in the shadow of the presidential contest. Despite change at the national level, low change was the theme at the state level: all eight incumbents were reelected; in only one state (Missouri) was there a partisan shift in gubernatorial control (from Republican to Democrat). In terms of issues, voters cited the economy, taxes, education, and ethics as the chief concerns. On the legislative side, Democrats gained control of five chambers to bring their total to sixty; Republicans added four, making their total thirty-six chambers. (Two chambers were evenly split.)

The focus in 2009 shifted to New Jersey, where incumbent Democratic governor Jon Corzine sought reelection, and Virginia with an open seat gubernatorial contest. Republican candidates were triumphant in campaigns dominated by basic economic issues such as unemployment, home foreclosures, and taxes. State-specific issues also played a role in the gubernatorial elections: corruption in New Jersey and transportation in Virginia.

## Nonpartisan Elections

**nonpartisan election**

An election without party labels.

A **nonpartisan election** removes the political party identification from the candidate in an effort to depoliticize the electoral campaign. Elections that have been made nonpartisan include those for many judicial offices and for many local-level positions. The special task of judges—adjudicating guilt or innocence, determining right and wrong—does not lend itself to partisan interpretation. The job of local governments—delivering public services—has also traditionally been considered non-ideological. Nonpartisan local elections are likely to be found in municipalities and in school districts and special districts (see Chapters 10 and 11).

Under a nonpartisan election system, all candidates for an office compete in a first election; if there's no majority winner, the top two vote-getters run in a second election (runoff). Although approximately three-quarters of cities use nonpartisan elections, some regional variation exists in their usage. The prevalence of nonpartisanship is somewhat lower in the Northeast and Midwest than it is in western cities.[25]

Most studies have concluded that nonpartisanship depresses turnout in municipal elections that are held independent of state and national elections. The figures are not dramatic, but in what are already low-turnout elections, the difference can run as high as 10 percent of municipal voters.[26] Recent research has found that lower turnout results in lessened representation of Latinos and Asian Americans on city councils and in the mayor's office.[27] Nonpartisan elections seem to produce a city council that is somewhat well-to-do by socioeconomic standards and a greater number of officeholders who consider themselves Republicans.

What does it take to get elected? In the absence of political parties, candidates are forced to create their own organizations to run for office. They raise and spend money (much of it their own), and they seek the support of business and citizen groups. Money matters, and according to studies of city elections in Atlanta and St. Louis, so do incumbency and newspaper endorsements.[28] In some communities, **slating groups** function as unofficial parties by recruiting candidates and financing their campaigns; citizens' groups can also be an important factor in local elections.[29]

**slating groups**
Nonpartisan political organizations that endorse and promote a slate of candidates.

## DIRECT DEMOCRACY

What happens when the government does not respond to the messages that the people are sending? More and more frequently, the answer is to transform the messages into ballot propositions and let the citizens make their own laws. As explained in Chapter 3, *initiatives* are proposed laws or constitutional amendments that are placed on the ballot by citizen petition, to be approved or rejected by popular vote. An initiative lets citizens enact their own laws, bypassing the state legislature. This mechanism for legislation by popular vote was one of several reforms of the Progressive era, which lasted roughly from 1890 to 1920. Other Progressive reforms included the popular referendum and the recall. The **popular referendum** allows citizens to petition to vote on actions taken by legislative bodies. It provides a means by which the public can overturn a legislative enactment. (A popular referendum is different from a general **referendum**—a proposition put on the ballot by the legislature that requires voter approval before it can take effect. Constitutional amendments and bond issues are examples of general referenda.) The **recall** election, another citizen-initiated process, requires elected officials to stand for a vote on their removal before their term has expired. Recall provides the public with an opportunity to force an official out of office.

**popular referendum**
A special type of referendum whereby citizens can petition to vote on actions taken by legislative bodies.

**referendum**
A procedure whereby a governing body submits proposed laws, constitutional amendments, or bond issues to the voters for ratification.

**recall**
A procedure that allows citizens to vote elected officials out of office before their term has expired.

The key characteristic shared by initiative, popular referendum, and recall is that they are actions begun by citizens. The Progressives advocated these mechanisms to expand the role of citizens and to restrict the power of intermediary institutions such as legislatures, political parties, and elected officials. Their efforts were particularly successful in the western part of the United States, probably due to the difficulty of amending existing state constitutions in the East and to an elitist fear of the working class (namely, the industrialized immigrants in the Northeast and the rural black sharecroppers in the South). The newer western states, by contrast, were quite open, both procedurally and socially. In 1898, South Dakota became the first state to adopt the initiative process; the initiative was actually used for the first time in Oregon in 1902 when citizens successfully petitioned for ballot questions on mandatory political party primaries and local option liquor sales. Both of the initiatives were approved.

Today, twenty-four states allow the initiative for constitutional amendments, statutes, or both; Mississippi is the most recent addition, having adopted it in 1992. A few of the twenty-four states use the indirect initiative, which gives the legislature an opportunity to consider the proposed measure. If the legislature fails to act or if it rejects the measure, the proposal is put before the voters at the next election. Popular referendum is provided in twenty-five states, and recall of state officials is provided in eighteen. These figures understate the use of such mechanisms throughout the country, however, because many states without statewide initiative, popular referendum, and recall allow their use at the local government level.[30] Table 4.2 lists some of the states that give citizens all three of the direct democracy mechanisms and some of the states with none of them.

## The Initiative

The first step in the initiative process is the petition. A draft of the proposed law (or constitutional amendment) is circulated along with a petition for citizens to sign. The petition signature requirement varies by state but usually falls between 5 and 10 percent of the number of votes cast in the preceding statewide election. To ensure that a matter is of statewide concern and that signatures have been gathered beyond a single area, some states set geographic

| TABLE 4.2 | Five States That Do, Five States That Don't | |
|---|---|---|
| **ALL THREE DIRECT DEMOCRACY MECHANISMS** | **NONE OF THE DIRECT DEMOCRACY MECHANISMS** | |
| Arizona | Alabama | |
| California | Iowa | |
| Colorado | North Carolina | |
| North Dakota | Vermont | |
| Wyoming | Virginia | |

SOURCE: Various Tables, *Book of the States 2008*, Lexington, KY: Council of State Governments, 2008.

distributional requirements. In Montana, for example, signature requirements must be met in at least one-third of the legislative districts and in Nebraska in two-fifths of the counties. Signatures can be gathered by door-to-door canvassing, buttonholing people at shopping malls and sporting events, posting downloadable petition forms on the Internet, and sending forms to a pre-selected list of likely signers.

**The Popularity of Initiatives** One of the most influential modern initiatives was California's Proposition 13 (1978), which rolled back property taxes in the state and spawned an immediate wave of tax-reduction propositions across the land. The increased popularity of initiatives has at least two explanations: (1) Some observers believe that wavering public confidence in government has led citizens to take matters into their own hands. The attitude seems to be that "if government can't be trusted to do the right thing, we'll do it ourselves." (2) New methods of signature collection have brought the initiative process within the reach of almost any well-financed group with a grievance or concern. An example from Massachusetts makes the point. When then-governor Paul Cellucci could not get the legislature to pass his tax-cut proposals, he took the issue straight to the voters. Using donations from supporters, he paid a company to collect sufficient signatures on petitions, and he got his issue on the ballot.[31] Massachusetts voters approved it. Figure 4.4 shows the use (and passage) of citizen initiatives by state from 1904 to 2008. Three states—Oregon, California, and Colorado—accounted for approximately one-third of the 2,305 ballot initiatives during this period.

**Recent Initiatives** If ballot questions are any indication of the public's mood, then the public has had quite an attitude lately. Listed below is a sampling of the fifty-nine citizen initiatives appearing on the 2008 ballots, and the outcomes. California and Colorado led the way with ten initiatives on their ballots; Oregon had eight. As is typically the case, more initiatives went down to defeat than passed; historically, the approval rate for statewide initiatives is around 41 percent.[32] The states, the proposed initiative, and the results included:

- Arizona, a proposal to require sellers of new homes to provide a ten-year warranty to buyers (failed).
- Arkansas, a measure that prohibits people cohabitating outside marriage from adopting children (passed).
- California, the Prevention of Farm Animal Cruelty Act, which requires a minimum living space for certain animals (passed).
- Colorado, a provision to allocate surplus revenue to public education rather than refunding it to taxpayers (failed).
- Massachusetts, a proposal to decriminalize possession of small amounts of marijuana (passed).
- Oregon's Kids First Act, which bases public school teachers' pay raises on classroom performance, not seniority (failed).
- Washington's Death with Dignity Act, which allows doctors to prescribe lethal doses of medication at the request of terminally ill patients (passed).[33]

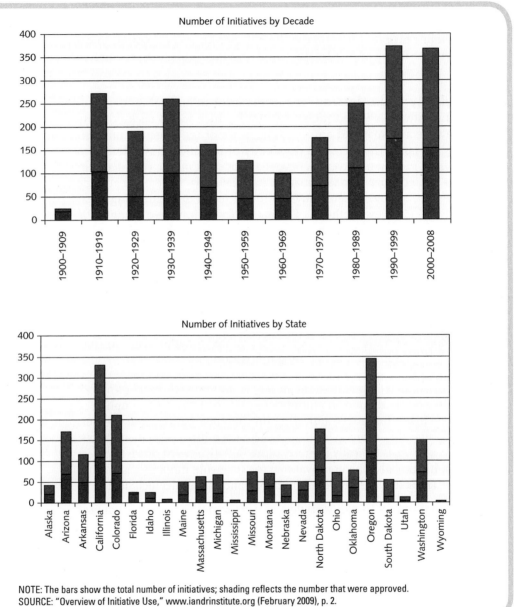

**FIGURE 4.4**

**Overview of Initiative Use over Time by State**

NOTE: The bars show the total number of initiatives; shading reflects the number that were approved.
SOURCE: "Overview of Initiative Use," www.iandrinstitute.org (February 2009), p. 2.

**Questions About the Initiative** By resorting to initiatives, citizens can bypass (or, in the case of indirect initiatives, prod) an obstructive legislature. And initiatives can be positive or negative—that is, they can be used in the absence of legislative action or they can be used to repudiate actions taken by the legislature. But is the initiative process appropriate for resolving tough public problems? Seldom are issues so simple that a yes-or-no ballot question can adequately reflect appropriate options and alternatives. A legislative setting, by contrast, fosters the negotiation and compromise that are likely to produce workable solutions.

A related concern is whether the public is too ill informed to make intelligent choices or to avoid susceptibility to emotional appeals. Ballot questions are considered low-information elections: Facing little information or conflicting claims, voters respond to readily available cues. Some initiative states have enacted laws requiring clear identification of financial sponsors of initiatives, on the assumption that the public is being hoodwinked by some initiatives. But, at the same time, initiatives have positive effects on the electoral process. For one, they seem to stimulate more citizen participation. Research has found that voters with frequent exposure to ballot questions are more likely to vote, donate money to political campaigns, and feel more politically efficacious.[34] However, amid these salutary effects, ballot initiatives seem to place citizens in an adversarial relationship with government and spur distrust of public officials.[35]

Legislators are of two minds when it comes to direct citizen involvement in policy making. On the one hand, having the public decide a controversial issue such as abortion or school prayer helps legislators out of tight spots. On the other hand, increased citizen lawmaking intrudes on the central function of the legislature and usurps legislative power. Given the popularity of initiatives, legislators must proceed cautiously with actions that would make them more difficult to use. So far, efforts to increase the signature requirements, as Oklahoma and Wyoming legislators tried to do in 2002 and 2008, respectively, or to reduce the amount of time citizens and groups have to get petitions signed, a change that Florida lawmakers considered in 2004, have been unsuccessful. A citizenry accustomed to the initiative process does not look kindly on its weakening. A survey of Oregon citizens found 81 percent agreeing with this statement: "Ballot initiatives enhance the democratic process in Oregon by allowing voters to decide important policy issues."[36]

Once an initiative is passed, the new law has to be implemented and, as research has shown, "under normal conditions, legislatures, bureaucrats, or other government officials will work to alter a winning initiative's impact on public policy."[37] Direct democracy enthusiasts should heed the words of political scientist Valentina Bali, who studied local compliance with a California initiative intended to dismantle bilingual education programs: "... the large number of constraints suggests that the final policy outcome of an initiative can be quite limited after the initiative's implementation."[38] Initiative sponsors have learned that if they want their initiative to have the desired impact, they have to keep the pressure on, even after the measure has been approved.

## The Recall

Recalls were once a little-used mechanism in state and local governments. Only eighteen states provide for recall of state officials, and in seven of them, judicial officers are exempt. City and county government charters, even in states without recall provisions, typically include a process for recalling local elected officials. In fact, the first known recall was aimed at a Los Angeles city council member in 1904. Recalls have a much higher petition signature requirement than initiatives do; it is common to require a signature minimum of 25 percent of the votes cast in the last election for the office of the official sought to be recalled. Kansas, for example, requires a 40 percent minimum.

Recall efforts usually involve a public perception of official misconduct. On occasion, however, simply running afoul of citizen preferences is enough to trigger a recall, as former California governor Gray Davis discovered in 2003. Californians unhappy with Davis's leadership in resolving the state's budget crunch and its problems with energy deregulation, collected sufficient signatures (a total of 986,874) to force a recall election. The ballot contained two sections: the recall question (a yes-or-no choice) and a list of candidates vying to replace the incumbent if the yeses prevailed. After a seventy-seven-day campaign, 61.2 percent of the Golden State's registered voters turned out to recall Davis by a 55 to 45 percent margin.[39] The winning candidate, a bodybuilder-turned movie star, Arnold Schwarzenegger, captured 49 percent of the vote in a 135-candidate race.

The rationale for the recall process is straightforward: Public officials should be subject to continuous voter control. Whether it is used or not, the power to recall public officials is valued by the public. A national survey several years ago indicated that two-thirds of those polled favored amending the U.S. Constitution to permit the recall of members of Congress.[40] It is unlikely that California's success will trigger a rash of recalls because most states with recall provisions require higher signature thresholds and allow less time to collect signatures than California does. In Nevada, in 2003, for instance, an effort to force a gubernatorial recall election fell well short of the necessary 25 percent of the voters.

Initiatives and recalls have helped open up state and local governments to the public. Yet ironically, increased citizen participation can also jam the machinery of government, thus making its operation more cumbersome. Advocates of greater citizen activism, however, would gladly trade a little efficiency to achieve their goal.

## CITIZEN ACCESS TO GOVERNMENT

As we saw in Figure 4.1, citizens have opportunities to participate in government in many nonelectoral ways. Because state and local governments have undertaken extensive measures to open themselves to public scrutiny and stimulate public input, citizen access to government has been increased. Many of these measures are directly connected with the policy-making process. At minimum, they enable government and the citizenry to exchange information, and thus they contribute to the growing capacity of state and local governments. At most, they may alter political power patterns and resource allocations.

| How to Participate in City Government, Tacoma-style | TABLE 4.3 |
|---|---|
| **CITIZENS' FORUM** | Citizens' Forum takes place at the first city council meeting of every month. During Citizens' Forum, citizens may address the council on any issue. |
| **VISION LINE** | The city manager maintains a twenty-four-hour voicemail line to record ideas, suggestions, issues, and concerns from citizens. Call 253-591-2020 to leave a message. The city manager's office will respond and/or forward the message to the appropriate department. |
| **CITYLINE** | CityLine is aired live Thursday at 9 a.m. TV Tacoma produces this one-hour, live, call-in talk show discussing issues related to city government. Viewers may call in at 253-591-5168 during the show to participate in the discussion. |
| **NEIGHBORHOOD COUNCILS** | The city council established the neighborhood council program in 1993 to provide a link between neighborhoods and city government. The neighborhood councils serve as advisory bodies to the city council and city staff on neighborhood matters. Call 253-591-5229. |
| **TACOMA CARES** | Tacoma CARES (Tacoma Cleanup And Revitalization EffortS) brings together several city services to help with clean-up efforts in Tacoma's neighborhoods. It involves immediate steps to work with neighbors to clean up garbage and debris, and involves a long-range plan to revitalize, improve, and maintain city neighborhoods. Call 253-591-5001. |
| **CITY COUNCIL MEETINGS** | Meetings are held Tuesdays at 5 p.m. in the council chambers, first floor of the Tacoma Municipal Building, 747 Market Street, Tacoma, Washington. TV Tacoma airs the meetings live and replays them during the following week on TV Tacoma, Channel 12. |

SOURCE: City of Tacoma, Mayor Bill Baarsma, Deputy Mayor Julie Anderson, Council Members Jake Fey, Connie Ladenburg, Mike Lonergan, Spiro Manthou, Marilyn Strickland, Rick Talbert, and Lauren Walker. Used by permission; http://www.cityoftacoma.org/Page.aspx?nid=52

An example of a local jurisdiction that has embraced citizen participation extensively is Tacoma, Washington, a city of 203,000 people and with a land area of 49 square miles. Table 4.3 lists six different participatory venues, ranging from a twenty-four-hour voicemail line that records citizen suggestions and complaints to more structured neighborhood council meetings. Through citizens' forums and the CityLine call-in talk show, Tacoma has worked to engage citizens and policy makers in meaningful conversations.

## Opening Up Government

Many of the accessibility measures adopted by state and local governments are the direct result of public demands that government be more accountable. Others have resulted from an official effort to involve the public in the ongoing work of government.

**open meeting laws**

Statutes that open the meetings of government bodies to the public.

**Open Meeting Laws** Florida's 1967 sunshine law is credited with sparking a surge of interest in openness in government, and today **open meeting laws** are on the books in all fifty states. These laws do just what the name implies: They open meetings of government bodies to the public, or, in Florida's parlance, they bring government "into the sunshine." Open meeting laws apply to both the state and local levels and affect the executive branch as well as the legislative branch. Basic open meeting laws have been supplemented by additional requirements in many states. Advance public notice of meetings is required in all states; most insist that minutes be kept, levy penalties against officials who violate the law, and void actions taken in meetings held contrary to sunshine provisions. These "brighter sunshine" laws make a difference. Whether a meeting is open or closed is irrelevant if citizens are unaware that it is occurring. If no penalties are assessed for violation, then there is less incentive for officials to comply.

Although some states would prefer to resist the sun's rays, the trend is toward more openness. But this is complicated by the fact that most states' sunshine laws were written for a world of paper-based records stored in metal filing cabinets. Colorado was one of the first states to make the archived e-mail files of the state's politicians open to the public. Now, eight states require that governmental e-mails be subject to their open-records laws, and four prohibit officials from using e-mails as meetings.[41]

**Administrative Procedure Acts** After state legislation is passed or a local ordinance is adopted, an administrative agency typically is responsible for implementation. This process involves the establishment of rules and regulations and hence constitutes powerful responsibility. In practice, agencies often have wide latitude in translating legislative intent into action. For example, if a new state law creates annual automobile safety inspections, it is the responsibility of the state's Department of Motor Vehicles to make it work. Unless the law specifies the details, bureaucrats will determine the items to be covered in the safety inspection, the location of inspection stations, and the fee to be charged. These details are just as important as the original enactment.

**administrative procedure acts**

Acts that standardize administrative agency operations as a means of safeguarding clients and the general public.

To ensure public access to this critical rule-making process, states have adopted **administrative procedure acts**, which usually require public notice of the proposed rule and an opportunity for citizen comment. All states provide for this notification and comment process, as it is known. These provisions offer the public and various political actors a way to influence the content of agency rules.[42] In addition, some states give citizens the right to petition an administrative agency for an adjustment in the rules.

**Advisory Committees** Another arena for citizen participation that is popular in state and especially local governments is the **advisory committee**, in the form of citizen task forces, commissions, and panels. Regardless of name, these organizations are designed to study a problem and to offer advice, usually in the form of recommendations. People chosen to serve on an advisory committee tend to have expertise as well as interest in the issue and, in most cases, political connections. Wisconsin's Task Force on Global Warming provides an illustration. In 2007, Governor James Doyle assembled a prominent and diverse group of Wisconsin leaders from business, industry, government, energy, and environmental fields to create a plan of action to reduce greenhouse gas emissions in the Badger State. Another option for policy makers is to use a **focus group**, which provides a small group setting for intense discussion and debate about public issues.[43]

Citizen advisory committees provide a formal structure for citizen input. Many cities have created community boards like Tacoma's neighborhood councils to provide a channel for communication between neighborhoods and city government. If officials heed public preferences, citizen advice can become the basis for public policy. Citizen advisory organizations also provide elected officials with a relatively safe course of action. In a politically explosive situation, a governor can say, "I've appointed a citizen task force to study the issue and report back to me with recommendations for action." The governor thus buys time, with the hope that the issue will gradually cool down. Another benefit of these organizations is that they ease citizen acceptance of subsequent policy decisions because the governor can note that an action "was recommended by an impartial panel of citizens." This is not to suggest that citizen advisory committees are merely tools for manipulation by politicians, but they do have uses beyond citizen participation.

## E-Government

The Internet has brought state and local governments into citizens' homes in a way earlier technology could not. States and localities have already incorporated electronic communications into their daily operations. Websites abound and e-mails proliferate. People can click on a city's homepage and find an array of useful information, such as the agenda for the next city council meeting, the minutes of previous council sessions, the city budget, the comprehensive plan, and the like. Some mayors use weblogs or "blogs" as a way to stay in touch with their constituents—and circumvent conventional media. A few, like Mayor R. T. Rybak of Minneapolis, featured in the Engaging Citizen Participation box, use Twitter as a means of connecting with the public. States have created elaborate websites that link the user to vast databases and information resources. In a clever twist, Pennsylvania was the first state to promote its Web address by emblazoning it across the bottom of its vehicle license plates.

**advisory committee**

An organization created by government to involve members of the public in studying and recommending solutions to public problems.

**focus group**

A small group of individuals assembled to provide opinion and feedback about specific issues in government. Participants are often paid for their time.

## Engaging Citizen Participation

## Twittering Politicians

Twitter is a social-networking phenomenon, which, since debuting in April 2007, has spread like wildfire throughout the United States with its one simple question, "What are you doing?" In 140 characters or less, you can update your friends immediately with your current status. The popularity with Twitter lies in its mobility. A "tweet" can be sent and received from many different platforms, such as the Internet, through a text message, an IM, RSS feed, and more. Individuals can receive updates from the friends, celebrities, special-interest groups, and news organizations that matter most to them. Politicians at all levels have discovered that Twitter can be a powerful tool for engaging citizens; many have created Twitter pages to connect personally with the people.

Newark, New Jersey, Mayor Cory Booker, connects with his constituents.

A great example would be Minneapolis Mayor R. T. Rybak, who has joined the social-networking frenzy with his own Twitter page. Since his first "twitter" in April 2008, he has amassed an impressive following of over 4,000 of his citizens. His followers are now able to stay on top of a range of affairs, such as local events happening in the city: "*Tonight you can see some of the city's best artists...music, dance...on the State and Pantages stages for FREE. www.min-neapolismosaic.com.*" He also keeps his citizens informed of state and federal initiatives that impact Minneapolis: "*To find out how we are using the federal Recovery dollars to help Minneapolis, go to www.minneapolisrecovery.us.*" Tweeting about his travel, Mayor Rybak said, "*I'm in China. Either I'm standing upside down on the globe or you are.*" He even includes candid comments about other politicians including Minnesota Governor Tim Pawlenty: "*Does anyone else think Gov. Pawlenty shouldn't be lecturing President Obama (or anyone) about budgeting?*" And Mayor Rybak does not shy away from

adding a personal note to his twitters from time to time. When did his youngest child graduate from high school? It was on June 4, as all his Twitter followers could tell you.

Yet the beauty of Twitter, at least as far as citizen participation is concerned, is that it connects the politicians with the people, and vice-versa. Mayor Rybak's followers are able to twitter back to him with any comments about his latest post, and many citizens do indeed take advantage of this outlet to voice their opinions. But does he read the responses? Absolutely! We know because he twitters his responses back for everyone to see.

If you would like to connect with your local politicians, search for them on Twitter, or any one of your favorite social-networking sites. Politicians are increasingly recognizing the important role these Web 2.0 sites play in citizen participation. In this information age, citizen involvement through the Internet is a trend that will only continue to expand as more of the internet-savvy young voters become engaged in politics.

SOURCES: Mayor R. T. Rybak Twitter Page. http://twitter.com/MayorRTRybak/ Tom Regan, "Twitter: How News and Politics Plays on a Popular Social Networking Service," Christian Science Monitor, www.csmonitor.com/2008/0213/p15s01-stct.html (February 13, 2008).

Now the task for states and localities is to expand their use of the Internet in dealing with the public. Jurisdictions have begun to realize the Internet's potential beyond simple information provision. It started with the downloading of public reports and generic forms and has moved into more highly individualized interaction such as filing taxes, applying for licenses and permits, and accessing personal information.

The Internet also offers an efficient way for government to gauge public opinion and preferences. This aspect of e-government was put to good use in 2003 when Maine's new governor confronted a $1 billion deficit. Clearly, cuts would have to be made, but in which programs? Governor John Baldacci came up with a novel idea: create a budget-balancing game that Pine Tree State residents could play on the state's website.[44] (The look of the game's webpage is displayed in Figure 4.5.) State programs, their costs, and their funding sources were listed. The simulation required players to choose which programs to cut and which taxes to increase as they tried to whittle away at the deficit and achieve a balanced budget. Players were encouraged to e-mail the governor with their suggestions once they made their way through the thicket of competing programs.

One of the major concerns as the push toward e-government grows is that the so-called technology have-nots will be left behind. Low-income Americans lag far behind middle- and upper-income groups regarding access to the Internet. This digital divide has led many communities to install personal computers in libraries as well as in government information kiosks located in shopping malls and transit stations. In an effort to get its rural communities wired, North Dakota spent over $3 million to connect more than sixty communities to a broadband network. Other concerns involve security and privacy. Fear that hackers might break into government computers or that personal information might be misused tempers some public enthusiasm for e-government.

## Volunteerism as Participation

Voluntary action is another constructive participatory activity unrelated to the ballot box. People and organizations donate their time and talents to supplement or even replace government activity. **Volunteerism** is a means of bringing fresh ideas and energy, whether physical or financial, into government while relieving some of the service burden. Washington created the first statewide volunteerism office in 1969, and within twenty years all states had volunteer programs in place.

One highly visible example of volunteerism is the Adopt a Highway program. Over the past fifteen years, the number of local businesses and civic clubs willing to pick up litter along designated stretches of state highways has skyrocketed. You have probably noticed the Adopt a Highway signs, with the names of volunteering groups listed on the signs. The state saves money, the roadsides stay cleaner, and the volunteering groups share good feelings and free advertising. For instance, Minnesota's Don't Waste Our State anti-littering campaign requires groups that volunteer to agree to work at least three times a

**volunteerism**

A form of participation in which individuals or groups donate time or money to a public purpose.

FIGURE 4.5 **An E-Game: Balancing a State Budget**

**The Budget**

My first priority as Governor is the state budget. As I began my term, Maine faces a projected shortfall of $1 billion over the next two years. I submitted a balanced budget to the Legislature on February 7th that eliminates this short-fall without raising taxes. This tool will allow you to view the most current budget projections and to send me your own balance budget proposal.

**The Budget Balancing Education Tool**

The Budget Balancing Tool was created without any General Fund spending, through an innovative partnership between the state and the Information Resource of Maine (InforME). InforME has been self-funding since its inception in 1999 and does not draw money from the state's General Fund Budget.

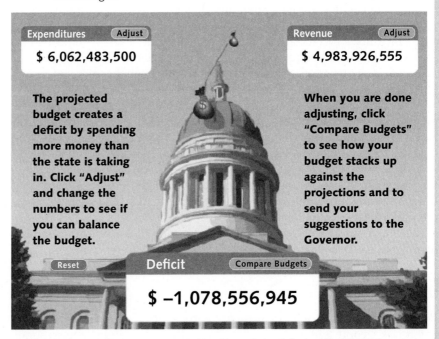

SOURCE: Office of the Governor, State of Maine, www.maine.gov/governor/baldacci/issues/budget/index.html (April 30, 2004).

year on a specific stretch of highway for a minimum of two years. In return, the state supplies equipment to the volunteers and handles removal of the filled trash bags.[45]

Successful volunteer programs like Adopt a Highway are emblematic of the concept of social capital, as mentioned earlier in this chapter. Stephen Knack's 2002 study showed a positive relationship between several indicators of social capital, especially the percentage of the public engaged in volunteerism, and state governmental quality.[46] States with a greater propensity toward volunteerism scored higher on several performance measures, including financial management, capital management, and information technology.

Local governments use volunteers in various ways. Generally, volunteerism is most successful when citizens can develop the required job skills quickly or participate in activities they enjoy, such as library work, recreation programs, or fire protection. In addition to providing services to others, volunteers can be utilized for self-help; that is, they can engage in activities in which they are the primary beneficiaries. For example, some New York City neighborhoods take responsibility for the security and maintenance of nearby parks. Residential crime-watch programs are another variety of self-help. In both these instances, the volunteers and their neighborhoods benefit. Overall, studies show that volunteerism is especially successful in rural areas and small towns.[47]

Important supplements to government volunteer programs are those of the nonprofit sector. Members of local faith-based groups and civic organizations, for example, often volunteer their time in support of community improvement projects such as Habitat for Humanity, Meals on Wheels, and Sistercare. Sometimes volunteerism has a political agenda, as does the Minutemen Civil Defense Corps, a group of volunteers who in 2005 launched a border watch program. Periodically, they mass along stretches of the border with Mexico to monitor illegal entry into the United States. Their actions have added fuel to the firestorm of debate over illegal immigration.

## THE EFFECTS OF CITIZEN PARTICIPATION

Consider again the four quadrants of Figure 4.1. Constructive participatory behaviors, whether active or passive, invigorate government. The capacity of state and local governments depends on several factors, one of which is citizen participation. Underlying this argument is the implicit but strongly held belief shared by most observers of democracies that an accessible, responsive government is a legitimate government. Some commentators held out hope that new media technologies such as cable television and the Internet would stimulate interest in politics and move more people into the constructive quadrants. However, recent research indicates that this has not happened. Instead, politically interested individuals use these technologies to become better informed, whereas the politically uninterested opt for entertainment programming.[48]

An active public, one that chooses the *voice* option in Figure 4.1, has the potential to generate widespread change in a community. The mobilization of lower class voters, for instance, is linked to more generous state welfare policies.[49] From the perspective of government officials and institutions, citizen participation can be a nuisance because it may disrupt established routines. Involving the public in policy making takes money and staff time, resources that are in short supply in most jurisdictions. The challenge is to incorporate citizen participation into ongoing operations. A noteworthy example is Dayton, Ohio, where neighborhood-based priority boards shape city services and policies. As a Dayton official noted, "Citizen participation in this city is just a way of life."[50] Durham, North Carolina, is another. The city hosts regular "coffee with council" meetings to get input from the citizenry regarding budget priorities.[51] Innovations such as the use of nonprecinct-based vote centers on election day in Larimer, Colorado stimulate participation, especially among infrequent voters[52] Perhaps other localities and states will emulate and expand upon these endeavors. Citizen involvement may not be easy or efficient, but in a democracy, it is the ultimate test of the legitimacy of that government.

## CHAPTER RECAP

- Citizen participation in the community can be active or passive, and constructive or destructive. Local governments have devoted much time and energy to encouraging active, constructive participation among the citizenry.

- Voter turnout rates vary dramatically from one state to another, and the reasons have to do with the political culture of the state, the competitiveness of the political parties, and the way elections are administered.

- After the 2009 elections, twenty-six gubernatorial offices were in Democratic hands; twenty-four were held by the GOP.

- Almost half of the states have an initiative process, and in those that do, it has become an important tool for policy making.

- Although it is difficult to mobilize the public in support of a statewide recall, it happened in California in 2003 when Governor Gray Davis was recalled from office.

- E-government is on the rise, with states and localities adopting more and more high-tech ways of interacting with citizens. This trend holds tremendous potential for increasing citizen participation in government.

- Volunteerism is a way of bringing fresh ideas and energy into government and helps connect citizens to their community.

- State and local governments continue to encourage their citizens in meaningful participation. Doing so seems to make government work better.

## Key Terms

participation (p. 80)
free rider (p. 84)
social capital (p. 85)
Voting Rights Act of 1965 (p. 85)
voting-age population (p. 86)
voting-eligible population (p. 86)
primary system (p. 88)

closed primary (p. 89)
open primary (p. 89)
blanket primary (p. 90)
runoff election (p. 90)
instant runoff (p. 91)
plurality (p. 91)
fusion (p. 91)
coattail effect (p. 92)
nonpartisan election (p. 92)

slating groups (p. 93)
popular referendum (p. 93)
referendum (p. 94)
recall (p. 94)
open meeting laws (p. 100)
administrative procedure acts (p. 100)
advisory committee (p. 101)
focus group (p. 101)
volunteerism (p. 103)

## Internet Resources

The website of the Federal Election Commission, **www.fec.gov**, contains information about U.S. elections, including laws, campaign financing, and results.

The League of Women Voters, a well-respected organization that encourages informed and active participation of citizens in government, maintains a website at **www.lwv.org**.

The organization established to stimulate interest in political participation among America's youth can be found on the Internet at **www. kidsvotingusa.org**.

A nonpartisan, nonadvocacy website providing up-to-the-minute news and analysis on election reform can be found at **electionline.org**.

An organization found at **www .americaspromise.org** encourages volunteers to create "communities of promise" in their hometowns.

You can find just about anything you want to know about ballot measures at **www.iandrinstitute.org** and **www.ballot.org**.

# Political Parties, Interest Groups, and Campaigns

**5**

- Political Parties
- Interest Groups
- Political Campaigns

**T**hree Republican state legislators in Iowa found themselves challenged in their bids for reelection in 2006—not by Democrats but by fellow Republicans. It turns out that the policy positions taken by the incumbent GOP legislators were a tad too moderate for some of their brethren in the party. A powerful group called Iowans for Tax Relief (ITR), a coalition of anti-tax folks, Christian right activists, and gun owners, targeted the incumbents for defeat. With the active support of ITR and its political arm, Taxpayers United, the conservative challengers were victorious in the party primary. This illustrates a truth about contemporary partisan politics: Sometimes party loyalty is in short supply.[1]

**political parties**

Organizations that nominate candidates to compete in elections, and promote policy ideas.

## POLITICAL PARTIES

The two major **political parties**, the Democratic Party and the Republican Party, offer slates of candidates to lead us. Candidates campaign hard for the high-profile jobs of governor, state legislator, mayor, and various other state and local positions. In some states, even candidates for judicial positions compete in partisan races. But party involvement in our system of government does not end on election day—the institutions of government themselves have a partisan tone. Legislatures are organized along party lines; governors offer Republican or Democratic agendas for their states; county commissioners of different ideological stripes fight over the package of services provided to local residents. Through the actions of their elected officials, political parties play a major role in the operation of government.

## The Condition of Political Parties

The condition of contemporary American political parties has been described with words such as *decline, decay,* and *demise.* In some ways, the description is accurate, but in other ways, it is overstated. True, the number of people who identify themselves as members of one of the two major parties is only about 60 percent of the electorate, whereas the number of people calling themselves independents is approaching 40 percent.[2] Furthermore, campaigns are increasingly candidate-centered rather than party-centered, and they rely on personal organizations and political consultants. But at the same time, the party organization has become more professionalized, taking on new tasks and playing new roles in politics and governance. Parties have more financial and technological resources at their disposal.[3] Thus, to some observers, political parties are enjoying a period of revitalization and rejuvenation. While the debate over the condition of political parties continues, it seems clear that they have undergone a transformation during the past twenty-five years and that they have proven to be quite adaptable.

American political parties are composed of three interacting parts: the party organization (party committees, party leaders, and activists), the party in government (candidates and officeholders), and the party in the electorate (citizens who identify with the party).[4] These parts interact to do many things, but among their central tasks are nominating and electing candidates, educating (some might say propagandizing) citizens, and, once in office, governing.

Parties in the United States function as umbrella organizations that shelter loose coalitions of relatively like-minded individuals. In terms of **ideology**, Republicans tend to be more conservative, favoring a limited role for government; Democrats tend to be more liberal, preferring a more activist government. A general image for each party is discernible: The Republicans typically have been considered the party of big business, the Democrats the party of workers. On many of the social issues of the day—gay rights, abortion, pornography, and prayer in schools—the two parties tend to take different positions. By 2009, approximately 35 percent of the voting-age public considered themselves Democrats while Republican identifiers slipped to 23 percent and the Independent segment climbed to 36 percent. Note, however, that typically about one-third to one-half of the Independents lean toward one of the two major parties. (See Figure 5.1, which tracks party identification during the recent past.) These national percentages mask tremendous variation: Washington, D.C., Rhode Island, Massachusetts, and Hawaii have substantially higher percentages of Democratic voters; Utah, Wyoming, and Idaho have significantly more Republicans.[5]

**ideology**
Core beliefs about the nature and role of the political system.

**Party Identification in the United States, 2003–2009**

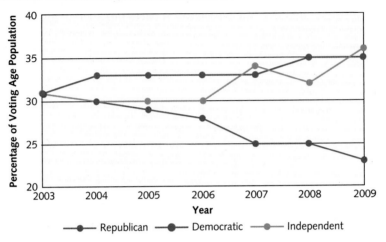

SOURCE: "GOP Party Identification Slips Nationwide and in Pennsylvania," *Pew Research Center for People and the Press*, pewresearch .org/pubs/1207/republican-party-identification-slips-nationwide-pennsylvania-specter-switch (April 29, 2009).

The geographical distribution of partisan loyalties has produced some interesting patterns. The South, where conservative political attitudes predominate, is no longer the Democratic stronghold it was forty years ago. In fact, it has become a region of so-called red states, that is, states that vote Republican in presidential elections. Other red states are found in the plains region and the Rocky Mountain west. States that are more reliably Democratic in presidential elections—usually the Northeastern region, the Pacific Coast, and the upper Midwest—are designated "blue" states. (The labels "red" and "blue" refer to the color-coded maps that television broadcasters use to show election returns.) States with greater partisan diversity have been called "purple" by some pollsters.[6] It is important not to overgeneralize from these colorful, but simple, descriptors of state-level partisanship. Within an individual state, various partisan configurations exist, as research on presidential voting at the county level has shown.[7] Voters display a remarkable penchant for **ticket splitting**—that is, voting for a Democrat for one office and a Republican for another in the same election. Many voters are fond of saying that they "vote for the person, not the party." West Virginians demonstrated this tendency in 2008 with their strong support for Republican John McCain in the presidential election and their reelection of a Democratic governor.

**ticket splitting**

Voting for candidates of different political parties in a general election.

## Party Organization

Political parties are decentralized organizations, with fifty state Republican parties and fifty state Democratic parties. Each state also has local party organizations, most typically at the county level. Although they interact, each of

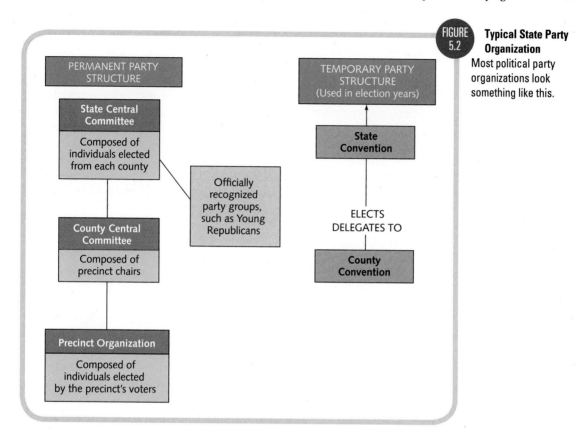

**FIGURE 5.2**

**Typical State Party Organization**
Most political party organizations look something like this.

these units is autonomous, a situation that promotes independence but is not so helpful to party discipline. Specialized partisan groups, including the College Democrats, the Young Republicans, Democratic Women's Clubs, Black Republican Councils, and so on, have been accorded official recognition. Party organizations are further decentralized into precinct-level clusters, which bear the ultimate responsibility for turning out the party's voters on election day.[8] Figure 5.2 shows a typical state party organization.

**State Parties** State governments vary in how closely and how vigorously they regulate political parties. In states with few laws, parties have more discretion in their organization and functions.[9] Each state party has a charter or bylaws to govern its operation. The decision-making body is the state committee, sometimes called a central committee, which is headed by a chairperson and is composed of members elected in party primaries or at state party conventions. State parties (officially, at least) lead their party's push to capture statewide elected offices. Although they may formulate platforms and launch party-centered fund-raising appeals, their value to candidates is in the services they provide.[10] In many states, parties host seminars for party nominees about campaigning effectively, they conduct research into the public's mood, and they advertise on behalf of their candidates.

State party organizations differ in their organizational vitality and resources. In nonelection years, the parties operate with limited staff and revenue; in election years, however, they employ, on average, nine full-time staffers and seven part-timers, and their funds increase dramatically.[11] Republican organizations generally outstrip Democratic ones in measures of organizational strength. Although partisan volunteers still canvass neighborhoods, knocking on doors and talking to would-be voters, these activities are increasingly supplemented by Web-based and e-mail appeals for funds and votes. To a candidate, one of the most valuable services the state party can provide is access to its database of party voters.[12]

**Local Parties** County party organizations are composed of committee members chosen at the precinct level. These workers are volunteers whose primary reward is the satisfaction of being involved in politics. But the work is rarely glamorous. Party workers are the people who conduct voter registration drives, drop off the lawn signs for residents' front yards, and organize candidate forums. On behalf of the party's candidates, they distribute campaign literature, organize fund-raising events, contact voters, and run newspaper advertisements. But what impact do these activities have on the campaign? State legislative candidates report that local parties are most helpful when providing traditional grassroots services such as rounding up volunteer workers and getting voters to the polls on election day.[13]

Local parties are less professionally organized than state parties. Although many local organizations maintain campaign headquarters during an election period, few operate year-round offices. County chairpersons report devoting a lot of time to the party in the months before an election, but otherwise the post does not take much of their time. Most chairpersons lead organizations without any full-time staff, and vacancies in precinct offices are common.

**Factions** As the vignette opening this chapter illustrates, political parties frequently develop factions—that is, identifiable subsets. They can be ideologically based, such as the struggle between moderates and liberals for control of state Democratic parties. They can be organized around particular political leaders, or they can reflect sectional divisions within a state. When factions endure, they make it difficult for a party to come together in support of candidates and on behalf of policy.[14] Persistent intraparty factions create opportunities for the opposing party.

Ohio offers a relevant example. Claiming that the leadership of the state's GOP was "out of touch with its base," conservative Christians launched the Ohio Restoration Project in 2005, an effort "to register half a million new voters, enlist activists, train candidates and endorse conservative causes."[15] The group's "patriot pastors" develop voter guides, hold rallies, set up e-prayer networks on the Internet, and raise funds to donate to selected candidates. Leaders of the Ohio Republican Party have cast a wary eye on the project, contending that if the party moves too far to the right on the ideological spectrum, its electoral success could be jeopardized.

For the Democrats, the public's increasing conservatism has forced the party to move more toward the center of the ideological spectrum. The emergence of candidates who refer to themselves as "New Democrats" and speak the language of **pragmatism** is evidence of that movement.

## The Two-Party System

General elections in the United States are typically contests between candidates representing the two major political parties. Such has been the case for the past century and a half. The Democratic Party has been in existence since the 1830s, when it emerged from the Jacksonian wing of the Jeffersonian Party. The Republican Party, despite its label as the Grand Old Party, is newer; it developed out of the sectional conflict over slavery in the 1850s.

**Why Just Two?** There are numerous reasons for the persistence of two-party politics. Explanations that emphasize sectional dualism, such as East versus West or North versus South, have given way to those focusing on the structure of the electoral system. Parties compete in elections in which there can be only one winner. Most legislative races, for example, take place in single-member districts in which only the candidate with the most votes wins; there is no reward for finishing second or third. Hence, the development of radical or noncentrist parties is discouraged. In addition, laws regulating access to the ballot and receipt of public funds contribute to two-party politics by creating high start-up costs for third parties. Another plausible explanation has to do with tradition. Americans are accustomed to a political system composed of two parties, and that is how we understand politics. The institutionalization of the two-party system is reflected in these numbers: In 2008, only twenty of the nation's 7,382 state legislators were not Democrats or Republicans—and eight of the twenty were in Vermont.

**Third Parties** The assessment of former Alabama governor George Wallace that "there ain't a dime's worth of difference between Democrats and Republicans," although exaggerated, raises questions about the need for alternative parties. Third parties (also called nonmajor or minor parties) are an unsuccessful but persistent phenomenon in U.S. politics. The Greens, Libertarians, Socialists, and the Constitution Party are some examples of third parties currently active in some states. The two major parties may not differ substantially, but for the most part their positions reflect the public mood. Third parties suffer because the two established parties have vast reserves of money and resources at their disposal; new parties can rarely amass the finances or assemble the organization necessary to make significant inroads into the system. Moreover, most states have erected barriers making it difficult for minor parties to get on the ballot; lawsuits challenging these barriers typically have been dismissed by

**pragmatism**
A practical approach to problem solving; a search for "what works."

## BREAKING NEW GROUND

### Opening up the Ballot to More Parties

Tired of Pennsylvania's restrictive ballot access laws, a group of individuals and organizations, including several third parties (Libertarian, Green, Constitution, and Reform, among others) formed an interest group called the Pennsylvania Ballot Access Coalition (PBAC). The goal of the group was simple: to change the state's laws to make it easier for minor parties to get on the ballot. They argued that it would create more political competition and give voters more choices. PBAC got the ball rolling in 2009, when a Pennsylvania state senator introduced the Voters' Choice Act. The bill relaxes the definition of a minor party and allows these parties to create their own rules for nominating candidates since they would be unlikely to hold primaries. "No state makes it tougher to get on the ballot than Pennsylvania, as independent and minor party candidates face significantly more difficult barriers than Republicans and Democrats," the senator said. "My bill would enhance our democratic process by leveling the playing field."

Pennsylvania is not the only state in which third parties are pursuing more political power. In Oregon, minor parties got a boost in 2009 when the legislature adopted a measure that allows candidates to list the nomination of more than one political party on their ballot line. Third parties can run their own candidates and, if they desire,

endorse candidates of other parties, both major and minor. As noted in the previous chapter, this is known as party fusion, a process that benefits minor party candidates. The West Virginia legislature recently passed a bill reducing the number of petition signatures needed for a third party to qualify for ballot position from 2 percent of the vote cast for that office in the previous election to 1 percent. This is important because high signature requirements depress third party candidacy. In Arkansas, a new law not only lowered the petition signature requirement for minor parties to 10,000, it increased the time frame in which to collect the signatures from sixty to ninety days. All in all, third party efforts to get more favorable rules for ballot access have been picking up steam. Around the country, voters are finding that their partisan options have expanded.

SOURCES: "Voter's Choice Act," Pennsylvania Ballot Access Coalition, www.paballotaccess.org/voters_choice_act.html (September 18, 2008); Jeff Mapes, "Kulongoski will sign fusion voting bill," blog.oregonlive.com/mapesonpolitics/2009/07/kulongoski_will_sign_fusion_vo.html (July 9, 2009); Bernard Tamas and Matthew Hindman, "Do State Election Laws Really Hurt Third-Parties? Ballot Access, Fusion, and Elections to the US House of Representatives" Paper presented at the annual meeting of the Midwest Political Science Association, Chicago, IL, April 12, 2007; Conor M. Dowling and Steve B. Lern, "Explaining Major and Third Party Candidate Entry in U.S. Gubernatorial Elections, 1980–2005," *State Politics and Policy Quarterly* 9 (Spring 2009): 1–23.

the courts. (The Breaking New Ground box discusses efforts in some states to ease minor party access to the ballot.) Furthermore, third parties receive scant attention from the news media, and, without it, their credibility wanes. Still, many third parties contest elections even with the odds stacked against them because a campaign provides an opportunity to promote the party's policy positions.

Public interest in partisan alternatives may be increasing. One national survey reported that 53 percent of the electorate believed that there should be a third major political party; scholarly research has found among self-described Independents support for the creation of more parties.[16] Many indicated that their estrangement from the Democratic and Republican parties had reached the point that they would willingly affiliate with a third party that reflected their interests. This sentiment makes it easier to understand why, in 1998, the Reform Party candidate, Jesse Ventura, was successful in his quest for the governorship of Minnesota, besting both the Democratic and the Republican candidates in the general election.

## Interparty Competition

A study comparing the amount of competition for state legislative seats arrived at some interesting findings.[17] Looking at the percentage of the popular vote given the winning candidate, the margin of victory, and the relative safeness of the seat, the research found wide variation across states. Topping the list with relatively high levels of competition for the legislature were North Dakota and Oregon; clustered at the bottom of the list were Georgia and Mississippi. In these southern states, as many as 60 percent of their legislative seats go uncontested; thus incumbents are returned to office again and again.[18]

The extension of interparty competition to states that had lacked it in the past is a healthy development in American politics. Citizens who are dissatisfied with the performance of the party in power have another choice. And there is an interesting twist to increased party competition and more choices for voters. Research has found that the amount of competition for legislative seats appears to be related to the policy outputs of the legislatures. States with higher levels of electoral competition tend to adopt more liberal policies than do states with less competitive legislative elections.[19] To be sure, the relative strength of the two parties helps explain partisan competition and legislative actions.

**Patterns of Competition** Another way of thinking about interparty competition is to examine which party controls the major policy-making institutions in the state: the governor's office and the state legislature. In the past, some states experienced long periods of institutional dominance by one party, but that trend has been on the decline for years. These days, party strength is fairly balanced. Based on gubernatorial vote margins and legislative seats held, as many as twenty-six states can be classified as two-party competitive and no states fall into the "one party" category.[20] Of the remaining states, thirteen are considered modified Democratic states (i.e., Democrats control more institutions more often); eleven are modified Republican states. During the period 2003–2006, Massachusetts was the closest to a one-party Democratic state; Idaho was the closest to a one-party Republican state.

Generally, there is a link between the partisan composition of the electorate and partisan control of a state's institutions. For instance, in Utah in 2009, the Republican Party had a voter registration advantage over the Democratic Party of more than 2 to 1. Not surprisingly, in the Utah legislature, Republicans outnumbered Democrats by a nearly 3 to 1 margin, and a Republican occupied the governor's office. But the electorate–institution relationship is not a simple one. Consider Maryland and Massachusetts, two of the states in which voter registration patterns give the Democratic Party a strong advantage. Both states elected Republicans to the governor's office in 2002 but sustained

**FIGURE 5.3**

**Party Control of State Government, 2010 Map**

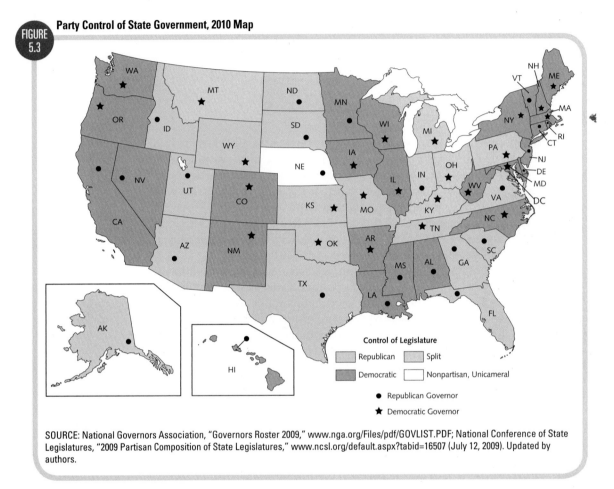

**Control of Legislature**

☐ Republican    ☐ Split

■ Democratic    ☐ Nonpartisan, Unicameral

● Republican Governor

★ Democratic Governor

SOURCE: National Governors Association, "Governors Roster 2009," www.nga.org/Files/pdf/GOVLIST.PDF; National Conference of State Legislatures, "2009 Partisan Composition of State Legislatures," www.ncsl.org/default.aspx?tabid=16507 (July 12, 2009). Updated by authors.

**divided government**

One party controls the governor's office; the other party controls the legislature.

the Democratic dominance in the legislature. That year, in Maryland and Massachusetts, and in many other states, voting produced an institutional outcome called **divided government**.

Before the 2010 elections, the Democratic Party controlled the governor's office and both houses of the legislature in sixteen states; the Republican Party had institutional control of nine states. Although **unified government** prevailed in these states, twenty-four states operated with divided government. Figure 5.3 shows the state-by-state patterns.

**unified government**

Both houses of the legislature and the governor's office are controlled by the same party.

**Consequences of Competition** Two-party competition has spread at a time when states are becoming the battleground for the resolution of difficult policy issues. Undoubtedly, as governors set their agendas and legislatures outline their preferences, cries of partisan politics will be heard. But in a positive sense, such cries symbolize the maturation of state institutions. Partisan politics will probably encourage a wider search for policy alternatives and result in innovative solutions.

In the view of many, two parties are better than one. Heated partisan competition turns a dull campaign into a lively contest, sparking citizen interest and increasing voter turnout. In governance, however, many believe that unified party control is preferable to divided government. When competitive elections produce unified party control of government institutions, it is easier for the public to hold the party accountable for what it does—or does not do—while in office.

## Is the Party Over?

Have political parties as we know them outlived their usefulness? Should they be cast aside as new forms of political organization and communication emerge? These impertinent questions are intended to spark debate.

As some have argued, a more educated populace that can readily acquire political information via the Internet is likely to be less reliant on party cues.[21] Today's generation is less loyal to political parties than its grandparents were and is not so likely to vote along party lines. The trend toward **dealignment**, or weakening of individual partisan attachments, slowed for a period but has begun to pick up again. For example, in New York, one-third of the 3 million new registered voters from 1992 to 2004 rejected the major parties and registered as unaffiliated or as Independence Party members.[22] These nonmajor party identifiers are difficult to categorize in ideological terms. According to one political consultant, "A large group of the electorate tends to be socially tolerant and more receptive to fiscally conservative methods. They don't have a home in either party."[23] This trend is not good news for the two major parties. Neither are the conclusions of a recent study showing that in states with an initiative process, political parties are less able to shape public policy than in non-initiative states.[24]

The Democratic and Republican parties are not sitting idly by as their role in the political system is challenged. Party organizations are making their operations more professional and have more money to spend and more staff to spend it. They are actively seeking to make their organizations more meaningful to younger voters, using various new technologies to engage the so-called "millennial generation." The past several years have seen the development of party-centered advertising campaigns and a renewed commitment to get-out-the-vote drives.[25] These activities present a special challenge to the GOP as polls show that the electorate is increasingly diverse, and in terms of partisanship, likely to be independent or leaning in the direction of Democrats.[26] In a few states that have publicly funded campaigns, parties as well as candidates have been designated as recipients of funds. All in all, parties are doing their best to adapt to the changing environment.

**dealignment**
The weakening of an individual's attachment to political parties.

# INTEREST GROUPS

**Interest groups** have become powerful players in our democratic system. Joining a group is a way for individuals to communicate their preferences—their interests—to government. Interest groups attempt to influence governmental decisions and actions by pressuring decision-making bodies to, for example,

**interest groups**
Organizations of like-minded individuals who desire to influence government.

put more guidance counselors in public schools, restrict coastal development, keep a proposed new prison out of a neighborhood, or strengthen state licensing of family therapists. Success is defined in terms of getting the group's preferences enacted—or blocking actions that are detrimental to the group's interests. In certain states, interest groups actually dominate the policy-making process.

In considering the role of groups in the political system, we must remember that people join groups for reasons other than politics. For instance, a teacher may be a member of a politically active state education association because the group offers a tangible benefit such as low-cost life insurance, but he may not be interested in or may even disagree with some of the political positions taken by the organization. In general, motivations for group membership are individually determined.

## Types of Interest Groups

Interest groups come in all types and sizes. If you were to visit the lobby of the state capitol when the legislature was in session, you might find the director of the state school boards association conversing with the chairperson of the education committee, or the lobbyist hired by the state hotel-motel association exchanging notes with the lobbyist for the state's restaurateurs. If a legislator were to venture into the lobby, she would probably receive at least a friendly greeting from the lobbyists and at most a serious heart-to-heart talk about the merits of a bill. You would be witnessing efforts to influence public policy. Interest groups want state government to enact policies that are in their interest or, conversely, not to enact policies at odds with their preferences.

The interests represented in the capitol lobby are as varied as the states themselves. One interest that is well represented and powerful is business. Whether a lobbyist represents a single large corporation or a consortium of businesses, when he talks, state legislators tend to listen. From the perspective of business groups (and other economically oriented groups), legislative actions can cost or save their members money. Therefore, the chamber of commerce, industry groups, trade associations, financial institutions, and regulated utilities maintain a visible presence in the state capitol during the legislative session. Table 5.1 documents the influential nature of business interests at the state level. It is important to remember, however, that business interests are not monolithic; occasionally they may find themselves on opposite sides of a bill.

Other interests converge on the capitol. Representatives of labor, both established AFL-CIO unions and professional associations such as the state optometrists' group or sheriffs' association, frequent the hallways and committee meeting rooms to see that the legislature makes the "right" decision on the bills before it. For example, if a legislature were considering a bill to change the licensing procedures for optometrists, you could expect to find the optometrists' interest group immersed in the debate. Another workers' group, schoolteachers, has banded together to form one of the most effective state-level groups. In fact, as Table 5.1 indicates, schoolteachers' organizations are ranked among the most influential interest groups in thirty-one states.

| | The Twenty Most Influential Interests in the States | TABLE 5.1 |
|---|---|---|

| RANK | INTEREST | NUMBER OF STATES IN WHICH THE INTEREST WAS SEEN AS VERY EFFECTIVE |
|---|---|---|
| 1 | General business organizations (chambers of commerce, etc.) | 39 |
| 2 | Schoolteachers' organizations (NEA and AFT) | 31 |
| 3 | Utility companies and associations (electric, gas, water, telephone/telecommunications) | 28 |
| 4 | Manufacturers (companies and associations) | 25 |
| 5 | Hospital/nursing home associations | 24 |
| 6 | Insurance: general and medical (companies and associations) | 22 |
| 7 | Physicians/state medical associations | 21 |
| 8 | Contractors/builders/developers | 21 |
| 9 | General local government organizations (municipal leagues, county organizations, elected officials) | 18 |
| 10 | Lawyers (predominately trial attorneys and state bar associations) | 20 |
| 11 | Realtors' associations | 20 |
| 12 | General farm organizations (state farm bureaus, etc.) | 14 |
| 13 | Bankers' associations | 15 |
| 14 | Universities and colleges (institutions and employees) | 14 |
| 15 | Traditional labor associations (predominantly the AFL-CIO) | 15 |
| 16 | Individual labor unions (Teamsters, UAW, etc.) | 13 |
| 17 | Gaming interests (race tracks, casinos, lotteries) | 13 |
| 18 | Individual banks and financial institutions | 11 |
| 19 | State agencies | 10 |
| 20 | Environmentalists | 8 |

NOTE: The influence ranking is determined by more than the "very effective" score.
SOURCE: Adapted from Anthony J. Nownes, Clive S. Thomas, and Ronald J. Hrebenar, "Interest Groups in the States," in Virginia Gray and Russell L. Hanson, eds., *Politics in the American States: A Comparative Approach* (Washington, D.C.: Congressional Quarterly Press, 2008), pp. 117–18. Copyright © 2008 CQ Press, a division of Congressional Quarterly Inc. Reprinted by permission of the publisher, CQ Press.

| TABLE 5.2 | Top Contributors to Michigan Senate Races, Aggregated, 2008 Cycle | |
| --- | --- | --- |
| **CONTRIBUTOR** | | **TOTAL CONTRIBUTIONS ($)** |
| Blue Cross/Blue Shield of Michigan PAC | | 95,675 |
| Michigan Beer and Wine Wholesalers Association PAC | | 76,257 |
| Auto Dealers of Michigan PAC | | 62,070 |
| DTE Energy Company PAC | | 60,030 |
| Michigan Association of Health Plans PAC | | 53,582 |
| Michigan Bankers Association | | 53,180 |
| Michigan Association of Realtors | | 48,050 |
| Michigan Health and Hospital Association PAC | | 43,550 |
| CMS Energy Employees for Better Government | | 34,325 |
| Meijer PAC | | 26,700 |

SOURCE: Michigan Campaign Finance Network 2008. Citizen's Guide to Michigan Campaign Finance, http://www.mcfn.org/pdfs/reports/MCFNCitGuide08.pdf (July 10, 2009).

Many other interest groups are active (but not necessarily influential) in state government, and a large number are ideological in nature. In other words, their political activity is oriented toward some higher good, such as clean air or fairer tax systems or consumer protection. Members of these groups do not have a direct economic or professional interest in the outcome of a legislative decision. Instead, their lobbyists argue that the public as a whole benefits from their involvement in the legislative process. Consider PennPIRG, which describes itself as a nonprofit, nonpartisan watchdog group working on behalf of consumers, the environment, and responsive government in Pennsylvania.

Looking at a specific state reveals a mix of active, effective interest groups. Table 5.2 displays the leading contributors to the campaigns of Michigan state senators in 2008. (Note that the actual contributions are made by arms of these groups known as political action committees or PACs.) The list of contributors reflects some of the interests that are among the most influential groups in state government and politics, as shown earlier in Table 5.1. Keep in mind however that much contemporary interest group research suggests that patterns of influence can be somewhat unpredictable and highly dependent on the state context.[27]

## Interest Groups in the States

Although states share some similarities, the actual interest group environment is different from one state to another. Variation exists not only in the composition of the involved groups but also in the degree of influence they exert. Research by political scientists Clive Thomas, Ronald Hrebenar, and Anthony

Nownes, along with a team of researchers throughout the country, provides fresh insights into the interest group scene. One of the important characteristics is the power of groups vis-à-vis the policy-making institutions in a state. States cluster into one of four different categories. In four states—Alabama, Florida, Hawaii, and Nevada—interest groups dominate state political institutions such as political parties, that is, groups wield an overwhelming and consistent influence on policy making.[28] On the other hand, interest groups are comparatively weaker in Kentucky, Michigan, Minnesota, South Dakota, and Vermont. In fifteen states, interest groups are one of many sources of power and they enjoy complementary relationships with other political institutions. The pattern is less stable in the remaining twenty-six states. Interest group power tends to ebb and flow in these states, with groups playing a dominant role in some instances, but not in others.

For the most part, interest group politics is defined by its state context. First of all, interest groups and political parties have evolving, multidimensional relationships. Typically, in states where political parties are weak, interest groups are strong; where political parties are strong, interest groups tend to be weaker.[29] Strong parties provide leadership in the policy-making process, and interest groups function through them. In the absence of party leadership and organization, interest groups fill the void, becoming important recruiters of candidates and financiers of campaigns; accordingly, they exert tremendous influence in policy making.

A second, related truth adds a developmental angle to interest group politics. As states diversify economically, their politics are less likely to be dominated by a single interest. Studies of state interest systems show that the number of groups has increased over time and the power of once-dominant economic interests has decreased.[30] As states increasingly become the arena in which important social and economic policy decisions are made, more and more groups go to statehouses hoping to find a receptive audience.

## Local-Level Interest Groups

Interest groups also function at the local level. Because so much of local government involves the delivery of services, local interest groups devote a great deal of their attention to administrative agencies and departments. Groups are involved in local elections and in community issues, to be sure, but much of their major focus is on the *actions* of government: policy implementation and service delivery. According to surveys of local officials in small cities, the two functional areas in which interest groups have the greatest influence are economic development and parks and recreation.[31]

As in states, business groups are influential in local government. Business-related interests, such as the local chamber of commerce or a downtown merchants' association, usually wield power in the community. These groups speak with a loud voice because business contributes both to the local tax base and to candidates for local offices. An increasingly important group at the local level is the neighborhood-based organization, which in some communities rivals business interests in influence. Other groups active at the local level include faith-based organizations, public employee unions, and ethnic minority groups.[32] Thus far, these groups have not achieved the degree of influence accorded business and neighborhood groups.

Neighborhood organizations deserve a closer look. Some have arisen out of issues that directly affect neighborhood residents—a nearby school that is scheduled to close, a wave of violent crime, a proposed freeway route that will destroy homes and businesses. Members of these groups devote much of their time to networking, to building relationships with policy makers and to recruiting more individuals to their cause.[33] Other neighborhood groups have been formed by government itself as a way of channeling citizen participation. In Los Angeles, for instance, the city established neighborhood councils as a way to increase governmental responsiveness to local needs. In practice these councils have been most active in opposing the city's land use and taxation decisions.[34]

**direct action**

A form of participation designed to draw attention to a cause.

Neighborhood groups, as well as others lacking a bankroll but possessing enthusiasm and dedication, may resort to tactics such as **direct action**, which might involve protest marches at the county courthouse or standing in front of bulldozers clearing land for a new highway. Direct action is usually designed to attract attention to a cause, and it tends to be a last resort, a tactic employed when other efforts at influencing government policy have failed. A study of citizen groups in seven large cities found that 34 percent of the groups engaged in protests or demonstrations at least occasionally.[35]

## Techniques Used by Interest Groups

Interest groups want to have a good public image. It helps a group when its preferences can be equated with what is good for the state (or the community). Organizations use slogans like "What's good for the timber industry is good for Oregon" or "Schoolteachers have the interests of New York City at heart." Some groups contend that their main interest is that of the public at large. Groups, then, invest resources in creating a positive image.

Being successful in the state capitol or at city hall involves more than a good public image, however. For example, interest groups have become effective at organizing networks that exert pressure on legislators. If a teacher pay-raise bill is in jeopardy in the senate, for instance, schoolteachers throughout the state may be asked by the education association to contact their senators to urge them to vote favorably on the legislation. To maximize their strength, groups with common interests often establish coalitions.

Sometimes related groups carve out their own niches to avoid direct competition for members and support.[36] For example, gay and lesbian groups, relatively new to state politics, tend to focus on narrow issues such as ending prohibitions on same-sex marriages rather than on broad concerns.[37] This targeting strategy allows more groups to flourish. Interest groups also hire representatives who can effectively promote their cause. To ensure that legislators will be receptive to their pressures, groups try to influence the outcome of elections by supporting candidates who reflect their interests.

Several factors affect the relative power of an interest group. In their work, Thomas, Hrebenar, and Nownes identify twelve characteristics that give some groups more political clout than others:

- The degree of necessity of group services and resources to public officials.
- Whether the group's lobbying focus is primarily defensive or promotional.
- The extent and strength of group opposition.
- Potential for the group to enter into coalitions.
- Group financial resources.
- Size and geographical distribution of group membership.
- Political cohesiveness of the membership.
- Political, organizational, and managerial skill of group leaders.
- Timing and the political climate.
- Lobbyist–policy maker relations.
- Legitimacy of the group and its demands—how these are perceived by the public and public officials.
- Extent of group autonomy in political strategizing.[38]

No single interest group is on the high end of all twelve of these characteristics all of the time. Many of the effective groups listed in Table 5.1, for example, possess quite a few of these factors. An indispensable group armed with ample resources, a cohesive membership, and skilled leaders, when the timing is right, can wield enormous influence in the state capitol. This is especially true when the group has taken a defensive posture—that is, when it wants to block proposed legislation. On the other hand, victory comes less easily to a group lacking these characteristics.

## Lobbying

**Lobbying** is the attempt to influence government decision makers. States have developed official definitions to determine who is a lobbyist and who is not. A common definition is "anyone receiving compensation to influence legislative action." A few states, such as Nevada, North Dakota, and Washington, require everyone who attempts to influence legislation to register as a lobbyist (even those who are not being paid), but most exclude public officials, members of the media, and people who speak only before committees or boards from this definition. Because of definitional differences, comparing the number of lobbyists across states raises the proverbial apples-and-oranges problem. But with that in mind, some cautious comparisons can be made. As of 2006, Florida, Illinois, and New York had more than 2,100 registered lobbyists. Smaller interest group universes exist in North Dakota and Rhode Island, each with fewer than 200 registered lobbyists.[39]

In most states, lobbyists are required to file reports indicating how and on whom they spent money. Concern that lobbyists would exert undue influence on the legislative process spurred states to enact new reporting requirements and to impose tougher penalties for their violation. Maine and New Jersey, for instance, require lobbyists to report their sources of income, total and

**lobbying**
The process by which groups and individuals attempt to influence policy makers.

categorized expenditures, the names of the individual officials who received their monies or gifts, and the legislation they supported or opposed. Despite stringent disclosure laws, legislator–lobbyist scandals have caused many states to clamp down even harder. In Iowa, for instance, each registered lobbyist is prohibited from spending more than $3.00 per day on a legislator; in Florida, lobbyists cannot give any gifts, regardless of value, to legislators.[40]

As state government has expanded and taken on more functions, the number of interests represented in state capitals has exploded.[41] The increase in the number of lobbyists has a very simple but important cause: Interests that are affected by state government cannot afford to be without representation. An anecdote from Florida makes the point. A few years ago, legislators supported a new urban development program that Florida cities had lobbied for but about which they could not agree on a funding source. After much debate, they found one: a sales tax on dry cleaning. Because the dry-cleaning industry did not have a lobbyist in Tallahassee, there was no one to speak out on its behalf. Indeed, because their views were not represented in the debate over funding sources, dry cleaners were an easy target. (The dry-cleaning industry learned its lesson and hired a lobbyist a few days after the tax was enacted.)[42]

To win over legislators in their decision making, lobbyists need access, so they cultivate good relationships with lawmakers. In other words, they want connections; they want an "in." There are many ways of establishing connections, such as entertaining, gift giving, and contributing to campaigns. Also, lawmakers want to know how a proposed bill might affect the different interests throughout the state and especially in their legislative districts, and what it is expected to achieve. And lobbyists are only too happy to provide that information. Social lobbying—wining and dining legislators—still goes on, but it is being supplemented by another technique: the provision of information. A new breed of lobbyists has emerged, trained as attorneys and public relations specialists, skilled in media presentation and information packaging.

A recent analysis of the lobbying environment in two states—Ohio and West Virginia—identified the kinds of techniques that lobbyists rely on. Table 5.3 lists the techniques that more than 75 percent of the 266 lobbyists surveyed said they used. Making contacts with key actors in the policy-making process—legislators, legislative and gubernatorial staff, and agency officials—are at the top of a lobbyist's "to-do" list. Moreover, a substantial 91 percent of the lobbyists indicated that they helped draft legislation, which makes them key actors as well. Notice that lobbying is not confined to the legislative process. Lobbyists regularly attempt to shape the implementation of policies after they are enacted.

The influence of lobbyists specifically and of interest groups generally is a subject of much debate. The popular image is one of a wheeler-dealer lobbyist whose very presence in a committee hearing room can spell the fate of a bill. But, in fact, his will is done because the interests he represents are considered vital to the state, because he has assiduously laid the groundwork, and because legislators respect the forces he can mobilize if necessary. Few lobbyists cast this long a shadow, but in many states, some of the most effective lobbyists are former legislators themselves. They know how the policy-making system works, thus making them valuable to myriad interests.

| | | TABLE 5.3 |
|---|---|---|
| **The Most Popular Techniques Used by Lobbyists** | | |
| 1 | Meeting personally with state legislators | |
| 2 | Meeting personally with state legislative staff | |
| 3 | Helping to draft legislation | |
| 4 | Meeting personally with executive agency personnel | |
| 5 | Meeting personally with members of the governor's staff | |
| 6 | Entering into coalitions with other organizations | |
| 7 | Testifying at legislative committee hearings | |
| 8 | Submitting written testimony to legislative committees | |
| 9 | Talking with people from the media | |
| 10 | Inspiring letter-writing, telephone, or e-mail campaigns to state legislators | |
| 11 | Submitting written comments on proposed rules/regulations | |
| 12 | Making personal monetary contributions to candidates for office | |
| 13 | Helping to draft regulations, rules, or guidelines | |

SOURCE: Anthony J. Nownes, Clive S. Thomas, and Ronald J. Hrebenar, "Interest Groups in the States," in Virginia Gray and Russell L. Hanson, eds., *Politics in the American States: A Comparative Approach* (Washington, D.C.: Congressional Quarterly Press, 2008), p. 107.

A not so new tactic that is enjoying a resurgence is **grassroots lobbying**, in which groups use their members to communicate with legislators (translation: bombard with mail, e-mail, faxes, and telephone calls) on behalf of the group's issue. Grassroots lobbying is not just a technique for outsiders. Citizen groups, unions, religious/charitable groups, corporations, and trade and professional associations all use grassroots techniques.[43] Are they effective? A recent study reached this unequivocal conclusion: "Grassroots lobbying by e-mail has a substantial influence on legislative voting behavior."[44]

**grassroots lobbying**
Group mobilization of citizens to contact public officials on behalf of shared public policy views.

**Political Action Committees** Political action committees (PACs) have become a regular feature of state politics since the 1980s. Narrowly focused subsets of interest groups, PACs are political organizations that collect funds and distribute them to candidates. PACs serve as the campaign-financing arm of corporations, labor unions, trade associations, and even political parties. They grew out of long-standing laws that made it illegal for corporations and labor unions to contribute directly to a candidate. Barred from direct contributions, these organizations set up political action subsidiaries to allow them legal entry into campaign finance.

**political action committees**
Organizations that raise and distribute campaign funds to candidates for elective office.

The impact of PACs on state politics is potentially far-reaching. Some Michigan legislators, for example, consider PACs a potentially dangerous influence on state politics because their money "buys a lot of access that others can't get."[45] And access can mean influence. Research on tobacco industry PACs suggests that their campaign contributions affect legislative behavior: "As legislators [in

California, Colorado, Massachusetts, Pennsylvania, and Washington] received more tobacco industry campaign contributions ... legislators were more likely to be pro-tobacco industry."[46] Similarly, in Florida, campaign contributions from teacher union PACs were shown to have influenced legislators' votes on a school vouchers bill.[47]

States have responded to the proliferation of PACs by increasing their regulation. In New Jersey, for instance, PACs are required to register and to provide information regarding their controlling interests. One likely possibility is that an independent interstate network of groups with money to spend could emerge as a real threat to political parties as a recruiter of candidates and a financier of campaigns. As a harbinger of tighter regulation of PACs, Alaska and Washington enacted a law that restricts contributions from out-of-state PACs. Most states have acted to limit PAC contributions, although the content of the laws varies. For example, Tennessee restricts the proportion of PAC contributions to fifty percent of a candidate's total contribution amount; Colorado allows "small donor" PACs to contribute more than "regular" PACs.[48] Some states have set absolute dollar amount ceilings on PAC contributions such as Nevada and New Mexico ($5,000 per candidate per election campaign); others differentiate by office and set lower amounts for legislative races than for statewide campaigns. States with extremely low-allowable contribution levels include Florida ($500 per candidate per election) and Rhode Island ($1,000 per candidate per election year). Fourteen states have taken a completely different approach and allow unlimited contributions from PACs to candidates (see Table 5.4).

| TABLE 5.4 Unlimited PAC Contributions |
| --- |
| **STATES WITH NO LIMITS ON PAC CONTRIBUTIONS TO CANDIDATES** |
| Alabama |
| Illinois |
| Indiana |
| Iowa |
| Mississippi |
| Missouri |
| North Dakota |
| Oregon |
| Pennsylvania |
| South Dakota |
| Texas |
| Utah |
| Virginia |
| Wyoming |

SOURCE: National Conference of State Legislatures, "State Limits on Contributions to Candidates," http://www.ncsl.org/Portals/1/documents/legismgt/limits_candidates.pdf (April 30, 2009).

# POLITICAL CAMPAIGNS

Political parties and interest groups bump into each other all the time, especially in political campaigns. Like so many things these days, political campaigns aren't what they used to be. But despite changes in campaign styles and technologies, the goal remains the same: attracting enough voters to win the election. Figure 5.4 diagrams the voting configuration in a hypothetical election district. This district typically splits its vote evenly between Democrats and Republicans. Thus, in any given election, each party can count on about 25 percent of the vote (labeled the "base" in the diagram), with another 17 percent that is fairly likely to vote for the party's candidate (the "soft" partisan vote). That leaves about 16 percent of the vote up for grabs (the toss-up vote).[49] The toss-up vote and the soft partisan vote comprise what is typically referred to as the swing vote. Candidates target their energies on the swing vote, the size of which varies with the distribution of the partisan base vote. It is important to remember that most districts are not so evenly divided in their partisan loyalties.

## A New Era of Campaigns

Campaigns of the past conjure up images of fiery oratory and county fairs. But campaigns orchestrated by rural courthouse gangs and urban ward bosses have given way to stylized video and electronic campaigning that relies on the mass media and political consultants. Direct contact with potential voters still matters, of course. Candidates for state legislative seats, for example, devote time to door-to-door canvassing, neighborhood drop-ins, and public forums. Yet more and more, they rely on direct mail and electronic media to deliver their messages to voters and on political consultants to help them craft the message.[50]

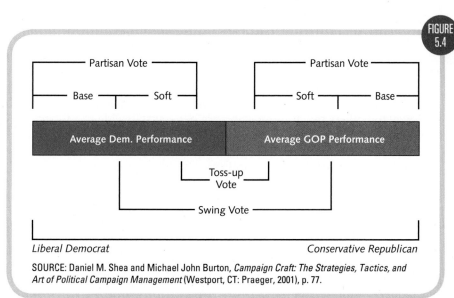

**FIGURE 5.4**

**The Voting Configuration of a Hypothetical Election District** Candidates rely on their partisan base and compete for the swing vote.

SOURCE: Daniel M. Shea and Michael John Burton, *Campaign Craft: The Strategies, Tactics, and Art of Political Campaign Management* (Westport, CT: Praeger, 2001), p. 77.

**Using Old and New Media** The mass media, especially television, are intrinsic aspects of modern statewide campaigns. Even candidates for legislative and local offices are increasingly using the mass media to transmit their messages. Campaigns can either buy their television and radio time and newspaper space for advertising or get it free by arranging events that reporters are likely to cover. These events range from serious (a candidate's major policy statement) to gimmicky (a candidate climbing into the ring with a professional wrestler to demonstrate his "toughness"); either way, they are cleverly planned to capture media attention. A candidate seeking free media attention needs to create visual events, be quotable, and relentlessly attack opponents or targeted problems. Televised debates, common in campaigns for statewide office, offer another opportunity for free media time.

Free media time is seldom sufficient. Candidates, particularly those running for higher-level state offices and for positions in large cities, rely on paid advertisements to reach the public. Paid media advertisements seem to be of two distinct varieties: generic and negative. Generic advertisements include the following:

1. *The sainthood spot*, which glorifies the candidate and her accomplishments.
2. *The testimonial*, in which other people (celebrities, average citizens) attest to the candidate's abilities.
3. *The bumper-sticker policy spot*, which emphasizes the campaign's popular and noncontroversial themes (good schools, lower taxes, more jobs).
4. *The feel-good spot*, which identifies and capitalizes on the spirit of a place and its people (e.g., "Vermont's a special place" or "Nobody can do it better than Pennsylvania").[51]

Media advertising is important because it is frequently the only contact a potential voter has with a candidate. A candidate's personal characteristics and style—important considerations to an evaluating public—are easily transmitted via the airwaves. And, indeed, advances in communications technology offer new options to enterprising candidates. For instance, more candidates are now using cable television to cut media costs and to target audiences.

The Internet has become a powerful campaign tool that can disseminate the candidate's message to far-flung audiences, mobilize potential supporters, and serve as a vehicle for attracting contributions. Since 2002, all of the major candidates for gubernatorial offices have maintained campaign websites, some rudimentary, others much more elaborate. Several statewide candidates pioneered the use of campaign e-cards (the electronic equivalent of chain letters) so that supporters could contact people in their e-mail address books about the candidate. One of the innovations for the 2006 round of statewide elections was the creation of interactive websites that engaged Web surfers and kept them coming back. By 2008, the advent of YouTube provided opportunities for candidates and for their opponents as videos of campaign high points—and low moments—made their way to the website. YouTube is easy to use, cost-effective for campaigns, and increasingly popular. Approximately 35 percent of Americans watched online political videos in 2008, compared with just 13 percent in 2004.[52] Social networking sites such as MySpace and Facebook hold tremendous potential for generating a fanbase for candidates and for raising money. Running for mayor of Houston in 2009, Annise Parker took to the Internet to ask supporters to click the "submit" box and send her at least five dollars. Within four months, she had raised $304,000 from 1,099 online donors.[53]

The value of the Internet in campaigns has only just begun to be tapped, but an example from Colorado underscores its potential. In a pre-emptive move, a Denver politician bought the domain names of his rivals in an effort to complicate their Web presence.[54] It is a far cry from the old days when a candidate's biggest worry during the campaign season was whether an opponent was stealing his yard signs!

New York City Mayor Michael Bloomberg campaigns for reelection in 2009.

**Political Consultants** An occupational specialty that sprang up during the 1970s and 1980s is clearly here to stay: political consulting. Individuals with expertise in polling, direct mail, fund-raising, advertising, and campaign management put their talents to work in political campaigns. These consultants form the core of the professional campaign management team assembled by candidates for state offices. They identify and target likely voters, both those who are already in the candidate's camp and need to be reminded to vote *and* those who can be persuaded to vote for the candidate. Consultants use survey research to find out what the public is thinking. They carefully craft messages to appeal to specific voters, such as the elderly, home owners, and environmentalists. Advertising on cable television, radio, and through direct mail are three popular means of getting a candidate's message to subsets of potential voters. In fact, recent research has found that much of the public actually prefers narrowcast messages, tailored to their interests.[55]

Any number of factors can influence the result of an election, such as the presence of an incumbent in a race and the amount of funds that a challenger has accumulated, but one significant factor is the ability to frame or define the issues during the campaign. Even in a quietly contested state legislative race, district residents are likely to receive mailings that state the candidates' issue positions, solicit funds, and perhaps comment unfavorably on the opposition. The candidate who has an effective political consultant to help set the campaign agenda and thereby put her opponent on the defensive is that much closer to victory. A study of legislative elections indicates that the use of campaign professionals is especially valuable to challengers who are hoping to unseat incumbents.[56]

**Negative Campaigning** Negative campaign advertising comes in three flavors: fair, false, and deceptive. A fair ad might emphasize some embarrassing aspect of an opponent's voting record or some long-forgotten indiscretion. A false ad, as the label implies, contains untrue statements. More problematic are deceptive advertisements. These misleading ads distort the truth about an opponent. The difficulty for states is to regulate negative campaign advertising without violating free-speech guarantees of the U.S. Constitution. False advertising that is done with actual malice can be prohibited by a state, but deceptive ads, replete with accusation and innuendo, are more difficult to regulate.[57]

Most states have enacted laws prohibiting false campaign statements; candidates who use false ads against their opponents can be fined. One of the problems with these laws is that the damage is done long before the remedy can be applied. Fining a candidate after the election is akin to latching the barn door after the horse has fled. Some states, such as California and Nevada, have adopted a fair campaign practices code. These codes typically contain broad guidelines such as "do not misrepresent the facts" or "do not make appeals to prejudice based on race or sex." The limitation of the codes is that compliance is voluntary rather than mandatory.

In addition to government action, many newspapers report regularly on the content, presentation, and relative accuracy of campaign advertising. Ad watches or truth boxes, as they are often called, occasionally have led to the retraction or redesign of ads. Despite the efforts of government and the media, negative campaign advertising persists because many candidates believe that, if done cleverly, it can benefit their campaigns. Research by political scientist Ted Braden has confirmed that negative messages, accompanied by fear-evoking music and images, trigger strong reactions in viewers.[58] People may not like negative ads, but they certainly seem to remember them.

## Campaign Finance

To campaign for public office is to spend money—frequently a lot of money. How do you define "a lot"? Thirty-six governors' seats were up for election in 2006 and, all told, campaign spending topped $728 million.[59] This was the second highest level of gubernatorial election spending, topped only by the $841 million spent in the 2002 gubernatorial election cycle. (The 2002 figure is actually $943 million in 2006 dollars. The difference between the 2002 and 2006 spending totals can be partially explained by the presence of twenty open-seat races in 2002, thus attracting more candidates willing to spend more money. In 2006, there were only nine open-seat gubernatorial contests.) In absolute terms, the campaign in California and, in 2005, in New Jersey cost the most, $129 million and $88 million, respectively. When the cost per vote is calculated, the gubernatorial campaigns in New Jersey and Louisiana are at the top of the list with $38.32 and $30.35, respectively.[60] Table 5.5 provides comparative figures on campaign spending in governors' races in ten states.

Big spending is not confined to gubernatorial contests. Spending in legislative races is climbing, and fast. Consider data from two neighboring

| | **Campaign Costs in Ten Gubernatorial Races, 2006** | | | TABLE 5.5 |
|---|---|---|---|---|

| STATE | EXPENDITURE TOTAL (ALL GUBERNATORIAL CANDIDATES) ($) | COST PER VOTE ($) | WINNER'S SHARE OF EXPENDITURES (%) | WINNER'S SHARE OF THE VOTE (%) |
|---|---|---|---|---|
| Races with an incumbent seeking reelection | | | | |
| Alabama | 18,542,577 | 14.83 | 65.1 | 57.4 |
| Kansas | 6,414,413 | 7.55 | 74.1 | 57.9 |
| Michigan | 52,816,237 | 13.89 | 56.3 | 56.3 |
| Pennsylvania | 40,993,556 | 10.02 | 74.4 | 60.4 |
| South Dakota | 1,295,714 | 3.86 | 22.8 | 61.7 |
| Open seat races, no incumbent | | | | |
| Arkansas | 9,953,116 | 13.27 | 65.0 | 55.4 |
| Florida | 41,947,768 | 8.69 | 47.4 | 52.2 |
| Iowa | 16,653,062 | 15.89 | 45.4 | 54.0 |
| Massachusetts | 42,313,712 | 18.86 | 21.0 | 55.0 |
| Nevada | 14,857,797 | 25.52 | 38.2 | 47.9 |

SOURCE: Thad Beyle, "Gubernatorial Elections, Campaign Costs, and Powers," in *The Book of the States 2008* (Lexington, KY: Council of State Governments, 2008), p. 170.

Midwestern states, Illinois and Indiana, with similar numbers of candidates competing for house seats in 2008. In Illinois, total spending by the 224 candidates for 118 house seats totaled $42,866,912, or $191,370 per candidate. Indiana's expenditures were lower by comparison but represented increases over previous election cycles. In 2008, 225 house candidates competed for 100 seats, and spent a total of $17,009,173, or $75,596 per candidate.[61]

Just how important is money? One knowledgeable observer concluded, "In the direct primaries, where self-propelled candidates battle for recognition, money is crucial. Electronic advertising is the only way to gain visibility. Hence the outcome usually rewards the one with the largest war chest."[62] This trend does not bode well for an idealistic but underfunded potential candidate. Winning takes money, either the candidate's or someone else's. If the latter, it may come with a string or two attached. And as noted earlier, that is the real concern: To what extent do campaign contributions buy access and influence for the contributor?

Recent research has confirmed several long-standing truths about the costs of campaigning.[63] For instance, close elections cost more than elections in which one candidate is sure to win because uncertainty regarding the outcome is a spur to spending. A candidate quickly learns that it is easier to get money from potential contributors when the polls show that she has a chance of winning. Also, elections that produce change—that is, in which an incumbent is unseated or the out-of-office party gains the office—typically cost more. Taking on an existing officeholder is a risky strategy that drives up election costs. And an open race in which there is no incumbent represents an opportunity for the party out of office to capture the seat, thus triggering similar spending by the in-office party in an effort to protect the seat. It is no wonder that campaign costs are exploding. But there may be a side benefit to more campaign spending: an increase in voter turnout. Research on state legislative elections revealed a link between expenditure levels and turnout.[64]

**State Efforts at Campaign Reform** Concern over escalating costs and the influence of deep-pocketed special interests in campaigns has led reform groups such as Common Cause to call for improved state laws to provide comprehensive and timely disclosure of campaign finances, impose limitations on contributions by individuals and groups, create a combined public–private financing mechanism for primaries and general elections, and establish an independent commission to enforce tough sanctions on violators of campaign finance laws.

States have performed impressively on the first of these recommendations; in fact, all states have some sort of campaign financing reporting procedure. Thirty-six states make information on campaign contributions available online in a searchable database; twenty-four states provide similar access to campaign expenditure data.[65] In response to the fourth recommendation, twenty-six states have established independent commissions to oversee the conduct of campaigns, although they have found it somewhat difficult to enforce the law and punish violators.

The other recommendations have proved more troublesome. States have grappled with the issue of costly campaigns but have made only modest progress in controlling costs. A 1976 decision by the U.S. Supreme Court in *Buckley v. Valeo* made these efforts more difficult; the Court ruled that governments cannot limit a person's right to spend money in order to spread his views about particular issues and candidates. In essence, then, candidates have unlimited power to spend their own money on their own behalf, and other individuals may spend to their hearts' content to promote their own opinions on election-related issues. In 1996, in a lawsuit from Colorado, the Court decided that independent spending by political parties, so-called **soft money**, could not be limited, either. The 2002 Federal Bipartisan Campaign Reform Act, typically referred to as the McCain-Feingold law, aims at controlling the flow of soft money, but reports from recent election cycles suggest that loopholes remain.[66] (The Engaging Parties and Groups in Campaigns box takes up the issue of soft money, organizations called 527s, and state campaign finance reform.) What the Court let stand, however, were state limits on an individual's contributions to candidates and parties; it also ruled that if a candidate accepts public funds, then he is bound by whatever limitations the state may impose.

Some states have established specific limits on the amount of money that organizations and individuals can contribute to a political race. In New York, for example, corporations are limited to a contribution maximum

**soft money**
Unregulated funds contributed to national political parties and nonparty political groups.

# Engaging Parties and Groups in Campaigns

Money is a necessary evil in campaigns, and efforts to reform campaign financing have frustrated the states. Vermont's law, which limited the amount that someone could contribute to a candidate for statewide office to $400 over a two-year election cycle, was struck down by the U.S. Supreme Court in 2006. The Court concluded that the law, which also included spending limits, made it too difficult for candidates to compete effectively and for groups to participate in the campaign process.

States continue to persevere in their attempts to regulate the flow of money in campaigns. The latest challenge comes from nonparty political organizations called **527 groups** (after a section of the U.S. tax code), which sprang up after the McCain–Feingold law took effect. These organizations have had a tremendous impact in state elections. For example, in West Virginia in 2004, a group called "For the Sake of the Kids" spent $3.6 million to defeat an incumbent state Supreme Court justice. How could it spend so extravagantly, given West Virginia's $2,000 limit on campaign contributions? It was a 527 group not connected to a candidate so the limit did not apply. In Washington, a 527 called the Voters Education Committee spent nearly $1.5 million to defeat a candidate for state attorney general. As it turned out, the Voters Education Committee was a front group funded solely by the U.S. Chamber of Commerce, which disagreed with the candidate's position on the regulation of business. West Virginia and Washington were only two of the states in

which 527s—both within the state and from outside the state—played a key role in election outcomes. Sometimes these groups do not focus on specific candidates but instead address issues of the day. But regardless of their focus, the intent is the same: to mold public attitudes. In the 2008 election cycle, 527 groups spent $232 million in support of (or in opposition to) state and local candidates and ballot issues.

Soft money via 527s weakens a state's campaign finance laws. It skews spending upward, and it circumvents disclosure provisions. The public has little inkling about who is behind the organization. What is the Coalition for Smaller Smarter Government or Arkansans for the Twenty-First Century? After its experience, West Virginia became the first state to enact a law that could rein in the activities of 527 organizations. Under the new law, a contributor to a 527 was limited to a maximum of $2,000 and the law required 527s to disclose their sources of funding. In 2009, Massachusetts tightened the reporting requirements for groups like 527s that make so-called "independent expenditures" during an election cycle. Expect to see more states take on the complicated issue of campaign finance.

SOURCES: Zach Patton, "Chasing the Shadow," *Governing* 19 (June 2006): 43–45; William Branigin, "High Court Rejects Vermont Campaign Law," *Washington Post,* www.washingtonpost.com (June 26, 2006); Center for Responsive Politics, "527s: Advocacy Group Spending in the 2008 Elections," www.opensecrets.org/527s/index.php (July 2, 2009).

of $5,000 per calendar year, and individuals (other than official candidates) are restricted to $38,000 in a gubernatorial election, and $9,500 and $3,800 in general elections for senate and house seats, respectively. Florida's approach is uncategorical: individuals (other than the candidate herself), political parties, corporations, labor unions, and PACs are allowed to contribute a maximum of $500 per candidate per election. Some states, such as Arizona, Connecticut, North Dakota, Minnesota, Pennsylvania, and Wyoming, have gone even further by prohibiting contributions from corporations and labor unions.[67] But a totally different philosophy pervades the politics of several states that continue

**527 groups**

Nonprofit, tax-exempt political organizations set up to accept contributions and make expenditures in campaigns, although not explicitly connected to candidates.

to operate their election systems without any limitations on contributions. In Illinois, Missouri, Oregon, and Virginia, to name just a few, organizations and individuals can contribute as much as they wish.

States have also considered the other side of the campaign financing equation: expenditures. All states require candidates and political committees to file reports documenting the expenditure of campaign funds. A few states impose limits on a candidate's total expenditures, but a 2006 U.S. Supreme Court ruling that Vermont's spending limits were too low to allow candidates to compete effectively has complicated that approach. Many have followed Hawaii's lead and set voluntary spending limits. Colorado, for example, adopted a non-binding $2 million spending cap for gubernatorial candidates. Michigan takes a different approach: Publicly funded candidates (governor and lieutenant governor) are restricted to $2 million per election, with additional spending allowable in certain circumstances. Florida has a similar system in place for candidates receiving public funds. In just over half of the states, however, candidates campaign without any spending limits.

## Public Funding as a Solution

Half the states have adopted some sort of public funding of some campaigns, although in most of these states, public financing supplements the private contributions candidates receive. Individuals voluntarily contribute to a central fund that is divided among candidates or political parties. As a condition of accepting public money, whether it is a matching grant (as in Florida and Nebraska) or a fixed subsidy (as in Minnesota and Wisconsin), candidates must abide by state-imposed spending limits. In states that have adopted a fully-funded "clean elections" system of campaign finance (Arizona, Connecticut, Maine, New Jersey, New Mexico, North Carolina, and Vermont), a candidate who wishes to participate must first demonstrate her viability by getting signatures on a petition and/or collecting a certain number of small dollar contributions. Once in the program, she may spend only public funds.[68] Not all elective offices are covered by public funding, however. For instance, Maryland's program covers the governor and lieutenant government, New Mexico's applies to the Public Regulation Commission and statewide judicial offices, and Connecticut's includes legislative campaigns as well as statewide races.

The system is fairly easy to administer and is relatively transparent for citizens. In most of the public funding states, citizens can use their state income tax form to earmark a portion (a dollar or two) of their tax liability for the fund. A check-off system of this sort does not directly increase taxpayers' tax burden. In a few states, the public fund is amassed through a voluntary surcharge, or additional tax (usually $1.00 or $5.00). In addition to check-offs and surcharges, some of the public-funding states, including Arizona, Ohio, and Virginia offer taxpayers a tax credit (usually a percentage of the contribution, up to a specific maximum) when they contribute to political campaigns. Another option is a state tax deduction for campaign contributions, an approach used in Hawaii and Oklahoma. In addition to taxpayer contributions some states also allocate money from specific sources such as Arizona's traffic and criminal fine surcharges.

Public campaign financing is supposed to rid the election process of some of its evils. Proponents argue that it will democratize the contribution process by freeing candidates from excessive reliance on special-interest money. Other possible advantages include expanding the pool of potential candidates, allowing candidates to compete on a more equal basis, and reducing the cost of campaigning. Not everyone has embraced public funding, however. Obviously, it represents a cost to taxpayers and some contend that incumbents will benefit from limits on campaign spending, and that non-serious candidates will be able to use public funds as their own personal treasury. In Arizona, in 2002, nearly 50 percent of the eligible candidates selected the public financing option. That same year, Governor Janet Napolitano became the first governor to be elected with full public financing of her campaign. In the next election cycle, 60 percent of state legislative candidates ran with public money and 93 percent of them were elected. Research on Arizona and Maine shows that clean elections programs deliver on the promise of increased competition.[69]

By contributing to the fund, average citizens may feel that they have a greater stake in state elections. Although more research needs to be done, studies suggest that public financing produces at least some of the benefits its supporters claim. For instance, an analysis of gubernatorial campaigns indicated that the use of public funds by incumbents and challengers holds down overall spending. It also narrows the expenditure gap between them.[70] In 2007, North Carolina adopted its version of clean elections, the "Voter-Owned Elections Act," amid high expectations. This following excerpt from the language of the act sets out the lofty purpose of the law:

> The purpose of this Article is to ensure the vitality and fairness of democratic elections in North Carolina to the end that any eligible citizen of this State can realistically choose to seek and run for public office. It is also the purpose of this Article to protect the constitutional rights of voters and candidates from the detrimental effects of increasingly large amounts of money being raised and spent in North Carolina to influence the outcome of elections.[71]

Public financing continues to be an important weapon in the state struggle to reform and control the influence of money in campaigns.

## CHAPTER RECAP

- Even though voter loyalties have weakened, political parties have proved remarkably resilient and have taken on new roles in politics and governance.

- The Democratic Party can claim about 35 percent of the voting-age public for itself and the Republican Party around 23 percent. The rest of the electorate is considered independents (although they might lean toward one of the major parties), with a small fraction affiliated with third parties.

- Interparty competition has increased over time. One result has been a rise in divided government.

- Interest groups exert a powerful force in state government, with business lobbyists and teachers' groups the most influential in the majority of states.

- The state interest group system is changing: A more diverse set of interests lobbies at the state capital; meanwhile, state governments have tightened their regulation of lobbyists.

- Groups are involved in local elections and in community issues, but their major focus is on the *actions* of government: policy implementation and service delivery.

- Campaigns for state office still involve door-to-door canvassing, neighborhood drop-ins, and public forums, but they increasingly use direct mail, various electronic media, and political consultants.

- Running for public office can be an expensive proposition. To try to level the playing field and diminish the role of private money, most states limit contributions and an increasing number provide public financing.

## Key Terms

political parties *(p. 108)*
ideology *(p. 109)*
ticket splitting *(p. 110)*
pragmatism *(p. 113)*
divided government *(p. 116)*

unified government *(p. 116)*
dealignment *(p. 117)*
interest groups *(p. 117)*
direct action *(p. 122)*
lobbying *(p. 123)*

grassroots lobbying *(p. 125)*
political action committees (PACs) *(p. 125)*
soft money *(p. 132)*
527 groups *(p. 134)*

## Internet Resources

The major political parties have official websites: the Democratic Party is at **www.democrats.org** and the Republican Party is at **www.rnc.org** or **www.gop.com**.

At the state level, illustrative websites are Hawaii's at **www.hawaiidemocrats.org** and Virginia's at **www.rpv.org**.

An interesting state-level, third-party website, **www.cagreens.org**, is the site for the Green Party of California.

Common Cause has a website, **www.common cause.org/states**, that tracks the activities of its thirty-six state offices and the progress of campaign finance reform.

A group devoted to cleaning up elections is Public Campaign. Their website is **www.publicampaign .org/**. Another group with a reform focus is the Center for Public Integrity at **www.publicintegrity.org**.

The National Institute on Money in State Politics provides an abundance of information on the subject at **www.followthemoney.org**.

To learn more about 527 groups, see **www .opensecrets.org/527s/**.

Different perspectives are reflected in the websites of the American Civil Liberties Union, **www .aclu.org**, and the Christian Coalition, **www .cc.org**.

**www.flchamber.com** and **www.ilchamber.org** are the websites for the chambers of commerce for Florida and Illinois, respectively. Other state chambers use similar URLs.

The Texas State Teachers' Association at **www .tsta.org** is an example of a state schoolteachers organization. A different but related perspective is provided by the Oregon PTA at **www .oregonpta.org**.

Other examples of state-level interest groups include the Mississippi Association of Realtors at **www.msrealtors.org** and the Arizona Hospital and Healthcare Association at **www .azhha.org**.

*SOURCE: AP Photo/Kelley McCall*

# State Legislatures

**6**

State legislators work hard during the session. In difficult economic times as in 2009, they hunker down to deal with tough questions. How to close a state budget gap? Which programs will be scaled back? Which taxes and fees will be increased? Which funds will be redirected or raided? Think about California, where the budget gap was more like a crevasse: $26 billion. It took months of intense wrangling, endless debate, and finally, secret agreements to craft a solution. In times like these, legislators welcome the end of the session. And they relish the traditions that adjournment brings. In Mississippi, a tomato seedling is placed on each legislator's desk to mark the end of the session. In Florida, North Carolina, and Washington, officials drop a handkerchief when they adjourn; in Hawaii, legislators join hands, form a circle and sing the state song to close the session. Missouri, Georgia, and Maryland lawmakers, awash in all of the paper that accumulates during a session, celebrate by tossing bills in the air, or shredding them and making confetti. These session-ending traditions help to sustain the otherwise serious legislative process in the states.[1]

## THE ESSENCE OF LEGISLATURES

The new year dawns quietly in Boise, Idaho; Jefferson City, Missouri; and Harrisburg, Pennsylvania, but it does not remain quiet for long: State legislators are set to converge on the state capitol. Every January (or February or March in a few states; every other January in a few others), state legislatures reconvene in session to do the public's business. More than 7,000 legislators hammer out solutions to intricate and often intransigent public problems. They do so in an institution that is steeped in tradition and governed by layers of formal rules and informal norms.

Legislatures engage in three principal functions: *policy making, representation,* and *oversight.* The first, policy making, includes enacting laws and allocating funds. The start of the second decade of the twenty-first century found legislators debating issues such as budget shortfalls, gun control, higher education, and global warming. These deliberations resulted in the revision of old laws, the passage of new laws, and changes in spending, which is what policy making is all about. Legislatures do not have sole control of the state policy-making function; governors, courts, and agencies also determine policy, through executive orders, judicial decisions, and administrative regulations, respectively. But legislatures are the dominant policy-making institutions in state government. Table 6.1 lists the issues that attracted legislative attention in 2010.

In their second function, legislators are expected to represent their constituents—the people who live in their district—in two ways. At least in theory, they

| Popular Legislative Issues in 2010 | TABLE 6.1 |
|---|---|
| **ISSUE** | **WHAT IT'S ALL ABOUT** |
| Dominant issues | |
| State budgets | Cutting expenditures and finding new revenue |
| Health care | Controlling costs and extending coverage |
| Unemployment | Creating jobs and funding benefits |
| Higher education | Keeping public higher education affordable |
| Corrections | Analyzing sentencing policies and lowering costs |
| Transportation/Infrastructure | Identifying new funding sources for construction and maintenance |
| State government | Changing agency structures, functions, and personnel |
| Alternative energy | Finding and using cleaner, renewable energy sources |
| Sex offenders | Complying with new federal policies for registration |
| Broadband coverage | Extending wired and wireless Internet access to rural areas |
| Other popular issues | |
| Distracted driving | Regulating cell phone usage while operating a motor vehicle |
| Voting | Standardizing voting procedures for military and overseas citizens |
| DNA technology | Exploring its uses and misuses, especially in criminal justice |
| Home ownership | Designing new programs to help people keep their homes |

SOURCE: National Conference of State Legislatures, "NCSL Annual Forecast: Construction Continues on Repairing State Budgets," www.ncsl.org (January 7, 2010).

are expected to speak for their constituents in the legislative chamber—to do the will of the public in designing policy solutions. This is not easy. On quiet issues, a legislator seldom has much of a clue about public opinion. And on noisy issues, constituents' will is rarely unanimous. Individuals and organized groups with different perspectives may write to or visit their legislator to urge her to vote a certain way on a pending bill. In another representative function, legislators act as their constituents' facilitators in state government. For example, they may help a citizen deal with an unresponsive state agency. This kind of constituency service (or casework, as it is often called) can be time consuming, but it pays dividends at re-election time because voters tend to look favorably on a legislator who has helped them.[2]

The oversight function is different from the policy making and representation functions. Concerned that the laws they passed and the funds they allocated frequently did not produce the intended effect, lawmakers began to pay more attention to the performance of the state bureaucracy. Legislatures have adopted several methods for checking on agency implementation and spending. The oversight role takes legislatures into the administrative realm. Not surprisingly, this role is little welcomed by agencies, although legislatures see it as a logical extension of their policy-making role.

# LEGISLATIVE DYNAMICS

State legislative bodies are typically referred to as the legislature, but their formal titles vary. In Colorado, it is the General Assembly that meets every year; in Massachusetts, the General Court; and in Oregon, the Legislative Assembly. The legislatures of forty-four states meet annually; in only six states (Arkansas, Montana, Nevada, North Dakota, Oregon, and Texas) do they meet every two years. (Kentucky had been among the biennial sessions group until 2000, when voters approved a switch to annual legislative sessions.) The length of the legislative session varies widely. For example, the Utah General Assembly convened in Salt Lake City on January 26, 2009, and left town on March 12, 2009, for a total of forty-five calendar days in session. By contrast, in states like Michigan and New Jersey, legislative sessions run nearly year-round.

The length of a state's legislative session can be a sensitive issue. In 1997, the Nevada legislature met for 169 days—the longest, most expensive session in its history.[3] Nevadans showed their displeasure the following year when they passed a measure limiting future legislative sessions to 120 days. Voters in the Silver State apparently believed that it should not take more than four months—every two years—to conduct their state's business.

## The Senate and the House

State legislatures have two houses or chambers, similar to those of the U.S. Congress. Forty-nine state legislatures are bicameral. (As noted in Chapter 3, the exception is Nebraska, which in 1934 established a unicameral legislature.) Bicameralism owes its existence to the postcolonial era, in which an upper house, or senate, represented the interests of the propertied class, and a lower house represented everyone else. Even after this distinction was eliminated, states stuck with the bicameral structure, ostensibly because of its contribution to the concept of checks and balances. It is much tougher to pass bills when they have to survive the scrutiny of two legislative houses. Having a bicameral structure, then, reinforces the status quo. Unicameralism might improve the efficiency of the legislature, but efficiency has never been a primary goal of the consensus-building deliberative process.

In the forty-nine bicameral states, the upper house is called the senate; the lower house is usually called the House of Representatives. The average size of a state senate is forty members; houses typically average about 100 members. As with most aspects of state legislatures, chamber size varies substantially—from the Alaska senate, with twenty members, to the New Hampshire house, with 400 representatives. Chamber size seldom changes, but in 2001 Rhode Island began implementing a voter mandate that by 2003 had reduced its 150-member legislature by one-fourth.

For senators, the term of office is usually four years; approximately one-quarter of the states use a two-year senate term. In many states, the election of senators is staggered. House members serve two-year terms, except in Alabama, Louisiana, Maryland, Mississippi, and North Dakota, where four-year terms prevail. The 2009 state legislative sessions found Republicans in control of both chambers in fifteen states, the Democratic Party controlling both houses in twenty-three states, and split control in the remaining twelve states.

There are 7,382 state legislators in this country: 1,971 senators and 5,411 representatives. As of 2009, the number of Democrats and Republicans was 55.2 percent and 43.8 percent, respectively; men outnumbered women 75.5 to 24.3 percent. Legislatures are becoming more racially and ethnically diverse. African Americans occupied 9 percent of all legislative seats; Latinos, 3 percent; Asian Americans, 1 percent; and Native Americans, 1 percent. (Table 6.2 displays the composition of each state legislative chamber in terms of diversity.) Yet even these small proportions of women and racial-ethnic minorities represent a substantial increase, relative to their near absence from most pre-1970s legislatures. The average age of legislators is fifty-six, but as the Engaging the Legislature box indicates, an occasional "Gen Y'er" can be found amid the lawmakers. In terms of occupations, full-time legislators are the single largest category (16.4 percent), overtaking attorneys (15.2 percent), which historically had been the dominant occupation. These two groups are followed by retirees (11.7 percent), business owners (9.2 percent), and business executives/managers (8.7 percent).[4]

## Legislative Districts

Legislators are elected from geographically based districts, with each district in a state containing approximately the same number of inhabitants. Most

**TABLE 6.2** Legislative Diversity, 2009

| STATE | SENATE | | | | HOUSE | | | |
|---|---|---|---|---|---|---|---|---|
| | TOTAL SEATS (%) | WOMEN (%) | AFRICAN AMERICAN (%) | LATINO (%) | TOTAL SEATS (%) | WOMEN (%) | AFRICAN AMERICAN (%) | LATINO (%) |
| Alabama | 35 | 11 | 23 | 0 | 105 | 12 | 26 | 0 |
| Alaska | 20 | 15 | 5 | 0 | 40 | 23 | 0 | 0 |
| Arizona | 30 | 40 | 3 | 20 | 60 | 27 | 2 | 7 |
| Arkansas | 35 | 20 | 11 | 0 | 100 | 25 | 10 | 0 |
| California | 40 | 33 | 5 | 25 | 80 | 25 | 9 | 21 |
| Colorado | 35 | 37 | 3 | 6 | 65 | 40 | 2 | 2 |
| Connecticut | 36 | 22 | 8 | 0 | 151 | 34 | 7 | 5 |
| Delaware | 21 | 38 | 5 | 0 | 41 | 17 | 10 | 2 |
| Florida | 40 | 23 | 18 | 8 | 120 | 24 | 16 | 10 |
| Georgia | 56 | 13 | 21 | 0 | 180 | 21 | 23 | 2 |
| Hawaii | 25 | 28 | 0 | 0 | 51 | 35 | 0 | 0 |
| Idaho | 35 | 23 | 0 | 0 | 70 | 26 | 0 | 1 |
| Illinois | 59 | 22 | 17 | 7 | 118 | 31 | 18 | 7 |
| Indiana | 50 | 26 | 8 | 0 | 100 | 20 | 8 | 1 |
| Iowa | 50 | 18 | 0 | 0 | 100 | 25 | 0 | 0 |
| Kansas | 40 | 33 | 5 | 0 | 125 | 27 | 4 | 3 |
| Kentucky | 38 | 16 | 3 | 0 | 100 | 15 | 6 | 0 |
| Louisiana | 39 | 21 | 23 | 0 | 105 | 13 | 19 | 0 |
| Maine | 35 | 23 | 0 | 0 | 151 | 30 | 0 | 0 |
| Maryland | 47 | 23 | 17 | 2 | 141 | 34 | 23 | 2 |
| Massachusetts | 40 | 30 | 3 | 3 | 160 | 25 | 6 | 3 |
| Michigan | 38 | 24 | 11 | 3 | 110 | 25 | 15 | 2 |
| Minnesota | 67 | 40 | 0 | 1 | 134 | 32 | 1 | 1 |
| Mississippi | 52 | 8 | 21 | 0 | 122 | 17 | 30 | 0 |
| Missouri | 34 | 24 | 9 | 0 | 163 | 20 | 10 | 1 |
| Montana | 50 | 20 | 0 | 0 | 100 | 29 | 0 | 1 |
| Nebraska | 49 | 20 | 2 | 0 | — | — | — | — |
| Nevada | 21 | 33 | 14 | 5 | 42 | 31 | 10 | 10 |
| New Hampshire | 24 | 54 | 0 | 0 | 400 | 36 | 0 | 0 |
| New Jersey | 40 | 25 | 5 | 3 | 80 | 34 | 13 | 9 |
| New Mexico | 42 | 26 | 0 | 40 | 70 | 33 | 3 | 46 |
| New York | 62 | 16 | 18 | 8 | 150 | 28 | 16 | 9 |

| (continued) | | | | | | | | TABLE 6.2 |
|---|---|---|---|---|---|---|---|---|
| North Carolina | 50 | 12 | 14 | 2 | 120 | 31 | 19 | 1 |
| North Dakota | 47 | 13 | 0 | 0 | 94 | 17 | 0 | 0 |
| **Ohio** | 33 | 18 | 15 | 0 | 99 | 22 | 14 | 0 |
| **Oklahoma** | 48 | 10 | 2 | 0 | 101 | 12 | 4 | 1 |
| Oregon | 30 | 37 | 10 | 0 | 60 | 23 | 0 | 2 |
| Pennsylvania | 50 | 20 | 8 | 0 | 203 | 13 | 8 | 0 |
| Rhode Island | 38 | 21 | 0 | 3 | 75 | 23 | 3 | 3 |
| South Carolina | 46 | 0 | 17 | 0 | 124 | 14 | 23 | 0 |
| **South Dakota** | 35 | 20 | 0 | 0 | 70 | 19 | 0 | 0 |
| Tennessee | 33 | 24 | 6 | 3 | 99 | 16 | 15 | 0 |
| Texas | 31 | 19 | 3 | 19 | 150 | 25 | 9 | 21 |
| Utah | 29 | 17 | 0 | 7 | 75 | 24 | 0 | 3 |
| Vermont | 30 | 33 | 0 | 0 | 150 | 38 | 0 | 0 |
| Virginia | 40 | 20 | 13 | 0 | 100 | 16 | 9 | 1 |
| Washington | 49 | 39 | 2 | 2 | 98 | 30 | 1 | 2 |
| West Virginia | 34 | 6 | 0 | 0 | 100 | 20 | 3 | 0 |
| Wisconsin | 33 | 21 | 6 | 0 | 99 | 22 | 0 | 1 |
| Wyoming | 30 | 3 | 0 | 3 | 60 | 25 | 2 | 2 |
| **TOTALS** | **1971** | **22** | **8** | **3** | **5411** | **25** | **9** | **3** |

NOTE: States in bold have legislative term limits.

SOURCES: National Conference of State Legislatures, www.ncsl.org/default.aspx?tabid=16507; "Number of African American Legislators 2009." www.ncsl.org/Default.aspx?TabId=14781; "2009 Latino Legislators." http://www.ncsl.org/Default.aspx?TabId=14766; "Women in State Legislatures, 2009." Center for the American Woman and Politics, www.cawp.rutgers.edu/fast_facts/levels_of_office/StateLeg-CurrentFacts.php (July 2009).

legislative districts are single-member districts (SMDs), that is, one legislator represents the district. In Nebraska, for instance, each member of the unicameral legislature represents 32,210 people, more or less. Dividing or apportioning a state into districts is an intensely political process that affects the balance of power in a state. In the 1960s, for example, the less-populated panhandle area of Florida was overrepresented in the legislature at the expense of the heavily populated southern areas of the state. Therefore, despite Florida's rapid urbanization during that period, public policy continued to reflect the interests of a rurally based minority.

Eight states, including Minnesota and the Dakotas, continue to use **multimember districts (MMDs)** containing more than one lower house seat. (Usually, it is a two-member district and the number of people in the MMD is approximately double that of an SMD.) There are two main types of MMDs.

**multimember districts (MMDs)**
Legislative districts containing more than one seat.

## Engaging the Legislature

# The Emergence of Generation Y

The average state legislator may be fifty-six years old, but the election of more Generation Y legislators is likely to lower the average. In 2006, voters in a legislative district in New Hampshire elected the youngest state legislator in the country: nineteen-year-old Jeff Fontas. A student at Northeastern University at the time, he put his academic schooling on hold for some real-world schooling in the Granite State's House of Representatives.

New Hampshire has a large legislature: 424 members. Lest one think that the state is peculiarly youth oriented, consider this: When Fontas began his term, the average age of his colleagues was sixty-one. The House included the oldest state legislator in the country, Angeline Kopka, who completed her term at the age of ninety-two.

Fontas' brought a fresh perspective to the legislature. Lawmakers are supposed to speak on behalf of the people in their districts, and the youngest members of society are often underrepresented in local and state offices. Recognizing this, Fontas periodically introduced bills tailored specifically for the younger demographic. He sponsored legislation that would allow first-time drug and alcohol offenders to participate in a state program that could eventually lead to their charges to be dropped. Another bill he sponsored would have decriminalized marijuana possession. And as a college student, he insisted that the education funding crisis was the most pressing issue for the state.

Fontas also brought to the lawmaking arena an ingenuity that is common to his demographic. Technologically savvy, he used the Internet and social-networking tools as his primary means of communication with his constituents. His high-energy style and his often differing opinions on the issues of the day created a healthy give-and-take among his colleagues.

Fontas's term provided him with an unparalleled opportunity. While his friends worked toward their undergraduate degrees, Fontas gained a professional experience that can put his political career on the fast track (if he so chooses to pursue this route after finishing college). Perhaps you could emulate Fontas and seek a legislative seat. Having such work listed on your resume is an excellent foundation for a career in local and state governments. It can also be a stepping

AP Photo/Seth Perlman

Former Illinios state representative Aaron Schock

stone to federal office. In 2008, Aaron Schock (pictured above), at age twenty-seven, was elected as the youngest member of the U.S. House of Representatives and the first Generation Y Congressman. He might be young, but he's no legislative novice having spent two terms in the Illinois State Legislature.

Before beginning your campaign, be sure to educate yourself on the minimum age requirements of the state where you live. These age requirements not only vary by state, but can also vary between the house and senate. In the house, the minimum requirements can range anywhere between eighteen and twenty-five years of age, with twenty-one being the most common age minimum (twenty-six states). In the sixteen states where eighteen years of age is the threshold, one is old enough to be a lawmaker even before being old enough to drink. State senates tend to have higher minimum age requirement on average, typically between eighteen and thirty years, with age twenty-five the most common minimum (nineteen states). And if you live in Kentucky, Missouri, New Hampshire, New Jersey, or Tennessee, you will have to wait until you are thirty to run for senate.

SOURCES: Morgan Cullen. "He's 21. She's 92," *State Legislatures* (July/August 2008), pp. 52–54; Randy James, "The First Gen Y Congressman," *Time* (January 8, 2009); www.time.com/time/politics/article/0,8599,1870301,00.html (July 18, 2009); "The Legislators: Qualifications for Election," *The Book of the States, 2008* (Lexington, KY: Council of State Governments, 2008), pp. 89–90.

In the first type, all candidates compete against one another and the two candidates with the most votes are elected. In the other type, candidates have to declare which of the district's two seats they are seeking. In both types, voters in the district vote in as many races as there are seats in the district. Once elected, the two legislators represent the entire MMD area. Does district structure matter? Is there any difference between legislators in MMDs and those in SMDs? The answer is a cautious yes, if research on the Arizona legislature can be extended to other states. Researchers found that lawmakers in the MMD House of Representatives tended to be more ideologically extreme than lawmakers in the SMD senate.[5]

**Malapportionment** Unequal representation, or **malapportionment**, has characterized many legislative bodies. In the past, for example, some states allocated an equal number of senators to each county. (This system calls to mind the U.S. Senate, which has two senators per state.) Because counties vary in population size, some senators were representing ten or twenty times as many constituents as their colleagues were. New Jersey offered one of the most extreme cases. In 1962, one county contained 49,000 residents and another had 924,000, yet each county was allotted one senator, and each senator had one vote in the senate. This kind of imbalance meant that a small group of people had the same institutional power as a group that was nineteen times larger. Such disproportionate power is inherently at odds with representative democracy in which each person's vote carries the same weight.

> **malapportion- ment**
>
> Skewed legislative districts that violate the "one person, one vote" ideal.

Until the 1960s, the federal courts ignored the legislative malapportionment issue. It was not until 1962, in a Tennessee case in which the malapportionment was especially egregious (house district populations ranged from 2,340 to 42,298), that the courts stepped in. In *Baker v. Carr*, the U.S. Supreme Court ruled that the Fourteenth Amendment guarantee of equal protection applies to state legislative apportionment. With this decision as a wedge, the Court ruled that state legislatures should be apportioned on the basis of population. Two years later, in *Reynolds v. Sims* (1964), Chief Justice Earl Warren summed up the apportionment ideal by saying, "Legislators represent people, not trees or acres."[6] Accordingly, districts should reflect population equality: one person, one vote. In the aftermath of this decision, which overturned the apportionment practices of six states, a **reapportionment** fever swept the country and district lines were redrawn in every state.

> **reapportion- ment**
>
> The reallocation of seats in a legislative assembly.

Reapportionment provided an immediate benefit to previously underrepresented urban areas, and increased urban representation led to a growing responsiveness in state legislatures to the problems and interests of cities and suburbs. Where reapportionment had a partisan effect, it generally benefited Republicans in the South and Democrats in the North. Other effects of reapportionment have included the election of younger, better-educated legislators and, especially in southern states, better representation of African Americans. All in all, reapportionment is widely credited with improving the representativeness of American state legislatures.

**Redrawing District Lines** State legislatures are reapportioned following the U.S. Census, which is taken every ten years. Reapportionment allows population fluctuations—growth in some areas, decline in others—to be reflected in redrawn district lines. Twenty-six legislatures **redistrict** themselves; twelve states attempt to depoliticize the process by using impartial commissions to develop their redistricting plans.[7] In the remaining states, the redistricting task involves the legislature and either a commission or another political institution such as the governor (Maryland) or the state supreme court (Florida). A state's decision to use a less politicized approach such as a commission often comes about after a well-publicized redistricting controversy that creates a climate for reform of the process.[8]

In states where the legislature redistricts itself (and the state's congressional districts), the party controlling the legislature controls the redistricting process. Therefore, district lines have traditionally been redrawn to protect incumbent legislators and to maximize the strength of the party in power. The art of drawing district lines creatively was popularized in Massachusetts in 1812, when a political cartoonist for the *Boston Gazette* dubbed one of Governor Elbridge Gerry's district creations a **gerrymander** because the district, carefully configured to reflect partisan objectives, was shaped like a salamander.

Gerrymandering has not disappeared and neither has the partisan politics surrounding the process. In 2003 redistricting was on the legislative agenda in Texas, where Republicans controlled both houses of the legislature for the first time since Reconstruction. Using their partisan advantage, the GOP drew a congressional redistricting map that would greatly benefit Republican candidates. Unhappy Texas Democratic senators responded with an unusual tactic: they left the state (first to Oklahoma, later to New Mexico) to prevent a **quorum** from being present in the chamber to take up the redistricting bill. The Republican governor, using a tactic available to him, dispatched a law enforcement unit, the Texas Rangers, to track down the absent senators. Much partisan hue and cry ensued but eventually the redistricting plan was passed. In Illinois, it was the Democrats who controlled the redistricting process. In 2002, the Democrats redesigned Senate district boundaries so that, based on the voting preferences of the citizenry, what had been relatively liberal Republican districts would become relatively conservative Democratic districts.[9] The goal, of course, is to maintain and grow the partisan majority.

Amid the politics, redistricting has become a sophisticated operation in which statisticians and geographers use computer mapping to assist the legislature in designing an optimal districting scheme. Although "one person, one vote" is the official standard, some unofficial guidelines are also taken into consideration. Ideally, districts should be geographically compact and unbroken. Those who draw the lines pay close attention to traditional political boundaries such as counties and, as noted, to the fortunes of political parties and incumbents. As long as districts adhere fairly closely to the population-equality standard (if a multimember district contains three seats, it must have three times the population of an SMD), federal courts tolerate the achievement of unofficial objectives. But redistricting does occasionally produce some oddly shaped districts resembling lobsters, spiders, and earmuffs. Dividing

---

**redistrict**

The redrawing of legislative district lines to conform as closely as possible to the "one person, one vote" ideal.

**gerrymander**

The process of creatively designing a legislative district, usually to enhance the electoral fortunes of the party in power.

**quorum**

The minimum number of legislators who must be present to transact business.

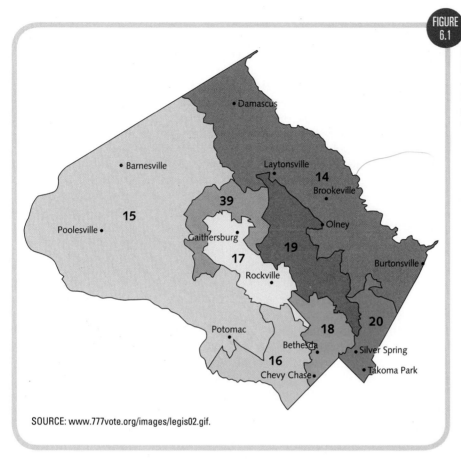

SOURCE: www.777vote.org/images/legis02.gif.

**FIGURE 6.1** **State Legislative Districts in Montgomery County, Maryland**
Although the districts have similar population sizes, their shapes and territorial sizes vary.

Montgomery County, Maryland, into legislative districts after the 2000 Census produced the shapes displayed in Figure 6.1.

Legislatures have to pay attention to the effects of their redistricting schemes on racial minority voting strength. In fact, amendments to the Voting Rights Act and subsequent court rulings instructed affected states to create districts in which racial minorities would have majority status. The intentional creation of districts more favorable to the election of African Americans had a partisan consequence. African Americans are more likely to be Democrats than Republicans; therefore, clustering black voters into specific districts diluted the potential Democratic vote of adjacent districts. This increased the likelihood that Republican candidates would win in those nearby districts. For instance, Florida drew thirteen heavily African American statehouse districts, leaving the other 107 districts with fewer black voters. Some observers contended that this situation made it easier for Republicans to win sixty-five of those seats and thus control the house.[10]

The courts have not spoken with crystal clarity on the question of reapportionment. The racial composition of districts should be taken into account, but racial considerations should not be the sole criterion. In *Vieth v. Jubelirer*

(2004), the Court ruled that reliance on partisan considerations remains an appropriate redistricting option. In *LULAC v. Davis* (2006), one of the newly-drawn congressional districts in Texas was found to violate the Voting Rights Act, but the rest of the state's plan, which favored Republicans, was acceptable to the Court. As one expert, political scientist Ronald Weber, put it, the strategy for line-drawers is "to determine the best way to waste the vote of the partisans of the other party."[11] Thus, the practice of redrawing district lines in response to population shifts is highly politicized, as a recent study of the Kansas legislature demonstrated.[12] Deals are made, interests are protected, and coalitions are built, all in an effort to craft an acceptable map, one that the legislature will adopt and the courts will uphold.

## Compensation

Legislative compensation has increased handsomely in the past three decades, again with some notable exceptions. Before the modernization of legislatures, salary and *per diem* (a daily amount to cover legislators' expenses while staying in the state capital during the session) levels were set in the state constitution and thus were impossible to adjust without a constitutional amendment. The lifting of these limits puts most legislatures, as the policy-making branch of state government, in the curious position of setting their own compensation levels. Recognizing that this power is a double-edged sword (legislators can vote themselves pay raises and the public can turn around and vote them out of office for doing so), almost half the states have established compensation commissions or advisory groups to make recommendations on legislative remuneration. Arizona carries it a step further, requiring that a commission-recommended pay raise for legislators be submitted to the voters for approval—or rejection.

As of 2009, annual salaries of legislators ranged from a low of $100 in New Hampshire to a high of $116,208 in California.[13] Other states at the top of the compensation list include Michigan ($79,650), New York ($79,500), Pennsylvania ($78,315), Illinois ($67,836), and Massachusetts ($61,440). Nine states pay their lawmakers between $30,000 and $50,000 annually. Compare these figures with the more modest yearly pay levels of legislators in Georgia ($17,342), Idaho ($16,116), Nebraska ($12,000), Texas ($7,200), and South Dakota ($6,000). (These figures do not include *per diem*.) As a general rule, states paying a more generous compensation typically demand more of a legislator's time than do low-paying states. And in most states, legislative leadership positions such as speaker of the house come with additional pay; in a few states the chairs of major committees get a salary supplement. New Mexico legislators cannot be accused of seeking elective office for the money. There, legislators receive no salary. What is their financial reward for legislative service? One hundred forty-four dollars per day for living expenses while in Santa Fe during the session, plus a travel allowance.

Legislative pay is but a fraction of the cost of operating a legislature. Legislative staff salaries consume a large chunk of institutional expenditures, as do building maintenance and technological improvements.

## Leadership

Legislatures need leaders, both formal and informal. Each chamber usually has four formal leadership positions. In the senate, a president and a president pro tempore (who presides in the absence of the president) are in charge of the chamber; in the house, the comparable leaders are the speaker and the speaker pro tempore. These legislative officials are chosen by the members, who almost always vote along party lines. (In four states, the post of senate president is occupied by the lieutenant governor.) Both houses have two political party leadership positions: a majority leader and a minority leader.

The leaders are responsible for making the legislature, a relatively decentralized system, run smoothly and for seeing that it accomplishes its tasks. In a typical chamber, the presiding officer appoints committee members, names committee chairs, controls the activity on the floor, allocates office space and committee budgets, and (in some states) selects the majority leader and the holders of other majority-party posts.[14] The actual influence of the leadership varies from one chamber to another. One factor that affects leaders' power is whether the positions are rotated or retained. Leaders who have the option of retaining their position can build power bases. In the case of rotation, however, one set of leaders is replaced with another on a regular basis, so the leaders are **lame ducks** when they assume the posts.

> **lame duck**
> An elected official who cannot serve beyond the current term of office.

On average, today's leaders are different from the caricatured wheeler dealers of the past. For one thing, in 2009, six women were senate presidents; five women served as speakers of the house.[15] New Hampshire scored two historic firsts in 2009: the first state with a female majority in a legislative chamber (the senate: 54 percent women) and the first state to have women occupy both the house speakership and the senate presidency. More evidence that legislative leadership has changed comes from Colorado, where, in 2009, it became the first state in which African Americans led both chambers of the legislature at the same time. Another indicator of change has less to do with diversity and more to do with process: rank-and-file members of the legislature are not as reluctant as they used to be to challenge their leaders on both procedural and policy matters. Confirmation of this point came from the New York senate in 2009 when two freshman Democrats defied the leadership and moved to the Republican side of the chamber for several weeks.

Leadership in legislatures is linked to political parties. Voting to fill leadership posts follows party lines. For example, the Florida senate began one term with twenty Democrats and twenty Republicans. Each time the chamber voted to select its president, the balloting was tied 20 to 20. To break the deadlock, the senators negotiated a novel solution: split the term into two one-year segments, with a Republican president the first year and a Democratic president the second year. The Michigan House of Representatives, also operating with partisan equality, opted for a different power-sharing arrangement. There, lawmakers decided to use cospeakers and co-committee chairs. The speakership rotated monthly between the Republican leader and the Democratic leader; the committee chairs did likewise.

As political parties become more competitive in the states, legislative behavior and decisions take on a more partisan cast, that is, the legislature becomes more "procedurally partisan."[16] There are Democratic and Republican sides of the chamber and Democratic and Republican positions on bills. Each party meets in a caucus to design its legislative strategy and generate camaraderie. In states where one political party continues to dominate, partisanship is less important; however, in one-party settings, the dominant party typically develops splits or factions at the expense of party unity. But when the outnumbered minority party begins to gain strength, the majority party usually becomes more cohesive.

In many states, legislative leaders have embraced a new function: fund-raising. Leaders tap interest groups and lobbyists for money and divide it among their party's candidates for legislative seats. California has led the way, with multimillion-dollar legislative **war chests**. In other states, the amount of money thus raised is not as great, of course, but it has become a significant source of campaign funding. Lobbyists find it difficult to say no to a request for funds from the leadership. The leaders allocate the funds to the neediest candidates—those in close races. If they are victorious, their loyalty to party leaders pays legislative dividends.

**war chest**

A stash of funds accumulated in advance of a campaign.

## The Committee System

The workhorse of the legislature is the committee. Under normal circumstances, a committee's primary function is to consider bills—that is, to hear testimony, perhaps amend the bills, and ultimately approve or reject them. A committee's action on a bill precedes debate in the house or senate. Along with the leadership, committees provide a structure for organizing the process of making laws.

All legislative chambers are divided into committees, and most committees have created subcommittees. Committees can be of several types. A *standing committee* regularly considers legislation during the session. A *joint committee* is made up of members of both houses. Some joint committees are standing; others are temporary (sometimes called ad hoc or select) and are convened for a specific purpose, such as investigating a troubled agency or solving a particularly challenging public policy problem. A *conference committee* is a special type of joint committee that is assembled to iron out differences between house- and senate-passed versions of a bill. Most states use *interim committees* during the period when the legislature is not in session to get a head start on an upcoming session. The number of committees varies, but most senates and houses have standing committees on the issues listed in Table 6.3. Most of these committees, in turn, have professional staffs assigned to them.

A substantive standing committee tends to be made up of legislators who have expertise and interest in that committee's subject matter.[17] Thus, farmers would be assigned to the agriculture committee, teachers to the education committee, small-business owners to the commerce committee, lawyers to the judiciary committee, and so on. These legislators bring knowledge and commitment to their committee assignments; they also may bring a certain bias because they tend to function as advocates for their career interests. Note, too,

| Standing Committees of the Legislature | | TABLE 6.3 |
|---|---|---|
| Both houses of state legislatures typically have standing committees dealing with these substantive issues: | | |
| Agriculture | Government operations | |
| Banking/financial institutions | Health | |
| Business and commerce | Insurance | |
| Communications | Judiciary and criminal justice | |
| Education | Local affairs | |
| Elections | Public employees | |
| Energy | Rules | |
| Environment and natural resources | Social/human services | |
| Ethics | Transportation | |
| In addition, both houses have standing committees that address the raising and allocating of state funds. These committees may have different names in different chambers: | | |
| Appropriations | Finance and taxation | |
| Ways and means | | |

that every chamber has at least one undesirable committee (usually defined as one whose substance is boring) to which few legislators want to be assigned.[18]

The central concern of a standing committee is its floor success—getting the full chamber to accede to its recommendations on a bill. Several plausible explanations exist for a committee's floor success. A committee with an ideological composition similar to that of the chamber is likely to be more successful than one whose members are at odds with the chamber. The leadership takes this situation into account when it makes committee assignments; thus, very few committees are ideological outliers.[19] Also, committees full of legislatively experienced members generally have more floor success than committees composed of legislative novices. And committees that have a reputation for being tough have more floor success with their bills than committees that are easy and pass everything that comes before them.

# LEGISLATIVE BEHAVIOR

Legislatures have their own dynamics, their own way of doing things. Senate and house rule books spell out what can and cannot be done, in the same way that an organization's bylaws do. Legislatures function as self-regulating institutions for the most part; it is especially important, therefore, that participants know what is expected of them. To make certain that the chamber's rules are understood, most legislatures conduct orientation sessions for new members.

## Norms of the Institution

An understanding of the legislature involves not only knowledge of formal structures and written rules but also awareness of informal norms and unwritten policies. For example, nowhere in a state's legislative rules does it say that a freshman legislator is prohibited from playing a leadership role, but the unwritten rules of most legislatures place a premium on seniority. A primary rule of legislative bodies is that you must "go along to get along," a phrase that emphasizes teamwork and paying your dues. Legislators who are on opposite sides of a bill to regulate horse racing might find themselves on the same side of a bill outlawing the use of cell phones while operating a motor vehicle. Yesterday's opponent is today's partner. For this reason, a legislator cannot make bitter enemies in the legislature and expect to flourish.

Those who aspire to rise from rank-and-file legislator to committee chairperson and perhaps to party leader or presiding officer find consensus-building skills quite useful. These skills come in handy because many norms are intended to reduce the potential for conflict in what is inherently a setting full of conflict. For instance, a freshman legislator is expected to defer to a senior colleague. Although an energetic new legislator might chafe under such a restriction, one day he will have gained seniority and will take comfort in the rule. Legislators are expected to honor commitments made to each other, thus encouraging reciprocity: "If you support me on my favorite bill, I will be with you on yours." A legislator cannot be too unyielding. Compromises, sometimes principled but more often political, are the backbone of the legislative process. Few bills are passed by both houses and sent to the governor in exactly the same form as when they were introduced.

Informal rules are designed to make the legislative process flow more smoothly. Legislators who cannot abide by the rules find it difficult to get along. They are subjected to not-so-subtle behavior-modification efforts, such as powerful social sanctions (ostracism and ridicule) and legislative punishment (the bottling up of their bill in committee or their assignment to an unpopular committee), actions that promote adherence to norms.

## Cue Taking and Decision Making

Much has been written about how legislators make public policy decisions, and several explanations are plausible. Legislators may adopt the policy positions espoused by their political party. They may follow the dictates of their conscience—that is, do what they think is right. They may yield to the pressures of organized interest groups. They may be persuaded by the arguments of other legislators, such as a committee chairperson who is knowledgeable about the policy area or a trusted colleague who is considered to be savvy; or they may succumb to the entreaties of the governor, who has made a particular piece of legislation the focus of her administration. Of course, legislators may also attempt to respond to the wishes of their constituents. On a significant issue—one that has received substantial media attention—they are likely to be subjected to tremendous cross-pressures.

A legislator reflecting on his years in the Massachusetts house tells this revealing story. During one session, he voted yes on corporate tax break legislation that he was opposed to because the speaker of the house favored the bill and wanted him to vote yes. Why was the speaker's position so compelling? Because the legislator's favorite bill was due to be voted on later and he wanted the speaker's support on it.[20] Another remarkably candid assessment of how legislators make public policy decisions was offered by a freshman in the Tennessee House of Representatives. He identified two often unspoken but always present considerations: "Will it cost me votes back home?" and "Can an opponent use it against me [in the] next election?"[21] These pragmatic concerns intrude on the more idealistic notions of decision making. They also suggest a fairly cautious approach to bold policy initiatives.

Assuming that legislators are concerned about how a vote will be received back home, it seems logical that they would be particularly solicitous of public opinion. In actuality, state legislators frequently hold opinions at odds with those of their constituents. They occasionally misperceive what the public is thinking; at such times, it is difficult for them to act as mere **delegates** and simply fulfill the public's will. To improve the communications link, some legislators use questionnaires to poll constituents about their views; others hold town meetings at various spots in the district to assess the public's mood.

It is quite probable that first-term legislators feel more vulnerable to the whims of the public than legislative veterans do. Hence, the new legislator devotes more time to determining what the people want, whereas the experienced legislator "knows" what they want (or perhaps knows what they need) and thus functions as a **trustee**—someone who follows his or her own best judgment. Since the vast majority of legislators are returned to office election after election, it appears that there is some validity to this argument. In fact, a study of legislators in eight states found that the members' personal opinions were consistently important in their decision choices.[22]

In the final analysis, the determining factor in how legislators make decisions depends on the issue itself. On one hand, "when legislators are deeply involved with an issue, they appear to be more concerned with policy consequences" than with constituency preferences.[23] In this situation, the legislators are focused on a goal other than re-election. On the other hand, if legislators are not particularly concerned about an issue that is important to their constituents, they will follow their constituents' preference. In that sense, they act as **politicos**, adjusting as the issues and cues change.

**delegate**
A legislator who functions as a conduit for constituency opinion.

**trustee**
A legislator who votes according to his or her conscience and best judgment.

**politico**
A legislator who functions as either a delegate or a trustee, as circumstances dictate.

# HOW A BILL BECOMES LAW (OR NOT)

A legislative bill starts as an idea and travels a long, complex path before it emerges as law. It is no wonder that of the 3,723 bills introduced in the Illinois legislature in 2008, only 324 had become law by the end of the session.[24] A legislative session has a rhythm to it. Minor bills and symbolic issues tend to be resolved early, whereas major, potentially divisive issues take a much longer time to wend their way through the legislative labyrinth. With the clock ticking at the end of the session, legislators try to broker compromises and build coalitions to get key bills passed.[25] The budget or appropriations bill typically generates several rounds of contentious debate among legislators. And if legislatures cannot get their work completed, they may end up back in the state capitol at a later date in a special session. In 2008, for example, thirty-seven special legislative sessions were called; some states held more than one extra session.

The lawmaking process has been described in many ways: a zoo, a circus, a marketplace. Perhaps the most apt description is a casino because there are winners and losers, the outcome is never final, and there is always a new game ahead.[26] Figure 6.2 displays a simplified version of a typical lawmaking process, showing at just how many points a bill can get sidetracked.

The diagram of the legislative process in Figure 6.2 cannot convey the dynamism and excitement of lawmaking. Ideas for bills are everywhere: with constituents, interest groups, and state agencies. Legislators may turn to other states for ideas or to their staffs. **Policy entrepreneurs**, people who are knowledgeable about certain issues and are willing to promote them, abound. Introducing a bill—"putting it in the hopper," in legislative parlance—is just the beginning.

A bill does not make it through the legislative process without a lot of effort and even a little luck. A bill's chances of passage rise as more legislators sign on as cosponsors, and if the cosponsors are legislative leaders, even better. Assignment of the bill to a favorable committee improves the likelihood that the bill will be scheduled for a hearing in a timely manner. Many bills get bottled up in committee and never receive a hearing. Strong support from key interest groups is a powerful advantage as is the emergence of only weak opposition to the bill. Sometimes bill passage is a matter of fortuitous timing. For example, a spectacular prison break from an overcrowded state penitentiary would help garner support for passage of a prison construction bill.

Controversial issues such as abortion raise the stakes. The former speaker of the Wisconsin Assembly, Tom Loftus, described abortion politics in his state as trench warfare in which compromise was almost impossible. Leadership on the issue came from legislators who felt strongly about the matter and who held safe seats. (In this instance, "safe" meant that taking a position was not likely to cost them too many votes or generate too many serious challengers when they ran for re-election.) As anti-abortion bills were introduced, battle lines were drawn. According to the speaker,

> The pro-choice side, which included the Democratic leadership, tried to keep the bill bottled up in committee, and the pro-life side, through political pressure on the Republicans and conservative Democrats, tried to pull it out so the whole assembly could vote on it on the floor of the chamber. If the pro-life people could get the bill to the floor for a vote, they would win. To accomplish this end, they needed to gain supporters from the pivotal middle group of legislators, usually moderates of both parties from marginal districts.[27]

**policy entrepreneurs**

People who bring new ideas to a policy-making body.

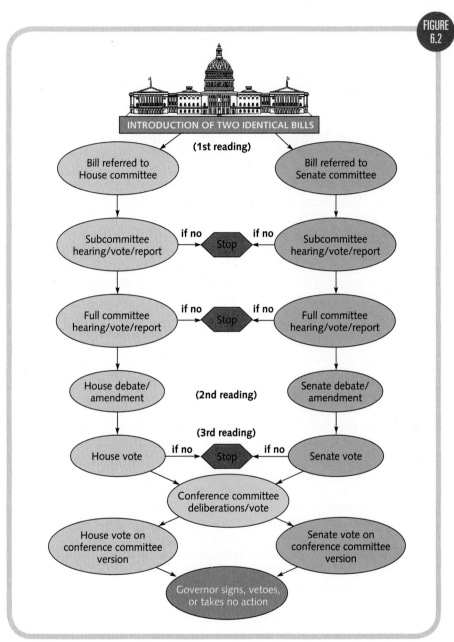

FIGURE 6.2

**How a Bill Becomes Law**
At each of the stages in the process, supporters and opponents of a bill clash. Most bills stall at some point and fail to make it to the end.

INTRODUCTION OF TWO IDENTICAL BILLS

(1st reading)

Bill referred to House committee — Bill referred to Senate committee

Subcommittee hearing/vote/report — if no — Stop — if no — Subcommittee hearing/vote/report

Full committee hearing/vote/report — if no — Stop — if no — Full committee hearing/vote/report

House debate/amendment — (2nd reading) — Senate debate/amendment

(3rd reading)

House vote — if no — Stop — if no — Senate vote

Conference committee deliberations/vote

House vote on conference committee version — Senate vote on conference committee version

Governor signs, vetoes, or takes no action

The powerful anti-abortion group, Wisconsin Citizens Concerned for Life, pressured vulnerable legislators. These legislators were in a tough position because they knew "regardless of how you voted, you were going to make a slew of single-issue voters mad."[28] Their strategy became one of parliamentary maneuvering and delay.

Even if a bill is successful in one chamber, potential hurdles await in the other chamber. Representatives and senators may see the same issue in very different terms. In Ohio a few years back, everyone agreed that the state's system for funding public education needed reform. (The Ohio Supreme Court had found the state's school-funding system unconstitutional and had given the legislature one year to devise a new system.) But initial efforts derailed when the house and senate could not agree on a plan. The senate approved a funding package that would have increased the sales tax, provided debt financing, and allowed local school boards to propose property tax increases.[29] The house, dominated by Republicans who had signed an anti-tax pledge the preceding year, approved a bill that did not include tax hikes. Each chamber rejected the other's plan. Hammering out a compromise agreeable to both chambers took a long time, even with the court's order as a spur to action.

Once conference or concurrence committees resolve differences and agreement is secured in both chambers, then the bill is enrolled (certified and signed) and sent to the governor. The governor may do one of three things: (1) sign the act (once passed, a bill is called an act) into law, (2) veto it (in which case the legislature has a chance to have the last word by overriding the veto), or (3) take no action. If the governor does not take action and the session has ended, then in most states the act will become law without the governor's signature. Why not simply sign it if the act will become law anyway? Sometimes it is a matter of political symbolism for the governor. In approximately one-third of the states, if the governor does not sign or veto the act and the legislature has adjourned, the act dies (a circumstance called a pocket veto).

During its 2008 session, the Illinois General Assembly passed only 9 percent of the bills that were introduced. Is this a sign of success or failure? Illinois's figures are lower than those of most states—20–25 percent is a common passage rate— but not necessarily a cause for alarm. Not all bills are good ones, and the inability to generate sufficient consensus among legislators may reflect that condition.

Colorado tried something new for one of its recent sessions: a process called "Getting to Yes."[30] A task force representing groups involved in education—teachers and their unions, administrators, school board members, business leaders, and legislators—met before the session to develop bills on procedures for evaluating and dismissing teachers. Participants agreed beforehand to focus on goals, not turf. Although the process was not conflict-free, it did produce two bills that participants could agree on.

## LEGISLATIVE REFORM AND CAPACITY

During the 1970s, fundamental reforms occurred throughout the country as legislatures sought to increase their capacity and become more professional. And, even though these reforms have had a substantial impact, the modernization process never really ends. The Breaking New Ground box discusses a novel proposal in California to redesign the professional, but highly partisan, legislature.

## BREAKING NEW GROUND

### Letting Citizens Redesign the Legislature, and Maybe the Rest of State Government, Too

California's legislature is a pretty partisan place. Some observers contend that it has become too "partisanized" to function effectively. Less than one-third of the public approves of the job that the legislature is doing. In fact, the word *dysfunctional* is frequently used to describe the legislature. To try to foster some bipartisanship within the institution and pump up the approval rating, two assemblymen came up with a novel idea in 2006. Democrat Joe Canciamilla and Republican Keith Richman advocated the creation of a "citizens' assembly" that would study the state's politics and, after one year, recommend changes in California's electoral process and its legislature. Everything, with the exception of the state's judicial elections, would be on the table. Unicameral legislature? Campaign finance reform? Changing term limits? These changes and more would be subject to consideration by the proposed eighty-person Citizens' Assembly. Any recommendation that the group might make would be voted on by the public.

Although the idea did not gain much traction in the legislature, among the public, the concept of a citizen's assembly struck a responsive chord. A new group, Repair California, sprang up and expanded the proposal, calling for a full-fledged constitutional convention to be held in 2011. This being California, the group bypassed the legislature and used the initiative process to get the question of holding a constitutional convention before the voters. Repair California convened a series of town hall meetings in 2009 and from them it was evident that the legislature itself would be a central topic at any constitutional convention in the Golden State.

SOURCES: Lynda Gledhill, "Lawmakers Promoted 'Citizens' Assembly' for California," *San Francisco Chronicle* (January 27, 2006); "The Mod Squad," *Governing* 19 (March 2006): 17–18; "California: The Ungovernable State," *The Economist* (May 14, 2009); "Repair California," www.repaircalifornia.org (July 25, 2009).

## The Ideal Legislature

In the late 1960s, the Citizens' Conference on State Legislatures (CCSL) studied legislative performance and identified five characteristics critical to legislative improvement.[31] Ideally, a legislature should be functional, accountable, informed, independent, and representative (FAIIR).

The *functional* legislature has almost unrestricted time to conduct its business. It is assisted by adequate staff and facilities and has effective rules and procedures that facilitate the flow of legislation. The *accountable* legislature's operations are open and comprehensible to the public. The *informed* legislature manages its workload through an effective committee structure, legislative activities between sessions, and a professional staff; it also conducts regular budgetary review of executive branch activities. The *independent* legislature runs its own affairs, independent from the executive branch. It exercises oversight of agencies, regulates lobbyists, manages conflicts of interest, and provides adequate compensation for its members. Finally, the *representative* legislature has a diverse membership that effectively represents the social, economic, ethnic, and other characteristics of the constituencies.

The fifty state legislatures were evaluated and scored by CCSL according to the FAIIR criteria. For the first time ever, the rankings offered a relatively scientific means of comparing one state legislature with another. Overall, the most effective state legislatures were found in California, New York, Illinois, Florida, and Wisconsin. The worst, in the assessment of CCSL, were those in Alabama, Wyoming, Delaware, North Carolina, and Arkansas.

The CCSL report triggered extensive self-evaluation by legislatures around the country. Most states launched ambitious efforts to reform their legislatures. The results are readily apparent. In terms of the CCSL criteria, states have made tremendous strides in legislative institution building. The evidence of increased professionalism includes more staff support, higher legislative compensation, longer sessions, and better facilities. Many legislatures revamped their committee systems, altered their rules and procedures, and tightened their ethics regulations. The consequences of these actions are state legislatures that are far more FAIIR now than they were thirty years ago.

## The Effects of Reform

Today's legislative institutions are different, but are they better? Although many observers would answer in the affirmative, the legislative reform picture is not unequivocally rosy. Political scientist Alan Rosenthal, who has closely observed legislative reform, warns that "the legislature's recent success in enhancing its capacity and improving its performance may place it in greater jeopardy than before."[32] Rosenthal's argument is that a constellation of demands pulls legislators away from the legislative core. That is, the new breed of legislators becomes caught up in the demands of re-election, constituent service, interest groups, and political careerism and thus neglects institutional matters such as structure, procedure, staff, image, and community. The legislature as an institution suffers because it is not receiving the necessary care and attention from its members. Minnesota, with a highly reformed legislature, exhibited relatively poor performance in the mid-1990s, described as a period of bitter partisanship and personal scandal. Some observers blame reform.[33]

Consider the idea of a citizen-legislator, one for whom service in the legislature is a part-time endeavor. Since the onset of reform, the proportion of legislators who are lawyers, business owners, or insurance or real-estate executives has dropped, and the number of full-time legislators has risen. In states such as Michigan, Pennsylvania, and Wisconsin, roughly two-thirds of the lawmakers identify themselves as legislators, with no other occupation. The critical issue is whether the decline of the citizen-legislator is a desirable aspect of modernization. Should a state legislature represent a broad spectrum of vocations, or should it be composed of career politicians? One perspective is this: "If I'm sick, I want professional help. I feel the same way about public affairs. I want legislators who are knowledgeable and professional."[34] Another view is represented by a Michigan legislator who believes that his careerist colleagues have lost touch with their constituents: "When you spend all your time in Lansing, you're more influenced by the lobbyists than by your constituents."[35]

**Legislative Professionalism**

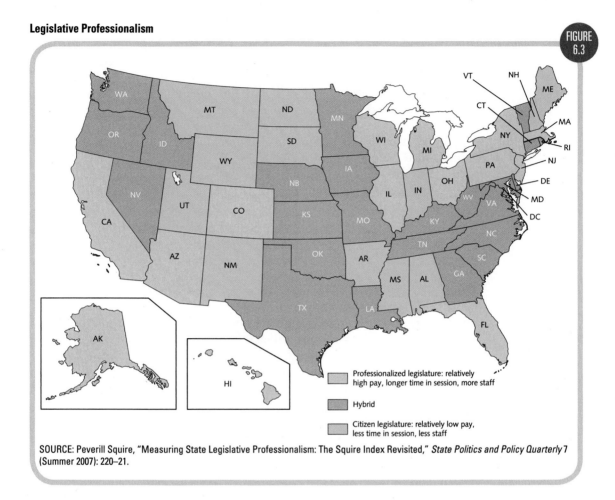

FIGURE 6.3

Professionalized legislature: relatively high pay, longer time in session, more staff

Hybrid

Citizen legislature: relatively low pay, less time in session, less staff

SOURCE: Peverill Squire, "Measuring State Legislative Professionalism: The Squire Index Revisited," *State Politics and Policy Quarterly* 7 (Summer 2007): 220–21.

In effect, state legislatures are becoming more like the U.S. Congress. Legislators are staying in the legislature in record numbers. Modernization has made the institution more attractive to its members, so turnover rates are declining. But do we really want fifty mini-Congresses scattered across the land? Today's legislatures are more FAIIR than in the past, but reform has also brought greater professionalization of the legislative career, increased polarization of the legislative process, and more fragmentation of the legislative institution.[36] Figure 6.3 shows the pattern of citizen, professional, and hybrid state legislatures throughout the land. The categories are derived from an index developed by political scientist Peverill Squire that reflects legislator salary and benefits, the time demands of legislative service, and the staff resources available to the legislature.

Change continues in state legislatures, but much of it is cloaked in an anti-reform guise. Term limits (discussed below) are, of course, a major component in the effort to limit the legislature. Other attempts to chip away at reform include Louisiana's approval of a constitutional amendment that, in even-numbered years, limits the legislature to a thirty-day session that addresses only fiscal issues. Also, as noted earlier, Nevada has trimmed the length of legislative sessions, whereas Illinois and Rhode Island have reduced the size of their legislatures.

To some analysts, the reforms of the past decades have produced a legislative monster. Richard Nathan, a veteran observer of the states, argues that the key to increased government productivity is the empowerment of the governor.[37] Nathan advocates term limits, unicameral legislative bodies, rotation of committee memberships, and reduction of legislative staff and sessions as a means of reining in the legislature vis-à-vis the governor. If adopted, Nathan's recommendations would undo thirty-five years of legislative reform. And the governor's political power would be significantly strengthened. The legislative–gubernatorial nexus is the subject of a later section of this chapter.

## Term Limits

In September 1990, Oklahoma voters took an action that has sent state legislatures reeling. Oklahomans overwhelmingly approved a ballot measure limiting the tenure of state legislators and statewide officers. And, as it turned out, limiting terms was not just a Sooner thing. Within two months, voters in California and Colorado had followed suit. With a close defeat in Washington State slowing it only slightly, the term-limits movement swept the country. In Oregon, a group called Let Incumbents Mosey into the Sunset (LIMITS) grew out of a tax limitation organization. In Wisconsin, a coalition known as Badgers Back in Charge took up the term limitation cause. And political activists of many stripes—populists, conservatives, and libertarians—found a home in the term limitation movements in Florida, Michigan, and Texas.[38] In time, twenty-one states slapped limits on state legislative terms. And they gradually bore the intended fruit: By 2009, more than 1,865 legislators had been barred from seeking re-election.[39] Table 6.4 compares the term-limit provisions of the states where legislative term limits remained in force in 2009. Note that Nebraska voters had approved term limits three times prior to the 2000 initiative, but the courts had invalidated the measures.

In most states, the measures limit service in each chamber separately. In Maine, for example, a legislator is limited to eight years in the house and eight years in the senate. It is quite possible, then, that an individual could serve a total of sixteen years in the legislature under this plan. In a few states, the restriction is on total legislative service. In Oklahoma, for instance, the limitation is twelve years, whether in the house, the senate, or a combination of the two. Some term limits are for a lifetime (as in Arkansas and Nevada); some simply limit the number of consecutive terms (as in Ohio and South Dakota).

Limiting legislative terms captured the fancy of a public angry with entrenched politicians. The measure offers voters a chance to strike back at an institution that they perceive as self-serving and out of touch. But not everyone favors limiting legislative terms. Opponents offer several arguments against them. On a theoretical level, they argue that term limits rob voters of

| STATE | YEAR ADOPTED | SENATE | HOUSE | YEAR LAW TOOK EFFECT | REFERENDUM VOTE | BALLOT STATUS |
|---|---|---|---|---|---|---|
| Arizona | 1992 | 8 | 8 | 2000 | 74 to 26 | Initiative |
| Arkansas | 1992 | 8 | 6 | 2000/1998 | 60 to 40 | Initiative |
| California | 1990 | 8 | 6 | 1998/1996 | 52 to 48 | Initiative |
| Colorado | 1990 | 8 | 8 | 1998 | 71 to 29 | Initiative |
| Florida | 1992 | 8 | 8 | 2000 | 77 to 23 | Initiative |
| Louisiana | 1995 | 12 | 12 | 2007 | 76 to 24 | Referendum |
| Maine | 1993 | 8 | 8 | 1996 | 67 to 33 | Indirect Initiative |
| Michigan | 1992 | 8 | 6 | 2002/1998 | 59 to 41 | Initiative |
| Missouri | 1992 | 8 | 8 | 2002 | 74 to 26 | Initiative |
| Montana | 1992 | 8 | 8 | 2000 | 67 to 33 | Initiative |
| Nebraska | 2000 | 8 | — | 2006 | 56 to 44 | Initiative |
| Nevada | 1994 | 12 | 12 | 2010 | 70 to 30 | Initiative |
| Ohio | 1992 | 8 | 8 | 2000 | 66 to 34 | Initiative |
| Oklahoma | 1990 | 12 | 12 | 2004 | 67 to 33 | Initiative |
| South Dakota | 1992 | 8 | 8 | 2000 | 63 to 37 | Initiative |

**Term Limits in the States**

TABLE 6.4

SOURCES: State Legislative Term Limits (2009), www.termlimits.org, and the National Conference of State Legislatures, "Members Termed Out, 1998–2006," www.ncsl.org/Default.aspx?TabId=14842.

their fundamental right to choose their representatives. In a related vein, they contend that these measures unfairly disqualify a subset of the population—legislators—from seeking office. And, finally, they claim that term limits are unnecessary, that sufficient legislative turnover occurs without them.

Term limits were expected to produce several consequences:

- Ending the domination of a chamber by powerful, entrenched veteran legislators.
- Increasing the proportion of first-term legislators in any given session.
- Increasing representation by groups underrepresented in the legislature, especially women and minorities, because of the guarantee of open seats.[40]
- Shifting power from the legislature to the governor and to lobbyists.

Term limits have changed the nature of the legislative process in affected states. The first two expected consequences have indeed come to pass. The exodus of veteran legislators and the influx of inexperienced members have some observers shaking their heads in dismay. Data from term-limit states reflect procedural difficulties, a slower-working institution, and less deliberation in committees.[41] One solution has been to increase the amount of training new legislators receive; another has been to increase the role of legislative staff. Clearly, replacing the lost institutional experience is a critical issue. The expectation that term limits would produce greater representation of under-represented groups has not been borne out, at least not yet. The number of women in term-limited legislatures has actually decreased slightly, and the increase in racial and ethnic minorities may be due more to their increased voting strength rather than to term limits.[42] As for shifting power to other actors, consensus seems to exist among researchers that governors, agency heads, legislative staff, and interest groups have benefited at the expense of the term-limited legislature.[43] Term-limit devotees who wanted to strike back at an out-of-touch institution would be surprised to learn that term-limited legisla-tors actually become less beholden to their constituents.[44] In sum, limiting the terms of legislators has consequences beyond simply forcing incumbents out of office.

Despite these effects, term limits remain popular with the public.[45] In 2008, South Dakota legislators asked voters if they wanted to repeal legislative term limits; the answer was a resounding "no"—76 percent to 22 percent. But the term-limit movement is losing steam. As Table 6.4 indicates, citizen initiatives are the primary vehicle through which the term-limit question has been placed before the voters. And the issue has just about run the gamut of states that allow initiatives. (The Utah legislature imposed term limits on itself in 1994, but it had a change of heart and repealed the law in 2003.) Court challenges have undone legislative term limits in Massachusetts, Oregon, Washington, and Wyoming (see Table 6.5). And in a surprising move, the Idaho legislature, bowing to an array of political pressures, repealed the term-limits law that was adopted via the initiative process in 1994.[46] (In Idaho, term limits were statu-tory, not constitutional; thus, the repeal was within the legislature's purview. The governor vetoed the legislature's action, but the house and senate overrode the veto.) Angry Idahoans gathered a sufficient number of signatures to place a question on the 2002 ballot asking whether the legislature's action should be upheld. After a heated campaign, the "Repeal the Repeal" question was defeated, thus ending term limits in Idaho before they took effect.

| TABLE 6.5 | Repeals of Legislative Term Limits | | | |
|---|---|---|---|
| **STATE** | **YEAR ADOPTED** | **YEAR REPEALED** | **REPEALED BY** |
| Idaho | 1994 | 2002 | Legislature |
| Massachusetts | 1994 | 1997 | State Supreme Court |
| Oregon | 1992 | 2002 | State Supreme Court |
| Utah | 1994 | 2003 | Legislature |
| Washington | 1992 | 1998 | State Supreme Court |
| Wyoming | 1992 | 2004 | State Supreme Court |

SOURCE: "Legislative Term Limits: An Overview," National Conference of State Legislatures, www.ncsl.org/default.aspx?tabid=14849.

# RELATIONSHIP WITH THE EXECUTIVE BRANCH

In Chapter 7, you will read about strong governors leading American states boldly in the twenty-first century. In this chapter, you have read about strong legislatures charting a course for that same century. Do these institutions ever collide in their policy making? You bet they do. Conflict between the legislature and the governor is inevitable, but it is not necessarily destructive. It is inevitable because both governors and legislators think that they know what is best for the state. It is not necessarily destructive because, during the posturing, bargaining, and negotiating that produces a consensus, governors and legislators may actually arrive at an optimal solution.

## Dealing with the Governor

The increased institutional strength of the legislature and its accompanying assertiveness have made for strained relations with a governor accustomed to being the political star. Institutional conflict is exacerbated under conditions of divided government, that is, when a legislature is controlled by one party and the governor is of the other party. The result of divided government is often gridlock, accompanied by finger pointing and blame-gaming. As the Republican governor of Mississippi, Haley Barbour, said to the Democratic-controlled legislature in his first "State of the State" address, "As Governor of Mississippi you have two choices…you can work with the Legislature, or you can fail. Well, I'm not into failure, so I look forward to working with each of you to make sure we all succeed."[47] As Governor Barbour quickly learned, that is much easier said than done. Figure 6.4 tracks the incidence

**Divided Government in the States, 1948–2008**

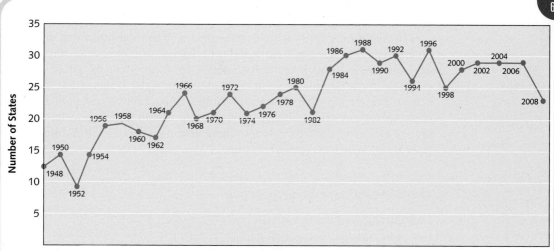

FIGURE 6.4

SOURCES: Data for 1948–1958 adapted from Morris Fiorina, "Divided Government in the States," in Gary Cox and Samuel Kernell, ed., *The Politics of Divided Government* (Boulder, CO: Westview Press, 1991), p. 180. Data for 1960 to the present calculated by National Conference of State Legislatures. States with nonpartisan elections (Minnesota prior to 1972 and Nebraska) are excluded. States with odd-year elections are included in the succeeding even-numbered year. Updated by the authors.

of divided government over a sixty-year period. The trend is clear: Divided government is more prevalent now than it was in the 1950s. One explanation for this trend is the notion of policy balance, that is, the preference of moderate voters for a government in which the two branches—a Republican governor and a Democratic legislature or vice versa—have to compromise to enact policies.[48]

A governor and a legislature controlled by the same party do not necessarily make for easy interbranch relations either. Especially in states where the two parties are competitive, legislators are expected to support the policy initiatives of their party's governor. Yet the governor's proposals may not mesh with individual legislators' attitudes, ambitions, and agendas. Idaho offers an illustration. In 2009, the Republican governor and the overwhelmingly Republican legislature battled long and hard over funding for highway maintenance.[49] Despite their partisan affinity, they saw the highway spending issue very differently.

Governors have a media advantage over deliberative bodies such as a legislature. The governor is the visible symbol of state government and, as a single individual, fits into a media world of thirty-second sound bites. By contrast, media images of the legislature often portray deal making, pork barrel politics, and general silliness. To be sure, those images can be quite accurate. "Gotcha" journalism, the term for media efforts to catch public officials in seemingly questionable situations, certainly complicates legislative life.

Sometimes governors who have previously served as legislators seem to have an easier time dealing with the lawmaking institution. For example, former governor Madeleine Kunin of Vermont assumed the office after three terms in the legislature and one term as lieutenant governor "knowing the needs of legislators, the workings of the legislative process, the sensitivities of that process."[50] Usually about two-thirds of the governors have had legislative experience, although the proportion has recently declined.

The legislature is not without its weapons. If the legislature can muster the votes, it can override a gubernatorial veto. Legislatures have also enacted other measures designed to enhance their control and to reduce the governor's flexibility in budgetary matters. For example, some states now require the governor to obtain legislative approval of budget cutbacks in the event of a revenue shortfall. Others have limited the governor's power to initiate transfers of funds among executive branch agencies. These actions reflect the continuing evolution of legislative–executive relations.

## Overseeing the Bureaucracy

Legislative involvement with the executive branch does not end with the governor. State legislatures are increasingly venturing into the world of state agencies and bureaucrats, with the attitude that after authorizing a program and allocating funds for it, they should check on what has happened to it. Legislative oversight involves four activities: policy and program evaluation, legislative review of administrative rules and regulations, sunset legislation, and review and control of federal funds received by the state.

**Policy and Program Evaluation** Legislatures select auditors to keep an eye on state agencies and departments. (In a few states, auditors are independently elected officials.) Auditors are more than super-accountants; their job is to evaluate the performance of state programs with respect to their efficiency and effectiveness, a task sometimes known as the postaudit function. Specifically, they conduct periodic performance audits to measure goal achievement and other indicators of progress in satisfying legislative intent, a process that has been credited with both saving money and improving program performance. In this respect, Virginia's Joint Legislative Audit and Review Commission (JLARC), is regarded as a model for the rest of the country. Throughout its thirty-five year history, JLARC has conducted hundreds of evaluations of state programs and saved the state millions of dollars. The key to a useful auditing function is strong legislative support (even in the face of audits that turn up controversial findings) and, at the same time, a guarantee of a certain degree of independence from legislative interference.

**Legislative Review of Administrative Rules** Forty-seven state legislatures conduct reviews of administrative rules and regulations, but they vary in their methods. They may assign the review function to a special committee (such as a rule review committee) or to a specific legislative agency, or they may incorporate the review function in the budgetary process. In this role, the legislature acts as a gatekeeper, striving to keep agency rules in line with legislative preferences.[51]

Legislative review is a mechanism through which administrative abuses of discretion can be corrected. Legislative bills frequently contain language to the effect that "the Department of Youth Services shall develop the necessary rules and regulations to implement the provisions of this act." Such language gives the agency wide latitude in establishing procedures and policies. The legislature wants to be certain that, in the process, the agency does not overstep its bounds or violate legislative intent. If it is found to have done so, then the legislature can overturn the offending rules and regulations through modification, suspension, or veto—depending on the state.

This issue is a true gray area of legislative–executive relations, and court rulings at both the national and state levels have found the most powerful of these actions, the **legislative veto**, to be an unconstitutional violation of the separation of powers. For example, in 1997, the Missouri Supreme Court ruled that the legislature's rule-review process was an unconstitutional intrusion into the functions of the executive branch.[52] Legislatures continue to use the budgetary process to review (and sanction) agency behavior. Increasingly, legislatures are requiring state agencies to furnish extensive data to justify their budget requests, and they can use their financial power to indicate their displeasure with agency rules and regulations.

**legislative veto**
An action whereby the legislature overturns a state agency's rules or regulations.

**Sunset Legislation** Half the states have established **sunset laws** that set automatic expiration dates for specified agencies and other organizational structures in the executive branch. An agency can be saved from termination only

**sunset laws**
Statutes that set automatic expiration dates for specified agencies and other organizations.

through an overt renewal action by the legislature. Review occurs anywhere from every four years to every twelve years, depending on individual state statute, and is conducted by the standing committee that authorized the agency or by a committee established for sunset review purposes (such as a government operations committee). The reviews evaluate the agency's performance and its progress toward achieving its goals.

During the 1970s, sunset legislation was widely hailed as an effective tool for asserting legislative dominion over the executive branch, but more than thirty years' experience with the technique has produced mixed results, and some states have repealed their sunset laws. Agency reviews tend to be time-consuming and costly. And the process has become highly politicized in many states, involving not only agencies and legislators but lobbyists as well. One Texas representative commented that she "never saw so many alligator shoes and $600 suits as when some agency is up for sunset review."[53] On the positive side, sunset reviews are said to increase agency compliance with legislative intent. Statistics show that, nationwide, only about 13 percent of the agencies reviewed are eventually terminated, thus making termination more of a threat than an objective reality.[54]

**Review and Control of Federal Funds** Since the early 1980s, legislatures have played a more active role in directing the flow of federal funds once they have reached the state. Before this time, the sheer magnitude of federal funds and their potential to upset legislatively established priorities caused great consternation among legislators. The executive branch controlled the disposition of these grant funds almost completely by designating the recipient agency and program. In some cases, federal money was used to fund programs that the state legislature did not support. Federal dollars were simply absorbed into the budget without debate and discussion, and legislators were cut out of the loop. By making federal fund disbursement part of the formal appropriations process, however, legislators have redesigned the loop.

If legislatures are to do a decent job in forecasting state priorities, some control of federal funds is necessary. In the face of reduced federal aid to states, it is critical for legislators to understand the role that federal dollars have played in program operation. When funding for a specific program dries up, it is the legislature's responsibility to decide whether to replace it with state money.

How effectively are legislatures overseeing state bureaucracies? As with so many questions, the answer depends on who is asked. From the perspective of legislators, their controls increase administrative accountability. A survey of legislators in eight states found legislative oversight committees, the postaudit function, and sunset laws to be among the most effective bureaucratic controls available.[55] Another effective device, and one that legislatures use in special circumstances, is legislative investigation of an agency, an administrator, or a program. But from the perspective of the governor, many forms of legislative oversight are simply meddling and, as such, they undermine the separation of powers.

# LEGISLATURES AND CAPACITY

State legislatures are fascinating institutions. Although they share numerous traits, each maintains some unique characteristics. Houses and senates have different traditions and styles, even in the same state. And across states, the variation in legislative systems is notable. As Alan Rosenthal writes, "Legislatures are interwoven in the fabric of their states."[56] As institutions, legislatures are dynamic; amid the layers of traditions and rules, they change and evolve.

The demands placed on state legislatures are unrelenting. Challenges abound. The ability of a legislature to function effectively depends on institutional capacity. The extensive modernization that almost all legislatures underwent in the 1970s is evidence of institutional renewal. Structural reforms and a new breed of legislator have altered state legislatures and are sending them in the direction of increased capacity. How ironic then that, with all their institutional success, reformed legislatures continue to struggle with their public image.[57]

One real concern is that the legislatures of some states are being marginalized through a citizen-empowering mechanism, the initiative, and an institution-weakening provision, term limits. It is no wonder then that, in several states, legislators have mounted efforts to increase public knowledge of and respect for the legislative process. For instance, in its 2003 session, the leadership of the New Jersey Assembly bundled bills into topic areas to be taken up on various theme days.[58] Some days were devoted to "Advocating for Consumers," and seven others were devoted to other topics, including Defending Our Families and Protecting Our Seniors. Theme days were preceded by public forums around the state on the upcoming topics. These forums were designed to increase public understanding of how the assembly conducts its business. Was it worth the time and energy? The speaker of the assembly summed it up this way: "The ultimate bottom line for any legislature is the quality of laws it enacts."[59]

## CHAPTER RECAP

- The three principal functions of legislatures are policy making, representation, and oversight.

- Reapportionment is a battleground for state legislatures because drawing district lines is a partisan process.

- Legislatures operate with their own formal and informal rules. Violations of institutional norms result in sanctions.

- The lawmaking process is a complex one, with multiple opportunities for delay and obstruction. Most bills never make it through; those that do seldom look like they did when they were introduced.

- Although legislatures perform more effectively than they used to, in 2010, fifteen states had term limits in effect. Term limits create open seats and thus increase competition for legislative seats. But when legislative terms are limited, other institutional actors such as the governor gain power.

- Legislators vie with governors in the policy-making process. Governors have the power to veto, but legislators have the power to override a gubernatorial veto. In addition, the legislature plays several oversight roles with regard to the bureaucracy.

- Legislative capacity has increased but at the same time, legislatures risk becoming marginalized in states with the initiative process and term limits.

## Key Terms

multimember districts
(MMDs) *(p. 143)*
malapportionment *(p. 145)*
reapportionment *(p. 145)*
redistrict *(p. 146)*

gerrymander *(p. 146)*
quorum *(p. 146)*
lame duck *(p. 149)*
war chest *(p. 150)*
delegate *(p. 153)*

trustee *(p. 153)*
politico *(p. 153)*
policy entrepreneurs *(p. 154)*
legislative veto *(p. 165)*
sunset laws *(p. 165)*

## Internet Resources

To find out what's up in state legislatures, visit the website of the National Conference of State Legislatures at **www.ncsl.org**.

Most states have websites that allow citizens to follow the progress of legislation during the session. See, for example, the legislative sites for Iowa and West Virginia at **www.legis.state.ia.us** and **www.legis.state.wv.us**, respectively.

The website **www.vote-smart.org** tracks the performance of political leaders, including state legislators.

Explanations and diagrams of how a bill becomes a law in several states can be found at **www.apic.org/Content/NavigationMenu/ GovernmentAdvocacy/Resources/how_bills_ to_laws.htm**.

To learn about model state laws, see the National Conference of Commissioners on Uniform State Laws at **www.nccusl.org**.

An advocacy website, **www.termlimits.org**, provides up-to-date coverage of the term-limits issue.

An avowedly conservative organization that drafts model legislation on various topics and reviews legislative activities across the states maintains a website at **www.alec.org**.

SOURCE: MIKE THEILER/epa/Corbis

# Governors

Problems of biblical proportions sometimes come crashing down on governors and the people of their states. Earthquakes, fires, tornados, floods, and hurricanes can ravage a state and devastate many of its residents. When such catastrophic events occur, people may first think of calling for help from the president of the United States, but it is often the governor who takes charge. The governor's actions may either draw praise or castigation from the afflicted and other citizens.

Identify a natural or man-made catastrophe and you'll also find a governor in charge of gathering and providing state resources. A governor will quickly visit the scene; demonstrate personal concern; reallocate money and personnel; call out the National Guard; coordinate the response of the Federal Emergency Management Agency (FEMA), state agencies, local governments, and nongovernmental agencies; and appeal to Congress, the president, and neighboring states for assistance.

But if a governor does not perform up to expectations, she suffers the consequences. On August 29, 2005, Hurricane Katrina tore into southern Louisiana and Mississippi during Louisiana governor Kathleen Babineaux Blanco's first term. Blanco arrived in the devastated areas with dispatch and showed compassion, including shedding tears on camera. Yet despite extensive government experience as lieutenant governor and state legislator, Blanco seemed hesitant and uncertain during the first days following the storm and the subsequent floods. Considering the more than one thousand fatalities, tens of thousands of stranded flood victims, and massive destruction, perhaps any governor would have seemed stunned. There was not much help from Washington, D.C., as FEMA and the Bush administration stumbled badly in offering their own responses.[1]

Today the governors speak with voices of authority on important national policy issues. Although they do not always agree on what they want, the governors have recently been influencing Congress and the president as never before in our history. Asserting themselves as a righteous third force in U.S. politics and speaking through the National Governors' Association (NGA) and the media, they have helped shape federal reform of welfare, education, and health care policies, and even led the response to combating global warming. And while Congress feuds along partisan and ideological lines over virtually all issues of significance, the governors preach—and often practice—partisan peace making to reach common policy ground with their own legislatures.

Members of Congress and leaders of the national Democratic and Republican parties have developed a healthy respect for the governors, for their ideas, and for their practical knowledge of policies and problems and of how federal actions play out at the state and local levels. Indeed, it is not unusual for governors to be invited to sit at the table to help congressional committees to draft laws that are of special consequence to the states.

The governors serve as catalysts for positive national policy change. But state policy responses have been made even more complicated than usual by the states' far-reaching financial problems, a voting public with no stomach for raising taxes, and state budgets in which some three-fourths of expenditures are dedicated to just three functions: education, Medicaid, and local government. The governors must make tough choices. Some bravely advance tax hikes, despite the possible electoral consequences. Others impose brutal spending cuts on prisons, Medicaid, social services, and higher education.

Their responsibilities are prodigious. But the governors' enhanced visibility and contributions in national politics are a tribute to their policy-making capacity and responsiveness to common—and uncommon—problems affecting the citizens of their respective states. It also reflects the policy leadership of the states in the U.S. federal system.

## THE OFFICE OF GOVERNOR

It has been said that the American governorship was conceived in mistrust and born in a straitjacket. Indeed, because the excesses of some colonial governors appointed by the English Crown resulted in strong dislike and distrust of executive power by the early American settlers, the first state constitutions concentrated political power in the legislative branch.

### History of the Office

Early governors were typically elected by the legislature rather than by the voters, were restricted to a single one-year term of office, and had little authority.

Two states, Pennsylvania and Georgia, even established a plural (multimember) executive. Slowly the governorships became stronger through longer terms, popular election, and the power to veto legislation, but power did not come easily. The movement for popular democracy during the Jacksonian era led to the election of other executive branch officials, and reaction to the excesses of Jacksonian democracy resulted in numerous independent boards and commissions in the executive branch. Although governors did gain some power, they were not able to exercise independent authority over these executive boards and commissions.

In the early 1900s, along with their efforts to democratize national politics and clean up the corrupt city political machines, Progressive reformers launched a campaign to reform state government. Their principal target was the weak executive branch. Efforts to improve the state executive branch have continued throughout the twentieth century. The essential goal has been to increase the governor's powers to make them more commensurate with the increased duties and responsibilities of the office. As a result, constitutional and statutory changes have fortified the office of the chief executive, reorganized the executive branch, and streamlined the structure and processes of the bureaucracy. The capacity of governors and the executive branch to apply state resources to the solution of emerging problems has thus been greatly enhanced.[2] And, as observed at the beginning of this chapter, the governors have become prominent players in national policy making.

## Today's Governors

Today, being governor is a high-pressure, physically demanding, emotionally draining job. As one political scientist states, "Governors must possess many skills to be successful. They are expected to be adroit administrators, dexterous executives, expert judges of people, combative yet sensitive and inspiring politicians, decorous chiefs of state, shrewd party tacticians, and polished public relations managers."[3] The job is also hard on the governor's private life. It consumes an enormous number of hours, at the expense of family activities; hobbies; and, in some cases, more significant moneymaking opportunities in law, consulting, or business.

Fortunately, governorships are attracting well-qualified chief executives, most of whom are a far cry from the figureheads of the eighteenth and nineteenth centuries and the stereotypical backslapping, cigar-smoking wheeler-dealers of the early twentieth century. Today's governors are better educated and better prepared for the job than their predecessors were. A large proportion of recent governors hold law or other advanced degrees. Most of today's governors paid their political dues in state legislatures, gaining an understanding of important issues confronting the state, a working familiarity with influential figures in government and the private sector, and a practical knowledge of the legislative process and other inner workings of state government (see Table 7.1). About one-third of governors have served previously as elected state executive branch officials, including lieutenant governor and attorney general (AG).

Several were once mayors. Although previous elected experience is a tremendous advantage in winning a governorship, a number have come straight from the private sector, touting their business credentials. The attractiveness of the governorship is evident in the fact that several of the 2009 chief executives had left a congressional seat to take statewide office. Why would someone desert the glamour of the nation's capital for the statehouse in Boise, Augusta, or Columbia? For political power and the opportunity to make a difference in one's own state. Simply put, being a state chief executive is just more rewarding and more fun.

Although still predominantly white males, today's governors are more representative of population characteristics than former chief executives were. Several Latinos have served as governors in recent years, including Bill Richardson of New Mexico and Bob Martinez of Florida. Two African Americans have been elected governor: L. Douglas Wilder, Virginia (1990–1994) and Deval Patrick, Massachusetts (2006–). A third, David Paterson, rose to the governorship in New York upon Eliot Spitzer's resignation in the aftermath of a prostitution scandal. Gary Locke, the first Asian American governor not from Hawaii, was elected governor of Washington in 1996. In 2007, Bobby Jindal was elected as the first Indian American (Asian) governor in 2007 in Louisiana. In early years, several women succeeded their husbands as governor, but a growing number are winning governorships on their own, including seven sitting governors today (Table 7.1).

The path to the governorship of Delaware's former governor Ruth Ann Minner makes a compelling rags-to-riches story. She had to drop out of school at sixteen to work on a tenant farm. At seventeen she was married. Widowed with three children when her husband died at age thirty-two of a heart attack, Minner worked two jobs, earned her high school equivalency degree, and eventually graduated from college. She remarried and took a job as a secretary for

| TABLE 7.1 | Women Governors, 2009 | | | | |
|---|---|---|---|---|---|
| NAME | STATE | PARTY | YEAR FIRST ELECTED | AGE FIRST ELECTED | PREVIOUS PUBLIC SERVICE |
| Jennifer Granholm | MI | Democrat | 2002 | 44 | Federal prosecutor, attorney general |
| Linda Lingle | HA | Republican | 2002 | 49 | Mayor |
| Jan Brewer | AZ | Republican | 2009* | 64 | Secretary of state, state legislature |
| Beverly Perdue | NC | Democrat | 2008 | 62 | State legislature, lieutenant governor |
| Jodi Rell | CT | Republican | 2006* | 58 | State legislature, lieutenant governor |
| Christine Gregoire | WA | Democrat | 2004 | 57 | State attorney general |
| Sarah Palin** | AK | Republican | 2006 | 42 | City council member, mayor |

NOTE: Rell was sworn in on July 1, 2004, following Governor John Rowland's resignation.

*Brewer assumed the governorship in 2009, when Governor Janet Napolitano became secretary of the U.S. Department of Homeland Security.

**Palin resigned her position in 2009, less than a year after a failed run for vice-president in the 2008 presidential election.

former Delaware governor Sherman Tribbet. A few years later, she won a seat in the statehouse, and later moved to the state senate and the lieutenant governorship. In 2000, Ruth Ann Minner, a former governor's secretary, was elected chief executive of Delaware.

## Getting There: Gubernatorial Campaigns

Without question, the governorship is an alluring office. Occasionally its luster attracts true wackos as candidates. One such case was Jonathan "The Impaler" Sharkey. A self-proclaimed PhD and "Satanic Dark Priest, Sanguinarian Vampyre and...Hecate Witch," Sharkey announced his candidacy for the 2006 governorship of Minnesota. A former pro-wrestler and co-owner of "Kat's Underworld Coven," the gubernatorial wannabe announced a unique plan for dealing with terrorists who might be tempted to infiltrate the Gopher State. Any such terrorist caught in Minnesota would "find out what the true meaning of my nickname "The Impaler" means." Literally, the unfortunate suspect would be impaled on a stake on the capitol grounds.[4] Another colorful candidate was Texas mystery writer, songwriter, and performer Kinky Friedman. His progressive country band in the 1970s called "Kinky Friedman and the Texas Jewboys" recorded various alternative hits, including "They Ain't Makin' Jews Like Jesus Anymore," "Asshole from El Paso," and "The Mail Don't Move Too Fast in Rapid City, South Dakota." While cracking jokes and one-liners, he also campaigned on serious issues, including election reform and education improvement. Friedman again placed his name in the Democratic primary in 2009. Georgia's 2010 gubernatorial candidate Neal Horsley, running on the Creator's Rights party ticket, revealed in an interview that "When you grow up on a farm in Georgia, your first girlfriend is a mule."[5]

If anyone ever said that running for governor was easy, they were profoundly wrong. The campaign is both expensive and humbling. As North Carolina governor Mike Easley observed during his successful race in 2000, "My mama taught me never to think I was better than anybody else, never to brag and never to ask for money. So you get into politics, and what do you do? Tell people you're better than someone else, brag about your accomplishments and ask for money."[6]

Certainly, the lure of the governorship must be weighed against the financial costs. Campaigning for the office has become hugely expensive. Because candidates no longer rely on their political party to support them, they must continuously solicit great sums of money from donors to pay for campaign costs—political consultants, opinion polls, air travel, media advertisements, telephone banks, direct mailings, websites, and interactive video links. The growing attractiveness of the office has led to more competitive (and costlier) primary and general election races.

To date, the most expensive governor's race was the 2002 election in New York, in which $146.8 million was spent by three candidates. Loser Thomas Golisano spent $76.3 million; the winner, George Pataki, spent "only" $44.2 million. In the 2004 Texas governor's race, loser Tony Sanchez spent

$81 million. These official figures do not include in-kind donations, such as free transportation, door-to-door canvassing, and other contributions from supporters. Generally, elections tend to cost more when they are close, are held in a non-presidential election year, involve a partisan shift (i.e., when a Democrat succeeds a Republican, or vice versa), and are held in highly populated and geographically large states (e.g., Florida, Texas, California, and New York).[7] On a cost-per-vote basis, races in the 2006 gubernatorial elections ranged from $38.32 in New Jersey to only $2.42 in Arizona.[8]

Money is the single most important factor contributing to winning a governorship, but it isn't the only important factor. As one veteran of political campaigns has reflected, "Everyone knows that half the money spent in a political campaign is wasted. The trouble is that nobody knows which half."[9] Other factors important in candidate success are state party strength and candidate profile, including incumbency. The strongest influence is the strength of the candidate's political party in the state electorate[10] because party identification usually translates into votes for a party's candidate. High-profile candidates stand an excellent chance of being elected because they possess campaign skills, political experience, and other characteristics that help them raise the campaign funds needed to get their message and persona across to the electorate.[11] Of course, being independently wealthy doesn't hurt either. Jim Corzine (2006–) tapped into an estimated $60 million of his own fortune in winning the New Jersey governorship.

Incumbency is a particularly important aspect of a candidate's profile. An incumbent governor running for re-election stands an excellent chance of victory; about three-quarters of incumbents have retained their seats since 1970. Incumbents enjoy a number of important advantages, including the opportunity while in office to cultivate popularity with the voters and collect campaign donations from interest groups. However, re-election is no sure thing. Budget and tax woes can lead voters to toss chief executives out of office, particularly those who, as candidates, pledged not to raise taxes but then do so after election.[12]

## BEING GOVERNOR: DUTIES AND RESPONSIBILITIES

In performing the duties of the office, the governor wears the hats of top policy maker, chief legislator, chief administrator, ceremonial leader, intergovernmental coordinator, economic development promoter, and political party leader. Sometimes several of these hats must be balanced atop the governor's head at once. All things considered, these roles make the governorship one of the most difficult and challenging, yet potentially most rewarding, jobs in the world.

### Developing and Making Policy

Montana's governor Brian Schweitzer pragmatically declared, "We don't care where the idea comes from. We'll steal the ideas from anybody."[13] Transforming that good idea from concept to practice is an exciting but extraordinarily difficult challenge for governors.

A governor is the leading formulator and initiator of public policy in his state, from his first pronouncements as a gubernatorial candidate until his final days in office. The governor's role as chief policy maker involves many other players, including those in the legislature, bureaucracy, courts, interest groups, and the voting public. Most major policies are initiated by the governor, and success or failure depends largely on how competently the governor designs and frames policy proposals and develops public support for them. The governor must also follow through to see that adopted policies are put into effect as originally intended.

Some issues are by nature transitory, appearing on the agenda of state government and disappearing after appropriate actions are taken. These issues are often created by external events, such as a federal court decision that mandates a reduction in prison overcrowding; a new national law requiring a state response; or an act of nature such as a hurricane, tornado, forest fire, or flood.

Most policy issues, however, do not emerge suddenly out of the mists. Perennial concerns face the governor each year: education, corrections, social welfare, health care, the environment, and economic development. Cyclical issues also appear, increase in intensity, and slowly fade away. Examples of the latter type are consumer protection, ethics in government, reapportionment, and budget shortfalls. Of course, national policy issues sometimes absorb the governor's time as well, such as preparing for and responding to acts of terrorism, coping with an influx of illegal immigrants, providing health care insurance to children and the working poor, and dealing with proposals to drill for oil and gas in national parks or just off state shorelines.

Several factors have contributed to stronger policy leadership from the chief executives in recent years, including larger and more capable staffs who are knowledgeable in important policy fields; a more integrated executive branch with department heads appointed by the governor; strengthened formal powers of the office, such as longer terms and the veto and budget powers; and the assistance of the NGA, which offers ideas for policy and program development. Of no small importance is the high caliber of individuals who have won the office in recent years.

## Marshaling Legislative Action

The gubernatorial role of marshaling legislative action is closely related to that of policy maker because legislative action is required for most of the chief executive's policies to be put into effect. In fact, the governor cannot directly introduce bills; party leaders and policy supporters in the statehouse and senate must put the bills in the hopper. Dealing with legislators is a demanding role for a governor, consuming more time than any other role and representing for many the single most difficult aspect of the job.

**Executive–Legislative Tensions** Developing a positive relationship with the legislature requires great expenditures of a governor's time, energy, and resources. Several factors hinder smooth relations between the chief executive and the legislature, including partisanship and personality clashes. Even the different natures of the two branches can cause conflict. Governors are elected by a statewide constituency and therefore tend to take a broad, comprehensive, long-range view of issues, whereas legislators, representing relatively small geographical areas and groups of voters, are more likely to take a piecemeal, parochial approach to policy making. Conflicts typically erupt during budget time, when critical spending decisions are at hand.[14]

According to one study, the amount of strife between the two branches is influenced by three factors: the size of the majority and the minority parties, the personalities of the governor and legislative leaders, and the nearness of an election year. Following the 2008 elections, there were twenty-eight Democratic governors and twenty-two Republicans. In a majority of the states today the governor has to deal with a one-or two-house majority from the opposing political party. When the opposition party is strong, the governor must seek bipartisan support to get favored legislation passed. Often a governor facing a large legislative majority from the opposing party has only the veto and the possibility of mobilizing public support as weapons against the legislature. Yet minority governors like Kathleen Sibelius of Kansas and Jodi Rell of Connecticut have earned reputations for being nonpartisan, while still getting their way on legislation important to them.[15] Arizona governor Janet Napolitano, a Democrat, assumed a combative posture with her majority Republican legislature. She vetoed more than 100 bills during her first term (2002–2006) but won favor with the voters and was re-elected to a second term in 2006.[16]

Independent governors don't even have a minority party to count on, but this situation doesn't preclude success. Former Independent governor Angus King of Maine asserted that not having a party affiliation brought some advantages. For instance, he says, "I have no automatic friends in the legislature, but I have no automatic enemies. I have 186 skeptics."

A governor who ignores or alienates members of the opposing political party can quickly find himself in the desert without a drink of water. New York governor David Paterson compared legislators in Albany to "a bunch of bloodsuckers" who cater to special interests during the day and go home without taking action on bills.[17] The ups and downs of gubernatorial–legislative relations were experienced in California by Arnold Schwarzenegger, who famously referred to opposing legislators as "girlie men" and "stooges" but then experienced contrition late in his first term when four ballot initiatives that he had staked his governorship on went down to resounding defeat by the voters (see the feature "Engaging Governors:").

Republican governor Mark Sanford of South Carolina antagonized legislators from both parties by bickering with them over issues big and small and taking vindictive actions against nonsupporters. The legislature responded by overriding hundreds of his vetoes. A low point in legislative relations was reached when Sanford brought two piglets into the statehouse to protest pork barrel spending. Most South Carolinians were deeply embarrassed by the episode, in which the porcine visitors defecated both on the governor's clothes

## Engaging Governors

# The Mercurial Governorship of Arnold Schwarzenegger

Former bodybuilder, Mr. Universe, and Hollywood celebrity Arnold Schwarzenegger became governor of California following a special election to replace Governor Gray Davis, who had been recalled from office by the voters. The "Governator" (from his lead role in Terminator movies) entered office in 2003 as a partisan Republican in a democratic majority state.

Early on, the Governor won some legislative battles including bills to repeal an unpopular vehicle registration fee and prevent illegal immigrants from obtaining drivers' licenses. His public approval ratings were reasonably high. But when he took on the public employee unions and other powerful political interests with a set of proposed initiatives, he suffered resounding defeats from the voters. His approval levels dropped to only 30 percent.

Realizing that he was on the right (or "wrong") side of a liberal, Democratic electorate and legislature, Schwarzenegger apologized for his missteps and moved strategically to the left, appointing Democrats to his staff and crossing partisan lines to work with democratic legislators on issues of common concern. Such issues included greenhouse gas reduction, infrastructure bonds, and universal health care. The Governor began referring to himself as "post partisan." When wildfires raged and other natural disasters struck the Golden State, the Governor was quick to respond, using a take-charge posture honed in the cinema. The turnaround was enough to win re-election in November 2006 with 56 percent of the popular vote. As late as January 2008 Schwarzenegger's approval ratings hovered around 60 percent.

But early rumblings of an economic earthquake had already begun. California's economy, the eighth largest in the world, was squeezed hard by a deepening national recession and by previous voter initiatives that severely constrained raising taxes. Revenues fell precipitously. The Governor's efforts to work with the legislature came to nought, with the legislature rejecting all spending and taxing bills sent to them. Schwarzenegger reacted angrily, threatening to veto all bills sent to his desk

until the legislature approved a new budget. During a relatively brief period in 2008 he rejected 415 pieces of legislation, including many that were not controversial.

As the budget deficit reached $11.2 billion and climbing in December, the Governor declared a fiscal emergency and called the legislators back into Sacramento. Under California law, the legislature must remain in session until agreement on a balanced budget is reached. But nothing seemed to be acceptable to the legislators. Spending cuts? Democrats were certain to object. Tax hikes? Over the Republicans' dead bodies. The Governor even ordered his agency heads to implement a furlough of state workers, but they refused. Schwarzenegger publicly chided and berated the legislators, telling them to "step up, compromise, get out of your rigid ideologies, and solve the problems."

By January 2009 the budget's red ink reached an estimated $34 billion. As the governor of a once proud state begged the Congress for a financial bailout, Schwarzenegger's approval ratings dropped to 30 percent. Ever resilient, the Governor attempted a legislative end run by proposing six measures to the voters, including a spending cap, changes to the state lottery system, and a tax increase. Only one of the six measures was approved: a measure to prohibit legislators and other state officials from receiving a pay hike during a budget deficit. Finally, in July, the legislature delivered a budget to the governor, who signed it after cutting nearly $500 billion with line item vetoes.

Despite prodigious personal skills and a willingness to work across party lines, Schwarzenegger was in many ways a victim of national and California-specific factors beyond his control or influence. The monumental national recession, financial crisis, housing market collapse, and soaring unemployment would have badly impacted California in any case. But when combined with an antiquated and poorly structured revenue system, onerous constitutional requirements of a supermajority of two-thirds of the legislature to enact a budget, extraordinarily powerful special interest groups, and a system of government-by-popular-initiative, few could reasonably blame the Governor for the state's misery.

SOURCES: Jennifer Steinhauer, "Seeking a Hollywood Ending in Sacramento," *NYTimes.com* (May 6, 2009); John Wildermuth and Wyatt Buchanan, "Schwarzenegger Declares Fiscal Emergency," *San Francisco Chronicle sfgate.com* (December 2, 2008); Timothy Egan, "Where's EuroArnold?" *The New York Times* (June 7, 2007) *NYTimes.com*; Louis Jacobson, "A Tale of Two Comebacks," *stateline.org* (January 30, 2008); Matthew Yi, "Governor sets Record for Vetoing Bills," *San Francisco Chronicle* (October 2, 2008) *sfgate.com*; Pamela Prah, "The Path to California's Fiscal Crisis," www.stateline.org (May 15, 2009).

and the house floor.[18] When Sanford refused to apply for $700 billion in federal stimulus dollars in June 2009, the legislature took the issue to the state supreme court, which ordered Sanford to take the funds. Shortly thereafter, Sanford again became the butt of national jokes for leaving the state without informing anyone where he was for four days. After his staff gave conflicting accounts of his whereabouts, the governor finally reappeared. Confronted by reporters in the Columbia airport, he admitted to having been to Argentina. After telling various versions of his story, Sanford finally conceded to having an extramarital affair with a woman there.

The approach of statewide elections can also bring gubernatorial–legislative deadlock because incumbents in both branches of government may become extremely cautious or overtly partisan in their efforts to please (or at least not to offend) the voters while discrediting their opponents. Gridlock may result. These three conflict-producing factors of partisanship, personalities, and proximity of an election are intensified during debates on the budget, when the principal policy and financial decisions are made.

Even in states in which the governor's own party enjoys a large majority in both houses of the legislature, factions are certain to develop along ideological, rural–urban, geographical, institutional (house versus senate), or other divisions. Ironically, a large legislative majority can create the greatest problems with factionalism primarily because a sizable opposition doesn't exist to unite the majority party. Apparently a legislative majority of 60–70 percent helps a governor; anything more than that percentage and the majority party tends to degenerate into intraparty rivalries beyond the governor's control. As one Democratic governor lamented in the face of a 4-to-1 majority of his own party in the legislature, "You've got Democrats, you've got moderate Democrats, you've got suburban Democrats, you've got urban Democrats, you've got rural Democrats...."[19]

**Executive Influence on the Legislative Agenda** Despite the difficulties in dealing with the legislature, most governors dominate the policy agenda, usually by working hand in hand with legislative leaders. The governor's influence begins with the "State of the State" address, which kicks off each new legislative session and continues in most states with the annual budget message. In 2009, governors stressed austere economic conditions and resultant budget problems, education improvements, health care, infrastructure, and energy development and conservation.[20] During the legislative session itself, the governor might publicly (or privately) threaten to veto a proposed bill or appeal directly to a particular legislator's constituency.

Most of the drama, however, takes place behind the scenes. The governor might promise high-level executive branch jobs or judgeships (either for certain legislators or for their friends) to influence legislative votes. Or she might offer some sort of **pork barrel** reward, such as arranging funding for a highway project in a legislator's district or approving an appropriation for the local Strawberry Festival. Private meetings or breakfasts in the governor's mansion flatter and enlist support from individuals or small groups of legislators. Successful governors can usually relate to representatives and senators on a personal level. Many are former members of the state legislature, so they can rely on personal connections and experiences to win over key members. One of the most successful governors today, for example, is Governor Mike Beebe of Arkansas, who labored in the state senate for twenty years and as attorney general for four, before winning the state's top office.

> **pork barrel**
> Favoritism by a governor or other elected official in distributing government monies or other resources to a particular program, jurisdiction, or individual.

In addition, all governors have legislative liaisons who are assigned to lobby for the administration's program. Members of the governor's staff testify at legislative hearings, consult with committees and individuals on proposed bills, and even write floor speeches for friends in the legislature. Some governors designate a floor leader to steer their priorities through the legislature.

Most governors, however, are careful not to be perceived as unduly interfering in the internal affairs of the legislature. Too much meddling in legislative affairs can bring a political backlash that undermines a governor's policy program. The role of chief legislator, then, requires a balancing act that ultimately determines the success or failure of the governor's agenda.

## Administering the Executive Branch

As chief executive of the state, the governor is (in name, at least) in charge of the operations of numerous agencies, departments, boards, and commissions. In the view of many voters, the governor is directly responsible not only for pivotal matters such as the condition of the state's economy but also for mundane concerns such as the number and depth of potholes on state highways. Most governors are sensitive to their chief administrative responsibilities and spend a great amount of time and energy attending to them. Constitutional and statutory reforms, including the concentration of executive power in the office of the governor and the consolidation of numerous state agencies, have considerably strengthened the governor's capacity to manage the state. (See Chapter 8 for additional discussion of public administration.) If governors are diligent and expeditious in appointing talented and responsive people to policy-making posts, they should feel no compulsion to micromanage the state's day-to-day affairs. Instead, they can focus their energies on leadership activities such as identifying goals, marshaling resources, and achieving results.

In many respects the governor's job is comparable to that of the chief executive officer (CEO) of a very large corporation. Governors must manage tens of thousands of workers, staggering sums of money, and complex organizational systems. They must establish priorities, handle crises, and balance contending interests. But there are important differences as well. For one, governors are not paid comparably for their responsibilities. In terms of expenditures and employees, most states are as big or bigger than Fortune 500 companies, whose CEOs typically earn tens of millions of dollars a year in salary, stock options, and other forms of remuneration. Yet the fifty governors average only about $128,700 in annual salary. (The highest paid is the governor of California, at $212,170; the lowest is Maine's, at $70,000.)[21]

In addition to being woefully underpaid, today's governors experience high levels of stress from interest group criticism, legislative sniping, extraordinarily long hours on the job, and constant media attention to every possible misstep. Arkansas governor Mike Huckabee and his First Lady even endured the ignominy of living in a manufactured home, or trailer, while the mansion underwent much-needed repairs and refurbishing. Plagued with unforgiving budget problems, South Carolina governor Mark Sanford was planning to shut down the governor's mansion and move his family out until a group of business supporters saved the day with a bailout. Governor Rick Perry's mansion in Austin, Texas, was torched by an arsonist.

**Restraints on Management** Reforms of the executive branch have allowed far more active and influential gubernatorial management, but significant restraints remain. For example, the separation-of-powers principle dictates that the governor share his or her authority with the legislature and the courts, either or both of which may be politically or philosophically opposed to any given action. Changes in state agency programs, priorities, or organization typically require legislative approval, and the legality of such changes may be tested in the courts.

The governor's ability to hire, fire, motivate, and punish is severely restricted by the courts; merit-system rules and regulations; collective bargaining contracts; independent boards and commissions with their own personnel systems; and other elected executive branch officials pursuing their own administrative and political agendas. Thus, most employees in the executive branch are outside the governor's formal sphere of authority and may challenge that authority almost at will. Career bureaucrats, who have established their own policy direction and momentum over many years of seeing governors come and go, usually march to their own tune. In sum, governors must manage through third parties and networks in the three branches of government as well as in the private and nonprofit sectors. They have little unilateral authority.

**Governors as Managers** Some governors minimize their managerial responsibilities, preferring to delegate them to trusted staff and agency heads. Others provide strong administrative and policy leadership in state government. Former Virginia governor Mark Warner (2001–2005), a Democrat with a strong Republican legislature, enjoyed unusual success by utilizing a collaborative decision-making style to address budget shortfalls, promote economic development, and improve public education, thereby earning the Government Performance Project's award for "Best Managed State." His successor, Tim Kaine (2006–), further contributed to Virginia's reputation by winning the same award in 2008.

But the constraints on the governor's managerial activities are not likely to lessen, nor are the potential political liabilities. The governors who courageously wade into the bureaucratic fray must invest a great deal of time and scarce political resources, yet they risk embarrassing defeats that can drag their administrations into debilitation and disrepute. After all, "Reorganized the State Bureaucracy" hardly resonates as a campaign slogan. Meanwhile, in the face of social and economic change, the management of state government has become increasingly complex, and the need for strong administrative leadership more critical than ever before.

## Master of Ceremonies

Some governors thrive on ceremony and others detest it, but all spend a large portion of their time on it because it helps garner re-election support. Former governors remember ceremonial duties as the second most demanding of the gubernatorial roles, just behind working with the legislature. Cutting the ribbon for a new highway, celebrating the arrival of a new business, welcoming potential foreign investors, receiving the queen of the Collard Green Festival, announcing "Respect your Parents Week," opening the state fair, and handing out diplomas are the kind of ceremonial duties that take a governor all over the state and often consume a larger portion of the workweek than does any other role.[22] Even a seemingly pleasant task can have its personal horrors. George A. Aiken, the late governor of Vermont, dreaded having to pin the ribbon on the winner of the Miss Vermont contest because he couldn't figure out how to put the pin in without getting his hand under the bathing suit.

## Coordinating Intergovernmental Relations

Governors serve as the major points of contact between their states and the president, Congress, and federal agencies. Everything from emergency response to settling disputes over cross-border water pollution issues are carried out through the governor's office. At the local level, governors are involved in allocating grants-in-aid, promoting cooperation and coordination in economic development activities, and various other matters. Governors also provide leadership in resolving disputes with Native American tribes involving casino gambling and related issues.

The role of intergovernmental coordinator is most visible at the national level, where governors are aided by the NGA and the state's Washington office. The NGA meets twice a year in full session to adopt policy positions

Bobby Jindal, Republican Governor of Louisiana, acknowledges a crowd of supporters.
*SOURCE:* LEE CELANO/Reuters/Landov

and to discuss governors' problems and "best practice" policy solutions. The governors also meet in separate regional organizations. (C-SPAN covers national meetings of the governors.) The NGA's staff analyzes important issues, distributes its analyses to the states, offers practical and technical assistance to the governors, and holds a valuable seminar for new governors. The NGA, however, has recently come under fire from conservative Republicans, who object to the organization's perceived "tax-and-spend" agenda, even when it benefits their own states. In fact, in 2003, Republican governors of Texas and Hawaii withdrew from the NGA over this concern. Gubernatorial sniping was also witnessed in 2009, as three Republican governors criticizing the federal stimulus package (designed to relieve state economic problems) were met with ridicule by Democratic governors happy to receive whatever money Congress and the President would hand over.[23]

Some thirty-five states have established Washington offices to fight for their interests in Congress, the White House, and, perhaps most important, the many federal agencies that interact with states on a daily basis. A governor's official inquiry can help speed up the progress of federal grant-in-aid funds or gain special consideration for a new federal facility. Washington offices are often assisted by major law and lobbying firms under contract to individual states.

The governor's role as intergovernmental coordinator is becoming more important with each passing year. It reflects the elevated position of the states in the scheme of American federalism and the increasing state importance in national and international affairs. It is also a reaction to provocations and intrusions from the national government, such as unfunded mandates, poorly framed laws, and unwelcome blundering into the affairs of the states. Acting together and as individuals, the governors have exercised national policy leadership on critical issues such as environmental protection, climate change, taxation of Internet sales, public education, welfare and health care reform, and economic development. Increasingly often, when the national government confronts a policy problem, it turns to the states for solutions.

## Promoting Economic Development

Unfairly or not, governors are held responsible by the voters for their state's economic health. As promoter of economic development, a governor works to recruit businesses and tourists from out of state and to encourage economic growth from sources within the state (see Chapter 14). Governors attend trade fairs; visit the headquarters of firms interested in locating in the state; telephone and e-mail promising business contacts; and welcome business leaders. The role may take the governor and the state economic development team to Mexico, China, Germany, and other countries as well as to other states. Governors also work hard to promote tourism and the arts. But mostly, development entails making the state's climate "good for business" by improving infrastructure, arranging tax and service incentives, and other strategies designed to entice out-of-state firms to relocate and encourage in-state businesses to expand or at least stay put. New Mexico governor Bill Richardson once proudly boasted that he calls corporate CEOs daily and "sucks up to them."[24]

When a state enjoys success in economic development, the governor usually receives (or at least claims) a major portion of the credit. Sometimes the personal touch of a governor can mean the difference between an industrial plum and economic stagnation. Success stories are heralded proudly. Washington governor Christine Gregoire promoted development of "two 21st Century technologies: life sciences and alternative fuels."[25] Are incumbent governors punished in a re-election effort when promised economic growth falls short? Research findings on this question are mixed.[26]

## Leading the Political Party

By claiming the top elected post in the state, the governor becomes the highest-ranking member of her political party. This role is not as significant as it was several decades ago, when the governor controlled the state's party apparatus and legislative leadership and had strong influence over party nominations for seats in the state legislature and executive branch offices. The widespread adoption of primaries, which have replaced party conventions, has put nominations largely in the hands of the voters. And legislative leaders are a much more independent breed than they were, for example, in Illinois, when Governor Richard Ogilvie (1969–1973) brought up the need for income tax legislation during a breakfast meeting at the mansion. Senate president Russ Arrington angrily asked, "Who is the crazy son of a bitch who is going to sponsor this thing?" The governor calmly replied, "Russ, you are." And he did.[27] Such an order is unlikely these days. Still, some governors get involved in legislative elections through campaign aid, endorsements, or other actions. If the governor's choice wins, the victor may feel a special debt to the governor and support him on important legislation.

The political party remains useful to the governor for three principal reasons.[28] Legislators and legislative leaders from the governor's own party are more likely to support the chief executive's programs. Communication lines to the president and national cabinet members are more likely to be open when the president and the governor are members of the same party. And finally, the party remains the most convenient means through which to win nomination to the governor's office.

As a growing number of states have highly competitive political parties, governors find that they must work with the opposition if their legislative programs are to pass. For Independent governors, a special challenge exists: how to govern without a party behind you to organize votes and otherwise push proposed laws through the convoluted legislative process. The recent record has been mixed. Maine's Independent governor, Angus King, demonstrated a talent for working with shifting legislative coalitions on various major issues. Reform Party governor Jesse Ventura did not experience the same level of success with his legislature in Minnesota.

# FORMAL POWERS OF THE GOVERNOR

**formal powers**
Powers of the governor derived from the state constitution or statute.

A variety of powers are attached to the governor's office. A governor's **formal powers** include the tenure of the office, power of appointment, power to veto legislation, responsibility for preparing the budget, authority to reorganize the executive branch, and the right to retain professional staff in the governor's office. These institutional powers give governors the *potential* to carry out the duties of office as they see fit. However, the formal powers vary considerably from state to state. Some governors' offices (Illinois, New York) are considered strong and others (Alabama, Georgia) weak. Also, the fact that these powers are available does not mean that they are used effectively. Equally important are the **informal powers** that governors have at their disposal. These powers are potentially empowering features of the job or the person that are not expressly provided for in the law. Many of the informal powers are associated with personal traits on which the chief executive relies to carry out the duties and responsibilities of the office. They are especially helpful in relations with the legislature.

**informal powers**
Powers of the governor not derived from constitutional or statutory law.

Both sets of powers have increased over the past several decades. Indeed, governors are more influential than ever before, primarily because of their enhanced formal powers; charisma, however, remains as important as ever. The most successful governors are those who employ their informal powers to maximize the formal powers. The term for this concept is *synergism*, a condition in which the total effect of two distinct sets of attributes working together is greater than the sum of their effects when acting independently. An influential governor, then, is one who can skillfully combine formal and informal powers to maximum effectiveness. Counted among the most effective governors in recent years are Michael Leavitt (Republican, Utah), Tim Kaine (Democrat, Virginia), and Tim Pawlenty (Republican, Minnesota). The Debating Politics box on the next page poses a conundrum that calls for exercising both types of powers.

## Tenure

The governor's tenure power has two characteristics: the duration (number of years) of a term of office and the number of terms that an individual may serve

## DEBATING POLITICS

## What Should the Governor Do?

Here is the situation: You have served successfully as governor for the past three years. With your re-election campaign just kicking off, however, you are facing what could be your greatest challenge: what to do about a $2 billion shortfall (about 5 percent of the state's budget).

You have already ordered emergency cuts in state expenditures on Medicaid and other programs, laid off 250 prison guards and 1,200 other state workers, signed off on a 20 percent tuition hike by public universities, and withheld state aid to local governments and state retirement plans. The cries of economic anguish are becoming deafening, and you can't find anything else to cut.

Raising new revenues appears to be the only alternative. Yet you were elected to office on a platform that promised no new taxes. In the legislature, support is growing for a one-penny sales tax increase. If the trend continues, you are quite likely to have a sales tax bill placed on your desk for signature or veto. A majority in the state senate has already committed to passing it.

You have mixed feelings about a tax hike. On one hand, it would solve the budget problems for at least the next few years, and in your heart you feel it is the optimal solution. On the other hand, negative taxpayer reaction could cost you re-election.

The speaker of the statehouse of representatives, a member of your own political party and someone with whom you have a good working relationship, has scheduled an appointment with you for tomorrow at 10:00 a.m. to discuss the proposed tax bill. You know that he personally favors it but that the floor vote is too close to call.

What will you do? What formal and informal powers are at your disposal to help resolve this dilemma?

as governor. Both have slowly but steadily expanded over the past two centuries. From the onerous restriction of a single one-year term of office placed on ten of the first thirteen governors, the duration has evolved to today's standard of two or more four-year terms (only New Hampshire and Vermont restrict their governors to two-year terms). In addition, gubernatorial elections have become distinct from national elections now that thirty-nine states hold them in non-presidential election years. This system encourages the voters to focus their attention on issues important to the state rather than allowing national politics to influence state election outcomes.

The importance of longer consecutive terms of office is readily apparent. A two-year governorship condemns the incumbent to a perpetual re-election campaign. As soon as the winner takes office, planning and fund-raising must begin for the next election. For any new governor, the initial year in office is typically spent settling into the job. In addition, the first-term, first-year chief executive must live with the budget priorities adopted by his or her predecessor. A two-year governorship, therefore, does not encourage success in matters of legislation or policy. Nor does it enable the governor to have much effect on the bureaucracy, whose old hands are likely to treat the governor as a mere bird of passage, making him almost a lame duck when his term begins. As Governor Alfred E. Smith of New York observed after serving four two-year terms during the 1920s, "One hardly has time to locate the knob on the Statehouse door."[29]

By contrast, Virginia's governor, the only one who is restricted to a single four-year term, is a bit less confined in carrying out his responsibilities. But he really has only two years to put his programs and priorities in place, sandwiched on one side by the initial learning year and on the other by the lame-duck period. The incumbent needs another four-year term to design new programs, acquire the necessary legislative support to put them into place, and get a handle on the bureaucracy by appointing competent people to top posts. Eight years in office also enhances the governor's intergovernmental role, particularly by giving him or her sufficient time to win leadership positions in organizations such as the NGA. The record of an eight-year chief executive stands on its own, untainted by the successes or failures of the office's previous inhabitant.

The average time actually served by governors has grown steadily since 1955 as a result of fewer restrictions on tenure. The gubernatorial graybeard is Illinois governor Jim Thompson, who stepped down after serving his fourth consecutive term in 1990—a twentieth-century record.[30] (North Carolina's Jim Hunt served four, nonconsecutive four-year terms, 1977–1985 and 1993–2001). Long periods in office strengthen the governor's position as policy leader, chief legislator, chief administrator, and intergovernmental coordinator, as shown by the policy legacies left in Illinois by Thompson and in North Carolina by Hunt. Another sort of gubernatorial record was set by Cecil H. Underwood, who in 1956 became West Virginia's youngest governor at the age of thirty-four. He was re-elected for a second term in 1996 as the state's *oldest* governor at seventy-four years of age (but lost in another bid for office in 2000).

There is still some resistance to unlimited tenure. More than one re-election creates fears of political machines and possible abuses of office. And, pragmatically speaking, a long period of a "safe governorship" can result in stagnation and loss of vigor in the office. Even in states that do not restrict governors to two consecutive terms, the informal custom is to refrain from seeking a third term.

## Appointment Power

Surveys of past governors indicate that they consider appointment power to be the most important weapon in their arsenal when it comes to managing the state bureaucracy. The ability to appoint one's supporters to top positions in the executive branch also enhances the policy management role. When individuals who share the governor's basic philosophy and feel loyal to the chief executive and her programs direct the operations of state government, the governor's policies are more likely to be successful. Strong appointment authority can even help the governor's legislative role. The actual or implicit promise of important administrative and especially judicial positions can generate a surprising amount of support from ambitious lawmakers.

Unfortunately for today's governors, Jacksonian-style democracy and the long ballot live on in the **plural executive**. Most states continue to provide for popular election of numerous officials in the executive branch, including insurance commissioners, public utility commissioners, and secretaries of agriculture. Proponents of popular election claim that these officials make

**plural executive**

A system in which more than one member of the executive branch is popularly elected on a statewide ballot.

political decisions and therefore should be directly responsible to the electorate. Opponents contend that governors and legislators can make these decisions more properly, based on the recommendations of appointed executive branch professionals who are not beholden to special interests.

Perhaps appointment authority should depend on the office under consideration. Those offices that tend to cater to special interests, such as agriculture, insurance, and education, probably should be appointive. Less substantive offices such as secretary of state or treasurer probably should be appointive as well. It makes sense to *elect* an auditor and an AG, however, because they require some independence in carrying out their responsibilities. (The auditor oversees the management and spending of state monies; the AG is concerned with the legality of executive and legislative branch activities).

Many governors are weakened by their inability to directly appoint the heads of major state agencies, boards, and commissions. These high-ranking officials make policy decisions in the executive branch, but if they owe their jobs in whole or in part to popular election or legislative appointment, the governor's authority as chief executive is significantly diminished. Although nominally in charge of these executive branch agencies, the governor is severely constrained in his ability to manage them. Such an arrangement would be unthinkable in a corporation.

The fragmented nature of power in the executive branch diminishes accountability and frustrates governors. Former Oregon governor Tom McCall once lamented that "we have run our state like a pick-up orchestra, where the members meet at a dance, shake hands with each other, and start to play."[31] When the assorted performers are not selected by the chief conductor, their performance may lack harmony, to say the least. And elected statewide offices provide convenient platforms for aspiring governors to criticize the incumbent.

Reformers interested in "good government" generally agree on the need to consolidate power in the governor's office by reducing the number of statewide elected officials and expanding the power of appointment to more policy-related, "unclassified" posts in the executive branch. Most states have increased the number of policy-making positions in the governor's staff and in top agency line and staff positions. But the number of elected branch officials has remained virtually the same for forty years. Table 7.2 shows the range and number of separately elected officials. North Dakota has the greatest number with twelve statewide offices filled through elections: governor, lieutenant governor, secretary of state, AG, agricultural commissioner, chief state school officer, treasurer, labor commissioner, tax commissioner, two insurance commissioners, and utility commissioner. At the bottom of the list are the reformer's ideal states: Maine, New Hampshire, New Jersey, and Tennessee, which elect only the governor. The average number of elected officials is about eight.

Why has it been so difficult to abolish multiple statewide offices? The main reason is because incumbent education superintendents, agricultural commissioners, and others have strong supporters in the electorate. Special-interest groups, such as the insurance industry, benefit from having an elected official—the insurance commissioner—representing their concerns at the highest level of

| TABLE 7.2 | Separately Elected State Officials |
| --- | --- |
| **OFFICE** | **NUMBER OF ELECTED OFFICIALS** |
| Governor | 50 |
| Lieutenant governor | 42 |
| Attorney general | 44 |
| Treasurer | 39 |
| Secretary of state | 37 |
| Education (superintendent or board) | 14 |
| Auditor | 24 |
| Secretary of agriculture | 13 |
| Controller | 14 |
| Public utilities commissioner | 6 |
| Insurance commissioner | 12 |
| Land commissioner | 5 |
| Labor commissioner | 4 |
| Mines commissioner | 1 |
| Adjutant General (National Guard) | 1 |

SOURCE: Adapted from *The Book of the States 2008* (Lexington, KY: Council of State Governments, 2005), Table 4.10.

state government. Such groups fiercely resist proposals to make the office appointive. Additional resistance may be credited to the fact that many citizens simply like having an opportunity to vote on a large number of executive branch officials.

**Professional Jobs in State Government** The vast majority of jobs in the states are filled through objective civil service (merit-system) rules and processes. Governors are generally quite content to avoid meddling with civil service positions (see Chapter 8), and a few have actually sought to transfer many **patronage** appointments—those based on personal or party loyalty—to an independent, merit-based civil service. Gubernatorial sacrifice of patronage power is understandable in view of the time and headaches associated with naming political supporters to jobs in the bureaucracy. There is always the possibility of embarrassment or scandal if the governor accidentally appoints a person with a criminal record, a clear conflict of interest, or a propensity for sexual harassment or other inappropriate behavior, or someone who causes harm through simple incompetence. Moreover, those who are denied coveted appointments may become angry. One governor is quoted as stating, as he was about to name a new member of a state commission, "I now have twenty-three good friends who want [to be] on the Racing Commission. [Soon] I'll have

**patronage**

The informal power of a governor (or other officeholder) to make appointments on the basis of party membership and to dispense contracts or other favors to political supporters.

twenty-two enemies and one ingrate."[32] Governors who abuse the merit hiring system can be prosecuted. Kentucky governor Ernie Fletcher and fifteen members of his administration were indicted in a hiring scandal in 2006. A governor benefits from a stable, competent civil service that hires, pays, and promotes on the basis of knowledge, job-related skills, and abilities rather than party affiliation or friendship with a legislator or other politician.

**The Power to Fire** The power of the governor to hire is not necessarily accompanied by the power to fire. Except in cases of extreme misbehavior or corruption, it is very difficult to remove a subordinate from office, even if such action is constitutionally permitted. For instance, if a governor attempts to dismiss the secretary of agriculture, he can anticipate an orchestrated roar of outrage from legislators, bureaucrats, and farm groups. The upshot is that the political costs of dismissing an appointee can be greater than the pain of simply living with the problem.

Several U.S. Supreme Court rulings have greatly restricted the governor's power to dismiss or remove from office the political appointees of previous governors. In the most recent case, *Rutan et al. v. Republican Party of Illinois* (1990), the Court found that failure to hire, retain, or promote an individual for reasons of political or party affiliation violates that person's First Amendment rights.[33]

A good appointment to a top agency post is the best way for a governor to influence the bureaucracy. By carefully choosing a competent and loyal agency head, the governor can more readily bring about significant changes in the programs and operations of that agency. Where appointment powers are circumscribed, the chief executive must muster his or her informal powers to influence activities of the state bureaucracy or rely on the seasoned judgment of professional civil servants.

## Veto Power

As we noted in Chapter 6, the power to veto bills passed by the legislature bolsters the governor as chief policy maker and chief administrator. A bill may be vetoed because its contents are contrary to a governor's principles or preferences, or for many other reasons. A veto accompanied by an explanation makes a powerful symbolic statement or can instruct the legislature about how the bill might be amended for the governor's signature. A veto can also punish an offending legislator or state agency by eliminating a favored program or severely cutting its budget. Often the mere threat of a veto is enough to persuade a recalcitrant legislature to see the governor's point of view and compromise on the language of a bill. Vetoes are not easy to override. Most states require a majority of three-fifths or two-thirds of the legislature.

**Types of Vetoes** The veto can take several forms. The **package veto** is the governor's rejection of a bill in its entirety. All governors hold package veto authority. The package veto is the oldest form available to governors, having been adopted in the original constitutions of New York and Massachusetts.

**package veto**
The governor's formal power to veto a bill in its entirety.

The **line item veto** allows the governor to strike out one or more objectionable sections of a bill, permitting the remaining provisions to become law. Only Nevada, Maine, and six other states forbid this gubernatorial power. Several states permit a hybrid form of line item veto in which the governor may choose to reduce the dollar amount of a proposed item to hold down state expenditures or cut back support for a particular program. In some states, the line item veto is permitted only in appropriations bills.

The **pocket veto**, which is available in fourteen states, allows the governor to reject a bill by refusing to sign it after the legislature has adjourned. In two states (Hawaii and Utah), the legislature can reconvene to vote on a pocket veto; otherwise, the bill dies. A governor might use the pocket veto to avoid giving the legislature a chance to override a formal veto or to abstain from going on record against a proposed piece of controversial legislation.

A fourth type of veto is the **executive amendment**, formally provided in fifteen states and informally used in several others. With this amendatory power, a governor may veto a bill, recommend changes that would make the bill acceptable, and then send it back to the legislature for reconsideration. If the legislature concurs with the suggestions, the governor signs the bill into law.

**Use of the Veto** The actual use of the veto varies by time, state, and issue. Some states, such as California and New York, often record high numbers of vetoes, whereas others, like Virginia, report few. On average, governors veto around 4 percent of the bills that reach their desks.[34] The variation among states reflects the tensions and conflicts that exist between the governor and the legislature. The largest number of vetoes typically occurs in states with divided party control of the executive and legislative branches. Occasionally, the governor stands as the last line of defense against a flawed bill backed by the legislature because of powerful interest groups or a bill passed just to score political points. It is not unknown for legislators to secretly ask the governor to veto a questionable bill they have just passed because the bill's contents, although undesirable, are politically popular.[35]

Although the overall rate of veto utilization has not grown significantly, the proportion of successful legislative overrides has increased in the past two decades. This trend is an indication of the growing strength and assertiveness of state legislatures, the increase in conflict between the executive and legislative branches, and the prevalence of split-party government. Differences in party affiliation between the governor and the legislative majority probably provoke more vetoes than any other factor, especially when party ideology and platforms openly clash. Republican governor Tim Pawlenty of Minnesota earned the moniker of the "Godfather of No" by vetoing a record number of Gopher State bills in 2008.[36]

Conversely, when mutual respect and cooperation prevail between the two branches, the governor rarely needs to threaten or actually use the veto. Most governors interact with the legislature throughout the bill-adoption process. Before rejecting a bill, the governor will request comments from key legislators, affected state agencies, and concerned interest groups. He may ask the AG for a legal opinion. And before actually vetoing proposed legislation, the governor usually provides advance notification to legislative leaders, along with a final opportunity to make amendments.

The veto can be a powerful offensive weapon that may be used to obtain a legislator's support for a different bill dear to the governor's heart, particularly near the end of the legislative session. The governor may, for instance, hold one bill hostage to a veto until the legislature enacts another bill that he favors. California governor Arnold Schwarzenegger did just that in 2008, when he began vetoing all bills sent to his desk until the legislature approved a budget bill; all told, he vetoed 35 percent of the bills sent to him that session.[37] Wisconsin's storied history includes the "Vanna White Veto" and the "Frankenstein Veto." The first, abolished in 1990, permitted the governor to delete individual letters and numbers to change a bill's content. The second, which took a stake in the heart in a 2008 voter referendum, allowed the governor to strike out some words and piece together others to alter a bill's content. For instance, Governor Jim Doyle (2003–) used the Frankenstein Veto to delete 752 words from a bill, which effectively shifted $427 million from transportation to education.[38]

## Budgetary Power

Whether one is a conservative Republican or a liberal Democrat, spending money is gratifying and even fun. By developing the executive budget, the governors effectively set the legislative agenda at the beginning of each session. By framing the important policy issues and attaching price tags to them, the governor can determine the scope and direction of budgetary debates in the legislature and ensure that they reflect her overall philosophy on taxing and spending. All but a handful of governors have the authority to appoint (and remove) the budget director and to formulate and submit the executive budget to the legislature. In Mississippi and Texas, budget authority is shared with the legislature or with other elected executive branch officials. And in these two states, two budgets are prepared each year, one by the governor and one by a legislative budget board.

Because full budgetary authority is normally housed in the office of the chief executive, the governor not only drives the budgetary process in the legislature but also enjoys a source of important leverage in the bureaucracy. The executive budget can be used to influence programs, spending, and other activities of state agencies. For example, uncooperative administrators may discover that their agency's slice of the budget pie is smaller than expected, whereas those who are attentive to the concerns of the governor may receive strong financial support. Rational, objective criteria usually determine departmental budget allocations, but a subtle threat from the governor's office does wonders to instill a cooperative agency attitude.

The governor's budget requests are rarely, if ever, enacted exactly as put forward. Rather, they are usually argued and debated thoroughly in both houses of the legislature. A legislature dominated by the opposing political party is nearly certain to scorn and disparage the governor's budget. Governors, who are elected statewide, must appeal to a large and diversified electorate. Legislatures must please localized geographic constituencies. Ultimately, "the governor proposes, but the legislature disposes." In fact, no monies may be appropriated without formal action by the legislature. (The budget process is discussed further in Chapter 8).

During state budget crises, governors find themselves in an extremely vulnerable political position, particularly if they promised "no new taxes" when running for office. Legislatures struggle with the governor over the question of who will assume primary responsibility for reducing state expenditures or hiking taxes. Usually, governors take the heat, and even light the match, by unilaterally cutting agency budgets, introducing tax increases, or both.[39] Such bold actions, though fully appropriate, are not taken without due caution by the governor because the electoral consequences can be direct and extremely negative.

## Reorganization Power

Reorganization power refers to the governor's ability to create and abolish state agencies, departments, and other offices and to reallocate administrative responsibilities among them. Reorganizations are usually aimed at the upper levels of the bureaucracy in an effort to streamline the executive branch and thereby make it work more efficiently and effectively. The basic premise is that the governor, as chief manager of the bureaucracy, needs the authority to alter administrative structures and processes to meet changing political, economic, and citizen demands. For instance, serious and recurring problems in coordinating the delivery of social services among several existing state agencies may call for a consolidated human services department with expanded powers. A governor with strong reorganization power can bring about such a department without approval of the legislature.

Traditionally, legislatures have been responsible for the organization of state government, and in the absence of a constitutional amendment to the contrary or a statutory grant of reorganization power to the governor, they still are. But today, more than twenty states specifically authorize their chief executive to reorganize the bureaucracy through **executive order**. Through an executive order, the governor can make needed administrative changes when he or she deems it necessary. All governors are permitted through the constitution, statute, or custom to issue directives to the executive branch in times of emergency, such as during natural disasters or civil unrest.[40]

Administrative reorganization today takes place under the assumption that streamlined government improves bureaucratic performance and saves money by cutting down on duplication, waste, and inefficiency. Achieving a more efficient and user-friendly government is a top priority of most governors. Initiatives to reinvent or reinvigorate government aim to make the bureaucracy more flexible and responsive by changing incentive systems for state employees, privatizing certain operations, reducing layers of bureaucracy, implementing e-government, and decentralizing personnel management agency activities.

**executive order**

A rule, regulation, or policy issued unilaterally by the governor to change executive branch operations or activities.

Executive branch reorganization is widely practiced, but its actual benefits may be ephemeral. Reorganization typically achieves modest financial savings, if any at all, and it can produce bureaucratic infighting, delays, unanticipated financial costs, and widespread confusion.[41] Reorganization is not a panacea for state fiscal ills. However, restructuring the executive branch may help to provide a clearer focus on a particular problem such as the needs of children, as illustrated by Georgia governor Sonny Perdue's executive order combining four child welfare agencies in 2008. It can also help to contain administrative costs, and it may serve various political purposes, such as rationalizing the pain of employee layoffs.

**The Politics of Reorganization** Reorganization is a politically charged process. Mere talk of it sounds alarms in the halls of the legislature, in the honeycombs of state office buildings, and in the offices of interest groups. Reorganization attempts usually spawn bitter controversy and conflict both inside and outside state government as assorted vested interests fight for favorite programs and organizational turf. Accordingly, comprehensive reorganization proposals are frequently defeated or amended in the legislature, or even abandoned by discouraged chief executives. One study of proposed state reorganizations discovered that almost 70 percent resulted in rejection of the plan either in part or in its entirety.[42] Even when enacted, reorganizations may generate extreme opposition from entrenched interests in the bureaucracy and, in the final analysis, be judged a failure. In the memorable words of former Kansas governor Robert F. Bennett,

> In the abstract, [reorganization] is, without a doubt, one of the finest and one of the most palatable theories ever espoused by a modern-day politician. But in practice . . . it becomes the loss of a job for your brother or your sister, your uncle or your aunt. It becomes the closing of an office on which you have learned to depend. . . . So there in many instances may be more agony than anything else in this reorganization process.[43]

Most governors who have fought the battle for reorganization would concur. Perhaps this fierce opposition helps explain the rarity of far-reaching state agency restructuring and the preference for small, incremental steps.[44]

## Staffing Power

The governor relies on staff to provide policy analysis and advice, serve as liaisons with the legislature, assist in managing the bureaucracy, and provide constituent services. Professional staff members are a significant component of the governor's team, composing a corps of political loyalists who help the governor cope with the multiple roles of the office. From the handful of political cronies and secretaries of several decades ago, the staff of the governor's office has grown in number, quality, and diversity (with respect to gender and color).[45] The average number of professional and clerical staff members is approximately sixty-two today. In some larger, more highly populated states, staff members number well over 100 (Florida lists 293).[46] The principal staff positions of the governor's office may include the chief of staff, legislative liaison, budget director, policy director, public relations director, legal counsel, scheduler, press secretary, and intergovernmental coordinator.

Perhaps the most important to the governor is her chief of staff. Among wide range of duties discharged by the chief of staff are gatekeeping access to the governor, representing the governor's views, protecting the governor's time and good name, recruiting and filling appointive executive branch positions, coordinating emergency planning and response, and acting as personal confidant to the governor.[47]

A question of serious concern, especially in the states whose governors have large staffs, is whether too much power and influence are being placed in the hands of nonelected officials. Clearly, professional staff members have been highly influential in developing and promoting policies for the governor in some states, particularly in states where the governor lacks a coherent set of priorities and lets the staff have free rein to advance their own agenda. In other states, the chief executive is very much in charge, relying on staff primarily for drafting bills and providing technical information. Given their physical and intellectual proximity to the governor, staff members are in a highly advantageous position to influence their boss. In their role as the major funnel for policy information and advice, they can affect the governor's decisions by controlling the flow of information and individuals into his office.

## The Relevance of the Formal Powers

In Table 7.3, the states are scored according to the strength of the governor's formal powers of office. As noted, governors have won stronger powers during

**TABLE 7.3** **Relative Power of the Governors' Offices**

| 2.5 | 2.6 | 2.7 | 2.8 | 2.9 | 3 | 3.1 | 3.2 | 3.3 | 3.4 | 3.5 | 3.6 | 3.7 | 3.8 | 3.9 | 4 | 4.1 | 4.2 | 4.3 |
|-----|-----|-----|-----|-----|---|-----|-----|-----|-----|-----|-----|-----|-----|-----|---|-----|-----|-----|
| VT | RI | | AL | IN | NV | WY | CA | ID | AZ | DE | AR | NM | IL | CO | UT | AK | | MA |
| | | | OK | MS | SC | | GA | KS | HI | MT | CT | | IA | ND | | MD | | |
| | | | NC | SD | | | NH | KY | LA | OR | FL | | NE | | | NJ | | |
| | | | | | | | TX | | | WI | ME | | PA | | | NY | | |
| | | | | | | | VA | | | | MI | | TN | | | WV | | |
| | | | | | | | | | | | MN | | | | | | | |
| | | | | | | | | | | | MO | | | | | | | |
| | | | | | | | | | | | OH | | | | | | | |
| U.S. Average: 3.5 | | | | | | | | | | | WA | | | | | | | |

NOTE: The scale is measured from 2.5 to 4.3. The measures of power are SEP (separately elected executive branch officials), TP (tenure potential of governors), AP (governor's appointment in six functional areas: corrections, K-12 education, health, highways/transportation, public utilities regulation, and welfare), BP (budget power), VP (veto power), and PC (gubernatorial party control).

SOURCE: Adapted from Thad Beyle, http://www.unc.edu/~beyle/gubnewpwr.html (accessed May 15, 2009).

the past three decades. But how helpful are the formal powers? Despite the major transformation of the governor's office, governors remain relatively weak because of the setting of state government. They must function within a highly complex and politically charged environment with formal authority that is quite circumscribed by the legislature, the courts, and constitutional and statutory law. Owing to the nature of our federal system, the national government effectively strips them of control over many policy and administrative concerns. Moreover, the business of state government is carried out in a fishbowl, open to regular scrutiny by the media, interest groups, talk-show hosts, and other interested parties. Notwithstanding the continued constraints on the exercise of their authority, however, today's governors as a group are more effective than their predecessors were in carrying out their varied responsibilities. Today, the formal powers of the office are substantially strengthened, and, in general, highly qualified people are serving as chief executives.

In theory, governors with strong formal powers, such as the governors in Alaska, New Jersey, and Massachusetts, should be more effective than their counterparts in Vermont and Rhode Island. In practice, that tends to be true—but not always. The potential for power and influence must not be confused with action. A governor with strong formal powers enjoys the capacity to serve effectively, but he may choose not to do so or, for various reasons, be unable to utilize the formal powers properly. This point is indirectly confirmed by a study that finds that formal gubernatorial power does not translate into greater success for incumbent governors seeking re-election.[48] Alternatively, a governor with weak formal powers can nonetheless be an effective, strong chief executive if she actively and skillfully applies the levers of power available in the constitution and in statutes.

# INFORMAL POWERS

No doubt a governor with strong formal powers has an advantage over one without them. But at least equally important for a successful governor is the exploitation of the informal powers of the office. These powers carry authority and influence that are not directly attached to the governorship through statute or constitution but rather are associated with the human being who happens to occupy the governor's mansion. Governors who can master these powers can be highly effective, even in the absence of strong formal powers.

The informal powers help transform the capacity for action into effective action. They react in synergy with the formal powers to create a successful governorship. An incumbent chief executive in the strong-governor state of Massachusetts will be hopelessly weak unless he also uses his personal assets in performing the multiple roles of the office. Alternatively, a chief executive in a weak-governor state such as Oklahoma can be remarkably successful if she fully employs her informal powers to excel in persuading the people in the state to adopt new ideas. The informal powers are not as easy to specify as the formal powers are. However, they generally include such tools of persuasion and leadership as popular support, prestige of the office, previous elected experience, public relations and media skills, negotiating and bargaining skills, pork barrel and patronage; and personal characteristics such as youth, ambition, experience, and energy.

## Tools of Persuasion and Leadership

*Popular support* refers to public identification with and support for the governor and his priorities. It may be measured in terms of the margin of victory in the primary and general elections or in terms of the results of public opinion polls. Governors with large victory margins and high levels of public support can lay claim to a popular mandate. They can parlay popular support into legislative acceptance of a policy mandate and otherwise channel the pressures of public opinion to their advantage. But popular support may erode when governors' actions alienate the voters. When governors Mark Sanford of South Carolina and Sarah Palin of Alaska rejected some of the federal stimulus money earmarked to help ease the financial crisis in their states in 2009, negative public opinion was fast and furious.

Indeed, popular support can quickly vanish when a governor's words or actions alienate voters and/or interest groups. Nevada governor Jim Gibbons' support dropped to just 28 percent within six months of taking office. Gibbons had made several poorly thought out policy proposals (e.g., to sell water rights under state highways when the state held no such rights) and endured an FBI investigation into helping a friend secure lucrative military contracts. Gibbons deftly outraged many Nevada women when, after his wife filed for divorce in 2009 alleging a history of marital infidelity, he compared her to "an enraged ferret."[49]

The *prestige of the office* helps the governor open doors all over the world that would be closed to an ordinary citizen. National officials, big-city mayors, corporate executives, foreign officials, and even the president of the United States recognize that the governor sits at the pinnacle of political power in the state, and they treat her accordingly. Governors of California, New York, and Texas—the largest states—almost automatically assume roles of national and even international prominence. Within the state, the governor typically makes use of the prestige of the office by inviting important individuals for an official audience, or perhaps to a special meal or celebration at the mansion.

Previous electoral experience is a valuable asset. Those who have made their way up the state's political ambition ladder by serving in the state legislature or serving as AG or lieutenant governor have learned how to find their way through political briar patches and avoid tar pits.[50] They can also take advantage of political friends and allies they cultivated along the way. Other informal powers may be defined in terms of leadership skills. *Public relations and media skills* help the governor command the "big mike": the captive attention of the press, radio, and television. Any governor can call a press conference at a moment's notice and get a substantial turnout of the state's major media representatives, an advantage enjoyed by precious few legislators. Some chief executives appear regularly on television or radio to explain their policy positions and initiatives to the people. Michigan governor Jennifer Granholm offered a weekly radio address and podcast. Others write a regular newspaper column, blog, Twitter, or Facebook message for the same purpose. Frequent public appearances, staged events, telephone calls, correspondence, and even state-funded "public interest" advertisements delivered through the mass media can also help develop and maintain popular support. Governors have used such techniques to attain statewide voter approval ratings of 85 percent and above. The ability to improvise in unpredictable, chaotic situations doesn't hurt. New York governor David Paterson illustrated that point effectively in 2009. When the wife of Jonathan Lippen, whom Paterson had just nominated as a judge, fainted at a press conference during Lippen's remarks, the governor quipped to the audience "It's the usual reaction when Jonathan is speaking."[51] Spontaneity may serve the governor well, but one must also weigh his words carefully before speaking. Former Oklahoma governor Frank Keating observed that "[t]he biggest mistake I made was saying things I thought were cute or funny, and very few other people did. Keep it to your wife and children."[52]

Effective governors know instinctively that the media can be a strong ally in carrying out their programs and responsibilities, and cultivate the press like a flower garden. But media relations are a two-way street. The media expect the governor to be honest, forthright, and available. If he instills respect and cooperation, the governor's media relations can be "of incalculable value in his contest for the public eye and ear."[53]

*Negotiating and bargaining skills* are leadership tools that help the governor to convince legislators, administrators, interest groups, and national and local officials to accept his point of view on whatever issue is at hand. These skills are of tremendous assistance in building voting blocs in the legislature, particularly in divided-power settings in which hyperpluralism (such as exists in national politics) must be avoided. They also help persuade new businesses to locate in the state and help the governor effectively represent a state's interests before the national government. Governor Ed Rendell used his persuasive powers in Pennsylvania to accomplish far-reaching change in education, children's health care, and alternative energy.[54] And Washington governor Christine Gregoire's reputation as a gifted negotiator and deal maker helped her attain ambitious education and economic development initiatives.[55]

*Pork barrel and patronage* are aspects of the seamier side of state politics. Although they are utilized much less frequently now than they were before the civil service reforms of the first half of the twentieth century, governors are still known to promise jobs, contracts, new roads, special policy consideration, electoral assistance, and other favors to influential citizens, legislators, donors, and others in return for their support. All governors have discretionary funds with which to help out a special friend who has constituents in need. And although patronage appointments are now severely limited in most jurisdictions, a personal telephone call from the governor can open the door to an employment opportunity in state government.

## Characteristics of a Successful Governor

The *personal characteristics* of an effective governor are nearly impossible to measure. As indicated earlier, however, leadership is generally agreed to be a vital quality of effective governors. Leadership traits are difficult to define, but former Utah governor Scott Matheson identified the best governors as "men and women who have the right combination of values for quality public service—the courage to stick to their convictions, even when in the minority, integrity by instinct, compassion by nature, leadership by perception, and the character to admit wrong and when necessary, to accept defeat."[56]

A successful governor achieves her objectives by blending these qualities with the formal and informal powers of office. For example, following the political campaign to win the election, the governor must conduct a "never-ending campaign" to win the loyalty and support of her cabinet, state employees, the legislature, and the people if she is to be effective.[57] Sixteen-hour days and one hundred-hour workweeks are not uncommon.

Successful governors, particularly those in weak-governor states, know how to limit their policy agendas. Realizing that to try to do everything is to accomplish nothing, they focus on a few critical issues at a time and marshal their formal and informal resources behind them. Eventually, a determined governor can wear down opponents. But more important, the successful governor exercises leadership by convincing the public that he is the person to pursue their vision and their interests. He prevails in the legislature by applying the pressure of public opinion and by building winning blocs of votes, and he leads the bureaucracy by personal example. Above all else, the successful governor must be persuasive.

In short, the formal powers of the office are important to any governor, but even strong formal powers do not guarantee success. As noted earlier, they must be combined with the informal powers to be effective. Whatever approach the governor chooses as chief executive, her individual skills are probably more important than formal powers.[58] Evidence of this conclusion is provided by governors who have won and held their state's top job and successfully pursued their policy agendas in the face of significant opposition. A notable example is Indiana governor Mitch Daniels, whose leadership led to dramatic improvements in the performance of state agencies, successful privatization efforts in highways and welfare, and even the legislature's reluctant approval of the Hoosier State finally adopting Daylight Savings Time.[59]

# REMOVAL FROM OFFICE

Upon leaving office, the vast majority of governors simply continue their public service in another venue. Four out of the last five presidents were ex-governors. Six former governors were appointed to cabinet-level positions by former president George W. Bush, and President Obama raided the ranks of sitting governors to fill several key federal cabinet positions. Former California governor Jerry Brown was elected mayor of Oakland; Colorado's Roy Romer became superintendent of Los Angeles, California's public schools; and Virginia's Douglas Wilder was mayor of Richmond. Eleven former governors are serving in the U.S. Senate.

Because state chief executives are held to higher standards today than ever before and are constantly under the microscope of the media and watchdog groups, illegal actions or conflicts of interest are likely to be discovered and prosecuted. Recently, such actions have occurred with alarming frequency.

All states but one provide in their constitutions for the impeachment of the governor and other elected officials (in Oregon, they are tried as regular criminal offenders). Impeachment proceedings are usually initiated in the statehouse of representatives, and the impeachment trial is held in the senate. A two-thirds vote is necessary for conviction and removal of the governor in most states. Of the more than 2,100 governors who have held office, only twenty-three have been either impeached and removed from office, or resigned under a cloud of legal problems. Besieged governors are much more likely to resign than face a lengthy public scourging through impeachment and legislative trial.

The most recent governors to leave office in disgrace were James McGreevey of New Jersey, Eliot Spitzer of New York, and Rod Blagojevich of Illinois. McGreevey resigned after a homosexual affair with an appointed agency head was revealed. Spitzer stepped down after getting snared in a federal prostitution sting operation. His dramatic rise and fall as AG and then governor of the Empire State shocked people across the nation. The Blogojevich saga involved a host of federal criminal charges, including trying to sell the U.S. Senate seat that was vacated when Barack Obama assumed the presidency.[60]

But these fallen governors are the gubernatorial black sheep—the political throwbacks of contemporary state government who spawn media feeding frenzies. They deflect proper attention from the vast majority of hard-working, capable, and honest chief executives who typify the American state governorship today.

When governors die, are removed from office for misconduct, resign, or take a position in the federal executive branch, they are normally succeeded by the lieutenant governor. For example, when President Obama appointed Utah Governor Jon Huntsman, Jr. as ambassador to China, lieutenant governor Gary Herbert assumed the state's top office. Lieutenant governors moved up to the governorship following the recent unpleasantness involving the three fallen governors noted above. States lacking the office of lieutenant governor specify alternative arrangements, such as succession by the president of the senate (New Jersey) or by other executive branch officials. When Janet Napolitano was appointed secretary of the Department of Homeland Security by the president in 2009, Secretary of State Jan Brewer took the gubernatorial reins.

# OTHER EXECUTIVE BRANCH OFFICIALS

The states elect more than 300 officials to their executive branches, not count-ing the fifty governors, ranging from AGs and treasurers to railroad commis-sioners. The four most important statewide offices are described here.

## Lieutenant Governor

This office was originally created by the states for two major reasons: to provide for orderly succession to a governor who is unable to fulfill a term because of death or other reasons, and to provide for an official to assume the responsi-bilities of the governor when the incumbent is temporarily incapacitated or out of the state. Seven states have not seen the need for the office: Arizona, Maine, New Hampshire, Oregon, Tennessee, West Virginia, and Wyoming. Others attach little importance to it, as indicated by an extremely low salary (e.g., $7200 in Texas) or the absence of official responsibilities. The historical reputation of the lieutenant governor was that of a corpse at a funeral; you are needed for the ceremony but no one is expecting much from you.

But since 2003, nine lieutenant governors have risen to occupy the execu-tive office because of a death, impeachment, or resignation. Even when a gov-ernor's unplanned exit is not the cause, the lieutenant governorship has been a springboard to the top elected office in the state.[61] The lieutenant governorship in the majority of states has become a more visible, demanding, and responsi-ble office. This trend is likely to continue as state governance grows increasingly complex and as additional states adopt the team election of governor and lieu-tenant governor. Many lieutenant governors hold important powers in the state senate, including serving as presiding officer, assigning bills to committees, and casting tie-breaking votes. They are official members of the cabinet or of the governor's top advisory body in sixteen states.[62] And virtually all lieutenant governors accept special assignments from the chief executive, some of which are quite visible and important. For example, Indiana's lieutenant governor acts as the state's commissioner of agriculture while performing forty-one other statutory duties, and Utah's is head of that state's homeland security efforts. In general, lieutenant governors' salaries, budget allocations, and staff have grown markedly during the past two decades.

A lingering problem is that seventeen states continue to elect the gover-nor and lieutenant governor independently. This system can result in conflict when, for example, the chief executive is out of state and the two officeholders are political rivals or members of opposing political parties. On several recent occasions, a lieutenant governor, assuming command, has proceeded to make judicial appointments, veto legislation, convene special sessions of the legisla-ture, and take other actions at odds with the governor's wishes.

To avoid partisan bickering and politicking in the top two executive branch offices, twenty-five states now require team election. In addition to avoiding embarrassing factionalism, team election has the advantages of promoting party accountability in the executive branch, making continuity of policy more likely in the event of gubernatorial death or disability, and ensuring a measure of compatibility and trust between the two state leaders. It doesn't entirely preclude problems, but team election does avoid situations in which a lieutenant governor, for political purposes, takes actions contrary to a governor's wishes.

## Attorney General

The AG is the state's chief legal counsel. The AG renders formal written opinions on legal issues, such as the constitutionality of a statute, administrative rule, or regulation, when requested to do so by the governor, agency heads, legislators, or other public officials. In most states, the AG's opinions have the force of law unless they are successfully challenged in the courtroom.

The AG represents the state in litigation in which the state government is a legal party, and he represents the state in federal and state courts. The AG can initiate civil and criminal proceedings in most states. AGs have actively represented their states more and more often in legal actions contesting national government statutes and administrative activities in controversial fields such as consumer rights, education reform, and business regulation. AGs today are bringing litigation against the national government that argues against the legality of unfunded mandates such as REAL ID (see Chapter 2). Activist AGs have initiated actions to protect consumers against mail fraud, cybercrime, Medicaid fraud, misleading advertisements by pharmaceutical companies, and other consumer rip-offs.

AGs also took on the powerful tobacco industry, winning $206 billion in reimbursements for state funds spent to provide Medicaid-related health care for residents with smoking-related illnesses. Their collective actions help to reform corrupt corporate behavior and to push the national government to regulate business more aggressively. Their litigation and arguments often push issues onto the policy agenda of Congress. Under the auspices of the National Association of Attorneys General, they work together as point persons to assert and defend state authority in the U.S. federal system. Predictably, the AGs' activism has spawned a growing corporate backlash that includes intense interest and participation in AG elections.

## Treasurer

The treasurer is the official trustee and manager of state funds and the state's chief financial officer. He collects revenues and makes disbursements of state monies. (The treasurer's signature is on the paycheck of all state employees and on citizens' state tax refunds). Another important duty is the investment of more than $3.2 trillion in state funds, including state employee pension monies. Treasurers are also responsible for managing college savings plans and unclaimed property programs. The failure to make profitable investments can cost the treasurer his job. West Virginia treasurer

A. James Manchin was impeached for losing $279 million in state funds through bad investments. Other treasurers have been criticized for taking lucrative private-sector jobs in the middle of their terms (Connecticut, New Jersey), accepting gifts from financial firms (Massachusetts), or using their post to raise large sums of money from investment companies for their next election (nearly all states in which the treasurer is elected rather than appointed).

### Secretary of State

In the past, the duties of the secretary of state were rather perfunctory, entailing record keeping and election responsibilities. But voting system reforms, e-government, and other changes in how states run elections have substantially elevated the responsibilities of the position. Secretaries of state typically register corporations, securities, and trademarks, and commission people to be notaries public. The typical secretary of state also maintains state archives, files agency rules and regulations, publishes statutes and copies of the state constitution, and registers lobbyists.

In their election-related responsibilities, they determine the ballot eligibility of political parties and candidates, receive and verify initiative and referendum petitions, supply election ballots to local officials, file the expense papers and other campaign reports of candidates, and maintain voter registration rolls. A function of growing importance in the secretary of state's offices is to protect citizens' Social Security numbers and other private identification data placed in public databases that put citizens at risk of identify theft.[63]

# THE CAPABILITY OF U.S. GOVERNORS

The states have reformed their executive branches to enhance the capability of the governor as chief executive and to make the office more efficient, effective, accountable, and responsive. Indeed, the reforms discussed in this chapter not only have extended the formal powers and capacity of the office but also have improved the contemporary governor's performance in his many demanding roles.

In addition, today's governors are better educated, more experienced in state government, and more competent than their predecessors. Unfortunate exceptions notwithstanding, their strength and policy influence impresses. They are better able to employ the informal powers of their office in meeting multiple and complex responsibilities. In sum, the governorships have displayed greater *capability* and *vigor* than ever before.

## CHAPTER RECAP

- The American governorship historically was institutionally weak, with limited formal powers.

- Today's governors are better qualified, better educated, and better prepared for the office than governors of the past. But winning the office is increasingly expensive.

- Duties of the governors include making policy, marshaling legislative action, administering the executive branch, serving as master of ceremonies, coordinating intergovernmental relations, promoting economic development, and leading their political party.

- Formal powers of the office, which have strengthened over time, are tenure, appointment, veto, budgeting, reorganizing the executive branch, and staffing.

- To be successful, a governor must master the informal powers of the office and integrate them with the formal powers. Among the informal sources of power are tools of leadership and persuasion, such as public relations skills and negotiating and bargaining skills.

- Governors who violate the law may be removed from office through impeachment.

- Other key executive branch officials are the attorney general, lieutenant governor, treasurer, and secretary of state.

## Key Terms

pork barrel *(p. 179)*
formal powers *(p. 184)*
informal powers *(p. 184)*
plural executive *(p. 186)*

patronage *(p. 188)*
package veto *(p. 189)*
line item veto *(p. 190)*
pocket veto *(p. 190)*

executive amendment *(p. 190)*
executive order *(p. 192)*

## Internet Resources

Each state's governor has his or her own website, which can be located through the state homepage or from links at **www.nga.org**, the NGA's website. It features, among other items, governors' biographies, the latest "State of the State" addresses, and a subject index on various state and local issues, including welfare reform.

For information about the attorneys general, see **www.naag.org**. State treasurers can be audited at **www.nast.org**, and lieutenant governors at **www.nlga.us**. Even secretaries of state have a national organization: see **www.nass.org/**.

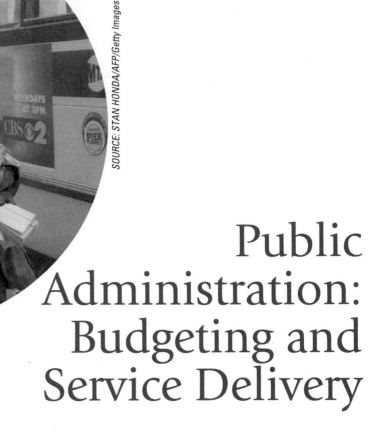

# Public Administration: Budgeting and Service Delivery

**8**

**Bureaucracy** is a paradox. On one hand, bureaucracy is portrayed as the problem with U.S. government at all levels. From the ponderous department of social services, to the dilatory department of motor vehicles, to the extractive county tax assessor's office, it is depicted as all-powerful, out of control, inefficient, wasteful, and drowning in red tape. Bureaucrats are often seen as insensitive and uncaring, yet they stay in their jobs forever. Nearly everyone, from elected officials—presidents, governors, mayors, and legislators at all levels—to talk-show commentators, television and film script writers, bloggers, and even product advertisers have stridently bashed the bureaucrats, blaming them for all imaginable sins of omission and commission (and all too often for their *own* personal shortcomings). The answer to the problem is no less than bureaucratic liposuction to "get the fat out."

On the other hand, bureaucracy can be beautiful.[1] Bureaucratic organization is indispensable to public administration. Legislative bodies and chief executives enact public policies through vague laws and then must depend on various state and local agencies to deal with the specifics, such as operationally defining key components of the policies and putting the policies into effect. Some bureaucracies make our lives more difficult, but others improve the quality of our existence by enforcing the laws and punishing the criminals, putting out the fires, repairing and maintaining the roads, and helping the poor and disadvantaged among us. Heroic, life-saving actions by police and firefighters are commonplace, but seldom recognized publically.

A theme of this chapter is that state agencies and local departments (the public administration) should not be treated as scapegoats for all the social, economic, and political maladies that befall society. The quality and capacity of public administration have improved markedly in the vast majority of the country's states, municipalities, and counties in terms of the characteristics of employees and the efficiency, effectiveness, and professionalism with which they perform their duties. In fact, studies comparing public employees with cohort groups in the private sector find few important differences between the "public-sector ethos" and the "private-sector ethos." Government workers are just as motivated, competent, and ethical as private-sector workers. Moreover, public employees tend to be more sensitive to other human beings, and more highly educated, than their counterparts in business and industry (see Table 8.1).[2]

**bureaucracy**
The administrative branch of government, consisting of all executive offices and their workers.

| Comparing Public- and Private-Sector Employees | | TABLE 8.1 |
|---|---|---|
| **CHARACTERISTIC** | **ADVANTAGE** | |
| Motivation | Equal (though public workers favor intrinsic rewards and private workers prefer extrinsic rewards) | |
| Work habits | Equal | |
| Competence | Equal | |
| Personal achievement | Private employees | |
| Educational Achievement | Public employees | |
| Values of civic duty and public service | Public employees | |
| Ambition | Private employees | |
| Compassion and self-sacrifice | Public employees | |
| Ethics | Public employees | |
| Helping other people | Public employees | |
| Making a difference | Public employees | |

An extensive analysis of published studies on the characteristics of public- and private-sector employees debunks certain stereotypes.

SOURCES: Adapted from Mary K. Feeney, "Sector Perceptions among State-Level Public Managers," *Journal of Public Administration Research and Theory* 18(3) (2008): 465–94; Richard W. Stackman, Patrick E. Connor, and Boris W. Becker, "Sectoral Ethos: An Investigation of the Personal Values Systems of Female and Male Managers in the Public and Private Sectors," *Journal of Public Administration Research and Theory* 16 (October 2006): 577–97; J. Norman Baldwin, "Public Versus Private Employees: Debunking Stereotypes," *Review of Public Personnel Administration* 11 (Fall 1990–Spring 1991): 1–27; James L. Perry, "Antecedents of Public Service Motivation," *Journal of Public Administration Research and Theory* 7(2) (1997): 181–97; Gene A. Brewer, Sally Coleman Selden, and Rex L. Facer, II, "Individual Conceptions of Public Service Motivation," *Public Administration Review* 60 (May/June 2000): 254–64.

State and local employees are responding to citizen demands by providing a wider range of services, in greater quantities, to more people than ever before, and publicly provided services are perceived to be just as good as the same services provided by private firms.[3] Public employees are much more accountable and responsive to political actors and to the public than they are popularly perceived to be. And contrary to popular opinion, government work does not consist of pay without labor. Public employees perform some of the most unpleasant (but necessary) tasks imaginable, from saving abused or threatened children from their parents to caring for the mentally ill and guarding prisoners who hurl feces at them. They must contend daily with clients who are criminals, deadbeats, emotionally disturbed, drug abusers, and worse,[4] and expand considerable quantities of "emotional labor."[5] They serve as our first—and continuing—response to disasters and terrorist events.

It is only on those rare occasions when someone fouls up that a public outcry is raised and a media investigation is launched; praise for consistency and excellence in public-service delivery is seldom heard. When government fails to perform effectively, blame can occasionally be laid at the feet of public employees. But more often than not, good government workers are the scapegoats for vague and poorly designed statutes and policies, failed political and corporate leadership, and other factors beyond the control of civil servants. It must also be pointed out that occasional lapses in government administrative ethics often pale in comparison to corporate scandals such as recent ones involving defense contractors, banking and finance companies, and pharmaceutical firms.

## PUBLIC EMPLOYEES IN STATE AND LOCAL GOVERNMENTS: WHO THEY ARE, WHAT THEY DO

More than 19.7 million employees work for states and localities. Their numbers have grown steadily since accurate counts were first compiled in 1929. The distribution of government employees is also of interest (see Figure 8.1). Government work tends to be labor-intensive. As a result of this fact and because of inflation, personnel expenditures for states and localities have risen even faster than the number of workers. Total payroll costs for state and local governments approach $750 billion.

Of course, the number of employees varies greatly among jurisdictions. Generally, states and localities with large populations and high levels of per capita income provide more services and thus employ larger numbers of workers than do smaller, less affluent jurisdictions. California, for instance, has some 1.8 million state and local employees on its payroll, compared with only 39,792 in Vermont. Employment figures are further influenced by the distribution of functions and ser-

**Distribution of Public Employment, 1929–2009** Since the end of World War II, the percentage of state and local employees, as a proportion of the total government work force, has increased.

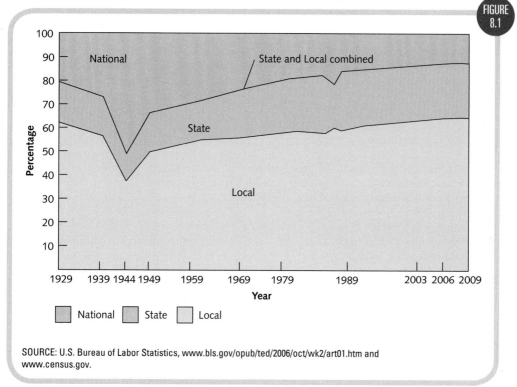

FIGURE
8.1

SOURCE: U.S. Bureau of Labor Statistics, www.bls.gov/opub/ted/2006/oct/wk2/art01.htm and www.census.gov.

vice responsibilities between states and their local jurisdictions. A state government may have hundreds of agencies, boards, and commissions. A municipality or county may have dozens of departments, boards, and commissions.

Such figures do not adequately represent the real people who work for states, cities, counties, towns, townships, and school districts. These workers include the police officer on patrol, the welfare worker finding a foster home for an abandoned child, the eleventh-grade English teacher, the state trooper, and even your professor of state and local governments (if you attend a public institution).[6] (See the Debating Politics box on the next page). Their tasks are as diverse as their titles: sanitation engineer, animal-control officer, heavy-equipment operator, planner, physician, and so on. The diversity of state and local government work rivals that of the private sector, although important distinctions are made in the nature of the work (see Table 8.2). From the sewer maintenance worker to the director of the public library, all are public servants—often known as bureaucrats. Approximately one of every six working Americans is employed by government at some level. If bureaucrats are the enemy, we have met them and they are us.

## DEBATING POLITICS

## Damned If You Do...

Welfare caseworkers are staffing the frontlines of the states' and localities' efforts to change the welfare system and its culture. Many of these individuals are highly educated and trained, with Master of Social Work (MSW) degrees and casework certificates. But sometimes they are called on to intervene or provide counseling in terribly difficult situations.

Put yourself in the following situation. You are a county welfare caseworker who specializes in the well-being of children who live in troubled households. Your office has received two telephone calls from the neighbors of a welfare mother complaining that her two young children (ages two and four) appear to have suffered bruises on their bodies, and that they are frequently heard crying when their mother's boyfriend is in their apartment. You visit the welfare mother's apartment, and the children look fine, except for a couple of minor bruises. The mother assures you that they are not in any danger from the boyfriend or from anyone else. Obviously, however, the children are not in an entirely healthy environment. Trash is strewn around the apartment, the children are not well clothed, and the older child seems to be a bit slow

or retarded. You tell the mother that you will be back next week to check on the situation and that she should let you know immediately if they are endangered in any way. She agrees.

Three days later, you receive a call from your department head. The boyfriend has disappeared, and the four-year-old is dead. The mother claims he fell down the stairs, but a neighbor reports that she heard the boyfriend, who often appeared to be high on drugs, screaming at and then beating the child.

Media reaction is immediate. Some are calling for your dismissal; others criticize departmental policy that did not require you to remove the child from his mother and place him in a foster home as soon as you heard allegations of trouble (departmental policy encourages caseworkers to give the benefit of the doubt to the family, so that the child can remain with his relatives).

In hindsight, did you make the right decision? Should you have acted differently? What principles of ethics or decision making should guide you in such decisions? How would you have handled criticism from the mother and welfare groups insisting that families be kept together?

Public- and private-sector management differ in terms of constraints, clients, accountability, and purpose.

| TABLE 8.2 | Public Management and Private Management: What Are the Distinctions? | |
|---|---|---|
| | **PUBLIC MANAGEMENT** | **PRIVATE MANAGEMENT** |
| **CONSTRAINTS** | Politics, public opinion, resources | Markets, competitors, resources |
| **CLIENTS** | Citizens, legislatures, chief executives, interest groups | Customers who purchase products or services |
| **ACCOUNTABILITY** | To citizens and elected and appointed officials. | To customers, boards of directors, and shareholders. |
| **PURPOSE** | To serve the public interest and the common good | To make profits and grow the organization |

# BUDGETING IN STATE AND LOCAL GOVERNMENTS

The budget is the very lifeblood of public administration. Without a budgetary appropriation, state and local organizations would cease to exist. The monies are allocated (usually on an annual basis) by legislative bodies, but the politics of the budgetary process involves all the familiar political and bureaucratic players: chief executives, interest groups, other government employees, the general public, firms and industries, and, of course, the recipients of legislative appropriations—the state highway department, the municipal police department, the county sanitation office, and so on. In a phrase, budgeting is a highly charged political poker game with enormous stakes. To understand public administration, one must have a grasp of budgetary politics.

An often-quoted definition of politics is Harold Lasswell's famous line: "Politics is who gets what, when, where, and how."[7] The budget document provides hard dollars-and-cents data in answer to this question. It is a political manifesto—the most important one you will find in state and local governments. It is a policy statement of what government intends to do (or not do), detailing the amount of the taxpayers' resources that it will dedicate to each program and activity. The outcomes of the budgetary process represent the results of a zero-sum game—for every winner there is a loser—because public resources are limited. An extra million dollars for corrections can mean that much less for higher education; an expensive new fleet of sanitation trucks requires higher taxes or trash collection fees from residents.

## The Budget Cycle

The process of governmental budgeting is best understood as a cycle with overlapping stages, five of which can be identified: preparation, formulation, adoption, execution, and audit (see Figure 8.2). Several stages are simultaneously taking place at any single time. For example, while the 2011 budget is being executed and revenues and expenditures are being monitored to guard against an operating deficit, the governor and the legislature are developing the 2012 budget. Meanwhile, the 2010 budget is being audited to ensure that monies were properly spent and otherwise accounted for.

Budgets are normally based on a *fiscal* (financial) *year* rather than on the calendar year. Fiscal years for all but four states run from July 1 through June 30 (the exceptions are Alabama, Michigan, New York, and Texas). Twenty-four states, including Montana, Indiana, and Kentucky, have biennial (two-year) budget cycles. Most local governments' fiscal years also extend from July 1 to June 30.

The initial phase of the budget cycle involves demands for slices of the budget pie and estimates of available revenues for the next fiscal year. State and local agency heads join the chorus of interest groups and program beneficiaries seeking additional funding. (With no concern for profits, agencies have little incentive to ask for less funding instead of more). Large state agencies are typically represented by their own lobbyists, or "public information specialists."

**The Budget Process**
The budget process has built-in checks and balances because all spending is approved or audited by more than one agency or branch.

FIGURE 8.2

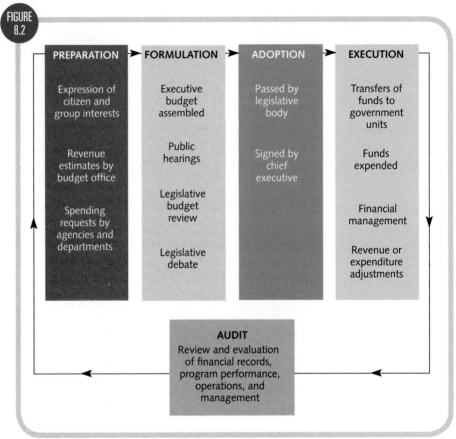

| PREPARATION | FORMULATION | ADOPTION | EXECUTION |
|---|---|---|---|
| Expression of citizen and group interests | Executive budget assembled | Passed by legislative body | Transfers of funds to government units |
| Revenue estimates by budget office | Public hearings | Signed by chief executive | Funds expended |
| Spending requests by agencies and departments | Legislative budget review | | Financial management |
| | Legislative debate | | Revenue or expenditure adjustments |

**AUDIT**
Review and evaluation of financial records, program performance, operations, and management

State and local finance administrators and analysts develop estimates of revenues based on past tax receipts and expected economic conditions, and they communicate them to their respective state agencies or municipal departments, which then develop their individual spending requests for the fiscal year. Such spending requests may be constrained by legislative and executive guidance, such as agency or program dollar ceilings, program priorities, or performance-based budgeting considerations.

Formulation, or initial development, of the budget document is the responsibility of the chief executive in most states and localities. Exceptions include states in which the balance of power rests with the legislature (such as Arkansas, Mississippi, and South Carolina) and local governments in which budgeting is dominated by a council or commission. The executive budget of the governor or mayor is submitted to the chief executive for the final touches.[8] The executive budget is then presented to the appropriate legislative body for debate, review, and modification. The lengthy review process that follows allows agencies, departments, interest groups, and citizens to express their points of view. Finally, the legislative body enacts the amended budget. Usually the budget moves forward in accordance with mandated deadlines. Sometimes, however, fiscal crisis or political disputes delay budget passage, forcing legislators into all-nighters and casting state and local operations into a sea of uncertainty over what they can and cannot afford to do.[9] For various reasons, New York is famously tardy in adopting its annual budget, chronically missing its April 1 deadline.

The state legislature or city council ensures that the final document balances revenues with expenditures. Balanced-budget requirements are contained in the constitutions or statutes of forty-eight states and operate through precedent in Vermont and Indiana.[10] These requirements usually apply to local governments as well and are also enforced through municipal ordinances in many localities. Balanced-budget requirements force state and local governments to balance projected expenditures with revenues, but they may be circumvented to some extent. Big-ticket items, for instance, may be funded in a capital budget with payments scheduled over several years. One popular device is the "off-budget," in which costs and revenues for public enterprises such as government corporations or for special projects are exempt from central review and are not included in budget documents and figures. Another accounting tactic is to borrow money from employee pension funds or next year's revenues to cover the current year's deficit. Perhaps the simplest way to balance a problematic budget is to assume extra revenues or savings (fiscal realism may take a back seat to political necessity). Before the budget bill becomes law, the chief executive must sign it. Last-minute executive–legislative interactions may be needed to stave off executive vetoes or to override them. Once the chief executive's signature is on the document, the budget goes into effect as law, and the execution phase begins.

During budget execution, monies from the state or local general fund are periodically allocated to agencies and departments to meet payrolls, purchase goods and materials, help average citizens solve problems ranging from a rabid raccoon in the chimney to a car-swallowing sinkhole in the front yard, and generally achieve program goals. Accounting procedures and reporting systems continually track revenues and outlays within the agencies. If revenues have been overestimated, the chief executive or legislative body must make adjustments to keep the budget in the black. They may draw on a rainy day fund to meet a shortfall (see Chapter 13) or, if the deficit is a large one, order service reductions, layoffs, unpaid furloughs, travel and hiring freezes, or across-the-board spending cuts. In a crisis the governor may call the legislature into special session, or the mayor may request a tax increase from the city council. Governments are forced into a series of Hobson's Choices to raise taxes, reduce expenditures, cut services, delay or cancel needed capital expenditures, or use some combination thereof to balance the budgets—unpopular choices all. Rainy day funds are tapped as well. Eventually, real pain is experienced by many different organizations and individuals.

The final portion of the budget cycle involves several types of audits, or financial reviews—each with a different objective. Fiscal audits seek to verify that expenditure records are accurate and that financial transactions have been made in accordance with the law. Performance audits examine agency or department activities in relation to goals, objectives, and outcomes, and ensure that the government is serving its citizens efficiently and effectively. Operational and management audits review how specific programs are carried out and assess administrators' performance.

A performance measurement and management trend has firm traction in state and local governments today, reflecting these jurisdictions' genuine determination to improve service provision to citizens.[11] Washington State, a leader in outcomes-based budgeting, develops a set of priorities to guide and inform agency spending. Those programs that accomplish their goals and objectives are funded; those that fail are not.[12]

## The Actors in Budgeting

Four main actors participate in the budget process: interest groups, agencies, the chief executive, and the legislative body. Interest groups organize testimony at budget hearings and pressure the other three actors to pursue favored policies and programs. The role of the agency or department is to defend the base—the amount of the last fiscal year's appropriation—and to advocate spending for new or expanded programs. Agency and department heads are professionals who believe in the value of their organization and its programs, but they often find themselves playing Byzantine games to get the appropriations they want, as set forth in Table 8.3.

| **TABLE 8.3** | **The Games Spenders Play** | |
|---|---|---|

The following are tactics used by state and local officials to maximize their share of the budget during negotiations and hearings with governors, local chief executives, and the legislative body.

| | | |
|---|---|---|
| **MASSAGE THE CONSTITUENCY** | Locate, cultivate, and utilize clientele groups to further the organization's objectives. Encourage them to offer committee testimony and contact legislative members on your behalf. | |
| **ALWAYS ASK FOR MORE** | If your agency or department doesn't claim its share of new revenues, someone else will. The more you seek, the more you will receive. | |
| **WHINING FOR DOLLARS** | Keep griping to your boss until his annoyance level is so high that he coughs up the money to shut you up. | |
| **SPEND ALL APPROPRIATED FUNDS BEFORE THE FISCAL YEAR EXPIRES** | An end-of-year surplus indicates that the elected officials were too generous with you this year; they will cut your appropriation next time. | |
| **CONCEAL NEW PROGRAMS BEHIND EXISTING ONES** | Incrementalism means that existing program commitments are likely to receive cursory review, even if an expansion in the margin is substantial. An announced new program will undergo comprehensive examination. Related to this game is *camel's nose under the tent*, in which low-program start-up costs are followed by ballooning expenses down the road. | |

| | |
|---|---|
| **"HERE'S A KNIFE; CUT OUT MY HEART WHILE YOU'RE AT IT"** | When told that you must cut your budget, place the most popular programs on the chopping block. Rely on your constituency to organize vigorous opposition. Alternatively, state that all your activities are critically important so the elected officials will have to decide what to cut (and answer to voters). |
| **A ROSE BY ANY OTHER NAME** | Conceal unpopular or controversial programs within other program activities. And give them appealing names (for instance, call a sex education class "Teaching Family Values"). |
| **"LET'S STUDY IT FIRST" (AND MAYBE YOU WON'T BE RE-ELECTED)** | When told to cut or eliminate a program, argue that the consequences would be devastating and should be carefully studied before action is taken. |
| **SMOKE AND MIRRORS** | Support your requests for budget increases with voluminous data and testimony. The data need not be especially persuasive or even factual, just overwhelming. Management writer James H. Boren calls this "bloatating" and "trashifying." |
| **A PIG IN A POKE** | Place an unneeded item in your budget request so you can gracefully give it up while protecting more important items. |
| **END RUN** | If the chief executive initiates a budget cut, scurry quickly to friends in the legislature. |
| **EVERY VEIN IS AN ARTERY** | Claim that any program cut would so completely undermine effectiveness that the entire program would have to be abandoned. |

Political scientist Aaron Wildavsky described the basic quandary of agency and departmental representatives as follows:

> Life would be simple if they could just estimate the costs of their ever-expanding needs and submit the total as their request. But if they ask for amounts much larger than the appropriating bodies believe is reasonable, their credibility will suffer a drastic decline.... So the first decision rule for agencies is: do not come in too high. Yet the agencies must also not come in too low, for the assumption is that if the agency advocates do not ask for funds they do not need them.[13]

What agency heads usually do is carefully evaluate the fiscal-political environment. They take into consideration the previous year's events, the composition of the legislature, the economic climate, policy statements by the chief executive, the strength of clientele groups, and other factors. Then they put forward a figure somewhat larger than they expect to get.

The chief executive has a much different role in the budget process. In addition to tailoring the budget to his program priorities as closely as possible, he acts as an economizer. Individual departmental requests must be reconciled, which means that they must be cut because the sum of the requests usually greatly exceeds estimated revenues. Of course, an experienced governor or mayor recognizes the games played by administrators; she knows that budget requests are likely to be inflated in anticipation of cuts. In fact, various studies on state and local budgeting indicate that the single most influential participant is the chief executive.[14] Not surprisingly, astute public administrators devote time and other resources to cultivating the chief executive's support for their agency's or department's activities.

The role of the legislative body in the initial stage of the budget cycle is essentially to respond to and modify the initiatives of the chief executive. The governor, mayor, or city manager proposes, and the legislature or council reacts. Later in the budget cycle, the legislative body performs another important function through its review of agency and department spending and its response to constituents' complaints.

What about the people whose salaries, homes, and vehicles will be taxed to fund the budget? In many jurisdictions, budgetary decision making remains a top-down enterprise, with elected officials deciding and then informing citizens what their hard-earned dollars will be spent on. But more and more state and local governments offer budget transparency by encouraging citizens to attend and speak in budget hearings, focus groups, coffees, and Web-based applications.[15] Unfortunately, few citizens avail themselves of the opportunity to participate, often preferring to carp and complain about "government taxing and spending." Nonetheless, the movement to "see-through government"[16] is real, and evidenced in public Web access to government revenues and expenditures in Kansas, Missouri, and Texas.

## Pervasive Incrementalism

In a perfect world, budgeting would be a purely rational enterprise. Objectives would be identified, stated clearly, and prioritized; alternative means for accomplishing them would be considered; revenue and expenditure decisions would be coordinated within the context of a balanced budget.

That is how budgeting *should* be done. But state and local officials have to allocate huge sums of money in a budgetary environment where objectives are unclear or controversial and often conflict with one another. It is nearly impossible to prioritize the hundreds or thousands of policy items on the agenda. Financial resources, time, and the capacity of the human brain are severely stretched.

To cope with such complexity and minimize political conflict over scarce resources, decision makers "muddle through."[17] They simplify budget decision making by adopting decision rules. For example, instead of searching for the optimal way to address a public policy problem, they search only until they find a feasible solution. As a result, they sacrifice comprehensive analysis and rationality for **incrementalism**, in which small adjustments (usually an

**incrementalism**

A decision-making approach in the budgetary process in which last year's appropriations are used as a base for the current year's budget figures.

increase) are made to the nature and funding base of existing programs. Thus, the policy commitments and spending levels of ongoing programs are usually accepted as a given—they become the base for next year's funding. Decisions are made on a very small proportion of the total budget: the increments from one fiscal year to the next. If the budget has to be cut it is done decrementally—as many were in 2009–2010—small adjustments are subtracted from the base. In this way, political conflict over values and objectives is held to a minimum.

The hallmarks of incremental budgeting are consistency and continuity: The future becomes an extension of the present, which is itself a continuation of the past. Long-range commitments are made, then honored indefinitely. This is not to say that state and local budgeting is a pedestrian affair. On the contrary, it is as tangled and intricate as the webs of a thousand spiders on crystal meth.

## Types of Budgets

A budget document can be laid out in various ways, depending on the purposes one has in mind: control, management, or planning. Historically, *control*, or fiscal accountability, has been the primary purpose of budgeting, incrementalism the dominant process, and the line item budget the standard document.

**Control Through Line Item Budgets**  The **line item budget** facilitates control by specifying the amount of funds each agency or department receives and monitoring how those funds are spent. Each dollar can be accounted for with the line item budget—which lists every object of expenditure, from police uniforms to toilet paper—on individual lines in the budget document. Line item budgets show where the money goes, but they do not tell how effectively the money is spent.

**line item budget**
A budget that lists detailed expenditure items such as personal computers and paper, with no attention to the goals or objectives of spending.

**Budgeting for Performance**  Budget formats that are intended to help budget makers move beyond the narrow constraints of line items and incrementalism toward more rational and flexible decision-making techniques and incremental procedures that help attain program results are popularly known as performance budgets. Chief executives and agency officials seek to ensure that priorities set forth in the budget are properly carried out by organizational units. Formal program and policy evaluations are necessary steps to ensure program performance and public accountability.

In **performance budgeting**, the major emphasis is on services provided and program outcomes. The idea is to focus attention on how effectively goals are attained rather than on what is acquired or spent. Whereas line item budgets are input oriented, performance budgets are output and outcome oriented. Governments and their managers decide what they want to accomplish and then measure these accomplishments versus expendi-

**performance budgeting**
Budgeting that takes into account the outcomes of government programs.

tures. For example, the performance of a fire department can be evaluated by response times to emergency calls and by how quickly a fire is contained once the firefighters arrive on the scene. Police departments can track arrests, clearance rates, crime rates, and citizen survey results. By focusing on program objectives and work performance, performance budgets can assist managers, elected officials, and citizens in improving the quality of government operations.[18]

**Capital Budgets** The budget formats described above apply to operating budgets, whose funds are depleted within a year. Capital outlays are made over a longer period of time and are composed of big-ticket purchases such as hospitals, university buildings, libraries, bridges, and new information systems. They represent one-time, nonrecurring expenditures that call for special

**capital budget**
A budget that plans large expenditures for long-term investments, such as buildings and highways.

funding procedures, or a **capital budget**. Because such items cannot be paid for within a single fiscal year, governments borrow the required funds, just as most individuals borrow when buying a house or an expensive automobile. The debt, with interest, is paid back in accordance with a predetermined schedule.

Capital projects are funded through the sale of general obligation or revenue bonds. *Bonds* are certificates of debt sold by a government to a purchaser, who eventually recovers the initial price of the bond plus interest (see Chapter 13). *General obligation bonds* are paid off with a jurisdiction's regular revenues (from taxes and other sources). In this instance, the "full faith and credit" of the government is pledged as security. *Revenue bonds* are usually paid off with user fees collected from use of the new facility (e.g., a parking garage, auditorium, or toll road). Payments for both types of bonds are scheduled over a period of time that usually ranges from five to twenty years. The costs of operating a new facility, such as a school or a sports arena, are met through the regular operating budget and/or user fees.

# HUMAN RESOURCE POLICY IN STATE AND LOCAL GOVERNMENTS: FROM PATRONAGE TO MERIT

Whether the tasks of state and local governments are popular (fighting crime, educating children), unpopular (imposing and collecting taxes and fees), serious (saving a helpless infant from an abusive parent), or mundane (maintaining the grass on municipal sports fields), they are usually performed by public employees. The 5.2 million state workers and 14.6 million city, county, and town employees are the critical links between public policy decisions and how those policies are implemented. Agencies and departments must be organized to solve problems and deliver services effectively, efficiently, and reliably. Human resource (personnel) rules and procedures must determine how public employees are recruited, hired, paid, and fired.

In the nation's first decades, public employees came mainly from the educated and wealthy upper class and, in theory, were hired on the basis of fitness for office. During the presidency of Andrew Jackson (1829–1837), who wanted to open national government jobs to all segments of white, male society, the *patronage* system was adopted to fill many positions. Hiring could depend on party affiliation and other political alliances rather than on job-related qualifications.

Patronage became entrenched in many states and localities, where jobs were awarded almost entirely on grounds of partisan politics, personal friendships, family ties, or financial contributions. This system made appointees accountable to the governor, mayor, or whoever appointed them, but it did nothing to ensure honesty and competence. By the beginning of the Civil War, the spoils system permeated government at all levels, and the quality of public service plummeted.

## The Merit System

The concept of the **merit system** is usually associated with the national campaign to pass the federal Pendleton Act of 1883. Two key factors led to its realization. First, Anglo-Saxon Protestants were losing political power to urban political machines dominated by new Americans of Catholic faith and Irish, Italian, and Polish descent. Second, scandals rocked the administration of President Ulysses S. Grant and spawned a public backlash that peaked with the assassination of President James Garfield by an insane attorney seeking a political appointment. The Pendleton Act set up an independent, bipartisan civil service commission to make objective, merit-based selections for federal job openings.

> **merit system**
> The organization of government personnel to provide for hiring and promotion on the basis of knowledge, skills, and abilities rather than patronage or other influences.

The *merit principle* was to determine all personnel-related decisions. Those individuals best qualified would receive a job or a promotion based on their knowledge, skill, and abilities. Far from perfect, the merit system was thoroughly overhauled by the Civil Service Reform Act of 1978. But as a result of the Pendleton Act, the negative effects of patronage politics in national selection practices were mostly eliminated. **Neutral competence** became the primary criterion for obtaining a government job, and public servants are expected to perform their work competently and in a politically neutral manner.

> **neutral competence**
> The concept that public employees should perform their duties competently and without regard for political considerations.

During the period of national merit system reform, the state and local governments were also busy. New York was the first state to enact a merit system, in 1883, and Massachusetts followed its example in 1884. The first municipal merit system was established in Albany, New York, in 1884; Cook County, Illinois, became the first county with a merit system, in 1895. (Ironically, both Albany and Cook County, Chicago, were later consumed once again by machine politics and spoils-ridden urban governance, a condition not entirely eradicated even today.)[19]

Many states and numerous local governments enacted merit-based civil service systems on their own. Congressional passage of the 1939 amendments to the Social Security Act of 1935 gave additional impetus to such systems. This legislation obligated the states to set up merit systems for employees in social service and employment security agencies, and departments that were at least partly funded by national grants-in-aid under the Social Security Act. Thus, all states are now required to establish a merit system for a sizable segment (around 20 percent) of their work force; most of them have in fact developed comprehensive systems that encompass almost all state employees. Common elements of these merit-based personnel systems include recruitment, selection, and promotion according to knowledge, skills, and ability; regular performance appraisals; and employee incentive systems.

Some merit systems work better than others. In a handful of states and localities, they are mere formalities around which a shadowy world of patronage, spoils, favoritism, and incompetence flourishes.[20] Such conditions came to public attention when terrorists boarded and hijacked two commercial aircraft at Boston's Logan Airport on 9/11. For years, gubernatorial patronage appointees with little or no experience in security or law enforcement had run Logan's security operations.[21] Rigid personnel rules, a lack of training programs, and inadequate salaries continue to plague some jurisdictions. Political control over merit-system employees is limited everywhere because most cannot be fired without great difficulty. Georgia and Florida are exceptions: In these states, new employees are hired on fixed-term contracts and not granted in tenure in the job.

## State and Local Advances

On balance, state and local personnel systems have been greatly improved, and the process continues. State and local governments are experimenting with progress recruitment and testing innovations, pay-for-performance plans and other incentive systems, participative management innovations, new performance-appraisal methods, the decentralization of personnel functions, and many other concepts. Almost every state is reforming its civil service in some way.[22] General public dissatisfaction with government at all levels, combined with increasing needs for government to become more sophisticated and responsive to its clients, means that efforts to "reinvent" human resource management are certain to grow.

These reforms are designed to make the executive branch leaner and more responsive to the chief executive; to improve service efficiency and effectiveness; to shift the overarching focus to outputs and outcomes from inputs and processing and, through decentralization of authority, to enhance flexibility for chief executives, agency heads, city managers, and other officials.[23] Reformers remain dedicated to the principle of protecting the civil service from unnecessary and gratuitous interference by politicians with patronage considerations in mind. But they also want to increase the capacity of government executives to manage programs and people in their organizations and to achieve desired results.

## Merit-System Controversies

As we shall see, state and local governments have taken the lead in addressing controversial questions that involve merit-system principles and practices, including **representative bureaucracy** and **affirmative action**, sexual harassment, and labor unions.

**Representative Bureaucracy** This controversial policy is related to another key concept—affirmative action. The concept of representative bureaucracy suggests that the structure of government employment should reflect major sexual, racial, socioeconomic, religious, geographic, and related components in society. The assumptions behind this idea are that (1) bureaucrats have discretion; (2) a work force representative of the values, points of view, and interests of the people it governs will be responsive to their special problems and concerns; and (3) a representative bureaucracy provides strong symbolic evidence of a government "of the people, by the people, and for the people." These assumptions have been widely debated. In some situations, representative bureaucracy has "active" dimensions through decisions that may favor a class of people, such as women and minorities.[24] However, empirical research indicates that the specific agency a person works for and the profession she belongs to are better predictors of public policy preferences than racial, sexual, and other personal characteristics.[25] The symbolic, or "passive," aspects of representative bureaucracy are also important. A government that demonstrates the possibility of social and occupational mobility for all sorts of people gains legitimacy in the eyes of its citizens and expands the diversity of views taken into account in bureaucratic decisions. For example, research shows that blacks are more likely to perceive interactions with police as legitimate when African American officers are involved,[26] and report greater satisfaction with police, education, and other services when blacks are represented on city councils or school boards.[27]

A controversial problem is how to *achieve* a representative work force, particularly at the upper levels of government organizations, without sacrificing the merit principle. *Equal employment opportunity (EEO)*—the policy of prohibiting employment practices that discriminate for reasons of race, sex, color, religion, age, disability, or other factors not related to the job—is mandated by federal law. This policy has been the law for well over a century, yet progress was slow until the past three decades or so, when affirmative action policies were adopted throughout government.

Affirmative action recognizes that equal opportunity has not been sufficient because employment discrimination persists. Governments must take proactive steps to hire and retain those categories of workers legally defined as "protected classes" who have suffered discrimination in the past. These measures may be adopted voluntarily, but they are required under certain conditions specified by the U.S. Equal Employment Opportunity Commission (EEOC), the regulatory body created to enforce EEO and, in some instances, by the courts. The measures include goals, timetables, and other preferential selection and promotion devices intended to make the work forces of public

**representative bureaucracy**

The concept that all major groups in society should participate proportionately in government work.

**affirmative action**

Special efforts to recruit, hire, and promote members of disadvantaged groups to eliminate the effects of past discrimination.

and private organizations more representative of the racial, sexual, and other characteristics of the available labor pool.

Under affirmative action, the absence of overt or intentional discrimination in employment is not sufficient; organizations may implement preferential recruitment, hiring, and promotion schemes to redress existing imbalances. The legitimacy of affirmative action policies imposed on employers by the EEOC was seriously questioned in a series of U.S. Supreme Court decisions during the past two decades and by state legislative actions and referendums.[28]

Obviously, affirmative action is highly controversial. Establishing specific numerical goals and timetables for hiring and promoting minorities does not necessarily correspond with selection or promotion of the best person for the job. In other words, affirmative action appears to conflict with the merit principle. It has also alienated many white males, who feel that they have become victims of reverse discrimination.

Legal clashes among the federal courts, Congress, and the states and localities continue but have not produced a coherent interpretation of affirmative action's legal standing. Three examples illustrate the complexity of the issues surrounding affirmative action policy. The first concerns a 1992 lawsuit against the University of Texas Law School, filed by four white applicants (three men and a woman), who alleged that they had not been admitted despite having LSAT scores higher than those of African American and Hispanic applicants who were accepted. The first federal judge to hear this case, in *Hopwood v. Texas*, ruled against the white applicants.[29] On appeal, however, the Fifth Circuit Court judges agreed that the university had violated the students' constitutional rights. According to the court, the use of race as a selection criterion "is no more rational…than would be choices based upon the physical size or blood type of applicants." The Fifth Circuit Court's decision applied to universities in Texas, Louisiana, and Mississippi.

Texas attorney general Dan Morales appealed to the U.S. Supreme Court, which refused to hear the case and thus kept the circuit court's ruling in effect. Yet to Texans' astonishment, the U.S. Department of Education warned the state, in an official letter, that Texas could lose all federal financial aid if it ended its affirmative action programs as ordered by the courts! After a furious reaction by the state's powerful congressional delegation, the Department of Education backed down.

National confusion and uncertainty about affirmative action are further illustrated by the 1996 passage of Proposition 209 in California, which amended the state constitution by prohibiting race and gender consideration in contracting decisions and in hiring for state and local jobs. The initiative was approved by nearly 55 percent of the voters. Soon, however, a federal judge blocked enforcement on grounds that Proposition 209 was discriminatory and therefore unconstitutional. About six months later, judges for the Ninth Circuit Court of Appeals reinstated Proposition 209, an action that was upheld by the U.S. Supreme Court. The debate in California presaged similar conflicts elsewhere. Following Proposition 209, Washington voters approved an anti–affirmative action initiative and Governor Jeb Bush of Florida eliminated racial preferences in college admissions in his state through an executive order.

The third example of confusion and complexity involves a pair of U.S. Supreme Court rulings in 2003 concerning the admissions procedures at the University of Michigan.[30] The Court invalidated a point system, used to select undergraduates, that awarded additional points for minority status, but it upheld the law school's consideration of race as a nonquantified "plus" in its admission decisions.

Despite such confusion and ugly political invective, substantial progress toward representative bureaucracy has been made, especially in recruiting and hiring protected-class individuals for entry-level positions. Indeed, African Americans are *over*-represented relative to their presence in the overall civilian labor force in a majority of state governments. Latinos, however, have had much less success in gaining public jobs at all levels.[31] Granted, some minorities and women continue to bump against a glass ceiling as they try to penetrate the upper levels of state and local agencies,[32] as well as glass walls that restrict their access to certain agencies, departments, or occupations.[33] But significant progress is being seen even with respect to these final barriers to representative bureaucracy, as indicated by descriptive data (for instance, the number of female, African American, and Latino city managers and other professionals in state and local governments has grown dramatically in recent years).[34]

Indeed, widely recognizing the need to recruit, motivate, and manage a work force that reflects an increasingly diverse general population, state and local governments today have recast EEO and affirmative action approaches as "diversity" policies.[35] Of course, when employees working together differ in terms of gender, color, religion, customs, and other key characteristics, misunderstandings and miscommunications are inevitable. The astute public manager helps employees recognize and accept such differences while leveraging the different experiences, perspectives, and knowledge of a diverse work force to maintain and even raise levels of organizational productivity and effectiveness.[36]

**Sexual Harassment** Sexual harassment has long been a problem in public and private employment. Sexual harassment can consist of various behaviors: unwanted touching or other physical contact of a sexual nature, implicit or overt sexual propositions, or (in one of its worst forms) extortion of a subordinate by a supervisor who demands sexual favors in return for a promotion or a raise. A "hostile working environment" that is pervasive and discriminates on the basis of gender also constitutes sexual harassment.[37] Examples in this category include repeated—and unwelcome—leering, sexual joking or teasing, or lewd calendars or e-mails at the workplace. Isolated incidents of sexual teasing or innuendo do not constitute sexual harassment. Sexual harassment is illegal according to federal and state laws, a form of punishable employee misconduct under civil service rules. It is also prosecuted in the courts. (See the Debating Politics box on the next page for a glimpse at its definitional complexity).

## DEBATING POLITICS

# Is this Sexual Harassment?

The EEOC has issued guidelines to combat sexual harassment. Such harassment is defined as unwelcome actions that are sexual in orientation, that subject the employee to adverse employment conditions or create a hostile work environment. Most state and local employers have similar laws, regulations, or policies that reinforce the EEOC guidelines.

Consider the following situations and decide if they constitute unlawful sexual harassment:

1. A male supervisor quietly tells a female employee that he will see that she is promoted if she agrees to "have a special dinner" with him at his house.
2. An employee who is accused of making sexually aggressive remarks to a coworker claims that he didn't understand that such speech was a problem.
3. Coworkers commonly tell dirty jokes and sexually oriented stories, and make lewd remarks, but no one has complained.
4. A woman frequently makes complimentary remarks about a male coworker's backside, which makes the man feel uncomfortable.
5. A man sexually comes on to another man.

Unwelcome touching in the workplace can be a form of sexual harassment.
SOURCE: Danwer Productions / Alamy

6. A female employee complains that she is experiencing a hostile work environment because coworkers often comment on her appearance. The employee typically wears sexually provocative clothing and behaves in a manner that male coworkers find flirty.
7. A woman who once participated in vulgar language and sexual horseplay around the office now maintains that she is offended by such activity.

Sexual harassment is common in the workplace.[38] Surveys of women discover that at least half of the respondents report being a victim. Approximately 15 percent of men have experienced sexual harassment. Such behavior subverts the merit principle when personnel decisions such as hiring or promotion are influenced by illegal or discriminatory considerations of a sexual nature, or when an employee cannot perform his or her assigned duties because of sexual harassment. Sexual harassment can exact a high price on organizational productivity, not to mention the cost of monetary settlements with victims. Unfortunately for the recipient of unwanted sexual attention, there are seldom any witnesses. The matter becomes one person's word against another's. And when one of the parties is the supervisor of the second party, a formal complaint may be decided in favor of the boss.

Much of the official activity aimed at stopping sexual harassment has been concentrated in the states, with local governments following suit. Michigan was the first to adopt a sexual harassment policy, in 1979; since then nearly every state has adopted a statewide policy through legislation or executive order. States offer employee-training programs that help workers and supervisors identify acts of sexual harassment, establish procedures for effectively addressing it, and enforce prompt, appropriate disciplinary action against offenders.

The consequences of sexual harassment go far beyond the personal discomfort, stress, or injury suffered by victims. The problem also results in significant financial costs to organizations whose employees lose productive work time. Such misconduct is unacceptable today in a national work force that is almost 50 percent female.

**Unions** Nearly always controversial in government, *public-employee unions* present a potentially serious threat to the merit principle. They usually insist on seniority as the primary criterion in personnel decisions, often seek to effect changes in merit-system rules and procedures that benefit their membership, and regularly challenge management authority. Moreover, unions aggressively seek higher pay and benefits, threatening to drive up the costs of government and, in some instances, prompting tax increases.

Until the 1960s, the growth and development of unions in the United States was a private-sector phenomenon. Federal legislation protected the rights of workers in industry to organize and engage in **collective bargaining** with their employers over wages, benefits, and working conditions. Workers then organized in record numbers. By the late 1950s, however, private-sector union growth began to decline for a number of reasons, including the shift in the U.S. economy from manufacturing to services and the globalization of labor markets.

Unionization in state and local governments developed and flourished in the 1960s and 1970s, some thirty years after the heyday of private-sector unionism. Why the sudden growth? In retrospect, several reasons are apparent.

First, the rise of unionism in government was spurred by the realization by state and local employees that they were underpaid and otherwise poorly treated in comparison with their counterparts in the private sector, who had progressed so well with unionization and collective bargaining. Second, the bureaucratic and impersonal nature of work in large government organizations encouraged unionization to preserve the dignity of the workers. A third reason for the rise of state and local unionism was the employees' lack of confidence in many civil service systems. Not only were pay and benefits inadequate, but grievance processes were controlled by management; employees had little or no say in setting personnel policies; and merit selection, promotion, and pay were often fraught with management favoritism.

Perhaps most important, the growth of unions in government was facilitated by a significant change in the legal environment. The rights of public employees to join unions and bargain collectively with management were guaranteed by several U.S. Supreme Court rulings, state legislation, local ordinances, and various informal arrangements that became operative during the 1960s and 1970s. Wisconsin was the first state, in 1959, to permit collective bargaining for state workers. Today, forty-three states specifically allow at least one category of state or local government employees to engage in collective bargaining, and most have taken advantage of the offer.

The extent of unionization and collective bargaining is greatest in the states of the Midwest and Northeast—the same areas so fertile for the growth of private-sector unions. A handful of traditionalistic states, including Mississippi, Utah, Virginia, and the Carolinas, continue to resist the incursion of

**collective bargaining**
A formal arrangement in which representatives of labor and management negotiate wages, benefits, and working conditions.

**FIGURE 8.3**

**Public Employee Collective Bargaining Rights in the States**

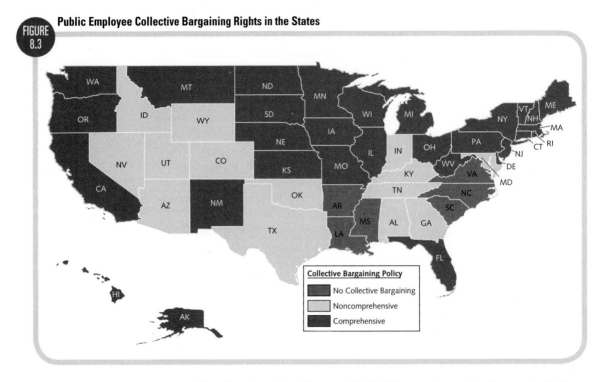

Collective Bargaining Policy

- No Collective Bargaining
- Noncomprehensive
- Comprehensive

state and local unions (see Figure 8.3). Public employees in these jurisdictions have the legal and constitutional right to join a union, but their government employers do not have a corresponding duty to bargain with them over wages, benefits, or conditions of work.

Approximately 32 percent of state and 42 percent of local government workers belong to unions, compared with only about 8.4 percent of workers in private industry. The highest proportions of union workers are found in education, highway departments, public welfare, police and fire protection, and sanitation.[39]

The surge in the fortunes of state and local unions was partially arrested by the taxpayer revolt of the late 1970s and by President Ronald Reagan's successful effort to "bust" a federal air traffic controllers' union. Additional resistance to unions developed in the 1990s and continues today as governments downsize, outsource, privatize, and seek greater efficiencies. Taxpayer resistance has helped stiffen the backbones of public officials, who have been criticized in some jurisdictions for giving the unions too much.

In the late 2000s, unionism in state and local governments has leveled off in some jurisdictions while others have experienced significant growth, largely due to a more facilitative legal environment. Unions remain an important and highly visible component of many state and local government personnel systems.

What is the impact of collective bargaining in state and local governments? Market forces largely determine the outcomes of bargaining between a union and a firm in the private sector, such as profit levels and the supply and demand for labor. In government, political factors are much more important. The technical process of negotiating over wages and other issues is very similar to that in business. But the setting makes government labor relations much more complex, mostly because the negotiating process culminates in the *political* allocation of *public* resources.

Four factors make government labor relations highly political. First, public officials are under greater pressure than private employers to settle labor disputes. Public services are highly visible and often monopolistic in nature; for example, there are no other convenient suppliers of police and fire protection. Accordingly, elected officials who confront a controversial labor dispute in an "essential service" may fear that negative developments will derail their opportunity for re-election.

Second, public-employee unions wield political clout. Their members can influence election outcomes, particularly at the local level. A recalcitrant mayor or city council member who opposes a hefty wage increase may suffer defeat at the polls in the next election if the municipal union members vote as a bloc. Unions actively engage in politics by raising money, writing letters to the editor about candidates, knocking on doors to get out the vote, formally endorsing candidates, or using any of the other electoral techniques employed by interest groups. Many unions have professional lobbyists to represent them at the state capitol or in city hall.

A third politicizing factor in government labor relations is the symbiotic relationship that can develop between unions and elected officials. In exchange for special consideration at the bargaining table and perhaps elsewhere, the unions can offer public officials two valued commodities: labor peace and electoral support.

Finally, a hard-pressed union can use the strike or a related job action (such as a slowdown or a picket line) as a political weapon. In the private sector, a strike is not likely to have widespread public repercussions unless it involves goods or services that the nation relies on for its economic well-being (such as air transportation, coal mining, or communications). In government, however, a strike can directly involve the health and safety of all the citizens of a jurisdiction. A 2005 strike by 33,700 subway and bus workers left millions of commuters in New York City on street corners and snarled in traffic. A general strike involving police officers, firefighters, and sanitation workers has the potential to turn a city into filthy, life-threatening anarchy. At a minimum, any strike leaves the public inconvenienced.

Strikes and other job actions by public employees are illegal in most jurisdictions, although thirteen states permit work stoppages by certain "nonessential" workers under strictly regulated conditions. Even where strikes are forbidden, teachers, health care workers, firefighters, and others sometimes walk off the job anyway. It is extremely rare for police or firefighters to strike today, and it is illegal everywhere. But parents angry about a teacher strike or commuters paralyzed by a transportation walk out have convinced many an elected official to seek prompt settlement of government–labor impasses.

Given these politicizing factors, one might expect unions in government to be extravagantly successful at the bargaining table, but quite the opposite is true. Public-employee unions have raised wages and salaries an average of 4–8 percent, depending on the service, place, and time period under consideration

Public employee strike— Chicago garbage strike.
*SOURCE:* Bettmann/CORBIS

(e.g., teachers earn around 5 percent more and firefighters around 8 percent more if represented by a union). These figures are much lower than the union-associated wage effects identified in the private sector. Greater success has come in the form of better benefits, particularly pensions and health care insurance. It should be noted that union-driven wage and benefit hikes in the private sector are absorbed through profits, layoffs, or higher product prices. In government, by contrast, the choices are to raise taxes or fees, cut services, increase productivity, or contract out.

Certain personnel impacts have also been associated with collective bargaining in government. Clearly, unions have gained a stronger employee voice in management decision making. All personnel-related issues are potentially negotiable, from employee selection and promotion procedures to retention in the event of a reduction in force. As a result of collective bargaining, many government employers have altered civil service rules, regulations, and procedures. In heavily unionized jurisdictions, two personnel systems coexist uncomfortably—the traditional merit-based civil service system and the collective bargaining system.[40] Certainly, the rights of public employees have been strengthened by unions.

Generally speaking, governments and collective bargaining have reached an uneasy accommodation. The principle of merit in making personnel decisions is still largely in place, and it is usually supported by the unions as long as seniority is fully respected as an employment decision rule. In an increasing number of jurisdictions, unions are cooperating with management to increase productivity in government services through participative decision-making techniques, labor–management partnerships, and worker empowerment programs.

## THE POLITICS OF BUREAUCRACY

In an ideal representative democracy, political officials popularly elected by the people would make all decisions regarding public policy. They would delegate to public administrators in the executive branch the duty of carrying out these decisions through the agencies of state and local governments. In the real world of bureaucratic politics, however, the line dividing politics (policy) and administration is difficult to discern. Politicians frequently interfere in administrative matters, as when a legislator calls an agency head to task for not treating a constituent favorably. Administrators practice politics at the state capitol and in city hall by participating in and influencing policy formulation decisions.

## Joining Administration and Politics

Bureaucrats are intimately involved in making public policy, from the design of legislation to its implementation. Government workers are often the seed bed for policy ideas that grow to become law, in large part because they are more familiar with agency, departmental, and clientele problems and prospective solutions than anyone else in government. It is not unusual, for instance, for law enforcement policy to originate with police administrators or higher education policy to be the brainchild of university officials.

Once a bill does become law, state and local employees must interpret the language of the legislation to put it into effect. Because most legislation is written in general terms, civil servants must apply a great deal of **bureaucratic discretion** in planning and delivering services, making rules for service delivery, adjudicating cases and complaints, and otherwise managing the affairs of government. All states have legal systems for hearing and acting on disputes over agency rules and regulations, such as environmental permitting and determination of social service eligibility. These administrative procedures allow individuals, firms, and local governments to challenge agency rules and regulations before an administrative law judge, who issues an order settling the dispute.

**bureaucratic discretion**
The ability of public employees to make decisions interpreting law and administrative regulations.

In a very real sense, the ultimate success or failure of a public policy depends on the administrators who are responsible for its implementation. Experienced legislators and chief executives understand this, and they bring relevant administrators into the legislative process at an early stage. The knowledge and expertise of these administrators are invaluable in developing an appropriate policy approach to a specific problem, and their cooperation is essential if a policy enacted into law is to be carried out as the lawmakers intend.

Thus, bureaucratic power derives from knowledge, expertise, information, and discretionary authority. It also comes from external sources of support for agency activities—that is, from the chief executive, legislators, and interest groups. Those who receive the benefits of government programs— the clientele, stakeholders, or customers—are also frequently organized into pressure groups. All government programs benefit some interest—agriculture policy for the farm community; tourism policy for the business community; public assistance policy for the poor; education policy for parents, students, teachers, and administrators—and these **clientele groups** are often capable of exerting considerable influence in support of policies that benefit them. Their support is critical for securing the resources necessary to develop and operate a successful government program. They serve as significant political assets to state agencies and municipal and county departments that are seeking new programs or additional funding from legislative and executive bodies and they can become fearsome political in-fighters when their program interests are threatened.[41] Often, clientele and other concerned interest groups form ad hoc coalitions with relevant government agencies and legislative committees to dominate policy making and implementation in a particular policy field.

**clientele groups**
Groups that benefit from a specific government program, such as contractors and construction firms in state highway department spending programs.

Thus the problem of politics and administration has two dimensions. First, elected officials have the duty of holding administrators responsible for their decisions and accountable to the public interest, as defined by the constitution and by statute. Second, political oversight and intrusion into administrative activities should be minimized so that administrative decisions and actions are grounded in objective rules and procedures—not in the politics of favoritism. For example, legislators have the duty of ensuring that decisions by a state department of environmental protection guard the public from the harmful effects of pollution while treating polluting companies fairly. Nevertheless, state representatives should not instruct agency employees to go easy on a favored business constituent. Most government agencies discharge their tasks competently and professionally, and therefore require little direct oversight. Occasionally, however, a rogue agency or department head may strike out in the wrong direction.

An example of the proper balance of politics and administration is the attempt by legislators to influence public administrators. This typically occurs when elected officials or their staff members perform casework for constituents. Although the legislator may occasionally seek favorable treatment that borders on illegality, the bulk of legislative casework comprises responses to citizens' inquiries or complaints, or requests for clarification of administrative regulations or decisions. Such legislative casework is useful because it promotes both feedback on the delivery of services and helpful exchanges of information between elected officials and administrators. If inquiries determine bias or error in the means by which services are delivered, corrective political actions can be taken.

In sum, state and local politics are intricately joined with administration. Public policy is made and implemented through the interaction of elected officials, interest groups, and public administrators. Nonetheless, the vast majority of administrative decisions are based on the neutral competence and professionalism of public employees. When the municipal transportation department must decide which streets to repave, for example, a formula is applied that takes into account factors such as the date of the last repaving, intensity of public usage, and the condition of the road.

This is not to say that such decisions are never made on the basis of political favoritism. Sometimes political pressures influence bureaucratic discretion. For example, a telephone inquiry from the mayor or city council member can advance the road-paving schedule in front of the house of a powerful constituent. On the whole, however, state and local services are provided in an unbiased fashion through applying professional norms and standards.

## NEW PUBLIC MANAGEMENT

State and local government employment has burgeoned at a rate much faster than that of population growth. In Texas, for instance, the number of state workers jumped from 223,000 in 1990 to 365,700 in 2008. The total state and local payroll in the Lone Star State exceeds $4 billion.[42] Explanations for this huge expansion in the size and costs of state governments are numerous, including federal mandates, expanding levels of services, partisan politics, and the power of incremental budgeting.

Are the quantity and quality of services better than ever? Not according to most citizens, as we pointed out at the beginning of this chapter. Instead, taxpayer ire and criticism of government are high at all levels. Still, approval of government began rising in 2001, when the heroic actions of public employees and military personnel in response to terrorist attacks helped citizens regain an understanding of the value of civil service. And it continued with the presidential campaign of Barack Obama, who helped to make public service cool again. Innovations that make government more efficient, effective, and responsive have also played a role. Many new strategies are being tried in an effort to solve this quite "vexing puzzle for public administrators since time immemorial"[42] by improving the performance, productivity, and responsiveness of state and local governments.

The most far-reaching approach is called **New Public Management (NPM)**.[43] It is a global movement, but in the United States, it is often associated with the widely read book *Reinventing Government*, by David Osborne and Ted Gaebler.[44] According to NPM proponents, governments today are preoccupied with rules, regulations, and hierarchy; their bureaucracies are bloated, inefficient, and altogether poorly suited for meeting the demands made on them. The solution is for governments to free up managers to tap their powers of entrepreneurship and market competition to design and provide efficient and effective services to state and local "customers." In short, governments should "steer, not row," by stressing a facilitative or cooperative approach to getting services to citizens rather than delivering all services directly. Among the alternative service-delivery systems are public–private partnerships, volunteerism, voucher plans, and technical assistance. Once transformed, the governments would be enterprising, mission driven, outcome oriented, focused on the needs of their customers, and prepared to "do more with less."

Among the formidable obstacles to such profound change in government activities and behavior are labor-intensive tasks such as teaching and policing that do not readily lend themselves to labor-saving technology; rule-bound civil service systems, which tend to discourage management and entrepreneurial risk taking; the inevitable inertia that plagues public organizations having no bottom line and few market-driven incentives; the difficulties of innovating in organizations created essentially to regulate; the need for politicians to buy into and support the movement, which implies greater autonomy and discretion for administrative agencies but more risks and more mistakes as well; and the certain opposition by powerful vested interests, such as public-employee unions, that feel threatened by change. Undeterred by the carping critics and maligning malcontents, many state and local governments have adopted a reinventing attitude in tackling

**New Public Management**
The argument that government should manage for results, through entrepreneurial activity, privatization, and improvements in efficiency and effectiveness.

various problems. Principally, they have placed their bets on (1) privatization of government services and (2) e-government.

## Privatization

Privatization shifts government functions to private or nonprofit organizations through service arrangements such as vouchers, franchises, public–private partnerships, and contracting out. It is a widely heralded reform that garners much support today, especially among conservatives, Republicans, and others who want to see a "businesslike" approach to government. Almost any government service is a candidate for contracting out (outsourcing), from jails to janitorial work, from teaching to trash collection. (In theory, most government facilities can even be sold to private interests and operated as businesses; airports and bridges are examples). The purported benefits of privatization include cost savings, higher-quality services, the acquisition of highly specialized skills, and more efficient service delivery. It is a popular strategy for reducing service costs. To date, privatization has been used most frequently to outsource vehicle towing, solid waste collection, building maintenance and security, street repair, ambulance services, printing, data processing, human resource management tasks, and social welfare services.[45]

In choosing the privatization route to reinventing government, Massachusetts has contracted out mental health care, prison health care, various highway maintenance functions, and operations of interstate highway rest stops, among many other functions. Florida has outsourced projects valued at $1.6 billion.[46] Riverside, California, has privatized operations of its public libraries, whereas Chicago outsources window washing, sewer cleaning, compost processing, and parking garages. Privately built and operated toll roads and bridges operate in a growing number of states. Indiana leased its main toll road to a private consortium, raising $3.85 billion (but the purchasers were foreign companies and tolls were soon set at much higher levels, spawning a sharp political backlash).[47]

Privatization isn't as easy as it sounds, and it doesn't always generate savings.[48] It usually elicits virulent opposition from public-employee unions, who fear the loss of their jobs or reductions in pay and benefits. Unless governments carefully negotiate and then monitor the quality and effectiveness of privatized services, performance may decline and costs may actually rise. Contracts that are vaguely worded or filled with loopholes, and insufficient contract oversight on the part of some jurisdictions, have resulted in cost overruns, shoddy services, and fraud or corruption by the contractors. Service disruptions have occurred when a firm's workers have walked off the job. Indeed, successful outsourcing requires not only careful government planning, design, and analysis of what the jurisdiction and its citizens need and want to have done, but also a recognition that government accountability cannot be negotiated. The state, county, or city must remember that ultimately *it* will be held accountable for long-term successful and reliable delivery of a service. If anything goes wrong, government officials—not the private provider—will be blamed and held responsible. Successful contract monitoring requires careful inspections, comprehensive performance reports, and assiduous investigations of citizen complaints, among many other factors.

To keep contractors honest, some governments use multiple, competing firms, government agencies, or nonprofit organizations to deliver the same service to different state or local activities. Arizona state workers, for instance, compete head-to-head with a national firm in administering public assistance programs. Inspired by pioneers such as Phoenix (Arizona) and Indianapolis (Indiana), other jurisdictions have developed public–private partnerships.[49] Such collaboration among governments, nonprofit organizations, and private firms saved Indianapolis some $100 million in four years through negotiated arrangements in waste-water treatment, recycling, sewer billing, street sweeping, and many other services.[50]

Is privatization worthwhile? Local officials believe that outsourcing improves service delivery in most cases, and some research indicates that it saves cities and states up to about 20 percent for some service categories, but little or nothing for others. After all, firms must figure a profit margin into their costs, whereas government providers do not. And there are many notable failures of privatization, particularly those involving sweetheart deals, no-bid contracts, or inept contract administrators.[51] It is not a cure-all for the problems besetting states and local governments, but privatization does represent one potentially useful alternative for reinventing government.

## E-Government

**E-government** involves re-engineering the way various government activities are conducted, and making the face of government more user-friendly. Some improvements are rather mundane and commonsensical. For instance, most states permit online tax filing and renewal of licenses and registrations. To both improve government–citizen communications and to relieve pressure on over-burdened 911 calls, Chicago, Denver, Charlotte, and other cities have launched 311 call centers for citizens to report service problems and determine where to direct their specific inquiries.[52] Other improvements are more futuristic. Arizonians can vote in primary elections on the Web and view live proceedings of the state legislature through their state's "digital democracy." New York City, Baltimore, and Washington State have mounted computer-coordinated attacks on crime that electronically track incidents and suspects, detect emerging crime patterns, and coordinate crime-fighting activities with other state and local jurisdictions. Arlington County, Virginia, sends mass alerts to its citizens on their Blackberries, cell phones, PCs, and iPhones through "Arlington alert."[53] Management of personnel systems has been vastly improved in Wisconsin through online job bulletins, walk-in testing services, and rapid hiring of employees for hard-to-fill positions. Delaware's podcasts allow downloads of breaking state news. Minneapolis gathers public input through an online tool called wiki (see Engaging Public Administration).

**e-government**
The use of information technology to simplify and improve interactions between governments and citizens, firms, public employees, and other entities.

## Engaging Public Administration

### Wiki World and Second Life

Adventuresome public administrators are taking e-government to a new dimension with wiki world and Second Life applications. A *wiki* is a Web page that permits any user to add content (most readers will be familiar with the popular online encyclopedia Wikipedia). In government, the idea is to use wiki to expand the range of new ideas and input on a problem or situation, sort of like a virtual suggestion box. The wiki thus encourages mass collaboration and group effort among a defined community of participants, which can range from a small internal task force to a public agency wiki open to anyone. For instance, a wiki can solicit ideas for saving money in parks and recreation services, or prioritizing budget cuts. Minneapolis invites citizens to provide wiki input for public meetings and the city's development plans.

Second Life is a virtual world in Web 2.0 that involves an "island" for customized use by personal "avatars"

(the participants), who can interact by speaking, moving about, or other actions. The actual participant is sitting at a PC or laptop while his or her avatar carries on in its virtual world. Second Life offers an inexpensive alternative to conferences, and a much more interesting approach to the traditional conference call or video meeting. It is also a useful technology for training exercises (e.g., an emergency response to a chemical spill on a major highway or a multi-vehicle traffic accident). Wikis and Second Life adoptions and applications in government are likely to pick up pace as young, tech-savvy people enter the labor force. Their potential as tools for public administration is only in the preliminary phases of testing.

SOURCE: Don Tapscott and Anthony D. Williams, *Wikinomics: How Mass Collaboration Changes Everything* (Expanded Edition) (New York: Portfolio, 2008); Ellen Perlman and Melissa Maynard, "Working in Wiki World." *Governing* (May 2008): 26–30.

Unmistakably, we are well on the road to electronic government. "Virtual offices" operating through the Internet are establishing convenient, 24–7 connections among citizens, businesses, nonprofit organizations, and their governments. From a home or office personal computer or one conveniently located PC in the neighborhood kiosk or library, citizens can obtain everything from English-language lessons online in Boston to free chats with online health care providers in Wyoming. Massive filing systems for documents and other hard copy are no longer needed. Instead, paperless offices use imaging technology to scan, store, and access important records of marriages, births, deaths, business licenses, and a host of other documents. Table 8.4 shows state rankings on the quality of e-government.

GIS systems can display visual data on crime incidence, transportation backups, water and sewer breaks, and other problems to help government employees analyze information and make decisions more quickly and less expensively. In addition to automating repetitive labor-intensive tasks, GIS facilitates interagency and interlocal cooperation on issues from land-use planning to social welfare services. Best of all, GIS turns abstract information into understandable visual displays.[54]

Despite much enthusiastic rhetoric, five hurdles are slowing the diffusion of e-government: the substantial investments required to pay for the computer

| Overall State E-Government Ratings, 2008 Ranking | | TABLE 8.4 |
| --- | --- | --- |
| **RANK** | **STATE** | **RATING OUT OF 100 PTS** |
| 1. | Delaware | 83.7 |
| 2. | Georgia | 78.3 |
| 3. | Florida | 77.9 |
| 4. | California | 70.9 |
| 5. | Massachusetts | 69.5 |
| 6. | Maine | 67.7 |
| 7. | Kentucky | 67.3 |
| 8. | Alabama | 66.4 |
| 9. | Indiana | 65.0 |
| 10. | Tennessee | 64.3 |
| 11. | Connecticut | 64.2 |
| 12. | Colorado | 62.2 |
| 13. | Arizona | 61.1 |
| 14. | Arkansas | 60.0 |
| 15. | Alaska | 59.1 |
| 16. | Pennsylvania | 58.2 |
| 17. | Texas | 55.1 |
| 18. | Oregon | 53.9 |
| 19. | Washington | 53.5 |
| 20. | New York | 51.4 |
| 21. | South Dakota | 51.4 |
| 22. | New Jersey | 51.0 |
| 23. | Ohio | 48.8 |
| 24. | Wisconsin | 48.6 |
| 25. | Rhode Island | 48.3 |
| 26. | Michigan | 47.4 |
| 27. | Virginia | 47.4 |
| 28. | South Carolina | 47.3 |
| 29. | North Carolina | 44.8 |
| 30. | Minnesota | 44.0 |
| 31. | North Dakota | 43.4 |
| 32. | Iowa | 43.2 |

**TABLE 8.4** (continued)

| RANK | STATE | RATING OUT OF 100 PTS |
|------|-------|-----------------------|
| 33. | Kansas | 43.1 |
| 34. | Oklahoma | 42.8 |
| 35. | Utah | 42.5 |
| 36. | New Hampshire | 42.3 |
| 37. | Nebraska | 42.2 |
| 38. | Illinois | 41.9 |
| 39. | Missouri | 41.6 |
| 40. | West Virginia | 41.2 |
| 41. | Montana | 41.1 |
| 42. | Louisiana | 39.8 |
| 43. | Indiana | 39.6 |
| 44. | Vermont | 39.5 |
| 45. | Nevada | 39.3 |
| 46. | Hawaii | 35.8 |
| 47. | Wyoming | 35.7 |
| 48. | Maryland | 32.9 |
| 49. | New Mexico | 32.5 |
| 50. | Mississippi | 31.1 |

SOURCE: Darrell M. West, *State and Federal Electronic Government in the United States, 2008*. The Brookings Institution, 2008.

hardware and trained personnel; absence of staff expertise; unresolved legal questions of liability, privacy, and security; the possibility of cyber attacks; and the difficulty of integrating software across multiple agencies and departments. Nevertheless, the potential of e-government to make government more accessible, understandable, and efficient is enormous.[55]

Is NPM simply a fad? Definitely not. Responsive states and localities have been reinventing their operations and services since they were created, and they will continue to do so for as long as they exist. In the short run, some governments may be reinvented or at least changed in fundamental ways, but others will continue to do things using old ways. Of course, sometimes "old ways" work just fine, as demonstrated by Chattanooga, Tennessee. When fast growing kudzu vines threatened to choke access to city property, the city summoned a herd of goats to eat the problem into remission.[56] Change is politically risky, and inertia is a powerful force. Ultimately, it is the responsibility of citizens and the elected officials who represent them to bring about change and reforms.

# THE QUALITY OF PUBLIC ADMINISTRATION

Despite the quantity of criticism hurled at government agencies, departments, and workers by the media, elected officials, and others, the quality of public administration in state and local governments has improved markedly. Of course, there is considerable variance among jurisdictions; that capacity generally is of a higher quality in affluent, highly educated, and urban jurisdictions.

Results of a study of state government administrative performance are found in Table 8.5. The Government Performance Project, conducted by the Pew Center on the States and *Governing* magazine, examined state performance in managing key administrative areas: money, people, infrastructure, and information.

Administrative quality is a critical factor in the support of revitalization and responsiveness of states and localities. State and local governments, particularly through partnership with private and nonprofit organizations, have the capacity to accomplish more on a grander scale than ever before, and this trend is continuing through the NPM movement. The basics of providing services, from disposing of dead animals to delivering healthy human babies, will continue to depend on government employees with high standards of performance and professionalism.

| State Administrative Report Card | | | | | TABLE 8.5 |
| --- | --- | --- | --- | --- | --- |
| **STATE** | **MONEY** | **PEOPLE** | **INFRAST.** | **INFO.** | **OVERALL** |
| Alabama | C– | B– | C+ | C | C+ |
| Alaska | C– | C– | C– | B– | C |
| Arizona | C+ | B– | B– | B– | B– |
| Arkansas | B– | C– | C+ | C– | C |
| California | D+ | C– | B– | C+ | C |
| Colorado | C+ | C | C+ | C | C+ |
| Connecticut | B– | B– | C+ | B– | B– |
| Delaware | A– | B | B+ | B– | B+ |
| Florida | B– | C– | A– | B– | B– |
| Georgia | B+ | A– | B | B+ | B+ |
| Hawaii | C+ | B– | C | C– | C+ |
| Idaho | B+ | C+ | B– | C+ | B– |
| Illinois | C– | C– | C | C+ | C |
| Indiana | B+ | B | B+ | B– | B |
| Iowa | B+ | B+ | C+ | B+ | B |
| Kansas | B– | C+ | C+ | B | B– |
| Kentucky | C+ | C+ | A– | B | B– |
| Louisiana | B | B | C+ | B+ | B |
| Maine | C | C– | C+ | C | C |

**TABLE 8.5**    (continued)

| STATE | MONEY | PEOPLE | INFRAST. | INFO. | OVERALL |
|-------|-------|--------|----------|-------|---------|
| Maryland | B+ | C+ | B+ | B– | B |
| Massachusetts | C+ | C | D+ | C | C |
| Michigan | C+ | B+ | A– | A | B+ |
| Minnesota | B+ | B– | C+ | B | B– |
| Mississippi | C+ | C | C+ | C | C+ |
| Missouri | B+ | B– | B+ | A | B+ |
| Montana | C+ | B– | C+ | C+ | C+ |
| Nebraska | A– | B– | B+ | B– | B |
| Nevada | C+ | C– | B– | B– | C+ |
| New Hampshire | C– | D | D+ | D+ | D+ |
| New Jersey | C– | B– | C+ | C– | C |
| New Mexico | B– | C | C+ | B | B– |
| New York | C+ | B– | B– | C+ | B– |
| North Carolina | B– | B | B– | B– | B– |
| North Dakota | B | C | B– | C+ | B– |
| Ohio | B | C+ | B– | B– | B– |
| Oklahoma | B– | C+ | C– | C | C+ |
| Oregon | C+ | C+ | C+ | B– | C+ |
| Pennsylvania | B | C+ | B– | B | B– |
| Rhode Island | D+ | D | C+ | C | C– |
| South Carolina | B– | A– | C– | B– | B– |
| South Dakota | B+ | C+ | B | D+ | C+ |
| Tennessee | B– | C | B | B | B– |
| Texas | B | B | B | A– | B+ |
| Utah | A– | B+ | A– | A | A– |
| Vermont | B– | C+ | B+ | C– | B– |
| Virginia | A– | A– | B+ | A | A– |
| Washington | A– | A– | B+ | A | A– |
| West Virginia | B | C | C– | C | C+ |
| Wisconsin | C+ | B– | B– | C+ | B– |

**Money** incorporates long-term outlook, budget process, structural budget balance contracting/purchasing, and financial controls/reporting; **People** includes strategic work force planning, hiring and retaining employees, training and development, and managing performance; **Infrastructure** includes capital planning, project monitoring, maintenance, internal and intergovernmental coordination; **Information** measures strategic direction, performance budgeting, managing for performance, performance auditing and evaluation, and online services/information.

SOURCE: The Quality of Public Administration source: http://www.governing.com/gpp/2008/al.htm

## CHAPTER RECAP

- The quality and capacity of public administration have greatly improved in the majority of the states and local governments.

- State and local government employment has grown rapidly.

- State and local operating budgets must be balanced each year.

- Interest groups, agencies, the chief executive, and the legislative body are the four principal actors in the budgetary process.

- Budgets tend to expand (or contract) incrementally.

- The trend in accounting for revenues and expenditures is performance-based budgeting.

- Most state and local jobs are part of a merit system and are filled based on knowledge, skills, and experience.

- Affirmative action led to gains in the advancement of minorities and women in state and local employment, but it is very controversial.

- States and localities are addressing the problem of sexual harassment in public agencies.

- Unions and collective bargaining present special challenges to many state and local governments.

- Bureaucratic discretion makes public employees important decision makers.

- The New Public Management, aimed at reinventing government through privatization, e-government, and other steps, is a long-term trend.

## Key Terms

bureaucracy *(p. 205)*
incrementalism *(p. 214)*
line item budget *(p. 215)*
performance budgeting *(p. 216)*
capital budget *(p. 216)*

merit system *(p. 217)*
neutral competence *(p. 217)*
representative bureaucracy *(p. 219)*
affirmative action *(p. 219)*
collective bargaining *(p. 223)*

bureaucratic discretion *(p. 227)*
clientele groups *(p. 227)*
New Public Management *(p. 229)*
e-government *(p. 231)*

## Internet Resources

All major municipalities and states have webpages. Many provide links to jobs, New Public Management initiatives, service-provision information, and other data. Innovative, award-winning websites include Indianapolis's "Electronic City Hall" at **www.indygov.org**, Service Arizona at **http://servicearizona.com**, NC@YourService at **www.ncgov.com**, AccessWashington at **www.access.wa.gov**, and Delaware's at **www.delaware.gov**.

An Internet-based clearinghouse on GIS is maintained by the Center for Technology in Government at **www.ctg.albany.edu/gisny.html**. Another interesting site on technology and government is located at **www.govtech.net**.

An informative public-employee union website is AFSCME's at **www.afscme.org**.

For a step-by-step illustration of a state budget process, see **http://www.budget.state.ny.us/citizen/process/process.html**. Check out Kansas, Texas, and Missouri "see through budget" sites at **http://www.kansas.gov/KanView/**; **www.window.state.tx.us/**; **www.mapyourtaxes.mo.gov**.

To view streaming videos of public meetings in Indiana, visit **www.stream.hoosier.net/cats**.

Information on the Government Performance Project is found at **www.governing.com**.

# The Judiciary

In the case of *Barnes v. Glen Theatre Inc.* (1991), a prudish U.S. Supreme Court ruled that nude dancing, being dangerous to "order and morality," is not protected as free expression under the First Amendment of the U.S. Constitution. This case, which arose in Indiana, was tried in the federal courts under national constitutional law. But in Ohio, strippers may freely cavort in their full birthday suits; patrons, however, are barred from touching the "naughty bits" at risk of six months in jail and a $1,000 fine.[1]

And in Boston, Massachusetts, a city once known for banning all manner of objects and activities deemed to be immoral, totally naked women grind, bump, and pirouette at tacky cabarets, fully confident that their activity is legal. In Massachusetts, the voluntary display of a naked body has been protected under the *state* constitution as a form of free expression since the state supreme court ruled it so in 1984.[2]

As the U.S. Supreme Court has become increasingly conservative since the chief justiceship of Earl Warren (1953–1969), state courts have become more open to individuals and groups advocating liberal causes such as civil rights, free speech, and freedom of expression. All sorts of conflicts and problems find their way to state and local courts, from the profound (abortion rights) to the profane (nude dancing). Decisions of state courts have a weighty "impact on the overall distribution of wealth and power in the United States and on the daily well-being of the citizens."[3] Courts at this level are busy; 99 percent of the nation's cases are filed in state courts—approximately 100 million cases a year! New York State's cases alone outnumber those filed in all federal courts by a factor of 9 to 1. Many of the state courts are innovative in their decision making and administration; in addition, all are far more accessible to the people and responsive to their concerns than are the federal courts.

State supreme courts sometimes act as policy makers. As the third branch of government, the judiciary is, after all, the final authority on the meaning of laws and constitutions and the ultimate arbiter of disputes between the executive and legislative branches. It also makes public policy through rulings on

9

- The Structure of State Court Systems
- How Judges are Selected
- Judicial Decision Making
- Judicial Federalism
- Administrative and Organizational Improvements in State Courts

**239**

questions of political, social, and economic significance and may serve as the last chance for minority interests to defend themselves from the decisions of the majority. As noted in Chapter 3, state courts have become more active policy makers in recent years and have increasingly based important decisions on state constitutions rather than on the national constitution. As with the other branches of state government, their structures and processes have been greatly reformed and modernized. In our lifetimes, nearly all of us will experience the judicial branch as direct participants (juror, plaintiff, defendant, or witness). At times, the courts are more accessible to us than are the other branches of government. Disputes that cannot be resolved through ordinary legislative, executive, and political processes frequently wind up before a judge as litigation.

The work of the fifty state court systems is divided into three major areas: civil, criminal, and administrative. In **civil cases**, one individual or corporation sues another over an alleged wrong. Occasionally, a governmental body is party to a civil action. Typical civil actions are divorces, property disputes, and suits for damages arising from automobile or other accidents. **Criminal cases** involve the breaking of a law by an individual or a corporation. The state is usually the plaintiff; the accused is the defendant. Murder, assault, embezzlement, and disorderly conduct are common examples. **Administrative cases** concern court actions such as probating wills, revoking driver's licenses, or determining custody of a child. Some administrative cases involve administrative law judges and quasi-judicial (less formal) proceedings. A government entity is usually a party to an administrative case.

State courts adjudicate (take actions to administer justice) by interpreting state statutes, the state and federal constitutions, and **common law**. In developing and deciphering the common law, courts are concerned with the legal rules and expectations that have developed historically through the citizens' custom, culture, and habits, and that have been given standing through the courts decisions rather than from statutes. The most important applications of common law today concern enforcing contracts (contract law), owning and selling property (property law), and establishing liability for death or injuries to people as well as damage to property (tort law).

## civil case
A case that concerns a dispute involving individuals or organizations.

## criminal case
A case brought by the state against persons accused of violating a law.

## administrative case
Usually, a case in which a government agency applies rules to settle a legal dispute.

## common law
Unwritten law based on tradition, custom, or court decisions.

# THE STRUCTURE OF STATE COURT SYSTEMS

State courts have evolved in response to changes in their environment. In colonial days, they developed distinctively, influenced by local customs and beliefs. Because of a shortage of trained lawyers and an abiding distrust of English law, the first judges were laymen who served on a part-time basis. It did not take long for the courts to become overwhelmed with cases: case overloads were reported as long ago as 1685.[4] More than three centuries later, case backlogs still plague our state judiciaries.

As the population and the economy grew, so did the amount of litigation. Courts expanded in number and in degree of specialization. However, their development was not carefully planned. Rather, new courts were added to existing structures. The results were predictably complex and confusing, with overlapping, independent jurisdictions and responsibilities. For instance, Chicago offered an astounding array of jurisdictions, estimated at one time to number 556.[5] State court systems were beset as well by a host of other serious problems, including administrative inefficiency, congestion, and excessive delays. In short, the American system of justice left much to be desired.

The organization of the state courts is important because it affects the quality and quantity of judicial decisions and the access of individuals and groups to the legal system. It also influences how legal decisions are made. An efficiently organized system, properly staffed and administered, can do a better job of deciding a larger number of cases than a poorly organized system can. Court structure is of great interest to those who make their living in the halls of justice—lawyers, judges, and court staff. It is also an issue of concern to citizens who find themselves in court.

## The Two Tiers of Courts

Most states today have a two-tiered court structure: trial courts and appellate courts. There are two types of trial courts: those of limited jurisdiction and major trial courts. Each tier, or level, has a different *jurisdiction*, or range of authority. *Original* jurisdiction gives courts the power to hear certain types of cases first, in contrast to *appellate* jurisdiction, which grants the courts the power to review cases on appeal after they have been tried elsewhere. Trial courts, which comprise the lower tier, include (1) minor courts of limited jurisdiction and (2) major trial courts of general jurisdiction.

**Limited jurisdiction trial courts**, also known as special trial courts, handle minor, specialized cases, such as those involving juveniles, traffic offenses, and small claims. Most states have three to five courts of limited jurisdiction, with names that reflect the type of specialized case: traffic court, police court, probate court, municipal court, and so on. Criminal cases here are usually restricted by law to misdemeanor violations of municipal or county ordinances that are punishable by a small fine, a short jail term, or both. Additional courts of limited jurisdiction, sometimes called "boutique" or "problem-solving" courts, have been created to deal with special types of cases or circumstances. For example, all states have created drug courts, with the dual aims of processing drug-related offenses

> **limited jurisdiction trial courts**
> Those courts with original jurisdiction over specialized cases such as juvenile offenses or traffic violations.

A judge in veterans' court instructs the participants.
*SOURCE:* AP Photo/Don Heupel

## Engaging the Courts

### Evidence-Based Sentencing

Our state prisons are spilling over even though millions of dollars are shoveled into new construction; the rates of released felons committing another crime and returning to prison (recidivism) are at a historic high of nearly 60 percent; court dockets, judges, and staff are slammed with work; parole and probation services are widely believed to be broken; and state budgets have been severely depleted as corrections costs ($50 billion a year) have become the fastest-growing segment of state budgets, second only to Medicaid. There seems to be no end to the problems besetting the courts and criminal justice.

However, a new approach to sentencing promises at least a modicum of relief to prison overcrowding, high-recidivism rates, and soaring caseloads. There is a growing body of research indicating that evidence-based sentencing (EBS) helps to reduce crime rates and save states money.

The driving principle of EBS is that all offenders are different: they may be drug addicted, alcoholic, mentally ill, violent, or generally like the rest of the non-criminal population. The goal is for the judge's sentence to provide the incarceration period, probation conditions, or treatment services called for. Through flexible sentencing, the judge can individually craft penalties or inducements to reduce recidivism risk in rehabilitative cases and to reduce risk to the public through swift and lengthy sentences in others. By using actuarial risk and assessment tools, the court can

statistically associate the offender's characteristics with those of past cases for which the recidivism outcomes are known and provide these data to the judge before sentencing. The judge can then impose the preferred degree of diversion from prosecution, probation, jail time, or other sanction. The goal is to motivate the offender to change his behavior.

What stands in the way of EBS are state legal provisions that mandate strict sentencing and/or prohibit judges from assigning offenders to treatment or probation, as well as inadequate offender record-keeping and tracking. Training in EBS is required for both judges and court personnel so that they are fully aware of sentencing alternatives and their likely implications.

Taking the lead in developing and funding EBS approaches are Oregon and Washington. Based on early evaluations in Washington, significant monetary savings have been achieved and recidivism rates reduced by 17 percent. Other states are taking notice.

SOURCES: Pew Center on the States, *Arming the Courts with Research: Ten Evidence-Based Sentencing Initiatives to Control Crime and Reduce Costs.* Public Safety Policy Brief 8 (May 2009). www.pewpublicsafety.org; Pew Center on the States, *One in 1000: Behind Bars in America,* 29 (Washington, D.C.: The Pew Charitable Trusts, 2008). D. A. Andrews, James Bonta, and J. Stephen Wormith, "The Recent Past and Near Future of Risk and/or Need assessment," *Crime and Delinquency* 7 (January 2006): 12–13.

more efficiently and reducing the recidivism rates of drug offenders on probation or parole. Domestic violence and mental health courts are common as well. "Water courts" in Colorado and Montana hear disputes over water rights. In Charleston, South Carolina, a "livability court" convenes regularly to hear complaints against those accused of damaging the quality of life, including barking dogs, homeowners with unkempt lawns, and parking violators.[6] Illinois and Wisconsin created special "veterans courts" in 2009 to hear minor offenses charged to Iraq and Afghanistan war vets.[7]

Present in almost all states are *small claims courts*, which offer a relatively simple and inexpensive way to settle minor civil disputes without either party having to incur the financial and temporal burdens of lawyers and legal procedures. Small claims courts are usually divisions of county, city, or district trial courts. In cases before small claims courts, the plaintiff (the person bringing the suit) asks for monetary recompense from the defendant (the individual or firm being sued) for some harm or damage. Claims are limited to varying amounts, usually around $1,000. The proceedings are informal. Each party presents to a judge the relevant facts and arguments to support his or her case. The party with the preponderance of evidence on his or her side wins. Most disputes involve tenant–landlord conflicts, property damage, or the purchase of goods (e.g., shoddy merchandise or the failure of a customer to pay a bill).

The plaintiff usually wins in small claims court. About half the time, defendants do not show up to plead their case and thereby lose by default. In contested cases, plaintiffs win around 80 percent of the time. Unfortunately for the plaintiff, winning a case is often easier than collecting from the defendant. It's the plaintiff's responsibility to get written court permission to extract the amount due from the debtor's wages, bank account, or other assets, and to retain the local sheriff or constable to deliver and enforce the court order.

The second type of trial court is the **major trial court**, which exercises general authority over civil and criminal cases. Most cases are filed initially under a major trial court's original jurisdiction. However, trial courts also hear cases on appeal from courts of limited jurisdiction. Major trial courts are often organized along county or district lines. Their names (circuit courts, superior courts, district courts, courts of common pleas) vary widely.

The upper tier of the two-tiered state court system consists of appellate courts: **supreme courts** (sometimes called courts of last resort) and, in most states, **intermediate appellate courts**. Oklahoma and Texas have two supreme courts: one for criminal cases and the other for civil disputes. Forty states have intermediate appellate courts; Nevada voters were to consider adding their own in a 2010 referendum. Alabama, Oklahoma, Oregon, Texas, Pennsylvania, and Tennessee have two, typically one each for criminal and civil cases. Most intermediate appellate courts are known as courts of appeals. Their work generally involves cases on appeal from lower courts. Thus, these courts exercise appellate jurisdiction by reviewing a trial court's interpretation and application of the law. By contrast, state supreme courts have original jurisdiction in certain types of cases, such as those dealing with constitutional issues, as well as appellate jurisdiction.

Intermediate appellate courts represent the most notable change in the landscape of state courts during the past three decades. They are intended to increase the capability of supreme courts by reducing their caseload burden, speeding up the appellate process, and improving the quality of judicial decision making. The weight of the evidence points to moderate success in achieving each of these objectives. Case backlogs and delays have been reduced, and supreme court justices are better able to spend an appropriate amount of time on significant cases. Counteracting this positive trend, however, is the growing number of mandatory appeals, such as for death penalty cases, which can make up more than half of the caseload.

If a state supreme court so chooses, it can have the final word on any state or local case except one involving a federal constitutional question, such as

**major trial court**
Court of general jurisdiction that handles major criminal and civil cases.

**supreme court**
The highest state court, beyond which there is no appeal except in cases involving federal law.

**intermediate appellate court**
A state appellate court that relieves the case burden on the supreme court by hearing certain types of appeals.

First Amendment rights. Some cases can be filed in either federal or state court. For example, a person who assaults and abducts a victim and then transports him across a state line can be charged in state court with assault and in federal court with kidnapping. Some acts violate nearly identical federal and state laws; possession or sale of certain illegal drugs is a common example. Other cases fall entirely under federal court jurisdiction, such as those involving treason, mail theft, or currency law violation.

Thus, there exists a *dual system* of courts that is sometimes referred to as *judicial federalism*. Generally, state courts adjudicate, or decide, matters of state law, whereas federal courts deal with federal law. The systems are separate and distinct. In some instances, however, there is jurisdictional overlap and even competition for a case. Following the arrests of Beltway snipers John Muhammad and Lee Malvo in 2003, Virginia, Maryland, and the U.S. Department of Justice all sought to bring the multiple murder case to trial first (six victims were killed in Maryland, three in Virginia, and one in the District of Columbia; Virginia was given the honor of first prosecution).

Although state courts cannot overturn federal law, they can base certain rulings on the federal constitution. Recently, state courts have decided cases governed by both state and federal laws in hate crimes, the right to die, and gay rights. It is very unusual for a case decided by a state supreme court to be heard by the U.S. Supreme Court or any other federal court. Even if such a review is done, the U.S. Supreme Court usually upholds the state high court decision. For instance, in 2004, the U.S. Supreme Court let stand a Massachusetts Supreme Court decision upholding the right of gay couples to marry.[8] An important exception to the custom occurred in the aftermath of the 2000 presidential election, when the U.S. Supreme Court overturned a Florida Supreme Court decision that had ordered a recount of ballots in three counties. The intervention of the nation's highest court in state election affairs effectively awarded the presidency to George W. Bush.

## Structural Reforms

The court reform movement that swept across the states in the 1960s and 1970s sought, among other things, to convert the state courts into more rational, efficient, and simplified structures. A driving goal was to increase the capacity and responsiveness of state and local judicial systems. An important legacy of that movement is the unification and consolidation of state court systems.

Although the two tiers of state courts appear to represent a hierarchy, in fact they do not. Courts in most states operate with a great deal of autonomy. They have their own budgets, hire their own staff, and use their own procedures. The decisions of major and specialized trial courts usually stand unchallenged. Only around 5 percent of lower-court cases are appealed, mainly because great expense and years of waiting are certain to be involved.

Unified court systems consolidate the various trial courts with overlapping jurisdictions into a single administrative unit and clearly specify each court's purpose and jurisdiction. The aim of this arrangement, which includes centralized management and rulemaking, is to make the work of the courts more efficient, saving time and money and avoiding confusion. Instead of a system whereby each judge runs his or her own fiefdom, such responsibilities as rulemaking, recordkeeping, budgeting, and personnel management are standardized and centralized, usually under the authority of the state supreme court or the chief justice.

Centralization relieves judges from some of the mundane tasks of day-to-day court management so that they can concentrate on adjudication. Additional efficiencies are gained from *offices of court administration,* which exist in all states. Court administration in most states involves actively managing, monitoring, and planning the courts' resources and operations.

Information technology is permitting tremendous improvements in the way the courts manage criminal cases. In Los Angeles County, which has the largest local government justice system in the country, Consolidated Criminal History Reporting System (called "Cheers") consolidates the databases of fifty law enforcement agencies, twenty-one prosecutor's offices, twenty-four municipal courts, and sixty-two other authorities. Judges and other law enforcement authorities have instant access to the case histories of defendants, as well as to computerized fingerprint-matching technology.[9] Responsiveness to the public is also growing. An increasing number of state courts are electronically disseminating court documents; judicial

After being a couple for twelve years, two gay men receive their marriage certificate in Boston, Massachusetts.
*SOURCE:* AP Photo/Steven Senne

rulings; and general information such as instructions for jury duty, maps showing directions to the courthouse, and answers to commonly asked questions about the courts. Some display photographs and biographies of judges, many permit interested citizens to ask questions via e-mail, and others even provide performance evaluations of judges and broadcast cases live over the Internet. (See Internet Resources at the end of the chapter).

Despite consolidation and centralization, court structures and processes continue to vary widely among the states, as shown in Figure 9.1. Generally, the most modern systems are found in the "newer" states, including Alaska and Hawaii, whereas some of the most antiquated are situated in southern states, among them Arkansas and Georgia.

**FIGURE 9.1**

**Complexity and Simplicity in State Court Systems**

### New York
(Court structure as of Calendar Year 2006)

**Court of Appeals**    COLR
*7 judges*

CSP Case Types:
- Mandatory jurisdiction in civil, capital criminal, administrative agency, juvenile, original proceedings cases.
- Discretionary jurisdiction in civil, criminal, administrative agency, juvenile, disciplinary, original proceedings cases.

**Appellate Divisions of Supreme Court**    IAC
*56 justices sit in panels in 4 departments*    A

CSP Case Types:
- Mandatory jurisdiction in civil, criminal, administrative agency, juvenile, lawyer disciplinary, original proceedings, interlocutory decision cases.
- Discretionary jurisdiction in civil, criminal, juvenile, original proceedings, interlocutory decision cases.

**Appellate Terms of Supreme Court**    IAC
*15 justices sit in panels in 3 terms*

CSP Case Types:
- Mandatory jurisdiction in civil, criminal, juvenile, interloctuory decision cases.
- Discretionary jurisdiction in criminal, juvenile, interlocutory decision cases.

**Supreme Court (12 districts)**    GJC
*326 justices plus 59 judges from the Court of Claims*    A
*Jury trials*

CSP Case Types:
- Tort, contract, real property, miscellaneous civil.
- Exclusive marriage dissolution.
- Felony, misdemeanor.

**County Court (57 countries outside NYC)**    GJC
*129 judges (of which 50 serve the Surrogates' Court and 6 serve the Family Court)*
*Jury trials*

CSP Case Types:
- Tort, contract, real property ($0-$25,000), civil appeals, miscellaneous civil.
- Criminal.

**Court of Claims (1 court)**    LJC
*86 judges (of which 59 act as Supreme Court justices)*
*No jury trials*

CSP Case Types:
- Tort, contract, real property involving the state.

**Surrogates' Court (62 counties)**    LJC
*31 surrogates plus 50 judges from the County Court*
*Jury trials in probate/estate*
CSP Case Types:
- Probate/estate.
- Adoption.

**City Court (79 courts in 61 cities)**    LJC
*158 judges*
*Jury trials for highest level misdemeanor*
CSP Case Types:
- Tort, contract, real property ($0–15,000), small claims (up to $3,000)
- Felony, misdemeanor, preliminary hearings.
- Traffic infractions, ordiance violations.

**Family Court (62 counties)**    LJC
*127 judges plus 6 judges from the County Court and 81 quasi-judicial staff*
*No jury trials*
CSP Case Types:
- Guardianship.
- Domestic relations.
- Exclusive domestic violence.
- Exclusive juvenile.

**District Court (Nassau and Suffolk counties)**    LJC
*50 judges*
*Jury trials except in traffic*
CSP Case Types:
- Tort, contract, real property ($0–15,000), small claims (up to $3,000)
- Felony, misdemeanor, preliminary hearings.
- Traffic infractions, ordinance violations.

**Town and Village Justice Court**    LJC
**(1,487 courts)**    Locally funded
*2,300 justices*
*Jury trials in most cases*

CSP Case Types:
- Tort, contract, real property ($0–3,000), small claims (up to $3,000)
- Misdemeanor, preliminary hearings.
- Traffic/other violations.

**Civil Court of the City of New York (1 court)**    LJC
*120 judges*
*Jury trials*
CSP Case Types:
- Tort, contract, real property ($0–25,000), small claims, (up to $3,000), miscellaneous civil.

**Criminal Court of the City of New York (1 court)**    LJC
*107 judges*
*Jury trials for highest level misdemeanor*
CSP Case Types:
- Misdemeanor, preliminary hearings.
- Traffic infractions, ordinance violations.

Legend
⬭ = Appellate level
⬭ = Trial level

COLR = Court of Last Resort
IAC = Intermediate Appellate Court
GJC = General Jurisdiction Court
LJC = Limited Jurisdiction Court
A = Appeal from Admin. Agency
↑ = Route of appeal

FIGURE
9.1

**Minnesota**
(Court structure as a Calendar Year 2006)

**Supreme Court**                                                              COLR
*7 justices sit en banc*                                                          A

CSP Case Types:
- Mandatory jurisdiction in criminal, administrative agency, disciplinary, certified questions from federal court cases.
- Discretionary jurisdiction in civil, criminal, administrative agency, juvenile, original proceedings cases.

**Court of Appeals**                                                            IAC
*16 judges sit en banc and in panels*                                             A

CSP Case Types:
- Mandatory jurisdiction in civil, criminal, administrative agency, juvenile cases.
- Discretionary jurisdiction in civil, criminal, juvenile, original proceeding cases.

**District Court (10 districts)**                                               GJC
*281 judges*
*Jury trials except in small claims and non-extended juvenile jurisdiction cases*

CSP Case Types:
- Tort, contract, real property, small claims (conciliation division; $0–7,500), mental health, probate/estate, miscellaneous civil.
- Domestic relations.
- Criminal.
- Juvenile.
- Traffic/other violations.

**Legend**

⬭ = Appellate level

⬭ = Trial level

COLR = Court of Last Resort
IAC = Intermediate Appellate Court
GJC = General Jurisdiction Court
LJC = Limited Jurisdiction Court
A = Appeal from Admin. Agency

↑ = Route of appeal

SOURCE: State Court Organization, 1998, Washington, D.C.: U.S. Bureau of Justice Statistics.

# HOW JUDGES ARE SELECTED

The quality of a state court system depends heavily on the selection of competent, well-trained judges. According to the American Bar Association (ABA), the leading professional organization for lawyers, judges should be chosen on the basis of solid professional and personal qualifications, regardless of their political views and party identification. Judges should have "superior self-discipline, moral courage, and sound judgment."[10] They should be good listeners. They should be broadly educated and professionally qualified as lawyers. (But five states—Arizona, New Mexico, New York, Texas, and Utah—have a large number of non-law-degreed judges.[11]) An appellate or general trial court judge should also have relevant experience in a lower court or as a courtroom attorney.

For a great many years, however, controversy has swirled around the selection of state judges. Should they be elected by popular vote? Should they be appointed by the governor? By the legislature? Many critics insist that judicial selection be free from politics and interest group influences. Others claim that judges should regularly be held accountable to a majority of the voters or to elected officials for their decisions.

The conflict between judicial independence and accountability is manifest in the types of selection systems used in the states: legislative election, partisan popular election, nonpartisan popular election, the merit plan, and gubernatorial appointment. Most states use a single selection system for all appellate and major trial court judges. The others take separate approaches to selecting judges, depending on the tier. Figure 9.2 shows the popularity of these selection techniques for appellate and major trial courts. Some states have rather elaborate systems that defy simple categorization. Oklahoma, for example, utilizes a merit plan for the supreme court and court of criminal appeals, nonpartisan elections for its other appellate courts and district courts, and city council appointment of municipal judges.

## Legislative Election

In South Carolina and Virginia, the legislature elects judges by majority vote from among announced candidates. Not surprisingly, a substantial majority of judges selected under this plan are former legislators (in South Carolina, the proportion has been close to 100 percent).[12] In these two states, a judgeship is viewed as a highly valued reward for public service and a prestigious cap to a legislative career.

Few people other than legislators approve of legislative election. Indeed, the method is open to criticism. The public has no role in either choosing judges or re-electing them, so democratic accountability is minimal. The judges may be independent, but because the major criterion for selection is service as a legislator, they often lack other qualifications. Legislative service has little connection to the demands of a judgeship.

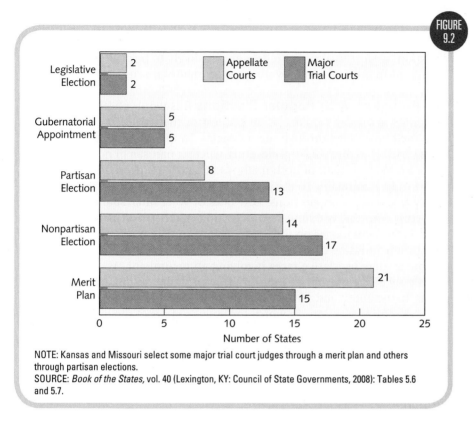

FIGURE 9.2 **State Appellate and Major Trial Court Selection Plans**

NOTE: Kansas and Missouri select some major trial court judges through a merit plan and others through partisan elections.

SOURCE: *Book of the States,* vol. 40 (Lexington, KY: Council of State Governments, 2008): Tables 5.6 and 5.7.

## Popular Election

Judges on one or more courts face elections in thirty-nine states. Some are listed on the ballot by party identification; others are not. In theory, elections maximize the value of judicial accountability to the people. Judges must run for office on the same ticket as candidates for other state offices. Like other candidates, they must raise and spend money for their election campaigns and deal publicly with political issues.

**Partisan Popular Election** This plan enjoyed enormous popularity during the Jacksonian era as a way to create a judiciary answerable to the voters. Most of the partisan election states are located in the South. In theory, partisan elections maximize the value of judicial accountability to the voters.

**Nonpartisan Popular Election** This plan won favor during the first half of the twentieth century, when reformers sought to eliminate party identification in the election of judges and certain other officials in state and local government. Political parties are prohibited from openly taking sides in nonpartisan judicial elections. In reality, they sometimes play a covert role in such contests. The vast majority of judges have a political party preference. Most list it in their official biographies that are available to interested voters during campaigns. A disadvantage of nonpartisan elections is that they tend to reduce voter participation because incumbent judges are less likely to be challenged and party identification is an important voting cue for many citizens.

**The Problems with Popular Elections** It is worth observing that electing judges is virtually unknown in the rest of the world, in which they are appointed or selected through merit systems. In the United States, voter turnout is very low in most judicial elections, whether partisan or nonpartisan. This fact is a major criticism of both methods of electing judges: The winners may not be truly accountable to the people, which is the principal advantage commonly associated with elections. Low rates of voter interest and participation frequently combine with low-key, unexciting, and issueless campaigns to keep many incumbent judges on the bench as long as they run for re-election. One recent study indicates that less than 10 percent are defeated.[13] Still, this is comparable to state legislative races involving an incumbent. And research finds that a state electorate can be mobilized by engaging candidates or distressing events. In the 2000s, judges have been more vulnerable, particularly in partisan elections, and in elections in which the voters's views of the death penalty are harsher than those of the judge.[14]

Two more problems have become increasingly troublesome: the politicization of judicial races and the creeping realization that campaign donations influence decisions from the bench. The ABA Code of Judicial Conduct forbids judicial campaigning on legal issues, but this prohibition is increasingly overlooked in close contests and in elections in which crime-related concerns, such as the death penalty or an accused murderer freed on a legal technicality, claim voters' attention. As in other electoral contests, negative campaigning is on the rise in judicial elections. Judicial candidates today energetically sling mud at their opponents for allegedly letting drug abusers free, being corrupt, or lazy, sympathizing with terrorists, and acting soft on crime. Several states have restricted aggressive judicial politicking through new ethics rules and other limitations. When challenged in federal or state courts, however, such restrictions are usually overturned as intrusions on the candidates' First Amendment rights to free speech.[15]

Even more serious is the problem that occurs when judges elected on a partisan ballot are accused of pandering to special interests during election campaigns and of favoring them in court decisions. In Texas, for instance, supreme court justices deciding a $10.5 billion judgment against Texaco in favor of Pennzoil were criticized for accepting huge campaign contributions from both parties. In some recent Ohio Supreme Court decisions all seven judges accepted money from lawyers for the plaintiffs or defendants.[16] Nonpartisan elected judges have been open to similar charges, especially because political action committees (PACs) have boosted their contributions to candidates for state court judgeships. Research has found systematic empirical evidence that judicial decisions have followed dollars. Similar conclusions have been drawn from case study research on judicial decision making in Alabama, Ohio, and Georgia.[17]

In addition, popular elections are criticized for the growing amount of money necessary to win a state judgeship. And as in legislative and executive branch contests, the candidate who spends the most is likely to win the election.[18] In some cases, the implication is that judges have sacrificed their independence and professionalism for crass electoral politics. Following the trend set in executive and legislative contests, judicial campaign spending in state elections surged to $34.4 million in 2006.[19] In a heated 2004 race for an Illinois state supreme court seat, two candidates spent $4.5 million each. The geographical district in which they ran had experienced high-profile tort litigation, including a $10.1 billion product liability award against Phillip Morris Tobacco Company. The largest campaign contributors are usually trial lawyers, corporations, and other groups with an interest in judges' decisions, such as labor unions; business interests desiring to limit the amount of jury awards for tort litigation; and various professions, such as insurance or medicine.[20] A supreme court incumbent was brought down in West Virginia largely through the efforts of a corporate CEO who had a lawsuit pending before the court. In "a race noted for money and malice,"[21] the CEO provided some $2.3 million to a "friendly" incumbent's opponent. The CEO in question, Don Blankenship of Massey Energy, had shamelessly vacationed with the justice whom he favored in the election.[22] Similarly, enthusiastic spending by business interests angry about large medical malpractice awards generated more than $1.4 million to unseat the first Wisconsin Supreme Court incumbent in forty years.[23]

It looks as though judges running for election are forfeiting their independence in certain legal disputes while offering accountability only to the highest bidders instead of to the general public. If justice is indeed for sale or rent, this trend is the case; neither independence nor accountability is achieved and faith in the legal system is being eroded. According to the president of the Ohio State Bar Association, "The people with money to spend who are affected by court decisions have reached the conclusion that it's a lot cheaper to buy a judge than a governor or an entire legislature, and he can probably do a lot more for you."[24] This sentiment is supported by research showing a positive correlation between campaign contributions and judges' decisions.[25]

If it is unethical for a judge to rule on a case in which he or she has accepted money from one or more of the interested parties, then it would be difficult to bring together enough judges to hear cases in some states. Increasingly, the general sentiment is that judges should be both qualified and dignified, and that elections do not further either objective. The winds of judicial reform are blowing. New Mexico has joined North Carolina and Wisconsin by launching public financing for judges' campaigns to help contain spiraling costs. Other states are imposing spending restrictions and penalties for false campaign advertising by judicial candidates.[26] Meantime, the U.S. Supreme Court ruled, in an important 2009 case involving the West Virginia saga mentioned above, that justices must recuse or disqualify themselves from ruling on cases in which interested or involved campaign donors have spent large sums of money.[27]

## Merit Plan

Dissatisfaction with other methods for selecting judges has led to the popularity of the so-called *merit plan*. Incorporating elements of gubernatorial appointment and elective systems, the merit plan attempts to provide a mechanism for appointing qualified candidates to the bench while permitting the public to evaluate a judge's performance through the ballot box.

First recommended by the ABA in 1937 and strongly supported today by almost the entire legal community, the merit plan has been adopted by nearly all of the states that have changed their selection systems since 1940. Missouri became the initial adopter in 1940. Since then, another twenty-one states have adopted the merit plan, and others are considering merit selection.

**Three Steps** Commonly referred to as the Missouri plan, the basic merit plan involves three steps:

1.  A judicial nominating commission meets and recommends three or more names of prospective judges to the governor. Members of this bipartisan commission usually include a sitting judge (often the chief justice), representatives chosen by the state bar association, and laypersons appointed by the governor. The nominating commission solicits names of candidates, investigates them, chooses those it believes to be the best-qualified individuals, and then forwards three or more names and their files to the governor.
2.  The governor appoints the preferred candidate to the vacant judgeship.
3.  A retention election is held, usually after one or two years, in which the newly appointed judge's name is placed before the voters on a nonpartisan, noncompetitive ticket. The voters decide whether or not the judge should be retained in office. If she is rejected by a majority vote, the judicial nominating commission begins its work anew. Subsequent retention elections may be held every eight or twelve years, depending on the merit plan's provision.

Various hybrids of the basic plan are also in use. For example, the California's plan for choosing appellate judges begins when the governor identifies a candidate for a vacancy on the bench and sends that person's name to the Commission on Judicial Appointments. The commission, composed of two judges and the attorney general, hears testimony regarding the nominee and votes to confirm or reject. The new judge is then accepted or rejected in a retention election in the next regularly scheduled gubernatorial contest. Thus, although the governor appoints, the new judge is subject to confirmation by both the Commission on Judicial Appointments and the voters. In New Mexico's multistage merit plan, a judge is nominated by a commission and appointed by the governor. During the next general election, the judge must run in a partisan election. If he wins, he must run unopposed in a nonpartisan retention election on the next general election ballot.

The object of the merit plan is to permit the governor some appointive discretion while removing politics from the selection of judges. If it works as intended, election or direct gubernatorial appointment is replaced with a careful appraisal of candidates' professional qualifications by an objective commission. The process is intended to ensure both the basic independence of judges and their accountability to the people.

**The Politics of Merit Selection** The merit plan looks great on paper, but in practice it has not fulfilled its promise. First, it has not dislodged politics from judicial selection. A judgeship is too important a political office in any state ever to be immune from politics. It is a prized job and an important point of judicial access for numerous individuals, firms, and interest groups, especially the powerful state bar association.

Studies of judicial nominating commissions show that politics—partisan or nonpartisan—are rampant in the review and nomination of candidates.[28] For better or worse, the legal profession often dominates the process. Counting the judge who presides over the nominating commission, lawyers make up a majority of the commission in most of the states. Bar association lobbying is often the prime reason that merit plans are adopted in the first place. However, the legal profession is not monolithic in its politics: it is often divided into two camps—plaintiff's attorneys and defendant's attorneys.

Furthermore, the governor's influence can be exceptionally strong. The laypersons he appoints to the nominating commission may hold the judge in awe, but they are there to represent the governor's point of view and sometimes to promote specific candidates or the agenda of the governor's political party. In six states, the majority of commission members are laypersons. The member who is a judge may also respect the governor's preferences, particularly if the judge owes her appointment to that chief executive.

A second criticism of the merit plan is that the procedure intended to ensure judicial accountability to the people—the retention election—rarely generates voter interest and seldom results in the departure of an incumbent judge from office. Turnout in retention elections is normally very low and, on average, favors the incumbent by more than 70 percent.[29] Few incumbent judges have been voted out in retention elections—only a handful in nearly sixty years. In most cases, merit selection means a lifetime appointment.

However, voter backlashes have occurred against judges whose decisions are distinctly out of step with public opinion. In 1986, California chief justice Rose Bird and two associate justices were swept from the state supreme court by large margins in retention elections, as voters reacted negatively to a series of supreme court rulings that significantly expanded the rights of the accused and of convicted felons. Bird had voted to overturn all sixty-one capital-punishment cases brought to the court during a period when polls showed 80 percent of the public supported the death penalty in California.[30] Ten years later, Tennessee Supreme Court Justice Penny White was rejected in a retention election for failing to support the death penalty for the perpetrator of a particularly heinous crime.[31]

The final charge leveled against the merit plan is that despite reformers' claims to the contrary, it does not result in the appointment of better-qualified judges or of more women and minorities. When background, education, experience, and decision making are taken into account, judges selected through the merit plan are comparable with those selected through other plans. A large majority are white males. Most leave private practice for the bench in their forties and stay on the bench until retirement. Approximately 20 percent come from a family in which the father or grandfather held political office (often a judgeship).[32] And a substantial majority were born, raised, and educated in the state in which they serve.

## Gubernatorial Appointment

All gubernatorial appointment states are former colonies, reflecting the early popularity of the plan. As a method per se, gubernatorial appointment rates fairly high on independence because the judge is directly appointed without an election, but it is weak on accountability because the judge is beholden to only one person for his or her job.

Although only a handful of states formally recognize it, gubernatorial appointment is in fact the most common method for selecting a majority of appellate and major trial court judges in the United States. Judges in states with popular elections or merit plans often resign or retire from office just before the end of their term.[33] Under most state legal systems, the governor has the power to make interim appointments to vacant seats until the next scheduled election or the commencement of merit-plan selection processes. The governor's temporary appointee then enjoys the tremendous advantage of running as an incumbent for the next full term. Gubernatorial appointment is also used to replace a judge who dies before the expiration of the term.

What criteria does a governor apply in making appointments to the bench? Political considerations usually come first. The governor can use the appointment to reward a faithful legislator, shore up support in certain regions of the state, satisfy the demands of party leaders and the state legal establishment, or appeal to women's groups or to minority groups.[34]

## Which Selection Plan Is Best?

The ongoing debate over which selection plan among the five formal selection systems best achieves a healthy balance of (1) judicial independence from interest groups, attorney organizations, the next election, and other influences and (2) accountability to the people is unlikely to be settled. Legislative election and gubernatorial appointment probably maximize the value of independence, but may be the least desirable because judges selected under these systems tend to come from a rather specific political occupation (the legislature), and the general public has little opportunity to hold them accountable. Judicial accountability is maximized when judges and judicial candidates must face voters, but few incumbents are defeated in elections. (Perhaps the vast majority of sitting judges are capable and competent)? However, significant policy issues involving the courts can rouse the voters to the polls in certain instances, meaning that elected judges who want to stay on the bench must pay attention to public opinion.

None of the prevalent selection systems produces "better" judges, although gubernatorial appointment is more likely to benefit women than the other selection systems are.[35] And minorities have not done particularly well under any selection plan. African Americans fill about 6 percent of state court seats and Latinos 2.5 percent.[36] Interim gubernatorial appointments and nonpartisan elections apparently increase the selection opportunities for African American judges, but significant gains probably await development of a larger pool of minority attorneys.

Politics, of course, is what raises all judges into office, regardless of the selection method. According to research by political scientists, what matters is the path a judge takes to the bench. Those chosen through elective systems tend to view the judiciary in more political—as opposed to juridical—terms than those who reach the bench through gubernatorial or merit appointment systems. Elected judges also tend to be more activist in their decision making and more attentive to voter concerns close to election time, and they are more likely to dissent from other judges in their opinions than are appointed judges.[37] Voter preferences carry extra weight in a judge's decision making when facing competitive elections, particularly with respect to issues of criminal justice, same-sex marriage, and abortion rights.[38] Those in merit-plan states have less to fear from an angry electorate; they can be guided more by personal ideological preferences and their interpretation of the law. In other words, judges who attain their jobs through electoral politics tend to behave like elected officials in the executive and legislative branches of state government by emphasizing political, rather than legal, factors in their decision making.[39] The irony is that voters prefer to elect their judges but they fear that campaign spending influences what judges decide in court.[40]

## Removal of Judges

Like anyone else, judges can and do break the law or become physically incapable of carrying out their responsibilities. If a judge displays serious deficiencies, he must be removed from the bench. Forty-five states provide for impeachment, wherein charges are filed in the statehouse of representatives and a trial is conducted in the senate. Other traditional means for removing justices include the legislative address and popular recall. In the legislative address, both houses of the legislature, by two-thirds vote, must ask the governor to dismiss a judge. Popular recall requires a specified number of registered voters to petition for a special election to recall the judge before her term has expired. Angry Nevada voters attempted to recall six supreme court justices in 2003 for ruling invalid a popular tax-limitation initiative. But these traditional mechanisms are cumbersome and uncertain, and hence seldom successful.

Today, states generally use more practical methods to remove judges. Problems related to senility and old age are avoided in at least thirty-seven states by a mandatory retirement age (generally seventy years) or by the forfeiture of pensions for judges serving beyond the retirement age. Such measures have the added benefit of opening the courtrooms to new and younger judges, even in situations where advancing age does not impair performance.

Most states have established special entities to address behavioral problems. *Courts of the judiciary*, whose members are all judges, and *judicial discipline and removal commissions*, composed of judges, lawyers, and laypersons, are authorized to investigate complaints about judges' qualifications, conduct, or fitness. These entities may reject allegations if they are unfounded, privately warn a judge if the charges are not serious, or hold formal hearings. Hearings may result in dismissal of the charges; recommendation for early retirement; or, in some states, outright suspension or removal. Finally, in some states, chief justices can suspend a lower-court judge indefinitely for misbehavior.

The discipline, suspension, or removal of state court judges is uncommon, but it becomes necessary in all states at one time or another. Judges have been found guilty of drunkenness and drug abuse, sexual misconduct with witnesses and defendants, soliciting and accepting bribes, buying and selling verdicts, and just about every other kind of misconduct imaginable, including taking kickbacks for sentencing teenagers to privately operated detention centers in Pennsylvania.[41] Sometimes judicial ethics seem to be in short supply. In Rhode Island, a state seldom celebrated as a paragon of political virtue, two consecutive supreme court chief justices vacated the bench when faced with impeachment. One resigned in 1986 following allegations and testimony that he associated with criminals and had adulterous relations with two women in a Mafia-linked motel, among other things. And in 1994, another pleaded guilty to using court money to pay for personal expenses, fixing friends' and relatives' speeding tickets, and ordering his secretary to destroy financial records.[42] In 2003, Alabama chief justice Roy Moore was removed by the Court of Judiciary for defying federal and state court orders to haul away a two-and-a-half-ton Ten Commandments monument he had installed in the state judicial building.

## JUDICIAL DECISION MAKING

What factors influence the rulings of state court judges? Why are some courts widely recognized as liberal (California, Hawaii) and others as tough on crime (Arizona, Mississippi)? Why does a prosecutor "judge shop," preferring to file a case before one judge rather than another? Isn't justice supposed to be blind, like its symbol of the woman holding the scales?

Judges, alas, are mortal beings like the rest of us. The formalities and legal jargon of the courtroom tend to mask the fact that judges' decisions are no less discretionary and subjective than the decisions of a governor, legislator, or agency head. Before we examine the factors that affect judicial decision making, however, we must distinguish between the legal settings of appellate courts and trial courts.

## In and Out of the Trial Court

Approximately 90 percent of all civil and criminal cases are resolved outside the courtroom or through guilty pleas. In many civil cases, the defendant never appears in court to defend himself, thereby implicitly admitting his guilt and therefore losing the case by default. Other civil cases are settled in a pretrial conference between the defendant and the plaintiff (where, for instance, payments on an overdue debt might be rescheduled) or through voluntary dispute resolution procedures.

The process of settling criminal cases out of court at the discretion of the prosecutor and the judge is called **plea bargaining**. Although some defendants plead guilty as originally charged, acknowledging guilt for a lesser charge is more typical in criminal proceedings. With the possible exceptions of the victim and the general citizenry, everyone benefits from plea bargaining, a fact that helps account for its extensive use. The accused gets off with lighter punishment than she would face if the case went to trial and she lost. The defense attorney frees up time to take on additional legal work. The prosecuting attorney increases his conviction rate, which looks good if he has political ambitions. The judge helps cut back the number of cases awaiting trial. Even police officers benefit by not having to spend time testifying (and waiting to testify) and by raising the department's clearance rate (the number of cases solved and disposed of).

Out-of-court settlements through plea bargaining are negotiated in an informal atmosphere in the judge's chamber, between attorneys in the halls of the court building, or over drinks in a neighboring pub. This is a disturbingly casual way to dispense justice. The process is secretive and far removed from any notion of due process. The prosecuting (district) attorney enjoys enormous discretion in making deals. Often the propensity to settle depends on the length of the prosecuting attorney's court docket or her professional relationship with the accused's attorney, not on the merits of the case. All too often an innocent person pleads guilty to a lesser offense for fear of being wrongly convicted of a more serious offense, or because he cannot post bail and doesn't want to spend any unnecessary time behind bars. Equally disturbing, particularly to a victim, is the fact that plea bargaining can soon put a guilty person back on the streets, perhaps to search for another victim.

Nonetheless, plea bargaining is widely practiced. It is almost inevitable when the prosecutor's case hinges on weak evidence, police errors, a questionable witness, or the possibility of catching a bigger fish. Negotiation of a guilty plea for a lesser offense can occur at any stage of the criminal justice process.

If the accused is unable to reach a compromise with the prosecuting attorney, he faces either a **bench trial** by a single judge or a **trial by jury**. Both involve a courtroom hearing with all the legal formalities. In some jurisdictions and for certain types of cases, the defendant has a choice. In other situations, state legal procedures specify which trial format will be utilized. A jury is always mandatory for murder cases.

In a bench trial, the judge alone hears all arguments, determines the facts, and makes rulings on questions of law. Jury trials depend on a panel of citizens who decide the facts of the case; the judge instructs the jury on the applicable

**plea bargaining**
Negotiation between a prosecutor and a criminal defendant's counsel that results in the defendant pleading guilty to a lesser charge or pleading guilty in exchange for a reduced sentence.

**bench trial**
Trial by a single judge, without a jury.

**trial by jury**
A trial in which a jury decides the facts and makes a finding of guilty or not guilty.

law. Although judges and juries would usually reach the same decision, the uncertainty introduced by twelve laypersons is usually great enough to convince a defendant to choose a bench trial or, if offered, alternative dispute resolution such as mediation to settle the dispute prior to trial. Only 2 percent of all cases are resolved by jury trial.[43]

When jury trials do occur, attorneys seek to limit the unpredictable nature of juries by extensively questioning individuals in the jury pool. Each side in the dispute has the right to strike the names of a certain number of potential jurors without giving a specific reason. Others are eliminated for cause, such as personal knowledge of the case or its principals. In high-stakes cases, the jury-selection process involves public opinion surveys, individual background investigations of potential jurors, and other costly techniques.

Many courts experience problems in getting people to perform their civic duty of jury service. Juror shortages can seriously impede the value of a speedy trial. Some individuals shirk from jury duty to avoid the accompanying loss of income from their regular job. Others may not be able to arrange day care or elder care. With increasing frequency, some people simply shirk their responsibility to serve. Judges may respond to those who ignore their summons by sending the sheriff or bailiff to round them up and haul them before the judge. In North Dakota, New Jersey, and elsewhere, their names are published in the local newspaper. Turning to positive incentives, some states are improving the jury duty experience by installing computer workstations, snack rooms, libraries, and other amenities in the jury lounge.[44]

## Inside the Appellate Court

Appellate courts are substantially different from trial courts: no plaintiffs, defendants, or witnesses are present; no bargaining or pre-decision settlement is allowed. The appeal consists of a review of court records and arguments directed by the attorneys, who frequently are not the same lawyers who originally represented the parties. Appellate court rulings are issued by a panel of at least three judges who are tasked with deciding if legal errors have occurred. Unlike decisions in most trial courts, appellate court decisions are written and published. The majority vote prevails. Judges voting in the minority have the right to make a formal, written dissent that justifies their opinion.

State supreme courts vary dramatically in ideology. Those in Hawaii, Rhode Island, and Maryland are much more liberal than those in Arizona, Mississippi, and New Hampshire. There is marked variation in the dissent rates of state appellate courts. Some courts maintain a public aura of consensus on even the most controversial matters by almost always publishing unanimous opinions. Justices may disagree, but they do not necessarily officially dissent. Other courts are rocked by public disputes over legal questions. Personal, professional, partisan, political, and other disagreements can spill over into open hostility over casework. As an Illinois chief justice observed, "Dissents are born not of doubt but of firm convictions."[45] Supreme courts in states such as

California, New York, Michigan, and Mississippi have a history of contentiousness, whereas others, like those in Rhode Island and Maryland, are paragons of harmony. Dissent rates appear to be positively related to a state's socioeconomic and political complexity, such as urbanization and partisan competition. More dissent occurs in courts with a large number of justices and with intermediate appellate courts. The more time justices have at their disposal, the more likely they are to find reasons to disagree.

## Influence of the Legal System

In addition to the facts of the case itself, judicial decision making is influenced by factors associated with the legal system, including institutional arrangements, accepted legal procedures, caseload pressures, and the ease with which certain interested parties gain access to the legal process.

**1. Institutional Arrangements** The level, or tier, of court is a structural characteristic that influences decision making. Trial court judges enforce legal norms and routinely *apply* the law as it has been written and interpreted over the years. The trial court permits direct interpersonal contacts among the judge, the jury, and the parties (usually individuals and small businesses). Divorce cases, personal injury cases, traffic-related cases, and minor criminal cases predominate in trial courts.

Appellate courts are more apt to interpret the law and create public policy. State constitutional issues, state–local conflicts, and challenges to government regulation of business are the kinds of issues likely to be found in appellate courts. Cases typically involve government and large corporations. A particular case in a high court sometimes has an enormous impact on public policy, for example, when judges depart from established precedent or offer new interpretations of the law. Recently, the Wisconsin Supreme Court essentially overturned a constitutional amendment guaranteeing the right to carry a concealed weapon, the supreme court of Massachusetts legalized same-sex marriages, and Nevada's highest court nullified a state constitutional provision that two-thirds of the legislature must approve tax increases. Florida's supreme court struck down an education voucher system that permitted children to attend private schools at the public's expense, and New Jersey's and New York's have instructed the legislature to recognize civil (gay) unions.

Another important institutional arrangement is the selection procedure for judges. For instance, judicial decisions may be influenced by partisan electoral competition. Especially when a judge facing re-election must vote on an issue highly salient to voters, public opinion can affect the judge's ruling.[46] Death penalty cases provide a good example of this point. A study of judicial decision making in Texas, North Carolina, Louisiana, and Kentucky found that judges seeking re-election tend to uphold death sentences. In these traditionally conservative states, a decision in support of the death penalty helps to avoid unwanted pre-election criticism from political opponents.[47]

**stare decisis**

A legal doctrine that precedent set in earlier cases should guide judges' decisions.

**precedent**

The legal principle that previous similar court decisions should be applied to future decisions.

**2. Legal Procedures and Precedent** Under the legal doctrine of *stare decisis* and on the basis of **precedent**, the principles and procedures of law applied in one situation are applied in any similar situation. In addition, lower courts are supposed to follow the precedents established by higher courts. An individual decision may seem unimportant, but when it is made in the context of other similar cases, it helps judicial precedent evolve. Through this practice, the doctrine of equal treatment before the law is pursued. When lower-court judges refuse to follow precedent or are ignorant of it, their decisions can be overturned on appeal. Of course, several conflicting precedents may relate to a case; in such instances, a judge is permitted to choose among them in justifying his ruling. A previous decision may become obsolete, may be manifestly absurd, or may simply clash with a judge's values or point of view.

Where do judges find precedent? Within a state, supreme court decisions set the norms. Supreme courts themselves, however, scan the legal landscape beyond state boundaries. In the past, decisions of the U.S. Supreme Court heavily influenced those of the state supreme courts. Increasingly, however, state supreme courts are practicing doctrinal diversity and looking to one another for precedent. State appellate judges borrow from and cite the experiences and decisions of other states. They especially tend to rely on the more professional, prestigious supreme courts, such as those of California, Colorado, and Washington.[48] State courts also tend to network with courts in the same region of the country, where cultural and other environmental factors are similar.[49]

**3. Caseload Pressures** Caseload affects judges' decisions. The number of cases varies in accordance with crime rates, socioeconomic characteristics of the jurisdictions, state laws, the number of judges, and many other variables. It stands to reason that the quality of judicial decision making is inversely related to caseload. Judges burdened by too much litigation are hard-pressed to devote an adequate amount of time and attention to each case before them.

**4. Access to the System** The final legal-system characteristic affecting judicial decisions is the access of individuals, organizations, and groups to the court system. Wealthy people and businesses are better able to pay for resources (attorneys, legal research, and so on) and therefore enter the legal system with a great advantage over poorer litigants. (Perhaps this helps account for the reason that African American and Latino defendants tend to receive harsher sentences than white defendants do.[50]) Special-interest groups also enjoy certain advantages in influencing judicial decisions. They often have specialized knowledge in areas of litigation, such as environmental or business regulation. Lobbying by interest groups is much less prominent in the judicial branch than it is in the legislative and executive branches, but groups can affect outcomes by providing financial aid to litigants in important cases and by filing *amicus curiae* (friend of the court) briefs supporting one side or the other in a dispute, or, in popular election systems, making monetary contributions to a judge's re-election campaign.

The states have implemented several reforms to increase access to the judicial system for those who are disadvantaged. For example, court interpreter training is now available in states with large Latino populations. Physical and communication barriers are being removed so that persons with disabilities can participate fully in all aspects of the legal system. Racial, ethnic, and gender biases against attorneys, plaintiffs, defendants, witnesses, and other court participants are being addressed (although women tend to receive less severe sentences than men who commit similar crimes).[51] Night courts remain open late for people who have difficulty getting off their day jobs to appear in court. And day care is being provided for children of plaintiffs, defendants, witnesses, and jurors. Gradually, the state courts are responding to changes in the nature of society.

### Personal Values, Attitudes, and Characteristics of Judges

Simply put, judges do not think and act alike. Each is a product of individual background and experiences, which in turn influence decisions made in the courtroom. Studies of state court justices have found that decisions are related to the judges' party identification, political ideology, prior careers, religion, age, and sex. In other words, personal characteristics predispose a judge to decide cases in certain ways.

For example, Democratic judges tend to favor the claimant in civil rights cases, the injured party in liability (tort) cases, the government in tax disputes, the employee in worker's compensation cases, the government in business regulation cases, the defendant in criminal contests, the union in disagreements with management, and the tenant in landlord–tenant cases. Republicans tend to support the opposite side on all these issues. Female judges, who now occupy one out of four seats on supreme courts, are more supportive of women on sex discrimination and other feminist issues; more likely to favor the accused in obscenity and death penalty cases; and, in general, are more liberal than their male colleagues.[52] And finally, the judge's race appears to have little effect on the sentences handed down to black and white defendants, although African American judges, according to one study cited above, tend to be tougher when sentencing all defendants than are Latino judges.[53] Obviously, these distinctions do not hold in all situations, but the point is that *justice* is an opaque concept. No wonder attorneys try to shop around for the most sympathetic judge before filing a legal action.

# JUDICIAL FEDERALISM

During the 1950s and 1960s, the U.S. Supreme Court was the leading judicial actor in the land. Under Chief Justice Earl Warren (1953–1969) and his liberal majority, the Court handed down a long series of rulings that overturned racial segregation, mandated legislative reapportionment, extended voting rights, and expanded the rights of accused criminals. Significant reversals of state court decisions were commonplace.

**judicial federalism**

A trend in which state constitutional and statutory laws are consulted and applied before federal law.

Beginning with Chief Justice Warren Burger (1969–1986) and a growing faction of conservative justices, however, the Supreme Court changed direction. Since 1988, a conservative majority has been in control. The Court has been less intrusive in state and local affairs and has, through its own caution, flashed a green light to state courts inclined to activism (see Chapter 2). The result is **judicial federalism**, in which state courts look first to state constitutional and statutory laws in rendering legal judgments on important state and local issues once addressed mostly by the federal courts.

## Judicial Activism in the States

**judicial activism**

The making of public policy by judges through decisions that overturn existing law or effectively make new laws.

**Judicial activism** is a value-laden term with ideological dimensions.[54] When associated with politically liberal court decisions, it is decried by conservatives. However, conservative judges are also activists. Whether liberal or conservative, all tend to show strong ideological tendencies.

An objective definition of judicial activism, then, points to court-generated change in public policy that is perceived as illegitimate by opponents who favor the status quo.[55] Judicial activism is in the eye of the beholder. All too often, an "activist" judge is one who doesn't decide a case the way one *thinks* he should.

Regardless of one's feelings on the matter, state supreme courts have clearly become *more* activist by expanding into new policy areas. They are more likely to be involved in the policy-making process by making decisions that affect policy in the executive branch, and many even appear to pre-empt the lawmaking responsibility of the legislature when, in exercising the power of judicial review, they invalidate a statute based on constitutional grounds.

Recent examples of judicial federalism include the following:

- California, Connecticut, and Massachusetts courts have expanded a woman's right to abortion on demand and the right to financial aid from the state for abortions. Virginia, acting to the contrary, requires parental consent before an abortion can be obtained by an underage girl.
- Although the U.S. Supreme Court has upheld state sodomy prohibitions, courts in New York, Pennsylvania, and other states have struck down sodomy laws as violations of the right to privacy, as spelled out in the state constitution. And, as noted earlier, the Massachusetts supreme court has recognized the state constitutional right of same-sex couples to wed.
- Oregon's supreme court rejected a U.S. Supreme Court decision that provided guidelines for declaring certain printed and visual materials to be obscene. The Oregon court noted that its state constitution had been authored "by rugged and robust individuals dedicated to founding a free society unfettered by the governmental imposition of some peoples' views of morality on the free expression of others." The court went on to declare, "In this state, any person can write, paint, read, say, show or sell anything to a consenting adult even though that expression may generally or universally be considered 'obscene.' "[56]

How can state courts override the decisions of the highest court in the United States? The answer is that they are grounding their rulings in their own constitutions instead of basing them on the national constitution. In several decisions, the U.S. Supreme Court has upheld the right of the states to expand on the minimum rights and liberties guaranteed under the national document. Of course, when there is an irreconcilable conflict between state and federal laws, the latter prevails.

## Current Trends in State Courts

The wave of state court activism is not carrying all the states with it. Many state supreme courts remain caught in the doldrums, consistently endorsing—rather than repudiating—U.S. Supreme Court decisions. Some of them are so quiet, as one wag suggested, "that you can hear their arteries harden." But even traditionally inactive courts in states such as Wisconsin and North Carolina have been stirred into independent actions recently, and the trend is continuing.[57] The U.S. Supreme Court is likely to have a conservative majority for the foreseeable future, permitting the state courts to explore the legal landscape further. However, state court activism seems to be contagious, as courts utilize their own information and case networks instead of those of the U.S. Supreme Court.

Of course, with rare exceptions, judges cannot seize issues as governors and legislators can; they must wait for litigants to bring them to the courthouse. Although judges can issue rulings, they must depend on the executive and legislative branches to comply with and enforce those rulings. Nonetheless, many state supreme courts are becoming more active in the policy-making process.[58] The reluctance of the federal courts to address important and controversial issues comprehensively has resulted in more cases for state supreme courts to decide.

State court activism does have some negative points. First, some courts may overstep their authority and try to go too far in policy making, intruding into the proper domain of executive and legislative actors—not to mention that of the voters. The Nevada Supreme Court's nullification of a two-thirds legislative majority on tax hikes is a rather extreme example. One problem is that judges have little knowledge or expertise in the substance of public policy or in the policy-making process. They have no specialized staff to perform in-depth policy research on particular policy issues, and they cannot realistically depend on lawyers to do policy research for them. After all, lawyers are trained and practiced in legal reasoning and process, not social or political science. Second, state courts are increasingly issuing policy decisions that have significant budgetary implications. Court rulings on school finance, prison overcrowding, and treatment of the mentally ill have severely affected state budgets. Such court actions rarely take into account their related financial effects. A third problem is that in the context of state constitutional rights, geography is limiting. A state-by-state approach may not be appropriate for policies in areas such as civil rights, clean air, or safe food, which should be equal for all citizens.

# ADMINISTRATIVE AND ORGANIZATIONAL IMPROVEMENTS IN STATE COURTS

We have already discussed several important judicial reforms: intermediate appellate courts, court consolidation and unification, merit-selection plans for judges, more practical means for disciplining and removing judges, and administrative and organizational improvements, including those of a financial nature. This last category deserves further consideration.

## Financial Improvements, Financial Pressures

The exorbitant costs of some trials can bankrupt local jurisdictions if state financial assistance is not forthcoming. For example, one child molestation case in Los Angeles County lasted two and a half years and carried a tab of $15 million. (Neither of the two defendants was convicted). The price tag for a murder trial and subsequent appeals can also be counted in the millions. A high-profile multiple murder case in Georgia effectively drained the public defender system of funds in 2007 and halted proceedings in seventy-two other capital cases.[59]

The national economic collapse of 2008–2009 resulted in substantial cuts to state court budgets, with serious consequences for indigent defendants and all parties interested in justice and speedy trials. New Hampshire suspended jury trials for a month in 2009, Florida laid off 10 percent of its court employees, and caseloads for prosecutors, public defenders, and judges soared nationally with rising numbers of foreclosures, civil disputes, and other filings.[60]

In response to such budget crises in the past, more than half of the states assumed full financial responsibility for the operation of state and local courts. Through centralized budgeting (also referred to as *unified court budgeting*), a consolidated budget for all state and local courts is prepared by the chief administrative officer of the state court system, detailing all personnel, supplies, equipment, and other expenditures. This enhances financial management and helps maintain judicial independence from the executive and legislative branches. Legislatures have been known to threaten and even implement court budget cuts because of displeasure with unpopular rulings.[61] A unified court system, centralized management and financing, and unified budgeting share the objective of bringing a state's entire court system under a single authoritative administrative structure, helping to discourage legislative underfunding.

## Dealing with Growing Caseloads

Recently, court reformers have recognized the need to deal more effectively with case backlogs. State trial courts alone entertain some 80 million new cases each year.[62] Some judges hand down more than 300 opinions annually. Delays of two years are not uncommon for appellate court hearings, and the unprecedented pressure is growing.

Excessive caseloads are caused by numerous factors, including the greater propensity of losing parties to appeal lower-court decisions, the tremendous growth in litigation, huge increases in drug-related and drunk-driving cases, and poor caseload-management procedures. Exacerbating the problem is the high demand for litigation aggravated by the prodigious quantity of lawyers in the United States, which accounts for nearly two-thirds of all the lawyers in the world—over 1.1 million at last count. Calls for tort reform to reduce the number of personal injury cases and the size of subsequent awards are common.

The larger concern is that long delays thwart the progress of justice. The quality of evidence deteriorates as witnesses disappear or forget what they saw, and victims suffer from delays that prevent them from collecting damages for injuries incurred during a crime or an accident. Innocent defendants can be harmed by the experience of being held in jail for long periods while awaiting trial. Increasingly, criminal cases are thwarted because of witness intimidation by the accused, his friends, or others who desire to end the prosecution and free the accused.

Reducing excessive caseloads is not a simple matter. Common sense dictates establishing intermediate appellate courts and adding new judgeships. But much like a new highway draws more traffic, intermediate appellate courts, by their very existence, tend to attract more appeals. Although additional judges can speed up the trial process in lower courts, they may also add to appellate backlogs. Expanding the number of judges in an appellate court is also problematic; hearings may take longer because of more input or factional divisions among judges.

The stubborn persistence of case backlogs has led to some interesting and promising new approaches.

1. *Alternative dispute resolution.* Almost all states today use mediation, arbitration, or other techniques to help settle litigation prior to or during formal courtroom proceedings. Mediation involves a neutral third party who tries to help the opponents reach a voluntary agreement. Arbitration consists of a binding ruling by a neutral party in favor of one party or the other. In a growing number of states, civil litigants in search of timely settlement hire private judges to arbitrate their disputes.
2. *Fines against lawyers and litigants.* New laws or court rules allow judges to levy monetary fines against lawyers and litigants guilty of delaying tactics, frivolous litigation, or standards violations that require cases to be heard within a specified time period.
3. *Case management systems.* Judges can take charge of their dockets and impose a no-nonsense case management system. Although individual systems vary widely, a typical approach is multitracking, or *differentiated case management.* It distinguishes between simple and complex cases, as well as between frivolous and potentially significant cases, and treats them differently. Complex and significant cases are waved down the traditional appellate track. Simple and frivolous cases take a shorter track, usually under the direction of staff attorneys. In Vermont, this case management system is referred to as the "rocket docket." Experiments with multitracking have been successful in reducing case delays in Arizona, Maine, New Hampshire, and other states. As noted earlier, another case management innovation designed to speed

the wheels of justice is problem-solving or *boutique* courts, in which environmental law disputes, drug cases, or others with special characteristics are heard by judges in specialized courts.

4. *New technology.* Technological innovations are also improving the quality and quantity of court operations. Electronic databases (e.g., LEXIS and WESTLAW) are used to store case information and legal research and to transmit information from law offices to courts. Electronic filing of court documents and online access to court information for attorneys and citizens helps track child support payments, store case data for legal research, transmit from law offices to courts, and, in general, saves the courts money and staff time. Videotaping of witnesses' testimony is becoming common. Arraignment procedures, during which suspects are formally charged, are videotaped to save time or to prevent potential problems from a disruptive defendant. Video courtrooms, in which trials are filmed, create a more accurate trial record and cost much less than a written transcript by a court stenographer. Lawyers in high-tech courtrooms speed up proceedings by using PowerPoint, video clips, and Internet sources, all displayed for jurors on individual monitors. Audiovisual technology permits hearings, motions, pleas, sentencing, and other proceedings to be conducted long distance between the jail and the courthouse, thereby saving money and enhancing security.

5. *Performance standards.* The National Center for State Courts has developed performance standards for state trial courts to aid self-assessment and improvement.[63] A growing number of states are not only adopting quantitative indicators of the speed with which cases are processed but are also trying to measure broader concerns such as access to justice, fairness and integrity, public trust and confidence, and the quality of judges' decision making.

## Compensating the Judges

At first glance, judicial salaries seem high enough. State supreme court judges earned an average of approximately $150,000.[64] The variation is great: California justices make $218,000, whereas their counterparts in Montana are paid only $106,185. Trial court judges are paid 10–20 percent less. However, these amounts are substantially below what an experienced, respected attorney can expect to make. A successful lawyer who gives up private practice and perhaps a lucrative partnership for the bench must be willing to take a considerable cut in income. Unlike legislators, state judges are permitted little outside income. Therefore, it is reasonable to ask whether the best legal minds will be attracted to judgeships, given that judicial compensation is relatively low. This dilemma exists at all levels and in all branches of public service, from the municipal finance officer to the highway patrol officer, because most state and local government compensation lags behind that for comparable jobs in the private sector. If we expect our judges, law enforcement officers, and other public employees to be honest, productive, and highly qualified, they must be compensated fairly. Recent salary increases for state judges seem to reflect this principle.

## Judicial Performance Evaluation

Who judges the judges? In popular election and merit system states, the voters hold judges accountable. But voters have no voice in gubernatorial and legislative selection states. And even when judicial elections are held, how much do the voters really know about the candidates?

Judicial performance evaluation (JPE) offers an objective process to assess the performance of judges. Voters are educated, and judges are encouraged to use evaluation results for self-improvement. First adopted by Alaska in 1975, JPE programs are now mandated in eighteen additional states and under active consideration in several others. JPE involves confidential surveys of attorneys, court professionals, witnesses, jurors, and other court participants. Respondents are questioned about how the judge interprets the law, manages her workload, and interacts with people in the courtroom, among other factors.[65]

Indications are that JPE can contribute to judicial self-improvement and provide valuable, job-related information on judges' performance to the voters. Used appropriately, JPE helps preserve the hallmark characteristics of independence and accountability of the judiciary.[66]

## State Courts Today

Like the other two branches of government, the state judiciary has been reformed significantly. Court systems have been modernized and simplified, intermediate appellate courts have been added, processes have been streamlined, and case delays have been reduced. Disciplinary and removal commissions now make it easier to deal with problem judges, and JPE furnishes useful data on judicial performance. But courts are still striving for greater independence from political pressures and favoritism and more accountability for their actions. Justice may appear at times to be an ephemeral ideal, and an expensive one at that, but it is more likely to be approximated in state judicial decisions today than ever before. The courts, like the rest of society, are no longer immune to the technological age. New innovations and approaches will follow the recommendations of commissions in states now studying the needs of state judicial systems in the future.

Court modernization and reform have been accompanied by increased judicial activism. The newly assertive state courts have far surpassed the federal courts in public policy activism. They sometimes blatantly disagree with federal precedents and insist on decisions grounded in state constitutional law rather than in the national constitution. In short, the state courts are proactively responding to public concerns with the administration of justice.

## CHAPTER RECAP

- State courts are organized into two tiers: appellate courts and trial courts.

- Structural reforms such as unified court systems have sought to make the courts more efficient and effective.

- The five methods for selecting judges are legislative election, partisan election, nonpartisan election, merit plan, and gubernatorial appointment. Each selection plan has certain advantages and disadvantages—there is no "one best way."

- Many factors influence judicial decision making, including institutional arrangements; legal procedures; case precedent; caseload pressures; access to the legal system; and the personal values, attitudes, and characteristics of judges.

- Judicial federalism is related to increased capability and judicial activism in many state courts.

- Efforts to reform state courts include financial improvements, better caseload management, and improved compensation for judges.

## Key Terms

civil case *(p. 240)*
criminal case *(p. 240)*
administrative case *(p. 240)*
common law *(p. 240)*
limited jurisdiction trial courts *(p. 241)*

major trial courts *(p. 243)*
supreme court *(p. 243)*
intermediate appellate court *(p. 243)*
plea bargaining *(p. 257)*
bench trial *(p. 257)*

trial by jury *(p. 257)*
*stare decisis (p. 260)*
precedent *(p. 260)*
judicial federalism *(p. 262)*
judicial activism *(p. 262)*

## Internet Resources

The National Center for State Courts (NCSC) maintains a list of courts and their websites. NCSC's website at **www.ncsconline.org** is a rich source of information on the courts, including state court decisions, caseload statistics, and court organization.

Interesting state sites include the following: California at **www.courtinfo.ca.gov**/, Florida at **www.flcourts.org**, and Alaska at **http://courts.alaska.gov**.

The American Bar Association's website at **www.abanet.org/** provides an analysis of current controversial cases and other legal information.

The Law Forum Legal Resources site at **www.lawforum.net** has links to all online state and local courts.

For a detailed examination of all states' judicial selection systems, see **www.ajs.org/**

To watch live performances of Indiana's court proceedings, see **www.in.gov/judiciary/webcast**.

# The Structure of Local Government

10

An article appearing in a 2006 issue of the magazine *Governing* posed a particularly provocative question: "Can Dallas govern itself?" The story went on to detail the "political chaos and bureaucratic mismanagement" that has plagued America's ninth largest city for years. A local columnist criticized the city's governmental structure as "the weak-weak-weak system—weak mayor, weak manager, weak city council."[1] So, it would seem that it was time for a change. However, when given the opportunity to replace their council–manager structure with a strong-mayor form of government, Dallasites voted no. It seems that residents did not want a new structure—they just wanted the one they had to work better.

What do citizens want from their local governments? The answer is, to be governed well. They want governmental structures that work and leaders who are effective. They want jurisdictions with adequate capacity to resolve the tough public problems of our times. But as this chapter demonstrates, "governed well" is hard to achieve. Even with improved capacity, local governments confront a series of challenges.

- Orientations to Communities
- County Government
- Municipal Government
- Towns and Townships
- Special Districts
- School Districts
- Communities and Governance

# ORIENTATIONS TO COMMUNITIES

Communities and their governments can be discussed in many different ways. Theoretically, at least three different orientations have some appeal. When you move from the theoretical realm to legal realities, five types of local governments can be differentiated.

## Theoretical Orientations

In the early days of the United States, communities were idealized as *civic republics*.[2] In a civic republic, community government is based on the principle of mutual consent. Citizens share fundamental beliefs and participate in public affairs. Their motivation for civic involvement is less materialistic self-interest than altruistic concern for community welfare. Although this idea continued to have theoretical appeal, its reality was threatened by the growing and diverse nineteenth-century populace, which preferred to maximize individual liberty and accumulation of wealth. An economically inspired conception of community, that of the *corporate enterprise*, gradually emerged. Economic growth and the ensuing competition for wealth sparked extensive conflict.[3] With the guidance of state government, local governments adopted policies and juggled the clashing interests.

These two theoretical orientations, the community as a civic republic and the community as a corporate enterprise, remain viable. A new orientation has emerged, however—one that portrays the community as a *consumer market*.[4] In a consumer market, citizens are consumers of public services and governments are providers. This idea places increased emphasis on quality of life and cost effectiveness. Individuals make choices about where they will live—in the heart of the city, a suburban jurisdiction, or a rural portion of the county. In each of these locales, the individual will encounter government, or, more accurately, *governments*. The range of government services and their cost vary from one place to another. Informed consumers seek communities that are in line with their preferences. You say that you want to live in the Los Angeles area? You have many jurisdictional choices: Twenty-one cities share a border with the city of Los Angeles. Each one provides a different package of services, in terms of type, quality, and cost—a consumer market, indeed.

**general-purpose local government**
A local government that provides a wide range of functions.

## Five Types of Local Governments

Local government is the level of government that fights crime, extinguishes fires, paves streets, collects trash, maintains parks, provides water, and educates children. Some local governments provide all of these services; others, only some. A useful way of thinking about local governments is to distinguish between general-purpose and single-purpose local governments. **General-purpose local governments** are those that perform a wide range of governmental functions. These include three types of local governments: counties, municipalities, and towns and townships. **Single-purpose local governments**, as the label

**single-purpose local government**
A local government, such as a school district, that performs a specific function.

implies, have a specific purpose and perform one function. School districts and special districts are single-purpose governments. Typically, single-purpose local governments coexist with the general-purpose local governments covering the same territory. For example, the boundaries of a school district may be coterminous with the county, they may cover smaller portions of the county, or even extend over sections of two or more counties.

In the United States, the number of local governments exceeds 89,000. Figure 10.1 shows the number of local governments at two points in time: 1952 and 2007. Among general-purpose local governments, the number of counties and towns and townships decreased slightly over the fifty-five-year period as the number of municipalities increased. In terms of single-purpose local governments, the trends are more dramatic. From 1952 to 2007, nearly 80 percent of America's school districts were abolished or consolidated with surrounding districts; in the same period, special districts have tripled in number.

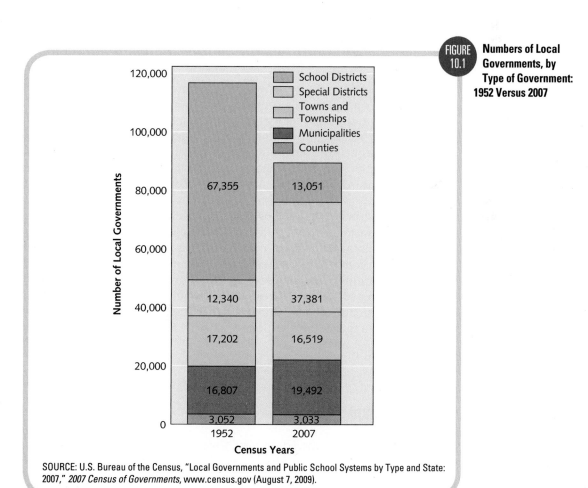

**FIGURE 10.1**  **Numbers of Local Governments, by Type of Government: 1952 Versus 2007**

SOURCE: U.S. Bureau of the Census, "Local Governments and Public School Systems by Type and State: 2007," *2007 Census of Governments*, www.census.gov (August 7, 2009).

Native American reservations are not considered a formal type of local government, even though they perform many local government functions. (Chapter 2 discusses the national–tribal–state relationship in more detail.) **Metropolitan areas**, which are composed of a central city and its surrounding county (or counties), are not local governments either. The label *metropolitan statistical area (MSA)* is used by the federal government to designate urban areas that have reached a minimum 50,000 population threshold. As of 2007, the United States contained 371 MSAs. Another federal designation, **micropolitan statistical area**, refers to places with populations between 10,000 and 49,999. The MSA and micropolitan labels are used for statistical data collection and, in some instances, in federal grant programs.

**metropolitan area**

A central city of at least 50,000 people and its surrounding county (or counties); often called an urban area.

Regardless of the purpose of a local government, we must remember that it has a lifeline to state government. In short, state government gives local government its legal existence. This relationship is not quite the equivalent of a hospital patient hooked up to a life-support system, but it is a basic condition of the local–state link. Local citizens may instill a community with its flavor and its character, but state government makes local government official. Over time, most states have gradually relaxed their control over localities through grants of **home rule**, which give local governments more decision-making power.

**micropolitan statistical area**

An urban cluster with a population between 10,000 and 49,999.

American local governments were not planned according to some grand design. Rather, they grew in response to a combination of citizen demand, interest group pressure, and state government acquiescence. As a consequence, no rational system of local governments exists. What does exist is a collection of autonomous, frequently overlapping jurisdictional units. The number of local governments varies from state to state. Consider the case of Pennsylvania and its 4,871 local jurisdictions. The state contains sixty-six counties, 1,016 cities, 1,546 townships, 1,728 special districts, and 515 school districts.[5] Nevada, on the other hand, has a grand total of 198 local governments.

**home rule**

A broad grant of power from the state to a local government.

Being so close to the people offers special challenges to local governments. Citizens know almost immediately when trash has not been collected or when libraries do not carry current bestsellers. They can contact local officials and attend public hearings. And they do. In a recent survey about interactions with government, over 40 percent of those surveyed said that they had contacted an elected official or attended a community meeting.[6] The interactive nature of local government makes the questions of capacity and proactivity all the more critical.

## COUNTY GOVERNMENT

State governments have carved up their territory into 3,033 discrete, general-purpose subunits called counties (except in Louisiana, where counties are called parishes, and Alaska, where they are called boroughs). Counties exist everywhere, with only a few exceptions: Connecticut and Rhode Island, where there are no functional county governments; Washington, D.C., which is a special case in itself; some municipalities in Virginia that are independent jurisdictions and are not part of the counties that surround them; and cities like Baltimore and St. Louis, which are not part of a county because of past political decisions. Also, some jurisdictions—Philadelphia and San Francisco, for example—are considered cities but are actually consolidated city–county government structures.

## Not All Counties Are Alike

Counties can be differentiated according to their urban/rural nature. Urban, or metropolitan, counties contain one or more large cities and surrounding suburbs and serve as the employment hubs for the area. Los Angeles County, California, with more than 9 million residents—and larger than most states—is the largest county. Even though most Americans live in metropolitan areas, most counties are actually nonmetropolitan; that is, they contain one or more small cities, with the rest of the area sparsely settled. More than three-fourths of American counties have fewer than 100,000 inhabitants. Counties that contain no incorporated places with more than 2,500 residents are the most rural of all. Loving County, Texas, with fewer than 100 people spread over its 673-square-mile territory, is an example of an extremely rural jurisdiction.

## The Role of County Government

Counties were created by states to function as their administrative appendages. In other words, counties were expected to manage activities of statewide concern at the local level. Their basic set of functions traditionally included property tax assessment and collection, law enforcement, elections, record keeping (pertaining to matters such as land transactions, births, and deaths), and road maintenance. The county courthouse was the center of government.

The twin pressures of modernization and population growth placed additional demands on county governments. As a result, their service offerings have expanded. In addition to their traditional responsibilities, counties today handle health care and hospitals, pollution control, mass transit, industrial development, social services, and consumer protection. Examples of the old and new functions of counties appear in Table 10.1. The more new services that a county provides, the more it is delivering city-type services to its residents and businesses.[7] As a result, counties are increasingly regarded less as simple functionaries of state government than as important policy-making units of local government. State governments have awarded greater decision-making authority and flexibility to counties through home rule. Thirty-eight states have adopted home rule provisions for at least some of their counties.[8] This has made it easier for counties to change their organizational structures and reform their practices.

Even with their gradual empowerment, counties, like other local governments, continue to chafe at the traditionally tight reins of state government

**TABLE 10.1    County Government Functions**

| FUNCTION | TRADITIONAL FUNCTION | NEW FUNCTION |
|---|:---:|:---:|
| Building and housing code enforcement | | X |
| Disaster preparedness | | X |
| Water supply/sewage disposal | | X |
| Parks and recreation | | X |
| Judicial administration | X | |
| County jail maintenance | X | |
| Planning and land-use control | | X |
| Record keeping: land transactions, births, deaths, marriages | X | |
| Airports | | X |
| Public hospitals | | X |
| Law enforcement | X | |
| Local roads and bridges, construction and maintenance | X | |
| Consumer protection | | X |
| Mass transit | | X |
| Property tax assessment and collection | X | |
| Election administration | X | |
| Natural resource preservation | | X |
| Welfare and social-service programs | X | |
| Libraries | | X |
| Stadiums, convention and cultural centers | | X |
| Pollution control | | X |
| Public health, including clinics | | X |
| Community development and housing | | X |

SOURCES: David R. Berman, *County Governments in an Era of Change* (Westport, CT: Greenwood Press, 1993); Tanis J. Salant, "Overview of County Governments," in Roger L. Kemp, ed., *Forms of Local Government* (Jefferson, NC: McFarland, 1999); J. Edwin Benton, et al., "Service Challenges and Governance Issues Confronting American Counties in the 21st Century: An Overview," *State and Local Government Review* 40 (2008): 54–68.

control. As will be explored further in Chapter 12, counties resent state requirements that the counties themselves have to pay for. In addition, they dislike the limits that states place on their authority. The issue of empowerment is unlikely to fade anytime soon.

## How Counties Are Organized

The traditional structure of county government is based on an elected governing body, usually called a board of commissioners or supervisors, which is the central policy-making apparatus in the county. The board enacts county ordinances, approves the county budget, and appoints other officials (such as the directors of the county public works department and the county parks department). One of the board members acts as presiding officer. Historically, this form of government has been the most popular; more than half of U.S. counties use it, although its predominance is decreasing. A typical county commission has three or five members and meets in regular session twice a month.

The board is not omnipotent, however, because several other county officials are also elected, forming a plural executive structure. In most places, these officials include the sheriff, the county prosecutor (or district attorney), the county clerk (or clerk of the court), the county treasurer (or auditor), the county tax assessor, and, in some states, even the coroner. These officials can become powerful political figures in their own right by controlling their own bureaucratic units. Figure 10.2 sketches the typical organizational pattern of county government.

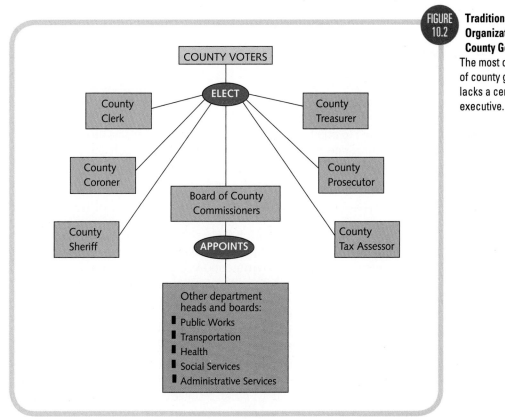

**FIGURE 10.2  Traditional Organization of County Government**
The most common form of county government lacks a central executive.

There are two primary criticisms of this type of organizational structure. First, it has no elected central executive official, like the mayor of a city or the governor of a state. County government is run by a board. Second, it does not have a single-professional administrator to manage county government, the way a city manager does in a municipality. Elected officials are responsible for administering major county functions.

These criticisms have led to calls for reform of the structure of county government. Two alternative county structures have grown in popularity over the past two decades. In one, called the *county council–elected executive plan*, the voters elect an executive officer in addition to the governing board. The result is a clearer separation between legislative and executive powers—in effect, a two-branch system of government. The board still has the power to set policy, adopt the budget, and audit the financial performance of the county. The executive's role is to prepare the budget, administer county operations (in other words, implement the policies of the board), and appoint department heads. More than 400 counties have adopted this arrangement. In the other alternative structure, the *council–administrator plan*, the county board hires a professional administrator to run the government. The advantage of this form of government is that it brings to the county a highly skilled manager with a professional commitment to efficient, effective government. Approximately 1,000 counties have variations of the council–administrator structure.

Determining the most effective structural arrangements for county government is an ongoing issue. Defections from the long-standing commission form of county government and experimentation with alternatives continue, especially in the most populous counties.[9] In 2007, Los Angeles County, which employs 100,000 people and has a budget of $20 billion, empowered its county administrator by giving him the power to hire and fire most department heads.[10] Does structure matter? If results from new research in Florida counties can be extended to other states, the answer is yes. Among fast-growing counties in the Sunshine State, the adoption of a reformed structure led to an expansion of the counties' services to its residents.[11]

## The Performance of County Government

The last word on counties has not been written. Granted, counties are now more prominent than they were in the old days when they were considered the shadowy backwaters of local governments. As urban populations spill beyond the suburbs into the unincorporated territory of counties, the pressure on all local governments grows. A county may do battle with the cities located within its boundaries on issues of service provision and regulation. A county may do battle with the state over the spiraling costs of state-imposed mandates for programs such as indigent services and long-term health care. In addition, counties are expected to tackle tough dilemmas of affordable housing and environmental compliance at the same time that they are expanding their services to include growth management, refugee resettlement, and homeland security.

The pressures on county government are many. One novel idea for relieving the burdens on counties was suggested in California awhile back, when the legislature considered a proposal to divide the state into seven regions that would be governed by thirteen-member elected boards.[12] These regional "super governments" would assume many of the development and infrastructure functions currently assigned to county governments. Although the bill did not pass, the performance of county government remains an issue in other parts of the nation. Massachusetts, where cities and towns provide most local services, took a completely different tack by abolishing several counties as functioning governments, contending that they were superfluous in the Bay State.[13] Clearly, county governments must continue to modernize and focus on the big picture or run the risk of being bypassed. With that in mind, voters in Allegheny County, Pennsylvania (the Pittsburgh area), approved a restructuring plan in 2005 that merged several elected county positions and made some elective offices appointed.[14]

# MUNICIPAL GOVERNMENT

*Municipalities* are cities; the words are interchangeable because each refers to a specific, populated territory, typically operating under a charter from state government. Cities differ from counties in terms of how they were created and what they do. Historically, they have been the primary units of local government in most societies—the grand enclaves of human civilization.

## Creating Cities

A city is a legal recognition of settlement patterns in an area. In the most common procedure, residents of an area in a county petition the state for incorporation. The area slated for **incorporation** must meet certain criteria, such as population or density minimums. In Alabama, for instance, 300 people are the population threshold necessary for incorporation; in Arizona, the number is 1,500. In most cases, a referendum is required. The referendum enables citizens to vote on whether they wish to become an incorporated municipality. If the incorporation measure is successful, then a **charter** is granted by the state, and the newly created city has the legal authority to elect officials, levy taxes, and provide services to its residents. Not all cities have charters, however. Most California cities, for example, operate under general state law.

New cities are created every year. For instance, during one six-year period, 145 places incorporated (and thirty-three cities disincorporated, or ceased to exist as official locales).[15] Although most new cities tend to be small, some begin with sizable populations. For example, more than 86,000 people were living in Sandy Springs, Georgia, when the city incorporated in 2005.

Like counties, cities are general-purpose units of local government. But unlike counties, they typically have greater decision-making authority and

**incorporation**
The creation of a municipality through the granting of a charter from the state.

**charter**
A document that sets out a city's structure, authority, and functions.

discretion. Almost all states have enacted home rule provisions for cities, although in some states, only cities that have attained a certain population size can exercise this option. (One of the few states without home rule for cities, New Hampshire, sought to provide it through a constitutional amendment in 2000. The measure was defeated by voters.) In addition, cities generally offer a wider array of services to their citizenry than most counties do. Police and fire services, public works, parks, and recreation are standard features, supplemented in some cities by publicly maintained cemeteries, city-owned and operated housing, city-run docks, city-sponsored festivals, and city-constructed convention centers. Municipal government picks up garbage and trash, sweeps streets, inspects restaurants, maintains traffic signals, and plants trees.

## City Governmental Structure

Nearly all city governments operate with one of three structures: a mayor–council form, a council–manager form, or a city commission form. In each structure, an elected governing body, typically called a city council, has policy-making authority. What differentiates the three structures is the manner in which the executive branch is organized.

**Mayor–Council Form** In the mayor–council form of government, executive functions such as the appointment of department heads are performed by elected officials. This form of government can be subdivided into two types, depending on the formal powers held by the mayor. In a **strong-mayor–council structure**, the mayor is the source of executive leadership. Strong mayors run city hall the way governors run the statehouse. They are responsible for daily administrative activities, the hiring and firing of top-level city officials, and budget preparation. They have a potential veto over council actions

The strong-mayor–council structure grew out of dissatisfaction in the late nineteenth century with the **weak-mayor–council structure**. The weak-mayor–council structure limits the mayor's role to that of executive figurehead. It has its roots in the colonial period of American history. The council (of which the mayor may be a member) is the source of executive power and legislative power. The council appoints city officials and develops the budget, and the mayor has no veto power. He performs ceremonial tasks such as speaking for the city, chairing council meetings, and attending ribbon-cutting festivities. A structurally weak mayor can emerge as a powerful political figure in the city, but only if he possesses informal sources of power. Figure 10.3 highlights the structural differences between the strong- and weak-mayor–council forms of city government.

Mayor–council systems are popular both in large cities (in which populations are greater than 250,000) and in small cities (with populations under 10,000). In large cities, the clash of conflicting interests requires the leadership of an empowered politician, a strong mayor. In small communities, however, the mayor–council structure is a low-cost, part-time operation. Large cities in which the administrative burdens of the mayor's job are especially heavy have

**strong-mayor–council structure**

The mayor is empowered to perform the executive functions of government and has a veto over city council actions.

**weak-mayor–council structure**

The mayor lacks formal executive power; the city council (of which the mayor may be a member) is the source of executive and legislative power.

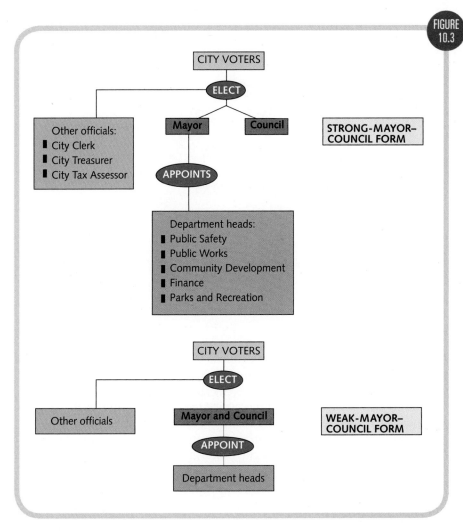

**FIGURE 10.3**

**Mayor–Council Form of Government**
The primary difference between these two structures concerns the power and authority possessed by the mayor. Strong mayors are more ideally situated to exert influence and control.

established the position of general manager or chief administrative officer to assist the mayor.

**Council–Manager Form** The second city government structure, the council–manager form, emphasizes the separation of politics (the policy-making activities of the governing body) from administration (the execution of the policies enacted by the governing body). Theoretically, the city council makes policy, and administrators execute policy. Under this structure, the council hires a professional administrator to manage city government. Figure 10.4 illustrates this structure.

The administrator (usually called a **city manager**) appoints and removes department heads, oversees service delivery, develops personnel policies, and

**city manager**
A professional administrator hired by a city council to handle the day-to-day operation of the city.

**Council–Manager Form of Government**

The council–manager form of government places administrative responsibility in the hands of a skilled professional. The intent is to make the operation of city government less political.

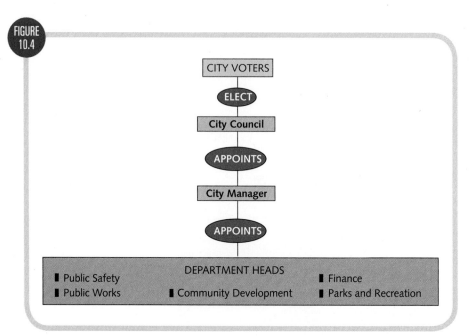

**FIGURE 10.4**

CITY VOTERS

ELECT

City Council

APPOINTS

City Manager

APPOINTS

DEPARTMENT HEADS
- Public Safety
- Public Works
- Community Development
- Finance
- Parks and Recreation

prepares budget proposals for the council. These responsibilities alone make the manager an important figure in city government. But add the power to make policy recommendations to the city council, and the position becomes even more powerful. When offering policy recommendations to the council, the manager is walking a fine line between politics and administration. Managers who, with the acquiescence of their council, carve out an activist role for themselves may be able to dominate policy making in city government.[16] In council–manager cities, the two entities typically have a working understanding about how far the manager can venture into the policy-making realm of city government.[17]

More than half of U.S. cities use the council–manager form of city government. Among cities of 25,000–75,000 people, the council–manager structure predominates; it is also popular in homogeneous suburban communities and in the newer cities of the Sunbelt. Examples of large cities with a council–manager structure include Phoenix, San Antonio, and Dallas.

**City Commission Form** Under the city commission form of government, illustrated in Figure 10.5, legislative and executive functions are merged. Commissioners not only make policy as members of the city's governing body, they also head the major departments of city government. In other words, they are both policymakers and policy executors. One of the commissioners is designated as mayor simply to preside over commission meetings.

The commission form of government was created as a reaction to the mayor–council structure. Its origins can be traced back to the inability of a mayor–council government in Galveston, Texas, to respond to the chaos caused

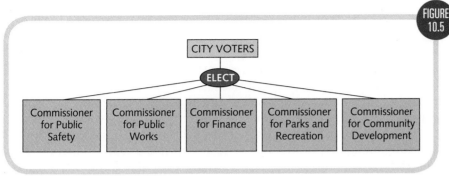

FIGURE
10.5
**City Commission Form of Government** Executive leadership is fragmented under a commission form of government. Each commissioner heads a department; together, they run city hall.

by a hurricane in 1900 that demolished the city and killed 6,000 people. Bowing to gubernatorial pressure, the Texas legislature authorized the creation of a totally new form of city government—a commission form—and by 1904, the new city government had entirely rebuilt Galveston. The success of the commission led to its adoption first by other Texas cities (Houston, Dallas, Fort Worth) and then, within a decade, by 160 other municipalities (such as Des Moines, Iowa; Pittsburgh, Pennsylvania; Buffalo, New York; Nashville, Tennessee; and Charlotte, North Carolina). Its appeal was its ostensible reduction of politics in city government.

But almost as fast as the commission form of government appeared, disillusionment set in. One problem stemmed from the predictable tendency of commissioners to act as advocates for their own departments. Each commissioner wanted a larger share of the city's budget allocated to her department. Another problem had to do with politicians acting as administrators: Elected officials do not always turn out to be good managers. By 1990, when Tulsa, Oklahoma, installed a mayor–council form in place of its commission system, only a few cities continued to use a commission structure. Notable among them was Portland, Oregon, which has retained its modified commission form of government.

## Which Form of City Government Is Best?

Experts disagree about which city government structure is best. Most would probably agree that structures lacking a strong executive officer are generally less preferable than others. By that standard, the weak-mayor–council and the commission forms are less favorable. The strong-mayor–council form of government is extolled for fixing accountability firmly in the mayor's office, and the council–manager system is credited with professionalizing city government by bringing in skilled administrators. Yet strong-mayor structures are criticized for concentrating power in one office; council–manager forms are taken to task for their depoliticization of city government. Thus, it is up to community residents to decide which form of government they want, and they have been doing just that.

In 2004, Richmond, Virginia, switched from a weak-mayor structure to a strong-mayor form; in 2006, San Diego replaced its city manager with a strong mayor. Sacramento, at the urging of its newly-elected mayor, put the question on its 2010 ballot. El Paso, Texas, however moved in a different direction and abandoned its strong-mayor structure and joined the ranks of council–manager cities. For some cities, a hybrid form that combines features of both structures may be the answer. Oakland, California offers a model of one hybrid structure. Oakland replaced its council–manager form of government with a modified strong-mayor structure that retained the position of city manager. In fact, the distinction between the mayor–council form and the council–manager form may be blurring as more cities tinker with their structures, designing entities that contain elements of both.[18] A recent study of Michigan cities found just such a pattern.[19] We will return to this issue in Chapter 11 in the discussion of local leadership.

## Pressing Issues for Cities

The pressing issues in city governments these days include planning and land use, annexation, finances, and representation. Although the issues are discussed separately in the following subsections, they are frequently intertwined. For instance, decisions about land use can affect the city's finances; the annexation of new territory may alter representation patterns. Note that county governments also face similar pressures.

**Planning and Land Use** Land is important to city governments for their economic and political well-being. City governments control land uses within their boundaries. They frequently use a comprehensive plan (often called a general or master plan) to guide them. The plan typically divides the city into sections for commercial, industrial, and residential uses. In addition, a city might set aside areas for recreation and open space. For example, the general plan for Santa Barbara, California, designates portions of the city for parks, bikeways, and a bird refuge.

**ordinance**

Enacted by the governing body, it is the local government equivalent of a statute.

New York City enacted the first modern zoning **ordinance** in 1916; since then, cities have used *zoning* to effect land-use planning and control. Through zoning, the designations established in a city's plan are made specific. For example, land set aside for residential use may be zoned for single-family dwellings, multifamily units, or mobile homes. Commercial areas may be zoned for offices, shopping centers, or hotels. Industrial sections of the city are often separated into "light" and "heavy" zones. In addition, cities can overlay special zones onto existing ones. For instance, cities bent on restoration of older sections of the commercially zoned downtown area may establish historic preservation zones. Once these zones are so designated, property owners are prohibited from tearing down old structures there and, instead, are encouraged to renovate them. A city eager to transform the appearance of a particular area may also create special zones so it can regulate architectural style or the height of buildings and thus achieve the right "look." Less desirable uses, such as pornographic bookstores and XXX theaters, are often clustered together in special adult entertainment zones.

Once set, zoning can be altered through applications for variances and rezoning, usually heard by a city's planning commission. A variance is a waiver of a zoning requirement such as a minimum lot size or a building height limit. Rezoning involves a change in zoning designation, either to allow more intense use of the land (an upzoning) or to restrict use (downzoning). Applications for variances and rezoning are often controversial. A study of fourteen years' worth of applications to upzone parcels in Wilmington, Delaware, demonstrated that community sentiment played an important role in the outcome.[20] Community resistance to the proposed construction of a Wal-Mart superstore in Inglewood, California, is the subject of the Breaking New Ground box.

Zoning is ultimately a political exercise with economic consequences. Cities use zoning to promote "good" growth such as upscale residential areas and to limit "bad" growth such as low-income housing.[21] Some cities have engaged in a practice that became known as *exclusionary zoning*. For example, a city might restrict its residential zones to 4,500-square-foot single-family dwellings on five-acre lots. The resulting high cost of housing would effectively limit the pool of potential residents to the wealthy. Court decisions have not only found exclusionary zoning illegal, they have also instructed local governments to provide housing opportunities for low- and moderate-income people.

**Annexation** **Annexation** has been a popular means of adding territory and population. In the past thirty years, many cities have found themselves squeezed by the rapid growth and incorporation of territory just outside city limits and hence beyond their control. What is worse (from a central city's perspective), some of these suburban cities have begun to threaten the central city's traditional dominance of the metropolitan area. People and jobs are finding suburban locales to their liking and many have left the central city. To counteract this trend and to ensure adequate space for future expansion, some cities have engaged in annexation efforts. During one six-year period, cities added nearly 3.5 million acres of land via 45,000 annexations.[22]

> **annexation**
> The addition of unincorporated adjacent territory to a municipality.

Not all cities can annex, however. They run up against two realities: the existence of incorporated suburbs (which means the territory cannot be annexed) and the strictures of state laws. State governments determine the legal procedures for the annexation process, and they can make it easy or hard.[23] Texas is a state that makes it easy for cities to annex and, not surprisingly, big Texas cities (in terms of population) have vast territories: Houston covers 580 square miles, San Antonio is 407 square miles, and Dallas is 385 square miles. Texas cities use their power of **extraterritorial jurisdiction (ETJ)** to supplement annexation. Under ETJ, they can control subdivision practices in unincorporated bordering territory. (The amount of territory varies from a half-mile for small cities to five miles for cities with over 250,000 people.) A Texas city can annex up to 10 percent of its territory annually without a referendum, simply by providing adequate notice to the about-to-be-annexed residents.

> **extraterritorial jurisdiction (ETJ)**
> The ability of a city government to control certain practices in an adjacent, unincorporated area.

Some states make it difficult for cities to annex. Cities may have to wait for landowners in an adjoining area to petition to be annexed. In some instances, a city bent on annexation will put pressure on landowners outside the city

## BREAKING NEW GROUND

### Wal-Mart versus Inglewood: Score 1 for the City

Inglewood, California, a city of 112,000 in southern California, took on Wal-Mart, the world's largest retailer, in a battle of mammoth proportions. It began as a typical developer–city council encounter: Wal-Mart, looking for new urban markets to expand into, decided on this well-situated suburb of Los Angeles for its newest superstore. A sixty-acre vacant lot near a racetrack seemed a perfect Wal-Mart location, so the corporation went about getting the necessary approvals from the city for its plan, which also included development of shops and restaurants on the site. Inglewood officials, however, were not willing to give the corporation the go-ahead to build the megastore. The city council had concerns about environmental impact, traffic congestion, labor standards, and the effect on local small businesses. The mayor, however, supported the new commercial complex because of its potential to add jobs and improve the city's tax base.

Not accustomed to hearing "No," Wal-Mart responded to the rebuff by mounting a campaign to take the issue directly to the citizens. The corporation succeeded in collecting enough signatures to get the question on the ballot, and it spent more than $1 million to promote its passage. Legal wrangling over whether an initiative process could be used to usurp the power of the city council to issue building permits brought the California attorney general into the picture. Wal-Mart's public relations firm bombarded city residents with mail, telephone calls, and advertisements on radio and television. Besides touting the new jobs and increased tax revenue, Wal-Mart targeted its appeal to consumers, promising low prices.

Opponents, including organized labor, church groups, and community organizations,

fought back. They organized the Coalition for a Better Inglewood, raised money, set up their own "vote no" phone banks, and took their Save Our Community from Wal-Mart campaign door-to-door. They contended that Wal-Mart pays low wages, offers minimal benefits, and fights employee attempts to unionize. They also argued that a Wal-Mart superstore would drain customers from locally owned shops and stores, which would close eventually, creating a net loss of jobs in the community.

The ballot measure would have exempted Wal-Mart from the city's planning, zoning, and environmental regulations. In many senses, it was a test case: If Wal-Mart was successful in Inglewood, it would open the door to similar tactics in other communities resistant to its plans. For example, in Contra Costa County, near San Francisco, voters had overturned a council-passed ordinance that would have banned the construction of superstores. In the end, the opponents of Wal-Mart were victorious in Inglewood: Voters rejected the ballot measure 60.6 to 39.4 percent. Wal-Mart, of course, moved on, searching for jurisdictions that might be a bit more enthusiastic about its presence. And it has found plenty: By 2009, Wal-Mart had won twenty-two of the twenty-seven ballot referenda in the Golden State.

SOURCES: John M. Broder, "Stymied by Politicians, Wal-Mart Turns to Voters," *The New York Times*, www.nytimes.com (April 5, 2004); Sara Lin and Monte Morin, "Voters in Inglewood Turn Away Wal-Mart," *Los Angeles Times*, www.latimes.com (April 7, 2004); Stephen Kinzer, "Wal-Mart's Big-City Plans Stall Again," *The New York Times*, www.nytimes.com (May 6, 2004); Emily Lambert, "Welcome Wal-Marts!," Forbes.com (January 13, 2009).

who use city services such as water or sewer. Agree to be annexed, they say, or the price of the service may skyrocket or, even worse, the service might be curtailed.[24] Even when a majority of the landowners request annexation, referendum elections must be held if the proportion is less than 75 percent. State law may require that the annexation be approved by referendum by both the existing city and the area to be annexed. This stipulation is known as a dual majority, and it complicates the annexation process.

Some of the most prominent U.S. cities have rather confined city limits. For example, of the fifty most populated cities in the country, twenty-two control fewer than 100 square miles of territory. The most extreme cases are Newark, New Jersey (covering 23.8 square miles); Miami, Florida (35.6); Buffalo, New York (40.6); San Francisco, California (46.4); and Boston, Massachusetts (48.4).[25] In the older, established metropolitan areas, a central city has little room to expand because it is hemmed in by incorporated suburbs. Suburban areas incorporate— that is, become legal municipal entities—for many reasons. The threat of being annexed by a neighboring city frequently stimulates the creation of new cities.

**Finances** City governments, like other local governments, must balance their fiscal resources against their fiscal needs. Unlike the national government, however, these governments have to operate within the constraints of a balanced budget. As a result, they have become fairly creative at finding new sources of revenue in hard times.

One standard approach to budget-balancing is to reduce the rate of growth in operational spending (expenditures related to service provision, such as city employee salaries). Another popular mechanism is to increase the level of fees and charges. For instance, a city might increase the cost of a building permit or charge more for health inspections at restaurants. It can also hike the cost of parking in a metered space or in a city-owned parking garage. (Commuting students at urban colleges with inadequate parking have probably marveled at how adept city officials are at the "make students pay" strategy.) Indeed, cities can boost revenues in several seemingly small ways. A city service that used to be free, such as a city park, may now have an admission fee. Cities can reduce their capital spending (expenditures for big-ticket items such as installation of sewer systems or the purchase of fire engines) and contract out services to private providers, for example, allowing a waste-disposal firm to collect residential garbage or a local charity to take over the operation of homeless shelters.

Cities and other local governments found the financial going tough in the early 2000s;[26] Figure 10.6 shows how rapidly the fiscal situation deteriorated in city governments. In 2007, 70 percent of city finance officers reported that they were better able to meet their city's financial needs than in the year before. By 2009, only 12 percent reported this to be the case, the lowest figure in decades.

**Representation** Representation in city government is another fundamental concern. How can citizens' preferences be represented effectively in city hall? In the colonial days of town meetings and civic republics, it was simple: A citizen showed up at the meeting hall, voiced his opinion, and the majority ruled. When this procedure proved to be unwieldy, a system of representative democracy seemed the perfect solution.

In city governments, city council members are elected in one of two ways: either at large or by districts (also called wards). In **at-large elections**, a city voter can vote in each council race. (One modification of the at-large approach requires candidates to compete for a specific seat or "place" on the council; however, the vote is citywide.) In **district (ward) elections**, a city voter can

**at-large elections**
Citywide (or county-wide) contests to determine the members of a city council (or county commission).

**district (ward) elections**
Elections in which the voters in one district or ward of a jurisdiction (city, county, school district) vote for a candidate to represent that district.

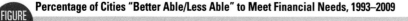

FIGURE
10.6

**Percentage of Cities "Better Able/Less Able" to Meet Financial Needs, 1993–2009**

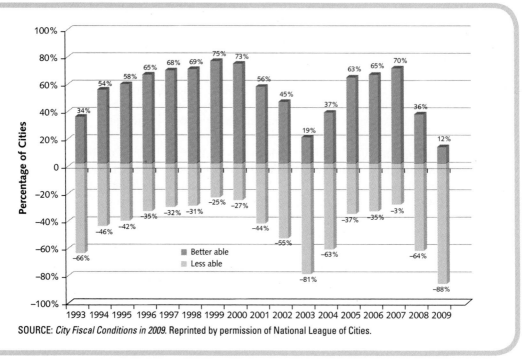

SOURCE: *City Fiscal Conditions in 2009*. Reprinted by permission of National League of Cities.

**reform movement**

An early twentieth-century effort to depoliticize local governments through nonpartisan elections, at-large representation, shorter ballots, and professional management.

vote only in the council race in her district. From the perspective of candidates, the at-large system means that a citywide campaign must be mounted. With districts, the candidate's campaign is limited to a specific area of the city. As discussed in Chapter 11, the structural **reform movement** during the Progressive Era advocated at-large elections as a means of weakening the geographic base of political machines. Candidates running in citywide races must appeal to a broad cross section of the population to be successful.

The use of at-large electoral systems has significant consequences. An in-depth study of almost 1,000 city council members across the country revealed that at-large members tend to be wealthier and more highly educated than council members elected from districts.[27] At-large council members also differ from district members in terms of their relationships with constituents. Council members elected at large devote less time to answering individual complaints and direct their attention to a citywide and business constituency.

Almost half of U.S. cities with populations of 2,500 or more use an at-large method for electing their council members, but the popularity of the method decreases as the size of a city's population increases. For example, only 15 percent of cities with populations above the half-million mark use at-large elections. This approach to city council representation is increasingly under attack for diminishing the likelihood that a member of a minority group can be elected. Research on more than 1,000 southern communities indicated that the abolition of at-large elections resulted in dramatic gains in black representation.[28] And the impact is not confined to the South. When New York City redrew city council district lines and increased the number of seats, the resulting council was composed of more African Americans and Latinos than ever before.

Although research on the topic continues, studies have shown that changing the electoral system from at large to districts has other effects such as an overall increase in citizen participation in terms of greater attendance at council meetings, higher voter turnout, and a larger number of candidates. These findings are not universal, however. For example, a recent study of fifty-seven cities compared voter turnout in the two different electoral systems and found that turnout in at-large elections actually outpaced turnout in district elections by nearly 6 percentage points.[29] Furthermore, it is not altogether clear that changing to districts will translate into policy benefits for the previously underrepresented sectors of the city. Earlier research suggested that in terms of attitudes toward public policy, there was really no significant difference between council members elected at large and those elected from districts.[30] However, this tendency may not hold up when it comes to minority employment. New research in Texas showed that school systems in which school board members were elected from wards hired more minority school administrators than at-large systems did.[31]

Modified at-large voting is seen as an alternative to district elections in jurisdictions where minority candidates have met with electoral defeat. In **cumulative voting**, candidates run at large, and voters cast as many votes as there are seats to be filled. The voter may allocate these votes as he wishes, either as a bloc for one candidate or spread out among the candidates. In a community with a history of racially or ethnically polarized voting, the chance of minority-candidate success increases under a cumulative-voting arrangement. For example, when Alamogordo, New Mexico, adopted cumulative voting, a Latino candidate who would have finished fourth in a standard at-large election placed third in total votes cast.[32] Because three seats were being contested, the difference between a third- and fourth-place finish meant the difference between winning and losing. Although interest in the cumulative voting option remains strong, its actual use is limited to seventy local jurisdictions in four states.[33]

**cumulative voting**
Candidates compete at large and voters can cast as many votes as there are seats to be filled, either as a bloc for one candidate or spread out among several candidates.

# TOWNS AND TOWNSHIPS

The word *town* evokes an image of a small community where everyone knows everyone else, where government is informal, and where local leaders gather at the coffee shop to make important decisions. This image is both accurate and inaccurate. Towns generally are smaller, in terms of population, than cities or counties. And the extent of their governmental powers depends on state government. But even where they are relatively weak, town government is increasingly becoming more formalized. (For a visual image of local government, see the Engaging the Structure of Local Government box.)

## Engaging the Structure of Local Government…Literally

What should the physical structure of a city hall or county courthouse look like? Should it resemble the grand buildings of nineteenth-century Europe or the more modern structures of twenty-first-century Asia? Or should it be less about "look" and more about function?

If you saw the 2008 film, *Milk*, shot in and around San Francisco's City Hall, you glimpsed a majestic edifice constructed during the early twentieth century in the aftermath of the area's devastating earthquake. If San Franciscans were constructing the same building today, it would cost in the $400 million range. In times of economic recession and fiscal stress, the least costly option is generally preferred. Is the era of impressive civic architecture behind us?

San Francisco City Hall building
SOURCE: aerialarchives.com/Aerial Archives/Alamy

Austin City Hall
SOURCE: Kim Karpeles/Alamy

Maybe not. Austin, the capital of Texas, built a new city hall in 2004 at a cost of approximately $57 million. Architects sought to create something that captured the city's style and natural surroundings. Here is how the city describes its new home:

> Reflecting Austin's natural beauty, Austin City Hall is a unique landmark gateway to Austin City government. The building and plaza serve as a gathering place for public discourse and community collaboration with informality, friendliness, environmental sensitivity and innovative technology. Built of Texas

limestone and sitting on the site of a once-raucous nineteenth-century bordello district, Austin's copper-clad City Hall is as unique as the community it serves.

The two structures, very different in design, have been successful at bringing the public together and creating an image of the city in which they are located. The next time you venture past public buildings in your community, stop for a moment and ponder their design.

SOURCES: Alan Ehrenhalt, "Stimulating Architecture," *Governing Magazine* 22 (January 2009): 9–10; "Austin City Hall," www.ci.austin.tx.us/cityhall/ (August 10, 2009).

## How Do We Know a Town When We See One?

Towns and townships are general-purpose units of local government, distinct from county and city governments. Only twenty states, primarily in the Northeast and Midwest, have official towns or townships. In some states, these small jurisdictions have relatively broad powers; in others, they have a more circumscribed role.

New England towns, for example, offer the kinds of services commonly associated with cities and counties in other states. Many New England towns continue their tradition of direct democracy through a **town meeting** form of government. At a yearly town assembly, residents make decisions on policy matters confronting the community. They elect town officials, pass local ordinances, levy taxes, and adopt a budget. In other words, the people who attend the town meeting function as a legislative body. Although the mechanism of the town meeting exemplifies democracy in action, it often falls short of the ideal, primarily due to the relatively low rate of citizen participation in meetings. Often, fewer than 10 percent of a town's voters attend the meeting. Those who do show up tend to be older and, not surprisingly, more engaged in politics in general. Some research has found that "some citizens are in fact turned off by the lack of civility of the face-to-face interactions at town meetings."[34] Larger towns in Connecticut and Massachusetts rely on representatives elected by residents to vote at the meetings.

Towns in New England, along with those in New Jersey, Pennsylvania, and, to some degree, Michigan, New York, and Wisconsin, enjoy fairly broad powers. In large measure, they act like other general-purpose units of government. In the remainder of the township states (Illinois, Indiana, Kansas, Minnesota, Missouri, Nebraska, North Dakota, Ohio, and South Dakota), the nature of township government is more rural. Rural townships tend to stretch across thirty-six square miles of land (conforming to the surveys done by the national government before the areas were settled), and their service offerings are often limited to roads and law enforcement. In one state, Indiana, townships actually cover the entire territory and population with other jurisdictional units superimposed

**town meeting**
An annual event at which a town's residents enact ordinances, elect officials, levy taxes, and adopt a budget.

on them. A part-time elected board of supervisors or trustees commonly rules the roost in townships. In addition, some of the jobs in government may be staffed by volunteers rather than salaried workers. However, the closer these rural townships are to large urban areas, the more likely they are to offer an expanded set of services to residents.

### The Future of Towns and Townships

The demise of the township type of government has long been expected. As rural areas become more populated, they will eventually meet the population minimums necessary to become municipalities. In 2000, for instance, residents of a Minnesota township decided to incorporate as a municipality to ward off annexation by a neighboring city.[35] Even in New England, questions of town viability have arisen. For example, many Connecticut towns with populations exceeding 15,000 have found it increasingly difficult to operate effectively through town meetings.[36] Accordingly, some are adding professional managers, whereas others are considering a shift to a strong-mayor form of government. Other towns face a different problem. Many are experiencing substantial population exodus and, in the process, losing their reason for existence. These towns may die a natural death, with other types of government (perhaps counties or special districts) providing services to the remaining residents. The question is: Do towns and townships make sense in contemporary America? Despite dire predictions, towns and townships have proved to be remarkably resilient. The U.S. Census Bureau counted 16,519 towns and townships in 2007, down only 110 from the 1997 figure. Most of the decline came in midwestern states.

Towns and townships have not been idle while commentators speculated on their dim future. They formed an interest group, the National Association of Towns and Townships (NATaT), to lobby on their behalf in Washington, D.C., NATaT spawned a spinoff organization, the National Center for Small Communities, to provide training and technical assistance to towns. Also, many small towns have embarked on ambitious economic development strategies—industrial recruitment, tourism promotion, and amenity enhancement—in an attempt to stimulate new growth.

## SPECIAL DISTRICTS

Special districts are supposed to do what other local governments cannot or will not do. They are established to meet service needs in a particular area. Special districts can be created in three different ways:

- states can create them through special enabling legislation,
- general-purpose local governments may adopt a resolution establishing a special district,
- citizens may initiate districts by petition, which is often followed by a referendum on the question.

Some districts have the power to levy taxes; others rely on user fees, grants, and private revenue bonds for funding. Taxing districts typically have elected governing boards; nontaxing districts—called **public authorities**—ordinarily operate with appointed boards.[37] The United States has approximately 37,000 special districts, and that number is increasing. In the ten-year period from 1997 to 2007, the number of special districts grew by nearly 2,700. As one might expect, the pattern of special-district creation (and abolition) varies from one state to another. For example, Illinois added nearly 200 new districts from 1997 to 2007, while Maryland and Pennsylvania actually reduced their numbers.[38]

Not all special districts are organized alike. Ninety-two percent of them provide a single function, but the functions vary. Natural resource management, fire protection, housing and community development, and water and sewer service are the most common. Most states have other, state-specific districts, such as Colorado's mine drainage districts and tunnel districts or Florida's beach and shore preservation districts and mobile home park recreation districts. The budget and staff size of special districts range from minuscule to mammoth. Some of the more prominent include the Port Authority of New York and New Jersey, the Chicago Transit Authority, the Washington Public Power Supply System, and the Los Angeles County Sanitation District. Illinois and California have the highest number of special districts (3,249 and 2,765, respectively). Alaska and Hawaii have the fewest by far, with fifteen each.

## Why Special Districts Are Needed

Special districts overlay existing general-purpose local governments and address deficiencies in them.[39] Three general categories of "deficiencies" are worth examining: technical conditions, financial constraints, and political explanations.

First are the technical conditions of a general-purpose local government. In some states, cities cannot extend their service districts beyond their boundaries. Moreover, the problem to be addressed may not fit neatly within a single jurisdiction. A river that runs through several counties may periodically overflow its banks in heavy spring rains—a problem affecting small portions of many jurisdictions. A flood control district covering only the affected areas may be a logical solution. Problems of scale must also be considered. A general-purpose local government simply may not be able to provide electric service to its residents as efficiently as a special utility district that covers a multitude of counties. Finally, some states prohibit the jurisdictional co-venturing that would allow counties to offer services jointly with other counties. In that case, operation of a two-county library would require the establishment of a special two-county library district.

A second set of deficiencies has to do with financial constraints. Local general-purpose governments commonly operate under debt and tax limitations. Demands for additional services that exceed a jurisdiction's revenue-raising ceiling or lead to the assumption of excessive debt cannot be

**public authority**

A type of special district funded by nontax revenue and governed by an appointed board.

accommodated. By using special districts, existing jurisdictions can circumvent the debt and tax ceilings. Special districts are better suited than general-purpose governments for service charges or user-fee financing, whereby the cost of the service can be directly apportioned to the consumer (as with water or sewer charges).

Technical and financial deficiencies of general-purpose local governments help to explain the creation of special districts, but political explanations shed even more light. Restrictive annexation laws and county governments with limited authority are political facts of life that encourage the use of special districts. For residents of an urban fringe area, a public-service district (which may provide more than one service) may be the only option. Some special districts owe their existence to a federal mandate. For example, national government policy has spurred the establishment of soil conservation and flood control districts throughout the country.

Once created, a special district may become a political power in its own right. In places where general-purpose governmental units are fully equipped legally, financially, and technically to provide a service, they may encounter resistance from special-district interests fighting to preserve the district.

## Concerns About Special Districts

The arguments in favor of special districts revolve around their potential for efficient service provision and the likelihood that they will be responsive to constituents whose demands are not otherwise being met.[40] For the most part, however, scholarly observers look at special districts with a jaundiced eye. The most frequently heard complaint is that special districts lack accountability. The public is often unaware of their existence, so they function free of much scrutiny. A recent study of 100 airport and seaport districts found that those with an elected governing board were no more likely to be responsive to public preferences than those with appointed boards.[41] And as research by Nancy Burns reminds us, the establishment of special districts is a costly political act.[42] Well-placed groups such as businesses, developers, and home-owners' associations are among the beneficiaries of special-district creation.

One thing is certain: The proliferation of special districts complicates the development of comprehensive solutions to public problems. It is not uncommon for cities and counties to be locked in governmental combat with the special districts in their area. All of these governmental units tend to be turf-protecting, service-providing rivals. Special districts may actually drive up the costs of service delivery. Research on 300 metropolitan areas, which compared services provided by special districts with those provided by general-purpose governments, found districts had a higher per capita cost.[43]

Cognizant of these concerns, state governments are looking more closely at special districts and the role they play in service delivery. Several states have taken actions that give their general-purpose local governments more input into the decision to create special districts.

# SCHOOL DISTRICTS

School districts are a type of single-purpose local government. They are a distinct kind of special district and, as such, are considered one of the five types of local government. The trend in school districts follows the theory that fewer is better. Before World War II, more than 100,000 school districts covered the countryside. Many of these were rural, one-school operations. In many small towns, community identity was linked to the local schoolhouse. Despite serving as a source of pride, small districts were so expensive to maintain that consolidations occurred throughout the nation, and by 2007 the number of districts was slightly over 13,000. Nebraska exemplifies the trend. In 1952, there were 6,392 school districts in the state; by 2007, the state had only 288. Currently, the states with the highest number of school districts are Texas (1,081) and California (1,044).

Consolidating schools can be a political hot potato, as the former governor of Arkansas, Mike Huckabee learned. In 2003, Governor Huckabee proposed a consolidation plan that would eliminate school districts with fewer than 1,500 students.[44] In effect, it was an efficiency issue. The state supreme court had ruled that the school finance system was inequitable and that a remedy had to be designed. Since raising taxes was a political no-no, the governor offered his consolidation plan. However, the governor's plan meant eliminating two-thirds of the school districts in the state and merging them to create larger districts. Folks in the rural, small-town areas of Arkansas were displeased, to put it mildly. Governor Huckabee's plan made for a lively legislative session in 2004, as lawmakers from affected areas fought to save their school districts. Legislators eventually agreed to allow the fifty-seven school districts that contained fewer than 350 students each to be absorbed by larger districts or to partner with other small districts to form a new, larger entity. Kentucky and West Virginia are among other states that have wrestled with the issue of merging small, rural school districts.

## School Politics

The school board is the formal source of power and authority in the district. The board is typically composed of five to seven members, usually elected in nonpartisan, at-large elections. Their job is to make policy for the school district. One of the most important policy decisions involves the district budget— how the money will be spent.

School districts are governed by these boards and managed by trained, full-time educational administrators. Like city governments, school districts invested heavily in the reform model of governance, and the average district has become more professional in operation in the past thirty years. An appointed chief administrator (a superintendent) heads the school district staff, the size of which depends on the size of the district. Finding the right person to take on the job of superintendent is crucial. Although some superintendents are home-grown, these days a superintendent's career path typically takes her from one school system to another. For example, in 2002, Philadelphia's troubled school system hired as its new chief executive the superintendent credited with turning around the public schools in Chicago.[45]

The 1980s were a time of rediscovery of public education, leading to a repoliticization of school districts. Since the 1990s, the focus has been on reforming and restructuring public education.[46] Many of the new reforms feature decentralized decision making such as school-based management, some increase the involvement of the private sector, and others enhance the role of parents. Regardless, they all share the same basic objective: improve the performance of public schools.

### School District Issues

Among the myriad challenges faced by school districts is one persistent conundrum: how to secure sufficient funding for public education. Although the relationship is a bit more complex than the old saying "you get what you pay for," there is widespread agreement that children in well-funded school districts are better off educationally than those in poorly funded ones.

Serious disparities in school funding, caused by wide differences in the property taxes that provide much of the revenue for public education, have led to the increasing financial involvement of state government in local school districts. State governments use an **equalization formula** to distribute funds to school districts in an effort to reduce financial disparities. Under this formula, poorer school districts receive a proportionately larger share of state funds than wealthier districts do. Although these programs have increased the amount of funding for education, they have not eliminated the inter district variation. Wealthier districts simply use the state guarantee as a foundation on which to heap their own resources. Poorer school districts continue to operate with less revenue. This situation prompted many state supreme courts around the country to declare their public-school finance systems unconstitutional. Legislatures struggled to design new, more equitable financial arrangements. Michigan lowered property taxes for schools and substituted sales taxes and other revenues. Other states have established lotteries and earmarked the proceeds for education. The issue of money for schools stays at the top of legislative agendas, year in and year out. This topic, along with school administration and innovations in education, is covered in more detail in Chapter 15.

**equalization formula**

A means of distributing funds (primarily to school districts) to reduce financial disparities among districts.

# COMMUNITIES AND GOVERNANCE

Let us return to the governance issue that was raised early in this chapter and has been alluded to throughout: How do we know when a community is well governed? This chapter is full of examples of communities restructuring their

| Public Opinion: Trust in Local Government | | | | | TABLE 10.2 |
|---|---|---|---|---|---|

Poll Question: How much trust and confidence do you have in the local governments in the area where you live when it comes to handling local problems—a great deal, a fair amount, not very much, or none at all?

| | Great deal (%) | Fair amount (%) | Not very much (%) | None at all (%) | No opinion (%) |
|---|---|---|---|---|---|
| 2008 | 23 | 49 | 17 | 9 | 2 |
| 2007 | 22 | 47 | 19 | 10 | 2 |
| 2005 | 23 | 47 | 23 | 7 | <1 |
| 2004 | 21 | 47 | 24 | 7 | 1 |
| 2003 | 18 | 50 | 23 | 8 | 1 |
| 2001 | 19 | 50 | 20 | 10 | 1 |

SOURCE: Gallup Poll, "Trust in Government," www.gallup.com/poll/5392/Trust-Government.aspx (August 10, 2009).

governments in hopes of improving governance. Voters oust incumbents and elect new council members in a similar effort. Conflict over local government spending priorities ensues. Local jurisdictions embark on innovative efforts to respond to their citizens' concerns. And on and on. Table 10.2 reports the results of Gallup polls conducted periodically that ask respondents about their trust and confidence in local government. Public opinion tends to be positive and stable over time with between 68 and 72 percent of respondents answering either "a great deal" or "a fair amount" of trust and confidence in localities.

Although there is no universally accepted set of criteria for evaluating the quality of governance, several organizations have come up with proxy measures. For example, the National Civic League bestows its "All-America City" designation on ten jurisdictions (cities, counties, and metro areas) that successfully tackle community problems in a collaborative way. Winning the accolade in 2009 were these jurisdictions:

- Phoenix, Arizona
- Inglewood, California
- Fort Wayne, Indiana
- Richmond, Indiana
- Wichita, Kansas
- Somerville, Massachusetts
- Albany, New York
- Kinston, North Carolina
- Statesville, North Carolina
- Caroline County, Virginia[47]

Three of the cities—Phoenix, Fort Wayne, and Wichita—must be doing something right because they have won the All-America City award more than once.

Back in 2000, the Government Performance Project conducted an extensive analysis of the management practices and performance of thirty-five major cities. One category on which cities were graded was managing for results. Researchers wanted to get answers to these questions: Does the city have a well-articulated strategic plan? Does the city actively involve the public in the goal-setting process? Does it monitor its progress and use the results in policy making? Collecting data from surveys and interviews, the researchers assigned grades to the cities.

Only Phoenix received an A; four cities received grades of A–: San Diego, Austin, Indianapolis, and Milwaukee. These five cities had well-developed visions for the future, they linked performance measures to goals, and they sought citizen feedback. At the other end of the grading scale were Buffalo, New York (D+); New Orleans, Louisiana (D+); and Columbus, Ohio (D).[48] One of the outcomes of the grading process—which received widespread publicity—was that low-scoring cities took a cue from their high-scoring counterparts and began efforts to improve. It is noteworthy that Columbus was able to convert its D grade on managing resources into an All-America City designation in the space of six years.

The governance question goes back to Plato and Aristotle, and we are unlikely to resolve it here. But the approaches used in identifying All-America cities and in the grades of the Government Performance Project offer some guidance for continued discussion about government structure and function.

## CHAPTER RECAP

- Theoretically, communities can be considered civic republics, corporate enterprises, or consumer markets. Legally, there are five types of local governments: counties, municipalities, towns and townships, special districts, and school districts. The United States has more than 89,000 local governments.

- Counties were created by states to serve as their local administrative extensions. Over time, they have taken on more functions and, especially in urban areas, they provide municipal-type services.

- The United States has more than 19,000 municipalities, or cities. The strong-mayor–council form of city government invests power in an elected mayor; the council–manager structure relies heavily on a professional administrator to run the city. The issue about which structure is better instigates much debate.

- Towns and townships are general-purpose local governments, like counties and cities. Twenty states, primarily in the Northeast and Midwest, have official towns or townships. Some have fairly broad powers;

others, especially rural midwestern townships, offer more limited services. Many have predicted that towns and townships will gradually disappear as the nation urbanizes.

- Special districts are the most prevalent and at the same time the least understood of the five types of local government. They provide a service to an area that other local governments do not provide because of technical, financial, or political considerations. Natural resource management, fire protection, housing and community development, and water and sewer service are the most common special districts. Their financing varies: Some have the power to tax; others rely on user fees, grants, or bonds.

- The number of school districts has declined because of mergers and consolidations to a current level of fewer than 13,000. School districts are typically governed by elected boards and managed by trained, full-time educational administrators. School politics can create rivalries as issues such as parental choice, neighborhood schools, and effective financing are debated.

- The public wants well-governed communities. Local governments redesign their structures in the hope of improving governance. Polls show that the public's trust and confidence in local government is fairly positive and stable. Analysts continue to develop criteria such as managing for results in an effort to identify the best performing localities.

## Key Terms

general-purpose local
  government (p. 270)
single-purpose local
  government (p. 270)
metropolitan area (p. 272)
micropolitan statistical area
  (p. 272)
home rule (p. 272)
incorporation (p. 277)
charter (p. 277)

strong-mayor–council
  structure (p. 278)
weak-mayor–council
  structure (p. 278)
city manager (p. 279)
ordinance (p. 282)
annexation (p. 283)
extraterritorial
  jurisdiction (ETJ) (p. 283)
at-large elections (p. 285)

district (ward) elections
  (p. 285)
reform movement
  (p. 286)
cumulative voting (p.287 )
town meeting (p. 289)
public authority (p. 291)
equalization formula
  (p. 294)

## Internet Resources

Most of the five types of government are represented by national associations, which have websites: **www .nacoonline.org** (National Association of Counties); **www.nlc.org** (National League of Cities); **www .natat.org** (National Association of Towns and Townships); **www.nsba.org** (for school districts, the relevant website is that of the National School Boards Association).

To explore a specific school district, see **www .philsch.k12.pa.us** (the website of the City of Philadelphia school district).

Special districts, by virtue of their specialized nature, tend to have function specific national organizations. For example, the National Association of Conservation Districts can be found at **www.**

**nacdnet.org**. A fifteen-county district, the Colorado River Water Conservation District, whose website can be found at **www.crwcd.org**, is an example of an individual special district. The website of one of the most famous special districts, the Port Authority of New York and New Jersey, is **www.panynj.gov**.

Over time, cities and counties have found that maintaining websites is a good way to connect with the public. See the website for consolidated Miami–Dade County at **www.miamidade.gov**.

The website for the city of Los Angeles can be found at **www.lacity.org**; the website for the county can be found at **www.lacounty.org**. The website for the largest county in Michigan is **www.waynecounty.com**.

You can find information about the Big Apple at **www.nyc.gov**; for the city of New Orleans, at **www.cityofno.com**. The websites for the cities of Houston and Boston are **www.houstontx.gov** and **www.cityofboston.gov**, respectively.

# Local Leadership and Governance

# 11

In 2009, Antonio Villaraigosa was reelected mayor of America's second largest city, Los Angeles. When he was sworn in for his second term, he declared,

> I stand, hopefully a little bit wiser as well, chastened and enlightened both by our successes and failures over the last four years. I stand renewed and reinvigorated, re-committed to the task before us. Above all, I stand determined to finish what we started, determined to find a second wind in our second term. I intend to lead with everything I have![1]

Among the items on the mayor's agenda were job creation, economic development, crime fighting, renewable energy, and rail transit. Mayor Villaraigosa—and mayors throughout the country—will need to use their leadership skills and build supportive coalitions to accomplish the tasks before them. And some good luck wouldn't hurt either.

Leadership goes hand in hand with governance. It can make the difference between an effectively functioning government and one that lurches from one crisis to another. The terms that conjure up images of leadership in local government circles these days include *initiative, inventiveness, risk taking, high energy level, persistence, entrepreneurship, innovation,* and *vision.* These words share a common element: They denote activity and

- Community Power
- Property Rights: A Matter of Power
- Local Executives
- Local Legislatures
- Leadership and Capacity

engagement. Leaders are people who make a difference. And there's an electoral payoff for doing a good job. Research findings have confirmed that higher job performance ratings translate into higher mayoral approval levels.[2] Not surprisingly, mayors with high approval are more likely to be re-elected.

One of the popular labels for contemporary leaders is *entrepreneur*. How do you know an entrepreneurial leader when you see one in local government? You can identify such leaders by their advocacy of innovative ideas. They are the people "who actively seek opportunities for dynamic changes in policy or politics."[3] Some may occupy positions of power in local government; others may emerge from the ranks of ordinary citizens. Regardless of their background, they share a commitment to new ideas and a willingness to take risks. The spirit of entrepreneurialism is not limited to individuals—communities exhibit leadership too. At some point, on some issue, a jurisdiction may try something new; it may "think outside the box." For instance, in 2007, New Haven, Connecticut, confronting an influx of illegal immigrants, decided to offer them city identification cards thus making them feel more welcome. The action did not set well with the federal government's Immigration and Customs Enforcement agency, but city leaders believed it was appropriate. Other cities with similar perspectives are looking closely at New Haven's program.[4] Leading cities become models for other cities.

# COMMUNITY POWER

**elite theory**

A theory of government that asserts that a small group possesses power and rules society.

Real questions about who is running the show in local government do arise. At the risk of sounding naive, we might suggest that "the people" run government; however, much of the evidence can persuade us otherwise. But we should not become too cynical, either. Citizen preferences do have an impact on public policy decisions.[5] Can we assume, therefore, that those who occupy important elected positions in government, such as the mayor and the city council, are in fact in charge? Are they the leaders of the community? These questions have interested scholars for a long time.

In sorting through the issue of who's running the show, we find that two theories predominate. One, **elite theory**, argues that a small group of leaders called an elite possesses power and rules society. Conversely, **pluralist theory** posits that power is dispersed among competing groups whose clashes produce societal rule.

**pluralist theory**

A theory of government that asserts that multiple, open, competing groups possess power and rule society.

## The Elite Theory

One of the earliest expositions of elite theory argued that any society, from underdeveloped to advanced, has two classes of people: a small set who rule and a large clump who are ruled.[6] The rulers allocate values for society and determine the rules of the game; the ruled tend to be passive and ill-informed and cannot exercise any direct influence over the rulers. This division is reflected elsewhere in society. In organizations, for example, power is inevitably concentrated in the hands of a few people. Given the pervasiveness of elite systems, should we expect decision making in communities to be any different?

A famous study of power in the community given the name of Middletown (actually Muncie, Indiana) in the 1920s and 1930s discovered an identifiable set of rulers.[7] The researchers, sociologists Robert and Helen Lynd, determined that Family X (the Ball family) was at the core of this ruling elite. Through their economic power, Family X and a small group of business leaders called the shots in Middletown. Government officials simply did the bidding of Family X and its cohorts.

Another widely read study of community power confirmed the basic tenets of elitism. Sociologist Floyd Hunter's study of Regional City (Atlanta, Georgia) in the 1950s and his follow-up research in the 1970s identified the top leadership—a forty-person economic elite—who dominated the local political system.[8] Hunter argued that an individual's power in Regional City was determined by his role in the local economy. Local elected officials merely carried out the policy decisions of the elite. To illustrate this point, Hunter compared the relatively limited power enjoyed by the mayor of Atlanta to the extensive power possessed by the president of a firm headquartered in Regional City, Coca-Cola.

Assume for a moment that elitist interpretations of community power are accurate; where do these interpretations take us? Do not be confused about the intent of an economic elite: They are not running the community out of a sense of benevolence. The following statement captures the larger meaning of elitism: "Virtually all U.S. cities are dominated by a small, parochial elite whose members have business or professional interests that are linked to local development and growth. These elites use public authority and private power as a means to stimulate economic development and thus enhance their own local business interests."[9] To many, this conclusion is disturbing.

## The Pluralist Theory

The findings of the studies discussed above did not square with the prevailing orthodoxy of American political science: pluralism. Not everyone saw community power through the elitist lens, and many questioned whether the findings from Middletown and Regional City applied to other communities.

Pluralist theory views the decision-making process as one of bargaining, accommodation, and compromise. According to this view, no monolithic entity calls the shots; instead, authority is fragmented. Many leadership groups can become involved in decision making, depending on the nature and importance of the issue at hand. Granted, the size, cohesion, and wealth of these groups vary, but no group has a monopoly on resources. Pluralism sets forth a much more accessible system of community decision making than the grimly deterministic tenets of elitism do.

A study conducted by Robert Dahl in New Haven, Connecticut, challenged the sociologists' findings, particularly those of Hunter.[10] According to Dahl, decisions in New Haven in the 1950s were the product of the interactions of a system of groups with more than one center of power. Except for the mayor, a single leader was not influential across a series of issue areas, and influential actors were not drawn from a single segment of the community.

Further explication of the pluralist model revealed that, although community decision making is limited to relatively few actors, the legitimacy of such a system hinges on the easily revoked consent of a much larger segment of the local population. In other words, the masses may acquiesce to the leaders, but they can also speak up when they are displeased. Success in a pluralistic environment is determined by a group's ability to form coalitions with other groups. Pluralism, then, offers a more hopeful interpretation of community power.

## New Haven: Is It All in the Approach?

New Haven, the setting for Dahl's affirmation of pluralist theory, has been examined and reexamined by skeptical researchers. Some of the debate between elitists and pluralists is a function of methodology—that is, the particular approach used in studying community power. Sociologists have tended to rely on what is called a **reputational approach**, whereby they go into a community and ask informants to name and rank the local leaders. Those whose names appear repeatedly are considered to be the movers and shakers. This approach is criticized on the grounds that it measures not leadership per se but the reputation for leadership. Political scientists approach the power question differently, through a **decisional method**. They focus on specific community issues and, using various sources, try to determine who is influential in the decision-making process. It is easy to see that the two different approaches can produce divergent findings.

Users of the decisional method claim that it allows them to identify overt power rather than just power potential.[11] In addition, it offers a realistic picture of power relationships as dynamic rather than fixed. Critics of the decisional method argue that when researchers select key issues to examine, they are being arbitrary. Also, a study of decision making may ignore the most powerful actors in a community—those who can keep issues *off* the agenda, who are influential enough to keep certain issues submerged. Table 11.1 reports the perceptions of members of a wide variety of citizen groups in seven large cities. Although 43 percent agree that business groups are powerful, their responses suggest, on balance, a relatively open local political system in which many groups are active. In their view, city officials pay attention to interest groups and their demands.[12]

New Haven was found by Dahl to be a pluralist's delight. Convinced that the finding was affected by Dahl's methods, another researcher, G. William Domhoff, examined New Haven and emerged with a contrary view of the power structure.[13] He claimed that Dahl missed the big picture by focusing

**reputational approach**

A method for studying community power in which researchers ask informants to name and rank influential individuals.

**decisional method**

A method for studying community power in which researchers identify key issues and the individuals who are active in the decision-making process.

| Citizen Groups' Assessment of Big City Politics | TABLE 11.1 |
|---|---|

| STATEMENT | PERCENTAGE AGREEING THAT THE STATEMENT IS A "GOOD" DESCRIPTION OF LOCAL POLITICS |
|---|---|
| Interest groups are active in city politics. | 60 |
| Business groups get what they want. | 43 |
| Elected officials oppose the aims of this organization. | 39 |
| Conflict erupts often in the policy area in which this organization is active. | 32 |
| Policy area in which this organization is active is marked by consensus. | 25 |
| City officials need not worry about interest groups. | 10 |

NOTE: Members of different types of citizen groups in seven large cities were surveyed.
SOURCE: Adapted from Christopher A. Cooper and Anthony J. Nownes, "Citizen Groups in Big City Politics," *State and Local Government Review* 35 (Spring 2003): 109.

on issues that were of minor concern to the New Haven elite, and that Dahl's finding of an accessible decision-making process in which many groups were involved was not an adequate test of the presence of an elite. Domhoff investigated the urban redevelopment issue and discovered that the long-time mayor, whom Dahl had seen as leading an executive-centered coalition, was in fact being actively manipulated by a cadre of local business leaders. Domhoff contended that New Haven was not quite the pluralistic paradise it was made out to be.

## The Dynamics of Power

The work of Hunter and that of Dahl remains significant, but neither elitism nor pluralism adequately explains who's running the show. Not all communities are organized alike; even within a single community, power arrangements shift as time passes and conditions change. One group of political scientists, Robert Agger, Daniel Goldrich, and Bert Swanson, has argued that an understanding of community power requires an assessment of two variables: the means by which power is distributed to the citizens and the extent to which ideological unity exists among the political leaders.[14]

Two examples offer insight into the dynamics of power. In Miami, a diverse city in which economic divisions are exacerbated by racial and ethnic tensions, an elite-dominated power structure continues to hold sway in important local decisions. According to Judith Gainsborough, who has studied the power structure in Miami, "The power to actually influence decision making is not widely dispersed."[15] Even so, the composition of the elite has changed over time, becoming more diverse itself. In Chicago, the city's political leaders joined forces with local economic leaders to create Chicago 2016, an organization devoted to bringing the Olympics to the city. Chicago 2016 formed a juggernaut, able to frame the issue and dominate debate. A fledgling anti-Olympics group, No Games Chicago, pushed back, raising questions about the potential cost to the taxpayers of hosting the Games, but to little avail.[16]

**Regime Theory** Is pluralism likely to triumph in communities across the land? Probably not. The penetration of the government's domain by private economic interests in American communities is deep. Consequently, to understand the dynamics of power in a community, one must look to the **regime**. Political scientist Clarence Stone defines regime as "the informal arrangements that surround and complement the formal workings of governmental authority."[17] Stone uses the concepts of *systemic power* and *strategic advantage* to explain why community decisions so frequently favor upper-strata interests.[18]

> **regime**
>
> The informal arrangements that surround and complement the formal workings of governmental authority.

The starting point of his argument is that public officials operate in a highly stratified socioeconomic system with a small upper class; a large, varied middle class; and a relatively small lower class. According to Stone, "Public officeholders are predisposed to interact with and to favor those who can reciprocate benefits."[19] Two considerations define the environment in which public officials operate: electoral accountability (keeping the majority of the public satisfied) and systemic power (the unequal distribution of economic, organizational, and social resources). Decision makers are likely to side with majority preferences on highly visible issues, but on less visible ones, the possessors of systemic power—the upper strata—will win most of the time. With their superior resources, they can set the agenda in the community and instigate (or block) change. In other words, they enjoy a strategic advantage. The Engaging Local Leadership and Governance box focuses on an unusual source of power and influence in one college town.

An urban regime brings a certain degree of stability to a community because key leaders share a vision for the future, that is, they have an agenda that they want to implement and they interact with one another. Chicago is a place in which a regime—actually a political machine—has held sway for decades. Figure 11.1 illustrates the connections between economic and political components of Mayor Daley's Chicago machine. An analysis of New Orleans found that the city's lack of a regime contributed mightily to the problems the city faced preparing for and responding to Hurricane Katrina in 2005.[20] In nonregime cities such as New Orleans, temporary coalitions spring up around various issues, but there is little shared understanding of the city's problems. Leaders do not communicate regularly and cooperation is in short supply. The result is haphazard governance, an outcome that was on display in New Orleans in the aftermath of Katrina. Ironically, the hurricane may have spawned an exercise in regime formation through Mayor Ray Nagin's Bring New Orleans Back Commission. Mayor Nagin was re-elected in 2006, despite a strong challenge from a member of one of New Orleans' leading political families.

# Engaging Local Leadership and Governance

## Who's Got The Power?

It all seemed so routine: a local hospital petitioning county government for permission to expand its facilities. But among the many opponents of the expansion attending the hearing was one unusual activist: Michael Stipe, lead singer for the band R.E.M. His presence at the hearing was one of several efforts by the band to block the hospital's plan. The band had made donations to a grassroots opposition group, Citizens for Healthy Neighborhoods (CHN), and had volunteered to foot the group's legal bills related to stopping the hospital.

The band's interest in local politics is both welcomed and resented in Athens–Clarke County, Georgia. Those who are on the same side of political disputes as the band are delighted with the musicians' activism. R.E.M. was formed in Athens and played its first gigs there. The band's world headquarters are in the city, and two members of R.E.M. still reside in the Athens area. Driving their activism is their interest in preserving what they consider to be the special qualities of the community. Athenians who are more supportive of growth and development contend that the band is too aggressive in pursuing its agenda. In the case of the hospital expansion, both sides got some of what they wanted, but not all. CHN was not able to stop the hospital's expansion but it was able to wrest

some concessions. Under the hospital's revised plan, only ten homes would be razed, not sixty as originally proposed, historic buildings would be preserved, and the impact of traffic changes would be minimized.

Lead singer Stipe argues that the band acts as a check on the good-old-boy network of conservative politicians and developers. Their clashes are most intense when the issue on the table is historic preservation or environmental protection. R.E.M.'s wealth and reputation give it standing in the community. Many Athenians are less enthusiastic, however, about the band's role in local politics, especially its support of liberal causes. One of the Republicans on the city–county governing board put it this way: "The average citizen does not realize how much funding R.E.M. has put into political campaigns in Athens." She continued, "They have an attitude of ultimately trying to control what happens in Athens government." That's what community power is all about. All places have their own set of interest groups; seldom, however, do they include world-famous rock bands.

SOURCES: Tom Lasseter, "Rock Group Takes on Ga. Town's Political Network," *The State* (July 25, 1999): A15; Deborah G. Martin, "Reconstructing Urban Politics: Neighborhood Activism in Land-Use Change," *Urban Affairs Review* 39 (May 2004): 589–612.

## Nonprofit Organizations as Power Players Nonprofit organizations

have become fully integrated into the government and politics of many communities. Four types of governmentally active nonprofit organizations can be identified:

- Civic nonprofits.
- Policy advocates.
- Policy implementers.
- Governing nonprofits.[21]

> **nonprofit organizations**
>
> Private sector groups that carry out charitable, educational, religious, literary, or scientific functions.

The first type, civic nonprofit organizations, plays a watchdog role, monitoring government and educating the public. A local citizen's league acts in this way, attending city council meetings and publicizing council decisions.

**Mayor Richard M. Daley's Chicago Machine. The Daley machine is about politics and economics.**

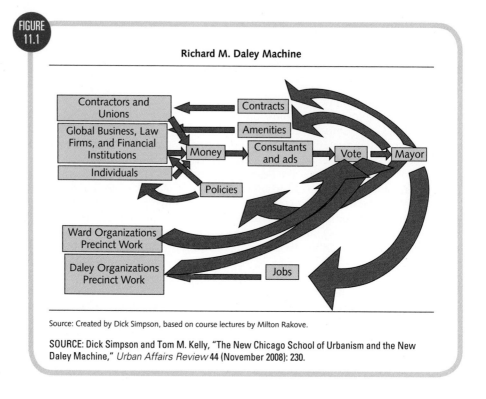

**FIGURE 11.1**

Richard M. Daley Machine

Source: Created by Dick Simpson, based on course lectures by Milton Rakove.

SOURCE: Dick Simpson and Tom M. Kelly, "The New Chicago School of Urbanism and the New Daley Machine," *Urban Affairs Review* 44 (November 2008): 230.

Policy advocates, the second type, move beyond the provision of information to become active supporters of particular policies or programs. For instance, if an education advocacy group endorses year-round schools, it would lobby the school board vigorously in support of such a policy change. The third type of nonprofit organization, policy implementers, actually delivers services, often through a contract with a local government. For example, homeless shelters in many communities are operated by nonprofit groups supported by city funds, federal grants, and charitable contributions. Governing nonprofits, the fourth type, are different because they may work through or with local government but they also act independently. These nonprofits are the most powerful of the four types because they offer an alternative venue for decision making.

Have nonprofit organizations upset community power structures? Policy advocates and governing nonprofits have the potential to reset agendas and effect real change. Research on the city of Detroit offers some insight into the long-term impact of nonprofit organizations. Richard Hula and Cynthia Jackson-Elmoore studied the influence of two nonprofits created in the aftermath of Detroit's civil disturbances of the late 1960s: New Detroit and Detroit Renaissance.[22] For more than thirty years, these organizations have been important players in the city's politics. Although they had a similar genesis—"both were born as an elite response to and fear of civil unrest"[23]—their styles and foci have varied. New Detroit has more of a social agenda, focusing on race relations and education reform. Detroit Renaissance, a smaller organization made up of the corporate elite from the Detroit area, has concentrated its energies on economic renewal. Both organizations have been active on the Detroit scene, advocating ambitious reforms and new policies over three decades. And although both organizations have enjoyed some successes, neither has been able to transform the local political agenda. Yet Hula and Jackson-Elmoore contend that the presence of New Detroit and Detroit Renaissance has had an important catalytic effect. When nonprofits join with local elected leaders, their impact increases. In other words, to become power players, nonprofit organizations must become part of the regime.

**Hyperpluralism** Our understanding of community power structures continues to evolve. What is certain is that some interests, especially those of the economically powerful, seem to prevail more often than others. Still, different communities have developed different arrangements for governance. In some places, weak political leadership and a dispersed business elite have resulted in a condition called **hyperpluralism**. In hyperpluralistic communities, where many interests clash, competing groups cannot form coalitions and the distribution of power tends to be unstable. Research on medium-size cities revealed at least seventeen different types of interest groups that were both active and influential on the local scene.[24] The range of interests represented by these groups is extensive, from taxes and traffic to economic development and public safety. The question of who's in charge remains an interesting one.

**hyperpluralism**
A condition characterized by a large number of groups and interests.

# PROPERTY RIGHTS: A MATTER OF POWER

The issue of property rights raises interesting questions about the exercise of power. You may have heard someone say, "I own this land; therefore, I can do anything I want with it," but that would be far from accurate. Through zoning and other regulations, government can limit what you can do with your property. Moreover, government can actually take that property away from you for a public purpose. All it has to do is follow proper procedures and compensate you, that is, pay fair market value, for the **taking**. Suppose you own a half-acre vacant lot near the central business district of your city. The city may be eyeing your lot as the site for the new library it plans to construct. If you are not willing to sell the land, the city can use its power of eminent domain, that is, it can take your property. You can haggle over the value of the lot, perhaps demand an administrative hearing, and maybe even file a lawsuit to try to stop the city, but in the end, if the taking is for a public purpose, the city has the power to do so. Where the issue gets a little dicey is over the notion of "public purpose." Obviously, a library is a public purpose but can the city use its eminent domain power to take that same lot and sell it to a developer so that he can construct an office building? The answer may surprise you.

**taking**
A government action assuming ownership of real property by eminent domain.

The city council of New London, Connecticut, had voted in 2000 to take 90 acres of land for a redevelopment project. The city's development corporation would redevelop the area with a hotel, marina, and upscale residences that would generate much needed jobs and tax revenue for the financially stressed city. Most of the property owners sold their land to the city but a small group refused and, instead, filed suit claiming that the action represented an illegal taking. The plaintiffs argued that the city's plans for the land would destroy an established neighborhood to benefit private developers. In essence, they contended that the city had violated the public purpose requirement of a taking. The case, *Kelo v. City of New London*, went all the way to the U.S. Supreme Court, which, in a 5 to 4 decision in 2005, ruled in favor of the city. The reasoning went like this: New London wanted to use the land to promote economic development, which is a traditional function of government; ergo, the city's plan fulfilled a public purpose.[25]

Property rights advocates deplored the Court's decision, arguing that working-class residents and small business owners were being displaced so that the city could pursue a more productive use of the land. They had an advocate in Justice Sandra Day O'Connor, who dissented, saying, "The beneficiaries [of the Court's ruling] are likely to be those citizens with disproportionate influence and power in the political process, including large corporations and development firms."[26] Localities, not surprisingly, welcomed the decision, claiming that eminent domain was an essential tool in their efforts to regain and maintain economic vitality. They pointed to other examples of the use of eminent domain to benefit private firms, particularly a Nissan automobile facility in Canton, Mississippi, and a speedway in Kansas City, Kansas.

The court did invite states to place restrictions on localities' use of eminent domain if they so desired and, as of 2009, forty-three states had done so, either by legislative action or by citizen initiative. Clearly, the exercise of eminent domain is costly, not only in terms of dollars but in terms of goodwill. A poll conducted in New Hampshire found that 93 percent of Granite State residents opposed governmental taking of private land for economic development. This sentiment is one of the reasons why Washington, D.C., as it acquired land for the construction of a new stadium for the Washington Nationals baseball team, explicitly refused to take property. But by the same token, New York City was not reluctant to condemn property and take it for a new basketball arena for the New Jersey Nets. The definition of *public purpose* is likely to continue to unleash a power struggle in many communities.

## LOCAL EXECUTIVES

The mantle of leadership in local government falls most often on chief executives: mayors and managers. Although it is possible for chief executives to eschew a leadership role, they rarely do.

### Mayors

Mayors tend to be the most prominent figures in city government primarily because their position automatically makes them the center of attention.

Occasionally, a city council member emerges as a leader on a specific issue or stirs up some interest with verbal attacks on the mayor (which many observers interpret as jockeying for position to run against the mayor at the next election). But for the most part, attention is drawn to the mayor.

A lot is expected of the mayor. In 2004, the city comptroller of New York described the incumbent mayor, Michael Bloomberg, positively: "He's hired a very talented group. He's run city services well. He's approached things in a balanced fashion." However, the comptroller continued, "But the mayor is not just a CEO. The mayor is an emotional leader, an inspirational leader, and in that regard I don't think he's done nearly as good a job."[27] A similar theme was echoed by Los Angeles city councilman Bernard Parks as he mulled a bid for the mayor's job. "This is a big city, a thriving city. The mayor's office doesn't make you a leader. You have to have a leader in the mayor's office."[28] The Breaking New Ground box looks at recently elected mayors who have taken an unusual route to City Hall.

**Differences Between Strong and Weak Mayors** Chapter 10 explained some of the differences between strong and weak mayors. It is important to note that these labels refer to the *position*, not to the person who occupies it. A structure simply creates opportunities for leadership, not the certainty of it. True leaders are those who can take what is structurally a weak-mayor position

## BREAKING NEW GROUND

### From the NBA to City Hall

There are many paths to the mayor's office. The most well-worn path is service on the city council. There politicians can make a name for themselves as they become familiar with the issues facing the city. Another path runs from the business world. Mayoral candidates often contend that their success in the private sector has equipped them with the skills necessary to run city hall. But the National Basketball Association? Is the NBA becoming another pathway to the mayor's office?

Consider the cases of Dave Bing and Kevin Johnson. Both were point guards when they played the game; Bing was with the Detroit Pistons and Johnson with the Phoenix Suns. Both were highly regarded players: Bing played in seven NBA All-Star games between 1968 and 1976; Johnson was a three-time NBA All-Star.

And what are they doing now? Bing is the mayor of Detroit and Johnson is the mayor of Sacramento. Perhaps being a point guard has something to do with it. Running the offense may be very good training for running a city. Both mayors face significant issues in their respective cities. Detroit is struggling with a local economy that is among the worst in the nation; Sacramento has its own budget problems.

But before concluding that the NBA is the fast-track to the mayor's office, think about James Donaldson, a former Seattle Supersonics player. He and others challenged incumbent Mayor Greg Nickels for the top spot in Seattle in 2009. At 7 feet, 2 inches tall, Donaldson would not be mistaken for a point guard. Ultimately, his bid for the mayoralty fell short as he finished in fourth place. Still, the popularity of professional athletes often gives them a leg up when they seek public office.

SOURCES: "Player," *Governing* 22 (June 2009): 56; Office of the Mayor, www.cityofsacramento.org/mayor (August 10, 2009); Chris Grygiel, "Former Sonic Donaldson Enters Seattle Mayor's Race," www.seattlepi.com/local/ (March 26, 2009).

and transform it into a strong mayorship. Some mayor–council systems have added a chief administrative officer (CAO) to their structures, thus blurring the distinction between them and council–manager systems.[29]

A *strong-mayor* structure establishes the mayor as the sole chief executive who exercises substantive policy responsibilities. In this kind of structure, the position of city manager, someone who can expand an administrative role and become a policy rival to the mayor, does not exist. As an ideal type, a strong mayor has the following features:

- is elected directly by the voters, not selected by the council,
- serves a four-year, not two-year, term of office,
- has no limitations on re-election,
- plays a central role in budget formulation,
- has extensive appointment and removal powers,
- has veto power over council-enacted ordinances.

The actual powers of a specific strong mayor may not include all these items, but the more of these powers a mayor can exercise, the stronger her position is and the easier it is for her to become a leader.

A *weak-mayor* structure does not provide these elements. Its design is such that the mayor shares policy responsibilities with the council and perhaps a manager, and serves a limited amount of time in office. (In an especially weak-mayor system, the job is passed around among the council members, each of whom takes a turn at being mayor.) A weak-mayor structure often implies strong council involvement in budgetary and personnel matters. The variation in mayoral power is reflected in mayoral remuneration—weak mayors receive token salaries. If a mayor in a weak-mayor structure is to become a leader, he has to exceed the job description.

Mayoral leadership has been the subject of discussion in the popular press.[30] An article, "The Lure of the Strong Mayor," argued that large, diverse communities grappling with complex problems are better served by a structure that fixes leadership and accountability in the mayor's office. In response, "Beware the Lure of the 'Strong' Mayor" contended that a too powerful mayor could run amok, building political machines based on the exchange of benefits. Structural differences can indeed have consequences. It is important to remember, however, that individuals who work within structures are the essential factor. Leaders can make structures work for them (sometimes by performing minor surgery on the structure). As David Morgan and Sheilah Watson note, "Even in council–manager communities—where mayors have the fewest formal powers—by negotiating, networking, and facilitating the efforts of others, mayors clearly rise above the nominal figurehead role."[31]

**Black Mayors** By 2009, African American mayors headed more than 700 cities and towns across the country. Not only can you find black mayors leading cities where the population is predominantly black, you can find them in majority white cities, too, as the listing in Table 11.2 shows. This new generation of African American mayors tends to be problem solvers, not crusaders;

| Black Mayors in Big Cities, 2010 | | TABLE 11.2 |
| --- | --- | --- |
| **CITY AND STATE**[a] | **BLACKS AS A PERCENTAGE OF CITY POPULATION** | **MAYOR** |
| Philadelphia, PA | 43.2 | Michael Nutter |
| Detroit, MI | 81.6 | Dave Bing |
| Columbus, OH | 24.5 | Michael Coleman |
| Charlotte, NC | 34.7 | Anthony Foxx |
| Memphis, TN | 61.4 | A. C. Wharton |
| Baltimore, MD | 64.3 | Stephanie Rawlilngs-Blake |
| Washington, DC | 60.0 | Adrian Fenty |
| New Orleans, LA | 67.3 | C. Ray Nagin |
| Cleveland, OH | 51.0 | Frank Jackson |
| Atlanta, GA | 61.4 | Kasim Reed |
| Oakland, CA | 41.7 | Ron Dellums |
| Cincinnati, OH | 42.9 | Mark Mallory |
| Buffalo, NY | 37.2 | Byron Brown |
| Newark, NJ | 53.5 | Cory Booker |
| Birmingham, AL | 73.5 | Roderick Royal |
| Baton Rouge, LA | 50.0 | Melvin Holden |
| Greensboro, NC | 37.4 | Yvonne J. Johnson |
| Shreveport, LA | 50.8 | Cedric Glover |

[a]Cities with populations of 200,000 or more, listed in descending order according to size.
SOURCES: Black Mayors of Cities with 50,000-plus Population, 2007, Joint Center for Political and Economic Studies, www.jointcenter.org (August 10, 2009); Factoid: Black Mayors of Cities with Population Over 50,000, allotherpersons.wordpress.com (August 25, 2008), updated by the authors.

political pragmatists, not ideologues.[32] For example, in his successful 2006 campaign for mayor of Newark, New Jersey, Cory Booker's message was about hard work...and hope. On his campaign website he proclaimed, "Working together we're going to make Newark's neighborhoods safe and our schools safe. ...Bringing real change to Newark won't be easy."[33]

Increased success by blacks in mayoral elections has led some observers to talk of **deracialization**, or the de-emphasis of race as a campaign issue in an effort to attract white voter support.[34] Instead of making racial appeals, candidates offer a race-neutral platform that stresses their personal qualifications and political experience.[35] In cities where the white electorate outnumbers the black electorate, such as Columbus and Buffalo, neither Michael Coleman nor Byron Brown could have been elected without the support of white voters. Even in cities where white voters constitute a minority, they often control the electoral balance when two African American candidates square off in the mayoral race.

**deracialization**

The de-emphasis of race in politics, especially in campaigns, so that there is less racial bloc voting.

Deracialization works both ways. Baltimore, a majority African American city, had a black mayor from 1987 to 1999, a white mayor from 1999 to 2007, and a black mayor since then. Deracialization of local campaigns, and the manner in which a mayor elected by a multiracial coalition governs once in office, is a compelling subject for research. For example, a study of Houston found that when minority mayors run for re-election, evaluations of job performance are more important to voters than racial group affiliation is.[36]

**Women Mayors** More women are running for and winning local elective offices. The data from cities with populations of 30,000 or more are instructive. In 1973, fewer than 2 percent of the cities in that population range had female mayors. A quarter-century later, the number of women mayors had increased to 202, or 21 percent, a level around which it has fluctuated. (In 2009, 17 percent of cities of 30,000 or more were governed by women.) Eleven women are at the helm of large U.S. cities (populations of 200,000 or more), as Table 11.3 shows.

The ranks of female mayors of major cities nearly increased by one in 2004 when Donna Frye, a member of San Diego's city council, ran against the incumbent mayor. Frye, competing as a write-in candidate, lost in a hotly disputed election. At issue were 5,547 ballots in which voters had written in Frye's name but neglected to fill in the small oval next to the write-in line. Election officials did not count these ballots because state law requires that the ovals be filled in for a write-in vote to count. Frye's supporters contended that regardless of the

**TABLE 11.3    Women Mayors in Big Cities, 2010**

| CITY AND STATE | MAYOR |
| --- | --- |
| Houston, TX | Annise Parker |
| Baltimore, MD | Stephanie Rawlings-Blake |
| Fresno, CA | Ashley Swearengin |
| Tulsa, OK | Kathryn L. Taylor |
| Tampa, FL | Pam Iorio |
| Stockton, CA | Ann Johnston |
| Greensboro, NC | Yvonne J. Johnson |
| Plano, TX | Pat Evans |
| Glendale, AZ | Elain M. Scruggs |
| Chula Vista, CA | Cheryl Cox |
| Scottsdale, AZ | Mary Manross |

NOTE: Cities with populations of 200,000 or more, listed in descending order according to size.
SOURCE: Center for American Women and Politics, "Fast Facts: Women Mayors in U.S. Cities 2009," www.cawp.rutgers.edu/fast_facts/levels_of_office/Local-WomenMayors.php (August 11, 2009), updated by the authors.

ovals, voter intent was clear: a vote for Frye. Had those ballots been counted, Frye would have won by 3,439 votes.[37]

Studies of female mayoral candidates have dispelled several electoral myths.[38] For example, women do not appear to experience greater difficulty in raising money or gaining newspaper endorsements than men do. Women mayors, however, do tend to be political novices. Few female mayors in Florida, for instance, had held elective office before their mayoral election; if they had, it was usually a city council seat. Other research indicates that mayors, regardless of gender, see their political environments similarly, which makes sense: Successful local politicians know their communities.

Pam Iorio, mayor of Tampa, Florida, holds a press conference.
*SOURCE: Doug Benc/Getty Images Sport/Getty Images*

**Visionary Mayors** For mayors to become leaders, they need to have vision; that is, they need the ability to identify goals for their city and achieve them, which is easier said than done. As a former Dallas mayor commented, "Mayors work in real time. You have to limit your agenda to the big stuff."[39] Three erstwhile mayors widely hailed as visionary when they were in office put their heads together recently to come up with a how-to list.[40] Their rules for creating and implementing successful city visions included several obvious items such as "borrow from everyone" and "build on existing strengths." But the list also instructed mayors to market their vision on a human scale so that local residents and business interests can understand its relevance to them. Getting cooperation from the community goes a long way in bolstering mayoral leadership. But the immediate tasks of keeping the city running smoothly can cause some mayors to lose sight of the vision or, at the least, put it aside as they worry about potholes, garbage collection, and budget deficits.

## City Managers

City managers (as well as county administrators and appointed school superintendents) exemplify the movement toward reformed local government. Local government reform was a **Progressive Era** movement that sought to depose the corrupt and inefficient partisan political machines that controlled many American cities. To the reformers, local government had become too political; what was needed, they believed, was a government designed along the lines of a business corporation. To achieve their goals, reformers advocated fundamental structural changes in local government such as the abolition of partisan local elections, the use of at-large electoral systems, and the installation of a professionally trained city manager. Altering the structure of local government

**Progressive Era**

A period in the early twentieth century that focused on reforming or cleaning up government.

has had profound consequences for local government leadership. City managers—the professional, neutral experts whose job is to run the day-to-day affairs of the city—have become key leaders.

In the original conception, managers were to implement but not formulate policy. Administration and politics were to be kept separate. The managers' responsibility would be to administer the policies enacted by the elected officials—the city councils—by whom they were hired (and fired). In other words, they were to act as the agents of their political principals. But it is impossible to keep administration and politics completely separate. City managers are influenced not only by their training and by the councils that employ them but also by their own political ideologies.[41] When it comes to making choices, they balance professional norms, the politics of the issue, and their own predispositions. Hence, city managers typically end up being far more influential on the local government scene than their neutral persona might suggest.

**Managers as Policy Leaders** According to the International City/County Management Association, the city managers' professional association, the role of the manager is to help the governing body function more effectively. "Managers—and their staffs—need to build political capacity so they can assist the elected body in framing community issues."[42] Ways in which the manager can assume a larger role in policy making include proposing community goals and service levels; structuring the budget preparation, review, and adoption process so that it is linked to goals and service levels; and orienting new council members to organizational processes and norms. This approach has had the intended effect. James Svara, who surveyed officials in large cities, concluded that managers have become "more assertive in attempting to focus the council on long-range concerns and in shaping the tone of the policymaking process."[43]

One indisputable role for the city manager is as an information source for the busy, part-time city council. For instance, suppose that some enterprising college students are requesting a change in a city ordinance that prohibits street vendors. The council asks the manager to study the pros and cons of street vending. At a subsequent meeting, he reports on other cities' experiences: Has it created a litter problem? Does it draw clientele away from established businesses? How much revenue can be expected from vendor licensing fees? The manager then offers alternative courses of action (allow street vending only at lunchtime, restrict pushcarts to Main Street) and evaluates their probable consequences. In some councils, the manager is asked to make a formal recommendation; in others, his recommendation is more along the lines of "Well, what do you think?" At some point, a vote is called and the council makes an official decision.

**Working with Councils and Mayors** City managers are not cut from one mold—they vary in terms of experience, outlook, and style. Ideally, a manager should be a near-perfect match for the community she serves. A manager who is focused on making the city function smoothly might be poorly suited for a community in need of an innovative, big-picture kind of leader. And the converse is true: A manager who wants to take on an expansive leadership role would find himself stymied in a city seeking a technical problem solver. Obviously, it is important that the city council and the city manager share similar views on the role the manager is expected to play. However, a good council–manager fit can be difficult to maintain. The composition of the city council can change, new issues will emerge, and managers may shift their orientation toward the job. It is no wonder that the average tenure of a manager in a city is between six and seven years. Some are fired, of course, but some are "ladder climbers" who move on to larger cities, whereas others are "lateral movers," relocating to similar size communities.[44] Consequently, the search for the "right" manager is nearly constant in many places.

A veteran city administrator in Missouri offered new managers this advice about dealing with elected officials:

- Don't substitute your political judgment for the judgments of the elected officials.
- Don't cut red ribbons, cut red tape...in other words, keep a low profile.
- Listen, count to three, and choose your words wisely.
- The council–manager relationship is not a game won on points.
- There's no great honor in being fired, but there's no shame in being fired for the right reason.[45]

As noted earlier, one new trend is the hiring of professional managers in cities that do not use the council–manager form of government. Cities are adapting their structures to employ officials with titles such as managing director or CAO.[46] These individuals have the educational credentials and professional experiences of city managers, and their role in a strong-mayor city is typically limited to administrative matters. For many years, the city of Tampa, Florida, used a structure in which the mayor had direct responsibility for the police and fire departments, along with offices such as art and cultural affairs, the city clerk, and the development office. To assist the mayor in running some of the city's large departments, a CAO was employed. The CAO supervised departments such as parks and recreation, public works, and water. But it remained a strong mayor system: The CAO served at the discretion of the mayor and reported to him. Wanting to handle things differently, Tampa's new mayor, Pam Iorio, replaced the CAO position with a more narrowly focused chief of staff when she took office, and reconfigured the agencies.

# LOCAL LEGISLATURES

Local legislatures include city councils, county commissions, town boards of aldermen or selectmen, special district boards, and school boards. They are representative, deliberative policy-making bodies. In this section, we focus on city councils because that is where most of the research has taken place, but many of the points are also applicable to the other local legislative bodies such as county commissions and school boards. Although the ensuing discussion focuses on patterns across councils, it is important to remember that significant variations may exist from one city to another. For example, in some communities, council members receive high salaries, are assisted by clerical and research staff, and have no limits on the number of terms they can serve. In Chicago, for instance, city council members (called **aldermen**) earn more than $110,000 per year, have office staffs, and can serve an unlimited number of four-year terms. (To put it in perspective, the mayor of Chicago has an annual salary of $216,000.) But in Oklahoma City, a council–manager city, the council receives a yearly salary of $12,000; the mayor earns $24,000. In many smaller places, council service is considered a volunteer activity, with members receiving virtually no compensation whatsoever.

> **aldermen**
>
> A label used in some communities for members of a local legislative body, such as a city council.

## City Council Members: Old and New

A former member of the city council of Concord, California, harkening back to an earlier time, commented, "When I first came on the city council, it was like a good-old-boys' club."[47] The standard description was that the city council was a part-time, low-paying haven for public-spirited white men who did not consider themselves politicians. Most councils used at-large electoral mechanisms, so individual council members had no specific, territorially based constituency. Council members considered themselves volunteers. Research on city councils in the San Francisco Bay area in the 1960s found that these volunteer members were fairly unresponsive to public pressures and tended to vote according to their own preferences.[48] In other words, there was not much representation going on.

Today, the circumstances have changed. City councils are less white, less male, and less passive than they were in the past. Now, city councilors are more engaged and active. Some of this change is due to modifications in the electoral mechanism such as the abandonment of at-large or citywide elections and the switch to district (or ward) elections. Figure 11.2 displays the district map for Boston, a city that, in 2002, redrew council district lines to conform to changes in population. Bostonians elect nine council members from districts and four at-large members. (Table 11.4 shows the wide variation in both council size and number of members elected at large and from districts in the twenty largest cities.) In many cities, including San Antonio, Texas, a council–manager city, only the mayor is currently elected at large. In cities across the nation, changes in election mechanisms signaled a change in council composition. More African Americans, Hispanics, and women serve on city councils than ever before, and not surprisingly, they are taking their governance roles quite seriously.

## Council Diversity

Racial and ethnic minorities are making inroads into local politics in increasing numbers. In 2006, for example, nearly 4,000 African Americans and 1,900 Hispanics served in elected city and county offices across the country.[49] (These

**Boston's City Council Districts**

FIGURE
11.2

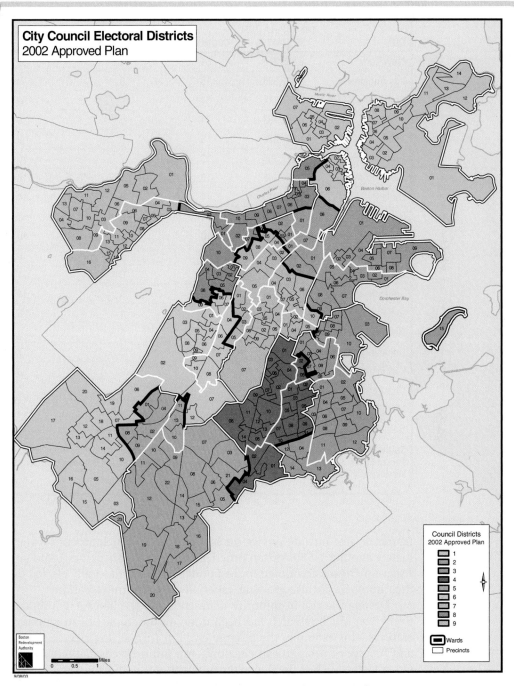

SOURCE: www.cityofboston.gov/citycouncil/pdfs/approved_planBmap.pdf (August 10, 2009).

| TABLE 11.4 | City Councils of the Twenty Largest U.S. Cities | | | |
|---|---|---|---|---|
| CITY | 2008 POPULATION ESTIMATES | COUNCIL SIZE | NUMBER ELECTED AT LARGE | NUMBER ELECTED FROM DISTRICTS |
| New York | 8,363,710 | 51 | 0 | 51 |
| Los Angeles | 3,833,995 | 15 | 0 | 15 |
| Chicago | 2,853,114 | 50 | 0 | 50 |
| Houston | 2,242,193 | 14 | 5 | 9 |
| Phoenix | 1,567,924 | 8 | 0 | 8 |
| Philadelphia | 1,447,395 | 17 | 7 | 10 |
| San Antonio | 1,351,305 | 10 | 0 | 10 |
| Dallas | 1,279,910 | 14 | 0 | 14 |
| San Diego | 1,279,329 | 8 | 0 | 8 |
| San Jose | 948,279 | 10 | 0 | 10 |
| Detroit | 912,062 | 9 | 9 | 0 |
| San Francisco | 808,976 | 11 | 0 | 11 |
| Jacksonville | 807,815 | 19 | 5 | 14 |
| Indianapolis | 798,382 | 29 | 4 | 25 |
| Austin | 757,688 | 6 | 6 | 0 |
| Columbus | 754,885 | 7 | 0 | 7 |
| Fort Worth | 703,073 | 8 | 0 | 8 |
| Charlotte | 687,456 | 11 | 4 | 7 |
| Memphis | 669,651 | 13 | 0 | 13 |
| Baltimore | 636,919 | 15 | 1 | 14 |

SOURCE: U.S. Census Bureau, "Table 1: Annual Estimates of the Population for Incorporated Places, Ranked by July 1, 2008 Population: April 1, 2000 to July 1, 2008" 2008 Population Estimates (July 30, 2009); individual city websites.

figures do not include service on school boards, which account for approximately another 1,550 African Americans and 1,650 Hispanics.) And although Asian Americans accounted for just under 1 percent of locally elected officials, their numbers are also growing, especially in California localities.

Despite the rise in minority representation, the percentages remain relatively low. Much research has been done on the impact of structural considerations—for example, the at-large election format, the size of the council, and the use of nonpartisan elections—on minority council representation.[50] Other factors such as the size of the minority group, its geographical concentration, and its political cohesiveness affect electoral success. In general, a higher proportion of African American council members can be found in central cities that use a mayor–council structure and in southern cities with large black populations. Councils with higher-than-average Latino representation tend to be found in the Southwest and Far West and in larger central cities that use council–manager structures. Thus far, Asian representation has been clustered primarily in the Pacific Coast area in larger council–manager central cities. Native American representation is highest in small communities using commission structures in the southwestern and Pacific Coast areas of the country. The increase in nonwhite representation on councils has policy consequences. Data from 351 city council members show nonwhites pursuing a more liberal agenda than whites do.[51]

Given the finite number of council seats in any community and the fact that more groups are now clamoring for representation, two outcomes are possible: Minority groups may try to build coalitions, or they may opt for a more independent, competitive approach. Although temporary electoral coalitions have emerged in a few cities, racial and ethnic minority groups have remained largely separate.[52] Politically, it appears that inter–minority group competition is on the rise. Research in ninety-six cities demonstrates, for example, that an increase in the Latino population has a negative effect on black representation on city councils.[53] Another interesting question is the extent to which the concept of deracialization can be extended to Latinos and Asian Americans in their bids for local offices. Research on the Little Saigon area of Orange County, California, showed evidence of racial bloc voting in every election for city council or school board between 1998 and 2002 in which a Vietnamese American competed against a white candidate.[54]

Local governing boards in cities and counties are becoming more diverse in another way: The number of local elected officials (the tally includes more than city council members) who are openly gay or lesbian has risen to more than 200.[55] The Gay and Lesbian Victory Fund is a political action committee that provides technical and financial support for openly gay and lesbian candidates, many of whom are seeking local offices. Christine Quinn, who in 2006 became speaker of New York City's council, is one of the most prominent; Sam Adams, formerly a city commissioner in Portland, Oregon, and now mayor, is another; so is Houston's newly elected mayor, Annise Parker. A study focusing on cities and counties that had anti-discrimination ordinances in place revealed several findings about the election of gays and lesbians. Based on that sample of jurisdictions, gay and lesbian electoral success was more likely in larger cities; in jurisdictions with higher numbers of nonfamily households (such as university communities); and in places with partisan, district election of council members.[56] The limited nature of the sample makes it difficult to generalize to all localities, but the research yields interesting findings about council diversity.

## Councils in Action: Increasing Conflict

In earlier times, when members of the council came from the same socio-economic stratum (in some communities, *all* members of the at-large council came from the same neighborhood) and when they shared a common political philosophy, governing was easier. Members of the council could come together before the meeting (usually at breakfast in a restaurant near City Hall) and discuss the items on the agenda. Thus, they could arrive at an informal resolution of any particularly troubling items and thereby transform the actual council meeting into a rubber-stamp exercise. No wonder that the majority of council votes were often unanimous; members were merely ratifying what they had already settled on.

**Intracouncil Conflict** Council members elected by districts report more factionalism and less unanimity than do their counterparts elected at large. The growing tendency of cities to move away from complete reliance on at-large electoral mechanisms suggests that council conflict will rise in the future. Fifty-five percent of the city council members responding to a recent national survey reported that council member conflict was a serious source of frustration to them.[57] Ten years earlier, only 33 percent voiced a similar concern.

High levels of council conflict have other consequences. Research on city managers has shown a link between council conflict and managerial burnout.[58] Burned-out city managers perform poorly and often leave the city or the profession itself. To minimize the deleterious effect of conflict, budding city managers are encouraged to develop conflict-management skills to assist in their dealings with the council.[59]

**Battles with the Mayor** Relationships between a city council and the mayor can be conflictive, to say the least. In fact, they can be downright hostile. A former mayor of Philadelphia did not pull any punches when he referred to the city council as "the worst legislative body in the free world."[60] Birmingham, Alabama, and Salt Lake City, Utah, offer lessons in council–mayor dealings. In Birmingham, the retirement of a veteran mayor had opened the top job; Bernard Kincaid, an erstwhile city councilor, won the post in 1999. The council, led by an unsuccessful candidate for mayor, saw the change in leadership as an opportunity to reassert its authority. Thus, the council passed ordinances limiting the scope of mayoral power. The mayor vetoed the ordinances; the council overrode the vetoes; the mayor took the council to court.[61] The jockeying for power between Mayor Kincaid and the council continued until council elections in 2001 changed the composition of the council somewhat.

In Salt Lake City, a new mayor, Rocky Anderson, took several actions at odds with the city council when he assumed office in 2000. He vetoed several of the council's pet projects, and he took action unilaterally through executive orders when the council was indecisive on an issue. In the mayor's words, "You don't ask the council...you just do it."[62] And what did the city council in Salt Lake City think of the mayor's approach? One council member put it this way: "It's not smart to treat us with such disdain."[63] The result for citizens of Utah's capital city was a tense political situation.

Council–mayor conflict is not necessarily unproductive. Conflict is expected in a political system that operates on the foundation of separation of powers. Clashes between the legislative branch and the executive branch can produce better government. But when the disagreements between the council and the mayor escalate to the point of gridlock, effective governance is stymied.

## Women on Local Governing Boards

Do women officeholders act differently from men and pursue different interests in public office? As the number of female officeholders in local government increases, this question becomes especially compelling. Nationally, women constitute 12 percent of county governing boards and 44 percent of school boards. Alaska and Hawaii consistently report female officeholding far above these national averages; Georgia and North Dakota are examples of states in which the proportion of women in local public office is substantially lower. In the South, a study of city councils in medium-size to large cities found that the percentage of councils without female members ranged from lows of 13 percent and 18 percent in Virginia and North Carolina, respectively, to highs of 70 percent in Arkansas and 73 percent in Alabama.[64] A national survey of city council members showed that, compared with males, female council members are much more likely to view the representation of women, environmentalists, abortion rights activists, racial minorities, and good-government organizations as extremely important.[65] In addition, men and women on the council see each other through different lenses. As Susan Adams Beck points out, "Men often express frustration that women ask too many questions, while women see themselves as well-prepared and think their male colleagues are often 'winging it.' "[66]

A review of the research suggests that women officeholders frequently differ not only from their male counterparts but also from one another. Four basic types of female political actors have been hypothesized:

- The traditional politician.
- The traditional liberal feminist.
- The caring humanist.
- The change-oriented feminist.[67]

Women who are traditional politicians articulate no particular gender differences and do not expect much divergence between men's and women's interests. Traditional liberal feminists, on the other hand, are concerned with what have been termed women's issues, such as abortion, rape, domestic violence, pornography, child care, and education. In addressing these issues, they work within the norms and practices of the established political system. Female officeholders of the caring-humanist type, although concerned with women's issues, place a higher priority on matters of social justice and ecological balance. They also tend to be somewhat estranged from the established order. And change-oriented feminists see sexism as a fundamental characteristic of our society and therefore have no interest in being assimilated into established male structures. Instead, they want to create a new order based on female sex-role expectations. Although all four types are represented among women holding local public office, most female officeholders have tended to cluster in the first two types.

# LEADERSHIP AND CAPACITY

In the final analysis, the concept of leadership remains somewhat ephemeral. Regardless of the difficulty we might have in defining it precisely, however, it is a central, critical concern in local government. Much is being made of a new pragmatism among America's big-city mayors, an orientation that is independent of race or ethnicity.[68] It is a back-to-basics approach to governing, one that emphasizes service delivery, balanced budgets, and working with the private sector to cure the city's ills. This new breed of mayor also seeks to build alliances with adjacent suburbs. Witness the pragmatism of Atlanta's former mayor, Bill Campbell, who wanted to greet visitors coming to his city for the 1996 Olympics with a sign reading "Welcome to Atlanta—a real city with real problems and real people working real hard every day to solve them."[69] Leave it to New York City mayor, Michael Bloomberg, to put it in perspective. When asked whether he would run for higher office, he responded, "I think I have a better job than the governor and the president."[70]

At the same time, local governments are becoming more entrepreneurial. Local governments are confronting their problems and challenges by trying new ideas, exploring alternatives, and reaching out for solutions. New approaches do not necessarily work and therein lies the risk. But when they do, other places are quick to embrace them. As a result, local governments change and, one hopes, improve.

Although our focus has been on formal leaders in government, remember that leadership can be bottom-up; that is, leadership can flow from the grass roots into and perhaps even around government. An example comes from comprehensive community initiatives (CCIs). These efforts seek to build neighborhood capacity through various means, such as leadership training and organizational collaboration. Participants in CCIs share a sense of connectedness and a commitment to solve neighborhood problems. The results are tangible: a street-lighting project in Hartford, Connecticut; a scholarship program in Memphis, Tennessee; recreational activity grants in Detroit, Michigan.[71] Just as important is the empowerment of the grassroots participants who are, in fact, community leaders on a smaller scale.

## CHAPTER RECAP

- Elite theory (a small group of leaders possesses power and rules society) and pluralist theory (power is dispersed among competing groups) have dominated the study of community power. Attention has been focused more recently on regime theory and the related concepts of systemic power and strategic advantage.

- Nonprofit organizations have become increasingly important in communities.

- Mayors tend to be the central figures in city politics and government, even if they operate in formally weak-mayor structures. One of the interesting features of mayoral politics is the deracialization of campaigns.

- City managers have become policy leaders. Even in cities without a formal city manager structure, chief administrative officers are being hired to take on some of the management responsibilities.

- City councils have changed from the good-old-boy clubs of the past. They are more active, they are more diverse, and more conflict occurs between city council members.

One of the reasons for these changes is the switch from at-large, or citywide, elections to district (or ward) election of council members.

- Leadership is the ability to realize goals. It varies from one place to another, as a function of the situation. Leadership also comes from the grass roots.

## Key Terms

elite theory *(p. 300)*
pluralist theory *(p. 300)*
reputational approach *(p. 302)*
decisional method *(p. 302)*

regime *(p. 304)*
nonprofit organizations
 *(p. 305)*
hyperpluralism *(p. 307)*

taking *(p. 307)*
deracialization *(p. 311)*
Progressive Era *(p. 313)*
aldermen *(p. 316)*

## Internet Resources

The association of mayors of cities with populations of 30,000 or more, the U.S. Conference of Mayors, has a website at **www.usmayors.org.**

Mayors in a single state frequently belong to a statewide organization such as **www.njcm.org** in New Jersey.

Specialized constituency groups often have their own organizations and websites, as does the National Conference of Black Mayors at **www.ncbm.org**.

The website for the Center for American Women and Politics at Rutgers University, **www.cawp. rutgers.edu**, contains a wealth of data on women and politics.

Information about the city and county management profession can be found at the International City/County Management Association's website: **www.icma.org.**

SOURCE: AP Photo/Tim Mueller

# State–Local Relations

# 12

Officials in Florida cities thought that they had come up with a clever way to issue citations to drivers who run red lights: use surveillance cameras to record the culprit's license tag. After all, more than twenty states already allowed such a program, and the data showed that the program results in fewer serious injury-causing crashes. Moreover, if the cameras catch enough red-light runners, they can generate much needed revenue for cash-strapped jurisdictions. Although Florida did not have a state law authorizing the use of surveillance cameras at intersections, the cities intended to adopt local **ordinances** to do so. Not so fast, the state's attorney general told the city; taking such an action would require the state to amend its own statutes.[1] And thus far, the state legislature has not been inclined to act. A few enterprising localities figured out a way to circumvent the state's ruling—for example, placing the cameras on private property—but most waited for the state to take action. This example underscores a central theme of this chapter: A state can supersede the local governments within its boundaries.

The relationship between states and their communities is often strained. On the one hand, state government gives local governments life. States create the rules for their localities. On the other hand, state governments historically have not treated their local governments well. Over time, states have realized that mistreating their governmental offspring is counterproductive, and many have launched a sometimes uncoordinated process of assistance and empowerment of local government.

Capturing this evolution is the statement of the National Conference of State Legislatures (NCSL) Task Force on State–Local Relations: "Legislators should place a higher priority on state–local issues than has been done in the past. The time has come to change their attitude toward local governments—to stop considering them as just another special interest group and to start treating them as partners in our federal system."[2] Stronger, more competent local governments are an asset to state government.

Chapter 13 will address the financial relationship between state and local governments. This chapter examines broader issues for the two entities and related trends. Let us first consider the most fundamental issue: the distribution of authority between the state and its constituent units.

**ordinance**

Enacted by the governing body, it is the local government equivalent of a statute.

# THE DISTRIBUTION OF AUTHORITY

In essence, local governments are creatures of their states. In the terminology of Chapter 2, the relationship is that of a unitary system: the state holds all legal power. Federal and state courts have consistently upheld the dependency of localities on the state since Iowa's judge John F. Dillon first laid down **Dillon's rule** in 1868. Dillon's rule established that local governments may exercise only those powers explicitly granted to them by the state, those clearly implied by the explicit powers, and those absolutely essential to the declared objectives and purposes of the local government. Any doubt regarding the legality of any specific local government power is resolved in favor of the state.[3] This perspective runs counter to the more Jeffersonian conception that local governments are imbued with inherent rights.[4]

In the words of the U.S. Advisory Commission on Intergovernmental Relations (ACIR), "State legislatures are the trustees of the basic rules of local governance in America. The laws and constitutions of each state are the basic legal instruments of local governance."[5] The ACIR statement denotes the essence of the distribution of authority between a state and its localities. In short, it is up to the state to determine the amount and type of authority a local government may possess. As specified by Dillon's rule, localities depend on the state to give them sufficient power to operate effectively.

**Dillon's rule**

A rule that limits the powers of local government to those expressly granted by the state or those powers closely linked to the express powers.

## The Amount and Type of Authority

The amount and type of authority that states give their local governments vary widely. Some states grant their localities wide-ranging powers to restructure themselves, impose new taxes, and take on additional functions. Others, much more conservative with their power, force local governments to turn to the legislature for approval to act. Empowerment also depends on the type of local government. As noted in Chapter 10, general-purpose governments such as counties, cities, and towns have wider latitude than special-purpose entities like school districts. Even general-purpose governments possess different degrees of authority; counties tend to be more circumscribed than cities in their ability to modify their form of government and expand their service offerings.

In general, states' regulatory reach is great. For example, states may regulate local governments'

- finances (by establishing debt limits and requiring balanced budgets),
- personnel (by setting qualifications for certain positions and prescribing employee pension plans),
- structure (by establishing forms of government and outlawing particular electoral systems),
- processes (by requiring public hearings and open meetings and mandating financial disclosure),
- functions (by ordering the provision of public safety functions and proscribing the pursuit of enterprise activities),
- service standards (by adopting solid waste guidelines and setting acceptable water-quality levels).

The preceding list makes the point: The state capitol casts a long shadow.

Building codes offer an illustration of the variability of state–local authority. Researcher Peter May examined all fifty states to determine the amount of discretion given local governments to adopt and enforce building codes.[6] He found several different patterns. Twelve states (Kentucky and Michigan among them) played an aggressive role by imposing mandatory building codes on their local governments and overseeing local compliance. Thirteen states (including Indiana and Wyoming) had mandatory local codes but stopped short of state review or oversight. The rest of the states gave their local governments more leeway. In eight states (Iowa and Nebraska among them), local governments themselves decided whether to enforce the state building code. And seventeen states (including Delaware and Oklahoma) had no comprehensive building codes; thus, local governments were free to design and enact their own. The building code example reflects an important point: States vary in their treatment of local government.

**second-order devolution**

A shift in power from state government to local government.

Devolution (the shift in power from the national government to the states) has also occurred between states and their local governments. In the state–local case, it is called **second-order devolution**. The more recently a state has adopted its constitution, the more likely the document is to contain provisions that strengthen local governments.[7] Many state constitutions set forth a provision for home rule (defined in Chapter 10). Although home rule falls short of actual local self-government, it is an important step in the direction of greater local decision making.[8] And local jurisdictions tend to be extremely protective of whatever power they have wrested from state government. For example, the beleaguered Baltimore school system rejected a state plan to take over the schools in 2004 because, in the words of the one local official, "the solution to the problems in Baltimore city starts with Baltimore city."[9]

## A State–Local Tug of War

Local governments want their states to provide them with adequate funding and ample discretion. Local officials are supremely confident of their abilities to govern, given sufficient state support. These same local officials express concern that neither their policy-making power nor their financial authority has kept pace with the increased administrative responsibilities placed on them by state government. The recognition and correction of such conditions are the state's responsibility. An extreme case of strained relationships is described in the Engaging State–Local Relations box.

States are not at all reluctant to exercise power vis-à-vis their local jurisdictions. Consider these examples:

- Multnomah County, Oregon, adopted a restaurant menu nutrition-labeling ordinance in 2009 only to see its effort superseded later when the state passed legislation on the subject.[10]
- In 2009, with the hole in Arizona's budget expanding, legislators decided to try to squeeze some money out of local governments, demanding that municipalities, counties, and special districts send the state $65 million. Not surprisingly, a lawsuit ensued.[11]
- After a local jurisdiction used its power to take property in an aggressive way in 2004, Colorado lawmakers introduced bills designed to restrict localities' power in this area.[12]

## Engaging State–Local Relations

## Killington, Vermont, Explores Its Options…In New Hampshire

Killington, Vermont, a place known as a skiing destination, may be heading down a slippery slope. At the annual town meeting in 2004, residents voted to explore the possibility of seceding from Vermont and becoming part of New Hampshire. To convey their seriousness, residents allocated $20,000 in the town's $2.5 million budget to get the secession movement underway. What fueled this unusual action? In a word: taxes. Killington residents were fed up with a Vermont tax system that, in their view, is inequitable, particularly with regard to funding for education. New Hampshire, their neighbor to the east, looks inviting in comparison. Buoyed by the support of their fellow citizens, the leaders of the secession movement sought an audience with the governor of New Hampshire to pitch their idea.

The decision by Killington to pursue secession made financial sense. One economic study projected a tax savings of $10 million annually if the town joined New Hampshire. However, one major logistical problem is that Killington is not on the Vermont–New Hampshire border; it is located twenty-five miles west of the Granite State. So, in effect, were it to join New Hampshire, Killington would be an out-of-state "island" in Vermont. Another problem is that any attempt to leave Vermont would have to be approved by the legislature in the Green Mountain State. The odds of that happening are slim to none. In New Hampshire, however, the idea of adding Killington got a boost when lawmakers created a commission to study the issue.

Ultimately, what Killington residents really hoped to accomplish with their bold exploit was to send a message to policy makers in the state capital, Montpelier. Threatening secession is an extreme action, but localities frustrated by state policies and actions have few tools at their disposal. And although Killington's threat of secession was more bluster than reality, it attracted extensive media coverage to the issue of tax reform, and state policy makers definitely took notice.

SOURCES: Seth Harkness, "Killington Voters Opt to Leave Vt., Join N.H.," *Rutland Herald* (March 4, 2004): 1; "Killington Residents Vote to Secede from Vermont," www.cnn.com (March 4, 2004); Kevin Forrest, "Killington Secession Not Too Popular in VT," *New Hampshire Public Radio* (March 16, 2005).

A persistent theme runs through the preceding list: State government can impose its will on local governments. These examples shouldn't suggest that states and localities are invariably at each other's throats. Plenty of examples of state–local partnerships exist, such as Florida's and Palm Beach County's joint effort to attract biotechnology industries. The county purchased the land to build a research facility ($200 million); the state is paying the facility's operating costs for seven years ($300 million).[13] Still, the relationship between a state and its local governments often involves conflict as each level tries to exert its will.

The diagram presented in Figure 12.1 reflects the two fundamental ways that states can influence the authority of local governments. One way is through the vertical state–local government relationship—states can choose to retain power (centralize) or disperse power (decentralize). The other way is horizontal—the centralized power relationships that local governments have with each other. Combining the two dimensions, vertical and horizontal, produces the four square-shaped boxes on the right half of the diagram.[14] Box A reflects a state that centralizes vertically and horizontally; box C is a state that decentralizes on both dimensions. In a metropolitan area in A states, there are few local governments, and they lack power. In states characterized by the pattern described in box C, many local governments exist and they enjoy substantial

**FIGURE 12.1**    **Typology of Governance Structure of Metropolitan Regions**

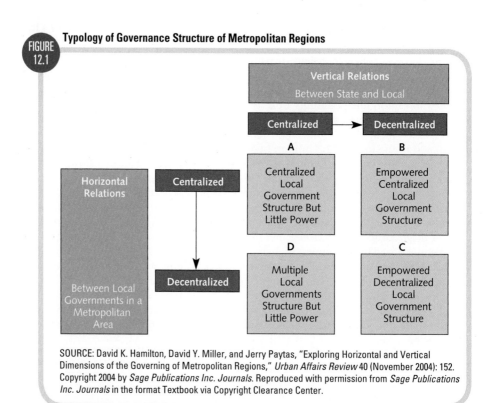

SOURCE: David K. Hamilton, David Y. Miller, and Jerry Paytas, "Exploring Horizontal and Vertical Dimensions of the Governing of Metropolitan Regions," *Urban Affairs Review* 40 (November 2004): 152. Copyright 2004 by *Sage Publications Inc. Journals*. Reproduced with permission from *Sage Publications Inc. Journals* in the format Textbook via Copyright Clearance Center.

power. The states depicted by boxes B and D have one centralizing feature and one decentralizing feature. Each state decided a long time ago the square in which it belongs.

The ability of states and localities to work together effectively has been tested by the issue of homeland security. Concerned that state and local governments were ill-prepared to respond to a disaster in a comprehensive and cooperative way, in 2005, the federal government funded two antiterrorism exercises. One simulation, a bomb and chemical weapons attack, took place in Connecticut; the other, a bioterrorism incident, was set in New Jersey.[15] The exercises exposed weaknesses in response capability, especially communications among responders. The results of the mock disasters sent state and local officials throughout the nation back to the drawing boards to try to determine how to improve their response systems. One outcome has been the creation of "all-hazards" emergency operations plans that identify and assign responsibilities to state and local agencies—and to nonprofit organizations—in the event of a disaster. These plans are designed to improve coordination and communication not only vertically (between the state government and localities) but also horizontally (among local jurisdictions).

## State Mandates

Although local governments generally want increased autonomy, state governments have shared their policy-making sphere with reluctance. Rather than let subgovernments devise their own solutions to problems, states frequently prefer to tell them how to solve them. For instance, when solid waste management became a concern in Florida, the state legislature's reaction was to require counties to establish recycling programs. Not only were counties required to initiate programs, they were ordered to achieve a recycling rate of 30 percent.[16] This kind of requirement or order is an example of a *mandate*. (The subject is discussed further in Chapter 13 in the context of state–local finances.) Unfunded mandates are a persistent source of friction between state and local levels of government.

From the perspective of state government, mandates are necessary to ensure that vital activities are performed and desirable goals are achieved. State mandates promote uniformity of policy from one jurisdiction to another (for instance, regarding the length of the public-school year or the operating hours of precinct polling places). In addition, they promote coordination, especially among adjacent jurisdictions that provide services jointly (as with a regional hospital or a metropolitan transportation system).

Table 12.1 provides some perspective on how those at the local level see the mandates issue. Based on a survey of local officials in Minnesota, the data in the table suggest that resistance to mandates is not uniform; that is, it depends on the policy area.[17] Mandates for infrastructure, public safety, and environmental protection, especially if funded at least partially by the state, are acceptable to local officials. But in areas such as recreation, economic development, and general government administration, a large subset of those surveyed

| TABLE 12.1 | Minnesota Local Officials' Views on State Mandates | | | |
|---|---|---|---|---|
| | MANDATES ARE APPROPRIATE… | | | MANDATES ARE NOT APPROPRIATE REGARDLESS OF STATE FUNDING |
| | …EVEN WITH NO STATE FUNDING | …IF THEY PARTIALLY STATE FUNDED | …IF THEY ARE FULLY STATE FUNDED | |
| Policy Area | | | | |
| Economic development | 6 | 30 | 24 | 40 |
| Environment | 6 | 40 | 48 | 6 |
| General government administration | 6 | 32 | 26 | 40 |
| Health services | 2 | 25 | 44 | 2 |
| Infrastructure | 2 | 56 | 31 | 11 |
| Public safety | 2 | 47 | 37 | 10 |
| Recreation | 2 | 33 | 21 | 41 |
| Welfare and human services | 1 | 20 | 25 | 2 |

NOTE: The numbers indicate the percentage of Minnesota local officials responding to the survey who agree with each statement.
SOURCE: Lawrence J. Grossback, "The Problem of State-Imposed Mandates: Lessons from Minnesota's Local Governments," *State and Local Government Review* (Fall 2002): 189. Reprinted by permission.

**mandate-reimbursement requirements**
Measures that take the financial sting out of state mandates.

believe that mandates are not appropriate. Recognizing that funding is one of the key considerations, many states have adopted **mandate-reimbursement requirements**. These measures require states either to reimburse local governments for the costs of state mandates or to give local governments adequate revenue-raising capacity to pay for them.

From their vantage point, local officials offer several suggestions for fixing the mandate problem. Three solutions supported by more than 80 percent of the respondents to the Minnesota survey are as follows:

- The state should provide a clear statement of the rationale behind the mandate; in other words, the state should justify its action.
- Localities should be given greater flexibility in implementing the provisions of the mandate.
- Financial aid to local governments should be increased so that they can deal with mandates effectively.[18]

As might be expected, these solutions are substantially less popular with state officials. But certainly, more communication between state policy makers and local officials, especially at the outset, would reduce some of the friction generated by mandates. Allowing local governments more leeway in implementation, either through extension of time or variation in rules, would lessen the punch that mandates pack. Even more central to any type of mandate reform is adequate state funding of mandates. This action would go a long way toward improving state–local relationships.

## State–Local Organizations

Legal, administrative, and financial ties link state and local governments. Additional interaction occurs when state governments establish organizations such as local government study commissions and advisory panels of local officials. Among the most prevalent structures are task forces, advisory commissions on intergovernmental relations, and departments of community affairs.

*Task forces* tend to be focused organizations set up by the governor or the state legislature in response to a perceived local-level problem. If a state wants to investigate the ramifications of changing its annexation statutes, the legislature might create a task force on annexation and boundary changes (or something similar). The task force would probably be composed of state and local officials, community leaders, and experts on the subject of annexation. First, the task force would collect information on how other states handle the annexation question; second, it would conduct a series of public hearings to get input from individuals and groups interested in the issue; finally, it would compile a report that included recommendations suitable for legislative action. Its work completed, the task force would then disband, although individual members might turn up as advocates when the task-force recommendations receive legislative attention. Task forces are quick organizational responses to local problems that have become too prominent for state government to ignore. A task force is a low-cost, concentrated reaction that undertakes specific tasks and, in some instances, actually influences legislative deliberations.

In an ongoing comprehensive effort at state–local cooperation, twenty-three states have created state-level *advisory commissions on intergovernmental relations (ACIRs)*, modeled after the commission, now defunct, created by the U.S. Congress in 1959. State-level ACIRs are designed to promote more harmonious, workable relations between the state and its governmental subdivisions. They are intended to offer a neutral forum for discussion of long-range state–local issues—a venue in which local officials can be listened to and engaged in focused dialogue; conduct research on local developments and new state policies; promote experimentation in intergovernmental processes, both state–local and interlocal; and develop suggested solutions to state–local problems. To prevent their recommendations from gathering dust on a shelf, many state-level ACIRs have added marketing and public relations to their list of activities.

Generally, state-level ACIRs return real benefits to local government. Whether in their narrowest form (as arenas for discussion of local issues) or in their broadest (as policy developers and initiators), ACIRs are useful to state and local governments. But their greatest impact occurs when they are given the authority and resources to do something more than simply discuss issues. Indiana's ACIR, for instance, has four primary duties:[19]

- To promote better understanding of the process of government and the outcomes of policy decisions;
- To improve communication between all levels of government and its citizens;
- To foster long-term planning between all levels of government; and
- To promote research on the impacts of mandates and policy changes.

Another way in which states can generate closer formal ties with their local governments is through specialized administrative agencies. All fifty states have created *departments of community affairs* (*DCAs*) that are involved in local activities. They have different names (Kentucky calls its DCA the Department for Local Government; Washington's is the Department of Community, Trade and Economic Development), but their function is similar: to offer a range of programs and services to local governments. DCAs are involved in housing, urban revitalization, anti-poverty programs, and economic development; they also offer local governments services such as planning, management, and financial assistance. DCAs vary on several dimensions: their niche in state government, the sizes of their budget and staff, and whether they include an advisory board of local officials. Compared with state-level ACIRs, DCAs function much more as service deliverers and much less as policy initiators. Therefore, these two types of organizations tend to complement rather than compete with one another. Both function as advocates for local government, however, at the state level.

## METROPOLITICS: A NEW CHALLENGE FOR STATE GOVERNMENT

State governments often find their dealings with local governments to be confounded by the side effects of urbanization. Regardless of which state we examine, its urban areas show the effects of three waves of suburbanization. An early wave occurred during the 1920s, when automobiles facilitated the development of outlying residential areas. Although the dispersion slowed during the Great Depression and World War II, its resurgence in the 1950s triggered a second wave during which retail stores followed the population exodus, the so-called malling of America. Now a third wave of suburbanization is upon us, one fueled by what has been called America's "exit ramp economy." Office, commercial, and retail facilities are increasingly located along suburban freeways.[20] This phenomenon is occurring nearly everywhere, from New York City to San Diego, from Milwaukee to Miami. This third wave of suburbanization has caught the attention of state governments.

As a result of the transformation of American metropolitan areas, central cities have lost some of their prominence as the social, economic, and political focal points of their areas. People have moved to surrounding suburbs and beyond; businesses and firms have sprung up in the hinterlands; communities have formed their own service and taxing districts. The outward flow of people and activities has fundamentally altered metropolitan areas. As noted above, these new boom towns are not simply residential but include business, retail, and entertainment activities.

The de-emphasis of the central city suggests the need for changes in outmoded state government policy toward metropolitan jurisdictions. A serious concern is that rapid, unplanned growth is producing sprawl and fostering what are called shadow governments. A logical question is, what is state government doing while all of this is occurring? More than it used to, as we shall see.

## Urban Sprawl Versus Smart Growth

Population growth is, of course, something that states and localities desire. But the consequences of rapid and unplanned population growth test the capability of governments to provide services efficiently and effectively. As growth spills beyond city limits into unincorporated areas, as **edge cities** spring up along interstate highways, the result is often traffic congestion and overcrowded schools. Far from the central city, subdivisions and strip malls sprout on land that was recently forests and farms. It costs a lot of money for government to provide infrastructure—streets, water and sewer lines, schools—to these new developments. Meanwhile, many inner cities, where the infrastructure is already in place, are plagued by empty storefronts, vacant lots, and abandoned factories. Many states and localities have struggled to balance the benefits of new growth against the attendant costs.

**edge cities**
New boom towns featuring retail shops and malls, restaurants, office buildings, and housing developments, far from the central city.

**Sprawling Growth** One of the hottest issues of the early twenty-first century is **urban sprawl**, a term that carries negative connotations. It refers to development beyond the central city that is characterized by low densities, rapid land consumption, and dependence on the automobile. It is often called leapfrog development because it jumps over established settlements. The exit-ramp communities mentioned earlier are a manifestation of sprawl. Urban sprawl is resource-intensive and costly, and it is also the subject of much political debate.

**urban sprawl**
Development characterized by low population density, rapid land consumption, and dependence on the automobile.

Until the mortgage crisis in 2008 and the subsequent recession, Las Vegas, Nevada, offered perhaps the best contemporary example of a fast-growing, sprawling city. According to the city's statistics, 200 new residents arrived in Las Vegas every day; a house was constructed every fifteen minutes.[21] Traffic congestion intensified as did concern over maintaining an adequate water supply in this desert city. As human settlement pushed ever outward to lower-cost land, local government was pressed to provide schools, parks, and roads. Growth quickly outstripped the infrastructure needed to support it. The mayor of Las Vegas proposed a $2,000 per house **impact fee** to mitigate the effects of growth, but the city lacked the authority to levy the fee. The Nevada legislature had to approve the proposal before it could take effect.

**impact fee**
A charge levied on new development to offset some of the costs of providing services.

Although the pace of growth has slowed in Las Vegas and the surrounding area, the issues related to planning and paying for new development remain. Even though revenues for local governments will increase as a result of development, costs of providing services will also rise and not necessarily commensurately. One study of Georgia counties found that for every $1.00 of revenue brought in by new housing developments, the cost of services was between $1.23 and $2.07.[22] Public education was the big-ticket item pushing up service costs. This is the primary explanation for the popularity of impact fees. Research on Florida counties found that rapid population growth stimulates the adoption of impact fees especially if nearby counties have adopted them already.[23] Only when commercial and industrial development complements subdivision growth, do local governments typically enjoy a net revenue gain.

Rapid growth can spark serious conflict in a community. Consider the case of Fillmore, a city of 13,000 in southern California. After losing many of its orange groves to new housing and commercial developments, concerned residents were able to place an initiative on the ballot that would require voter approval for development beyond the current city limits. It was called Save Open-space and Agricultural Resources (SOAR). City officials countered with their own less restrictive initiative: Vision 2020. Pundits characterized it as citrus groves versus Starbucks and sport-utility vehicles.[24] The campaigns for and against the measures were intense and, in the end, *both* initiatives were defeated by voters. In the aftermath, Fillmore's city council decided to establish **greenbelts** on two sides of the town to preserve some of the city's open space and agricultural base.

**greenbelts**

Open spaces in which development is limited.

The relentless creep of urban sprawl has prompted reactions in many states and communities. In 2008, 128 open-space protection measures appeared on ballots throughout the country; 99 of them passed. These measures committed more than $8 billion for land conservation; much of it in the form of tax increases.[25] One of the most extensive measures was adopted in Minnesota: a constitutional amendment that increases the state sales tax three-eighths of a percent to provide $5.5 billion for conservation over the next 25 years.

**Smart Growth** The majority of land-use decisions occur at the local level, and many states offer guidance and provide localities with tools to manage growth. Hawaii was a pioneer in this effort with its State Land Use Law, adopted in 1961; Vermont and Oregon got on board in 1970 and 1973, respectively, with growth management acts designed to control the pace of development and protect environmentally sensitive areas. The **smart growth** movement represents the new generation in state growth management. It is an effort by governments to reduce the amount of sprawl and minimize its impact. One of the key aspects of these new smart growth approaches is a stronger link between land use and infrastructure planning. (See Table 12.2 for a list of the states that have adopted comprehensive growth management and smart growth programs.)

**smart growth**

Government efforts to limit urban sprawl by managing growth.

Maryland was one of the first states to take action to limit sprawl. Calling sprawl "a disease eating away at the heart of America," Governor Parris Glendening signed the Smart Growth Areas Act into law in 1997.[26] In effect, the state rewards local governments that target new growth in areas that already have infrastructure, and it denies state funding for infrastructure projects that encourage sprawl. Several other states moved quickly to follow Maryland's lead. The following year, Arizona adopted a Growing Smarter Act; by 2003, another twenty states had taken antisprawl actions of one sort or another.[27] A particularly ambitious plan was New Jersey's Blueprint for Intelligent Growth (BIG). Had BIG been adopted as originally drafted, huge portions of the Garden State would have been off-limits to additional development, much to the dismay of many local officials and builders.[28] Although the far-reaching antisprawl proposal was eventually pared down, it was clear that in New Jersey, as in many other places, state governments are reestablishing themselves as major influences in local governments' land-use decisions.

A word of caution is necessary. Not everyone thinks that sprawl is so bad. In fact, to some, sprawl is simply the consequence of the unfettered workings

| States with Comprehensive Growth Management Programs | TABLE 12.2 |
|---|---|
| **STATE** | **YEAR ADOPTED** |
| Hawaii | 1961 |
| Vermont | 1970 |
| Oregon | 1973 |
| Florida | 1985 |
| New Jersey | 1987 |
| Rhode Island | 1988 |
| Georgia | 1989 |
| Washington | 1990 |
| Maryland | 1997 |
| Arizona | 1998 |
| Tennessee | 1998 |
| Colorado | 1999 |
| Wisconsin | 1999 |

SOURCE: Adapted from Jerry Anthony, "Do State Growth Management Regulations Reduce Sprawl?" *Urban Affairs Review* (January 2004): 381.

of a free-market system.[29] Given a choice, they contend, Americans prefer a spread-out, car-centered lifestyle. Obviously, there is some truth to that argument. Smart growth inevitably means higher density, that is, smaller lot sizes and taller buildings to accommodate more people. High-rise condominium complexes and soaring office towers appeal to some folks, but to most suburbanites, increased density is not something they want.[30]

## Shadow Governments

As new development pushes into the hinterlands, new forms of governance are emerging. They have become known as **shadow governments**, and although they may not be official government units, in many important ways they behave as if they were. They levy taxes, regulate behavior, and provide services. Three types of shadow government exist:

**shadow governments** Entities, especially unofficial ones, that function like governments

- private enterprise shadow governments, such as homeowners' associations;
- public–private partnership shadow governments, common examples of which are development corporations and business improvement districts; and
- subsidiaries of conventional governments with unusual powers, such as area-wide planning commissions.

Shadow governments exist within the confines of state law, but most states have not taken an active role in overseeing them.

Estimates place the number of private enterprise shadow governments at about 200,000, the majority located in suburban areas. A condominium community provides an illustration. The property owners' association makes rules for residents (from the speed limit on community streets to the color of the condo), provides services (security, maintenance, landscaping), and assesses fees (based on the size of the unit). Residents typically vote for the board of directors of the association (in some instances, developers of the project retain seats on the board), and votes tend to be weighted according to the value of the housing unit. Owners with a greater financial investment have a greater say in the governing of the community, which is a far cry from the one-person, one-vote principle.

Shadow governments, especially the first two types, raise questions about matters of power and equity (but not about their efficiency because, by most accounts, they tend to operate fairly efficiently). The power issue centers on information, influence, and accountability. Shadow governments control information, restrict influence to those who belong or can pay, and have little public accountability. They are not subject to the same legal standards as are typical governments.[31] The equity issue addresses the class discrimination inherent in these governments. A poor family out for a Sunday drive may be able to traverse public streets in their ramshackle automobile, but if they turn their car onto a private street patrolled by private police, they are likely to be followed and perhaps even stopped, questioned, and escorted out of the neighborhood.

Whatever our uneasiness over power and equity issues related to shadow governments, their number is increasing. Shadow governments are especially popular in metropolitan areas, because local government boundaries do not necessarily jibe with economic realities and development patterns. Their vaunted efficiency makes them a force to be reckoned with. Research on private enterprise shadow governments in California, Florida, and New Jersey showed each state taking vastly different approaches to their regulation.[32]

The social and economic changes in U.S. metropolitan areas have had a tremendous impact on urban governance. Urban expansion and shadow governments make up extended webs of interdependent jurisdictions. How can these places be governed best? Idealistic metropolitan reformers have called for regional government; more pragmatic observers have advocated regional coordination.

## Regional Governance

**regional government**

An area-wide structure for local governance, designed to replace multiple jurisdictions.

A **regional government** is a structure put in place because of the interdependence of proximate communities. A typical metropolitan area is fragmented, that is, comprised of many local governments. Under a regional government, local jurisdictions give up some of their power and authority to a larger government in exchange for area-wide solutions to local problems. State legislatures are important players in this process because, aside from the state constitution, they create the rules of the game. Their actions either facilitate or hinder local government reorganization into regional units.

**City–County Consolidation** In the United States, the closest thing to regional government is **city–county consolidation**, whereby area jurisdictions are absorbed into a single countywide government. In a pure form of consolidation, one police department, one fire department, and one water and sewer system exist for the area. The functions of local government—public safety, public works, health and human services, community and economic development, and recreation and arts programs—are provided by a single jurisdiction. Thirty-two consolidated city–county governments exist in the United States. Some of these consolidated jurisdictions reflect political decisions of the nineteenth century, such as the combined city–county governments of Philadelphia, San Francisco, and New Orleans. Among the most prominent mergers of the past forty years are those in Indianapolis–Marion County, Indiana; Jacksonville–Duval County, Florida; Nashville–Davidson County, Tennessee; and more recently Louisville–Jefferson County, Kentucky.

> **city–county consolidation**
> The merger of city and county governments into a single jurisdiction.

Regional government seems so rational, yet it has proven to be quite difficult to achieve. Voters usually defeat proposals to consolidate city and county government. At various times, voters have rejected the mergers of Des Moines and Polk County, Iowa; Spokane and Spokane County, Washington; Wilmington and New Hanover County, North Carolina; and Knoxville and Knox County, Tennessee; just to name a few. Opponents of jurisdictional consolidation often include city and county governing boards, city and county employees, and taxpayer organizations. Support for merging governments typically comes from the local chamber of commerce, real-estate developers, local newspapers, and civic organizations.[33]

To reformers, this lack of success is perplexing. The logic is straightforward: If small local governments in a metropolitan area merge to form a larger local government, two positive outcomes will occur. First, stubborn public policy problems can be tackled from an area-wide perspective. For example, the pollution generated by City A that affects City B can be handled as a regional problem rather than as a conflict between the two cities. Second, combining forces produces *economies of scale* in service delivery. Instead of each jurisdiction constructing and operating separate jails, for example, one large regional facility can be maintained. Jail service can be provided at a lower cost to each participating jurisdiction. These anticipated outcomes are persuasive arguments in favor of consolidation.

Regional government does not always perform as expected, however. Research has shown that city–county consolidation does not necessarily reduce the costs of government, and may even increase them.[34] Another criticism of regional government is that it can be inaccessible and destructive of the hard-won political gains of minorities. Compared with a city or town government, regional government is farther away, both literally and figuratively. Residents of small towns fear the loss of identity as their community gets swept into bigger government. The effect on minority political strength is no less troublesome. Because the proportionate number of minorities may be lessened when jurisdictions are combined, their voting strength can be diluted. For instance, African Americans made up 34 percent of pre-merger Louisville but only 19.5 percent of consolidated Louisville–Jefferson Metro Government.[35]

**public choice theory**

The theory that individuals shop around to find a local government whose taxes and services are in line with their own preferences.

A competing perspective on regional government comes from **public choice theory**. According to this theory, the existence of many jurisdictions in a metropolitan area gives people options, that is, they can choose to live in the central city, in nearby suburbs, or in the county. Each of these jurisdictions offers a particular mix of tax rates, policies, and public services. In deciding where to reside or open a business, individuals seek places that are in line with their own tax, policy, and service preferences.[36] To public choice theorists, consolidating cities and counties or creating regional governments robs people of important choices and creates inefficiencies. The consolidation of the city of Louisville and Jefferson County borrowed a page from public choice theory when, in a political compromise, it left eighty smaller jurisdictions in the county out of the merger. Figure 12.2 shows the boundaries of preconsolidated Louisville and Jefferson County, as well as the other jurisdictions.

**A City and Its Suburbs** The former mayor of Albuquerque, New Mexico, David Rusk, after thinking long and hard about the relationship between a central city and its suburbs, jumped into the regionalism debate with this statement: "The real city is the total metropolitan area—city and suburb."[37] He uses the concept of elasticity (and inelasticity) to signify the ability of a city to expand its city boundaries (or not). In a sense, a city's elasticity is its destiny. Elastic cities have been able to capture suburban growth; by adjusting their boundaries through annexation, they can keep pace with urban sprawl. Conversely,

**FIGURE 12.2**

**Map of Louisville, Jefferson County, and Small Cities**

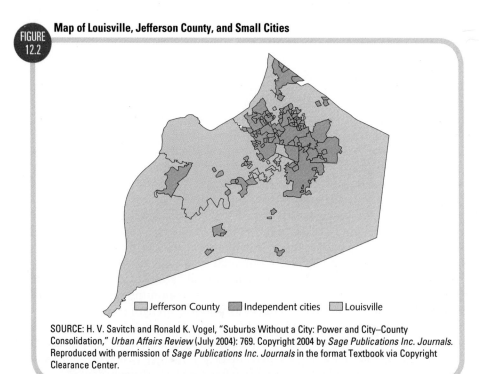

☐ Jefferson County   ■ Independent cities   ☐ Louisville

SOURCE: H. V. Savitch and Ronald K. Vogel, "Suburbs Without a City: Power and City–County Consolidation," *Urban Affairs Review* (July 2004): 769. Copyright 2004 by *Sage Publications Inc. Journals.* Reproduced with permission of *Sage Publications Inc. Journals* in the format Textbook via Copyright Clearance Center.

inelastic cities trapped in existing boundaries have suffered population loss and tax-base erosion, resulting in higher levels of racial and class segregation.

The solution offered is a familiar one: regional government. But to be effective, the regional government must include the central city and at least 60 percent of the area's population. The characteristics of the metropolitan area determine how this could be accomplished. In single-county metropolitan areas, empowerment of the urban county would effectively create regional government, as would city–county consolidation. And in multicounty metropolitan areas, a single regional government could be created out of existing cities and counties. Obviously, the restructuring of local governments in these ways would engender substantial opposition; as Rusk contends, however, few alternatives are available to areas with low elasticity.

The argument for a metropolitan-wide government is simple: Because economies are essentially regional in nature, governance can (and should) be, too. As discussed earlier, however, regional governance has never been a popular alternative in this country. Overcoming traditional anti-regionalism sentiment will not be easy, but regional approaches may be necessary for effective competition in an increasingly global economy. Maybe the mayor of Missoula, Montana (population 57,000), said it best when he commented: "It is not possible for Missoula to understand itself, or its future, except in a regional context. The city draws its strength from the region."[38] The Breaking New Ground box tells the story of two very different cities that are gradually becoming connected.

**It's Up to the States** Both Portland, Oregon, and the Twin Cities area of Minnesota have embraced regionalism. In Oregon, Portland joined with its suburbs and outlying jurisdictions to develop a region-wide vision for the future. The 2040 Plan, as it is called, aims at accommodating orderly growth while maintaining a desirable quality of life in the region. The planning process involved extensive public participation, including citizen surveys and public forums. In addition, the plan's backers launched media campaigns and loaned videos to acquaint residents with the proposal. The 2040 Plan is enforced by an elected, region-wide council that works to secure the compliance of local governments.[39]

In the Minneapolis–St. Paul area of Minnesota, jurisdictions contribute 40 percent of their new commercial and industrial tax base to a regional pool. The money in this pool is redistributed to communities throughout the region on the basis of financial need, thereby reducing fiscal disparities across jurisdictions. Thus, for instance, a new industry locating in one city becomes a benefit to neighboring cities as well. With regional tax-base sharing as a start, Minnesota went even further in 1994 when the state legislature placed all regional sewer, transit, and land-use planning in the hands of a regional organization— the Metropolitan Council of the Twin Cities.[40] This significantly empowered council makes crucial decisions about growth and development in the Twin Cities area from a regional perspective.

In the final analysis, it is up to state government to provide a sufficiently supportive environment in which regionalism can take root. It was Oregon and Minnesota that created the legal environment for Portland and the Twin

## BREAKING NEW GROUND

### Rocky Mountain Growth

Back in the nineteenth century, Cheyenne, Wyoming, lost out to Denver in the growth sweepstakes. True, Cheyenne had a railroad running through it, but Denver had good water supplies, gold strikes, and the civic derring-do to build a spur to the railroad. Only 100 miles separate the two cities, but their development trajectories took them in different directions. Over time, Denver became the leading city in the Rocky Mountain region complete with a U.S. Mint facility, professional sports teams, and a population of 600,000. Cheyenne, the capital of the Cowboy State and its largest city, grew slowly by comparison, with its population reaching 57,000 by 2008. But the city relished its relative isolation and its "real" Western culture. The distance between the two cities seemed greater than 100 miles.

But this may be changing as the suburbs of fast-growing Denver reach farther north into Wyoming. An interstate highway connects the two cities, and the metropolitan areas along it in northeastern Colorado are among the nation's growth leaders. The number of daily commuters between the two states is estimated to be around 2,200 and increasing. The National Center for Atmospheric Research based in Colorado has decided that its next-generation supercomputer center will be built in Cheyenne. This has local development officials salivating over the potential ripple effects, wondering whether the city could become a high-tech mecca. There is even talk of building a commuter rail line to facilitate transportation between Denver and Cheyenne. But not everyone embraces the change that is coming to Cheyenne. As the president of the Cheyenne Area Convention and Visitors Bureau said, "There would be...in some quarters, resistance to losing too much of the Cheyenneness—there would be some push back." Still, the forces favoring growth are strong and that 100-mile distance is gradually shrinking.

SOURCES: Kirk Johnson, "Cheyenne of Two Minds about Denver-Like Growth," *New York Times*, www.nytimes.com (November 4, 2008); Bruce Finley, "Thirsty Cities Eye Wyoming Water," *Denver Post*, www.denverpost.com (August 16, 2009).

Cities, respectively. As political scientists Margaret Weir, Harold Wolman, and Todd Swanstrom declared in their research on city–suburban coalitions, "States are critical players; they set the terms and conditions under which regionalism occurs."[41] They have to because the natural tendency for officials in cities and their suburbs is to see each other as rivals rather than allies or partners.

**councils of government**

Formal organizations of general-purpose governments in an area, intended to improve regional coordination.

**Regional Coordination** **Councils of government** (COGs) or regional planning commissions are examples of regional coordination. They do not involve a formal merger or combination of governments; instead, COGs are loose collections of local governments designed to increase communication and coordination in an area. They provide a neutral forum in which local leaders can come together to identify and discuss issues of common concern.[42] As noted earlier, they can become shadow governments. State governments were not active in the creation of COGs; national government programs spurred their development. For example, the federal government requires states to create metropolitan planning organizations (MPOs) to coordinate transportation programs in urban areas.[43] Currently, there are more than 500 COGs active in the United States.

Although area-wide planning is the most common activity of COGs, they also perform other tasks. Member governments can turn to them for technical assistance (such as help in writing federal grant applications), professional services (planning, budgeting, engineering, legal advice), and information (economic data for the region). The effectiveness of COGs varies, generally those with greater fiscal stability and staff competencies are more successful.

The impact of these councils has been less significant than their creators hoped, but they have had two positive effects. First, COGs have elevated the concept of area-wide policy planning from a pipe dream to a reality. They have been heavily involved in criminal justice, water quality, housing, and especially transportation planning. Second, councils have substantially improved the operational capacity of rural local governments by providing expertise to small local jurisdictions that cannot afford to hire specialized staff.

Some localities have taken a more informal route to regional coordination through service sharing. In service sharing, jurisdictions agree to consolidate specific services, cooperate in their provision, or exchange them. For instance, recreational facilities may be provided jointly by several jurisdictions, one government may rent jail space from another, or county residents may use the city library in return for city residents' use of the county's solid waste landfill. Service-sharing arrangements are popular because they hold the promise of greater efficiency in service delivery *and* they do not threaten the power and autonomy of existing jurisdictions the way consolidation does. Recent research suggests that local officials may be more receptive to this type of interjurisdictional cooperation than is commonly thought.[44] Still, the ability to hammer out agreements that benefit all participating governments is contingent upon numerous factors related to the problem itself and the jurisdictional context.[45] COGs and service-sharing agreements provide for a modicum of regional governance...without a regional government.

# STATES AND URBAN POLICY

If you had attended an urban policy conference recently, you would have heard the phrase *state government* used repeatedly. Many states have replaced some of their policies that had a negative impact on urban areas with urban-friendly programs. Michigan was one of the leaders when, in 1998, its Urban Caucus began a process of identifying state programs that hindered investment in central cities. Since then, other states have followed suit. Three significant contemporary issues—housing, infrastructure, and new urbanism—are of particular interest in an urban environment. Let us consider each of these contemporary issues in terms of state–local interaction.

## Housing Policy

For middle- and upper-income city residents, the housing market can be counted on to produce affordable units, but what is affordable to these residents is out of reach for low-income households. The mechanics of market economics effectively shut them out of the system. Low-cost housing does not generate the return that higher-cost housing does. As a result, governments have intervened to create incentives for developers to produce low-income housing units and, where incentives do not work, to become providers of housing themselves. One of the aims of the federal Housing Act of 1949 was "a decent home in a suitable living environment" for all Americans.

Over time, the national government has backed away from this goal and altered its approach to housing. In 1968, it was willing to become the nation's housing provider of last resort, but by the 1980s the push was to deregulate and let market forces prevail. Modifications of national tax laws have had a negative effect on rental housing stock. Deliberate actions and inaction resulted in a decline in home ownership, an increase in the proportion of household income that is spent on housing, a decrease in the number of affordable rental units, an increase in the number of physically inadequate and abandoned structures, and an increase in the number of homeless people.[46]

In response, state governments have set up housing finance agencies, nonprofit corporations have entered the low-income housing market, and local governments have adopted regulations to preserve their affordable housing stock. New Jersey, for example, mandated that all of its 567 communities provide their fair share of affordable housing for low- and moderate-income people. In some places, housing vouchers—a form of consumer subsidy that would open currently unaffordable housing to low-income residents—have been instituted. Another approach is for local governments to require developers to include a fixed proportion of affordable units in their market-rate projects as a condition for approval of a building permit. This approach works, however, only where developers are clamoring for access.

Connecticut has been particularly innovative in addressing its affordable-housing problem. As part of its statewide plan, the state conducted a housing needs assessment. In a pilot program, Connecticut entered into mediated negotiations with local jurisdictions in a specified area to develop a fair-housing compact for the area. To encourage communities to pursue the goals of the compact, it established a housing infrastructure fund to provide state financial assistance. As a result, thousands of new affordable housing units were constructed.[47] Connecticut's effort to address the scarcity of affordable housing has been emulated by other states.

Some local jurisdictions are also playing active roles. Montgomery County, Maryland, has been successful in generating affordable housing even as housing prices in the area have skyrocketed. The county requires developers to build low-cost housing in the suburban subdivisions they create.[48] In return for complying with this policy, developers receive a **density bonus** that allows them to build more homes than the zoning would have otherwise permitted. So-called moderately priced dwelling units (MPDUs) may look the same as other homes in the area, but they are sold (or rented) at below-market rates to lower-income people. The outcome has two positive effects: The county's supply of affordable housing increases, and neighborhoods become more economically diverse.

In states hit particularly hard by the downturn in the housing market in 2008 and 2009, problems of a different sort arose. In California, Arizona, Nevada, and Florida, plunging home values and mortgage foreclosures meant

**density bonus**

A provision that allows a developer to increase density (i.e., build more homes) in a development in return for complying with a government regulation.

lower-property tax revenues for local jurisdictions. In addition, the number of homeless people rose in many cities, straining the capacity of shelters and leading to the creation of tent cities and encampments.

## Infrastructure Policy

Infrastructure—public works projects and services—is the physical network of a community, that is, its roads and bridges, airports, water and sewer systems, and public buildings. Its importance lies in its connection to development; the simplest equation is no infrastructure = no development. Infrastructure has become an issue in many communities because of its crumbling condition and the high cost of repair or replacement. For example, it will cost Baltimore nearly $940 million over fourteen years to fix defective sewer pipes and connections that discharge untreated waste into the Chesapeake Bay.[49] The price tag in Atlanta is even higher: $3 billion to overhaul its sewer system and upgrade its water-treatment facilities.[50] But the granddaddy of all recent infrastructure projects is the Big Dig in Boston: a $14.6 billion transportation project that, among other things, replaced an elevated highway with underground roads, bridges, and green space. It is no wonder that in 2009, states and localities greeted the $787 billion federal stimulus package—intended to boost economic recovery and targeted at shovel-ready infrastructure projects—with great enthusiasm.

States take different approaches in financing local public works, and tradition is a powerful explanation of this behavior. Generally, they are providing more financial support for local public works today than they did in the early 1980s, through grants, dedicated revenues (the money collected from a particular tax), loans, and bonds. States that have been particularly inventive in public works assistance include Pennsylvania, Massachusetts, Virginia, Wisconsin, and Wyoming. Pennsylvania, for instance, allows cities to become financial partners in constructing roads to shopping malls and industrial sites. Massachusetts, through its Aquifer Land Acquisition Program, purchases property or development rights to protect public drinking-water supplies. In the aftermath of the I-35 bridge collapse in Minneapolis in 2007, several states launched new programs to repair and replace bridges. Missouri's Safe and Sound bridge program tried a novel approach: rather than bidding out the repair work for each bridge separately, it allowed a single firm to work on 550 of the state's bridges. The state figured that economies of scale would result, thus lowering the total cost.[51]

The stock of aging, sometimes unsafe infrastructure has prompted states to cast about for solutions. In the area of transportation infrastructure, one approach receiving greater scrutiny is privatization. Nearly one-quarter of the states have allowed the construction of private toll roads. Private highway projects are criticized on two counts. Some argue that private roadways will produce a have/have-not distinction, with the affluent traversing pay roads and the poor being dispatched to congested freeways. Others claim that privatization offers a Band-Aid solution to the enormous transportation problems facing the nation. Despite these concerns, privatization remains an attractive option to governors and legislatures intent on holding down highway taxes.

## New Urbanism

One of the most intriguing efforts at transforming the urban experience has its roots in architecture and urban planning. Called new urbanism, the approach rejects the suburban model of development in favor of a traditional small-town style. Proponents of **new urbanism**, especially Miami-based architects Andres Duany and Elizabeth Plater-Zyberk, have advocated what is essentially a high-density, pedestrian-friendly, environmentally sensitive design for communities.[52] In theory, residents of these new urban places will acquire a sense of community and become engaged in civic life. One of the first experiments with new urbanism was the development of Seaside, Florida. (Movie buffs will remember it as the town where *The Truman Show* was filmed.) Another, called Celebration, has been created by the Walt Disney Company on 5,000 acres on the fringe of Orlando, Florida. It is a corporate-planned town with a private government.

The real test for new urbanism will be in an existing city, not in a geographically separate enclave. Can new urbanism work in a place plagued by social disorder and disinvestment? The answer to that question will not be known for years, and many observers are skeptical. But the Congress for the New Urbanism (CNU), a nonprofit organization committed to promoting the concept, is forging ahead. Annually CNU selects exemplary projects, both in the United States and abroad, that embrace new urbanism principles. Table 12.3 lists four of the projects that won the 2009 award.

> **new urbanism**
>
> An anti-suburban, pro-small-town version of city planning.

**TABLE 12.3** — **Award Winning Projects, Congress of New Urbanism, 2009**

| CITYWIDE SCALE: | |
|---|---|
| Buffalo, New York | Adopted an interlocking array of plans for downtown, waterfront, and parks rationalized under the umbrella of a city-wide master plan. The plans contain smart growth features in the context of the economic realities of the region. |
| **NEIGHBORHOOD SCALE:** | |
| Orlando, Florida | Transformed a closed-down military training base into a traditional neighborhood development. The developer partnered with Audubon of Florida to help plan the parks and water edges, creating viable ecosystems where none existed before. What was once an environmentally-stressed brownfield site became a thriving, green, sustainable neighborhood. |
| Savannah, Georgia | Developed a civic master plan for a large tract of vacant, formerly industrial land on the border of the city's historic center. Working with the private sector, new city streets, a park, public spaces, and riverwalk extension are being constructed in an effort to expand the historic core into an underutilized area. |
| San Antonio, Texas | Initiated the planning effort for a blighted 377-acre area north of the historic downtown core. The goal is to create a shared community vision for the place to attract high-quality, high-value, urban development, and to create an urban code that would ensure coordinated development of public and private improvements. |

SOURCE: Congress for the New Urbanism, "Winners of the Charter Awards," www.cnu.org/awards/winners (August 2, 2009).

So far, states have not taken new urbanism to heart. But as states seek ways to revitalize declining central cities, new urbanism may be seen as a promising approach.

# STATES AND THEIR RURAL COMMUNITIES

When the local Dairy Queen closes its doors, a small town in rural America knows that it is in trouble. The Dairy Queen, like the coffee shop on Main Street, serves as a gathering place for community residents. Its demise symbolizes the tough times that a lot of rural communities face. In fact, some analysts argue that the major distinctions in regional economics are no longer between Sunbelt and Frostbelt, or East Coast and West Coast, but between metropolitan America and the countryside.[53] People are leaving many rural areas, with the most relentless decline occurring in a broad swath stretching northward from west Texas through North Dakota.[54]

The decline of rural America has provoked a question: What can state governments do to encourage the right kind of growth in rural areas? Short of pumping enormous amounts of money into the local economy, they can encourage the expansion of local intergovernmental cooperation, whereby small rural governments join together to increase their administrative capacity to deliver services and achieve economies of scale. Two state actions facilitate such cooperation. One is reform of state tax codes so that jurisdictions can share locally generated tax revenues, similar to the Twin Cities model discussed earlier. Rather than competing with one another for a new manufacturing plant or a shopping mall, local governments can cooperate to bring the new facility to the area; regardless of where this facility is located, all jurisdictions can receive a portion of the tax revenue. A second useful state action is the promotion of statewide land-use planning. As one observer has noted, "Currently too many rural local governments engage in wasteful inter-community competition, mutually antagonistic zoning, and contradictory development plans."[55]

Twelve small towns in Kansas have embraced a new strategy to reverse population loss: offering free land to relocating families. By early 2009, Marquette, a central Kansas town of 500 people a few years ago, had given away 40 free residential lots and had seen its population reach 682.[56] Others of these proverbial one-stoplight towns offer additional inducements to new residents: free water and sewer hookups, no-cost building permits, and memberships at nearby golf courses.

In an effort to find new ways to compete, rural places are getting entrepreneurial. For instance, an action that may bear fruit is the attempt to foster business by installing high-speed Internet connections to isolated rural areas. Indiana created its I-Light program to bring broadband to its farming communities; Alabama and Alaska give tax credits to broadband firms committed to investing in rural areas.[57] Also, the abundance of wind in the Great Plains region has spurred talk of the possibilities of developing large-scale wind farms

Wind farms in rural America
*SOURCE: aerialarchives.com/Aerial Archives/Alamy*

to provide an alternative energy source to other parts of the country. And music festivals—Wakarusa in the Arkansas hills; Dfest, Rocklahoma, and Country Fever in rural Oklahoma; and Bonnaroo in south central Tennessee—provide a significant shot in the arm to rural economies.

In 1990, the federal government offered states a means of redesigning their approaches to rural development. In selected states, newly established rural development councils brought together—for the first time—federal, state, and local officials involved in rural development. Rather than mandating the structure of the councils and their agendas, the federal government assumed a hands-off posture and simply provided the necessary start-up funds. During the ensuing years, each of the councils designed its own initiative aimed at specific conditions and problems confronting the state. Mississippi, for example, worked on a tourism and recreation project, South Dakota developed an online resource database, and Washington undertook the issues of affordable housing and job retraining.[58] The promise of these state-based interorganizational networks is substantial, and during the decade many successful projects were completed. Thinking optimistically, the federal government extended the initiative to thirty-seven states.

## THE INTERACTION OF STATE AND LOCAL GOVERNMENTS

Constitutionally, state governments are supreme in their dealings with local governments. New York City, Los Angeles, and Chicago are large, world-class cities but even they have to follow the dictates of their respective state governments. For example, when the mayors of these cities sought to increase their control over local public schools, it took action by their respective state legislatures to make it happen. Even so, power does not flow in only one direction. The political realities are such that these cities and their smaller counterparts influence what happens in their state capitols. Suffice it to say, the state–local relationship is subject to constant adjustment. A Governor's Task Force to Renew Montana Government, for instance, adopted several provisions aimed at diminishing the influence of the state in what are considered purely local issues. But in a different vein, when Philadelphia's mayor proposed closing some fire stations to cut costs, state legislators intervened, passing a bill to prevent the city from doing so.[59] (The governor of Pennsylvania, a former mayor of Philadelphia, vetoed the bill saying it infringed on the city's home rule power.)

Some issues or problems require a statewide, uniform response, whereas others are the particular concern of a single local jurisdiction. Consider the problem of drought, a condition that has affected most of the western states since 2000. Some areas of Colorado, such as Denver, have been especially hard hit. A local agency, Denver Water, is responsible for water management in the city; a state agency, the Colorado Water Conservation Board, has statewide authority. To address the drought problem, both agencies had to work together. The comments of a hydrologist capture the situation, "There needs to be a state coordinating mechanism, but it needs to be sensitive to the local context."[60] Thus, even with the constitutional superiority of the state, the state–local relationship is much more nuanced.

The words of former New York governor George Pataki are apropos: "As a former mayor, I know firsthand the importance of freeing our cities, towns, and counties from the heavy hand of state government."[61] But as Governor Pataki quickly learned, a governor has to engage in big-picture, statewide thinking, and it is awfully tempting to impose the state's will on those same localities. To make sure their voice is heard, many local governments do what those in California do: hire lobbyists to represent their interests in the state legislature. Localities in the Golden State spent nearly $40 million lobbying lawmakers in 2006.[62] Even so, cities and counties found themselves on the losing side of several key measures, including one that diverted funds for local transportation projects to the state. The state–local relationship can be rocky indeed.

## CHAPTER RECAP

- States vary in the amount and type of authority they give their local governments. The general trend has been toward increased state assistance and empowerment of localities, but some states continue to keep their local governments on a short leash.

- The issue of mandates is a particularly contentious state–local matter.

- Three types of state–local organizations are common: task forces, advisory commissions on intergovernmental relations, and departments of community affairs.

- Urban sprawl has become a major issue in state–local relations. States have begun to adopt smart-growth laws that are designed to help localities manage growth.

- Regionalism continues to be advocated as a solution to many local problems. More jurisdictions are creating regional organizations to link their local governments.

- States are looking for innovative solutions to challenging housing and infrastructure problems.

- New urbanism promotes a back-to-the-future community that appeals to a particular segment of the market.

- With many rural communities in decline, states are seeking ways of revitalizing them.

- Even as the interaction of states and localities becomes more positive, the tug of war between the two levels continues.

## Key Terms

ordinance *(p. 324)*
Dillon's rule *(p. 325)*
second-order devolution *(p. 326)*
mandate-reimbursement requirements *(p. 330)*
edge cities *(p. 333)*

urban sprawl *(p. 333)*
impact fee *(p. 333)*
greenbelts *(p. 334)*
smart growth *(p. 334)*
shadow governments *(p. 335)*
regional government *(p. 336)*

city–county consolidation *(p. 337)*
public choice theory *(p. 338)*
councils of government *(p. 340)*
density bonus *(p. 342)*
new urbanism *(p. 344)*

## Internet Resources

The National Association of Regional Councils maintains a website at **www.narc.org/**. It shows the differences and similarities of regional councils across the country.

The Association of Bay Area Governments' award-winning site can be found at **www.abag.ca.gov**.

The website for the regional planning agency that deals with 189 cities and six counties in Southern California is **www.scag.ca.gov**.

For information on the activities of a state-level ACIR, see the Tennessee ACIR at **www.state. tn.us/tacir**. Utah replaced its ACIR with the Utah Intergovernmental Roundtable at **www.cppa. utah.edu/uir/**.

The Urban Institute's site for research on economic and social policy can be found at

**www.urban.org**. It is a useful source of information on states and localities.

The Sierra Club presents its case against urban sprawl at **www.sierraclub.org/sprawl**.

To learn more about new urbanism, see **www. cnu.org**, the website for the Congress for the New Urbanism.

The Kansas Free Land program is described at **www.kansasfreeland.com/**.

Georgia's rural development council maintains an informative website at **www.ruralgeorgia. org**. Other states with rural development councils have similar websites.

# Taxing and Spending

**13**

Vallejo, California, a city of 117,000 situated about thirty-five miles north of San Francisco, rocked the municipal finance world when it declared Chapter 9 bankruptcy on May 6, 2008. Vallejo's role as a municipal poster child for the national economic crisis's impacts on local governments was the result of several factors, including closure of the city's major employer, a major slump in housing values, precipitously declining revenues, and very generous pay and benefits packages for police and firefighter unions. Nearly three-quarters of Vallejo's $80 million municipal operating budget deficit was dedicated to the police and firefighters. Severe service and payroll cuts were not sufficient to reverse the city's $16 million budget shortfall, and contract negotiations with the public safety unions failed to gain relief.

By declaring Chapter 9 bankruptcy, Vallejo gained the ability to maintain basic services while doing a "do-over" of its finance system, including a good possibility that the bankruptcy judge would void the city's union contracts. However, bankruptcy comes with harsh consequences, including extremely low-bond ratings, making future borrowing very difficult and expensive; a possible exit of concerned homeowners; and lengthy legal proceedings that could take several years and millions of dollars to conclude.

Across the country, similarly challenged municipalities and counties were watching closely. Some observers believed that Vallejo could be the leading wave in a tsunami of local government bankruptcies.[1] Fiscal drama was typical in city halls and state capitals in 2009. Budget shortfalls were astonishingly high and widely spread across the United States.

This chapter deals with state and local finance: the politics and policies of taxing and spending. Finance is a topic of continuing, visceral interest in state and local jurisdictions, and an activity characterized by much change and experimentation. From taxpayer revolts to spending mandates, the fiscal landscape has changed profoundly. More change is certain as state and local governments strive to meet taxpayer service demands economically and creatively.

# THE PRINCIPLES OF FINANCE

A major purpose of government is to provide services to citizens. But this costs money: Equipment must be purchased and employees must be paid. Governments raise needed funds through taxes, fees, and borrowing. In a democracy, the voters decide what range and quality of services they desire, and they register their decisions through elected representatives. Sometimes, when elected officials don't listen, voters revolt and take matters directly into their own hands.

Two basic principles describe state and local financial systems: *interdependence* and *diversity*. State and local fiscal systems are closely interlinked and heavily influenced by national financial activities. Intergovernmental sharing of revenues is a pronounced feature of our interdependent federal fiscal system. Yet our state financial structures and processes are also highly diverse. Though affected by national activities, their own economic health, and competitive pressures from one another, the states enjoy substantial autonomy in designing individual revenue systems in response to citizens' policy preferences.

**own-source revenue**

Monies derived by a government from its own taxable resources.

**intergovern-mental transfers**

The movement of money or other resources from one level of government to another.

## Interdependence

U.S. governments raise huge amounts of money. The states and localities collected about $2.3 trillion in 2008. Most of this money is **own-source revenue**, garnered from taxes, charges, and fees applied to people, services, and products within the jurisdiction of each level of government. Nonnational governments also benefit from **intergovernmental transfers**. The national government contributes about one-quarter of all state and local revenues; however, more than 60 percent of this federal money is "passed through" to *individual* recipients such as those receiving Medicaid. For their part, states pass on some $400 billion to their cities, counties, and special-purpose governments.[2] Some states are economic powerhouses. California's beleaguered economy still exceeds $1.8 trillion, making it the eighth largest in the world.

Local governments rely heavily on the states, and to a lesser degree on the national government, for financial authority and assistance. *Only the states* can authorize localities to levy taxes and fees, incur debt, and spend money. State constitutions and laws place many conditions on local government taxing and spending. States provide monetary support of local governments through state grants-in-aid and revenue sharing; they also assume financial responsibility for activities carried out by localities—in particular, school and social welfare costs. Most local governments are fine with this arrangement. But the role of the states as senior financial partners in state–local finance is criticized in some quarters as being unduly restrictive of local financial flexibility.

State–local finances are linked closely to activities of the national government. For instance, when the federal government changes the tax code, it can wreak havoc on those thirty-five states that base their own income taxes on the federal tax code. Congress's phase out of the estate tax was expected to cost the states upward of $5 billion a year.

When the national economy falls into a recession, state and local governments suffer most. They cannot, after all, print money or run an operating budget deficit into the future. This fact is sometimes recognized by Congress, which may send substantial amounts of **countercyclical aid** to the states and localities to help them recover from the ravages of recession. Special aid is targeted to states suffering natural disasters such as hurricanes, floods, and fires. Federal largess can be a life saver—the 2008–2009 federal stimulus package alleviated about 40 percent of the massive state budget deficits.

**countercyclical aid**

A transfer of federal dollars to states and localities to counteract a downturn in the economic cycle.

## Diversity

The second basic principle of state and local finance systems is diversity of revenue sources. Each level of government depends on one type of revenue device more than others. For the national government, it is the income tax; for the states, the sales tax; and for local governments, the property tax. But diversity triumphs among the states. Differences in tax capacity (wealth), tax effort, and tax choices are obvious even to the casual traveler. Most states tax personal income and merchandise sales, but a handful do not. Several states garner substantial revenues from severance taxes on oil, gas, and minerals.

Some states, such as New Jersey and New York, tax with a heavy hand. Others, including Nevada and Alaska, are relative tax havens. Most fall somewhere in the middle. If the basic objective of taxing is to pluck the maximum number of feathers from the goose with the minimum amount of hissing, the wealthy states hold a great advantage. They can reap high-tax revenues with much less effort than can poor states, which must tax at high rates just to pull in enough money to pay for the basics. Per capita state and local tax revenues vary from $7,864 in Alaska to $2,949 in Alabama. The U.S. average in 2008 was $4,294.

There is a close relationship between state wealth (as measured by personal income) and tax burden (see Table 13.1). Tax levels also reflect factors such as citizen attitudes, population characteristics and trends, business climate, limitations on tax increases and/or expenditures, and the quality as well as

| TABLE 13.1 | State/Local and Total Taxes by State, as a Percentage of Personal Income, Per Capita 2008 | | | | |
|---|---|---|---|---|---|
| STATE | STATE/LOCAL TAXES AS A % OF INCOME | STATE/ LOCAL TAX COLLECTIONS PER CAPITA RANK | STATE | STATE/LOCAL TAXES AS A % OF INCOME | STATE/LOCAL TAX COLLECTIONS PER CAPITA RANK |
| US average | 9.7 | – | Oregon | 9.4 | 26 |
| New Jersey | 11.8 | 1 | Michigan | 9.4 | 27 |
| New York | 11.7 | 2 | Indiana | 9.4 | 28 |
| Connecticut | 11.1 | 3 | West Virginia | 9.3 | 29 |
| Maryland | 10.8 | 4 | Illinois | 9.3 | 30 |
| Hawaii | 10.6 | 5 | Iowa | 9.3 | 31 |
| California | 10.5 | 6 | Missouri | 9.2 | 32 |
| Ohio | 10.4 | 7 | North Dakota | 9.2 | 33 |
| Vermont | 10.3 | 8 | Colorado | 9.0 | 34 |
| Wisconsin | 10.2 | 9 | Washington | 8.9 | 35 |
| Rhode Island | 10.2 | 10 | Mississippi | 8.9 | 36 |
| Pennsylvania | 10.2 | 11 | South Carolina | 8.8 | 37 |
| Minnesota | 10.2 | 12 | Alabama | 8.6 | 38 |
| Idaho | 10.1 | 13 | New Mexico | 8.6 | 39 |
| Arkansas | – | 10.0 | Montana | – | 8.6 |
| Maine | 10.0 | 15 | Arizona | 8.5 | 41 |
| Georgia | 9.9 | 16 | Louisiana | 8.4 | 42 |
| Nebraska | 9.8 | 17 | Texas | 8.4 | 43 |
| Virginia | 9.8 | 18 | Tennessee | 8.3 | 44 |
| Oklahoma | 9.8 | 19 | South Dakota | 7.9 | 45 |
| North Carolina | 9.8 | 20 | New Hampshire | 7.6 | 46 |
| Kansas | 9.6 | 21 | Florida | 7.4 | 47 |
| Utah | 9.6 | 22 | Wyoming | 7.0 | 48 |
| Massachusetts | 9.5 | 23 | Nevada | 6.6 | 49 |
| Delaware | 9.5 | 24 | Alaska | 6.4 | 50 |
| Kentucky | 9.4 | 25 | | | |

SOURCE: www.taxfoundation.org.

quantity of government services. And taxing is only one means of plucking the public goose. State and local governments increasingly rely on fees and charges for services provided. Examples include entrance fees for parks and recreation facilities, sewer and garbage fees, and motor vehicle fees.

There is an important difference between **tax capacity**, the potential ability to raise revenues from taxes, and **tax effort**, the degree to which a state exploits its fiscal potential. High-tax capacity is associated with high levels of urbanization, per capita income, economic development, and natural resources. But simply because a state has high-revenue-raising capacity does not necessarily mean that it will maximize its tax-collecting possibilities. Indeed, many states with high-revenue potential, such as Alaska and Wyoming, actually tax at relatively low rates, indicating low-tax effort.[3] Tax effort depends largely on the scope and level of services desired by the people.

**tax capacity**
The taxable resources of a government jurisdiction.

**tax effort**
The extent to which a jurisdiction exploits its taxable resources.

## REVENUES

Although the state and local finance systems have their own strengths, weaknesses, and peculiarities, certain trends can be found in all of them. The property tax is always unpopular. It is no longer a significant source of state revenue; its contribution to total own-source local coffers, though, is still strong. User fees and other miscellaneous charges are gradually growing. States continue to depend heavily on the sales tax, but alternatives are being used more widely. In fact, tax diversification is an important trend in all state and local tax systems (see Figure 13.1).

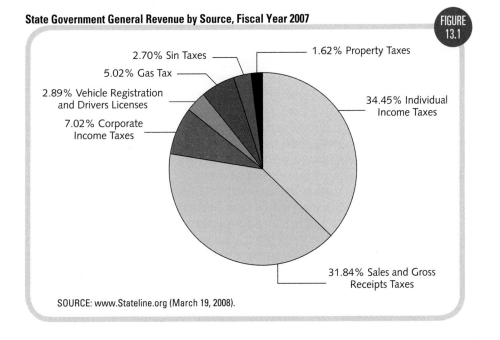

**State Government General Revenue by Source, Fiscal Year 2007**

FIGURE 13.1

- 2.70% Sin Taxes
- 5.02% Gas Tax
- 2.89% Vehicle Registration and Drivers Licenses
- 7.02% Corporate Income Taxes
- 1.62% Property Taxes
- 34.45% Individual Income Taxes
- 31.84% Sales and Gross Receipts Taxes

SOURCE: www.Stateline.org (March 19, 2008).

## Criteria for Evaluating Taxes

Numerous criteria can be used to evaluate taxes. What one person or interest group likes about a tax may be what another dislikes. Nevertheless, most political scientists and economists agree that among the most important criteria are equity, yield, elasticity, political accountability, and acceptability.

**Equity** If citizens or firms are expected to pay a tax, they should view it as fair. In the context of taxation, equity usually refers to distributing the burden of the tax in accordance with ability to pay: high income means greater ability to pay and therefore a larger tax burden. Equity includes other dimensions as well, such as the relative tax burden on individuals versus firms and the impact of various types of taxes on income, age, and social class.

> **regressive tax**
> A tax in which the rate falls as the base or taxable income rises.

Taxes may be regressive, progressive, or proportional. A **regressive tax** places a greater burden on low-income citizens than on high-income citizens. Thus, the ability-to-pay principle is violated, with the result that upper-income groups contribute a smaller portion of their incomes than do other lower-income groups. Most state and local levies, including property and sales taxes, are considered regressive. For example, both low-income and high-income people would pay, say, a 7 percent sales tax. The latter will likely make more purchases and contribute more total dollars in sales tax, but at a lower percentage of their total income, than the low-income individuals.

> **progressive tax**
> A tax in which the rate rises as the base or taxable income rises.

A **progressive tax** increases as a percentage of a person's income as that income rises. The more you make, the greater proportion of your income is extracted by the progressive tax. Thus, those better able to pay carry a heavier tax burden than do the poor. California's personal income tax is the most progressive, varying from 2 to 10.3 percent of taxable income. The more you earn, the higher your *income tax bracket*.

> **proportional (flat) tax**
> A tax in which people pay an identical rate regardless of income or economic transaction.

A **proportional tax**, sometimes called a **flat tax**, burdens everyone equally, at least in theory. For instance, a tax on income of, say, 10 percent that is applied across the board is a proportional tax. Whether you earn $100,000 or $10,000, you pay a flat 10 percent of the total in taxes. Of course, it can be argued that a low-income person is more burdened by a proportional income tax than is a high-income person (as is true of the sales tax).

> **benefit principle**
> The principle that taxes should be levied on those who benefit directly from a government service.

In place of ability to pay, some people advocate the **benefit principle**. Under this principle, those who reap more benefits from government services should shoulder more of the tax burden than people who do not avail themselves of service opportunities to the same degree. As a hypothetical example, it might be argued that parents whose children attend public schools should pay higher taxes for education than should senior citizens, childless couples, or single people without children. The benefit principle is the theoretical underpinning for user fees, which charge a taxpayer directly for services received. The unfortunate downside is that it disadvantages those who have the least ability to pay.

**Yield** Taxes can also be evaluated on the basis of efficiency, or how much money they contribute to government coffers compared to the effort expended to administer and collect them. The administrative and other costs of applying a tax must be taken into consideration when determining yield. Taxes that return substantial sums of money at minimal costs to the government are preferred to taxes that require large outlays for moderate revenues. Income and sales taxes have high yields because they raise large sums of money at low expense. They are simple to understand and fairly easy to collect. Property taxes, however, have lower yields because they are more expensive to assess and collect. Property values must be regularly appraised, which involves a certain degree of subjectivity.

Yield depends on base and rate: the broader the tax base and the higher the rate, the higher the yield. As a simple example, a sales tax applied to all purchases yields much more than a sales tax on cigarette purchases, and a $1.00-per-pack tax produces more money than a 25¢ tax.

**Elasticity** This criterion is related to yield. Tax yields should be automatically responsive to changes in economic conditions, and revenue devices should expand or contract their yields as government expenditure needs change. Specifically, as per capita income grows within the state and its localities, revenues should keep pace without increases in the tax rate. Tax reductions should accompany economic recession and declines in per capita income so that citizens' tax burdens are not increased during hard times. The progressive income tax is considered to be elastic because revenues increase as individuals earn more money and move into higher-tax brackets and decline as income falls. User fees, for example, generally do not move in tandem with economic conditions and are therefore considered to be inelastic.

**Political Accountability** Tax increases should not be hidden. Instead, state and local legislative bodies should have to approve them deliberately—and publicly. Citizens should know how much they owe and when it must be paid. For example, some state income taxes are silently hiked as wages rise in response to cost-of-living increases. After inflation is accounted for, taxpayers make the same real income as they did before, but they are driven into a higher-income bracket for tax purposes. This phenomenon, known as bracket creep, can be eliminated by **indexing** income tax brackets to changes in the cost of living.

**indexing**
A system in which tax brackets are automatically adjusted to account for inflation.

**Acceptability** The type and mix of taxes imposed should be congruent with citizen preferences. No tax commands wild enthusiasm, and a portion of the citizenry will always be opposed to *any* tax or fee increase, but some devices are less disagreeable than others. Tax acceptability varies depending on numerous factors, including equity implications and the perceived pain of paying. Large, direct payments, such as the annual property tax, inflict greater pain than small, frequently paid sales taxes. And a tax on someone else is always preferable. As Senator Russell Long of Louisiana put it many years ago, "Don't tax me, don't tax thee; tax that man behind the tree."

## Major State and Local Taxes

The principal types of taxes are those on property, sales, and income. Various miscellaneous taxes also provide revenue for state and local governments.

**Property Tax** In 1942, taxes on personal and corporate property accounted for 53 percent of all state and local tax revenues. Today, they represent only 27 percent of tax revenue. States hardly utilize the property tax at all today (it accounts for less than 2 percent of their total revenues), but local governments continue to depend on this fiscal workhorse for three-quarters of all their own-source revenues. Other revenue sources have augmented the property tax so its proportionate contribution has diminished. As always, there is considerable state-by-state variation. New Hampshire, which has no sales or income taxes, depends on property taxes for more than 18 percent of its total state tax revenues and approximately 75 percent of local revenues.

Property taxes are widely reviled. Assessments of value may seem to change suddenly or appear to stack up unfavorably against similar properties, and, when appealed, such taxes involve a frustrating process. Acceptability and accountability rank low in relations to other taxes. The best feature of the property tax is that it is certain; owners of property must pay it or the government may seize and sell their land, buildings, or other taxable possessions. But it tends to be regressive and sometimes must be paid in a large lump sum. At first thought, it seems that property taxes cannot be truly regressive because only those people who own property pay taxes on it directly; however, renters pay property taxes indirectly through their monthly rent checks to the landlord. When property tax assessments climb, so do rental charges. Property taxes can also violate the ability-to-pay principle when housing values spiral upward, as they did in the mid-2000s in Utah, Colorado, Nevada, and Arizona. Retirees and other home owners on fixed incomes discovered with alarm that their annual property tax bills were doubling or tripling as housing prices escalated. Then, as property values plummeted in the Great Recession of 2008–2009, tax values remained the same until the next scheduled reassessment.

Just this sort of situation helped precipitate Proposition 13 in California, which was credited with kicking off a taxpayer revolt across the United States. In the Los Angeles and San Francisco Bay areas during the 1970s, property taxes doubled and then tripled in only a few years. Some senior citizens were forced to sell their homes to pay their property tax. Proposition 13 reduced property tax bills by approximately $7 billion in the first year, and it imposed strict limitations on the ability of local governments to raise property and other taxes in the future. California dropped from the eighth-highest property tax state to the twenty-eighth. This example illustrates the problem of political accountability: When property values rise to lofty heights, taxpayers' bills keep pace (unless they revolt), even though elected officials do not explicitly vote to hike property taxes.

Property taxes are difficult to administer and somewhat arbitrary. The process of levying an annual fee on "real property" (land and buildings) begins with a government assessor making a formal appraisal of the market value of the land and the buildings on it. Then property values are equalized so that similarly valued real estate is taxed at the same level. Time is set aside to make corrections and to review appeals on appraisals that the owner believes are too high. Next, an assessment ratio is applied to the property. For instance, houses might be assessed for tax purposes at 80 percent of market value. A rate is placed on the assessed value to calculate the annual tax amount. (Assessed at a market price of $100,000, taxed at a ratio of 0.80 and a rate of $3 per $100 [30 mils], a house would produce a tax due of $2,400). Determining market value may seem fairly straightforward, but ultimately the appraised market value depends on the findings of the assessor, who may or may not be properly trained for the job or fully aware of conditions in the local housing market (statistical models remove some of the guesswork). Property can thus be under-appraised or over-appraised. For the sake of equity, property should be appraised regularly (e.g., every two or three years). Otherwise, property that does not change ownership becomes increasingly undervalued or overvalued, depending on the local real estate market.

Property tax systems are further criticized for exempting certain types of real estate and buildings. Government buildings such as hospitals and state offices are not taxed, even though they utilize police and fire protection, trash collection, and other local government services. Churches, synagogues, mosques, and related property used for religious purposes are also partly or wholly exempted in the vast majority of jurisdictions, as is property owned by charitable and nonprofit organizations. In some counties, as much as 60 percent of the property tax base is exempted. States make payments in lieu of taxes (PILOTs) to help offset the effects of exemptions for state property, but at rates below what local governments would have collected in tax payments.

In an effort to make property taxation more equitable and more in keeping with ability to pay, most states have enacted some form of **circuit breaker**. For instance, the property of low-income individuals is excluded from taxation in some states; others assign lower-assessment ratios to the homes of senior citizens or set a top limit on the tax according to the owner's income (e.g., 4 percent of net income). Many states have "truth-in-taxation" laws that roll back property tax rates as appraised values rise rapidly. Most also offer homestead exemptions, in which owner-occupied homes are taxed at lower rates or assessed at lower values than are rental homes or business property. Massachusetts municipalities permit seniors to earn credits against their tax bills through public service activities.

**circuit breaker**
A limit on taxes applied to certain categories of people, such as the poor or elderly.

Despite such attempts to make the property tax fairer, differences in property values among cities, counties, and school districts still have important implications for the quality and distribution of services. Jurisdictions with many wealthy families, capital-intensive industries, or rapid construction growth can provide high levels of services with low-tax rates, whereas areas with weak property tax bases must tax at high rates merely to yield enough revenue to maintain minimal services. Residential property tax rates vary widely from city to city. For example, the tax rate is $25.93 per $1,000.00 of assessed value in Buffalo, New York, but only $2.90 in Dothan, Alabama. Altering the unequal distribution of property values is essentially beyond the control of local governments. As a result, "wealthy suburbs remain wealthy, poor communities remain poor, and services remain unequal."[4] As discussed in Chapter 15, inequity in school funding has been the target of litigation in all except for a handful of states. In Michigan, the legislature significantly reduced taxes for public education and asked voters to substitute either sales tax increases or higher-income taxes. Voters opted overwhelmingly for a 2¢ sales tax increase accompanied by a 50¢-per-pack cigarette tax hike. Dramatic property tax–relief measures have also been adopted in Florida, Maine, and Washington.

**Sales Tax** Mississippi was the first state to adopt this form of taxation in 1932. Others followed suit rapidly, and states currently collect more of their revenues today from the general sales and gross receipts tax than from any other source. It accounts for about one-third of total state own-source taxes. Only five states do not levy a general sales tax: Alaska, Delaware, Montana, New Hampshire, and Oregon. State sales tax rates vary from 7.25 in California to 2.9 percent in Colorado. Some states, particularly those that do not have personal income taxes, are exceptionally dependent on the sales tax: Florida, South Dakota, Tennessee, and Washington derive approximately 60 percent of their own-source revenues from the sales tax.

The sales tax has remained in favor for two major reasons. First, citizen surveys have consistently shown that when a tax must be raised, voters reluctantly prefer the sales tax. Although the reasons are not entirely clear, this tax is perceived to be fairer than other forms of taxation. Second, there is an abiding belief that high-state income taxes depress economic development.[5]

Thirty-nine states authorize at least some of their municipalities and counties to levy local sales taxes. When state and local sales taxes are combined, the total tax bite can be painful. In Arkansas cities, the purchase of a $1.00 item requires up to 11.5¢ in sales tax. The rate on the dollar is 10.5¢ in Oklahoma City. Sales taxes are usually optional for the local jurisdiction, but may require state legislative approval in some cases. Typically, states impose ceilings on how many pennies the localities can attach to the state sales tax; states also specify which sizes and types of local governments are permitted to exercise this option.

When applied to all merchandise, the sales tax is clearly regressive. Poor folks must spend a larger portion of their incomes than rich people spend on basics, such as food and clothing. Therefore, the sales tax places a much heavier burden on low-income people. Most of the forty-five states with a sales tax alleviate its regressive nature by excluding certain "necessities." Twenty-nine states do not tax food purchased from the grocery store, only six states tax prescription drugs, most exempt consumer electric and gas utilities, and six states exclude clothing.[6] New Jersey excludes paper products. When the sales tax was extended to paper products in 1990, enraged Jerseyites mailed wads of toilet paper—some of it used—to horrified legislators, who quickly rescinded the tax.

States can improve the yield of the sales tax by broadening the base to include services. In this way, more of the burden is passed on to upper-income individuals, who are heavier users of services. More than half of the states tax services such as household, automobile, and appliance repairs; barber and beauty shop treatments; printing; rentals; dry cleaning; and interior decorating. Hawaii, Texas, and South Dakota tax almost all professional and personal services. New Jersey taxes hair transplants and tummy tucks, and Arkansas taps into tattoos and nose rings. Maryland residents must pay a "flush tax" of $30.00 on their sewer bills to help clean up polluted Chesapeake Bay. However, states can move too far and too fast with taxes on services. Florida, Massachusetts, and Michigan broadened the base of their sales tax to services, only to have it repealed shortly afterward through lobbying efforts by the business community.

These setbacks were likely to be temporary. Services are the largest and fastest growing segment of the U.S. economy. Eighty-five percent of new jobs are in services. As one political commentator asked, "How can one rationalize taxing autos, videocassettes, and toothpaste, but not piped-in music, cable TV, parking lot services, or $100 beauty salon treatments?"[7] Pet-grooming services, legal and financial services, and many others from landscaping to legal work were losing their tax-favored status in 2009 as states extended sales taxes to services incrementally, fighting industry and lobbyists one at a time.

A big fight has erupted over state and local governments' right to tax an enormously promising revenue stream—electronic commerce on the Internet. Twenty-one states were levying taxes or fees on Internet access, data downloads, or goods purchased on the Internet. Then pressures from Internet interests, including servers (e.g., America Online), media companies, and retail businesses, led Congress to pass the Internet Tax Freedom Act, which imposed a moratorium on taxing Internet access and online sales. State and local officials strongly opposed such limitations, estimating that it costs them as much as $20 billion in annual revenues because more and more goods are purchased on the Internet. Already states estimate that they forfeit $5 billion a year in uncollected taxes from interstate catalog sales. Only sales to citizens living in the same state as a catalog or mail-order firm that has a physical presence in the state are now taxed. Many states require citizens to declare and pay such sales taxes in their annual state income tax returns, usually to little avail because of the difficulty of enforcement.

Internet taxation is both complicated and controversial, and it has become a compelling issue for the states. A 1992 U.S. Supreme Court ruling blocked taxation of catalog sales on the grounds of violating the Interstate Commerce Clause, a ruling that has obvious applicability to taxing Internet commerce today.[8] Congress has been tied in knots on the issue. No less than the fiscal integrity of state revenue systems is at stake. If states continue to lose billions of dollars to a tax-free Internet, how will the gaping budget holes be filled? What about Main Street brick-and-mortar retailers whose prices are made less competitive by the amount of the sales tax? Despite protestations by Internet vendors that compliance with state and local sales taxes is a heavy burden, available software programs can calculate amounts due each jurisdiction relatively easily.

A compromise is the streamlined sales tax (SST), wherein states collapse all their local sales tax rates into one (or just a few) statewide rates, resulting in a manageable number of Internet tax jurisdictions.[9] This approach has the added advantage of laying the foundation for taxing mail-order catalog sales.

Seemingly a straightforward proposition, simplification of multistate sales systems has presented Zen-like puzzlers: Are marshmallows food or candy? What about a Twix bar? Are "fruit beverages" that contain only 10 percent juice a food or a soft drink? Still, as of 2009, twenty-two states had passed the SST model legislation. States are facilitating compliance by providing and setting up new tax collection software for Internet and catalog vendors. Meantime, sixteen states have adopted a sales tax on online purchases of music, games, ring tones, and other video entertainment. Vendors are required to apply the state sales tax when a product is sold and remit it to the state.[10]

Elasticity is not a strong point of the sales tax, although its productivity falls when consumer purchases slow, and rises as consumers boost their spending. Broadening the base helps. States attempt to make the sales tax more responsive to short-term economic conditions by increasing it on a temporary basis, to make up for lower-than-anticipated revenues, and then reducing it when needed monies are collected. A problem with these tactics, however, is that consumers tend to postpone major purchases until the tax rate falls.

The sales tax is relatively simple for governments to administer. Sellers of merchandise and services are required to collect it and remit it to the state on a regular basis. Political accountability is also an advantage because legislative bodies must enact laws or ordinances to increase the sales tax rate. And, as we have observed, the sales tax is the least unpopular of the major taxes.

**Income Tax** Most states tax personal and corporate income. Wisconsin was the first, in 1911, two years before the national government enacted its own personal income tax. Forty-one states have broad-based taxes on personal income; two states (Tennessee and New Hampshire) limit theirs to capital gains, interest, and dividends. Only Texas, South Dakota, Nevada, Washington, and Wyoming leave all personal income untaxed. The latter four states also abstain from taxing corporate income. Personal income taxes garner 22 percent of all state and local own-source taxes, and the corporate tax brings in about 4.0 percent. Seventeen states permit designated cities, counties, or school districts to levy taxes on personal income.

State and local income taxes are equitable when they are progressive. Progressivity normally entails a sliding scale, so that high-income filers pay a greater percentage of their income in taxes than do low-income filers. Most states do not levy a personal income tax on people whose earnings fall below a certain floor—say, $10,000. Overall, state personal income taxes are moderately progressive and are gradually becoming more so. Seven states, however, tax income at a flat rate varying from 3 percent in Illinois to 5 percent in Massachusetts.

Personal and corporate income taxes are superior to other taxes on the criteria of yield and elasticity. By tapping almost all sources of income, they draw in large sums of money and respond fairly well to short-term economic conditions. Through payroll withholding, income taxes are fairly simple to collect. Also, many states periodically adjust income tax rates in response to annual revenue needs. In 2009 a new sort of income tax adjustment was under state consideration. The huge federal stimulus package contained a number of new federal tax cuts. Those states coupling their state income tax to the federal tax faced significant reductions in revenues, as much as $760 million over two years in North Carolina.[11] As a result, decoupling was under active legislative consideration.

As mentioned earlier, political accountability can be problematic with respect to income taxes during periods of rising prices. Unless income tax rates are indexed to inflation, as they are in seventeen states, cost-of-living increases push salaries and corporate earnings into higher-tax brackets.

**Miscellaneous Taxes** A wide variety of miscellaneous taxes are assessed by state and local governments. "Sin taxes" raise a small—but growing—percentage of all state revenues. All states tax cigarettes and more than twenty states boosted this tax in 2009. Rhode Island discourages smoking with a $3.46 per-pack tax and New York posts a tax of $2.75. Some cities levy additional taxes on smokes, bringing the price of some premium brands up to $8.00 a pack. South Carolina charges only 7¢ per pack; not surprisingly, it is a tobacco-growing state.[12] This startling disparity in prices has led to a flourishing trade in Internet vending, cigarette smuggling from low- to high-tax states, and treks to nearby Indian reservations (where cigarettes are not taxed at all) to purchase tobacco.

In 1991 the states experienced the equivalent of winning the lottery. A court settlement with tobacco companies is sending as much as $246 billion into state coffers over a period of years. Ideally, the funds should be used for public health and smoking prevention programs. But few strings are attached, and many states have spent the windfall on economic development initiatives or to balance the budget. Seventeen states have taken the fiscally unsound step of selling bonds to be paid off with tobacco settlement money expected to appear in the state treasury. Ironically, the amount of tobacco settlement dollars pledged to the states is based on the number of packs of cigarettes sold. But high-tobacco tax states and others as well are experiencing shrinking sales as smokers beat the habit or take advantage of Indian reservations or Internet sales.

Alcoholic beverages are also taxed in all fifty states, although rates vary according to classification: beer, wine, or spirits. Beer guzzlers should steer clear of Alaska, where the tax per gallon of beer is $1.07; frequent imbibers are invited to visit Missouri, where the tax is only 6¢ per gallon, or Colorado (8¢). (These low rates could perhaps be related to the fact that Missouri hosts the headquarters of Anheuser-Busch, whereas Colorado hosts Coors). Wine lovers should consider New York, where the tax is 19¢ per gallon, or California (21¢). As drinking and smoking have declined during the past few years, so have their tax-based revenues. Clearly, raising alcohol and tobacco taxes helps to curtail these "sins." It is regularly suggested that marijuana and other "recreational" drugs be legalized so that they, too, can be taxed.

Though not a "sin," gasoline falls under taxation's shadow as well. The highest state tax on gasoline in 2009 was in Washington (37.5¢ per gallon). The lowest was in Alaska (8.0¢). Alas, the gas tax is running on empty as motorists reduce the number of miles they drive in response to high-gas prices and vehicles become more fuel efficient. The result is depletion of road mainte-

New York Yankees 3rd baseman Alex "A- Rod" Rodriguez picks up a ball he has just booted for an error. To add financial injury to insult, A-Rod was forced to pay thousands of dollars in taxes to host city Detroit.

SOURCE: Raul Sancya/AP Images.

nance and improvement funds for which gasoline taxes are earmarked. Several states are studying taxing miles driven instead of gallons purchased. Most states tax death in one form or another. Estate taxes must be paid on the financial assets and property of a deceased person before the remainder is disbursed to the survivors. Sixteen states tax those who inherit substantial assets (typically valued at more than $675,000). Rates are generally staggered according to the value of the estate and the relationship to the deceased. As noted above, however, a reduction of the federal estate tax foretells a decline for such state taxes as well, unless the states amend their estate tax laws.

Other miscellaneous sources of revenue include hunting and fishing licenses, business licenses, auto license fees, parking tickets, traffic violation fines, and telecommunications fees. Utah imposes a 10 percent tax on nude dancing clubs and on escort services. One interesting device is the "jock tax." Some twenty states and several cities require professional athletes to pay a prorated income tax for games played in their jurisdiction. California, for instance, takes 9.3 percent of athletes' daily pay when they are in state. For highly paid baseball, basketball, and football players, the jock tax burns. New York Yankees star Alex "A-Rod" Rodriguez must fork over to an estimated $267,859 a season in jock tax to California.

## User Fees

Setting specific prices on goods and services provided by state and local governments is one method that clearly pursues the *benefit principle*: Only those who use the goods and services should pay. User fees have been in existence for many years. Examples include college tuition, water and sewer charges, and trash collection assessments. Toll roads and bridges are coming back in fashion as well. Today, user fees are being applied broadly as state and especially local officials attempt to tie services to their true costs. Such fees are increasingly being levied on "nonessential" local government services, such as parks and recreation, libraries, airports, and public transit. The average American pays more than $1,803 a year in user fees,[13] which make up approximately 40 percent of local governments' own-source revenues.

User fees offer several advantages. If priced accurately, they are perfectly fair under the benefit principle and they enjoy a relatively high level of political acceptability. But those people who do not have enough money to purchase the goods and services may have to do without—a circumstance that violates the ability-to-pay principle. A good case in point is higher education, which is shifting increasingly from state funding to tuition and fee-based funding. (Fortunately, rebates, scholarships, fee waivers, and reduced-fee schedules help mitigate ability-to-pay difficulties among low-income residents). User fees are structured to yield whatever is needed to finance a particular service. An added benefit is that service users who do not live in the taxing jurisdiction must also pay the price, say, for a day in the state park. Elasticity may be achieved if the amount of the charge is varied so that it always covers service costs. In many instances, user fees can be levied without specific permission from the state.

Because service users must be identified and charged, some user fees can be difficult to administer. Political accountability is low because the charges can be increased without legislative action. However, a special advantage of user fees is that they can be employed to ration certain goods or services. For instance, entrance charges can be increased to reduce attendance at an overcrowded public facility, or varied according to the day of the week to encourage more efficient utilization. If the municipal zoo has few visitors on Mondays, it can cut the entrance fee on that day of the week by one-half.

An increasingly popular and specialized form of user charge is the local impact fee, or exaction, requiring private land developers to contribute roads, sewers, and other infrastructure as the price for local regulatory approval for subdivision, factories, or other development projects. The cost of infrastructure is thus shifted to firms and, ultimately, to those who purchase or use their buildings or facilities. A related concept applied through a special sales tax on travel-related services is the travel tax. Here, taxes on lodging, rental cars, and other services paid largely by out-of-towners are imposed at rates averaging 12 percent.

Table 13.2 rates various taxes and fees based on the five criteria discussed at the beginning of this section.

## Severance Tax

States blessed with petroleum, coal, natural gas, and minerals tax these natural resources as they are taken from the land and sold. A fortunate few (Alaska and

| Rating State and Local Taxes According to Five Criteria | | | | | TABLE 13.2 |
|---|---|---|---|---|---|
| TAX | EQUITY | YIELD | ELASTICITY | POLITICAL ACCOUNTABILITY | ACCEPT ABILITY |
| Property | C | C | C | D | D |
| Sales | D | B | B | A | B |
| Personal and corporate income | B | A | B | C | C |
| User fees | C | B | A | C | B |
| NOTE: A = excellent, B = good, C = fair, D = poor. | | | | | |

Wyoming among the most fortunate) are able to "export" a substantial portion of their tax bite to people living in other states. However, in-staters must pay the same tax rate as out-of-staters.

A large majority of states (thirty-nine) place a severance tax on some form of natural resources, but just ten states collect 90 percent of all severance tax revenues. Taxes on oil and natural gas account for around 50 percent of total state revenues in Alaska. Wyoming brings in about 45 percent of its revenues from severance taxes on coal, oil, and gas (which may explain why these states are able to forgo personal income taxes). Several states are rather creative in applying the severance tax. Washington levies the tax on oysters, salmon, and other food fish, and Louisiana on freshwater mussels.[14]

Severance taxes are popular in states rich in natural resources because they help keep income, property, and sales taxes relatively low. Severance tax revenues also help to pay for environmental damage resulting from resource extraction operations, such as strip mining. The major disadvantage is that a state economy too dependent on severance taxes can be damaged badly when the price or supply of its natural resources declines, as Alaska experiences from time to time with depressed crude-oil prices. Even so, natural resources have been individually enriching for Alaskans. For more than twenty years, every man, woman, and child resident of Alaska has received a rebate from the state's Permanent Fund. Checks totaled $3269.00 per person in 2008, the highest ever. Established primarily with severance taxes on petroleum, the Permanent Fund's reserves are diversified through investments in office buildings, industrial complexes, stocks, and bonds.[15]

## Gambling: Lotteries and Casinos

The lottery is an old American tradition; initially established in the 1600s, it was popular from the colonial days until the late 1800s. Lotteries flourished throughout the country as a means of raising money for good causes such as new schools, highways, canals, and bridges. But scandals and mismanagement led every state and the national government to ban "looteries." From 1895 to 1963, no legal lotteries operated. Then New Hampshire established a new one, followed in 1967 by New York. Since then, forty-one more states have created lotteries.

Several factors account for the rebirth of "bettor government." First, lotteries can bring in meaningful sums of money—some $23 billion in "profits" in 2008 and nearly 14 percent of Nevada's total revenue.[16] Second, they are popular and entertaining. And they are voluntary—you do not have to participate. In addition, lotteries help relieve pressure on major taxes. In some states, net lottery earnings take the place of a 1¢ increase in the sales tax. Finally, state ownership of a game of chance offers a legal and fair alternative to illegal gambling operations, such as neighborhood numbers games or betting (parlay) cards.

But lotteries also have disadvantages. They are costly to administer and have low yields. Prize awards must be great enough to encourage future ticket sales—the higher the payout, the more people play. New games must be created to retain enthusiasm. Ticket vendors must be paid commissions. And tight (as well as expensive) security precautions are required to guarantee the game's integrity. As a result, lotteries generate only a small percentage of most states' total revenues, usually less than 3 percent of own-source income. Although Rhode Island's lottery has provided more than 10 percent of its total revenues in some years, the average yield for players is low: about 50 percent of the total revenues is returned to players in prize money. This amount is far below the returns of other games of chance, such as slot machines, roulette, or craps. Although many states earmark lottery proceeds for popular programs, especially education, the result is often a shell game. For instance, Florida's lottery officially benefits schools and colleges, but in reality lottery money simply *replaces* general-fund revenues rather than actually enhancing education funding.[17]

Lotteries can also be attacked on the grounds of equity and elasticity. Although the purchase of a ticket is voluntary and thus seemingly fair, studies indicate that low-income individuals are more likely to play. Participation is also higher among African Americans, Latinos, males, seniors, and those with low levels of education.[18] The lottery, then, is a regressive way to raise money.[19] Furthermore, lotteries also tend to encourage compulsive gambling (one could further assert that states themselves become addicted to gambling revenues). In recognition of this problem, some states earmark a portion of lottery proceeds for treatment programs. Lotteries are considered inelastic because earnings are cyclical and generally unstable. Sales depend on such factors as the legalized gambling activities in neighboring states, the size of jackpots, the effectiveness of marketing efforts, and the level of competition from other gambling options.

As interstate lottery competition saturates markets and depresses profits, states have adopted other forms of legalized gambling, including pari-mutuel betting on horse and dog races; "racinos," with slot machines at the tracks; as well as gaming on river boats, Indian reservations, and at Old West historical sites. In a persistent quest for more revenues, many states have legalized casino gaming and other gambling. Once restricted to Atlantic City and Las Vegas, casino gambling now occurs in twenty-six states, including operations on about 400 Native American reservations. Gambling establishments virtually blanket Minnesota and Mississippi. Touted as producers of jobs, tourist attractions, and generators of higher revenues, casinos share many of the same disadvantages as lotteries, including diminishing returns as new casinos open monthly across the country. And little, if any, state revenue is derived from most tribal casinos.

Thwarting state-sponsored gambling activities are hundreds of illegal Internet gambling sites offering Texas Hold'em and other betting opportunities, even though the federal government has banned them. In coastal states, "cruises to nowhere" cast off in which the dice are rolled and blackjack is dealt as soon as the ship enters international waters. Interactive systems permit couch potatoes to place bets over the Internet with their personal computers. Kansas has an online "e-scratch" game.

# THE POLITICAL ECONOMY OF TAXATION

## Spending

Taxes lead to spending. The principle of diversity in state and local finance is evident, given what state and local governments choose to do with their revenues. First, these governments spend a great deal of money. State and local spending has been ascending much faster than the gross national product and the level of inflation. The functional distribution of spending varies from state to state. As indicated in Figure 13.2, education consumes the largest portion of total state and local spending, followed by social services, which includes public assistance and health care.

Within each of these functional categories lies a wide range of financial commitments. For instance, higher-education expenditures in a recent year ran from 25.1 percent of total state spending in Iowa to only 3.6 percent in Maine. Alaska dedicated 17.2 percent to highways, whereas Alabama set aside just 3.4 percent for the same purpose.[20] Such differences represent historical trends, local economic circumstances, and citizens' willingness to incur debt to pay for services. Demographic factors also play a role. For instance, states with high populations of children invest more money in schools than do states with large proportions of senior citizens. Population growth drives up expenditures for services such as water and sewer systems, street maintenance, and law enforcement. The largest expenditure gains in recent years have been registered in corrections and Medicaid, as populations of prisoners and the medically indigent have swelled.

One of the most difficult decisions for an elected official is to go on record in favor of raising taxes. The political heat can scorch even the coolest incumbent. But when revenues do not equal service costs and citizens do not want to cut services, raising taxes may be the only answer. However, most people do not want higher taxes. This dilemma is the familiar **tax–service paradox**: People demand new, improved, or at least the same level of government services

**tax–service paradox**

Situation in which people demand more government services but do not want to pay for them through higher taxes.

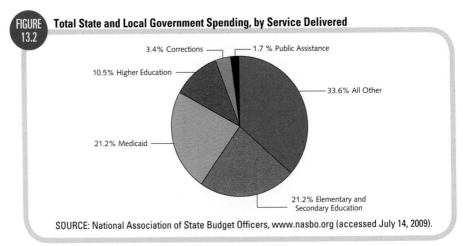

**FIGURE 13.2**  **Total State and Local Government Spending, by Service Delivered**

3.4% Corrections

1.7 % Public Assistance

10.5% Higher Education

33.6% All Other

21.2% Medicaid

21.2% Elementary and Secondary Education

SOURCE: National Association of State Budget Officers, www.nasbo.org (accessed July 14, 2009).

but do not want to pay for them through higher taxes. For instance, the people of Washington, in their collective wisdom, voted in a 1999 constitutional initiative to slice taxes. But the very next year, they passed another initiative to reduce class sizes and boost teacher pay—without, of course, providing any new money. Voters in a dozen other states have taken similar actions. As a former legislator put it, "I wouldn't say voters are stupid. But the same voter who wants unlimited services also does not want to pay for it. There is a disconnect."[21] Is it any wonder that user charges have become a popular option?

The tax–service paradox reflects a certain alienation between government and its citizens. The widespread belief that government at all levels has become too big and wasteful undoubtedly has some basis in fact. The size and responsibilities of state and local governments have grown dramatically, and waste and inefficiency have sometimes accompanied this growth. But the unwillingness of citizens to accept the inevitable reductions in services that follow tax cuts borders on mass schizophrenia.

Helping promote the tax–service paradox are the news media, which "commonly paint government with the broad brush of incompetence."[22] Prime-time television news capsules on "how government wastes your money" and typical reporting on actions of states and localities search for and emphasize the negative while ignoring the positive. Government bashing is a popular talk-radio sport. Meanwhile, state and local government functions have become much more complex and technical, tending to make government more difficult to understand, interact with, and communicate with.

State and local governments are responding with outreach efforts designed to educate citizens about what their governments are doing for them and where their tax dollars are going. There are indications that the "dollars and sense" message has been received in a growing number of states. Taxation and expenditure limits (TELS) have recently been defeated by voters in Maine, Nebraska, and Oregon and rolled back in Colorado. New York City's website provides personalized tax receipts, showing what each citizen's tax dollars paid for. Local governments everywhere are striving to write their annual budgets in reader-friendly formats.

Thus, the **political economy**—the set of political choices that frames economic policy—has become enormously perplexing for state and local officials. Several features of contemporary state and local economies merit additional discussion: the tax revolt, fiscal stress, limited discretion in raising new revenues, and underfunded retiree benefits.

**political economy**
Political choices that have economic outcomes.

## Tax Revolt

Taxpayer resentment of property taxes and changes in assessment practices, and the general perception that government is too big, too costly, and too wasteful, first took on a tangible form in 1978 with the passage of Proposition 13 in California. Its most Draconian embodiment was adopted by Colorado voters in 1992 as the Taxpayer's Bill of Rights, known as TABOR.[23] Some of TABOR's most restrictive provisions were diluted in a subsequent referendum alluded to above. Today, some twenty-seven states have enacted statutory or constitutional limitations on taxing and spending by slashing personal or corporate income taxes, indexing their income taxes to the cost of living, and cutting the sales tax. In most instances, citizens have taken tax matters into their own hands through the initiative process. In other cases, state legislators jumped in front of the parade and cut taxes and spending themselves. The taxpayer revolt continues at a slower pace today. Its legacy, however, remains enormously important. Watchdog organizations such as the Americans for Tax Reform, led by famous taxophobe Grover Norquist, insist that candidates for elective office sign a "no-tax" pledge. Public officials must work hard to justify tax increases; otherwise, they risk a citizen uprising and perhaps political death.

Indeed, the stirrings of new tax revolts are constantly in evidence. The prairie fire of tax revolt is never dead—only smoldering. Responding to citizen pressure, the Florida legislature rolled back property taxes in 2007. Oregon voters fanned the tax-revolt flames in 2003 by soundly defeating a proposal to raise personal and corporate income taxes, choosing instead to accept prisoner releases, layoffs of state troopers, a shortened school year, and other serious budget balancing measures. In desperation, the state legislature passed a plan to impose a three-year income tax surcharge. At least Beaver State voters acted civilly. Angry protesters in Tennessee once stormed the capitol building, screaming insults and hurling rocks at legislators.

**taxation and expenditure limitations (TELs)**

Restrictions on state and/or local government taxing and spending.

Most state and local jurisdictions managed the fallout of the tax revolt reasonably well. Many of them held large budget surpluses that they utilized to ameliorate the immediate effects of **taxation and expenditure limitations (TELs)**. TELs are restrictions on government taxing and spending, such as limiting the growth in spending to no more than the latest year's growth in per capita income. For example, California had a $3 billion surplus with which it temporarily replaced property tax revenues forgone by local governments. Only a handful of states followed California's stringent TELs, which cut property taxes by 60 percent. Forty-one states have some sort of property tax restriction in effect, and many place limitations on other forms of taxation as well. Raising taxes now requires a constitutional amendment, voter approval, or an extraordinary legislative majority in quite a few states. States and localities usually resist reducing service levels, opting instead to shift tax burdens or find new sources of revenues, such as user charges.[24]

Political and economic consequences of the tax revolt have been much studied. In many cases, TELs have made state and local finance an extraordinarily difficult undertaking: Voters insist on passing spending mandates for education, law enforcement, or other popular programs while at the same time tying the hands of legislatures with restrictions on new revenue-raising. This, in turn, can spawn bureaucratic imposition of new fees in attempts to gather sufficient funds to pay for essential services.[25] So far, TELs have not significantly reduced the size and cost of government, as had been advertised.[26] However, TELs have led local governments to depend more on the states and to greater recognition by public officials of the continuing need to measure the taxpaying public's pulse on tax issues.[27]

## Fiscal Stress

During national and regional economic downturns, many state and local jurisdictions experience severe **fiscal stress**: They struggle to pay for programs and provide services that citizens want and need without taxing the citizens at unacceptably high levels. Many factors contribute to fiscal stress. Typically, adverse social and economic conditions, mostly beyond state and local government control, establish an environment conducive to financial problems. The unwinding of the national economy in 2008–2009 was largely due to the deregulation of the financial industry and corporate greed, as well as to a housing bubble and resultant mortgage loan meltdown. In other words, state and local governments had reasonably clean hands in the crisis. Yet, they have paid the greatest financial price.

Older industrial cities are particularly vulnerable. Many jobs and manufacturing industries have been lost because of the gradual but compelling shift to a service- and information-based economy and company relocation to the Sunbelt and foreign countries. In cities such as Detroit, Philadelphia, and New York, the exodus of jobs and firms has eroded the value of taxable resources (mostly property), yet citizens left behind have growing service demands. In New Orleans and other Gulf Coast communities, the local tax base was essentially wiped out by hurricane Katrina in 2005 (but then sales tax revenues boomed in the aftermath as residents rebuilt).

Concentration of the poor and minorities in deteriorating housing, the shortage of jobs, high levels of crime, the illegal drug trade, homelessness, large expanses of blighted property, and related factors have produced crisis-level situations. Declining infrastructure also plagues older cities: Water and sewer lines, treatment plants, streets, sidewalks, and other components of the urban physical landscape are in dire need of restoration or replacement. The estimated amount needed to replace Atlanta's crumbling and leaking drinking water and wastewater systems alone is an astounding $3.9 billion over seven years. Pennsylvania needs $11 billion to replace failing bridges. The compelling need for serious attention to our aging national transportation infrastructure was punctuated by the catastrophic collapse of a Mississippi River bridge on Minnesota's I-35 in 2007, killing thirteen motorists. The Minnesota Department of Transportation was heralded for its outstanding job in beating an ambitious deadline to erect a new bridge in just over one year while meeting budget targets.[28]

> **fiscal stress**
> Financial pressure on a government from factors such as revenue shortfalls and taxing and spending limitations.

A collapsed Minnesota bridge visually illustrates the problems of aging infrastructure
SOURCE: SCOTT COHEN/Reuters/Landov.

Most of these problems, it should be noted, will require national government attention if they are to be addressed effectively. Special factors contributing to state fiscal stress include weak local real-estate markets; rapid increases in energy prices; unfunded federal and state mandates; and court- and congressionally-mandated spending increases in corrections, education, and other areas.

Political sources of fiscal stress typically compound the economic problems of cities. Mismanagement of resources and inefficient procedures and activities are common complaints. For example, mismanagement and fraud in the San Diego municipal pension system sent the city to the brink of bankruptcy in 2005 and led to the resignation of the mayor and federal charges against various former elected officials and their staffs.[29] Pressures from city workers and their unions have also driven up service-provision costs in some localities. Thus, service demands and the costs of providing services grow while taxes and intergovernmental revenues decline. This is a well-tested recipe for fiscal stress that evokes fears of bond defaults and even bankruptcy.

New York City offers a thirty-year-long saga of fiscal stress. People, jobs, and industry fled the city for the suburbs and the Sunbelt in the early 1970s, thereby reducing fiscal capacity. Yet public employees' pay and pensions grew to some of the highest levels in the United States, and welfare payments to the poor and unemployed were generous. The tuition-free City University of New York (CUNY) had an enrollment of 265,000 students.

As revenues tumbled and lagged behind expenditures, the city government played fiscal roulette with the budget and borrowed huge sums through municipal notes and bonds. Eventually it was on the brink of bankruptcy. Defaults on the city's bonds, notes, and other debt instruments seemed imminent. City officials cried out to the national government and New York State for help, but some people had little sympathy for a city that had lived beyond its means for so long.

Aided by national guarantees of new long-term loans, New York State and other large holders of New York City debt finally agreed to a bailout. Had this immense urban financial center collapsed, the fiscal shocks would have threatened New York State's economic stability and even resulted in serious fiscal repercussions for other states and localities throughout the United States.

Unfortunately, the Big Apple once again risked being reduced to a seedy core in 1992. It faced a budget deficit of $3.5 billion, a mass exodus of jobs, and the enormous cost of thousands of AIDS and crack babies. Seventy percent of the city's more than 2,000 bridges desperately needed expensive repairs, and water and sewer lines were rupturing regularly. Mayor David Dinkins responded with several actions, including massive city employee layoffs, closure of libraries and clinics, and shutdown of 25 percent of the city's street lights.

New York City's fiscal problems cannot be solved overnight. Its 250,000 employees and $59 billion operating budget serve 8.3 million people spread throughout five boroughs. The city itself is the area's biggest landlord, owning television and radio stations, a huge higher-education system, and four hospitals. When Mayor Rudolph Giuliani took office in 1994 (with most of the country enjoying economic growth), the operating deficit was pegged at $2.3 billion. Giuliani, too, cut city employment and targeted various services for budget reductions.

New York City continues to struggle with its vast fiscal problems with no relief in sight. As the ashes of the Twin Towers cooled in 2001, Mayor Michael Bloomberg, wrestling with a deficit of approximately $4 billion in his $43 billion budget, entertained the idea of a state takeover of city finances.[30] His "doomsday budget" included tens of thousands of layoffs, significant service cuts, and large property tax increases. Distressingly, the debt that New York City is still paying off from the 1970s had to be refinanced. The good news is that the city's huge budget deficit had been cut to "only" $3 billion by 2005; the bad news is that in 2009, revenues plummeted by $5 billion, prompting a city sales tax hike and 2,000 layoffs of city workers.[31]

Most jurisdictions have not experienced the misfortune faced by New York City and Vallejo, California. The taxpayer revolt and fiscal stress notwithstanding, budgets have been balanced, payrolls met, and most services maintained. When necessary, state officials have swallowed hard, held their noses, and raised taxes.

Recessions notwithstanding, many states and localities face chronic fiscal shortfalls because of structural problems deeply embedded in their revenue systems. Structural imbalances result from out-of-date tax systems developed for radically different state economies of fifty years past.[32]

## Limited Discretion

TELs have placed ceilings on the rates and amounts of taxation and spending, thus limiting the discretion of the nonnational governments. Other constraining factors, too, keep state and local governments from falling prey to the temptation of taxing and spending orgies. One important factor is interstate competition for jobs and economic development. High-tax states run a risk of having jobs, firms, and investments "stolen" by low-tax states (a principal reason for state and local tax incentives designed to attract and retain firms).

Earmarking taxes for popular programs also limits state and local taxing and spending discretion. Earmarking is well established: Gasoline taxes have been set aside for road and highway programs since automobiles first left ruts in muddy cow pastures. What differ today are the levels of specificity and creativity in earmarking. Surpluses may accumulate in some dedicated funds, such as highways, whereas other important needs such as education or law enforcement are not sufficiently met. The hands of government officials are tied, however, because they cannot move the funds around. Typical state earmarks fund local drainage, water, or sewer projects; enhance fisheries or environmental cleanups; or pay for municipal or county building improvements. Cigarette buyers in Washington cough up millions of dollars each year to help clean up Puget Sound. Several states earmark penny increases in the sales tax for public education. Connecticut earmarked $100 million for stem cell research in 2009.

Financial discretion is partly determined by one's position on the fiscal food chain. The national government can essentially tax and spend as it wishes, subject only to its highly underdeveloped capacity for self-discipline. States must meet federal spending mandates for Medicaid, education, and other functions while somehow balancing their budgets each year. Local governments, in addition to suffering reductions in state aid during tough times in this game of "shift and shaft federalism,"[33] must comply with an increasing number of state spending mandates, even though their legal authority to raise revenues remains severely circumscribed in most states. In some ways, local governments are not masters of their own fiscal fate.[34]

**Pensions and OPEB** When the U.S. General Accounting Standards Board (GASB) issued standards requiring state and local governments to publicly report the funding status of employee pension and health care benefits, most jurisdictions were caught with their financial pants down. As noted above, for many years most states and many localities have been underfunding the future liabilities of employee retirement benefits. Illinois owes some $54 billion in pension benefits to state employees and retirees; In 2009, California was $48 billion in debt to state workers; San Diego's pension liabilities were tallied at $1.4 billion,[35] a situation negatively compounded by substantial losses in pension plan investments during the equity market crash of 2008.

Even more serious are the estimated $558 billion in unfunded future liabilities for state health care for retirees and their families. California is in the red for $70 billion, New Jersey for $69 billion, and New York for $50 billion. The larger the state employment numbers, the higher the future debt in most cases. But on a per capita basis, other states are hard hit. New Jersey's obligation is nearly $8,000 per capita, Connecticut's is $6,200 per person, and Hawaii owes $7,650 per resident.[36]

There are several reasons for these huge pension and retiree health care debts, which, added together, total some $20,000 for each working American.[37] The baby boom bulge in the government work force is becoming a mass exit as retirement age is reached. Unwise state borrowing from pension funds during difficult economic times is a major cause in some jurisdictions. And, of course, legislators have a tendency to spend today and worry about the future tomorrow (or let the next generation of lawmakers worry about it).

Addressing the problem will require innovative thinking as well as aggressive pre-funding of future liabilities. The good thing about the GASB standards is that states and localities must now publicly account for future liabilities now. The downside is that in some cases tax increases and reductions in promised benefits for government employees will have to be implemented.

# MANAGING MONEY

Every state except Vermont is constitutionally or statutorily required to balance their operating budgets each fiscal year. In turn, the states require that local governments balance *their* budgets. However, these requirements apply only to operating budgets, which are used for daily financial receipts and disbursements. Capital budgets, used for big purchases that must be paid for over time (for instance, a new bridge or school building), typically run substantial deficits. Operating budgets may also run in the red during the fiscal year, so long as expenditures equal revenues at the end of the year. Consequently, the reliability of revenue estimates is a vital consideration.

## Estimating Revenues

Until fairly recently, state and local governments estimated their annual revenues simply by extrapolating from past trends. This approach is simple, inexpensive, and works well during periods of steady economic growth, but it fails miserably during years of boom or bust.[38] The finance officers of states and most larger cities and counties are much more sophisticated today. Using computer software, they employ econometric modeling to derive mathematical estimates of future revenues. Economic forecasting firms and/or academics commonly assist or provide independent projections.

Econometric modeling places key variables in equations to predict the fiscal-year yield of each major tax. A wide variety of variables are used, including employment levels, food prices, housing costs, oil and gas prices, consumer savings levels, interest rates, intergovernmental aid projections, and state and local debt obligations. Because state and local economies are increasingly linked to national and international factors, estimates often include measures for the value of the dollar, international trade and investment, and national fiscal policy.

Two critical factors determine the accuracy of revenue estimates: the quality of the data and the validity of the economic assumptions. Indeed, econometric modeling of state and local economies can be a voyage into the unknown. Data problems include difficulty in measuring key variables; periodic revisions of historical economic data, which require new calculations; and modifications in tax laws or fee schedules. But the major sources of error are the economic assumptions built into the models. Examples are legion: The national economy may not perform as expected; energy prices may plummet or soar; natural or human disasters may disrupt state or local economic growth. Recessions are particularly damaging to fiscal stability because state and local taxes are highly sensitive to economic downturns.

## Rainy Day Funds

Because a balanced budget is mandatory but estimation errors are inevitable, forty-seven states and many localities have established contingency, "stabilization," or reserve funds. Popularly known as rainy day funds, these savings accounts help insulate budgets from fiscal distortions caused by inaccurate data or faulty economic assumptions; they are also available for emergencies. In years of economic health, the funds accumulate principal and interest. When the economy falters, governments can tap into their savings accounts to balance the budget and avoid imposing tax and fee increases.[39] Deposits are made automatically in budget surplus years or, in some cases, in any year in which revenues grow by a certain amount. Nearly all states impose a limit on the size of the rainy day fund.

During sunny days of the mid-2000s, the states replenished their contingency funds to an average of 4 percent of general fund spending. Amidst the recessionary storms of 2008–2009, they were forced to draw them down. The task of balancing the budget is especially daunting to local governments, given their lack of economic diversity, dependency on state taxes and financial aid, and sensitivity to economic dislocations. The departure of a single large employer can disrupt a local economy for years. So the potential advantages of rainy day funds are numerous in the fragile fiscal context of cities and counties.

## Other Financial Management Practices

State and local governments, of necessity, are becoming more knowledgeable about how to manage cash and investments. Cash reserves that once sat idly in non-interest-bearing accounts or a desk drawer are now invested in short-term notes, money market accounts, U.S. Treasury bills, certificates of deposit, and other financial instruments so that governments can maximize interest earnings. Most states have local government investment pools that manage billions of dollars in short-term assets. The process of spending and collecting monies is also manipulated to advantage. For example, large checks are deposited on the day they are received; conversely, payable checks are drawn on the latest date possible. In general, state and local financial management today resembles that of a large corporation instead of the mom-and-pop approach of years ago. After all, the nonnational governments spend and invest some $3.0 trillion annually.

The most important state or local investment is usually the public-employee pension fund. These retirement accounts comprise about $3 trillion in assets. In the past, they were conservatively managed and politically untouchable. Today, however, they tend to be invested in more aggressive instruments such as corporate stock. They also represent a tempting honey pot for financially strapped states, whose governors have dipped their hands in the funds and pulled out billions to balance the budget. They are also of considerable interest to investment firms. More than one state treasurer has been convicted of corruption charges for taking cash kickbacks in return for investing millions in state pension funds with certain investment firms.

State and local investments must not be managed too aggressively, as the case of Orange County, California, demonstrates. One of the nation's biggest (fifth largest county) and wealthiest local jurisdictions, Orange County became the largest in history to file for federal bankruptcy in 1994. The county's financial nightmare commenced when its investment pool manager, Robert L. Citron, placed millions of dollars in financial instruments called derivatives. These instruments "derive" their value from underlying assets such as stocks, bonds, or mortgages. The derivatives' value changes when the price of the underlying assets changes. Orange County lost $1.5 billion when its derivatives, which were tied to interest rates, declined precipitously in value. In effect, Citron was borrowing money from stocks, bonds, and other assets to bet on the direction of interest rates. He lost, and so did Orange County's taxpayers.[40]

**Long-Term Borrowing** Like corporations, state and local governments issue long-term debt obligations, typically for five to twenty-five years. Bonds are the most common form of long-term borrowing. Because of federal and state tax breaks for investors, the nonnational governments are able to finance bonded indebtedness at significantly lower rates than corporations. There are three conventional types of bonds—general obligation bonds, revenue bonds, and industrial development bonds.

The principal and interest payments on **general-obligation bonds** are secured by the "full faith, credit, and taxing power" of the state or local jurisdiction issuing them. General-obligation bonds are used to finance public projects such as highways, schools, and hospitals. Lenders are guaranteed repayment so long as the bond-issuing government is solvent; defaults are nearly nonexistent, but downgrades of cities' credit worthiness occur from time to time.

**Revenue bonds** are backed by expected income from a specific project or service; examples include a toll bridge, a municipal sewer system, or sports complex. Revenue bonds are payable only from the revenues derived from the specified source, not from general tax revenues. Because they typically represent a riskier investment than general-obligation bonds, they command a higher rate of interest.

The **industrial development bond (IDB)** is a type of revenue bond. The payment of principal and interest on IDBs depends solely on the ability of the industry using the facilities financed by the bond to meet its financial obligation. If the user fails to make payments, creditors can seize and sell any real or personal property associated with the facility. Private interests, such as developers and retailers, are the primary beneficiaries of IDBs. Conventionally, these private-purpose bonds are issued by local governments to attract economic activity and investments; in fact, they are frequently used to furnish loans at highly favorable interest rates to small or medium-size firms.

**Limits on Borrowing** Almost all states place constitutional or statutory restrictions on their own and local government borrowing. Some have set maximum levels of indebtedness; others require popular referenda to create debt or to exceed specified debt limits. They tightly restrict local government debt, especially general-obligation bonds. (State-imposed constraints normally do not apply to revenue bonds).

The bond market places its own informal limitations on debt by assessing the quality of bonds, notes, and other debt instruments. Investors in government bonds rely on Moody's Investors Service, Standard and Poor's Corporation, Fitch Ratings, and other investment services for ratings of a jurisdiction's capacity to repay its obligations. Criteria taken into consideration in bond ratings include existing debt levels, rainy day funds, market value of real estate, population growth, per capita income, employment levels, and other measures of overall financial health and solvency. Highly rated bond issues receive ratings of *Aaa*, *Aa*, and *A*. Variations of *B* indicate medium to high risk. A rating of *C* is reserved for bonds in immediate danger of default. The average interest rate on low-rated bonds usually exceeds that of top-rated ones by 1½ to

**general-obligation bond**

A debt instrument supported by the full financial resources of the issuing jurisdiction.

**revenue bond**

A bond paid off from income derived from the facility built with the bond proceeds.

**industrial development bond (IDB)**

A bond issued to fund the construction of a facility to be used by a private firm.

**bond bank**

A state-administered fund that aggregates local government debt instruments and sells them as a package at a reduced interest rate.

2 percentage points, which translates into a considerable difference in interest payments. Bond ratings tend to rise during periods of economic growth but can fall rapidly during recessions, driving up borrowing costs. California's bond-rating drop from A– to BBB in 2009 cost the Golden State billions in borrowing costs.

States can consolidate the bond sales of smaller municipalities and counties through a **bond bank**. These banks help provide increased management capacity to less-experienced local governments and, through economies of scale, save them significant amounts of money because of economies of scale.

# STATE AND LOCAL FINANCIAL RELATIONS

Dollars and cents define state and local relations. Local governments today recognize that their financial future depends more on the states than on Washington, D.C.

## An Uneasy Relationship

A conflicted relationship exists between states and local governments when it comes to money. The status of localities is not unlike that of an eighteen-year-old boy with a part-time job. Because he still lives and eats at home, he remains dependent on his parents. He fervently wants to assert his independence, but his parents often rein him in when he does. As long as he dwells in his parents' house, he must bend to their authority. If he acts irresponsibly with his finances, he can expect parental intervention. Financial misbehavior and mismanagement in Flint, Michigan, and Pittsburgh, Pennsylvania, led the respective states to take control of the city governments.

Cities, counties, and other local governments will always live within the constitutional house of their parents, the states. They enjoy their own sources of revenue—property taxes, user fees, and business license fees—but they depend on the states for the bulk of their income. They suffer the frustration of having to cope with rising expenditure demands from their residents while their authority to raise new monies is highly circumscribed by state law. No wonder they turn to their "grandparent"—the national government—to bail them out when times are tough.

But by far the single largest source of local revenues is the state. About 40 percent of all state expenditures goes to local governments. Like federal grants-in-aid, however, state grants come with lots of strings attached. Most state dollars are earmarked for public education and social welfare. Other state assistance is earmarked for roads, hospitals, public safety, and public health. The result is that local governments have little spending discretion. And during bad economic times, states have a tendency to push a portion of their own budget shortfalls down to their already struggling local governments.

Naturally, great diversity characterizes the levels of encumbered (earmarked) and unencumbered (discretionary) state assistance to local jurisdictions, much of which is related to the distribution of functions between a state and its localities. Highly centralized states such as Hawaii, South Carolina, and West Virginia fund and administer at the state level many programs that are funded and administered locally in decentralized states such as Maryland, New York, and Wisconsin. In states where TELS have hampered the ability of local jurisdictions to raise and spend revenues, the trend has been toward fiscal centralization. Greater centralization has also resulted from state efforts to reduce service disparities between wealthy and poor jurisdictions and to lessen the dependence of local governments on the property tax.

## What Local Governments Want from the States

What local governments want from their states and what they actually get may be worlds apart. States and their local jurisdictions conduct nearly constant dialogue over financial matters. Typically, the states recognize and try to respond to local financial problems—subject, of course, to their own fiscal circumstances, citizen demands for tax relief, and their judgment about what is best for all state residents.

Simply put, what localities want most is *more money*. But they also want more control over how it is spent and the independent power to raise it. Taxpayer resistance, unfunded federal and state mandates, and pressing infrastructure needs have left many local jurisdictions in a financial bind. State governments must provide help. State aid for all local governments has grown steadily, substantially outstripping inflation over the past three and one-half decades.

Most increases in state aid are devoted to education, corrections, health care, and social services. But many states also distribute a portion of their tax revenues based on local fiscal need, thus tending to equalize or level economic disparities between local jurisdictions.

The specific means for sharing revenues takes many forms. Most of the states make special PILOT (payments in lieu of taxes) transfers to local governments where state buildings or other facilities are located. These buildings and facilities are exempt from property taxes but cause a drain on local services. Such payments are of particular importance to capital cities, in which large plots of prime downtown property are occupied by state office buildings.

In addition, local governments want the *legal capacity to raise additional revenues themselves*, especially through local option sales and income taxes. A share of gasoline, tobacco, and other tax benefits is greatly appreciated, as is the authority to impose impact fees on developers of residential property. The key is local option, whereby jurisdictions and their voters can decide for themselves which, if any, taxes they will exact. More than two-thirds of the states have authorized an optional sales or income tax for various local governments, and some permit localities to adopt optional earmarked taxes. Local option taxes are attractive because they provide jurisdictions with the flexibility to take action as they see fit in response to local needs. What protects citizens against "taxoholic" local legislative bodies in the aftermath of the taxpayer revolt is the state requirement that local tax hikes must be approved by the voters in a referendum.

Local governments also want *limitations on and reimbursements for state mandates* that require them to spend money. Through constitutional provisions, statutes, and administrative regulations, all states require localities to undertake certain activities and operate programs in accordance with state standards and rules. These mandates, which accumulate over the years, are similar to the strings attached to federal grants-in-aid (which also affect local governments), and they are just as distasteful to local governments as federal mandates are to states. Many state mandates are associated with local human resource policies, such as minimum wages, pensions, and safe working conditions. Others entail special-education programs, environmental-protection standards, and tax exemptions. Most are designed to achieve uniformity in the levels and quality of local government services throughout the state. Sometimes, however, state mandates appear to be nitpicking. Examples include requirements that public libraries carry a certain number of books per resident or that school buses be refueled daily, whether their tanks are empty or not.

Local governments believe that they should not have to both obey *and* pay, and that states should reimburse them for expenses incurred in carrying out such mandates. Most states have responded to this request by attaching fiscal notes to any proposed legislation or administrative regulation or rule that involves local governments; these notes estimate the local costs and fiscal impact of implementing the legislation. Some states are required by law to go one step further and reimburse local governments in full for mandated expenditures.

## CURRENT ISSUES IN STATE AND LOCAL FINANCE

A major theme of this chapter is the rapid and severe deterioration of state and local revenues in the 2008–2009 recession and their efforts to maintain essential services and balance budgets until the financial crisis passes. Debilitating economic problems are expected to continue plaguing state and local governments through 2010 and into 2011, as tax revenues fall short of desired expenditures and federal stimulus funds are expended. (It must be noted that a small number of energy and natural resource-rich states have been managing quite well, principally New Mexico, Alaska, Montana, North Dakota, and Wyoming). Engaging State and Local Taxing and Spending 16.1 notes some of the steps being taken by other governments to address a financial situation not far removed from that of the Great Depression.

The fiscal problems of many of the most hard-hit states and localities are not short term. Rather, they are systemic. For many years legislatures have conveniently ignored the developing chronic, structural problems of state revenue systems and other aspects of the political economy, stumbling as they

## Engaging State and Local Taxing and Spending

### Coping with the "Great Recession"

In the short term, state and local governments have coped as they normally do in a recession by imposing hiring and travel freezes, unpaid furloughs, and lay-offs, and reducing or eliminating non-essential services. A number of states have enacted tax increases to garner more revenues, particularly through sin taxes but also with hikes on sales and income taxes as well as various fees and charges.

Among the notable actions in 2009 were the following:

- California eliminated over 17,500 state jobs, severely pruned K-12 and higher education, imposed a three-days-per-month furlough on state workers; Washington imposed 7000 of layoffs in agencies, universities and public schools; Alabama adopted mandatory, unpaid, twenty-four day furloughs.
- Many local governments shut down libraries and park and recreation facilities; school counselors and nurses were laid off.
- States sliced Medicaid payments, closed prisons, and released prisoners early.
- Some local governments began assessing "accident response fees" for responding to traffic accidents ("cash-per-crash"), and charging for fire calls, hiking license fees for marriages, and raising charges for HIV/AIDS testing.
- Tuition hikes at public universities were popular.
- Some governors, in a desperate hunt for new revenues and budget fixes, proposed selling off state assets, including toll roads and bridges, parking lots, Interstate service plazas, and state buildings. California actually considered selling the Los Angeles Coliseum, San Quentin State prison, the Orange County Fairgrounds, and

scores of other assets. Arizona legislators considered selling the State Department of Public Safety Headquarters buildings, the state fairgrounds, prisons, and even the very buildings that the House and Senate meet in, and then leasing them back over a lengthy period of time.
- With an eye to helping staunch the tidal wave of housing foreclosures, some states offered restructured mortgage loans to hard-pressed homeowners and mediation services for owners and lenders.
- North Carolina raised the sales tax by a penny and imposed a 2 percent income tax surcharge on those making over $100,000 per year; Florida's desperate straits convinced lawmakers to propose that voters revoke a tax exemption on ostrich feed!
- Many state and local agencies and departments deferred routine maintenance on vehicles, buildings, and equipment; schools delayed purchasing new buses and police and sheriff's departments made do another year with high-mileage squad cars.
- Detroit's mayor proposed privatizing the city's payroll and tax collection systems.

Most of these steps were more like kicking the can down the road rather than the sorts of changes needed to wrestle the state revenue systems out of the early1900s and into the 2000s. As the recession wore on, even more severe actions were being weighed, despite the $200 billion in stimulus funds flowing from the federal government to the states. Indeed, forty-six states were anticipating budget shortfalls totaling $350 billion well into 2011.[41]

were confronted with demographic and economic changes. The U.S. economy has evolved from a manufacturing base to services, yet most state sales taxes are only now beginning to extend to services. E-commerce is supplanting bricks-and-mortar transactions, but the states have found it very difficult to win congressional approval to tax Internet and catalog sales. Property tax revenues fall dramatically with foreclosures and market variables, yet few local governments have other significant revenue sources to lean on.

What the state and local governments need is fiscal sustainability, so that future revenues are stable, predictable, and adequate for service needs.[42] However, fiscal restructuring requires a certain level of public understanding and support. Truth-in-taxation campaigns can educate citizens that reducing or eliminating taxes may result in fewer services. It is also important that citizens and elected officials fully recognize that the current tax codes of the states are geared to yesterday's economy. They will need to be rewritten to capture revenues efficiently in a changing economic and demographic environment. To gain citizen buy-in , state and local governments are starting to provide full budget transparency so that interested citizens have online access to spending and taxing data. The online data bases in Iowa, Kansas, Texas, and at least a dozen additional states encourage public understanding of financial complexities and solicit interaction through budget calculators and simulations.[43]

The spiraling costs of health care, corrections, and public education cannot be shouldered by a single level of government. Mandates without money are certainly not the answer. When mandates and program responsibilities are pushed to a different rung of the government ladder, funds should follow. Local governments, particularly, require more revenue-raising authority and broader tax bases to pay for the services they deliver. The need has never been greater for increasing state and local capability and responsiveness by reinventing and reinvigorating the financial equipment of government. The financial structures and processes of state and local governments must be made more appropriate to the social and economic environments in which they operate, which includes a service-based economy; international markets; aging baby-boomers; and the changing gender, racial, and ethnic composition of the labor force. Most states have been receptive to these principles; the federal government requires further education.

## CHAPTER RECAP

- The two basic principles of state and local financial systems are the interdependence of the three levels of government and the diversity of revenue sources.

- Among the criteria for evaluating taxes are equity, yield, elasticity, ease of administration, political accountability, and acceptability.

- The major state and local taxes are those assessed on property, sales, and income. Other taxes and fees are also imposed.

- Legalized gambling and gaming also raise money.

- Taxpayer resistance has produced tax and expenditure limitations in many states, increased sensitivity of state and local officials to taxpayer preferences, and in some cases fiscal stress for governments.

- State and local governments estimate annual revenues and set aside money in rainy day funds for emergencies and contingencies.

- State and local financial relationships are characterized by sharing and cooperation, but also by conflict over mandates and limited local discretion.

## Key Terms

own-source revenue *(p. 350)*
intergovernmental
    transfers *(p. 350)*
countercyclical aid *(p. 351)*
tax capacity *(p. 353)*
tax effort *(p. 353)*
regressive tax *(p. 354)*
progressive tax *(p. 354)*

proportional (flat) tax *(p. 354)*
benefit principle *(p. 354)*
indexing *(p. 355)*
circuit breaker *(p. 357)*
tax–service paradox *(p. 366)*
political economy *(p. 367)*
taxation and expenditure
    limitations (TELs) *(p. 368)*

fiscal stress *(p. 369)*
general-obligation
    bond *(p. 375)*
revenue bond *(p. 375)*
industrial development
    bond (IDB) *(p. 375)*
bond bank *(p. 376)*

## Internet Resources

The National Conference of State Legislatures' Principles of a High Quality Tax System are available for viewing at **www.ncsl.org**.

One of the best individual sites on state tax and budget information is "where the money goes" at the Texas State Comptroller at **www.window. state.tx.us**.

For current reports in developments, trends, and policy changes in state government

finances, see the website of the Center for the Study of the States at SUNY–Albany, **www.stateandlocalgateway.rockinst.org**.

Comparative state and local revenue, tax, and expenditure data may be found at the U.S. Census Bureau's website (**www.census.gov**) and at the Tax Foundation's website (**www.taxfoundation.org**).

See **www.taxsites.com** for general tax resources and official state tax sites.

SOURCE: Ronald Martinez/Getty Images Sport/Getty Images

# Economic Development

**14**

Virginia won a big economic plum in 2007 when it was selected by the British manufacturer Rolls-Royce as the site of its new $500 million jet engine facility. Initially, eight states were in the running for the plant: Georgia, Indiana, Mississippi, North Carolina, Ohio, South Carolina, Texas, and Virginia. Each of the competing states set about identifying possible sites and assembling incentive packages in an effort to attract Rolls-Royce. Several factors worked in the Old Dominion State's favor including the availability of a large (1,025 acres) site in an industrial zone and the presence of a skilled work force. The value of the incentives—land, infrastructure development, job training, and tax breaks—offered by the state to Rolls-Royce total $56.8 million over a multi-year period. Why was the state willing to provide these sweeteners? There are several reasons. First, the Rolls-Royce plant will bring several hundred jobs to the area. Second, the state hopes that this investment will have a ripple effect and attract other advanced manufacturing facilities to Virginia. And last but not least, Virginia was compelled to offer a generous incentive package because the other competing states were. As one official commented, "If you're going to play in the big leagues, you have to come to the field with more than your glove."[1]

Attracting new investment like the Rolls-Royce facility is what **economic development** is all about these days. Capital investment, employment, income, tax base, and public services—all are linked to economic development. And it is a competitive process, often pitting one state against another. State leaders are well aware of the stakes involved, as indicated in the salvo fired a few years back by New Jersey's governor: "No more losing our employers to job raids by low tax states. New Jersey is open for business."[2] Resurgent state and local governments are pursuing economic development with a vengeance.

> **economic development**
> A process by which a community, state, or nation increases its level of per capita income, high-quality jobs, and capital investment.

## REGIONAL DIFFERENCES IN ECONOMIC PROSPERITY

The United States continues to be a nation of diverse regional economies. When the headline in *USA Today* trumpets "Nation's economy improves," be assured that not all places are experiencing the same level of improvement. As economist Mark Crain notes, during the last three decades of the twentieth century, living standards (measured by real income per capita) in the United States increased by 50 percent.[3] However, this average figure masks a considerable range in the data: from a low of 28 percent in Alaska to a high of 64 percent in North Carolina. Even within regions, economies can vary. Detroit and Columbus are both located in the Midwest, but the largest city in Michigan and the largest city in Ohio are worlds apart economically. Different economic mixes of manufacturing, services, and retail employment mean different economic conditions. The effects of global economic restructuring coupled with a prolonged national recession hit states and communities hard in the early twenty-first century. When the nation's unemployment rate climbed to 9.7 percent in June 2009, eight California metropolitan areas had rates exceeding 15 percent; the lowest unemployment figures were recorded in Bismarck, North Dakota, at 3.8 percent.[4] Some places have done better than others in adjusting to the new economic realities.

The business network CNBC evaluates the states annually on forty different measures related to business competitiveness.[5] The individual measures—tax burden, training programs, wage rates, regulatory environment, venture capital, among others—are weighted and aggregated to produce scores and rankings. The map in Figure 14.1 organizes the states into quintiles based on these rankings. Virginia was the top scoring state in CNBC's 2009 survey; Alaska had the lowest score.

Remember that economies are dynamic; that is, economic momentum can slow down and speed up. The personal income growth in a state, the change in unemployment rates, and the level of population change are three indicators that can be combined into a useful index of economic momentum, or change. The figures for 2008 showed Louisiana, Utah, and Texas at the top of the list, with Rhode Island and Michigan at the bottom.[6] The index for the same period in 2006 found Nevada, Arizona, and Utah leading the way, with Louisiana and Washington at the end.

**FIGURE 14.1**

**State Business Competitiveness, 2009**

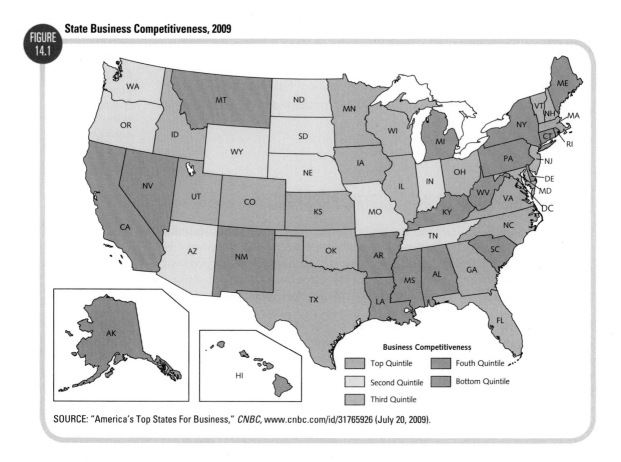

Business Competitiveness

- Top Quintile
- Second Quintile
- Third Quintile
- Fouth Quintile
- Bottom Quintile

SOURCE: "America's Top States For Business," *CNBC*, www.cnbc.com/id/31765926 (July 20, 2009).

Local economies are also dynamic. To illustrate, consider the cities of Denver, Colorado, and Salt Lake City, Utah, both of which boomed in the 1990s with surging high-tech and telecommunication industries. As the economy weakened in 2001, both cities were especially hard hit because technology and telecom firms began rounds of layoffs and closures.[7] The bloom was definitely off the economic rose—but only for awhile. Both cities began to rebound within a couple of years and their economic engines were humming again. As some cities decline, others surge. The Breaking New Ground box on the next page discusses some cities that have become magnets for what has been called the "creative class."

## APPROACHES TO ECONOMIC DEVELOPMENT

Governments devise elaborate strategies *and spend a lot of money* to promote economic development within their boundaries. The approaches they use have evolved over time, but even some of the oldest tools remain viable today.

## BREAKING NEW GROUND

## THE CREATIVE CLASS AND COOL CITIES

What's the hottest thing for cities these days? Well, to be cool. Metropolitan areas across the country are in a race for the informal title of the coolest city in America. They want to be considered hip, trendy, and sophisticated. This is because the cool cities attract well-educated, talented young professionals to their environs. They are magnets for the creative class, people whose work involves producing new ideas, new technology, or new creative content. It is this demographic of innovators that is, some contend, the driving force for economic development. And with a recent study showing that two-thirds of college graduates will choose where to live before looking for employment, this gives states and localities considerable leverage in attracting the urban crowd.

Cool cities possess what Richard Florida calls in his book, *The Rise of the Creative Class*, the three T's: technology, tolerance, and talent. Their economies are knowledge based, their policies promote social tolerance, and their communities nurture the arts and culture. Jobs are plentiful, gays and lesbians are welcomed, and the nightlife is lively. Cities that embrace such a culture experience an influx of entrepreneurial, ambitious, and creative young people. And this trend has a snowball effect, attracting a continual stream of well-educated, mobile fun-seekers to cool cities. Consequently, cities lacking in some or all of the three T's fall more and more behind, out of step with the cool places.

This three T's framework has proven so insightful that many state and local governments are implementing its precepts. Florida's consulting agency has helped begin thirty-three initiatives across seven cities, all with the end goal of developing a local "cool" culture. There are initiatives that promote the work of local artists, such as the creation of a sculpture garden in El Paso, Texas, which features exclusive work from the area's most talented sculptors. Promoting local events and workshops is another popular initiative, such as Tacoma's "Love Tacoma" social networking program, which sponsors cultural activities like glass blowing, boutique tours, and farmers' markets. As well, environmental awareness and such initiatives that cater to the eco-friendly crowd are gaining a lot of momentum. And it doesn't take a formal consulting firm to point this out to cities. The mayors of Chicago, New York, and San Francisco are battling for the reputation as America's "Greenest City." Pedestrian-friendly downtowns, public transit systems, trails, bike paths, and local parks are all selling-points to the creative class.

So, based on the above criteria of what defines cool, which cities top the list? According to a 2009 study, the top five cities for young singles are Boulder, Colorado; San Francisco, California; Washington, D.C.; Madison, Wisconsin; and Boston, Massachusetts. Their colorful social events and local flair give them a unique cultural personality tailored just for the creative class. Meanwhile, many other cities are implementing their own "cool" initiatives that could rival the current leaders.

SOURCES: CEOs for Cities National Meeting, "Attracting the Young, College-Educated to Cities," http://www.ceosforcities.org/files/CEOsforCitiesAttractingYoungEducatedPres2006.pdf (July 28, 2009); Tim Holt, "Ecofriendly is Good Business," *The Christian Science Monitor*, http://features.csmonitor.com/environment/2008/10/24/ecofriendly-is-good-business (October 24, 2008); "Best Cities for Gen Ys," *Business Week,* http://images.businessweek.com/ss/09/06/0609_top_gen_y_cities/1.htm (July 26, 2009); Richard Florida, *The Rise of the Creative Class* (New York: Basic Books, 2002).

## Early Approaches: First and Second Waves

Community efforts to spur economic development have a long history, but the first statewide program of industrial recruitment was created during the Great Depression. Mississippi, with its Balance Agriculture with

**subsidy**
Financial assistance given by a government to a firm or enterprise.

**venture capital pools**
Special funds earmarked for new, innovative businesses that cannot get conventional financing.

**small-business incubators**
Facilities that provide services aimed at nurturing start-up businesses.

**enterprise zone**
Areas of a community that offer special government incentives aimed at stimulating investment. Also called an empowerment zone.

**clusters**
Geographically concentrated firms that compete and trade with each other and have similar needs.

Industry plan, made it possible for local governments to issue bonds to finance the construction or purchase of facilities for relocating industry. Other southern states followed suit, luring businesses from elsewhere with tax breaks, public **subsidies**, and low wages. Called smokestack chasing, aggressive industrial recruitment had spread beyond the South by the 1970s. By the end of that decade, as states raided other states for industry, statistics showed that between 80 and 90 percent of new jobs came from existing firm expansions and start-up businesses, not from relocating businesses. About the same time, pressure from foreign competition intensified. Policy makers feverishly cast about for strategies that would spawn new businesses and keep state economies strong. These efforts began a new era, or second wave, in economic development. States established **venture capital pools**, created **small-business incubators**, and initiated workforce training programs in an attempt to support homegrown enterprise. Even with these new initiatives, many states continued to chase out-of-state industry.

## Newer Approaches: Third and Fourth Waves

The 1990s saw a third wave gather strength. This wave represented a rethinking of the role of government in promoting economic growth. Second-wave programs, well-intentioned perhaps, simply did not have sufficient scale or focus to transform state economies. An **enterprise zone**, for example, may revitalize a neighborhood, but unless an extensive network of such zones exists throughout the state, the overall impact is marginal. Third-wave efforts sought to correct some of the deficiencies of second-wave programs. One of the keys to the third wave was moving economic development programs out of state agencies and into private organizations. Rather than directly supplying the program or the service, as it had done in the first and second waves, government would provide direction and seed capital.

The latest ripple flowing from the third wave is called **clusters**. It reconfigures the economy as clusters of firms that compete and trade with one another and have common needs. By focusing on interconnections and working relationships among businesses, nonprofit organizations, and government, a state gets a better sense of its economic foundations.[8] Arizona pioneered the concept in its Strategic Plan for Economic Development. The state identified ten clusters ranging from food, fiber, and natural products to environmental technologies, to mining and minerals.[9] Each cluster has spawned an organization in which ideas can be shared, common strategies developed, and joint ventures negotiated. In Connecticut, the clusters are tourism, aerospace, and bioscience. To nurture and support its clusters, the Connecticut legislature redesigned the state's research and development tax credits. High technology remains an important cluster in many places around the country despite the slowdown the industry experienced in the early 2000s.

Third-wave thinking continues to influence states and localities, but a fourth wave has already developed. Political scientist Susan Clarke and geographer Gary Gaile contend that a distinctively different set of strategies lies ahead.[10] This new set, or fourth wave, is more attuned to global markets, especially localities' use of trade and telecommunications to their economic advantage. The fourth wave is also more focused on human capital, that is, on educating and training its work force. Even as states and localities turn to these third- and fourth-wave approaches, however, they continue to use strategies from the first and second waves. How to pursue economic development remains a hotly debated subject.

A leading figure who has headed economic revitalization efforts in three states points to five key trends that states must understand as they design their economic development policies:

- The economic playing field is the world, not the neighboring county or state.
- The new infrastructure is technology and telecommunications.
- Regionalism provides an opportunity for states and others to work together. Boundaries are falling.
- Sustainable development strategies that recognize the interdependence of the economy and the environment are necessary.
- Successful economic development efforts are built on a high-quality work force.[11]


## The Fourth Wave and the "New Economy"

The fourth wave in economic development approaches is linked to what some are calling the **"new economy."** The list of trends at the end of the preceding section identifies fundamental changes in the U.S. economy. According to adherents of the new economy, states that fail to adapt their development strategies to these new circumstances will be left behind. A public policy think tank, the Information Technology and Innovation Foundation (ITIF), lays it out: "The New Economy is a global, entrepreneurial, and knowledge-based economy in which the keys to success lie in the extent to which knowledge, technology, and innovation are embedded in products and services."[12] ITIF recently evaluated the states according to how close each one is to achieving a new economy. A total of twenty-nine indicators was used, among them were items such as state export capacity, in-migration of knowledge workers, number of fast-growing companies, residential use of broadband technology, and industry investment in research and development. Weighting each of the twenty-nine indicators according to its importance, ITIF calculated scores for each state. The map in Figure 14.2 groups the states into quintiles based on the aggregate scores. Leading new economy states are Massachusetts, Washington, and Maryland; at the other end of the score sheet are Arkansas, West Virginia, and Mississippi.

**new economy**
An economy based in global technology and knowledge, as opposed to the old economy based in national manufacturing.

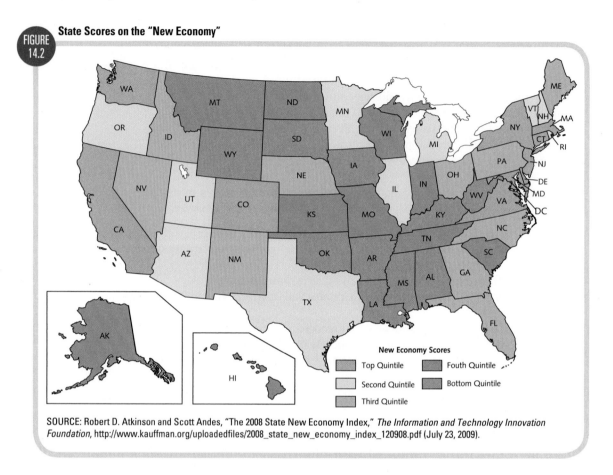

**FIGURE 14.2**

**State Scores on the "New Economy"**

**New Economy Scores**
- Top Quintile
- Second Quintile
- Third Quintile
- Fouth Quintile
- Bottom Quintile

SOURCE: Robert D. Atkinson and Scott Andes, "The 2008 State New Economy Index," *The Information and Technology Innovation Foundation*, http://www.kauffman.org/uploadedfiles/2008_state_new_economy_index_120908.pdf (July 23, 2009).

# THE POLITICS OF ECONOMIC GROWTH

Economic development occupies a central role in campaigns for state and local elective office. Like reducing crime and improving education, it is a consensus issue: Everybody is in favor of it. Thus, each candidate tries to convince the voters that his or her approach to economic development will be the most effective. At both the state and local levels, candidates' campaign rhetoric typically emphasizes jobs and employment, and candidates talk in terms of "sustaining and expanding economic growth."

Most states have created several mechanisms to implement economic development strategies. Ideally, a state government should be internally united for its economic development effort, but several natural cleavages—partisan politics, legislative–executive disputes, and agency turf battles—make cohesion difficult. Because economic development is a central issue, it inspires a lot of political posturing. In the end, a state government with a unified, cohesive approach to economic development is likely to be more successful than a state without one.

As a state's top elected official and chief executive, the governor commonly takes the lead in economic development. For example, Utah governor Jon

Huntsman reorganized state agencies to create a new Governor's Office of Economic Development (GOED), declaring, "Economic development is the cornerstone of my administration."[13] Organizations like GOED try to come up with fresh ideas and new tactics, maximizing the state's strengths and minimizing its weaknesses. And states are more than willing to borrow ideas that are successful in other states. Once an economic development strategy is in place, the next challenge is implementation. During what we earlier referred to as the first wave of economic development strategies, the responsibility for implementation belonged to state agencies. Adherents to the third wave argue, however, that state agencies have not responded creatively and effectively to the

Local officials break ground for a new manufacturing facility.
*SOURCE: Top Choice/Alamy*

challenges confronting them. Third-wave advocates want government agencies out of the economic development business, with more flexible, public–private hybrids or private-sector organizations as their replacements. Florida was the first state to replace its Department of Commerce with a public–private organization, which it named Enterprise Florida (or eFlorida).

Greater involvement by nongovernment organizations in providing economic development programs and services is risky. State governments have always had a complex relationship with the private sector. They must contend with demands from various interests, of which business is only one (albeit a powerful one). Nevertheless, state policy makers have generally tried to accommodate the demands of the business community. In fact, one persistent criticism of state legislatures is that they have been *too* receptive to the entreaties of business. Business leaders believe that because their success is central to a state's economy, they ought to be treated as a public-interest rather than as a special-interest group. A state may thus feel that it is less a partner than a prisoner. In response to the question "Who runs Massachusetts?" one state legislator responded, "The businesses that threaten to move out of the state. They have a chokehold on us."[14] This statement may be extreme in tone, but it conveys the frustration that some state officials feel about their government's relationship with business. It also highlights the skepticism with which many state policy makers greet calls for less government involvement in economic development. One successful partnership that has emerged in some states is the one between industries and universities. The Committee for Economic Development, a national group of prominent business executives and educators, identifies five ways in which states can facilitate these partnerships: through state-established centers, state grants to university research centers, research incubators, small-business development centers, and research parks.[15]

One emerging, potentially fertile area for industry–university collaboration is bioscience, especially stem-cell research. Minnesota was one of the first states to take action when it established a Stem Cell Institute at the University of Minnesota and set up tax-free zones for bioscience companies; Wisconsin, another pioneer, has its nonprofit WiCell Research Institute. New Jersey passed legislation in 2004 that legalized stem-cell research in the Garden State and promptly budgeted $6.5 million a year through 2010 in support of it. California, where many biotech companies are located, approved a massive spending initiative on its 2004 ballot. The California Stem Cell Research and Cures Initiative allocates a whopping $300 million a year for ten years. Stem-cell research could lead to significant advances in health, but for states the economic development benefits are just as—and maybe more—appealing. Accordingly, when President Obama lifted the federal ban on funding stem-cell research in 2009, the promise of new federal grants had many states paying attention. In the words of former Missouri governor Bob Holden, "Whether it's pharmaceuticals, biotechnology, or medical research—life sciences technologies will create the jobs of tomorrow."[16]

# CURRENT APPROACHES

State governments, aware that their economic development activities have appeared incoherent and even counterproductive to the outside world, have attempted to clarify their role. In doing so, many states have engaged in strategic planning. Economic sectors commonly targeted by states include travel and tourism, the arts, sports, and international trade.

## Strategic Planning

**strategic planning**

An approach to economic development that emphasizes adaptation to changing conditions and anticipation of future events.

**Strategic planning** can be useful for several reasons. First, it produces an understanding of the state's economic bedrock. Second, it provides a venue in which public- and private-sector leaders can exchange perspectives and develop a consensus about the state's economic future. In addition, strategic planning moves the economic development issue from goal setting to implementation. Finally, it provides a mechanism for adjusting and correcting the state's actions to match emerging economic trends.

Wisconsin was one of the first states to engage in strategic planning for economic development. A twenty-three-member strategic development commission was established by the governor during a time of economic turmoil in the state that resulted mostly from the loss of industrial jobs. The commission's assignment was to analyze the Wisconsin economy and identify avenues for government action. Eighteen months and half a million dollars later, it produced its strategic plan. The focus was on preserving the existing job base, fostering new jobs, and adopting the ethos that "Wisconsin is first in quality."[17] More than 100 specific recommendations were included in the plan.

Since then, most states have undertaken strategic planning exercises. Indiana's 2006 Strategic Economic Development Plan is typical. The theme of the plan, revamping the state's economy for the twenty-first century, sets out three overarching goals:

- Make Indiana a national leader for innovation and entrepreneurship in the global economy.
- Create a Hoosier work force whose capability, productivity, and flexibility are globally competitive and nationally superior.
- Make Indiana one of the most investment-friendly states in the nation.[18]

Indiana's plan identifies a series of actions intended to accomplish these goals. As with most strategic plans, the biggest hurdle is translating rhetoric into reality. And Indiana has its work cut out for it, as the state's position in Figure 14.2 suggests.

Strategic planning is an important first step. The actual programs and tools that state and local governments employ to accomplish their economic development objectives are many and varied. Four that have maintained their popularity are travel and tourism, the arts, sports, and international trade.

## Travel and Tourism

Travel and tourism are big business. According to the U.S. Travel Association, spending by travelers reached $738 billion in 2007, generating 7.7 million jobs and contributing $116 billion in tax revenue.[19] To attract big-spending tourists, states spend big—and some states spend really big. Wisconsin promotes its "Travel Green Wisconsin" program in several of its regions, whereas Tennessee and Nebraska host agri-tourism conferences to acquaint farmers with the benefits of attracting city slickers to their farms.[20] At the local level, convention and visitors' bureaus, which are frequently the joint ventures of the chamber of commerce and city government, have been created to promote individual communities and their assets.

States are actively marketing the virtues of their coasts, mountains, Revolutionary War battlefields, national parks, regional cuisine, casinos—whatever might attract a tourist dollar. States develop advertising campaigns around a catchy slogan: Come See for Yourself (New Jersey), Restart Your Engines (Indiana), Possibilities...Endless (Nebraska). As Iowa's tourism director noted, "We're looking for a type of kick-butt theme that gets on people's minds."[21]

Appealing images abound on state travel and tourism websites. For example, read how Maine's beaches are described in the state's Office of Tourism website: "Maine beaches come in many sizes and shapes. White sand ocean beaches cover much of the southern Maine coast and dot the rest of the 5,500 miles of Maine coastline. By day, beaches are teeming with people building sandcastles, body surfing, searching for seashells and just soaking in the sun. In the evening, the low rumble of the surf crashing upon the shore offers a soothing backdrop for a romantic stroll."[22] Pennsylvania took a different tack on its tourism website. They asked "celebrities, experts, and the people next door [about] what they love most about Pennsylvania" and posted their recommendations in the PA Playlists.[23] Michigan, battered by the recession and eager for both an economic jumpstart and an image boost, turned to tourism in 2009. The state launched a $10 million national tourism campaign that featured scenes of beauty and tranquility, action and excitement.

Travel and tourism are especially appealing because of the tax yield. Most states levy an **accommodations tax** (commonly referred to as a bed tax), and the money spent by travelers and tourists is also subject to state as well as local sales taxes. All in all, nonresidents contribute a significant sum to the tax base of tourism-rich locales. In fact, the tax sensitivity of tourists is much debated. At what point does the tax burden drive tourists away?

## The Arts

Throughout the country, in medium-size to large cities, performing arts lovers (patrons of dance, opera, theater, and orchestra) are joining with business leaders to forge a coalition. Their intent is to use the arts as a development strategy. Promoting the arts as a development tool may not be as far-fetched as one might initially think.[24] Cities hope that, by sponsoring world-class concerts in acoustically perfect arenas, they can bring audiences of white-collar workers back to the city's center. Such events would also generate secondary spending by the audience (and participants) at restaurants, retail shops, parking garages, and hotels. And just as important, a new sense of liveliness and vitality would infuse the nightlife. In fact, the accessibility of community **amenities** such as the arts is a factor that frequently contributes to business-relocation decisions. Members of arts coalitions argue that company officials might look more favorably on their city if it regularly attracts Broadway shows and the Bolshoi Ballet. They point out that a successful performing arts center could stimulate additional physical development in the downtown area. Indeed, a community might invest in an arts strategy for many reasons.

Aware that the arts can provide a valuable boost, several cities have cast an envious eye at Chicago's Millennium Park, a sculpture garden that opened to rave reviews (and a lot of visitors) in 2004. St. Louis took a page from the same book and created Citygarden in 2009, a three-acre sculpture park on downtown land that was previously vacant. Both San Francisco and Minneapolis invested in massive overhauls of their art museums, and Louisville built a brand-new performing arts and educational center. Denver sports a new opera house, and Atlanta advertises the Georgia Aquarium, billed as the largest indoor fish tank in the world.[25]

Providence, Rhode Island, has undergone a revival in its downtown area after the creation of an arts and entertainment empowerment zone that offers special tax breaks. Artists and performers who live in the one-square-mile area pay no state income tax on what they sell; their customers pay

Citygarden in St. Louis.
*SOURCE: AP Photo/Jeff Roberson*

**accommodations tax**

A tax on hotel- or motel-room occupancy, with the revenues usually earmarked for tourism-related uses.

**amenities**

Comfort and conveniences that contribute to quality of life.

no sales tax on what they buy.[26] The city also offers tax incentives to property owners who convert old, unused buildings in the zone into residential units.

But the arts need not be highbrow to affect development. Popular culture—be it multiplex theaters, theme restaurants, sports arenas, or entertainment-oriented stores—is turning around many central cities.[27] Street art, especially sculptural displays, is another popular art form that many places have embraced. Chicago kicked it off with that city's colorful and clever Cows on Parade: 320 life-size fiberglass bovines. Cultural leaders in other cities took the idea and ran with it. There were pigs in Cincinnati, Ohio; horses in Lexington, Kentucky; geckos in Orlando, Florida; and cornstalks in Bloomington, Illinois. Clearly, the arts have become an important economic development tool.

## Sports

Professional sports and big-league cities go hand in hand. Hosting a professional sports franchise is evidence that a city has arrived—that it is not simply a large city but a major-league city. Only sixty cities in the country host a top-level professional baseball, basketball, football, or hockey team. Smaller cities eagerly court minor-league teams to enhance the quality of life in the community.

Acquiring or retaining professional sports teams has become an important element in local economic development plans. Cities want professional sports franchises, but they don't come easily. In fact, ownership groups have to bid for franchises, typically through some sort of public subsidy. This subsidy usually comes in the form of below-market-rate leases and tax breaks for the stadium (depending on whether the facility is publicly or privately owned). City leaders defend these subsidies, arguing that the return, both economically and symbolically, is worth it. But the public is increasingly skeptical. Even in football-friendly Texas, some residents of Arlington, the home of the Dallas Cowboys new $1.12 billion mega-stadium, balked at the use of local tax revenue ($325 million) and the city's **eminent domain** power in support of the stadium.[28]

When public financial support is not forthcoming, team owners frequently threaten to relocate. The threat can be a potent one, as Cleveland found out when their beloved Browns left town to become the Baltimore Ravens. Baltimore, still smarting from the departure of the Colts in the 1980s, built a brand-new $200 million stadium for its new team. But owners are beginning to find their relocation options narrowing. When the owner of the Minnesota Twins threatened to move his team south after the legislature failed to come up with financing for a new stadium, he found a welcome mat but no cash. The electorate in North Carolina's Greensboro area had turned down plans for a publicly financed baseball facility. In Rhode Island, which once had hoped to become the new home of the New England Patriots, the governor concluded that the state could not afford to provide land and infrastructure, valued at $140 million, for the $250 million stadium complex.[29] However, few politicians want a treasured professional team to relocate. Thus, the governor of Minnesota, an opponent of stadium bills when he was

**eminent domain**

The right of a government to seize private property for public use, in exchange for payment of fair market value.

| TABLE 14.1 | Public Financial Support of Sports Stadiums | | | | | |
|---|---|---|---|---|---|---|
| **MAJOR LEAGUE BASEBALL** | | | **NATIONAL FOOTBALL LEAGUE** | | | |
| | | **PUBLIC FUNDS** | | | | **PUBLIC FUNDS** |
| TEAM | YEAR | (%) | TEAM | YEAR | (%) | |
| Cincinnati Reds | 2003 | 96 | Arizona Cardinals | 2006 | 76 | |
| Detroit Tigers | 2000 | 32 | Cincinnati Bengals | 2000 | 89 | |
| Florida Marlins | 2011 | 69 | Denver Broncos | 2001 | 73 | |
| Houston Astros | 2000 | 68 | Detroit Lions | 2002 | 36 | |
| Milwaukee Brewers | 2001 | 75 | Houston Texans | 2002 | 73 | |
| Minnesota Twins | 2010 | 72 | Indianapolis Colts | 2008 | 50 | |
| New York Mets | 2009 | 27 | New England Patriots | 2002 | 0 | |
| New York Yankees | 2009 | 17 | Philadelphia Eagles | 2003 | 39 | |
| Oakland Athletics | 2012 | 0 | Pittsburgh Steelers | 2001 | 69 | |
| Philadelphia Phillies | 2004 | 50 | Seattle Seahawks | 2002 | 83 | |
| Pittsburgh Pirates | 2001 | 70 | | | | |
| San Diego Padres | 2004 | 57 | | | | |
| San Francisco Giants | 2000 | 5 | | | | |
| St. Louis Cardinals | 2006 | 12 | | | | |
| Washington Nationals | 2008 | 100 | | | | |

SOURCE: *Sports Facility Reports*, 2008. National Sports Law Institute. Marquette University, http://law.marquette.edu/cgi-bin/site.pl?2130&pageID=3626.

a state legislator, proposed the construction of new stadiums for the Twins (baseball) and the Vikings (football). Governor Tim Pawlenty explained his flip-flop this way: "Bottom line: I don't want to lose the Twins or the Vikings on my watch."[30] Table 14.1 shows the wide range in the percentage of recent stadium construction paid for with public funds.

A study on the impact of sports stadiums on local economies found that the stadiums had negligible effects on jobs and development; instead, they diverted economic development from manufacturing to the service sector.[31] And a cost–benefit analysis of minor-league stadiums turned up negative.[32] But economic analyses of hosting the Olympics are more positive. Called by some the "world's largest economic development opportunity," the Olympic Games are the ultimate sports prize. This is why Chicago launched an ambitious but ultimately unsuccessful effort to beat out Madrid, Tokyo, and Rio de Janeiro to host the 2016 Summer Olympic Games. The 1996 Summer Olympics in Atlanta produced an estimated $5.1 billion for Georgia's economy. And the tax revenues were put at $165 million. Those kinds of numbers help in creating a broad base of support for the Olympics. When opposition does arise, it tends to be piecemeal and sporadic, aimed at diverting development from a specific location or mitigating negative consequences.[33] Environmental groups, neighborhood groups, taxpayer organizations, and citizen advocacy groups fought against certain aspects of the 2002 Salt Lake City Winter Olympics and even enjoyed occasional successes in having venues relocated. But there was no anti-Olympic coalition intent upon stopping the games. The very successful Winter Games brought international media attention to Salt Lake City (and to Utah) and long-lasting economic benefits.

## International Trade

States are no longer content to concentrate on domestic markets for the goods and services produced in their jurisdictions—they are venturing abroad. States pursue international trade for two reasons. First, foreign markets can be important consumers of state goods. Second, foreign investors may have capital to commit to projects in a state. Thus, the promotion of international trade is a two-way street: State products are exported and investment capital is imported.

One highly visible means by which state governments pursue international markets and investments is through trade missions in which the governor, top business leaders, and economic development agency officials make formal visits, most often to Europe and Asia. The state delegation exchanges information with representatives of the country's public and private sectors and establishes ties that delegation members hope will lead to exports and investments.

State governments perform three important roles in export promotion:

- brokering information,
- offering technical support,
- providing export financing.[34]

As information brokers, states conduct seminars and conferences, sponsor trade shows, provide market research, publish export handbooks, and offer individual counseling to American businesses. Oklahoma, for instance, has set up an international division in its commerce department to encourage export activity. One of its key functions is to identify export opportunities for Oklahoma's business firms. Once an opportunity has been identified, the division provides technical support to help the relevant firm become more knowledgeable about the exporting process.

Technical support is critical because U.S. firms may not be aware of the details involved in exporting: working with international banks, complying with another country's laws and regulations, securing the necessary licensing agreements, designing appropriate packaging for products, and the like. Thus, states conduct seminars to inform businesses of the details. Export finance is also important because without it, a state's information brokerage and technical support functions are weakened. The first state to tackle the export finance issue was Minnesota; it provides a firm with operating capital for the period between the signing of a sales agreement and the delivery of a product. In addition to working capital, some states offer insurance and export credit. The availability of financing converts the fantasy of exporting into reality. Texas and California, not surprisingly, lead the other states in terms of the value of exports, with 14.2 and 12.9 percent of the U.S. total, respectively.[35]

State government is also involved in promoting the state as a place for foreign investment. According to the U.S. Bureau of the Census, more than 5.1 million jobs are a direct result of foreign investment. (More than 10 percent of them are in California.)[36] Delaware leads all states with 7.2 percent of its work force in foreign-owned businesses; followed by South Carolina (7 percent) and Connecticut (6.9 percent). The value of foreign-owned property, plants, and equipment was over $1 trillion in 2007, with one-fifth of this investment located in two states: California and Texas.

The enactment of foreign trade agreements such as the North American Free Trade Agreement (NAFTA) and the decrees of the World Trade Organization (WTO) add another dimension to the globalization of trade for states and localities. NAFTA gradually eliminates trade barriers and investment restrictions among the United States, Canada, and Mexico. NAFTA opens new markets to a state's industries, but it also puts pressure on those industries to remain competitive. States with a heavy reliance on low-wage, low-skill industries have the most to fear about a NAFTA-inspired job drain. The agreement also imposes new limitations and duties on state governments.[37] Under NAFTA, for example, states may no longer discriminate in favor of homegrown service providing firms, nor can they restrict foreign ownership of land, unless these policies are specifically grandfathered into the agreement. The WTO picks up where NAFTA leaves off by, in effect, knocking down protectionism and opening borders throughout the world. California got schooled on the ins and outs of NAFTA and WTO when it adopted a new law that would recycle old tires into paving materials for use in highway construction projects. At issue was whether the requirement that the recycled tires be of U.S. origin violated NAFTA by discriminating against Canadian and Mexican tire manufacturers.[38] After multiple interpretations and reinterpretations of the new law and the treaty, the Golden State's law was allowed to stand.

# PERSISTENT QUESTIONS

A robust economy provides jobs for residents and revenues for governments. Therefore, economic health is a central public policy concern. Government actions intended to spark economic development are typically considered to be in the public interest. Still, three questions in particular are associated with government involvement in the economy, and they pertain to the impact, the extent, and the fairness of government action.

## Do State and Local Government Efforts Make Much Difference?

Views about the impact of government actions on the economy diverge widely. Some studies suggest that many of the important factors that affect an economy are beyond the control of state and local governments, whereas others contend that government action can greatly influence the fate of a local economy.[39] Both views contain a kernel of truth. One widely cited study of the location decisions

## Engaging Economic Development

### U.S. Car Dealerships: Small Pieces in a Large Puzzle

In the summer of 2009, a car dealership in Cissna Park, Illinois, was notified by General Motors that it would be forced to close. Rust Chevrolet was a family-run business and had been a local landmark since 1916, and the news of the closure was a major blow to the community of 800 residents. The company, with annual sales at just about 100 vehicles, made up half the town's annual sales tax and 20 percent of its yearly budget. Without this revenue source, the town government would be forced to cut services and restructure its budget substantially.

Rust Chevrolet is only one example of the more than approximately 2,000 car dealerships in the United States—representing an estimated 100,000 jobs—that have shut, or are about to shut, their doors. And it isn't going to stop there, for more closings are projected as the General Motors Corporation and the Chrysler Corporation struggle to get back on their feet. What's the perceived benefit to this restructuring of the automobile industry? Automakers and the remaining dealerships are expected to enjoy increased profits as the more unprofitable dealerships close. This should position the industry to better compete with foreign car companies such as Toyota. A more competitive American auto industry means sustainable employment and spillover effects for the economy in the long term. What's the downside? A drop in consumer confidence in American-made cars, a temporary increase in unemployment, a decrease in tax revenue, and inconvenienced car owners who will have to travel farther to find a dealership that will honor their warranty.

It is true that the number of dealerships in the United States represented an older era when American-made vehicles held a larger percentage of the market. As foreign companies continue to dominate the industry, their American counterparts must restructure in order to compete. What we are seeing in the auto industry is similar to other private industries where short-run sacrifices during restructuring must be realized for the sake of long-term survival. Some of the controversy lies in federal government's involvement during restructuring. Having accepted federal loans, automakers are forced to comply with stringent timetables for dealership closings. This has put the franchise dealership owners at the mercy of the government—claiming that politics, and not free-market economics, is picking the winners and the losers.

So what's your take on the auto industry's makeover? It may make sense in the aggregate, but to a local community defunct dealerships can be devastating. Many large jurisdictions had invested heavily, albeit indirectly, in dealerships by subsidizing the creation of auto malls, a mile-long stretch of highway lined with competing auto dealers. Anxious to collect the sales tax revenue generated by the sale of automobiles, some localities had made infrastructure improvements at auto mall sites and provided land to dealers at below-market cost. But with folks increasingly willing to car shop on the Internet, the auto mall has become less of a destination. Now, in small towns and large cities, empty dealerships dot the landscape and a once important mainstay of the local economy fades. What can local governments do about it?

SOURCES: Terrell Brown, "A Dealership at the Heart of a Town," *CBS Evening News,* www.cbsnews.com/stories/2009/07/11/eveningnews/main5152765.shtml?tag=cbsnewsTwoColUpperPromoArea (July 11, 2009); William Fulton, "The Dying Auto Mall," *Governing,* www.governing.com/node/429/ (March 1, 2009); Mark Trumbull, "Fewer Car Dealers: Good for GM, Bad for America?" *Christian Science Monitor,* features.csmonitor.com/economyrebuild/2009/06/12/fewer-car-dealers-good-for-gm-bad-for-america/ (June 12, 2009).

of large firms found that a favorable labor climate and proximity to suppliers and consumers were important criteria to most firms.[40] Governments can affect the first factor but not the second. Also, states vary in the degree to which their economies are influenced by external forces.[41] The Engaging Economic Development box takes up the issue of auto dealership closings, a situation over which localities have no control.

Questions about impact and return on investment continue to haunt state and local development officials. Can the actions of states and localities affect employment levels, income, and investment? Statistical tests suggest that the outcomes are both mixed and marginal. Research by political scientists Margery Ambrosius and Paul Brace has shown that, in some places, at some times, some economic development tools produce the intended outcomes.[42] A study of forty government-assisted development projects in ten medium-size cities reached similar conclusions.[43] Regardless of the modest results, however, governments continue to intervene in their economies. This behavior may rest in the political benefits of successful development projects to elected officials. Or it may be an outgrowth of business influence in public policy making. Whatever the explanation, the behavior continues.

An example demonstrates the inherent risk. Hoping to create jobs and stimulate investment in a poor county, the Mississippi legislature guaranteed a $55 million loan to a beef-processing firm in 2003. When the plant ceased operation at the end of 2004, the state was stuck with the $55 million loan.[44] What had seemed like a good idea at the time turned out to be ill-advised—and costly. Public officials were left with a shuttered facility and a lot of taxpayers wanting an explanation.

The comments of former Maryland governor Parris Glendening are apropos: "We are all having to learn new rules for the new economy. Under the old rules, states attracted businesses based on tax structures or incentive packages. But the high-tech companies that are the driving engines in this new economy can locate anywhere. They are motivated by the quality of the work force and the quality of life that is offered."[45] Thus, states may have to reorient themselves to fourth-wave thinking. Initial research findings are encouraging, suggesting that grants and loans in support of technology development can increase an area's share of high-technology employment.[46] Other fourth-wave approaches such as increased local–global links and investment in human capital may, in fact, make a difference.

## Does Government Spend Too Much?

Some observers claim that government gives away too much in its pursuit of economic health. This concern develops out of the fundamental relationship between a federal system of government and a capitalistic economic system. Governmental jurisdictions cover specific territories, but capital is mobile, so business firms can move from one location to another. Because these firms are so important to a local economy, governments offer incentives to influence their location decisions. As noted, the impact of these incentives on firms' decisions is not clear, but most jurisdictions believe that they cannot afford *not* to offer them. Concern is increasing, however, that competition among jurisdictions to attract business may be counterproductive and costly to government. As a consequence, citizens are beginning to look more closely at the **incentive packages**—tax breaks, low interest loans, and infrastructure development—that their governments offer to business.

Examples of government concessions to the automobile industry abound—the Honda plant in Ohio, the Mazda facility in Michigan, the General Motors Saturn operation in Tennessee, and the BMW plant in South Carolina. The fundamental

**incentive packages**
The enticements that state and local governments offer to retain or attract business and industry.

question is, how extensive should incentives be? The answer typically involves calculation of the return on the state's investment. In the late 1980s, Kentucky put together one of the first big automotive deals when it attracted a new Toyota assembly plant to the community of Georgetown. Twenty years later, the investment seems to have paid off—the facility is credited with spurring the creation of an additional 460 motor vehicle–related firms that employ 88,000 people in the state.[47]

Jurisdictions compete for major investments such as automobile manufacturing facilities, and that competition has the effect of ratcheting up the value of incentive packages. When German automaker Mercedes-Benz announced that it was seeking a location for its first U.S. facility, more than thirty-five states expressed interest. Five states—Alabama, Iowa, Nebraska, North Carolina, and South Carolina—survived the winnowing process. Each state tried to outdo the others by offering generous packages of tax breaks and low-cost land. In the end, Mercedes selected Vance, Alabama, as the site of the $300 million facility. But the price that Alabama paid was a dear one. The state provided $92.2 million in land and facility construction costs, $77.5 million in infrastructure development, $60 million in training, and a twenty-five-year tax abatement. Estimates put the state costs at approximately $179,000 per job. The extravagant bidding for the Mercedes plant raised some eyebrows, but in the words of one Alabama economist, "The symbolism [of winning the Mercedes facility] may be as important as the direct economic impact."[48]

Concern about government overspending lingers, and it extends beyond the automobile industry. New York City, for example, has provided almost $200 million in tax breaks and utility concessions to keep the three major television networks in the city. And Tootsie Roll Industries and a Nabisco plant agreed to remain in Illinois after the state offered loans, tax exemptions, and job-training funds that totaled $52 million in value.[49]

But even as governments continue to offer these packages, they are becoming more savvy about the potential risks.[50] Concern that a government-supported development project might turn sour has led to the imposition of **clawbacks**. Clawbacks require a subsidized firm that fails to deliver on its promises (regarding number of jobs, say, or amount of investment) to repay some or all of its subsidy. In this way, generous states and localities are not left holding the bag. Consider the case of United Airlines and its new maintenance facility in Indianapolis. To attract United to Indiana, the state offered the company a deal that included $300 million in assorted tax breaks and several clawback provisions. When it failed to create the number of jobs the agreement called for, United Airlines had to return more than $30 million to the Hoosier State.[51]

**clawbacks**
Requirements that subsidized firms repay some or all of the subsidy if they fail to deliver on their promises.

## Does Government Spend Fairly?

Traditionally, government involvement in economic development has taken the form of efforts to reduce costs to business. According to economic development professionals, the central business district, local developers, the local labor force, and existing business firms derive the greatest benefit from city-sponsored economic development activity.[52] As citizens began to ask *who* benefits, however, some state governments refocused their efforts toward direct investments in human resources. An illustration of this reorientation can be found in Arizona—a model of successful economic revitalization. At the top of the Arizona agenda for economic development are the goals of strengthening education, improving health care, and increasing skills training.[53] Based on research on minority entrepreneurs, this approach should pay dividends: investment in human capital and access to financial resources can lead to the creation of new firms.[54]

**linkaging**

A method by which local governments use large-scale commercial development projects to accomplish social objectives.

Local governments have been especially active in expanding the concept of economic development beyond a narrow concern with business investment. Led by the pioneering efforts of San Francisco and Boston, some U.S. cities are tying economic development initiatives to the achievement of social objectives, an approach called **linkaging**. For instance, local governments have linked large-scale commercial development (office and retail buildings and hotels) to concerns such as housing and employment. This movement grew out of frustration over the disappearance of older low-income neighborhoods from revitalized, commercially oriented downtown areas.[55] The upscaling of formerly low-income neighborhoods—a process known as **gentrification**—displaces existing residents. With linkaging, developers are required to provide low- or moderate-income housing or employment to targeted groups or to contribute funding to programs that support these objectives. In return for the opportunity to enter a lucrative local market, a developer pays a price. This process has been called "the cities' attempt to share the profits of their prospering sectors with their poor."[56]

**gentrification**

An urban revitalization process that replaces low-end land uses with upscale uses.

Linkaging works best in cities with booming economies. But even in cities with more stable economies, local government can negotiate with developers for social concessions. In Richmond, Virginia, for example, city officials convinced developers to provide substantial minority participation in a major retail project in the downtown area. In return for city approval of a massive redevelopment project in Jersey City, New Jersey, developers agreed to reserve a certain percentage of dwelling units for low- and moderate-income individuals.

Some states have taken a different direction in addressing the fairness issue: They have adopted legislation that increases the minimum wage paid to hourly workers in their jurisdictions. Table 14.2 lists the states that, as of 2009, had set the highest minimum wage rates. Some cities with relatively high costs of living, such as San Francisco, have raised the wage in their communities even higher. Although these actions are popular with workers, owners of small businesses such as restaurants are decidedly less enthusiastic. But supporters contend that without such increases, many people cannot afford to live in the city.

## THE IMPLICATIONS OF ECONOMIC DEVELOPMENT POLICY

A healthy economy is central to the functioning of government. State and local officials know this and act accordingly. The slogan for Rhode Island's economic development campaign several years ago sums up the attitude: "Every state says they'll move mountains to get your business. We're moving rivers."[57] The ad did not exaggerate: Rhode Island redirected two rivers as part of a $200 million redevelopment project in its capital city of Providence.

| States with Higher Minimum Wage Rates | | TABLE 14.2 |
|---|---|---|
| **STATE** | **DOLLARS/HOUR MINIMUM WAGE** | |
| Washington | 8.55 | |
| Oregon | 8.40 | |
| Connecticut | 8.25 | |
| Vermont | 8.06 | |
| California[a] | 8.00 | |
| Illinois | 8.00 | |
| Massachusetts | 8.00 | |
| Maine | 7.50 | |
| New Mexico | 7.50 | |
| Michigan | 7.40 | |
| Rhode Island | 7.40 | |
| Ohio | 7.30 | |
| Colorado | 7.28 | |

[a]By city ordinance, San Francisco's minimum wage is $9.79/hour.

SOURCE: "Minimum Wage Laws in the States—July 24, 2009," *U.S. Department of Labor*, www.dol.gov/esa/minwage/america.htm#Consolidated (July 25, 2009).

Yet when an observer steps back and ponders such strategies and deals, a degree of skepticism is inevitable. Could New York City have better spent the millions it committed to Chase Manhattan Bank to keep the financial institution from moving 4,600 office workers to New Jersey? The deal involved $235 million worth of tax abatements, discounted utilities, site improvements, and job-training tax credits over the next twenty years.[58] And which state really won when a division of Eastman Kodak turned down Maryland's $4.5 million package of subsidized land, tax breaks, and employee training in favor of Pennsylvania's $14 million deal? Some might conclude that corporations are staging raids on public treasuries. But many state and local government officials would argue that concessions for business serve an important function by creating jobs and generating economic activity, thus improving the local tax base, which in turn funds public services. Maybe the third and fourth waves of economic development will be characterized by more creative and productive efforts at achieving this outcome.

Local economies are evaluated, compared, and ranked also. *Forbes* magazine compiles a list yearly of the best metropolitan areas for business and careers, based on several measures of business costs, quality of life, and projected employment growth. Table 14.3 shows the top ten places in 2009, categorized by population size.[59] North Carolina cities fare particularly well in the rankings, as do Colorado cities among larger metro areas and Indiana and North Dakota cities in the smaller classification.

As one might expect, states and localities scoring high on these rankings place far more value on them than their low-scoring counterparts do—at least

**TABLE 14.3    The Best Places for Business and Careers, 2009**

| BEST METROS | | BEST SMALL METROS | |
|---|---|---|---|
| 1 | Raleigh, NC | 1 | Sioux Falls, SD |
| 2 | Fort Collins, CO | 2 | Greenville, NC |
| 3 | Durham, NC | 3 | Morgantown, WV |
| 4 | Fayetteville, AR | 4 | Bloomington, IN |
| 5 | Lincoln, NE | 5 | Columbia, MO |
| 6 | Asheville, NC | 6 | Bismarck, ND |
| 7 | Des Moines, IA | 7 | Fargo, ND |
| 8 | Austin, TX | 8 | Lafayette, IN |
| 9 | Boise, ID | 9 | Iowa City, IA |
| 10 | Colorado Springs, CO | 10 | Auburn, AL |

SOURCE: "The Best Places for Business and Careers," *Forbes.com,* www.forbes.com/2009/03/25/best-cities-careers-bizplaces09-business-places_lander.html (March 25, 2009).

publicly. But allowing for the inherent biases in the rankings, they certainly suggest that some communities are faring quite well in the economic development wars.

Critics claim that competition for economic development is nothing more than the relocation of a given amount of economic activity from one community to another, with no overall increase in national productivity. Mercedes-Benz was going to open a U.S. manufacturing facility anyway; the question was simply, where? By playing states against one another, Mercedes-Benz was able to exact a subsidy of unheard-of proportions.[60] Many critics call for increased cooperation among jurisdictions in their quest for economic development. However, this objective has been elusive at both the state and local levels, and jurisdictions continue to use financial carrots to gain an edge in the competition. A case in point: The new headquarters for the Boeing Company. Three areas—Denver, Dallas-Ft. Worth, and Chicago—were in the running for the facility. Denver and Dallas-Ft. Worth developed cooperative regional efforts to try and land Boeing; Chicago did not but offered an incentive package worth up to $51 million.[61] Which jurisdiction did Boeing select? Chicago.

Thus far, the courts have not been receptive to legal challenges seeking to outlaw the use of corporate tax incentives. The U.S. Supreme Court rejected the arguments of a group of Ohio taxpayers who sought to undo a $281 million package of tax breaks given to Daimler Chrysler for a Jeep plant in Toledo.[62] Even when jurisdictions agree not to steal companies from each other, the agreements can unravel. Within months after signing a cooperative no-poaching pact, Miami-Dade, Broward, and Palm Beach counties in south Florida reverted to their old competitive behaviors.[63] Economic development continues to be a singular proposition, with each jurisdiction pursuing its own destiny.

## CHAPTER RECAP

- The economic performance of the states varies. Even in an individual state, its economic health changes over time. The same is true for localities: Their economies are dynamic.

- Economic development has had four waves of different approaches or strategies. The first wave was characterized by smokestack chasing. The latest, or fourth, wave emphasizes globalization and human capital. Even now, states continue to use approaches from the earlier waves.

- The relationship between state government and the private sector can be complicated. Some states have begun to use public–private hybrid organizations in economic development functions.

- States have offered huge incentives to attract automobile manufacturers. But with trends showing a decline in manufacturing as a proportion of the job base, the emphasis is shifting toward research and technology. Many states have begun to invest in bioscience research.

- States have taken on many different economic development initiatives, including strategic planning, travel and tourism, the arts, sports, and international trade.

- Three major questions continue to surface with regard to government involvement in the economy: Do state and local government efforts make much difference? Does government spend too much to attract and grow new business and to retain old business? Does government spend fairly; that is, does reducing costs for business come at a cost to other groups?

- Many organizations rank states and localities on aspects of economic development. In evaluating these rankings, it is important to consider the criteria used in their compilation.

- Economic development is a competitive activity, pitting one jurisdiction against others. Efforts are underway to foster more cooperative behavior among jurisdictions.

## Key Terms

economic development
  (p. 383)
subsidy (p. 386)
venture capital pools (p. 386)
small-business incubators
  (p. 386)

enterprise zone (p. 386)
clusters (p. 386)
new economy (p. 387)
strategic planning (p. 390)
accommodations tax
  (p. 392)

amenities (p. 392)
eminent domain (p. 393)
incentive packages (p. 398)
clawbacks (p. 399)
linkaging (p. 400)
gentrification (p. 400)

## Internet Resources

Two economic development organizations, one with a national focus, the other with an international emphasis, maintain useful websites. These are the Corporation for Enterprise Development (CFED) at **www.cfed.org** and the

International Economic Development Council at **www.iedconline.org**.

All states have a Web presence in economic development, typically through a state agency.

The comprehensive website of Arizona's Department of Commerce can be found at **www .azcommerce.com**.

Explore a more targeted approach to economic development at **www.idahoworks.com**, which is a part of Idaho's Department of Commerce website.

Other examples of states with less traditional economic development websites are the state of Kentucky's new economy website at **www.thinkkentucky.com/dci** and Enterprise Florida at **www.eflorida.com**.

A statewide organization devoted to local economic development is the California Association for Local Economic Development, **www.caled.org**.

**www.nycedc.com** is the website for the New York City Economic Development Corporation.

For economic development from a private sector perspective, check out the website of *Site Selection* magazine at **www.siteselection .com**. It tracks new business activity around the nation.

SOURCE: Glyn Jones/Corbis/
Jupiter Images

# Education Policy

Can you interpret a bus schedule? Follow a map? Balance a checkbook? Fill out a job application? Were you able to follow the last chapter? If not, you are functionally illiterate, like one in four of your fellow adult Americans. Convincing evidence reports that too many students cannot read, write, and do math at grade level. And a substantial proportion of U.S. teenagers are shockingly ignorant of history and government. Unqualified teachers, school violence, and crumbling infrastructure also generate concern. In its much-cited report *A Nation at Risk*, the National Commission on Excellence in Education lamented the erosion of the educational foundations of society "by a rising tide of mediocrity that threatens our very future."[1]

Disturbing studies document the performance of U.S. students in comparison with students in other developed countries. Despite much higher per-pupil spending on schools, scores in mathematics, science, and reading earned by U.S. fifteen-year-olds consistently rank poorly; U.S. students scored below average in science and math, and their comparative underperformance grows as grade level rises.[2] U.S. firms corroborate these concerns with stories about their frustration in finding new employees who can read, write, and perform basic math functions. But the other side of the coin is that many public school systems are doing an outstanding job of preparing youngsters for college and the work world, especially those in middle-class and upper-middle-class communities where funding is adequate and education is considered important. Much of the alleged crisis in public education is a product of demographics—poverty, culture, dysfunctional or unsupportive families, and poor health and nutrition. These societal problems are factors that cannot be corrected by teachers or principals.

**15**

- The Crisis in Education
- Intergovernmental Roles in Education
- The Education Policy Actors
- Educational Innovation in the States
- The Continuing Challenges of Public Education

In the opinion of many Americans, education is the most important function performed by state and local governments. The facts support this point of view. Education consumes more of state and local budgets than any other service. More than $631 billion is spent on elementary and secondary schooling by the states and localities. That translates to around $9,963 per pupil.[3] The importance of education is also demonstrated by the sheer number of people involved in it as students, parents, teachers, administrators, and staff. Citizens have high expectations for their schools, assuming that they will teach everything from good citizenship and driving skills to safe sex. Schools have served at the frontlines in the battle against racial segregation. To a great extent, the future of this country and its economy is linked to the quality of free public education.

In 2002, Congress overwhelmingly passed, and President George W. Bush signed, a bill that promised to transform public education. The No Child Left Behind (NCLB) law, a $12 billion reauthorization of the Elementary and Secondary Education Act (ESEA), saddled the states and their schools with significant new (and mostly unfunded) mandates, including mandatory and frequent testing and a stipulation that failing schools not making sufficient progress in any one of numerous student demographic categories would have to offer students a transfer and even private tuition.

The broad goals of NCLB were admirable and widely accepted: no child would be neglected and left behind in school, and all would have an equal chance to succeed. But the devil was in the details of implementation. Teachers, principals, chief state school officers (CSSOs), governors, and state legislators soon howled like scalded hounds as they became aware of their predicament. The costs of annual testing amounted to millions of more dollars than what Congress provided. Established, and demonstrably effective, state standards and testing programs were threatened with replacement by cumbersome federal mandates. Local control of public education appeared to be the victim of a "regime change" replete with federal mandates and regulations.

## THE CRISIS IN EDUCATION

As the heated debate over NCLB illustrates, education policy has always been controversial and frequently proclaimed to be in crisis. Policy makers, parents, teachers, and others have perennially debated how schools should be organized and financed, and what should be taught. Our present education crisis, however, is different in three respects. First, education policy must be constantly reformulated and altered if schooling is to be relevant and the United

States is to remain a dominant player in the international sphere. In this sense, the crisis is now a permanent condition. Second, improved analysis and data collection have provided a clearer picture of our specific shortcomings in education, and they have generated greater public awareness about them. Third, despite billions of additional dollars in federal, state, and local government spending in recent years, along with a spate of institutional and classroom reforms, this education crisis is not easily resolved.

One seemingly straightforward sign of deterioration in the quality of schooling makes headlines in newspapers throughout the country each year: student performance on standardized college entrance exams. Scholastic Aptitude Test (SAT) and American College Test (ACT) scores on verbal and math sections dropped almost annually from 1963 to 1982, to levels below those existing at the time of the last declared crisis in education (see Figure 15.1). Following a brief rally during the mid-1980s, scores again began eroding slowly, then stabilized. The recent trend has been tilting downward.

Striking differences in SAT scores among the states reflect population characteristics such as race and ethnicity, immigration, poverty levels, and urban–suburban–rural population. But the greatest variation is accounted for by the percentage of high school students taking the SAT. Generally, the higher the percentage of high-schoolers who take the test is, the lower the state scores will be. A more comprehensive assessment of the quality of education in the states is found in Table 15.1, which grades them on four different measures not related to the SAT.

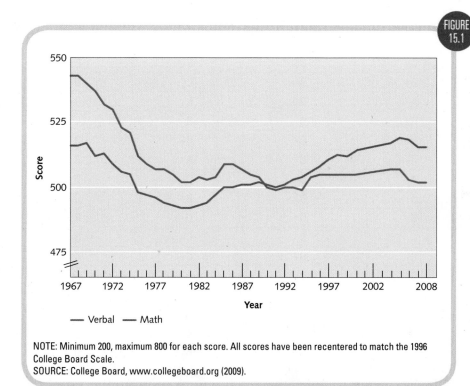

**FIGURE 15.1**

**Average SAT Verbal and Mathematics Scores, 1963–2008**

Average SAT verbal and math scores began a prolonged period of decline in the early 1960s but turned upward in 1982. The current trend is moderately to the downside.

NOTE: Minimum 200, maximum 800 for each score. All scores have been recentered to match the 1996 College Board Scale.
SOURCE: College Board, www.collegeboard.org (2009).

**TABLE 15.1 Quality Counts Grades for State Education Quality**

| STATE | STANDARDS, ASSESSMENTS, AND ACCOUNTABILITY | THE TEACHING PROFESSION* | CHANCE FOR SUCCESS | K-12 ACHIEVEMENT |
|---|---|---|---|---|
| Alabama | A– | B– | C– | F |
| Alaska | B | D– | C | D+ |
| Arizona | A– | D+ | C– | D |
| Arkansas | B+ | B+ | C– | D |
| California | A– | C– | C | D |
| Colorado | B– | D+ | B | C– |
| Connecticut | C | C– | A– | D |
| Delaware | B+ | C+ | B– | C– |
| District of Columbia** | C+ | D– | C+ | F |
| Florida | A– | B | C+ | C |
| Georgia | A– | B | C | D+ |
| Hawaii | B– | C+ | C+ | D |
| Idaho | C | D | C+ | C– |
| Illinois | C+ | D+ | B– | D+ |
| Indiana | A | C– | C+ | C– |
| Iowa | D+ | B– | B | C– |
| Kansas | C+ | D+ | B | C |
| Kentucky | B+ | B– | C | D+ |
| Louisiana | A | B | D+ | D– |
| Maine | C+ | D | B– | C |
| Maryland | B | C– | B+ | B |
| Massachusetts | A– | C | A | B |
| Michigan | A– | D+ | C+ | D |
| Minnesota | C | D+ | B+ | C |
| Mississippi | B | D | D+ | F |
| Missouri | C | C | C+ | D |
| Montana | C– | D+ | C+ | C– |
| Nebraska | D | D+ | B | D+ |
| Nevada | C+ | C– | D+ | D– |
| New Hampshire | C | D | A– | C |
| New Jersey | B– | C | A– | B– |
| New Mexico | A– | C+ | D+ | D– |

| Quality Counts Grades for State Education Quality (continued) | | | | TABLE 15.1 |
|---|---|---|---|---|
| New York | A | C+ | B | C− |
| North Carolina | B+ | B | C+ | D+ |
| North Dakota | C | D+ | B | C |
| Ohio | A | C+ | B− | C− |
| Oklahoma | A− | B− | C− | D |
| Oregon | C+ | F | C | D |
| Pennsylvania | C− | C+ | B | C+ |
| Rhode Island | B+ | D | B− | D |
| South Carolina | A | A− | C | D |
| South Dakota | C+ | D | B− | C− |
| Tennessee | A− | C | C− | D+ |
| Texas | B+ | C | C | C |
| Utah | C+ | C− | B− | C− |
| Vermont | B− | C− | B+ | C+ |
| Virginia | A | B− | B | C |
| Washington | B− | C | B− | C− |
| West Virginia | A | C+ | C− | F |
| Wisconsin | C+ | C− | B | C− |
| Wyoming | C+ | D− | B− | C− |

*The Teaching Profession includes state efforts to attract, develop, and retain teachers.
**Because the District of Columbia does not have a state revenue source, it did not receive a grade for equity. The District of Columbia is a single-district jurisdiction.

SOURCE: "Quality Counts," *Education Week* 27(18) (January 10, 2008).

Is the U.S. education system failing? Or is perception more pessimistic than reality? Public opinion surveys reveal that Americans are mostly satisfied with their own public schools but highly critical of everyone else's. The media bombardment about failing public schools notwithstanding, many school systems are academically strong and most others have shown improvements. State scores on the National Assessment of Educational Progress (NAEP), given to fourth- and eighth-graders, have also shown modest gains since 1992 in reading and math, but little or no improvement in the scores of twelfth grade students.[4] Dropout rates have stabilized at about 5 percent a year, and students are staying in school longer. But few would dispute that the U.S. education system suffers serious problems and needs improvement. The most widely recognized policy problems can be reduced to four major variables: standards, students, teachers, and the education bureaucracy.

## Standards

Schools have suffered from a malady that might be called curriculum drift. Courses designed to teach basic reading comprehension, writing, and mathematics are sometimes deemphasized as nonessential topics become popular. State legislatures and school boards have mandated courses on slavery, the Holocaust, genocide, and the Irish potato famine—worthy topics, perhaps, but no substitute for the basics. To many critics, education sometimes seems to neglect instruction in basic skills and the ability to think analytically. Business, military, and university leaders complain about having to invest millions of dollars in remedial education before ill-prepared high school graduates are ready to work, serve in the armed forces, or succeed in college. They further lament the prevalence of social promotions and a basic ignorance of history, culture, and government. Many students graduate from high school prepared for neither college nor the job market. The argument that the native intelligence of U.S. youth has declined has no basis, so considerable blame has been placed on vacillating educational standards for curricula and courses.

## Students

Students themselves have not escaped criticism. Some choose to soften their curriculum with easy nonacademic courses rather than English, math, science, social studies, and foreign languages. Today's students are said to be poorly motivated and lazy in comparison with their predecessors. They are faulted for seeking instant gratification through television, video games, the Internet, drugs, alcohol, and sex instead of seriously applying themselves to coursework. In a typical year and depending on the school, anywhere from 10 to 40 percent of students give up high school altogether by dropping out.[5]

Clearly, however, the legal and moral responsibility for providing direction to a young person's life rests with his or her parents; school readiness starts at home.[6] This responsibility includes encouraging the child to complete homework assignments and regulating television, video game, cell phone, and Internet access. Researchers have found that U.S. children start the first grade with fewer academic skills than their Asian counterparts, whose parents give them a head start by regularly working with them at home before they enter school. Coaching after school helps children in several Asian countries maintain their early advantage. But U.S. parents tend to abdicate to the schools the responsibility for educating their children. Often parents have little choice; as a result of the high percentage of single-parent and two-worker households, parents have little time, and less energy, to spend helping their children. The shortage and expense of professional day care and after-school learning opportunities compound the problem.

## Teachers

Teachers are the linchpins between students and the learning process. Effective teaching can bestow lifelong learning skills, whereas poor teaching can result in academic indifference among good students and dropping out for marginal students. One problem with teaching is that, for many years, the quality of individuals who choose to enter the teaching profession has declined. The gradual decline in the quality of teachers is partly due to changes in the nature of the work force and the elevated expectations for teachers. (Although social and behavioral expectations have certainly changed for the better, as shown by the socially repressive teacher contract reproduced in Figure 15.2)

Many top-notch young men and women enter the noble profession of teaching. But academically gifted women who once would have chosen the

**Thou Shalt Not**

FIGURE
15.2

## THOU SHALT NOT
*1922 Contract, Salisbury, N.C.*

Miss_____ agrees:

1. Not to get married. This contract becomes null and void immediately if the teacher marries.
2. Not to have company with men.
3. To be at home between the hours of 8:00 pm and 6:00 am unless in attendance at a school function.
4. Not to loiter downtown in ice cream stores.
5. Not to leave town at any time without the permission of the Chairman of the Trustees.
6. Not to smoke cigarettes. This contract becomes null and void immediately if the teacher is found smoking.
7. Not to drink beer, wine, or whiskey. This contract becomes null and void immediately if the teacher is found drinking beer, wine, or whiskey.
8. Not to ride in a carriage or automobile with any man except her brother or father.
9. Not to dress in bright colors.
10. Not to dye her hair.
11. To wear at least two petticoats.
12. Not to wear dresses more than two inches above the ankles.
13. To keep the classroom clean:
    (a) to sweep the classroom floor at least once daily.
    (b) to scrub the classroom floor at least once weekly with soap and hot water.
    (c) to clean the blackboard at least once daily.
    (d) to start the fire at 7:00 am so that the room will be warm at 8:00 am when the children arrive.
14. Not to wear face powder, mascara, or to paint the lips.

**From "North Carolina Women: Making History" by Margaret Supplee Smith and Emily Herring Wilson. @1999 by University of North Carolina Press. Used by permission of the publisher. For more information, visit http://www.uncpress.unc.edu.**

## Engaging Education Policy

### Guns in the Schools?

In August 2008 the school board in rural Harrold, Texas, became the first in the United States to permit teachers and administrators to carry concealed weapons into a school. After receiving forty hours of weapons training and a permit to carry a concealed handgun, a teacher would be "certified" to take his or her weapon into the classroom, lunchroom, or bathroom.

Why? To prevent a Columbine High School (twelve dead, twenty-three wounded in 1999) or a Virginia Tech (thirty-two dead, numerous wounded in 2007) type massacre by gunmen. According to the school board's logic, a teacher could pull out a Glock 9 mm and waste a potential assassin before he unloaded his own weapon, thereby saving innocent lives. Even the public *knowledge* that old Mr. Crotch the English teacher or Ms Slink the attractive music teacher might be carrying a pistol would probably be sufficient to deter an armed attack.

The reactions ranged from shock on the part of teacher organizations and many teachers, administrators, and parents to enthusiastic endorsement by Texas governor Rick Perry, who supported similar statewide legislation proposed in the legislature. The National Rifle Association was ecstatic, as were gun rights supporters across the United States.

School violence is a problem in some schools, though students are much more likely to suffer harm at home or otherwise away from school. But school shootings capture the public attention and evoke feelings of horror and fear for one's own children. School kids—particularly boys—have always fought but what is different today is the easy availability of firearms and the willingness to use them to settle a dispute. But if we cannot keep guns out of schools, is armed teachers and staff the best alternative—fighting fire with fire?

Thirty-seven states currently ban guns from school. Only two states permit them. Utah allows concealed weapons on college campuses, and South Carolina permits a student, teacher, administrator, or any other school employee or visitor to carry concealed weapons in their vehicle on school grounds.

However, Michigan, Ohio, Alabama, Virginia, and several other states were considering permitting guns on school property in 2009. Federal law prohibits taking a gun within 1,000 feet of a school under the Gun-Free School Zones Law of 1996. The practical effects of the federal law on state and local policies that appear to be in conflict are not yet known.

Are concealed weapons in schools a good idea? Perhaps at first blush the concept has appeal, but like most everything else in the public policy world, the devil is in the details.

- Do teachers and administrators want the tremendous responsibility of carrying a weapon and possibly using it against an armed or threatening student?
- At what point in a potentially violent conflict should a teacher actually deploy and use his gun? When a credible threat is communicated? A weapon revealed? A knife pulled? A shot fired?
- Will teachers be asked to purchase and maintain their own pistol, or would the school board or state purchase and maintain it instead? Who pays?
- Who will be responsible for ensuring that weapon-carrying teachers maintain their permits and receive regular weapons training?
- What happens when a teacher's firearm accidentally discharges and injures someone?
- Who is responsible and what should be done when a teacher's weapon is misplaced or stolen?
- What about potential liability for teachers, administrators, and the school district if an innocent person is harmed by a permitted gun?
- And most important: are there other, better policy options for handling violence in the schools?

SOURCES: Brad Knickerbocker, "Should Teachers Be Able to Bring Guns to school?" *The Seattle Times* (September 18, 2007); James C. McKinley, Jr., "In Texas School, Teachers Carry Books and Guns," *nytimes.com* (August 29, 2008); www.schoolsecurity.org (accessed July 27, 2009); www.safeyouth.org (accessed July 27, 2009).

teaching profession are now more likely to seek out higher-paying, more prestigious positions in government, the legal, medical, and other professions, and the private sector. In their place, less able college graduates elect to become teachers, resulting in a severe shortage of qualified teachers in some states. In 2008, verbal and math SAT scores for education majors averaged 960 versus 1,017 for other subject majors.[7] Also reflecting the drop in quality of the teaching labor pool is that many of those hired to teach each year lack the proper qualifications and preparation for the courses they teach.

Part of the blame must also be placed on university and college education schools that continue to emphasize educational methodology courses, which teach prospective instructors how to teach rather than giving them substantive knowledge of their subject matter. Another reason it has been difficult to find good teachers is that, in some states, teaching remains a low-wage occupation, with the starting salary comparing unfavorably with starting salaries in other professional fields.

In an effort to help improve pay and working conditions, most teachers have joined unions such as the American Federation of Teachers (AFT) and the National Education Association (NEA). According to some critics, these unions have become part of the problem with public education because they further teachers' narrow self-interest instead of encouraging more effective schools and because they protect incompetents from being fired.

Meanwhile, many of those who do become teachers quickly exit the profession. An estimated one-half of all teachers and one-half of those in urban schools quit their jobs within five years, making the teacher dropout rate exceed that of students![8] Many discouraged teachers also feel that they are not valued or respected. The frustration of teaching is perhaps best illustrated by the responses of teachers when they are asked to identify the biggest problems inhibiting public-school children's ability to learn in their community.

Topping the list are lack of parental interest and support, students' lack of discipline, and use of drugs. Noisy, disruptive behavior by a handful of students spoils the learning environment for all. Teachers are assaulted in the classroom, and violent crimes occur on or near school grounds. Empty gestures by elected officials such as mandating posting of the Ten Commandments (Jackson County, Kentucky) on classroom walls, requiring uniforms (Memphis, New York City), or requiring students to address teachers as ma'am and sir (Louisiana) do not help. Teacher stress is augmented, especially in poor schools, by crumbling buildings, chronic supply and equipment shortages, overcrowded classrooms, and crushing paperwork burdens.[9]

Further longstanding problems with the supply of teachers are being worsened by the retirement of baby boomers. Because of these demographic facts and the dissatisfactions noted above, severe shortages of teachers have developed, especially in the fields of mathematics, science, foreign languages, and special education. Meanwhile, the number of students is growing rapidly. Shortages are most severe in the booming Sunbelt. The acute teacher shortfall has forced too many school districts to hire unqualified, ill-prepared people simply to put a warm adult body in the classroom.

### The Education Bureaucracy

Bureaucracy is publicly vilified everywhere, and the schools are no exception. A strong case can be made that the United States has too many school administrators, rules, and restrictions and too few teachers. The ratio is as high as one nonteaching employee for every eight teachers in some districts. Critics say that school districts and their bureaucracies act like classic monopolies. They are guaranteed customers (students) and income (tax revenues), and they face little or no competition because parents have limited choice about where to send their children to school. The results of these monopolistic school bureaucracies allegedly include a lack of accountability to parents and the community (and ultimately to students and teachers), unnecessary rules and red tape, inefficient use of human resources, and time constraints and odious mounds of paperwork for teachers. Like most bureaucracies, those in the schools are reactive and resistant to innovation and change and therefore viewed as recalcitrant enemies of reform.

A scholarly debate has been joined over the bureaucracy issue. Some research finds that large, centralized bureaucracies with restrictive rules and red tape tend to reduce school effectiveness.[10] Findings of other political scientists show no significant effects of bureaucracy and that school bureaucracies tend to grow larger when schools perform poorly because administrators take actions to improve performance. In other words, bureaucracy does not harm school performance; rather, it is a rational response intended to arrest decline and boost performance by developing and putting into place new policies, programs, and oversight.[11]

Before reviewing the responses of the national, state, and local governments to these critical problems in public education, we look at how the complex intergovernmental relationships in education have evolved.

# INTERGOVERNMENTAL ROLES IN EDUCATION

The responsibility of establishing, supporting, and overseeing public schools is reserved to the states under the Tenth Amendment and expressly provided for in the state constitutions. Day-to-day operating authority is delegated to local governments by all states except Hawaii, which has established a unitary, state-run system. Ninety percent of U.S. primary and secondary school systems are operated by independent school districts, but cities, counties, towns, or townships run the schools in some states. Although local control is the tradition, the states have always been the dominant policy makers, deciding important issues such as the duration of the school year, curriculum requirements, textbook selection, teacher certification and compensation, minimum graduation requirements, and pupil–teacher ratios. The selection and dismissal of teachers, certain budget decisions, and management and operating details are carried out locally.

State involvement has intensified, largely because of recognized inequalities among schools and school districts, the accountability demands of NCLB, and forceful actions by governors and legislatures to address the perceived education crisis. Centralization of state authority in education policy has been greatest in the South, where poverty and race relations have called for high levels of state intervention. Conversely, the tradition of local autonomy is strongest in New England. But in the final analysis, it is difficult to identify a single important school policy issue today that is not subject to state or federal, rather than local, determination.

More state and federal involvement in the public schools has occurred because some citizens and policy makers have lost confidence in the schools' ability to provide a quality education and because local school districts are hard-pressed to cope successfully with political and financial pressures. In several instances, local school systems have essentially lost their independence as the states and some municipalities have assumed full operational responsibilities—an especially likely outcome when the local school districts are unable to respond adequately to political and financial pressures. States and some cities have imposed the ultimate sanction on failing schools by assuming full operational responsibility or shutting them down entirely. Maryland recently seized state control over several low-performing Baltimore schools; mayors did the same in New York, Boston, Chicago, and Cleveland.

## The National Government Presence in Education

The federal government has traditionally played a minimal role in primary and secondary education, especially when compared with the governments of most other countries, where public education is treated as a national responsibility. The first grant of money for education came only in 1917, when the Smith–Hughes Act financed vocational education in secondary schools. Much later, the National Defense Education Act provided funds to improve math, science, and foreign-language education.

The national role was substantially enlarged during the 1960s and 1970s, primarily through the Elementary and Secondary Education Act (ESEA of 1965). The ESEA established a direct national subsidy for education, providing funds to almost every school district in the United States. Amounts were allocated for library acquisitions, audiovisual materials, teachers' aides, and compensatory programs for children of poor families and for the mentally and physically handicapped. Parochial (religious) schools also benefit from ESEA funding, although no funds are provided for religious materials courses or teacher salaries. With each reauthorization of ESEA, Congress has taken the opportunity to pile on all manner of mandates about how the money must be spent.

During the 1960s and 1970s, the federal government exercised policy leadership in education. The Head Start program helped prepare poor children for school and provided many of them with their first medical, dental, and nutritional care. Matching grants encouraged states and localities to experiment with other programs, and research findings, statistics, and new policy information were disseminated by the National Institute of Education and the National Center for Education Statistics. The national commitment to public schools received an important symbolic boost in 1979 with the creation of the U.S. Department of Education.

These new commitments brought the national share of total school expenditures from 4.4 percent in 1960 to 9 percent in 1980. The federal government's proportion of education expenditures today is about 9.2 percent. Under President Bill Clinton, Head Start—demonstrated to be successful in several evaluations—was reauthorized and expanded to Early Head Start: all-day, all-year programs for low-income, at-risk infants and toddlers. Meanwhile, the Goals 2000: Educate America Act placed into statute six national education goals; the Community and National Service Act established scholarships and tuition reimbursements for community service. New federal monies were also provided for school modernization and construction, to improve technological literacy of teachers and students, and to promote charter schools.

The most recent reauthorization of ESEA, NCLB of 2002, insinuated the federal government in the schools debate as the "national schoolmarm, hovering over state school reform efforts and whacking those states that fail to record satisfactory and timely progress toward federal education goals with financial penalties and mandatory corrective actions."[12] NCLB was viewed as particularly onerous in its testing and performance mandates. The law significantly increases federal financial support for the schools, but it also requires substantial new state and local education spending.[13]

Implementation of NCLB has not gone smoothly as intergovernmental conflict immediately erupted. Michigan, Texas, Vermont, and the NEA filed suit against the federal government in 2004 on the grounds that NCLB illegally imposed unfunded mandates on the states. Other states, including Connecticut and Utah, also litigated or threatened to refuse to comply with NCLB. Gradually, accommodations to state and local concerns were made by the U.S. Department of Education.

The state and school district issues with NCLB are many, including a deadline for all schools to bring 100 percent of students up to reading and math proficiency (one writer called this akin to setting a date by which police are to end all crime),[14] burdensome annual testing requirements, and a "one size fits all" accountability system that undermines effective systems already in place in some states. A particularly vexing NCLB glitch is that schools can elevate overall student performance but if a single category of students, such as special needs children or non-native English speakers, struggles, the school can be declared to be impaired or "in need of improvement," meaning that students are eligible to transfer to a different, high-performing school. When schools and districts fail to meet their goals for a certain period of time, the U.S. Department of Education can declare them "failed," leading to closure or a state takeover. In early 2009, 6,000 schools had been officially declared to be failing or "needing improvement." NCLB was up for reauthorization by Congress in 2007 but state and local objections pushed Congress into a deadlock that still existed in late 2009.

Without question, the requirements of NCLB have caused an education regime change and interjected a loud federal voice in the education debate. No matter how strenuously state and local school districts may object, the federal role in public education is now that of policy leader. For the foreseeable future, federal education assistance will flow based on demonstrated improvements in teacher quality, academic standards, and performance, with testing as the principal means of data collection. The Obama administration's intentions were made clear in 2009 when $100 billion in federal stimulus money was earmarked for education. Strings attached included state assurances that they would make progress in collecting and using performance data, improving standards and assessment, supporting struggling schools, and attaining equity in the distribution of qualified teachers.[15]

**The Political and Financial Pressures on Public Schools** Political pressures constantly roil the waters of public education as teacher organizations, minority groups, and parents make new and controversial demands on their schools. Teachers and their unions want more control over what goes on in the classroom. Minority groups are concerned with inequities and poor performance of heavily minority schools. Bilingual education is an issue in states with large Hispanic or other non-English-language populations. And religious groups fight to keep prayer, abstinence education, anti-drug programs such as DARE, and "intelligent design" in the classroom and Charles Darwin and secular values out. None of this pressure has changed. If local school boards wilt under the crescendo of demands, then teachers, minority groups, parents, and other parties interested in education policy take their demands to higher political levels—the governor, the state legislature, the courts, and the state board of education, none of which may be in agreement on what to do about any given issue. In this way, school politics, once the province of local school boards and professional educators, has evolved into highly contentious interest group politics.

**Financial Pressures** Increased financial pressures on the schools are a second factor producing education policy centralization. Historically, schools have been funded mostly through revenues derived from the property tax. A school district can assess taxes only on property within its local boundaries, so wealthy districts with much highly valued residential and/or commercial property can afford to finance public schools at generous levels, whereas poor districts (even though they often tax their property at much higher rates than wealthy districts) tend to raise fewer dollars because of their lower property values. The consequence of such financial inequities is that some children receive a more expensive, and probably higher-quality, education than other children do, even though the parents of the advantaged group of children may contribute fewer tax dollars. Frequently, it is the children of the poor and minorities who fare the worst.

The states' assumption of primary financial responsibility for public schools has an important constitutional component. In the landmark case of *Serrano v. Priest* (1971), the California Supreme Court declared that inequalities in school-district spending resulting from variations in taxable wealth were unconstitutional. The court observed that local control is a "cruel illusion"; poor districts simply cannot achieve excellence in education because of a low tax base, no matter at how high a rate property is taxed.[16] Therefore, education must be considered a fundamental interest of the state; in other words, the state must ensure that expenditures on education are not determined primarily by the taxable wealth of the school district.

Following *Serrano*, lawsuits were filed in other states by plaintiffs who sought to have their own property tax–based systems declared unconstitutional. One of these cases, *San Antonio Independent School District v. Rodriguez* (1973), made its way to the U.S. Supreme Court. A federal district court had found the Texas school finance system to be unconstitutional under the equal protection clause of the Fourteenth Amendment. However, the Supreme Court reversed the lower court, holding in a landmark decision that education is not a fundamental right under the U.S. Constitution (in which it is not even mentioned).[17] The issue was thus placed exclusively in the constitutional domain of the states, which would have to rely on their own constitutions—and courts—to prevent arbitrary circumstances from predetermining the quality of a child's education.

All but a handful of state supreme courts have heard cases on educational financing; litigation is ongoing in approximately half the state courts. At least twenty-seven states have determined that existing funding schemes were unconstitutional because they did not provide an adequate education for all children or give them reasonable opportunity to attain state education goals, and have ordered equal funding for poor districts Alaska, Nebraska, Massachusetts, and Montana have been recently involved in such litigation.[18] A study of these cases found that courts declaring intergovernmental roles in unconstitutional spending disparities and ordering greater revenue equity tend to have more liberal justices than courts that uphold school-finance systems and that these courts are most likely to be situated in states with a politically liberal populace. Thus, politics matters in explaining school-funding equity in the states.[19]

All states have made efforts to equalize funding among school districts, usually by applying distribution formulas (the equalization formulas noted in Chapter 11) for state aid that take into account property values and property-tax effort in individual districts. Most increased state financing has been targeted to districts with low property values through **foundation programs**, which ensure all school districts receive a minimum level of funding per pupil. State education allocations also take into account the characteristics of students. For instance, a 2009 New Jersey formula distributes state aid based on enrollment, with additional funds designated for districts with high concentrations of students who are poor, have special needs, or have limited English-language abilities.[20] The tendency over time is for states to "level up" so that aid to poor districts does not come at the expense of more affluent districts.[21]

Figure 15.3 displays the increasing state revenue contributions for public schools over time. Note that the federal portion, averaging only about 9.0 percent since 1970, increased a bit to around 9.2 percent as a result of NCLB.

**foundation program**

A means of state education funding that allocates a basic level of funding to all districts.

Trends in Revenue Sources for Public Elementary and Secondary Education, 1920–2007. Elementary and secondary education receives the greatest portion of revenues from state government. The national contribution is just over 9 percent.

FIGURE
15.3

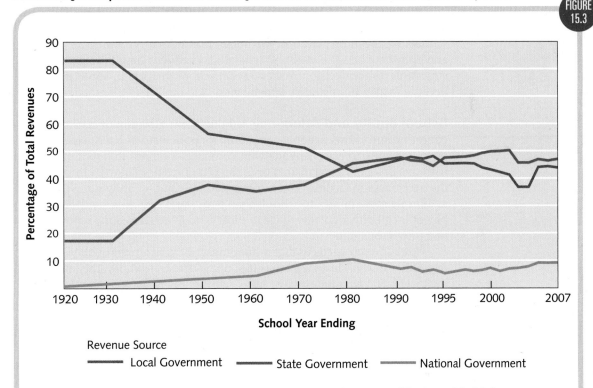

Revenue Source

———— Local Government ———— State Government ———— National Government

SOURCE: U.S. Department of Education, Center for Statistics, *Digest of Education Statistics, 2008* (Washington, D.C.: U.S. Government Printing Office, 2008).

**The Impact of Property-Tax Cuts** Additional impetus to the state assumption of school costs was provided by Proposition 13 in California and by similar state legacies of the taxpayer revolt. Statutory and constitutional limitations on taxing were typically aimed at the increasingly unpopular property tax. If public schools were to avoid such draconian measures as closing their doors in an effort to adjust to revenue shortfalls, the states had to increase their education contributions.

One state, Michigan, completely tossed away its property tax–based school-financing system. Prompted by numerous voter defeats of proposed property-tax increases to fund public schools and the actual closure of one school system (in Kalaska), the Michigan legislature repealed all property taxes supporting the public schools. The legislature then gave voters a choice: increase the state sales tax from 4 to 6 percent and triple the cigarette tax, or raise the state income tax.[22] In a statewide constitutional referendum, voters picked the first option. Vermont replaced its school-funding system, which relied on local government for 70 percent of funding, with a statewide property tax that made the state's share more than 70 percent.

An important principle of education policy today is that state centralization and control follow financial responsibility. A long tradition of local control of schools has been displaced in Michigan, Minnesota, New Mexico, Vermont, and elsewhere because state and federal governments have become the prime education policy decision makers. Local school districts in some states have become weak administrative appendages.

**School Equity and Adequacy** Although centralization of state control of education and efforts to equalize funding for poor districts have helped,[23] inequities continue to exist. Anyone who compares a school in a wealthy suburb with one in a poor rural district or urban center cannot fail to be impressed by the differences in facilities and resources. Simply put, wealthy states can afford to allocate more money to schools than poor states can. This invidious geography of inequality is an advantage to those who live in a wealthy school district in a prosperous state.[24]

Common sense tells us that money must be related to the quality of schooling. Modern, well-designed buildings, up-to-date technology, the latest learning materials, low pupil–teacher ratios, and well-paid teachers should enhance student achievement, as should a rich offering of honors and advanced placement (AP) courses. But research has revealed an astonishing paradox: There is no consistent, significant statistical relationship between school resources and student performance. Table 15.2 lists average state expenditures per pupil and teacher salaries along with performance of high school students on college admission tests.

The first research to reach this conclusion was the so-called Coleman Report in 1966.[25] Sociologist James S. Coleman examined thousands of school situations and discovered that curricula, facilities, class size, expenditures, and other resource factors were not associated with achievement. He *did* find that the family and socioeconomic backgrounds of students influenced performance, with children of well-off, well-educated parents outperforming those brought up in less-advantageous surroundings, a finding supported in more recent research.[26] Also, black students performed better in predominantly white schools than in predominantly black schools—a finding that later served as the grounds for implementing busing to put an end to school segregation. Coleman's staggering conclusions were re-examined in an extensive review of 120 studies; only eighteen found a statistically significant positive relationship between school expenditures and student performance. The overall conclusion is that no strong or systematic relationship exists between them.[27] However, the research consistently finds that minority students perform at lower levels than white students,[28] and the black–white performance gap worsens with grade level.[29]

The racial achievement gap is a stubborn and troubling issue. It is complicated, for example, by the fact that the achievement gap for African Americans who are early high achievers grows faster across the grades than it does for initially low-performing children.[30] And overall, the racial achievement gap expands as all

| | | | TABLE 15.2 |
|---|---|---|---|
| **Average Teacher Salaries and Expenditures per Pupil, and Composite SAT/ACT Scores 2008** | | | |

| SALARY RANK | STATE | AVERAGE SALARY ($) | EXPENDITURE PER PUPIL ($) | EXPENDITURE RANK | COMPOSITE SAT/ACT SCORES |
|---|---|---|---|---|---|
| 1 | Connecticut | 58,688 | 11,893 | 4 | 275 |
| 2 | District of Columbia | 58,456 | 15,073 | 1 | 244 |
| 3 | California | 57,876 | 7,815 | 32 | 261 |
| 4 | Michigan | 56,973 | 8,909 | 20 | 269 |
| 5 | New Jersey | 56,682 | 13,370 | 2 | 279 |
| 6 | New York | 56,200 | 12,879 | 3 | 272 |
| 7 | Illinois | 55,629 | 9,591 | 16 | 272 |
| 8 | Massachusetts | 54,325 | 11,681 | 5 | 286 |
| 9 | Rhode Island | 53,473 | 10,641 | 9 | 267 |
| 10 | Pennsylvania | 53,258 | 9,638 | 14 | 277 |
| 11 | Alaska | 52,424 | 10,042 | 11 | 271 |
| 12 | Maryland | 52,331 | 9,762 | 12 | 275 |
| 13 | Delaware | 50,869 | 11,016 | 7 | 274 |
| 14 | Ohio | 48,692 | 9,557 | 17 | 276 |
| 15 | Oregon | 48,330 | 7,842 | 31 | 275 |
| 16 | Minnesota | 46,906 | 9,249 | 19 | 280 |
| 17 | Indiana | 46,591 | 8,723 | 21 | 275 |
| 18 | Georgia | 46,526 | 8,451 | 24 | 267 |
| 19 | Hawaii | 46,149 | 8,622 | 22 | 260 |
| 20 | Washington | 45,724 | 7,858 | 30 | 275 |
| 21 | Virginia | 44,763 | 8,577 | 23 | 277 |
| 22 | Vermont | 44,535 | 11,608 | 6 | 282 |
| 23 | Wisconsin | 44,299 | 9,619 | 15 | 275 |
| 24 | Colorado | 43,949 | 8,337 | 25 | 276 |
| 25 | New Hampshire | 43,941 | 9,642 | 13 | 279 |
| 26 | Nevada | 43,394 | 6,525 | 46 | 262 |
| 27 | North Carolina | 43,348 | 7,350 | 39 | 272 |
| 28 | Arizona | 42,905 | 5,474 | 50 | 265 |
| 29 | South Carolina | 42,207 | 8,161 | 27 | 269 |
| 30 | Idaho | 42,122 | 6,743 | 45 | 274 |
| 31 | Tennessee | 42,072 | 6,856 | 44 | 267 |
| 32 | Florida | 41,587 | 7,035 | 41 | 269 |
| 33 | Texas | 41,009 | 7,142 | 40 | 273 |

(Continued)

| TABLE 15.2 | Average Teacher Salaries and Expenditures per Pupil, and Composite SAT/ACT Scores 2008 (Continued) | | | |
|---|---|---|---|---|
| SALARY RANK | STATE | AVERAGE SALARY ($) | EXPENDITURE PER PUPIL ($) | EXPENDITURE RANK | COMPOSITE SAT/ACT SCORES |
| 34 | Kentucky | 40,522 | 7,906 | 29 | 270 |
| 35 | Arkansas | 40,495 | 6,202 | 49 | 266 |
| 36 | Wyoming | 40,392 | 10,198 | 10 | 277 |
| 37 | Utah | 39,965 | 5,245 | 51 | 272 |
| 38 | Maine | 39,610 | 10,723 | 8 | 278 |
| 39 | Nebraska | 39,456 | 7,608 | 34 | 275 |
| 40 | New Mexico | 39,391 | 8,236 | 26 | 259 |
| 41 | Iowa | 39,284 | 7,477 | 37 | 276 |
| 42 | Kansas | 39,175 | 7,558 | 36 | 279 |
| 43 | Missouri | 38,971 | 7,451 | 38 | 272 |
| 44 | Louisiana | 38,880 | 7,589 | 35 | 263 |
| 45 | Montana | 38,485 | 8,025 | 28 | 279 |
| 46 | West Virginia | 38,360 | 9,448 | 18 | 263 |
| 47 | Alabama | 38,186 | 6,886 | 43 | 259 |
| 48 | Oklahoma | 37,879 | 6,269 | 48 | 267 |
| 49 | Mississippi | 36,590 | 6,452 | 47 | 257 |
| 50 | North Dakota | 36,449 | 7,033 | 42 | 280 |
| 51 | South Dakota | 34,040 | 7,618 | 33 | 279 |
| | U.S. average | 47,808 | 8,618 | | 271 |

SOURCE: Data from the National Education Association, *Rankings and Estimates: Update,* www.nea.org (Fall 2009).

African American students move through the grade levels. These racial disparities, which also exist between Latino and white students, are as resistant to a cure as the common cold. Desegregation of the schools has not been the answer, and a recent U.S. Supreme Court decision, along with persistent segregated housing patterns, dilutes school diversity efforts.[31] Money has not helped, either.[32] But some important research findings have recently been reported that could help narrow the achievement gap. For example, it appears that the achievement gap might widen because of more extensive summer learning opportunities for white children than for children of color.[33] Another intriguing finding is that some high-achieving African American students experience negative peer pressure for "acting white."[34]

Thus, equity in school financing and boosting school spending do not necessarily generate superior student performance. Controlling for the effects of inflation, total spending on K-12 education has grown significantly over the past two decades, yet measurable quality improvements have been only marginal, as shown by SAT scores and other tests and indicators. Obviously, money, however necessary, is not the only answer. Neither is financial equity.

**Relationship Between Student Performance and School Spending, by State**

FIGURE
15.4

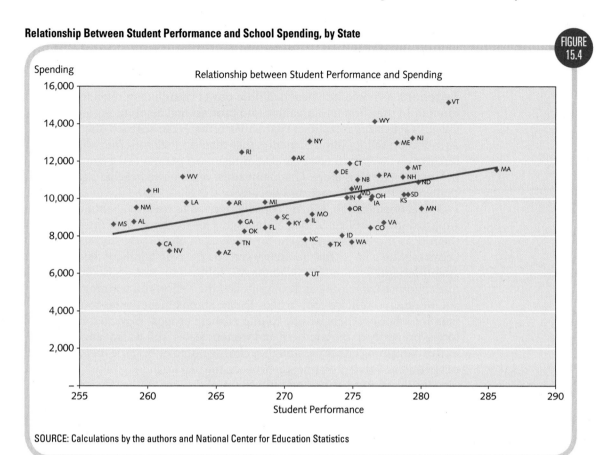

SOURCE: Calculations by the authors and National Center for Education Statistics

# THE EDUCATION POLICY ACTORS

The proliferation of independent school districts in the latter part of the nine-teenth century was accompanied by intensive politicization. School districts in both big cities and rural areas alike were as likely to hire teachers and principals on the basis of patronage as on the basis of professional competence. Reformers (mostly professional educators) struggled to remove partisan politics from the public schools by electing school boards on a nonpartisan, at-large basis, and by giving the professionals the primary responsibility for running school systems. These efforts were successful, but a new type of politics arose as teachers, school administrators, and state-level education actors began to dominate policy decisions as the "education establishment."

## The Education Establishment

In the past, the members of the education establishment, popularly referred to as the education bureaucracy, tried to dominate school policy making by resolving issues among themselves and then presenting a united front before legislative bodies and the governor. They constituted a powerful political coalition that managed to win substantial financial commitments to the schools. Because of the political pressures already mentioned, however, the education establishment is fractured today.

**Teachers** As noted, teachers had little power or influence outside the classroom until they began to organize into professional associations and unions. Once, teacher organizations, particularly the NEA, focused their primary attention on school improvement rather than on the economic well-being of teachers themselves. Teachers and administrators maintained a common front before the state legislature. Gradually, however, a newer teacher organization challenged the dominance and docility of the NEA, especially in large cities. This rival organization, the AFT, openly referred to itself as a labor union and struggled to win collective bargaining rights for teachers. With the election of the AFT as the bargaining agent for teachers in New York City, the teachers began carving a home for themselves outside the cozy family of the education establishment. Both the NEA and the AFT lobbied for state legislation permitting collective bargaining and concentrated their efforts on winning better pay and working conditions for teachers. Today, approximately three-fourths of the nation's schoolteachers belong to one of these groups. However, many NEA locals, primarily in the southern and western states, still do not engage in collective bargaining either because they choose not to or because their state does not permit it. This key distinction between the two teachers' groups, along with organizational turf battles and philosophical differences, has prevented them from merging, although it has been seriously considered on many occasions.

Teacher militancy accompanied unionization. Strikes and other job actions disrupted many local school districts as teachers battled for higher pay, fewer nonteaching duties, and other demands. The explosion of teacher's unions forever fragmented the education lobby in most states as teachers sought to look out primarily for their own interests rather than the interests of school administrators. Teachers remain the most powerful of education interest groups at the state level, although they regularly draw fire from citizens and other education stakeholders.[35] (Former U.S. secretary of education Rod Paige famously referred to the NEA as a "terrorist organization" in 2004) Each year, the opening day of school must be delayed in some districts because teachers go out on strike over critical concerns such as pay and benefits, working conditions, and education quality issues.

**Local School Boards** Another member of the education establishment, the local school board, is a legislative body responsible for governing and administering public education at the local level. About 14,000 of these local bodies exist. Local school boards are made up of laypeople, not representatives of the professional education community. Board members are elected by voters in independent school districts in most states, although some or all of them are appointed by local legislative delegations in several southern states and by the governor or, in a few large cities, the mayor.

The original American ideal of local control of public schools lodged its faith in local school boards, which were being popularly elected and were therefore responsive to citizens' opinions and points of view. In fact, their true authority has never equaled the myth of local control. The status and influence of local boards have diminished in recent years, except perhaps for those boards that have the authority to adjust property tax rates. Some school boards have contracted with private entities to run their schools. Others, rife with patronage practices and scandals, have been pushed aside and effectively replaced by city governments (e.g., Boston, Chicago, New York City, Philadelphia).[36] One critic recently called local school boards "the worst kind of anachronism.... ripe for corruption, as a springboard for aspiring politicians, and a venue for disgruntled former school employees to air their dirty laundry."[37]

School boards still commonly do financial planning and oversight, and as noted above, some set school taxes on property in the district. They also hire district superintendents of education and school administrators, approve teacher appointments, determine building and facility needs, and debate program needs. In fact, some local boards are criticized for trying to micromanage the daily minutiae of school operations instead of properly focusing on broad policy issues. Policy issues, however, are increasingly settled by state and federal standards and regulations, collective bargaining contracts, and court decisions.

Many local school boards suffer from yawning public apathy, extremely low turnouts for board elections, and widespread ignorance of what such boards are supposed to be doing. About the only events that focus citizen attention on local boards are the occasional bond or tax referendum that proposes to raise property taxes in the school district (and research indicates that school board financial decisions do reflect public opinion in the district),[38] especially in vitriolic debates over conflicting goals and values such as school redistricting, funding equity, sex education, and the respective place of Darwinian evolution and the Bible in the classroom.

**Other Policy Actors** Also known as the state education agency, the state board of education (SBE) exercises general supervision over all primary and secondary schools. The SBE members are appointed by the governor or legislature in thirty-two states, elected in thirteen, or selected through some combination of processes.[39] Like local boards, state boards sometimes become consumed by values debates. The Texas and Kansas state boards of education have been arguing for years about the proper roles of science and creationism in the classroom and in school texts.

Most SBEs make policy and budget recommendations to the governor and legislature. With few exceptions, however, they are not significant policy actors. They tend to lack political clout, policy expertise, and public visibility. Like local school boards, state boards of education defer to the authority and expertise of another policy actor—in this case, the chief state school officer (CSSO. This CSSO, known as the state superintendent of schools or the commissioner of education in some states, establishes and enforces standards and accountability for local school curricula, teacher certification, standardized student testing, and certain other matters and provides technical and other assistance to the schools. She may be appointed by the SBE, popularly elected on a statewide ballot, or appointed by the governor. Although the formal relationship between the CSSO and the SBE varies, nearly all CSSOs serve as executive officers and professional advisers to their state boards of education. As governors and state legislatures have increasingly provided policy leadership for the schools, the influence of CSSOs has declined.

An interesting North Carolina example illustrates some of the confusion over who should run the state school system. In the Tar Heel State, the superintendent of public instruction is elected on a statewide ballot. Superintendent June Atkinson had been administering the public schools since her election in 2004 and reasonably assumed that she would continue to do so after her reelection in 2008. But Governor Beverly Perdue appointed her own person to run the Department of Public Instruction and to chair SBE meetings. Atkinson filed suit and won in superior court; Perdue's appointee resigned.[40]

Yet another administrative creature, the state department of education, is responsible for rulemaking and for furnishing administrative and technical support to the CSSO and the SBE. It also administers national and state-aid programs for public schools. The state department of education is almost exclusively the habitat of education professionals. State departments have grown in size, competency, and power. They have taken on the difficult job of monitoring state education reforms, and they have significantly increased their capacities for research, program evaluation, performance measurement, and testing.

## The State Education Policy Leaders

Financial and political pressures on the education establishment, coinciding with a loss of public and business confidence in the schools, have fragmented the coalition of actors described above. Simultaneously, state-level education actors and community and business organizations have increased their interest in school issues and their capacity to respond to them, and governors and legislatures have added staff and augmented their ability to collect data and conduct research. The strengthened state departments of education are now handmaidens of the governors and legislatures. Education policy making today orbits around state and federal governments rather than local education professionals, although the demand for, and tradition of, local control remains important.

**Governors** The American people usually turn to their chief executives in times of crisis. Today, state chief executives are deeply involved in all major aspects of education policy making. Education issues often receive considerable attention during campaigns, in State of the State addresses, and throughout a governor's term of office. Occasionally, education clearly dominates governors' policy agendas. Education policy is the most important perennial issue in most states.

In formulating, lobbying for, and implementing education policy, the governors rely heavily on their staff. Many governors have special divisions of education. Staff members facilitate the flow of information to and from the governor's office and the desks of other key education policy makers. They analyze information from all levels of government, in and out of state, and from national organizations such as the National Governors' Association and the Education Commission of the States. They also draft proposed legislation, lobby legislators and education and business groups, and attempt to influence public opinion on education issues. The most successful governors have managed to weave delicate advocacy coalitions among all significant education policy actors to increase their chances of winning substantial reform programs.

**State Legislatures** Legislatures have always had the final responsibility for enacting broad education policy and for determining state funding of public schools. They were the leading state policy actors until governors upstaged them, but the critical policy battles are still fought on legislative turf.

Lobbyists for the education establishment are quite busy in the statehouse, but their influence has diminished because issue conflicts have precluded a united front. Numerous other interests, including business, minority groups, the disabled, community organizations, and the economically disadvantaged, also receive a hearing from legislators.

Although governors are the education policy leaders in most states, legislatures have expanded their capabilities. They have added their own education staff specialists, enhanced their research capabilities, and extended efforts to oversee the actions of governors and education agencies.

**Courts** Federal and state courts, especially the U.S. Supreme Court, are important factors in public education. They have issued rulings on several issues affecting students, such as censorship of school newspapers, personal dress and grooming standards, female participation in sports programs, student discipline, student drug testing, and school prayer. Federal courts imposed desegregation policies on public schools through a series of decisions beginning with *Brown v. Board of Education of Topeka* (1954), which declared that racial segregation violated the Fourteenth Amendment's equal protection clause.[41] Court-ordered busing to achieve school desegregation was mandated in *Swann v. Charlotte-Mecklenburg County Schools* (in North Carolina) in 1971 and in other decisions involving districts that had practiced government-approved racial segregation.[42] These decisions, and the subsequent busing, were highly controversial and contributed to white flight to the suburbs in many places. In some cities, such as Boston, Massachusetts, court-ordered busing led to violent protests.

Racial segregation of the schools remains just as serious and intractable a problem as it was when *Brown* was decided. Clearly, busing has been a failure: Research confirms that more school segregation exists now than it did twenty years ago.[43] Racial and social disparities from housing segregation have created "islands of immunity" to school integration.[44] It appears that a tipping point is reached when nonwhite enrollment surpasses 25 percent, triggering white flight. Remaining behind are the children of poverty and color.[45] African

Americans in particular continue to live in segregated housing and attend segregated schools. But with the endorsement of a conservative majority of the U.S. Supreme Court, many school districts, including Charlotte–Mecklenburg and Boston, have dismantled desegregation plans in favor of combining neighborhood schools with various "choice" options such as charter and magnet schools.

State courts, too, have ordered changes in education policy. As we have noted, many state supreme courts have mandated school-finance reform to attain greater equity in the funding of public education. State courts increasingly are also asked to resolve various legal disagreements spawned by education reforms. Individuals and groups representing minority positions can often capture the attention of top policy makers only through the legal system.

**The Corporate Community** Of necessity, businesses have become involved in the public schools. Many high school graduates lack the basic skills and knowledge to succeed in the contemporary workplace. Consequently, some firms have developed their own training and education programs, often incorporating fundamental reading and writing skills.

To members of the education establishment, business leaders are partly to blame for the sad state of the schools. Some industries based primarily on low-wage labor and unsophisticated skills historically opposed education reform as an unnecessary expense. Firms are also criticized for negotiating local property-tax breaks that deprive school districts of much-needed revenues, then complaining about the poor quality of education in those very districts they are starving financially. Today, however, due to the changing nature of work, most corporate leaders are vocal proponents of education improvement at all levels, from preschool to college.

Corporate involvement encompasses a broad range of activities, from purchasing computers and supplies for local school and adopt-a-school programs to sponsoring opportunities in which students may concentrate on a specially designed curriculum in areas such as finance, tourism, or biotechnology, and then work in paid summer internships. Overall, the role of business varies from state to state, but in most locations its contribution is largely rhetorical and episodic. Commercialization of the classroom is a growing problem. Product advertisements, exclusive lunchroom franchises for soft-drink bottler and fast-food chains, and even advertising on school buses raise questions about the true interests of business in the schools.

**Private Schools** The widespread presence of private schools, most of them church sponsored, makes them influential policy leaders. They enroll approximately 11 percent of K-12 students nationwide. To their supporters, the superiority of private schools in providing quality education is taken on faith. Private schools do provide a superior education in some instances, but in others, private schools are inferior, or they are little more than "seg academies" used by parents to keep their children in predominantly white classrooms. Because private schools stand to reap substantial gains from voucher programs, they are strong supporters of this alternative to public schools.

# EDUCATIONAL INNOVATION IN THE STATES

In the time since *A Nation at Risk* called national attention to the acute need for educational reforms, the states have responded on a large scale. Hundreds of task forces have thoroughly studied school problems and issued recommendations for resolving them. Many of these recommendations have been enacted into law as innovative programs to improve the quality of public education. The federal NCLB incorporated many principles and innovations first adopted by the states.

State financial support for schools has risen dramatically—by more than 50 percent over a recent eight-year period.[46] A broad and powerful coalition of state and local elected officials, professional educators, community organizations, parents, and business interests has been important in the reform drive. Improvement in education is a nonpartisan issue; Democrats, Republicans, and Independents agree that the economic future of the United States depends on the quality of schooling.

The states have been busily innovating in the four critical areas of standards, students, teachers, and the education bureaucracy. Every state has recorded remarkable program achievements in at least one of these categories, and, in some instances prodded by NCLB, a majority have implemented reforms in all four. But incremental reforms have not been bold enough to reverse the strong tide of school mediocrity in many troubled settings, opening up a growing demand for more far-reaching restructuring of public education.

## Standards

Standards and levels of assessment have been raised in almost every state. Curriculum and graduation requirements have been strengthened, instructional time has been increased, steps have been taken to minimize overcrowding, and technology has been ushered into the classroom. Special programs have been developed to encourage gifted students.

Minimum competency testing for basic skills has been another widely adopted reform. All states now test students at several grade levels to monitor progress in the basics, and most require students to pass a competency test (or exit exam) before graduating from high school. All states require school "report cards" to hold schools accountable for student performance. Successful schools and their teachers may receive financial rewards. Low-performing schools may be overhauled, receive special assistance, or, if hopeless, even be taken over or closed. Yet many teachers, parents, and students openly wonder if, prodded by the federal government, schools have gone overboard with frequent—and often intrusive—testing, much of it required by NCLB. And evidence is emerging that at least fifteen states have actually lowered their testing standards to comply with NCLB requirements that all schools be proficient in math and reading.[47]

Year-round schooling is required for millions of students in public schools—a substantial increase during a relatively brief period of time.[48] Three-month summer breaks—the legacy of an agrarian economy in which children were needed to plant and bring in the crops—are being replaced with multi-tracking arrangements in which students and teachers are divided into several groups, or tracks. They attend classes for forty-five, sixty, or ninety days, and then go on break for a two- or three-week intersession. Although the research remains inconclusive, year-round schooling may improve learning by ensuring that children keep their mental sharpness and do not forget much of what they have learned over the summer. It also saves money by maximizing the use of school buildings and resources. Certain problems must be addressed by schools and parents, however. For example, it is difficult to schedule maintenance on buildings and equipment, and extended schooling can interfere with sports and other extracurricular activities and disrupt family vacations and day-care arrangements. A more effective—though unpopular—approach would be to increase the length of the school day or academic year to pack in more time for teaching and learning.

## Students

Of course, students are the intended beneficiaries of the improvements and strengthening of standards. In general, expectations for student academic performance and classroom behavior have been raised. However, based on SAT and ACT scores and results of the National Assessment of Educational Programs tests, there are only modest indications of improvement. Great disparities remain among states, suburban and urban districts, racial groups, and family-income categories.

One common-sense approach is to better prepare students to begin school in the first place. The federal Head Start program is one such program, and states are also helping to build first-graders' learning foundations through highly structured and innovative preschool programs. Kindergarten is one step removed from first grade and can be very helpful in preparing kids for school. But the trend is pre-kindergarten initiatives that can involve children as young as three years. Early childhood programs boost reading and math skills for entering kindergarteners by four to six months ahead of those who remain at home[49] and help to identify medical and social service needs. Importantly, they also involve parents in the learning process.[50]

Course requirements for students to graduate from high school have been raised in virtually all states since *A Nation at Risk* was published. Students are required to take more upper-level math and science courses and more foreign-language classes, and a larger proportion of students are enrolling in honors and AP courses than ever before.

The national education paradigm today is known as **outcomes-based or performance-based education**. National standards, such as a national curriculum and achievement test on the basics for all students, are said to enhance school accountability by helping to determine and test for levels of student knowledge, skills, and abilities, as well as curriculum and teacher development needs. Although almost everyone agrees that standards must be raised and many think that national testing is a good idea, moving beyond broad goals and relatively painless incremental changes is proving to be difficult. Negative reactions to the NCLB demonstrate that many Americans support national standards, but they distrust the national government and fear federal intrusion into the schools. However, outcomes-based education is here to stay. With federal government encouragement, mandates, and monetary incentives, every state is developing or revising curricula to emphasize what children should know and be able to do regarding key subjects and testing them on that knowledge.

Student classroom behavior has been a target of reformers in many states. Strict discipline codes are being enforced, as are stronger attendance policies. In especially difficult school settings, police officers, closed-circuit television monitors, metal detectors, and other devices help maintain order. Most of the states that have adopted more stringent discipline policies in the past few years have made it easier for teachers to remove troublemakers from the classroom. Many school districts are using zero-tolerance policies to expel violent students. As the Engaging feature on the question of allowing guns in schools illustrates, some jurisdictions have decided to legalize firearms for teachers and administrators. Other violence prevention programs teach conflict-resolution and anger-

management skills to reduce fighting and discourage gang membership. Some implement policies to reduce the incidence of bullying. Ironically, corporal punishment (paddling, usually) remains legal in twenty-one states and is still used (mostly in the Bible Belt states) to discipline unruly students.[51]

Student drug testing is an active issue in some districts. The U.S. Supreme Court has ruled that schools may perform drug tests on students participating in extracurricular activities. (Before that ruling, public-school students were presumed to be excluded from drug testing by the Fourteenth Amendment's

> **outcomes-based or performance-based education**
> A reform that strives to hold schools, teachers, and administrators accountable for student performance, primarily based on standardized test scores.

Bob Daemmrich/The Image Works

Elementary school children being screened by metal detectors.

protection against illegal search and seizure). Presumably, drug (urine) testing would identify trouble-prone students and send a discouraging message to those contemplating smoking weed or getting involved with more serious substances. Professional educators and health groups oppose drug testing, arguing that students engaging in extracurricular activities are less likely to use drugs, and that requiring screening as a condition of participation in sports, band, clubs, and other activities would deter students from participating. At a more fundamental legal level remains the matter of overcoming *state* constitutional provisions regarding privacy and illegal search and seizure. More court actions, this time at the state level, are developing. The Washington Supreme Court held in 2008 that random drug testing of students is not permitted by that state's constitution.

As a positive incentive to stay in school (and, therefore, stay out of prison and off public assistance), students who graduate from high school with a B or better average in Georgia, New York, California, and several other states are guaranteed state payment of full tuition at a state college or university, as long as they maintain a B average or better. Such scholarship programs have the added benefit of helping stem the brain drain of top students who attend college out of state and never move back. New York City, Atlanta, Baltimore, Chicago, and other cities are also paying kids for performance. Incentives for regular, punctual attendance are being offered in many locales, including guarantees of a job or admission to college to all graduating seniors with a minimum grade point average and having regular attendance. Some offer cash for high attendance or for passing AP exams.[52] Taking a punitive tack, North Carolina and other states revoke the driver's license of any high school student who drops out or fails to pass 70 percent of his or her courses. Naugatuck, Connecticut, fines truant students or their parents $25.00 a day. The goal, of course, is to keep in school some of the hundreds of thousands of students who drop out each year, at a huge cost in lost tax revenues and increased expenditures associated with welfare, unemployment, and crime.

### Teachers

Of the many factors influencing student learning, the quality of the teacher in the classroom usually makes the greatest difference. Teachers have been the beneficiaries (or victims, depending on one's standpoint) of the most extensive and far-reaching educational reforms. They welcome higher pay, improved fringe benefits, and more opportunities for professional improvement. Smaller class sizes are particularly desirable, giving teachers more time to interact with each student. Voters agreed with their teachers in Florida, having approved an initiative to cap class size at twenty-five in high school and at eighteen in grades K–3 by 2010. Class size has also been reduced by law in California, Nevada, and other states. Teachers have been much less pleased with paperwork and accountability requirements, performance appraisals, testing of teachers, and teacher merit-pay schemes.

The national average of teacher salaries has basically tracked increases in the cost of living over the past ten years. But variations among the states continue to be rather pronounced, in response to differences in local cost of living, labor market conditions, and other factors (see Table 15.2). In 2008, teachers in California earned an average salary of $64,424; those in South Dakota averaged only $36,674.

**Teacher Shortages** Because of retirements, attrition, and the spurt in public-school enrollment, critical shortages of qualified teachers, particularly for math and science courses, continue to exist in almost all states. Baby boomer retirements, which are expected to peak at 100,000 a year in 2010–2011, could result in the absence of half of America's classroom teachers in the next few years.[53] Projections of new classroom teacher needs indicate even worse problems to come. The states are experimenting with several strategies to relieve teacher shortfalls. Most are taking steps to entice former teachers and education majors who are working in other fields back into the classroom, and nearly all have relaxed or set up streamlined teacher certification requirements. One particularly promising pool of new teachers consists of people who have retired early from military service, business, or government. Such nontraditional recruiting not only helps alleviate the teacher-supply problem but has the added benefit of elevating the quality and diversity of the teaching pool. Material incentives other than competitive salaries can be helpful in attracting and retaining teachers. Many states offer special scholarships, signing bonuses, or loans to attract college students into the teaching profession.

Research finds that many education problems stem from the failure to recruit, train, and retain good teachers. Some schools serve as retirement homes for the inept. Some teachers' colleges do an inadequate job of preparing teachers for the classroom. Some schools require teachers to teach out of their field of expertise and training. And once in the classroom, many teachers, especially in urban and poor rural schools, soon lose their enthusiasm and confidence in their own abilities when faced with at-risk children.

States are taking steps to solve these and related problems. State education statutes and collective bargaining contracts are being modified to make it easier to dismiss teachers who should no longer be in the classroom. Teachers of at-risk students are receiving much-needed assistance. State teacher-licensing requirements are being tightened up to include longer classroom internships and mastery of material in the subject area they will teach. Gradually, schools are learning the importance of the mentoring of new teachers by experienced teachers. NCLB stipulates that all teachers in core student classrooms be "highly qualified." The exact meaning of this term remains vague, but states were required to demonstrate that all teachers hold subject matter competence in their courses.

Several states have experimented with merit-pay plans that seek to reward high-performing teachers with special pay increases. Career ladders, which promote outstanding teachers up several levels to higher job classifications, have also been tried. For various reasons—including budget cuts, teacher dissatisfaction with the plans, and fierce union opposition—these initiatives generally

**school choice**

A market-based approach to education improvement that permits parents and students to choose which school the child will attend. Examples include charter schools and voucher programs.

have not been successful. An alternative approach, used in California, New York, North Carolina, and elsewhere, is to award teachers school wide bonuses when their school's standardized test scores exceed goals set by the state.

## Bureaucracy and School Choice

A single, boilerplate plan does not exist for reducing or avoiding the education bureaucracy, but all strategies hold one factor in common: **school choice**. Its most essential elements include a market-based, decentralized approach that permits individual selection of the school that the child will attend, while providing tax dollars to accompany the student to the chosen school. The expectation is that, in the scramble to attract tuition dollars, heretofore fossilized schools will try new ideas, offer new or specialized curricula, and take other steps to reinvigorate public education. Schools unable or unwilling to adapt to and compete within the education marketplace would be forced to consolidate with more successful schools or close their doors altogether.

**magnet school**

A public school whose curriculum emphasizes a specialized area, such as performing arts or science, to attract students from different ethnic and income groups.

**Magnet Schools** A common school-choice program, found in nearly all large urban school districts, is the **magnet school**. A form of public school, the magnet school offers specialized curricula to attract students from various backgrounds who share a common interest in areas such as dance, theater, science and technology, or foreign languages. Successful magnet schools help attract affluent children to the inner city and poor children to the suburbs. Related to magnet schools are **open enrollment programs** that permit students either to select schools only inside the existing school district or to choose any public school in the state. Within-district choice keeps resources and tax dollars in the same local jurisdiction. Between-district enrollment allows children to attend a school in a different district, perhaps many miles away. Open enrollment plans are intended to increase educational opportunities for students regardless of race, ethnicity, or socioeconomic status.

**open enroll-ment program**

An option that permits students to attend a public school of their choice within a designated jurisdictional area. The intent is to increase educational options for all children.

Open enrollment is not without its problems, however. An important shortcoming is that white and middle-class children tend to "choose" to flee inner-city schools for those in suburban or rural areas. An example of this "creaming effect" is found in Iowa. Such an outcome has obvious implications for racial and social-class balance in the schools. School-choice proponents claim that children of poor parents can also transfer to more desirable schools in the suburbs, but without special assistance, many poor children cannot afford transportation to outlying districts. This problem has been at least partially eliminated in states that furnish or help pay transportation costs for poor children. However, students still face the additional hurdle of gaining admission to their school of choice, which might be fully enrolled.

**charter school**

An alternative public school established by contract with a sponsoring agency, organization, or school district.

**Charter Schools** Unlike open enrollment programs, which provide greater choice among existing schools, **charter schools** expand the total number of school possibilities for parents to choose from. Charter schools are independent entities operating within the public-school system under charters, or contracts, that specify operating procedures and performance indicators. The charters are negotiated between their organizers and a sponsoring organization. The sponsor may be a local school board, teachers, parents, or other entity.

Charter schools promise to deliver results in exchange for being unleashed from the bureaucratic chains of the education establishment. Flexibility and innovation are their strong suits. Most design their own curricula, hire and fire teachers, and generally run their own show. Some feature a back-to-basics curriculum; others target high school dropouts or math and science whizzes. In actuality, however, their degree of autonomy varies widely, depending on the state authorizing legislation. Using public (mostly state) tax dollars to compete with private and traditional public schools, charter schools are intended to improve responsiveness to parents and enhance the quality of education throughout the jurisdiction.

Charter school laws have been adopted in thirty-nine states. They are particularly popular in Arizona, California, and Florida. In 2009, some 4,600 charter schools were operating throughout the United States. The concept remains unproven, however, and teacher's unions and some school boards are skeptical of charter-reform efforts. Across the United States, a growing number of charter schools have been closed for various reasons, from poor performance to unsanitary health conditions. Reliable evaluative research is only now appearing on how well they measure up, and the results are not particularly favorable for charter schools.[54]

**Voucher Plans** In a system using a **voucher plan**, parents receive a certificate from the state or from their local school district that may be used to subsidize the tuition for a public, private, or religious school of their choice. The concept is quite similar to that of the G.I. bill and Pell grants for federal reimbursements to colleges and universities. Voucher legislation has been introduced in more than half the states, but as of 2009 they were operating only in Milwaukee, Wisconsin, Cleveland, Ohio, Washington, D.C., and Utah. Despite an early display of public enthusiasm for voucher programs, they have gone down to defeat in every state initiative and referendum vote, and are being phased out in the nation's capital. Support for using public money for private-school tuition is about 40 percent.[55] In addition to voter and legislative resistance, several state courts have proven to be less than friendly to voucher plans, having blocked them from operating in Arizona, Florida, Maine, Pennsylvania, and Vermont, among other states.

The *federal* constitutional legitimacy of spending public money on religious schools was established by the U.S. Supreme Court in 2002 in *Zelman v. Simmons-Harris et al.*, a decision heralded as the most important ruling on religion and the schools in forty years.[56] The Court's 5–4 majority concluded that Cleveland's plan offered "a genuine choice between religious and nonreligious schools," despite the enrollment of 96 percent of voucher recipients in religious schools.[57] Left undetermined is the constitutionality of such vouchers according to the *state* courts.

The Florida program, enacted by the legislature in 1999, offered opportunity scholarships to students in chronically low-performing schools, permitting

**voucher plan**
An arrangement in which the state or school district subsidizes tuition for students to enroll in a school of student/parent choice.

them to transfer to a better-performing public school or to any private school. The Florida voucher program was struck down as unconstitutional by the state supreme court in 2006, on the grounds that public money cannot be used to finance private schools.[58] The Arizona Court of Appeals issued a negative ruling using similar logic in 2008.

The largest and most-examined voucher experiment began in 1999 in Milwaukee. The Milwaukee school-choice program provides low-income parents with vouchers to send their children to private schools. It is used by about 18,000 low-income students, who receive about $6,501 each. The majority are enrolled in religious (mostly Catholic and Lutheran) schools.[59]

Evaluations of the Milwaukee program have become politicized by the highly controversial spending of public tax dollars for private schools. Separation of church and state became a volatile issue when the program was extended to religious schools. Unlike in Florida, the Wisconsin state supreme court permitted vouchers to be applied to parochial schools. The court's reasoning was that the voucher money was going to parents, not to schools.

Overall, it does appear that voucher programs have encouraged parents to participate more in their children's education and that parental satisfaction with schools has increased. And there is no shortage of voucher champions, chiefly among political conservatives and religious supporters.[60] But no one has yet determined that vouchers improve student achievement. In Milwaukee and Cleveland, the most thorough analyses to date indicate that school-choice students have not performed any better than similar nonchoice students.[61] Also undetermined is the effect of public spending for private schools on the quality of public schools. Will public schools improve so that they can compete with private schools, or will they become education hovels for the remaining poor children? Will vouchers truly benefit children of low-income families who, even with a voucher, still must come up with thousands of dollars annually to pay private-school tuition? Or will vouchers disproportionately help upper- and middle-income families? What will be the impact on racial and social-class segregation?

## Privatization

Perhaps the most radical restructuring plan of all involves turning over management and operation of the public schools to a private firm. Some fifty private firms manage public schools in twenty-five states. Edison Schools, Inc., operates for-profit schools in twenty-four states, including large contracts in Pennsylvania and Minnesota. One of the most interesting privatization experiments is in Philadelphia. Following a state takeover of Philadelphia's troubled school system in 2002, thirty-eight failing public schools were transferred to seven outside administrators, including Edison, Temple University, St. Joseph's University, and the University of Pennsylvania.[62] Results from the City of Brotherly Love were mixed. Six of the schools were retaken by the Philadelphia School District in 2008 because of poor performance, and several others were placed on notice that they faced the same fate unless improvements were made.[63]

Noteworthy failures in school privatization have also occurred in Hartford, Connecticut, and Dallas, Texas, because of high financial costs and disappointing student performance. In an analysis by the U.S. General Accounting Office, comparing student test scores in public schools with privately run schools in six cities, results again were mixed. Students in traditional schools did better on standardized reading and science tests in Cleveland and St. Paul, but did worse than test takers in privately managed schools in Denver and San Francisco.[64]

## Homeschooling

In addition to the large number of children enrolled in private schools (approximately 10 percent of the student population), it is estimated that up to 3 percent of school-age children are taught at home by their parents.[65] Many homeschoolers are from religious families uncomfortable with the public school's environment, performance, or secular values. The homeschool curriculum, testing, and other factors are regulated by most states. Some states accommodate homeschooling by permitting selected public-school activities. For instance, Idaho public schools must allow homeschooled children to participate in any school activity, including sports. Studies of homeschooled children generally show positive results, with stay-at-home kids outperforming their public-school counterparts on standardized achievement tests.[66]

## Virtual Schools

Computer technology makes it possible for high school students to learn at home from long-distance teachers. California's Choice 2000 program enrolls middle school and high school students in a twenty-four-hour distance education program. The Florida Virtual School serves more than 63,000 students across the state through Internet-based instruction.

The virtual school could be particularly appropriate for rural states with great distances between schools, such as Alaska and Wyoming. During the swine flu epidemic of 2009, virtual education was one means to ensure that teaching and learning continued while kids were isolated at home to avoid spreading the virus. It has also attracted attention from charter schools. Issues with virtual schooling include test security, student performance assessment, parental involvement, and the potentially negative effects of education without interpersonal interaction.

## The Report Card on School Choice

Will the school-choice movement save the public schools or destroy them? Is the most salient issue the quality of education, or is it a desire for racial homogeneity and religious instruction?[67] Are parents truly capable and do they have sufficient information to make the best educational choices for their children?[68] Arguments are proffered from both perspectives. So far, relatively small numbers of students participate in school-choice programs. As a result, the data are insufficient, precluding comprehensive assessment of student performance or possible unintended consequences of school-choice programs.

One thing is certain: School choice is highly controversial and, except for the charter- and magnet-school options, is perceived as a threat by almost the entire education establishment, especially teachers and school board members, who fear losing funding from reduced enrollment and being saddled with the most difficult, at-risk children. When school-choice proposals involve parochial schools, they are especially controversial. The U.S. Supreme Court ruling notwithstanding, constitutional issues concerning the separation of church and state are now taken to state courts.

## THE CONTINUING CHALLENGES OF PUBLIC EDUCATION

The states are serious about excellence in education, and they are providing national direction and leadership. The vitality, innovation, and capability of the states are prominent in education policy.

But we should not be overly generous in our praise. A wide gap separates policy goals and enactment from policy implementation. More time must pass before we can accurately gauge the consequences of new state initiatives and the federal NCLB. It will take a tremendous act of political will and much hard work to bring to fruition the state and national educational improvement goals.

The continuing problems in public education are manifold and daunting, and reform is extremely complex and elusive. For example, most experts agree that school resources are best expended in the classroom, yet mandates and other legal requirements force administrators and teachers to complete hundreds of reports and other paperwork each year. As education reform seemingly plods along, many frustrated parents opt for alternative arrangements. The number of private schools and the number of children instructed at home have grown significantly. Meanwhile, during this prolonged crisis of legitimacy for the public schools, many thorny dilemmas persist. Students and teachers must learn how to utilize information technology productively, billions must be invested in much-needed building repairs and new construction, and the special problems of at-risk children must be addressed more effectively.

Putting state education reforms into practice requires the cooperation of many fragmented interests, including teachers, school administrators, superintendents, students, parents, and levels of government, each with their own interests and turf to defend. Triumph over this fractured policy subsystem will come only through civic action that mobilizes a vast array of public, private, and nonprofit actors and interests into a united front committed to reform over the long term—decades or more.[69] The unfinished portrait for educational excellence has been framed by governors, legislatures, the state education community, and the national government. The local schools must now fill in the details. And the states must encourage innovation and creative thinking at the local level while maintaining standards and accountability.

The national government has an important and legitimate role. State and local reform efforts are hobbled by childhood poverty, single-parent families, and other social problems that the national government can help address. And by funding and disseminating the results of research and experimental projects, the national government can elevate capacity and stimulate state and local innovation by state and local school districts. So far NCLB, though its premises are laudable, has been perceived as unduly intrusive and costly. It certainly provides no final answer to the persistent problems of public education. If the incremental education reforms fail to move us toward these objectives, radical rethinking and restructuring of American public education may well be needed.

## CHAPTER RECAP

- Education is the single most important—and most costly—function in state and local governments.

- The public perceives a crisis in the public schools; criticism involves standards, student performance, teachers, and the education bureaucracy.

- The activities of state and local actors and the education establishment largely determine policy development and outcomes.

- Despite much political rhetoric in the past, the role of the national government in education policy has become more important with No Child Left Behind.

- The education establishment has fragmented, and the new key policy actors are governors, legislatures, courts, private

schools, the business community, and the national government.

- A wave of education innovations in the states has raised standards, attempted to improve student retention and performance, hiked teacher salaries and benefits, and attempted to address a critical shortage of classroom teachers.

- The most controversial innovations have involved various school-choice programs, including magnet and charter schools and vouchers.

- The problems of reforming public education are multifaceted and complex, requiring the continual attention of government at all levels.

## Key Terms

foundation program *(p. 418)*
outcomes-based or performance-based education *(p. 431)*
school choice *(p. 434)*

magnet school *(p. 434)*
open enrollment program *(p. 434)*

charter school *(p. 434)*
voucher plan *(p. 435)*

## Internet Resources

For the National Report Card on state school systems, see **www.edweek.org**. This site, which may require payment for access, can also be used to find informative articles on school reform. School finance data are available from the National Center for Education Statistics at **www.nces.ed.gov** and on the U.S. Department of Education's website at **www.ed.gov**.

State education agencies may be explored at **www.ccsso.org**, home for the Council of Chief State School Officers.

One of the best places to go for education policy information and trends is the website of the Education Commission of the States at **www.ecs.org**.

Teacher salary data and education policy analysis may be found on the American Federation of Teachers' website at **www.aft.org** and at **www.nea.org**, the website of the National Education Association.

Check out the Governance and Finance Institute website for information on policy research, including charter schools, at **www.ed.gov/offices/OERI/GFI/index.html**.

# Criminal Justice

If you watched the local television news lately, odds are that the lead story was about a murder, rape, or other violent crime. The lead headline in your local newspaper today might well be on the same sort of subject. Crime shows abound on TV: COPS, NYPD, CSI, and many other such programs, along with courtroom dramas, cover the entire spectrum of law enforcement from commission of a felony to sentencing and incarceration. TV and print media, understandably, present us with the news that sells advertising. Perhaps less forgiveness should be granted to the politicians and candidates for office who exploit the fear of crime for their personal political gain. The result, however, is the same: the extent and danger of crime are highly exaggerated.

Just over twenty years ago, crime was seemingly out of control throughout the United States. As Figure 16.1 illustrates, however, a remarkable turnaround has occurred. The national violent crime rate has fallen to its lowest level in decades. Property crime has dropped nearly as dramatically. Why? The answers are complex and multifaceted, and sometimes contradictory. But states and local governments are responding creatively and forcefully to the crime challenge and making headway in the fight against crime. More police officers on the streets, more criminals behind bars, fewer guns in the hands of violent criminals, community policing programs, and improved technology are some of the effective items in the law enforcement toolkit, but there are other, unknown factors that may be pushing the crime rate down as well.

# 16

FIGURE 16.1

**Top 20 City Crime Rates, 2008**

| RANK | CITY | SCORE | RANK | CITY | SCORE |
|------|------|-------|------|------|-------|
| 1 | New Orleans, LA | 441.40 | 11 | Cleveland, OH | 255.80 |
| 2 | Camden, NJ | 381.84 | 12 | Baltimore, MD | 243.12 |
| 3 | Detroit, MI | 381.24 | 13 | Miami Gardens, FL | 239.51 |
| 4 | St. Louis, MO | 355.01 | 14 | Memphis, TN | 236.10 |
| 5 | Oakland, CA | 328.82 | 15 | Youngstown, OH | 234.56 |
| 6 | Flint, MI | 297.59 | 16 | Atlanta, GA | 230.58 |
| 7 | Gary, IN | 283.41 | 17 | Compton, CA | 229.22 |
| 8 | Birmingham, AL | 278.72 | 18 | Orlando, FL | 223.95 |
| 9 | Richmond, CA | 276.76 | 19 | Little Rock, AR | 219.20 |
| 10 | North Charleston, SC | 257.88 | 20 | Minneapolis, MN | 200.18 |

SOURCE: City Crime Rankings 2008–2009, http://os.cqpress.com/citycrime2008/citycrime2008.html.

## HOW MUCH CRIME IS THERE?

Crime data are available from two major sources: the Federal Bureau of Investigation's (FBI's) *Uniform Crime Reports* and victimization surveys. The FBI's annual crime index, drawn from state and local law enforcement agencies nationwide, covers four kinds of violent crime (assault, murder, rape, robbery) and four categories of property crime (arson, burglary, larceny, motor vehicle theft) (see Figure 16.1). It tracked a sharp increase in criminal behavior between 1960 and 1980, during which time the rate of violent crime tripled and that of property crime more than doubled. Since that time, the rates of both types of crime have dropped. It is a paradox that fear of crime persists even in the face of declining crime rates.

The FBI's statistics are suspect, however—for three reasons. First, they reflect only those crimes reported to local police departments. It is estimated that only 50–60 percent of total crimes committed are reported to the police. Second, some types of crime are more likely to be reported than others. Police have an incentive to underreport crime to make jurisdictions appear safer than they are. Murders, auto thefts, robberies, and aggravated assaults are usually reported, whereas larceny and rape victims, whether out of embarrassment, fear, or other reasons, may remain silent. Third, the FBI's crime data include only eight types of criminal behavior. Most white-collar crimes and drug crimes are excluded, despite their high numbers. Thus, the index provides only a partial picture of actual criminal activity.

Because of these disadvantages, a second, more accurate approach to measuring crime is used. *Victimization surveys* scientifically poll approximately

75,000 residents of jurisdictions in some 41,000 households across the country, asking them whether they or members of their households have been victims of crime during a specified recent time period. Long utilized by large metropolitan areas and some states, victimization surveys have been conducted on a nation-wide basis by the U.S. Bureau of the Census since 1973. Victimization statistics show identifiable patterns. Men are more likely to be crime victims than women are, blacks more than whites or Latinos, young people more than old, urban residents more than rural. According to the National Crime Survey, the true rate of crime is nearly two-and-one-half times greater than that reported by the *Uniform Crime Reports*. Yet even with this measure, the rates of nearly all types of crime have declined markedly.

Prediction is problematic because we do not really know what *causes* crime. We can state authoritatively, however, that it is associated with certain factors. From a broad perspective, criminal activity is normally associated with economic recessions, joblessness, and opportunity. Crime is most likely to be committed by young males, many of them from impoverished and/or broken families. Crime rates are higher in densely populated cities and states than in rural areas. Urban areas present more targets of opportunity, various sociocultural problems that promote criminal behavior, a better chance of escape for criminals, and a haven for gangs. Crime also appears to be related to poverty, unemployment, low levels of education, marital instability, drug abuse (particularly of crack cocaine and methamphetamines), and race.[1] A recipe for crime and incarceration is to take a male, unemployed, African American high school dropout from a low-income, unstable family background and place him within an urban setting. Approximately 60 percent of such individuals have served time by their mid-thirties.[2]

But crime is complex. Businesspeople are convicted of insider trading, fraud, kickbacks, Ponzi schemes, and other white-collar crimes that cost their victims millions of dollars. Some contractors rig bids on government construction projects and Pentagon defense contracts; some bankers embezzle money; some judges accept bribes; the occasional priest or minister sodomizes a child. The underlying causes of these and other sad cases cannot be attributed to economic deprivation, age, neighborhood, race, or the entertainment industry. Greed certainly contributes to many crimes, as does opportunity; the origins of others remain unknown.

Although reasonable people disagree about the causes of crime, most agree that law enforcement is not as effective as it should be in apprehending and deterring criminals. Fewer than 17 percent of all property crimes reported to the police are "cleared" by an arrest. For violent crimes, the record is better: approximately 44 percent.[3] Probably two-thirds of the arrests, however, do not result in a conviction or in any sort of punishment for the offender. Extrapolation from these somewhat rough estimates indicates that a criminal has only a slight chance—maybe one in a hundred—of being arrested and punished for a crime.

Throwing money at the problem does not seem to be the final answer; research has been unable to find a strong link between higher police expenditures on personnel and materials and a subsequent reduction in crime. Obviously, *how* the money is spent makes a difference. Most criminal activities cannot be prevented by law enforcement officials, and unreported crimes are very difficult to investigate. More prisons and longer sentences appear to have some effect on crime rates, as do gun control laws. Other factors that appear to be associated with higher arrest rates, and lower crime rates as well, are related to the attitude, tactical deployment, and tools of police officers. Aggressive and active police work in responding to calls from citizens and in investigating criminal events seems to help, as does the use of one-officer instead of two-officer patrol units for a more widespread police presence (Figure 16.1).

*Community policing* is the popular terminology for a hands-on law enforcement approach. Typically, officers are assigned specific territorial areas of responsibility and encouraged to use their imagination, experience, and personal touch in fighting crime. Police work directly with citizens and with relevant government and nonprofit organizations to identify problems and solve them creatively. If drug houses, junkies, and prostitutes infest a community, the citizens and community police officer find a way to run them out. Minor troublemakers are dealt with before they become big-time offenders. To be effective, officers must add community organizing and social work to their law enforcement duties to make their assigned neighborhood one in which they would themselves be willing to live.

Political scientist James Q. Wilson developed the concept underlying community policing in a 1982 article he wrote with George L. Kelling entitled "Broken Windows." In the authors' words, "If a window in a building is broken and is left unrepaired, all the rest of the windows will soon be broken."[4] The message of a broken window is that no one cares. Of course, the metaphor doesn't apply only to broken windows, but extends to all manifestations of neighborhood decay, including public consumption of alcohol and drugs, drug dealing, hookers on street corners, aggressive panhandlers, graffiti, and gang activity. Visual deterioration of a neighborhood leads to social degeneration. By preventing or correcting visible manifestations of neighborhood decline, or by "repairing" the "broken windows," neighborhoods will host fewer criminal activities, and positive forces can take root and flourish. Community policing and attention to "broken windows" appear to be at least partly responsible for the dramatic decline in violent crime in New York City, Boston, Fort Worth, and other large cities during the 1990s.

More controversial, but also believed to be effective, is "stop and frisk." The connection between guns and violence should be obvious, so one straightforward approach to reducing violent crime is to remove guns from the street. In New York City, Cleveland, Philadelphia, and other cities, officers are trained to profile individuals on the street for the likelihood of packing a weapon. Constantly hitching one's trousers, tightening one's belt, patting an inside pocket, wearing a heavy coat in warm weather are all indicators of a weapon. Hundreds of handguns have been seized in high-crime neighborhoods using stop and frisk tactics.[5] The tactic won approval by the U.S. Supreme Court,[6] but it is very controversial in African American neighborhoods and opposed by civil rights groups.

Innovative activity by police agencies is on the rise. Imaginative and surprisingly effective sting operations lead dimwitted fugitives to turn themselves in to

## Engaging Criminal Justice

## New Technology, New Approaches

While police still use common sense, hands-on community policing as described in the text, new advances in technology have given law enforcement new and increasingly imaginative approaches to locking up the bad guys.

San Diego's bait-and-switch-off operation nabs car thieves who try to steal specially equipped vehicles. Once the thief breaks into the vehicle, police are notified electronically. Via remote control, police officers can lock the doors, close the windows, and turn off the engine. Audio monitors have the added benefit of recording the criminal's sometimes humorous—and abundantly profane—verbal reactions to his plight.[7]

Technological applications for crime fighting are developing rapidly and show much promise. Computer-based fingerprint identification systems and other data-sharing systems track criminals across multiple jurisdictions. CSI-type labs perform forensic work to identify criminals and victims. Twenty states now require police to take DNA swabs of any individual charged with a felony. Computer mapping of crime hot spots and trends, as pioneered by New York City's COMPSTAT approach, facilitates police planning and response by linking crime statistics to geographic information systems. Commercial cell-phone translation services help police break through language barriers almost instantaneously.

Closed circuit TVs are deployed in Baltimore and other major cities to keep a 24–7 eye on crime-prone areas. Retired cops or officers assigned to light duty man them, notifying officers when something threatening or suspicious occurs. A senior citizen walking alone at night with youths clustered nearby bears watching, as does an apparent drug handoff or weapon display. The cameras produce a constant stream of police intelligence data and are believed to reduce crime rates.[8] In San Francisco, gunfire sensors have been installed around the city to

*SOURCE: Walter G Allgöwer/PhotoLibrary*

Security cameras oversee public areas in many U.S. cities

detect instances in which a firearm is discharged. Police can proceed immediately to the location to investigate.

Richmond, Virginia, criminal activity models track variables statistically correlated with crime. (For instance, a full moon is associated with a rise in crime, and Super Bowl Sundays is an unusually low-crime day.) Using such data as time of day, place, season, and previous crime patterns, police can anticipate new activity and assign officers appropriately.[9] The result? A "stunning drop in crime."[10] Similarly, Chicago's CLEAR system (Citizen and Law Enforcement Analysis and Reporting) uses GIS technology and software to map crime, cross-reference variables in a massive database on criminal activity and criminals, and predict when and where the next incident is likely to occur. A neighborhood crime alert may be issued if the situation calls for it. CLEAR is credited with significantly reducing property and violent crime in the Windy City.[11] To be effective, law enforcement must stay one step ahead of the bad guys. The examples above, as well as many other new approaches and technology, show that some cities are indeed one step ahead.

law enforcement officials. In Ohio, more than 100 fugitives showed up in person to collect a phony cash award from a class-action lawsuit, only to be handcuffed by waiting sheriffs' deputies. At New York's Rikers Island jail, fugitives who come to visit their buddies are commonly apprehended. As noted in the Engaging feature, the application of advanced technology to crime is also on the rise.

## INTERGOVERNMENTAL ROLES IN CRIMINAL JUSTICE

The problems with the U.S. system of criminal justice cannot be attributed to a lack of human and material resources. About 1.6 million employees work full-time in state and local police and corrections agencies. Total state and local expenditures are $168 billion.[12]

The states and localities hold jurisdiction over more than 95 percent of all crime that occurs in the United States. Municipal and county police and sheriff's departments carry much of the load of law enforcement, employing a large majority of all sworn police employees; the state law enforcement organizations (highway patrol and special agencies) employ many fewer.[13] These state and local entities enforce state laws and local ordinances. Federal crimes such as treason, kidnapping, and counterfeiting are dealt with by the FBI and processed through the federal courts and correctional system. The two systems are separate, but some cooperation occurs. For instance, the FBI and state law enforcement agencies exchange information such as fingerprints and details of the movements of fugitives, suspected terrorists, and drug smugglers; they also sometimes work together in criminal investigations, as they have in numerous drug busts and anti-terrorist activities.

Nine out of every ten dollars spent on police protection and corrections come from the coffers of state and local governments—an illustration of the decentralized nature of criminal justice spending in the United States. The national government's resources are concentrated on its own homeland security, enforcement, and corrections agencies. However, Washington provides certain forms of direct financial assistance to the states and localities.

Greater national involvement in state and local law enforcement appears necessary, given the rise in new types of cybercrime; the growing economic, political, and global dimensions of organized crime and drug trafficking; the ever-present threat of terrorist acts; and the fact that criminal activities do not respect national, state, or local jurisdictional boundaries. States and localities can only do so much to combat the poverty, poor housing, inadequate education, and other social and economic conditions that are conducive to crime.

## THE ONGOING CHALLENGE OF CRIME FIGHTING

As noted, the vast proportion of dollars spent on law enforcement comes from the coffers of states and localities. Congress and the president provide plenty of rhetoric but relatively little material assistance. In the majority of jurisdictions, crime is under control and citizens feel relatively safe. But many jurisdictions, particularly in urban poverty areas, are victims of demographics. High poverty rates, dysfunctional families, free-flowing illegal drug markets, and violent gangs are all factors invariably associated with high rates of crime. The hard-pressed police often find themselves simply trying to cope with the worst crimes. There may be scant opportunity for crime prevention activities, and law enforcement agencies acting alone lack the capability to improve socioeconomic and other conditions conducive to criminal activity. As for politicians, it is easy for them to talk "tough on crime" then to offer little extra financial assistance for fighting crime. For the cop on the street, tough and immediate judgment calls must often be made: arrest or mediate in a domestic dispute? Call for backup now or deal with the situation first? Does this berserk moron have a gun? Should I draw and fire now?

What about suspicious behavior in a vehicle? Black men driving through a wealthy white neighborhood raise suspicions, but does stopping them without cause amount to racial profiling for "driving while black"? Such profiling of African Americans and Latinos has been well documented anecdotally and in several empirical studies,[14] but the tactic is highly questionable in terms of constitutionality and fundamental fairness. Perception of racial bias corrodes public faith and trust in the criminal justice system. And it is firmly established that black men are much more frequently apprehended, arrested, and prosecuted than white men.

# ACTORS IN CRIMINAL JUSTICE POLICY

There is a large cast of actors in state and local criminal justice systems. State policy leadership is exercised by the governor, who sets the tone for the pursuit of law and order through State of the State addresses, proposed legislation, and public presentations. During the past several years, few governors have not announced a new crime prevention and law enforcement program.

Besides being involved in judicial selection in several states, legislative bodies decide what a crime is and prohibit it through legislation and law enforcement, establish the structure of the legal system, and determine sentencing parameters including the option of capital punishment. Legislatures tend to be responsive (to citizen pressures on law enforcement issues), as demonstrated by legislative activity in areas such as gun control, the death penalty, and sentencing reform.

## Law Enforcement Officials

The state attorney general formally heads the law enforcement function in most states; county and city attorneys and district attorneys generally follow the attorney general's lead. These positions call for a great deal of discretion in deciding whom to prosecute for what alleged crimes or civil violations. The prosecution of offenses is a politically charged endeavor, particularly when it is within the authority of people who aspire to higher political office. On the other side of the courtroom are public defenders and private defense attorneys, who try to get their clients declared innocent or negotiate a favorable plea bargain.

State troopers (highway patrol), special state law enforcement divisions modeled on the FBI, county sheriffs, police chiefs, local line and staff officers and civilian employees are also important. They are responsible for enforcing the policies decided on by elected officials and for carrying out the basic day-to-day activities connected with enforcing the law. But it is the highway patrol, the county sheriff, and the cops on the street who are the front line law enforcers. Just a few years ago, policing was a profession in high demand. More than 100 applicants would apply for each opening. Today, despite starting salaries of $50,000 and above and generous benefits, many police organizations have shortages of 10 percent or more. Military and paramilitary jobs have greater appeal to young people.[15] Therefore, we can add personnel shortfalls to the list of law enforcement challenges.

## The Courts

State and local courts decide the innocence or guilt of defendants brought before them, based on the evidence submitted (see Chapter 9). In the great majority of cases, however, plea bargaining prevails and the case never goes to trial. Courts can also influence criminal justice through rulings that specify correct police procedures in criminal cases. U.S. Supreme Court decisions, in particular, have shaped the criminal justice process. The federal courts have the final word on cases in which the defendants claim that their federal rights have been violated by state or local law enforcement personnel. State courts handle alleged violations of state constitutional rights.

Critics have asserted that the Supreme Court under Chief Justice Earl Warren made it more difficult to convict criminals through decisions that expanded the rights of the accused. The first of these famous cases was *Gideon v. Wainwright* (1963), in which the Warren Court ruled that all accused persons have a constitutional right to be defended by counsel. If they cannot afford to pay an attorney, the state or locality must provide one free of charge.[16] The second ruling, *Escobedo v. Illinois* (1964), required that the accused be informed of the right to remain silent at the time of arrest.[17]

The often-cited case of *Miranda v. Arizona* (1966) further expanded the rights of the accused. It requires police officers to inform anyone suspected of a crime of the right to remain silent; the fact that anything said can and will be used against him or her in a court of law; and the right to be represented by counsel, paid for by the state if necessary.[18] Evidence obtained when the accused has not clearly indicated his understanding of these *Miranda* warnings or explicitly waived his rights is not legally admissible in the courtroom because it is considered a violation of the Fifth Amendment right not to incriminate oneself.

The U.S. Supreme Court also influenced state and local criminal procedures in the case of *Mapp v. Ohio* (1961). Basing its decision on the due process clause of the

Fourteenth Amendment, the Warren Court ruled that evidence obtained illegally by the police cannot be introduced in court.[19] This exclusionary rule extended the Fourth Amendment's protection from illegal search and seizure. The police must have a search warrant specifying what person or place will be searched and what will be seized. Over time, these and other Warren Court decisions favoring the accused have been relaxed by subsequently more conservative Supreme Courts.

## The Public's Involvement

Another participant in justice policy is the voting public. Citizens make demands on officials (the governor, legislators, judges, police, and so on) to conform to public opinion on crimes and criminals. Generally, the pressure is for more law and order, and it results in stricter criminal codes and correctional policies. Citizens also participate directly in the criminal justice system by serving on juries. Most citizens consider it their public duty to serve on a jury from time to time, and such service does tend to be an interesting (if not always edifying) experience. Trials usually last fewer than four days. But occasionally, a jury trial will drag out over a lengthy period; one of the longest was concluded in Belleville, Illinois, after a forty-four-month marathon concerning liability for a toxic chemical spill. Attorneys for the losing party then announced that they would appeal.[20]

Citizens also participate in criminal justice by sitting on grand juries. A **grand jury** (which is typically composed of twelve members) serves as a check on the power of the state or local prosecutor by considering evidence in a case, then deciding whether to indict the accused. Twenty states require a grand jury **indictment** for serious crimes. In other states, it is optional, or a preliminary hearing of charges and evidence before a judge is used instead. Grand juries are usually organized on a county or district basis. In practice, they are inclined to rubber-stamp whatever course of action is recommended by the prosecutor. Rarely does one question the professional legal opinion of the district attorney or attorney general.

An additional function of the grand jury is to act as an investigatory body for certain types of crimes, especially vice, political and corporate corruption, and organized crime. In this capacity, it is empowered to issue subpoenas for suspects and evidence that it wishes to examine. A statewide grand jury is most appropriate for criminal investigations because it can deal with activities that cross county or district boundaries. Among the states that provide for statewide grand juries are Arizona, Colorado, Florida, New Jersey, South Carolina, and Virginia.

Finally, the public may become involved in the criminal justice process by tackling crime on their own. Telephone and Web-based crime report lines; neighborhood complaints of prostitution, drug dealing, or gang activity; and similar actions to report "broken windows" help take a bite out of crime. Neighborhood watches and patrols help detect and deter criminal presence.

## The Victim

The last influence on criminal justice policy is the one most frequently ignored in the past—the victim. Many victims are left psychologically, physically, and/or financially damaged after a crime. States have responded to this sad fact

**grand jury**
A group of citizens appointed to determine if there is enough evidence to bring a person to trial.

**indictment**
A formal, written accusation submitted to a court by a grand jury, alleging a specified crime.

by developing victim compensation programs. These programs are typically administered by a board, which assesses the validity of victims' claims and decides on a monetary award to help compensate for hospital and doctor bills, loss of property, and other financial needs resulting from the crime. Maximum benefits, paid for in part by the federal Victims of Violent Crime Act (VOCA), usually vary from $10,000 to $25,000, depending on the state. Rarely is a victim made whole by these limited payments, but at least some assistance is provided to help the person deal with the various traumas of the crime.

All states now permit use of victim-impact statements in court before sentencing a convicted criminal. The statements may include victims' and family members' views on how the crime has affected them, and their feelings about the crime and the accused. Most states and many counties now provide victim notification systems so that crime victims are made aware of their assailants' subsequent prison release. In Kentucky, victims can call a toll-free hotline to check on a prisoner's status,[21] while in Alaska, sex offenders must post their name and addresses to an online database. Finally, the 2007 federal Megan's Law requires notification of a community when a convicted sex offender moves into the neighborhood. (Megan was a seven-year-old girl who was sexually assaulted and murdered by a neighbor who had recently been released from prison after serving time as a sex offender).[22] States post their sex offender registry on the Web the names and whereabouts of offenders.

## HOW POLICY PARTICIPANTS INTERACT: TWO POLICY AREAS

All states do not define or treat crimes in the same manner. The states' handling of crimes in two policy areas—victimless crimes and capital punishment—illuminates this point.

### Victimless Crime

Prostitution, pornography, illegal drug use, music and movie pirating, and flouting mandatory seatbelt and motorcycle helmet laws are all examples of victimless crimes. Statutes enacted by legislative bodies define what constitutes criminal behavior, and public opinion usually influences what activities the legislatures treat as criminal. **Victimless crimes** are voluntary acts that violate the law but are perceived by some to present little or no threat to individuals or society. Up to 50 percent of all arrests in urban areas is estimated to be on charges of victimless crimes.

Some people argue that such crimes should be wiped off the books because those who engage in these activities suffer willingly (if at all). A strong case can be made for legalizing, regulating, and taxing prostitution and recreational drugs. People will pursue these activities anyway, the argument goes, so why criminalize a large portion of the population unnecessarily? Instead, why not

**victimless crimes**

Illegal acts that, in theory, do no one any harm.

get a little piece of the action for the public purse? State regulation of gambling helps diminish the role of organized crime in gambling, and regulation of prostitution could help prevent the spread of sexually transmitted diseases by requiring regular medical checkups for prostitutes. Almost every state permits some form of gambling, such as casinos, lotteries, bingo, and betting on horse or dog racing. Though "massage parlors" and "escort services" exist in all major cities, only Nevada has legalized and regulated prostitution.

Finally, legalizing drugs promises to take the profits out of the drug trade and to reduce drug-related crime and corruption. An estimated one-third of all new state prisoners have been convicted of drug-related crimes. The tens of billions of dollars spent annually by the United States on the War on Drugs have resulted in a pathetic failure, leaving us today with just as many addicts, swelling prison populations, an enormously profitable importation and distribution system that lures young people and even grade-school children into the trade, and a great deal of drug-related violence. By shifting drug enforcement money and efforts to medical and psychiatric treatment of addicts and users, perhaps legalization would even lead to less addiction. For example, research indicates that treatment is much more effective in reducing the consumption of cocaine than is attacking its supply channels.[23]

In states where legislative bodies define the scope of criminal behavior broadly to include victimless crimes, an extra burden is placed on other actors in the criminal justice system. Prosecutors and law enforcement authorities find much of their time consumed by these relatively minor and nonthreatening activities when they could be concentrating on more serious crimes, such as murder, rape, and robbery. The courts must also spend a great deal of time processing these cases. The legalization of victimless crimes would immediately shorten the dockets of prosecutors, police, and judges; render the process more manageable; and reduce the burgeoning prison and jail population. A less radical strategy is *decriminalization*—the prescribing of a minor penalty (usually a small fine) for certain crimes. For example, a growing number of states and localities have decriminalized possession of small amounts of marijuana; even more have legalized the use of marijuana for medical purposes.

Opponents claim that *victimless* is the wrong word to describe these actions. For example, with the selling of sex, prostitutes and their clients can become infected with the HIV virus and other communicable diseases. It is not uncommon for prostitutes to commit other types of crime and endure serious emotional and physical costs. Legalization of drugs such as methamphetamines, heroin, or crack cocaine might lead to a significant rise in addiction rates and require higher taxes for treatment and health care. And if legalization were selective (say, only marijuana, cocaine, and ecstasy were made available legally), then new, more powerful designer drugs would likely debut on the market.

In practice, hard-pressed prosecutors often drop charges against perpetrators of victimless crimes, judges dismiss the least offensive cases or administer a small fine or a suspended sentence, and law enforcement personnel tend to look the other way when passing near a prostitute or a pot smoker. De facto decriminalization is the norm for many victimless crimes in much of the

United States, especially in the case of prohibited sexual behavior between consenting adults, including sodomy, adultery, and the ever-popular fornication.

## Capital Punishment

Capital punishment offers a second example of how states vary in their approach to crime. In this area, the interactions among individuals and institutions are critically important. Public opinion helps determine a legislature's propensity to enact a death penalty statute. Prosecutors must decide under what circumstances to seek the death penalty. Only juries can find a defendant guilty or innocent in a capital case. Judges must enforce the penalty of death, subject to lengthy appellate review. Governors have the power to commute a sentence of execution. And the federal courts have played an important role in determining the conditions under which a state can legally put a person to death for a crime.

Criminal executions were once commonplace in the United States. In colonial days, public hangings were considered appropriate for adulterers, religious heretics, blasphemers, and thieves. A total of 717 people were legally executed during the 1950s. But public opinion slowly began to turn against capital punishment and so did the U.S. Supreme Court. In the 1972 case of *Furman v. Georgia*, a 5-to-4 majority held that the death penalty had been applied in a cruel, arbitrary, and racist manner by the states.[24] The Supreme Court expressly declared unconstitutional the capital punishment statutes in Louisiana and North Carolina and implicitly invalidated similar laws in many other states. It held that death penalty laws could be valid only if used in accordance with correct procedures and standards and could be invoked solely for lethal crimes.

The Supreme Court later ruled that the use of the death penalty for those who committed crimes while juveniles is unconstitutional.[25] In one seemingly bizarre 2003 case, the Court let stand lower court rulings that Arkansas could forcibly administer drugs to an insane murderer to render him sane enough to be executed.[26] However, the Court did prevent the execution of a retarded murderer in 2002 and of a man who raped, but did not kill, his eight-year-old stepdaughter in a 2008 decision.[27]

Several states voluntarily abolished capital punishment in the 1960s and 1970s. The majority, however, rewrote their statutes to conform to the Supreme Court's guidelines (see Figure 16.2). In 2008, the U.S. Supreme Court held in *Baze v. Rees* that the three-drug cocktail used to lethally inject the accused in Kentucky (and by implication in many other states) was constitutionally valid; executions then recommenced in several states following an unofficial six month moratorium while the case was under review.[28] A total of thirty-five states permit executions today. The most commonly used technique is lethal injection. Several states permit the condemned to choose his method of execution, adding to lethal injection the possibilities of lethal gas (five states), hanging (two states), or firing squad (only Utah). Those states supportive of the death penalty tend to have both a politically conservative population and a high murder rate. Some 3,297 inmates were languishing on death row in state penitentiaries in mid-2009. While statutes were being rewritten and clarified between 1968

## States with Capital Punishment

Most states permit capital punishment, although some have not actually carried out the death penalty for many years. For states that have allowed executions since 1977, the number executed is indicated in the map.

FIGURE 16.2

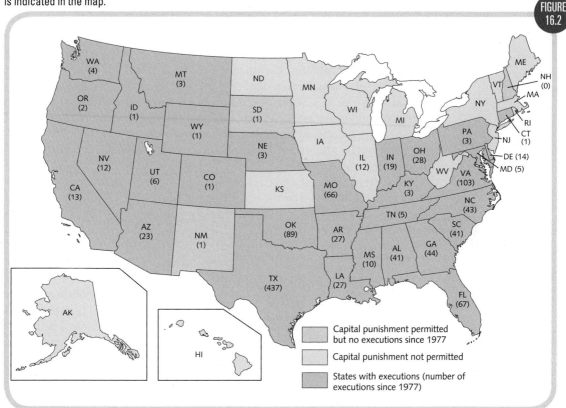

Capital punishment permitted but no executions since 1977

Capital punishment not permitted

States with executions (number of executions since 1977)

and 1976, no executions were carried out. Since January 1977, however, 1,171 people have made the long walk from death row to the death chamber, more than 80 percent of them in the South. Texas is the leading executioner; the state used lethal injection to execute 437 people between 1976 and June 2009.[29]

Recent public opinion polls indicate that 69 percent of the American people favor capital punishment. But when presented with the alternative of life without parole, the "in favor" group drops to less than 50 percent.[30] Execution remains a rather tedious and enormously expensive endeavor. The prisoners executed today have spent, on average, around eleven years on death row. The appeals process presents numerous opportunities for delay, and it is not unusual for an inmate, after languishing for a decade or more on death row, to escape the death penalty through the legal process. The price tag on death is shocking, averaging millions of dollars per execution; the price in Maryland has averaged $37.2 million for each of five executions since 1976. During the states budget travails of 2008–2009, arguments were made that abolishing the death penalty would help balance state budgets.

One troublesome aspect of the death penalty is that African Americans receive this form of punishment well out of proportion to their numbers. Although black people make up about 13 percent of the U.S. population, 34 percent of those executed since 1977 have been black, and 42 percent of death-row inmates are black. Blacks who kill whites are significantly more likely to be sentenced to death. Latinos have been executed in rough proportion to their presence in the overall population—7 percent, but they make up 11 percent of death-row inmates. Less than 2 percent of those condemned to death since 1977 have been women, and very few women have been executed.[31]

Under various U.S. Supreme Court rulings, states are required to write sentencing guidelines that consider factors related to the offender and the nature of the offense when deciding between a life sentence and death, yet the ultimate sentence must not be idiosyncratic or capricious. Critics of the death penalty claim, however, that it is applied capriciously, from the decision of a prosecutor to ask the jury to determine that a given crime is a capital offense to the requisite review of a jury's death sentence by the state supreme court. The offender's race is definitely a consideration, as noted earlier. And according to one study, those who murder police officers, women, the elderly, or multiple victims are more likely to be sentenced to death, as are those who kill after a sexual assault a robbery.[32]

Obviously, a great deal of controversy continues to surround the issue of executing criminals. Researchers generally agree that if punishment is to discourage future criminal behavior, it must be swift and certain. Neither of these conditions is met by the death penalty in the United States. And few reasonable and informed people today argue that capital punishment acts as a deterrent, except in the specific case of the individual who is executed. Studies comparing homicide rates in states with and without death penalties either find no significant differences in homicide rates or find that states with capital punishment actually have higher rates of homicide.

Also disturbing is the fact that the personal characteristics of judges influence their decisions. Republicans are much more likely to vote for the death penalty, as are older judges and those with previous experience as a prosecutor.[33] In this sense, the death penalty resembles a lottery. Application of the death penalty can also be cruel and unusual punishment in more ways than one. Florida's "Old Sparky" overheated, causing flames and smoke to erupt from a leather mask worn by the unfortunate murderer, Pedro Medina. (This gruesome scene helped to convince Florida officials to replace the electric chair with lethal injection). As noted above, even lethal injection has come under fire as a cruel and unusual cause of death. Typically, three chemicals are injected into the prisoner: a barbiturate, a paralytic, then a heart-stopping substance. If the first chemical is improperly administered and therefore ineffective, the other two can cause extreme agony.[34]

The public has become increasingly ambivalent about the death penalty because of growing evidence of serious problems in the justice system. Studies have found that two of every three death sentences are eventually overturned, usually due to errors by incompetent defense attorneys or evidence withheld by prosecutors and police officers. Calls for an end to executions have grown louder and some states have heeded them. New Jersey's supreme court issued an injunction against the death penalty in 2006, and then the Garden State legislature wrote the epitaph of the death penalty in a 2007 statute. New Mexico repealed the death penalty in 2009 while high courts in Kansas, Nebraska, and New York ruled executions to be unconstitutional. A number of states in which the death penalty is legally condoned have not put anyone to death for years. Concern is growing that innocent people are being put to death. DNA testing makes identification of a killer a statistical certainty when such evidence is available, and more states are demanding that DNA evidence be submitted before extinguishing a person's life and that inmates proven to be innocent are freed. It is estimated that 129 men and women have been exonerated since 1973, many of them as a result of negative DNA tests, and others because of incompetent defense attorneys or prosecutorial or police misconduct.[35]

On the side of those favoring the death penalty is the argument for the legitimacy of *lex talionis*, the principle that the punishment should fit the crime. According to this view, some crimes are so heinous that only the death of the perpetrator can balance the scales of justice and relieve the moral outrage of society. This argument for justice as retribution cannot be validated on empirical grounds; it is an ethical question that each individual must personally resolve.

# CORRECTIONAL POLICY

A person convicted of a crime in a court of law becomes the object of correctional policy, which, as its name implies, aims to correct behavior that society finds unacceptable. In theory, an offender should first be punished, for retribution and to serve as a lesson for other potential criminals. Second, convicted lawbreakers should be rehabilitated so that they can become productive law-abiding citizens after fulfilling the terms of their punishment. Third, criminals who represent a danger to society should be physically separated from the general public.

If correcting criminal behavior is the overarching goal of correctional policy in the states, we have a terrible policy failure on our hands. As already noted, most crimes do not result in an arrest. Even when an offender is detained by the police, she stands a good chance of avoiding conviction or incarceration. Thus, deterrence is a dubious proposition at best. Remember that the best way to prevent undesirable behavior is through swift and certain punishment. Those of us who quizzically stuck a foreign object into an electrical outlet in childhood received the shock of swift punishment. If we were foolish enough to try it a second time, we discovered that the punishment was certain. Only morons or masochists would subject themselves to such abuse a third time. That is how our correctional policy would have to work if deterrence is to be achieved. But for various reasons, swift and certain punishment is unlikely.

The U.S. Department of Justice has estimated that 70 percent of former inmates released from state prisons commit another serious offense within three years and return to prison because of it. It appears that prisons actually increase the likelihood that an individual will commit additional crimes when he is freed. Our state prisons have been called breeding pens for criminals. Instead of being rehabilitated, the first-time offender is likely to receive expert schooling in various criminal professions. Overcrowding, understaffing, physical and sexual brutality, gangs, and rampant drug abuse also make it unlikely that an offender will become a law-abiding citizen. Many approaches have been tried—counseling, vocational training, basic education, and others—but none has consistently been able to overcome the criminalizing environment of state prison systems.

Without doubt, most incarcerated offenders see deprivation of their freedom as punishment, and so retribution does occur. Just as surely, prison effectively removes undesirable characters from our midst. These two objectives of correctional policy are achieved to some degree, although cynics point out that sentencing tends to be rather inconsistent and a significant proportion of criminals are released before serving out their sentences. Most important, and contrary to the conventional wisdom, research consistently shows that state imprisonment rates are not significantly related to crime rates. In fact, supporting the notion that prisons are colleges for criminals, incarceration might actually boost crime. Figure 16.3 shows the relationship between incarceration rate and crime rate for the states.

**FIGURE 16.3**

**Relationship Between Crime Rate and Incarceration Rate, Controlling for Population, 2009**

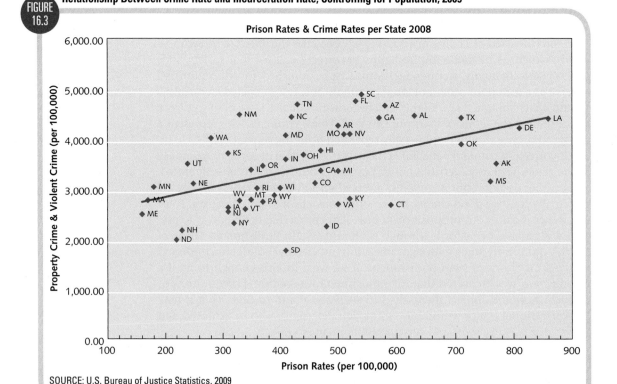

SOURCE: U.S. Bureau of Justice Statistics, 2009

## Sentencing

Sentencing reform has recently received a great deal of attention in the states. The inconsistency of criminal sentencing is obvious if we examine incarceration rates. In 2007, they varied from one of every fifty-five adults in Louisiana to one in 226 in Maine (see Figure 16.4). Southern states tend to be toughest on crime: They are more than twice as likely as other states to convict people arrested on felony charges, and their sentences are more severe than those in other regions. As observed above, however, crime rates and incarceration rates are not closely related. Some states with relatively high rates of crime lock up fewer people than do other states with lower crime rates.

One striking inconsistency is the extremely high lockup rate of African Americans in state and federal prisons: Blacks make up some 40 percent of all such inmates but only about 13 percent of the nation's population. One out of every eleven African American men is incarcerated or on parole or probation today. This trend has been attributed to poverty, poor education, and other

**Prisoners per 100 Residents in State and Federal Correctional Institutions, by State, as of 2008**

FIGURE
16.4

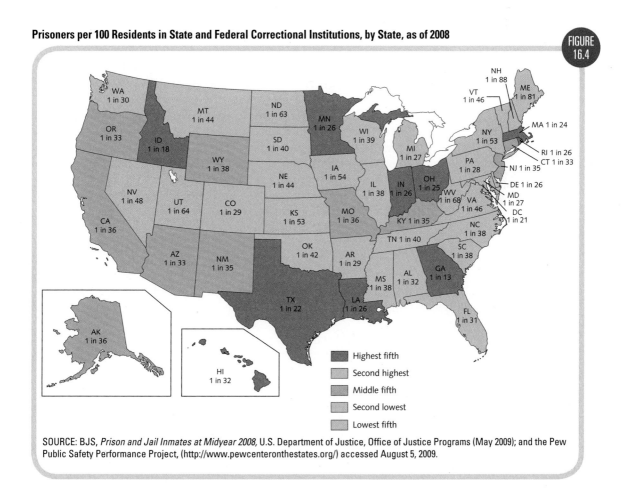

SOURCE: BJS, *Prison and Jail Inmates at Midyear 2008*, U.S. Department of Justice, Office of Justice Programs (May 2009); and the Pew Public Safety Performance Project, (http://www.pewcenteronthestates.org/) accessed August 5, 2009.

demographics of criminal activity, which drive up the black crime rate, as well as law enforcement's focus on crack cocaine, which is found predominantly in the inner-city black communities.[36] Possession of crack is punished more severely in the courts than offenses involving other illegal drugs. The political climate also matters: States dominated by conservative Republicans tend to imprison disproportionate rates of blacks.[37] Similarly, Latino defendants tend to receive harsher sentences than whites.[38] It should not come as a surprise that Blacks and Latinos are much more suspicious of police and distrustful of criminal justice systems than are whites.[39] With more than 2.3 million prisoners, the United States has the highest incarceration rate in the world by far; with only 5 percent of the earth's people, the United States has about one-quarter of the world's prisoners. One of every thirty-one American adults is behind bars or under supervision.

> **indeterminate sentencing**
>
> Sentencing in which a judge exercises discretion when deciding on the number of years for the sentence.

Why is our incarceration rate so high? First, prison sentences are harsh compared with those in other countries. Historically, state courts applied **indeterminate sentencing**, whereby judges have great discretion in deciding the number of years for which an offender should be sentenced to prison. The offender then becomes eligible for parole after a minimum period is served, based on good behavior and meeting prison goals. For instance, a ten- to twenty-year sentence for armed robbery may require the inmate to serve at least five years. After that time, he becomes eligible for parole, subject to the judgment of a parole board, which reviews the case and the prisoner's behavior in prison.

> **determinate sentencing**
>
> Mandatory sentencing that is determined by law, not a judge's discretion.

But the trend has been **determinate sentencing**, in which offenders are given mandatory terms that they must serve without the possibility of parole. Under so-called truth-in-sentencing laws, about half the states require violent offenders to serve at least 85 percent of their sentences, or even "life without possibility of parole." Determinate sentencing is designed to reduce the sentencing disparity among judges. It also eliminates the need for parole. Naturally, determinate sentencing keeps prisoners incarcerated for longer periods than indeterminate sentencing does.

Another explanation is public opinion, which tilts toward a punitive approach for criminals. Opportunistic politicians tend to assume a "law and order" posture and attempt to validate it by enacting strict sentencing laws.[40] This punitive attitude that the public has taken toward criminals has helped stiffen not only the sentences awarded by judges but also the judgments of parole boards.

The "lock-'em up'" syndrome is perhaps best shown by the three-strikes-and-you're-out legislation that has been enacted in a majority of states. Such laws mandate tough sanctions for habitual felons who are convicted of a third violent or serious crime. In California, even a *minor* conviction can invoke a twenty-five-year to life sentence; one felon who stole a pizza in Redondo Beach is now doing twenty-five years. Another received life for stealing three golf clubs. The price tag for "three strikes" has been projected at billions of dollars annually for new prisons and their operating costs. New judges have to be hired and more courtrooms built to hear the increased number of jury trials.

Despite the widespread media attention surrounding three-strikes laws, they are rarely applied. Why? Because all states have long had statutes on the books that increase prison time for repeat criminals, so three-strikes laws have had little practical effect. States are rethinking mandatory minimum sentences for drug offenders. Connecticut, Louisiana, Maryland, Texas, and other states have rolled them back, favoring drug treatment programs instead. California voters passed Proposition 36, an initiative that mandates treatment rather than prison for first and second drug offenses.

A third contributing factor to high imprisonment rates is drug enforcement penalties. Most drug-related offenses do not involve violence and are "victimless," yet they have been severely punished as part of the "War on Drugs." Michigan mandates life without parole for a first-time offender who possesses more than 650 grams (about one and one-half pounds) of cocaine or heroin. One could muster convincing arguments that we "lost" the war on drugs many years ago. Drug supplies are ample although large proportions of our jails and prisons hold nonviolent drug offenders.

But more criminals *are* doing more time, and prisons are increasingly serving as expensive geriatric hospitals for relatively harmless criminals who are senior citizens. Already, states are grouping aging inmates within correctional facilities for their special health care needs as well as to protect them from younger, more violent inmates. The average yearly cost of housing a sickly, geriatric prisoner can run two to three times the $27,000 for a younger, healthy inmate. Yet "criminal menopause" apparently afflicts felons in their twilight years, making them unlikely to commit a new crime if released.

## Prison Conditions

As noted above, 2.3 million people are confined to state prisons and local jails in the United States. The number of prisoners has been growing by about 4 percent annually. Prisons continue to operate beyond official capacity in many states, despite the construction of numerous new facilities to reduce the problems of prison overcrowding and its accompanying conditions of poor sanitation, inadequate health care, and high levels of violence. The courts once assumed a hands-off policy toward offenders once they were behind prison walls. The administration of state correctional systems was the sole responsibility of corrections officials, but in a series of decisions, the federal courts applied the Eighth Amendment prohibition on cruel and unusual punishment and the Fourteenth Amendment provision for due process and equal protection of the laws to prison inmates. In addition, the Supreme Court permitted inmates of state and local facilities to bypass less sympathetic state courts and file suits alleging violations of their civil rights in federal courts. Later, such suits were restricted by a 1996 federal law, but various federal court rulings have altered the nature of correctional policy and changed it greatly.

Much of the litigation has concerned overcrowding. As more and more people were sentenced to prison, corrections officials responded by doubling, tripling, and even quadrupling cell arrangements. It was not unusual for inmates to be crowded together at the rate of one per ten square feet of floor space. Drastic improvements were long overdue in Arkansas and Alabama, for instance. At Arkansas's dreaded maximum-security institution, Cumming Farms, inmates were worked in the fields like slaves, ten hours a day, six days a week, in all types of weather. At night they slept in 100-man barracks. Rapes and other forms of physical violence occurred regularly. A federal lawsuit led to the finding that Arkansas's entire penal system was in violation of the Eighth Amendment.

The adult prison systems of several states are presently being overseen under federal court orders. The most recent federal intervention was in 2009 in California, when a panel of federal judges ordered state officials to reduce the state prison population by 40,591 inmates within two years. By operating prisons at 190 percent of capacity, California was found to be in violation of the Eight Amendment's prohibition of cruel and unusual punishment, particularly for sick and mentally ill inmates.[41] State officials now face the choice of balancing the stringent law-and-order approach sought by the public and elected representatives with court orders that, to critics, sometimes seem to pamper inmates and turn convicted criminals out onto the streets to relieve overcrowding.

The intrusion of the federal courts into state correctional policy is quite controversial, particularly when they have taken over full operating responsibility or ordered increased state and local expenditures or mass inmate releases for prisons. Important questions concerning the proper division of power between the national government and the states have been raised, as have questions about the competence of federal court officials to run state prison systems.

However these important issues in federalism are ultimately resolved, the immediate problem for most states is producing adequate space for their growing prison populations and finding the money to pay for it. The only short-term options are to release inmates, find new space for lockup, or sentence newly convicted offenders to something other than incarceration.

Prisons have become financial albatrosses, diverting state expenditures from education, highways, and social services. Most state prison populations have quadrupled over the past twenty years. State and local spending on prisons and jails, currently estimated at over $44 billion a year, has risen at the startling rate of 127 percent over the past ten years (adjusted for inflation)[42] 15–20 percent annually. Room, board, and care for one state prison inmate averages about $79.00 per day. A huge number of prison and jail guards must be paid. And each new prison bed space for the growing ranks of confined criminals costs up to $100,000.[43] Prison costs are also escalating as a result of health care inflation. Prisoners are a particularly unhealthy subset of the population: Most smoke, many are drug abusers, some have acute mental problems, a troubling proportion is HIV positive, and a growing number are seniors. There seems to be no easy end in sight for prison spending, because of "Murphy's Law of Incarceration:" The number of inmates expands to fill all available space, or "if you build them, you'll fill them." However, the prison-building boom is tapering off because many new prisons have already come on line, and states are adopting alternatives to incarceration.

# POLICY ALTERNATIVES FOR STATES AND LOCALITIES

In addition to the immediate responses made necessary by federal court actions, states and localities are attempting to devise a more comprehensive approach to coping with the problem of prison overcrowding. Whatever their past failings, and primarily for reasons of budget rather than conscience, they are demonstrating today an increasing propensity for experimentation and innovation. Three basic strategies are being employed to bring and keep inmate populations in line with institutional capacity: back-door strategies, front-door strategies, and capacity enhancement.

## Back-Door Strategies

Back-door strategies include several methods for releasing offenders from prisons on probation or parole before they have served their full sentences. This strategy is the most conventional of the three, but some interesting innovations are being tested.

One of the less imaginative but nonetheless quite effective ways to deal with prison overcrowding is to grant early release. Most states have early-release programs in place, but the method of implementation varies. In some states, the governor or parole board simply pares off the last few months or weeks of sentences that are nearly completed, until the necessary number of inmates have left the prison. Other states apply a risk analysis approach that predicts the likelihood that certain inmates, if released, will not commit another serious offense. For example, nonviolent offenders are freed before violent offenders, larcenists before burglars, marijuana users before heroin dealers, and so on. An inmate's personal characteristics, prison behavior, and work history may also be taken into consideration. Early release reduces inmate populations quickly, but public outcries are certain to follow if an offender released before expiration of his or her sentence commits a highly publicized violent crime.

Ex-cons discharged without oversight and assistance are not likely to become model citizens overnight. Old habits and felonious friends tend to return and most employers hesitate to hire a convicted felon. Today, felons incarcerated during the lock-'em-up mentality of the 1990s are returning home in record numbers. Past patterns indicate that most will become repeat offenders within three years, a problem that states and localities ignore at their own peril.

**Reinventing Parole** An increasing number of states are taking a close look at new reentry approaches for convicts to boost their chances for successful transition from behind prison walls to the streets. Job-related skills training, placement services, and alcohol and drug counseling (80 percent of ex-cons are released with substance abuse problems) are typical. New, more comprehensive programs are also receiving experimentation. Maryland's Reentry Partnership develops collaborative transition plans for inmates. The state corrections and parole division, local police and health departments, and community organizations work together to determine (with the prisoner's input) individual needs, including counseling, transportation, and housing. Caseworkers and a prisoner's advocate coordinate the services. Programs such as these are costly, but they are much cheaper than the $25,000 per year to keep an inmate locked up—a daily cost of $3.42 for probationers and $7.47 for parolees, versus $79 to keep an offender behind bars.[44]

**parole**

Program in which offenders are released from prison to serve the remainder of their sentence under community supervision.

Conventional **parole** or **probation** has not been particularly effective, although these programs account for three out of four individuals in the corrections population. In most states that utilize this technique, the parole and probation officers (whose duty it is to keep up with the progress of the released offender) are terribly overworked. It is not unknown for a parole officer to be responsible for 200 offenders—a nearly impossible task. (The average is about 60 parolees per case officer and about 100 probationers.)[45] Most probationers and parolees are supposed to receive substance abuse counseling, pay restitution to their victims, or comply with other terms of their release, but many do not. And a large proportion end up back behind bars.

**probation**

Instead of incarceration, this program permits minor offenders to remain in the community under supervision.

Several states are determined to improve probation and parole. Texas has expanded drug treatment programs, reformed parole practices, and established drug courts. As a result, it saved nearly $1 billion in new prison costs.[46] Kansas provides grants to community organizations to train and monitor parolees.

**Electronic House Detention** A relatively new approach to parole takes advantage of technology to monitor parolees' whereabouts. Sometimes called *electronic house detention,* this technique requires released inmates to wear a transmitter (usually on the ankle) that steadily emits signals to a receiver in their home. Failure to detect a signal causes the receiver to contact a central computer automatically. The computer is programmed to know when the inmate is permitted to be away from home (usually during work hours). If an unusual signal appears, the computer notifies law enforcement officers. Removal of the transmitter also triggers an alarm at the central computer. A more advanced "active tracking" method is to use GPS to monitor the person's exact position round the clock.

Electronic monitoring is a popular way to cope with prison overcrowding. It is much cheaper than jail or prison, and it enables a working prisoner to pay his or her own share of the program and, in some cases, to repay the victim of the crime as well. It has also been found to significantly reduce new offenses and escapes.[47] But it is not appropriate for an escape-minded individual, who can cut off the anklet and walk away, perhaps to commit more crimes.

**Vocational Programs** Another back-door strategy reduces the sentences of prisoners who participate in educational and vocational programs. These programs are intended to teach convicts skills that can help them obtain jobs once they are out of prison, and they have the added benefit of keeping inmates involved in productive, rather than destructive, activities while behind prison walls.

The idea of profiting from prison work has considerable appeal. In addition to using their time productively and learning marketable skills, inmates earn wages that can help defray the cost of their room and board, provide monetary restitution to victims, and fund savings accounts for the inmates to use after their release. Several programs have had encouraging results, including the making of stained-glass windows and restoring of classic cars by Nevada prisoners, training and socializing rescued dogs for adoption in Oklahoma and Kansas, fighting forest fires in Oregon and Georgia, saddle-making in Colorado, and the sewing of everything from bed covers to Victoria's Secret lingerie in South Carolina. Prison industries usually include more conventional activities like printing, metalworking, textiles, signs and license plates, and basic manufacturing. South Carolina has used prison labor to build new correctional facilities, saving the state millions of dollars. Prison labor is not a bad deal for the inmates either. They may get paid only 25¢ to $1.50 an hour, but they can earn time toward early release for each week they work.

## Front-Door Strategies

The second basic strategy used to balance the number of prisoners with the supply of beds is the front-door approach, which aims to keep minor offenders out of prison in the first place by directing them into alternative programs.

**Creative Sentencing** One front-door strategy is to grant judges more flexibility in determining sentences. **Creative sentencing** permits judges or community boards to match the punishment with the crime while keeping the nonviolent offender in society. A common option is community service—sentencing the offender to put in a specified number of hours cleaning up parks or streets; working in a public hospital; painting public buildings; or performing specialized tasks related to the person's professional expertise, such as dentistry or accounting.

Another option is to link the sentence to available prison space. This about-face from determinate sentencing is applied in an elaborate grid in North Carolina that helps judges balance the seriousness of a crime and the perpetrator's past criminal record with the number of beds available in the prison system. In determining the length of the sentence, the judge refers to the grid for mini-

**creative sentencing**
Sentencing in which the punishment matches the crime and the characteristics of the convicted person.

mum and maximum terms. Offenders must serve at least the minimum term without the possibility of parole. Nonviolent offenders such as petty thieves, embezzlers, and minor drug offenders are assigned to halfway houses, drug treatment, or other programs.

Yet another strategy is for judges to assess fines in lieu of prison for relatively serious nonviolent crimes. A substantial fine, some argue, is just as strong a deterrent as a short stay in jail. So is the loss of a valued personal belonging. In Wake County, North Carolina, a juvenile court judge can confiscate a favorite item of clothing, a stereo, jewelry, or other possession from young larceny or breaking-and-entering offenders. A Texas judge recently ordered a father who physically abused his son to spend the next thirty nights sleeping in the family doghouse (no explanation is offered of where the dog slept). Those convicted of the serious offense of child molestation in California and Florida can be given the choice of surgical or chemical castration. The first option removes some of the offending male equipment permanently. The second requires regular injections of a female contraceptive that reportedly shrinks male organs for as long as the drug is taken.[48]

A municipal court judge in Los Angeles provided an especially pertinent example for any renter who has ever lived in a substandard building ignored by the landlord. A Beverly Hills neurosurgeon who had earned the nickname Ratlord because of numerous city citations for health, fire, and building code violations in his four apartment buildings was sentenced to move into one of his own apartments for a term of thirty days. The apartment contained mounds of rodent droppings, an army of cockroaches, inadequate plumbing, faulty wiring, and other problems. Ratlord was fitted with an electronic anklet to ensure that he remained in his "cell" from 5:30 p.m. to 8:30 a.m. Permanent residents soon noted improvements in the building conditions.[49]

**Regional Restitution Centers** Another front-door strategy used in Florida, Arizona, Georgia, Missouri, and other states is the *regional restitution center* (also known as diversion centers), a variation on the standard work-release center. Nonviolent offenders are housed in restitution centers near their homes and work in the community during the day; they receive regular supervision. Their paychecks are turned over to center staff members, who subtract expenses for food and housing and distribute the remainder to the offenders' victims as restitution, to the court for payment of fines, and to the offenders' spouses and children for support. Anything left over belongs to the inmates. Missouri's program of intensive counseling and treatment centers for juvenile offenders has significantly lowered the recidivism rate.[50]

**Intensive Probation Supervision** A third front-door strategy is *intensive probation supervision (IPS)*. IPS is somewhat like house arrest because it is designed to keep first-time offenders guilty of a serious but usually nonviolent crime (e.g., drunk driving or drug possession) out of state institutions. Those who qualify for the program face intense, highly intrusive supervision and surveillance for a prescribed period. Among other things, IPS requires face-to-face contacts between offenders and the IPS staff each week in the office, on the job, or in the home; random alcohol and drug testing and mandatory counseling for abusers; weekly employment verification; and an early nightly curfew (usually 8:00 p.m.). The program is basically self-supporting because probationers pay money into the program, in addition to the restitution they provide to their victims. Prisons get much-needed breathing space and save a substantial sum of money for each offender diverted from prison.

A front-door approach to easing prison overcrowding now losing favor is boot camps, or *shock incarceration*. Young (seventeen- to twenty-five-year-old) first-time felony offenders are given the option of serving their prison term or spending several months in a shock incarceration center, which resembles boot camp in the U.S. Marine Corps. In fact, former Marine drill instructors are often in charge. Those inmates who successfully complete the three- to six-month program win early release. Those who fall short are assigned to the regular prison population.

Shock incarceration is aimed at more than just relief of prison overcrowding. It is also intended to teach self-control and self-discipline to young people who come from dysfunctional homes or from selfish, undisciplined personal backgrounds. If shock incarceration has the long-term impact its advocates claim, it should keep thousands of young offenders from becoming recidivists; however, skeptics have challenged the results of boot camps. Boot-camp drop-out rates are high, and in most states the recidivism rate for graduates is only marginally lower than that for the regular prison population. Of course, drop-outs and recidivists end up in prison, canceling any savings generated from boot camp. Savings are also canceled out when judges assign youths to boot camp instead of probation.

Juvenile abuses and even deaths have been reported in boot camps in Arizona, South Dakota, and Texas. A review of Connecticut's program discovered gang infiltration, gambling, drug use, and other problems, leading the governor to close it down. Disappointing results have led several states, including Arizona, Florida, and California, to close their camps.

## Capacity Enhancement

Capacity enhancement is the third major strategy for matching available prison beds with the number of inmates. Usually it entails construction of new prison facilities, which is indeed costly, and operating them is even more so. Some states have completed new facilities, but have not been able to afford to staff and run them. Many taxpayers resent spending so much money on the care and feeding of criminals—although, ironically, they want convicted criminals to be locked up. Others oppose having a new prison located in their community. But poor, rural areas often perceive prisons to be a desirable form of economic development. A new prison typically brings 300 institutional jobs with 1,000 inmates. Prisons are supply-driven, and the flow of criminals is dependable. Prisons also purchase local goods and services. They pay sales taxes, water and sewer fees, and landfill charges. Also, because inmates are considered residents of local jurisdictions, their presence means more federal and state funding.[51]

The prison construction boom seems to have paused for now. Texas built so many new prisons so fast that it had a surplus of about 20,000 county jail cells, which it proceeded to rent to states with too many prisoners. Several states, from Hawaii to Massachusetts, sent nearly 4,000 inmates to the Lone Star State, at daily rates of as little as half those in states where the offender was sentenced.[52] But Colorado, Kansas, and Michigan have recently closed prisons, primarily for financial reasons. To help cover the costs of incarceration, states are imposing "pay to stay" fees, charging prisoners for room and board (most are unable to pay).

**Private Prisons** One increasingly popular long-term capacity enhancement innovation is private prisons, or prisons for profit, an idea spawned from the near-hopelessness of many overcrowded state correctional systems. The private sector has long provided certain services and programs to prisons, including health care, food services, and alcohol and drug treatment. Privately operated prisons existed more than 100 years ago in Louisiana, New York, and a handful of other states, but they were closed down amid revelations of prisoner abuse.

About 7.4 percent of incarcerated adults and juveniles are held in privately run correction institutions today. These institutions include medium-security prisons in Virginia, Texas, Oklahoma, and Tennessee. The two largest prison management firms, Corrections Corporation of America and Geo Group,[53] control 75 percent of the private corrections market (see the Debating Politics box on the next page).

**Does Prison Pay?** The construction and operation of prisons is the fastest-growing budget item in many states, even faster than the growth of Medicaid.

Arraigned men await trial in crowded holding cell, Maricopa County Jail, AZ

## DEBATING POLITICS

## Who Should Operate Our Prisons?

Despite its rapid growth, prison privatization is a controversial idea. Those who support it claim that prisons built and operated by the private sector save the taxpayers money. Because of less red tape, facilities can be constructed and operated more economically. Most important, advocates point out, private prisons reduce overcrowding. Opponents of privatization, however, question whether firms can in fact build and operate correctional facilities significantly less expensively than state or local governments can. They believe that the profit motive is misplaced in a prison setting, where firms may skimp on nutritious food, health care, or skilled personnel to cut operating costs. A "prison-industrial complex," whose businesses benefit from constructing and filling up cell space, lobbies and contributes campaign dollars to legislators in the interest of stricter sentencing requirements and additional prisons.[1]

Evidence on the economics of prison privatization is mixed. Most of the facilities house juveniles, illegal aliens, and minimum- and medium-security offenders. The majority of studies indicate that operating cost savings have been marginal or nonexistent.[2] Corrections Corporation of America and other private prison firms have reported significant financial losses. And although overcrowded conditions may be relieved more promptly through privatization, the burden on the taxpayers appears to be about the same.

Who should be responsible for prisons? Economic considerations are obviously important, but constitutional and legal issues challenge prisons for profit. A basic question is whether the delegation of the corrections function to a private firm is constitutionally permissible. The U.S. Supreme Court and state courts will have to determine not only whether incarceration, punishment, deterrence, and rehabilitation can properly

be delegated, but also who is legally liable for a private facility. The Supreme Court spoke on one such issue by declaring that private prison guards who violate inmates' rights are not entitled to qualified immunity—unlike public-sector guards.[3]

Another set of legal considerations concerns practical accountability for the day-to-day operation of jails and prisons. Who is responsible for developing operational rules, procedures, and standards and for ensuring that they are carried out? Who is responsible for maintaining security at the institutions and using "reasonable force" against prisoners? Who will implement disciplinary actions against inmates? What happens if prison employees strike? (Strikes by state correctional employees are illegal, but those by their private-sector counterparts are not). What if the corporation hikes its fees substantially? Or declares bankruptcy because of financial mismanagement or a liability suit? Who is liable if prisoners are abused and have their civil rights violated by a firm's guards, as happened with Missouri felons doing time in a Texas prison run by a Mississippi company? Consider this case: In Texas, two men escaped from a private prison near Houston. They nearly made it to Dallas before they were caught. But Texas authorities couldn't prosecute because by breaking out of a private facility, the men had not committed an offense under Texas law. The men, who had been sent to the private facility from Oregon, could not be prosecuted for escape in Oregon because the event happened in Texas.

Economic and legal issues aside, perhaps the most important question is, who *should* operate our jails and prisons? Legal scholar Ira Robbins suggests that we should remember the words of the novelist Fyodor Dostoevsky: "The degree of civilization in a society can be judged by entering its prisons." The state, after all, administers justice in the courtroom. Shouldn't it also be responsible for carrying out justice in the correctional facilities? Should profits be derived from depriving human beings of their freedom?

[1] B. E. Price, *Merchandizing Prisoners: Who Really Pays for Prison Privatization* (Westport, CT: Praeger, 2006).

[2] Anne Morrison Piehl and John J. DiIulio, Jr., "Does Prison Pay?" *The Brookings Review* (Winter 1995): 21–25.

[3] *Richardson v. McKnight* 138 L. Ed. 2d 540 (1997).

Yet every dollar sunk into correctional facilities is one less to pay for highways, social services, higher education, and the needs of children. Our priorities seem skewed indeed when we invest only $4,000–$8,000 per year for a child's education, whereas a prisoner costs tens of thousands of dollars more each year to keep incarcerated.

Does prison pay by keeping repeat offenders out of action? Benefit–cost analyses comparing the costs of incarceration with estimated savings to society from foregone burglaries, larcenies, murders, and rapes do indicate a net benefit to society. Taking into account crimes not committed by inmates in Wisconsin, researchers Piehl and DiIulio calculate "that imprisoning 100 typical convicted felons cost $2.5 million, whereas leaving them on the streets to commit more crimes would cost society $4.6 million." In a study of New Jersey, the same researchers confirm that "prison pays for most state prisoners," especially those who are either repeat or violent offenders who pose an immediate danger if released.[54]

Prison does not pay, however, for drug offenders, most of whom could be placed under supervision or substance abuse counseling, or released altogether. And it doesn't pay for older offenders who are no longer high-risk individuals. And as noted earlier, incarceration appears to have no measurable effect on the crime rate. States with the highest incarceration rates also have among the highest crime rates.

## THE CONTINUING CHALLENGE IN CRIME AND CORRECTIONS

The idea of placing people in prisons to punish them with deprivation of their freedom was devised only 200 years ago. Until fairly recently, brutality was the operating norm. Deliberately painful executions, maiming, flogging, branding, and other harsh punishments were applied to both serious and minor offenders. Misbehavior in prison was likely to be met with beatings or with more elaborate tortures such as stretching from ropes attached to a pulley in the ceiling or long confinement in an unventilated sweat box. By contrast, prison conditions in the states today seem almost luxurious. Inmates typically enjoy recreational activities; training and educational opportunities; the use of televisions, stereos, and videocassette recorders (VCRs, and DVDs) in their cells; and other amenities. Rules enforcement is also much more civilized and respectful of inmates' human rights. But a backlash is evident in some states. Surveys show that most citizens don't want criminals coddled.[55] They agree with former Massachusetts governor William Weld that prisons should offer "a tour through the circles of hell"—not the easy life. Today, shackled work crews can be seen along the highways of Alabama, Arizona, and Wisconsin.

Crime and corrections present major challenges to state and local governments. Certainly any long-term success will have to come from the recognition that all major components of the criminal justice system are interrelated to some extent. Thus, a broad approach to court, crime, and corrections is called for. That means beginning with the identification of at-risk children, creating an educational and social welfare support system for them, providing alcohol and drug abuse rehabilitation for prisoners and minor offenders, and helping to repair families and communities that are lacking in resources. It means addressing homelessness, poverty, gangs, and organized crime.

Some policies do seem to be driving down the crime rate. The aging of the U.S. population is an important factor, but so are technology enhancements and community-based activities such as community policing, drug treatment, and citywide crackdowns on gang leaders and serial offenders. Before the states can fully cope with the challenges described in this chapter, we must understand such complex relationships more fully and attack the causes of crime as well as its effects.

## CHAPTER RECAP

- Crime data are collected through the FBI's *Uniform Crime Reports* and victimization surveys. Both sources show a reduction in crime.

- Criminal justice is overwhelmingly a state and local government responsibility, with modest federal involvement.

- Key actors in criminal justice policy are law enforcement officials, the courts, the public, and victims.

- Victimless crimes and capital punishment are two policy issues that illustrate the variation in state approaches to criminal justice policy.

- Corrections policy deprives some criminals of their freedom, but little rehabilitation occurs.

- Policy alternatives for addressing prison capacity problems include back-door and front-door strategies and making additional prison cells available. Prison privatization is one controversial approach.

- Crime and corrections have become perennial challenges for state and local governments.

## Key Terms

grand jury *(p. 449)*
indictment *(p. 449)*
victimless crimes *(p. 450)*

indeterminate sentencing *(p. 458)*
determinate sentencing *(p. 458)*

parole *(p. 462)*
probation *(p. 462)*
creative sentencing *(p. 463)*

## Internet Resources

Hundreds of law enforcement and corrections-related sites appear on the Web. A few of the more interesting include the Federal Bureau of Investigation (FBI) homepage at **www.fbi.gov** and the Police Guide at **www.policeguide.com**.

For community policing, see the Office of Community Oriented Policing (COPS) at **www.cops.usdoj.gov**.

Links to most major criminal justice policy issues are available at **www.corrections.com**.

Statistics on prison privatization can be found at **www.crim.ufl.edu/pcp**.

**www.sentencingproject.org** is a nonprofit organization that promotes alternatives to prison.

For corrections and sentencing data, and other valuable information, see **www.ojp.usdoj.gov/bjs/** and **www.ncjrs.org**. Another general source is the Web address of the National Archive of Criminal Justice Data at **www.icpsr.umich.edu/NACJD**.

The Death Penalty Information Center (**www.deathpenaltyinfo.org**) provides a wealth of statistics and reports on capital punishment.

SOURCE: Tony Freeman/Photo Edit

# Social Welfare and Health Care Policy

**17**

Mary Harris, a thirty-year-old mother of two young children, is in desperate straits. Her husband left her eighteen months ago with nothing but a rented trailer and a fifteen-year-old Dodge. Unable to find work and the car broken down, Mary sells everything of value she has. With rent six months overdue, and following numerous eviction notices, she is now on the street with her kids. The youngest child, a girl six years old, is ready to join her eight-year-old sister in school—but to what school district do they belong? The local homeless shelter looks to be unsafe for the children, and they cannot stay there for more than a few weeks anyway. Where should they go? What should they do? What resources are offered by the city, community organizations, state, or federal offices to help them in this time of need?

The state and local governments must interact with people and situations such as these every day. There will always be people who, for various reasons, need help coping with poverty or other burdens that afflict them either temporarily or permanently. Most of those who need assistance actively seek it out through federal, state, local, and nonprofit social welfare and health care programs. Some do not receive welfare benefits but choose to fight their battles themselves, some need temporary help until they get back on their feet again, and some will be dependent on government assistance for the rest of their lives. Many of the poor work full-time jobs at low wages; others have never drawn a paycheck.

471

Welfare and health care reform programs are under way in every state today. With the Congress bogged down in a swamp of rhetoric and partisan mudslinging, the states have embarked on a path of unprecedented health and welfare innovations. The growth in the states' capacity to design, develop, and administer such programs is remarkable. It is confirmation of their increased responsiveness to problems besetting their citizens and improved capability to address some of the most difficult and persistent problems of our time both creatively and effectively.

# THE MEANING OF POVERTY

There are very few cases of absolute deprivation in this country. The necessities of life—food, clothing, housing—are available to all through government programs and nonprofit organizations (the homeless represent a perplexing and painful exception). The extreme, life-threatening poverty found in Sudan or Haiti simply does not occur here. Instead, poverty in the United States consists of relative deprivation: People are poor when they have relatively less wealth and income than most others, and despite their best efforts, they have difficulty making ends meet. Within this wealthy nation, relative differences in wealth and income equality are profound, and worsening. The United States has the highest degree of economic inequality among all advanced nations and greater than many Third World countries.[1]

The federal government uses a statistic called the *poverty line* (also called the *poverty threshold*) to define poverty in quantitative terms. The line has been set at three times the amount of income necessary to purchase essential food. The official poverty line changes each year as the cost of food rises (or, very rarely, falls). In 2009, it was pegged at $22,050 for a family of four and at $10,830 for an individual.[2] The poverty line is important because it helps determine who qualifies for various forms of public assistance. More than 37 million "officially" poor people lived in the United States in 2007, or around 13 percent of the population. In Mississippi, 20.6 percent of the state's population is officially poor; in New Hampshire, 7.1 percent of the population is. In race and ethnicity comparisons, poverty rates ranged from 24.5 percent for African Americans and 21.5 percent for Latinos, to less than 10.5 percent for whites and 10.2 percent for Asians and Pacific Islanders.[3]

Measuring poverty is far from an exact science. Government statistics fail to account for regional cost-of-living differences; variations in states' ability and willingness to fund welfare programs; a decline in the inflation-adjusted value of the minimum wage; a significant change in consumption patterns; the cost of housing, energy, and health care; in-kind benefits such as food stamps and the earned income tax credit; and the value of off-the-books income and barter income earned by individuals. And the poverty line is based on outdated assumptions about relative food costs and preferences taken from the year 1963! It is widely acknowledged that the official poverty numbers significantly understate the actual degree of poverty. Poverty in America was once associated largely with old age, but this view is no longer true. As the population has grown older, senior citizens have organized as a formidable interest group. Higher Social Security benefits, federal programs such as Medicare, and age-based preferences in local property and state income taxes have eased elderly people's financial burdens. Today, only 9.7 percent of those aged sixty-five and older are considered poor. The most alarming poverty victims are children: Some 18 percent live in poverty, including a shocking one-third of African American children from birth to age eighteen. In the context of limited government resources, a generational reckoning is inevitable; society will have to decide how to allocate its resources between the old and the young. Social Security and Medicare outlays to seniors are growing rapidly as a proportion of federal spending, while children's poverty statistics remain disturbingly high.

# SOCIAL WELFARE AND IDEOLOGY

Intense debates over political ideology and values have always stormed across the social welfare policy landscape, resulting in confused policy goals, a faulty patchwork of programs, and perpetual crisis. Conservatives and liberals have propounded starkly opposing points of view on the causes of poverty and the appropriate government response.

Conservatives, who generally believe in a restricted role for government, have tended to accept a modern version of the nineteenth-century view that "the giving of relief is a violation of natural law."[4] According to this viewpoint, the poor are victims of their own deficiencies. If they are to rise above poverty, they must hoist themselves up by their own bootstraps. From this perspective, the poor get what they deserve. Conservatives attack the social welfare system for interfering with "the free market," discouraging more productive allocations of public funds, undermining the work ethic, encouraging immoral behavior, and creating a permanent "underclass" of dependent welfare recipients. Conservatives favor policies that encourage marriage; discourage illegitimacy, unmarried sex, and teen pregnancy; promote individual responsibility; and cut welfare spending and dependency on public support.

For liberals, who generally believe in a broad and active role for government, poverty is a structural problem. People fall into poverty because of factors essentially beyond their control, such as inadequate schooling, poor and/or dysfunctional parents, divorce, lack of jobs, various forms of discrimination, and the up-and-down cycles of a capitalistic economy. According to this view, people cannot help being poor; and so it becomes the responsibility of government not only to relieve their poverty through public assistance programs but also to provide the poor with the appropriate skills and physical environment to enable them to become self-sufficient.

What does the typical American think about welfare? Contrary to conventional wisdom, most Americans favor government efforts to help the poor and are willing to pay higher taxes to assist them. But people tend to make a distinction between the "deserving" poor and those who are not willing to work and be personally responsible for their behavior. Media reports and racial stereotyping contribute to the widespread—but erroneous—belief that most welfare recipients are African Americans who lack a work ethic and behave irresponsibly.[5]

## The Origins of Social Welfare Policy

Social welfare programs developed later in the United States than in Western European nations. The U.S. programs in place today are also less uniform and less generous than those in Western Europe. These differences have been attributed to the federal system and especially to the competition among states for economic development. States attempt to create an attractive business climate characterized by low taxes and limited social program expenditures. This means less money for social services.

Our fragmented social welfare policy is a reflection of shifting conservative and liberal control of Congress and the presidency, and the inherently controversial nature of redistributive policies—those that result in taking from one group of people to give to another.

Although its roots may be traced back to pensions for Revolutionary War veterans and their widows, the basic foundations of the welfare system were laid by the liberal Democratic administration of Franklin D. Roosevelt in response to the Great Depression of the 1930s. Private charity and state and local relief programs were completely inadequate for combating a 25 percent unemployment rate and a collapsed national economy. The federal government responded with massive programs designed to provide temporary relief through public assistance payments, job creation, and Social Security. Since the 1930s, competing political parties and ideologies have sewn together a patchwork of programs to help the poor and unfortunate.

## A Social Welfare Consensus

A social welfare consensus emerged among conservatives and liberals and led to a new coalition for reform in the late 1980s. Conservatives admitted government's responsibility to help the truly needy and economically vulnerable, and liberals saw the need to attach certain obligations to welfare and to address the behavioral dependency of the underclass. Behavioral dependency means that poor people become dependent on government for their economic well-being by reason of their own choices, and it is a serious problem for this country's underclass, which is disproportionately young, male, minority, and urban. Many of these people are school and societal dropouts—borderline illiterates with no job skills. A disproportionate number become involved in drugs and crime. Agreement exists that welfare dependency must be reduced so that people can get off the dole and on the job. For those involved in crime and illegal drug activity, aggressive law enforcement, substance abuse counseling and treatment, or social work is called for.

This new consensus may reflect a somewhat common view of poverty, but disagreement about how to solve the problem persists. For example, which will most effectively encourage recipients to work: positive incentives or negative ones? Most agree that different types of poverty should be treated distinctively. For example, children, seniors, the disabled, single parents, working adults, and nonworking adults all have different needs. Many also agree that government should help those who can climb out of poverty through job training and other programs and that able-bodied welfare recipients have an obligation to seek and secure a job or perform public work.

Beyond these basic elements, the consensus tends to unravel. Conservatives seek better behavior from the poor, admonishing them to complete high school, find employment (even at low wages), and either get married and stay married or not have babies and get off welfare. Liberals are more willing to utilize social programs to transfer government resources to the poor, with fewer conditions. Despite these differences, the social welfare consensus was broad enough to enable congressional passage of the Family Support Act of 1988. This law incorporated conservative principles of personal responsibility with liberal principles of poverty relief. Then, in 1996, President Clinton made good on his promise to end welfare as we know it by signing a law that eliminated the nation's largest welfare program, Aid to Families with Dependent Children (AFDC). In doing so, he also threw down an enormous challenge to state and local governments to assume the lead in helping the poor exchange welfare checks for paychecks.

## CURRENT SOCIAL WELFARE POLICY

During and after the Great Depression, social welfare policy became primarily the responsibility of the federal government, with limited roles reserved to the states and localities. The states brought the various federal programs into action, administered them, and drew up rules to determine who was eligible for benefits. But with the 1996 welfare reform bill, entitled the Personal Responsibility and Work Opportunity Reconciliation Act (PRWORA), the federal government ceded a large portion of the policy field to the states and localities. Replacing AFDC was a new program, **Temporary Assistance for Needy Families (TANF)**, which emphasized maximum state discretion. As a consequence, state and local governments are in the vanguard of innovation and program experimentation, even more so than in other public policy fields.

Dramatic variations among the states exist in levels of social welfare spending. New York spends more than $2,239 per capita on welfare—the highest in the United States. Alaska, Rhode Island, and Delaware follow closely. The stingiest state is Nevada, at only $719, followed by Colorado ($736).[6] Some states pay relatively high benefits for one program, such as Medicaid, but relatively

**Temporary Assistance for Needy Families (TANF)**
A provision of the Personal Responsibility and Work Opportunity Reconciliation Act (PRWORA) of 1996, which replaced AFDC with a flexible program that allows states to set their own conditions and benefit levels for welfare recipients to help them secure and maintain employment.

low benefits for another, such as TANF—the result of battles among various constituencies over a limited social welfare pie. States controlled by the Democratic Party tend to be more generous than Republican dominated states, and strong party competition within a state drives up benefit levels. Race is important: Eligibility policies are stricter and benefits are lower in states with high African American caseloads.[7] Political beliefs have an impact as well. The relationship between a dominant liberal or conservative ideology and state welfare spending levels should be obvious.

# TYPES OF SOCIAL WELFARE PROGRAMS

Social welfare programs may be sorted into two categories: public assistance and social insurance. Public assistance programs, such as food stamps or TANF, involve government payments of money or in-kind benefits to poor people who meet various qualifying criteria. Social insurance programs, such as Social Security, include recipient contributions (e.g., the Social Security payroll tax) as well as government payments. Our concern in this chapter is primarily with public assistance programs.

To convey a basic understanding of complex intergovernmental social welfare policies, we examine the most significant ones individually. For purposes of discussion, we divide social welfare policies into three types: direct cash transfers, in-kind benefits, and social insurance (see Table 17.1). Most are public assistance, so-called "entitlement programs," meaning that these are government spending programs with eligibility criteria. If a recipient meets the criteria (age, income, and so on), he or she is entitled to the money.

## Direct Cash Transfers

**direct cash transfer**

The transfer of cash, such as in the form of a disability check, from one level of government to an individual citizen beneficiary.

**Direct cash transfers** are welfare programs that directly convey money, in the form of government checks, to qualified recipients. Administrative arrangements vary by type of program. *Aid to Families with Dependent Children* was included in the Social Security Act of 1935 to furnish financial aid to poor children whose fathers had died. By 1996, however, AFDC payments went almost entirely (90 percent) to single-parent families in which the living father was absent.

AFDC was the most costly and most controversial social welfare program in the United States. Critics claimed that it caused marriages to break up or to be consciously avoided; encouraged young, nonworking, unwed women to have babies; promoted migration of the poor to states paying higher AFDC benefits; and perpetuated dependency into future generations. No one professed fondness for AFDC, not even the recipients.

As noted earlier, AFDC was abandoned in 1996 with passage of the new welfare reform act, PRWORA, which replaced AFDC grants to individuals with block grants to the states. The states in turn designed programs for promoting

| PROGRAM CATEGORY AND NAME | NUMBER OF RECIPIENTS (IN MILLIONS) | WHO FUNDS | WHO ADMINISTERS | TOTAL EXPENDITURES (IN BILLIONS OF DOLLARS) |
|---|---|---|---|---|
| **DIRECT CASH TRANSFER** | | | | |
| TANF | 4.1 | National | State | 14.1 |
| SSI | 8.6 | National | National, state | 38.9 |
| Earned Income Tax Credit | 24.6 | National | National | 45.4 |
| **IN-KIND PROGRAM** | | | | |
| Food stamps | 30.3 | National | State, local | 35.6 |
| Medicaid | 58.7 | National, state | State, local | 335.0 |
| Child Nutrition | 30.5 | National | State, local | 11.5 |
| State Children's Health Insurance Program (S-CHIP) | 7.4 | National, state | State | 25.0 |
| **SOCIAL INSURANCE** | | | | |
| Social Security (OASDI) | 41.2 | National | National | 544.0 |
| Medicare | 44.8 | National, state | National, state | 303.4 |
| Unemployment compensation | 5.2 | State, private | State | 33.0 |
| Worker's compensation | 1.7 | State, private | State | 57.0 |
| Veterans' Benefits | 23.8 | National | National | 69.9 |

**TABLE 17.1** Major Social Welfare and Social Insurance Programs

SOURCE: U.S. Bureau of the Census, *Statistical Abstract of the United States,* 2009 (Washington, D.C.: U.S. Government Printing Office, 2009); www.census.gov; Medicare and Social Security Administration reports; and data from the Rockefeller Institute of Government. Various years (most recent data available) are reported above.

work and individual responsibility. The states received vast new authority and flexibility for reinventing welfare, subject to certain federal requirements. States submit TANF plans outlining how the state will assist needy families with children and help prepare parents to become self-sufficient. The law stipulates that adults have up to two years to find a job without losing benefits and a lifetime limit of five years to receive benefits. Up to 20 percent of the state's welfare population may receive hardship exemptions for circumstances such as mental or physical disabilities. This "tough love" approach to getting people off public support also has a financial stick to move any recalcitrant states ahead. Under 2006 congressional amendments to TANF, states must demonstrate that at least 50 percent of TANF recipients are engaged in work or work-related activities, for twenty to thirty hours per week, depending on the age of children; two-parent families must record a total of thirty-five to forty hours per week.

The states combined TANF requirements with previously existing state welfare-to-work programs to drop welfare caseloads dramatically (by 50–90 percent in the states, and by three-quarters nationwide). Many diverse options are being pursued by the states, including family caps that limit or eliminate additional payments for children born after a mother begins receiving benefits; transferring impaired clients to disability programs; and individual development accounts, which permit recipients to establish savings accounts to pay for items such as college or technical education, a new home, or the start of a business. Most states provide some form of child-care assistance, job training, and transportation aid (so that workers can have a dependable way to get to and from their jobs). Some states use TANF funds to provide post-employment services to help clients keep their jobs and even win promotions. States also vary in their approach to the controversial question of how to treat immigrants and citizens moving from other states.

Following the initial years of success, the states are now hard-pressed to find jobs for the less able of the welfare population, who experience serious, and often multiple, barriers to employment, even while the federal government has tightened up its demands that they do so. The states, however, believe that they are much better suited than the national government to handle welfare-to-work programs and that they will be successful in all except the most difficult cases, such as individuals with the most serious physical, mental, or emotional problems.

*Supplemental Security Income (SSI)* is financed and operated by the national government, except that state officials determine who is eligible for the program. Created in 1974, SSI combined three existing programs: Old Age Assistance, Aid to the Blind, and Aid to the Disabled. Its recipients are people who are unable to work because of old age or physical or mental disabilities and, increasingly, children with behavioral or learning disabilities.

The *Earned Income Tax Credit* provides cash assistance to low-income, working individuals and families through a refundable federal income tax credit. It was created in 1975 to offset the burden of Social Security taxes and to encourage work.

*General Assistance* is a state and local program intended to help poor people who do not qualify for other direct cash or in-kind transfer programs, such as the nonworking but physically able poor. State benefit levels vary greatly. Some states do not offer the program at all.

## In-Kind Programs

**in-kind program**

The payment of a noncash social welfare benefit, such as food stamps or clothing, to an individual recipient.

**In-kind programs** provide benefits in goods or services, rather than in cash, as a way to address specific problems of poverty, hunger, illness, and joblessness. *Food stamps*—essentially debit cards that can be used to purchase food—are paid for by the national government. The program was established in 1964, and benefit levels are uniform throughout the United States. Both the working and nonworking poor are eligible if their income falls sufficiently close to the poverty level.

*Medicaid* is a health care assistance program for the poor (SSI recipients automatically qualify). It is jointly funded by the national (57 percent) and state (43 percent) governments, and it is enormously expensive (more than $320 billion in 2007), constituting more than 21.5 percent of state budgets. The

Medicaid program provides free health care services to uninsured poor people and is the principal source of assistance for long-term institutional care for the physically and mentally disabled and the elderly. It must be distinguished from Medicare, which is an entitlement program that grants health care assistance to those aged sixty-five years or older. Since the inception of Medicaid in 1965, it has been wracked with scandals: Doctors, pharmacists, dentists, and other professionals have been charged with everything from performing unnecessary surgery and inflating fees to filing reimbursements for imaginary patients. Medicaid has also placed an increasingly onerous burden on state budgets.

*State Children's Health Insurance Program* (S-CHIP) is jointly funded by the federal and state governments to provide health insurance to children in families who cannot afford private insurance but who earn too much income to qualify for Medicaid. The program was reauthorized and significantly enhanced with new federal funding in 2009, as part of the national economic relief efforts. Under S-CHIP the states enjoy great flexibility in designing and implementing their own plans.

*Housing programs* exist in several forms today. The federal housing program helps pay for public housing or provides rent subsidies directly to the poor, who apply them to private rental units. States administer a portion of approximately 1.3 million subsidized apartment units; the U.S. Department of Housing and Urban Development administers the rest. As homelessness rates soared across the country in 2008–2009, emergency shelters were overwhelmed. Tent cities arose in Phoenix, Arizona, Reno, Nevada, Sacramento, California, and many other cities. Of an estimated 3.4 million Americans homeless in 2009, a majority were families with children.[8] States responded with expanded shelters, new subsidized housing, and other attempts to relieve the problem until the economy—and its innocent victims—recovered.

Max Whittaker/Getty Images News/Getty Images

Tent City in 2009, Reno Nevada.

*Other in-kind programs* include numerous types of public assistance, such as the *Child Nutrition*, or school lunch program, Head Start, energy assistance for low-income families, legal services, supplemental food programs, family planning, foster care, and services for the physically and mentally disabled. National, state, and local participation depends on the specific program in question. Under TANF, states have great flexibility in offering in-kind aid to help move welfare recipients into jobs and keep them working. Examples include child-care services, job training, transportation, technical and college education, and workshops on how to find and keep a job. The diversity of in-kind programs is compelling evidence of the complexity of the poverty problem.

Recent policy reforms have shifted welfare spending from cash assistance to in-kind services designed to help poor people acquire gainful employment and stay off government assistance. Very few receive any form of cash assistance today.

## Social Insurance

**social insurance**

A jointly funded benefit program made available by a government to its citizens as a right of its citizens.

**Social insurance** is distinguished from public assistance programs by the fact that recipients (or their relatives or employers) contribute financially through the Social Insurance Trust Fund, established by the Social Security Act of 1935. In effect, participants pay in advance for their future well-being. Although not generally considered to be a public assistance program, social insurance does help in the broad effort to relieve poverty. Contributions to social insurance come from Social Security payments by individual workers and by their employers.

*Social Security* (officially known as Old Age, Survivors, Disability, and Health Insurance) is run entirely by the national government and is paid for through a payroll tax on employers and employees. Monthly checks are sent electronically to retired people; to the disabled; and to the spouses and dependent children of workers who retire, die, or become disabled. It is the largest entitlement program.

*Medicare* provides federal health care, hospital, and prescription drug benefits for people over the age of sixty-five in exchange for a monthly premium and co-payments. It was created in 1965 through an amendment to the Social Security Act. Medicare costs have escalated rapidly as a result of the growing number of senior citizens and ballooning health care bills and prescription drug prices.

*Unemployment compensation* was mandated by the Social Security Act of 1935. It requires employers and employees to contribute to a trust fund administered by the states. Those who lose their jobs through layoffs or dismissals could draw combined state and federal unemployment benefits for as long as fifty-nine weeks during the recent economic crisis.

*Worker's compensation* is also part of the Social Security Act. Financed by employers and administered by the states, it establishes insurance for workers and their dependents to cover job-related accidents or illnesses that result in death or disability. Its cost, which is closely associated with the price of health care, has escalated rapidly.

Social welfare policy clearly demonstrates the interdependent nature of the federal system. The national government pays for and operates some programs on its own; Social Security is one example. State and local governments take care of others. The states and localities perform key administrative roles in most social welfare efforts and serve as incubators for new ideas and programs, many of which have later been incorporated into national policy. The private and nonprofit sectors contribute through charities such as United Way agencies and institutions such as hospitals, clinics, nursing homes, and myriad community-based organizations. Contracting by all levels of government with nonprofits has made hidden partners of these nonprofit organizations, which attend to Americans' problems from cradle to grave.

# STATE INNOVATIONS IN SOCIAL WELFARE

Public assistance policy today has two critical goals. One pertains to the well-being of children and necessity of the family. The other goal is to end welfare dependency. The respective roles of national, state, and local governments in these two policy goals are continually being sorted out. A perplexing array of welfare traps snares even the most carefully devised policy proposals (see Figure 17.1). Undeniably, however, the states and localities are the prime innovators in social welfare policy and the governments most responsive to the needs of the poor and disadvantaged.[9]

## Saving the Children

Several important reasons explain the plight of children. Many children live with a single parent because of high divorce rates (almost half of all children experience life with a divorced parent during childhood), births to unwed mothers (some 40 percent of all infants), and irresponsible fathers who refuse to support their offspring. Even if single mothers have the necessary education or skills to secure employment, their children often must be placed in the care of older siblings or left on their own if family or friends cannot care for them. Opportunities for affordable, subsidized, or free day care are generally limited to Head Start and oversubscribed state-run and charitable programs. Finally, too many children are born not only into poverty but also into sickness. Because of inadequate diets, lack of health insurance, ignorance about prenatal care, drug abuse, and the spread of sexually transmitted diseases such as acquired immune deficiency syndrome (AIDS), many mothers give birth to premature, underweight, and sickly children. Some infants do not survive.

Children's issues have risen to the top of national and state policy agendas. Historically, the national government has addressed these problems, and it

**FIGURE 17.1**

**Ten Welfare Traps**

*The policy objective seems simple: Make welfare a reciprocal arrangement in which the poor must look for and accept a job in exchange for government assistance in preparing for work. If recipients refuse, they should lose their benefits. Welfare should offer a helping hand, not a lifetime handout. But many traps make achieving this seemingly simple objective both complex and elusive, and they present significant roadblocks to state policy innovation.*

**Trap 1:** Some people *cannot* work. A large number of welfare recipients are simply incapable of holding down a job. Whether because of substance abuse, emotional problems, physical or learning disabilities, or other conditions, these people need long-term support for themselves and their children. It is not always easy to distinguish members of this group from the able-bodied.

**Trap 2:** Providing financial and other support may actually reduce the potential rewards of working. Taking even a low-wage job forces people to forgo the safety net of Medicaid, food stamps, and other programs.

**Trap 3:** The creation of community service or make work jobs for the poor is opposed by labor unions and other groups that fear welfare recipients will displace workers in low-wage, low-skilled jobs, sending *them* onto the welfare rolls.

**Trap 4:** Unless the government separates children from their parents and places them in foster homes, or other care facilities, help for poor children also means help for their parents. If welfare recipients are denied benefits for not working, their children may suffer hardships. The denial of additional assistance for the single welfare mother's second or third child unfairly punishes the innocent child.

**Trap 5:** "Deadbeat Dads" who do not pay court-ordered child support present a conundrum. If jailed, they cannot work to pay the support. If laboring in a low-wage job, they cannot afford to shelter and feed themselves plus turn over hundreds of dollars a month to the mother.

**Trap 6:** To get people off welfare and thus save money in the long term means spending money today. Most welfare reform proposals require spending for education, job training, child care, and related services. Failure to invest sufficiently can result in public assistance programs that are underfunded and doomed to fail. It is cheaper in the short run to send the poor their welfare checks. The long-run solution requires a large financial investment.

**Trap 7:** Bureaucracy can get in the way of compassion and good sense. The average length of a federal food-stamps form—which is designed by individual states—is twelve pages. Some run more than thirty pages. Confusing legalese and intrusive questions inhibit applications. Some states ask applicants to list the value of a burial plot, or what a child earns from cutting grass. Maryland requires applicants to list "deemor expenses" (a phrase not in the working vocabulary of most Americans).

**Trap 8:** Welfare policy sets a double standard: It pushes the poor mother to exercise "parental responsibility" by leaving her children for a job to support them, yet the middle-class woman is praised for staying home to raise her children.

**Trap 9:** The typical job-training program requires that participants be job-ready, have a high school diploma, read at the eighth-grade level or higher, and provide their own day care and transportation. But the typical unemployed person has little or no work experience, has a tenth-grade education, reads at the sixth-grade level, has limited access to day care, and has no personal transportation. As a result, job training may not help.

**Trap 10:** Most new jobs are found in the suburbs, but the vast majority of the poor live in central cities. Low-income housing is not available or is rare in many suburbs, and many of the poor do not have access to reliable transportation.

SOURCES: The authors; also Kent Weaver, "Old Traps, New Twists," *Brookings Review* (Summer 1994): 14–21; Clare Nolan, "States Use Red Tape to Shrink Food Stamp Program," www.stateline.org (August 14, 2000): 1–2.

continues to do so today through programs such as Head Start, which provides preschool education and medical, dental, and social services for approximately 910,000 children up to five years of age. Head Start is a popular program that also promotes parental self-sufficiency. In addition, the states and some local governments have their own agendas. Successful programs that assist children now should eventually help reduce welfare expenditures for future adults and the elderly.

To deal with the growing problem of absentee fathers (97 percent of nonpaying parents are male), the states withhold court-ordered child support payments from the wages of absent parents, even if the parent has not fallen behind in payments. States are also required to establish paternity, through blood tests and DNA techniques, for children born out of wedlock. The result is that more fathers are being held financially responsible for their offspring. The states have additional authority to speed up judicial and administrative procedures for obtaining paternal support, to establish guidelines for judges to determine the appropriate size of child support awards, and to monitor support payments. Many states use a "deadbeat dad" approach to publicize and prosecute delinquent fathers. A national database has been established, consisting of each person newly hired by every U.S. employer. States can plug into the database to track down deadbeat parents across state lines.

## Day Care

The issue of day care for children of working and single parents has received a great deal of attention from the state and local governments, while the national government has struggled in vain to produce child-care legislation. Hundreds of thousands of youngsters aged eleven and under are home alone each day from the time they return from school until a parent arrives. State and local governments are subsidizing day-care programs through tax breaks and are offering various child-care arrangements under TANF. Nearly all states partly or fully fund child-care expenses for TANF recipients. States are also taking the lead in improving prenatal care, gradually reducing the nation's shameful infant mortality rate, which exceeds the rate of most other industrialized nations. Certainly it is less costly to invest at the front end of a person's life than to try correcting medical and other ailments later.

## Teenage Mothers

Teenagers are highly likely to produce at-risk children (children more likely to experience school failure than other children). The rate of births to teen mothers accelerated during the 1970s and 1980s, and now stands at 42.5 births for every 1,000 girls today. About 86 percent of births to teen mothers are out of wedlock.[10] Most of these children and their mothers live in poverty. The annual taxpayer bill for aiding these almost certainly dysfunctional families is staggering.

The high teen birthrate represents a strong argument for greater use of counseling, sex education, contraception, and even abortion. Federal law prohibits using federal Medicaid funds for abortions for poor women unless their pregnancies are the result of incest or rape. Abortion is an extremely controversial "hot stove" issue in the states. State-paid abortions for poor women would undoubtedly reduce the number of illegitimate births and provide a family-planning option that is widely available to middle- and upper-class women. It would also save taxpayers the expense of supporting a substantial number of children born into poverty, perhaps with serious and costly health problems. But abortion is highly distasteful to many and sinful to pro-life advocates. To its most rabid opponents, it is grounds for assassinating physicians who perform abortions.

State programs to reduce teen pregnancy take several directions. Minnesota integrates teen pregnancy prevention with human immunodeficiency virus (HIV) and sexually transmitted disease (STD) awareness and prevention. North Carolina targets middle-school adolescents and teens who are at risk of sexual activity. Catawba County's Teen Up program, for example, provides classes in sexual abuse, sexuality, drug abuse, handling peer pressure for sex, managing emotions and conflict, and other topics for students identified by school counselors.

California, Delaware, Florida, and many other states are attacking teen pregnancy by strengthening enforcement of long-neglected statutory rape laws. The goal is to discourage "sexual predators"—older males who prey on girls under the legal age of consent (fourteen years in Hawaii, eighteen in California and a dozen others, and sixteen in most states).

Improvement in teenage birth rates was recorded in most states from 1991 to 2005. Fear of AIDS and other STDs played a part in the decline, as did more reliable birth control techniques, including long-lasting implants and injections. But the problem remains serious and perplexing, and it is getting worse again. Teen pregnancy is a mother's recipe for a lifetime of poverty. It encourages dependency and greatly reduces career and life choices for the mother. Teen pregnancies cost taxpayers billions of dollars for social welfare and health care support for the child and the mother, most of whom receive no assistance from the father. The vast majority of teen mothers never complete high school.

The states are a beehive of experimentation and creative activity, but they have learned that a great chasm exists between establishing a new program and making it work effectively. Policy implementation is hindered by the complexities of our federal system, the waxing and waning of elected officials' attention, and the enormity of our social welfare problems. Government programs such as abstinence education, no matter how well intended, sometimes cannot cause desired behavioral changes in target populations. The ravages of drugs, crime, and poverty; the lack of parenting skills; and low self-esteem place many Americans at risk of long-term welfare dependency. And once unmarried teens have given birth, it is an uphill struggle for public policy to help most of them become productive citizens.

# TURNING WELFARE CHECKS INTO PAYCHECKS

Until the 1996 Welfare Reform Act and TANF, checks were handed over to AFDC recipients, and little was required of them in return. The driving idea now is to help people find jobs and become independent. Jobs should produce more household income, along with improved self-image and self-reliance for recipients, and financial savings for taxpayers.

The states have taken two different approaches to moving clients from welfare to work. With an eye to meeting required federal work-participation rates, many states have "work-first" strategies that stress immediate job searches. Others, more concerned about the long-term reduction of poverty, focus on helping recipients develop necessary job skills through education, training, and other pre-employment preparation. TANF has evolved into additional efforts to help recipients retain jobs, and earn promotions and pay increases. Examples of work-first approaches are the widely praised Greater Avenues for Independence (GAIN) program in Riverside County, California, and Wisconsin Works.

In a change of direction, several states have privatized all or most major components of public assistance programs. Private firms or nonprofit organizations were given contracts to process forms and applications in Arizona and elsewhere. Some county job centers in Wisconsin are run by private companies and nonprofits. Indiana contracted out management of its entire TANF program as well as the food-stamps program, and terminated its $1.16 billion privatization contract because of excruciatingly long client waiting periods for food-stamps processing.[11] Privatization has not proven to be a panacea. Texas' ambitious effort to privatize public assistance program client intake and screening "turned into a dark comedy of bungled work and unanswered and dropped phone calls; applications lost, ignored, and misdirected."[12]

Many additional state and local efforts are under way. "Individual development" accounts encourage the poor to save. A rising number of states and cities have set minimum wages substantially above the $7.25 per hour the federal government imposed in 2009.

As indicated by the welfare traps discussed in Figure 17.1, however, divine intervention in settling the welfare conundrum would not be unwelcome. State and local efforts to significantly reform welfare—courageous and well intentioned as they may be—encounter enormous difficulties. Complicating factors abound in snarled webs. For example, what should be done about welfare recipients who truly want but cannot find a job? And what about the high proportion of TANF recipients who have physical or mental impairments?[13] Make-work or community service sounds promising, until one examines the costs of arranging, monitoring, and paying for it. What if a recipient is addicted to drugs and cannot hold a job? Detoxification and counseling are not cheap, but kicking the recipient off assistance could well result in a new enlistee in the ranks of criminals or the homeless. Evidence suggests that some welfare checks indirectly subsidize drug trade and addiction. Thirty-five states presently deny TANF benefits to convicted drug felons, and a growing number of jurisdictions require their general assistance recipients to undergo drug tests. Those testing positive must submit to treatment or forgo their assistance.

After six decades of public assistance as an entitlement under AFDC, a different regime, grounded in work and self-sufficiency, is in place. Rapidly declining welfare caseloads in nearly every state elated supporters of TANF and state and local innovators. But the early job placements essentially removed the better-educated and job-ready people from the welfare rolls. Those who simply do not want to work also dropped off public assistance. Those still seeking a declining number of low-skill jobs are those with few employment skills, physical and emotional disabilities, and limited English-language abilities. Welfare roles have been cut, but many—particularly single moms and their kids—remain in precarious circumstances.[14]

Fears of a race to the bottom, in which states seek to drive out the poor by cutting welfare benefits to the bare bone, and a magnet hypothesis, which predicted that poor people would move to states with relatively generous welfare benefits, have not been realized.[15] But unanswered questions and severe challenges remain for state and local governments: What happens as lifetime limits on cash assistance expire? Will more children be pushed into poverty? Will the numbers of homeless multiply? Are most of the newly employed in dead-end jobs that pay little and offer nothing in terms of advancement, or will former welfare recipients remain self-supporting? What happens to people who refuse to comply with work requirements and voluntarily drop out of welfare? Will the national government refrain from undermining state programs with new mandates? Much is at stake, and state and local governments are engaging the issues, as shown in this chapter's Engaging feature.

# HEALTH CARE

A national debate has raged over health care reform for nearly two decades, with promise of congressional action in 2009 or 2010. The interest groups' hysteria and hand-wringing reach a fever pitch with each new proposal. Americans have learned a lot about the problems and politics of health care, along with a new vocabulary of health care terms (see Table 17.2). Meanwhile, as the national government continues to struggle with health care policy, the states have moved into the breach with innovative policies of their own, the results of which are serving as a road map for future national reform efforts.

## The Problem

Nearly everyone agrees that, although the quality of health care technology in the United States is unsurpassed, the U.S. health care system is too expensive for most and dysfunctional for many. Costs have been soaring since the early 1980s. The nation's total annual health care bill exceeds $2.4 trillion, or 17 percent of the economy—by far the highest in the world.[16] Medicare alone pays medical bills for more than 47 million aging citizens. Medicaid costs (funded by states at a rate of 47 percent of total program costs) have skyrocketed and

## Engaging Social Welfare and Health Care Policy

### Strengthening and Expanding the Safety Net

As job losses and home foreclosures mounted during the Great Recession of 2008–2009, and the long-term effects of TANF pushed most people off any sort of cash assistance, the national safety net to catch people from falling into the financial abyss suffered some tears. A daunting, disconnected array of non cash programs are available, including Food Stamps (now called Supplemental Nutrition Assistance), S-CHIP, Medicaid, nutrition programs for women and infants, subsidized child care, home energy assistance, unemployment assistance, and job training and placement. All told, an estimated 200 federal, state, and local programs are available.[1] But each program has its own frustrating application and paperwork requirements and usually involves a different state office. A large proportion of state and federal assistance is never accessed by qualified individuals who cannot negotiate the health and welfare labyrinth. Those who face multiple barriers to employment, such as a high-school dropout with a young child and domestic violence and substance abuse issues, often don't know where to begin. Making the situation worse has been the need for governors and legislatures to lay off staff in social service organizations.[2]

State and local governments are sensitive to these problems and they are trying to address them. New York City's WeCare program furnished one-stop service centers to comprehensively assess an individual and his or her situation and develop a plan for coordinated assistance.[3] Utah has a similar approach using "storefront" service centers. Nearly every state and local jurisdiction has worked to eliminate bureaucratic obstacles to acquiring services. For example, a new Medicaid enrollee might be automatically placed in the home heating assistance program and job training. More than half the states have put into place online applications for benefits as well as call centers to help people make their way through the social welfare system. ACCESS Florida permits residents to apply for various benefits online 24–7 and then automatically distributes the information to relevant offices. To enable those without personal computer access to participate, the state refurbished hundreds of its old PCs and distributed them to local community centers and nonprofit service providers to be made publicly available. Wisconsin and Pennsylvania offer similar one-stop online shopping for services.[4]

A very different plan to sew up the safety net is found in Arkansas. Most of those TANF clients who find employment are in a job with low wages that might not include health benefits. To help such working poor succeed, Arkansas provides working parents with $204 a month in cash, plus a bonus for staying employed for up to two years. Oregon lays out $150 monthly for up to a year, and Virginia $50. Other states provide health insurance, subsidized day care, and even transportation to help clients stay on the job. Early evaluations indicate that such efforts to prop up the working poor do help keep them in the workplace.[5]

[1] Christine Vestal, "Policy Challenge: How to Expand Safety Net," stateline.org (January 8, 2009).
[2] ibid.
[3] Jonathan Walters, "Is Welfare Working?" Governing (February 2008): 46.
[4] Jonathan Walters, "The Struggle to Streamline," Governing (September 2007): 28–34.
[5] Rachel L. Swarms, "State Programs Add Safety Net for the Poorest," nytimes.com (May 12, 2008).

now gobble up 20–22 percent of state budgets. These costs include millions of elderly people in nursing homes, children in low-income families, physically disabled individuals who require daily living assistance, and the mentally disabled. State government spending on health coverage for the needy surpassed $151 billion in 2007.[17] The Great Recession of 2008–2009 pushed large numbers of new enrollees into Medicaid as people lost their houses, cars, and jobs.

**TABLE 17.2    An Essential Dictionary of Health Care Terms**

**MANAGED CARE:** Involves several types of health plans that seek to contain costs by restricting the physicians and services that patients can access, promoting preventive health care, and capping hospital and physician payments. Managed care is available through *health maintenance organizations* (HMOs), consisting of gatekeeper physicians who direct patients to approved hospitals and other providers, and *preferred provider organizations* (PPOs), which are networks of approved doctors and hospitals.

**MANAGED COMPETITION:** Market-driven insurance plans that create incentives for competing insurance companies to provide health care services at low prices through negotiated fees.

**PORTABILITY:** The ability of individuals to take health care coverage with them wherever they work or live.

**SINGLE PAYER:** A government agency administering a health care system financed through taxes. Called "socialized medicine" by its critics, this system is prevalent in Great Britain, Canada, and several European countries. An example in the United States is the federal Medicare program.

**UNIVERSAL COVERAGE:** A national plan that offers comprehensive health care coverage to all citizens, typically through a single-payer national health insurance program. The concept has been proposed and debated in the United States since the turn of the twentieth century.

Inflating health care costs are the aging U.S. population, which means more people with illnesses directly associated with old age; the obesity epidemic; and increased use of expensive medical technology such as MRI. Expansions of eligibility for health care entitlement programs drive up costs. So do fraud and abuse. For example, some physicians sell prescriptions for narcotics. Some nursing homes charge for services not provided, and some home health care companies bill for nursing visits never made. (In some Florida nursing homes, patients in comas were billed for speech therapy)[18]. In pill mills, a conspiracy of doctors, clinic owners, and pharmacists prescribe drugs and obtain government reimbursements, yet no drugs actually change hands. All told, Medicare overpayments may run as high as 25 percent of all Medicare costs.[19]

Even though per capita U.S. health care spending far exceeds that of other countries, a large and growing portion of the population (estimated to be 18 percent of people under age sixty-five) does not have health insurance. Consequently, the U.S. health care system is inferior to those of most other advanced nations in terms of access, mortality rates, patient safety, efficiency, equity, and many other measures.[20] A recent ranking by the World Health Organization (WHO) placed the United States at a rank of thirty-seven out of 190 countries. Uninsured Americans must spend their personal resources to the point of bankruptcy before they can qualify for government aid through Medicaid. For many, a layoff or job change results in the loss of insurance coverage, meaning entire families court financial disaster. Others among the nation's 47 million working uninsured simply cannot afford to make insurance payments for plans offered by their employers, which have been raising monthly premiums, deductibles, and co-payments. When uninsured, sick, or injured people take advantage of free government health care programs, usually in hospital emergency rooms or free clinics, individuals with health care insurance are the ones who pay. Doctors, hospitals, and others simply garner revenue lost from the uninsured through higher fees charged to those who can pay. The result is a fragmented, profit-driven, two-tiered system in which the insured receive state-of-the-art health care and the uninsured experience health care services that are equaled or surpassed by those of some Third World countries.

Medical malpractice suits complicate the financial issues of health care policy. Physicians and other health care providers bemoan astoundingly high jury awards for pain and suffering, and soaring insurance premiums. Some doctors in New Jersey, Florida, and West Virginia have literally walked off the job in protest. Trial lawyers fight caps on jury awards and defend victims' rights to seek fair and just compensation for preventable medical mistakes. With no action forthcoming from Congress or the president, states are left to grapple with the issue, and a growing number (twenty-four as of 2008) have set limits on jury awards for "pain and suffering" and other noneconomic claims.[21]

If nearly everyone agrees that the U.S. health care system is broken, why doesn't Congress fix it? The answer is that the United States is ideologically and institutionally unable to develop a comprehensive solution acceptable to a sufficient number of interests. The current system richly benefits the health care status quo—hospitals, insurance companies, drug companies. Only a political campaign of extraordinary proportions could overcome the culture of incrementalism and interest group politics in this particular policy field.

Of course, health care problems endure and—for better or for worse—will be revisited by Congress. Meanwhile, managed care and managed competition are resulting in mergers and consolidation in the health care industry and monetary efficiencies as doctor, hospital, and pharmaceutical fees and prices are squeezed. But most of the juice is out of the orange, and state Medicaid costs are expected to grow at an average annual rate of about 8 percent for the next ten years.[22] The states, frustrated with delay in Washington and facing the immediate health care problems and costs of their own citizens, are busily engaged in reforming health care.

## State Innovation

State efforts have been aimed at expanding health care coverage to the uninsured, particularly children from low-income families, containing escalating costs (including prescription drugs), and maintaining or enhancing the quality of health care. All states are involved in some way in reforming health care, but each state has its own perspective on what is wrong with health care and its own approach to fixing it.[23] State actions are also guided by economics and special circumstances. For example, huge variations exist in state health care spending. Per capita health care spending varies from $6,683 in Massachusetts to $3,972 in Utah.[24] The southeastern states present special health care problems because of the high prevalence of obesity, diabetes, and stroke. In the

Southwest, especially Utah, teetotaling, nonsmoking Mormons enjoy good health and help keep costs down. Florida's large aging population is a heavy consumer of nursing homes and other health care facilities, driving these costs up. Table 17.3 shows state health rankings. States that spend relatively high amounts per capita do not necessarily rank high on state health indicators.

State and local governments have always been concerned with the health of their citizens and indeed are delegated this responsibility in the U.S. Constitution. Colonial towns assumed responsibility for impoverished sick people in the 1600s, providing almshouses and primitive medical treatments involving leeches and native herbs. Cities and counties, along with private charities, built and operated public hospitals for the poor in the 1800s. Many states formally considered compulsory health insurance legislation before 1945.

Today, in the absence of systematic national government action, the states are hard at work extending quality health care protection to uninsured children and to the poor who are not currently covered by Medicare or Medicaid. Nearly all the states have enacted patients' rights laws to help patients appeal the decisions of health insurers and sue their health care providers for poor service. States are trying to offer expanded coverage while controlling escalating health care costs.

These rankings, from most healthy to least healthy, are based on various health indicators, including unemployment, smoking, availability of health services, and death rates.

**TABLE 17.3 State Health Rankings, 2008**

| | | |
|---|---|---|
| 1. Vermont | 18. New Jersey | 35. Delaware |
| 2. Hawaii | 19. Colorado | 36. North Carolina |
| 3. New Hampshire | 20. Virginia | 37. Kentucky |
| 4. Minnesota | 21. South Dakota | 38. Missouri |
| 5. Utah | 22. Kansas | 39. West Virginia |
| 6. Massachusetts | 23. Montana | 40. Alabama |
| 7. Connecticut | 24. California | 41. Georgia |
| 8. Idaho | 25. New York | 42. Nevada |
| 9. Maine | 26. Maryland | 43. Arkansas |
| 10. Washington | 27. Michigan | 44. Oklahoma |
| 11. Rhode Island | 27. Pennsylvania | 45. Florida |
| 12. North Dakota | 29. New Mexico | 46. Texas |
| 13. Nebraska | 30. Alaska | 47. Tennessee |
| 14. Wyoming | 31. Illinois | 48. South Carolina |
| 15. Iowa | 32. Ohio | 49. Mississippi |
| 16. Oregon | 33. Arizona | 50. Louisiana |
| 17. Wisconsin | 34. Indiana | |

Rank in order from most healthy to least healthy.
SOURCE: "America's Health Rankings," www.unitedhealthfoundation.org (accessed October 10, 2009).

Among the state actions providing instructive "lessons learned" for the Congress and President to consider are the following:

- Disease management and prevention
- Electronic record-keeping
- Healthy lifestyle promotion
- Results-based reimbursements for health care providers
- Health information exchanges within communities, states, and regions
- "Virtual visitations" with doctors via videoconferencing (telemedicine)
- Evidence-based medicine incentives that emphasize treatments and technologies that are proven to be effective in similar cases
- Expanded health care services for children
- Transparency laws that require health care providers to publicly release hospital infection rates and medical outcome data.

To implement significant health care changes and innovations, however, states must apply for and receive waivers of federal Medicare and Medicaid regulations. Most states, for instance, have received Health Care Financing Administration approval to convert their Medicaid programs to managed-care programs. Several states are pursuing radical reform that would pool funds from Medicaid (which serves the poor) with funds from Medicare (serving the elderly and disabled) to care for dually eligible people, those 6–7 million people who qualify for both. This group, composed of mostly low-income elderly and disabled people, accounts for only one-third of the total Medicaid population, but it makes up two-thirds of all Medicaid spending. Below we consider three states that have developed some of the most far-reaching health care reforms: Maine, Tennessee, and Massachusetts.

**Maine** In 2004, Maine began enrolling uninsured residents and small businesses in its trailblazing Dirigo (Latin for "I lead"). A public–private collaboration between the state and health care firms, Dirigo offers enrollees prescription drug discounts, low deductibles, and other benefits. By mid-2009, 30,000 people were signed up. Dirigo was the brainchild of Governor John Baldacci, who campaigned on the issue of universal health care coverage in his state. It has not come cheaply, but state contributions to Dirigo are augmented with a fee on insurance carriers and by employer contributions, hospital savings from lower numbers of charity cases, and federal dollars. Costs are held down by price caps on hospitals and other health care providers and premiums paid by the uninsured or their employers. Individual premiums are based on a sliding scale, with low-income people paying less. Maine also uses the state's purchasing power to force drug companies to deeply discount prescription drug prices for the working poor, elderly, and others.[25]

**Tennessee** Beginning in 1994, TennCare replaced Medicaid as the Volunteer State's health care program for the poor. The program was also extended to other uninsured residents. More than 1.3 million Tennesseans are enrolled, nearly all of the state's uninsured population. TennCare's managed-care approach involves health care networks with regional and statewide coverage. Pharmacy and dental benefits are also offered through 2006 changes called "Cover Tennessee."

TennCare's unique plan pays each managed-care organization (MCO) a set amount of money for each covered person who is enrolled. The money funds doctor visits, hospitalization, diagnostic tests, physical therapy, and all other standard health services. Participants share the costs based on a sliding scale that is determined by their income. In this way, a strong incentive is provided to hold down medical costs by reducing waste and inefficiencies. Conventionally, doctors and hospitals have been rewarded financially by providing more services, whether necessary or not. For example, the more tests a doctor orders for a Medicaid patient, the larger the federal–state reimbursement will be. TennCare makes health care providers think carefully before ordering questionable services because their profits depend on keeping per-patient expenditures under the cost ceiling.[26]

This dramatic departure from health care business as usual emerged from a Medicaid-induced budget crisis in which Tennessee's inefficient system had become one of the most expensive in the nation. Few resources were available for other pressing needs, such as education and corrections. Former governor Ned McWherter implemented TennCare through executive order, which was soon ratified by the legislature in the face of a frantic lobbying assault by physicians and various health care specialists who feared a loss of income.

Ironically, another budget crisis, this one in 2005 sprinkled generously with politics and MCO mismanagement and financial problems, caused Tennessee to authorize removal of 323,000 adults from TennCare's rolls, as rising Medicaid costs threatened to consume nearly all the state's revenue growth.

**Massachusetts** The Bay State's far-reaching "Commonwealth Care" plan for universal health insurance coverage has the goal of covering all residents. Firms with more than ten workers must either furnish health coverage or pay a "fair share" contribution to the state for each employee. The state subsidizes coverage for uninsured workers earning up to three times the federal poverty level who do not have either personal or employer coverage. What happens to those who fail to comply? Individuals lose their personal state income tax exemption and face a $219 fine unless they can demonstrate that they cannot find affordable coverage. A special feature of the Massachusetts universal coverage plan is "The Connector," which links individuals and small companies to state-subsidized private health coverage. Once obtained, health insurance coverage is portable if the employee changes jobs.

The Massachusetts plan has not come cheaply. Estimates that 57,000 would initially enroll were exceeded when 76,200 enlisted in the plan right away; today there are 177,000 members. Estimated cost for the first three years was $1.2 billion.[27] This figure was soon surpassed. Budget shortfalls meant that 30,000 legal immigrants (i.e., legally in the United States but not a citizen) had to be trimmed from program rolls in 2009.[28]

The bold Bay State experiment has been cited often as a national model. In terms of providing universal coverage, Commonwealth Care is a success, as

Massachusetts now records the lowest percentage of uninsured residents in the United States at 2.6 percent. And public support remains strong among Bay Staters.[29]

## State Health Care Reform Moves Forward

In mid-2009 all eyes were on President Obama and the Congress as they attempted to carve out a compromise national health care bill. How such a plan would affect the various state programs was unknown. Meanwhile, Medicaid continues to burden the states financially. Although state reforms, particularly managed care, have cut the rate of growth in Medicaid costs, this entitlement program now comprises the second largest portion of state expenditures, surpassing higher education. Medicaid costs are not the only serious problem. The ranks of the uninsured are increasing nationally. Prescription drug prices are escalating. A disturbing and deleterious nurse shortage threatens the quality of medical care. The nursing-home industry is riddled with problems, as is care for the mentally disabled.

State health care reform will continue at a lively pace until Congress finally enacts universal health care coverage, as twenty-eight other industrial countries have done. Even then, states will be service integrators, implementers, and innovators in their classic "middleman" role in U.S. federalism, and meanwhile, they are clearing new trails that will inform and greatly influence future federal policy making. The federal government could make the job of the states much easier by giving them greater authority or at least minimizing the conditions for federal waivers of state Medicaid changes. The attendant waiver requirements are cumbersome and slow, thus inhibiting innovation. Greater flexibility is needed if the states are to be given a full opportunity to deliver health care services to their citizens. One after another, they are voyaging into the foreign land of health care reform. The least the federal government can do is provide a passport.

## CHAPTER RECAP

- Social welfare and health care are major entrees on the federal–state policy menu. The national government may own the restaurant, but the cooks who turn out the policy dishes are the state and local governments.

- Poverty in the United States is measured, somewhat inaccurately, using a statistic called the poverty level.

- A social welfare policy consensus has yet to produce a coherent national policy, but the state and local governments are fully engaged in program design, experimentation, and administration.

- Programs to help poor children and to move adults from welfare rolls to payrolls have received special attention through state innovations.

- In the face of policy gridlock in Washington, the states are developing innovative approaches to providing affordable health care to all of their citizens.

## Key Terms

Temporary Assistance for
Needy Families (TANF)
*(p. 475)*

direct cash transfer *(p. 476)*
in-kind program *(p. 478)*

social insurance *(p. 480)*

## Internet Resources

The Institute for Policy Research at Northwestern University's website focuses on the causes of poverty and the effectiveness of policies aimed at reducing it. The website is located at **www.northwestern.edu/ipr/research/respoverty/html**.

For information on federal and state health care, see the Centers for Medicaid and Medicare Services at **www.cms.hhs.gov**. The Administration for Children and Families (ACF), within the U.S. Department of Health and Human Services (DHHS), is responsible for federal programs that promote economic and social well-being. Information about their programs can be obtained from their website at **www.acf.hhs.gov**.

Families USA is a nonprofit organization that works at the national, state, and local levels to achieve high-quality, affordable health care and long-term care for all Americans. Their website, **www.familiesusa.org**, serves as a clearinghouse for information about the health care system.

For information on children's issues, see the Children's Defense Fund at **www.childrensdefense.org**.

For general information and links on welfare programs and initiatives, see **www.welfareinfo.org**.

SOURCE: Justin Sullivan/Getty Images News/Getty Images

# Environmental Policy

18

Visitors to downtown Chattanooga, Tennessee, can stroll the city's tree-lined Riverwalk and watch blue herons feeding along the shore. In the river, fish are jumping. Tourists board one of the city's electric shuttle buses for a ride to the Tennessee Aquarium, which features freshwater ecosystems. A bridge that once carried cars is now reserved for walkers, joggers, and cyclists. Chattanooga, according to one environmentalist, is "a model for the nation and the world."[1] But what makes the Chattanooga story so compelling is that thirty-five years ago, the Environmental Protection Agency (EPA) called it "the dirtiest city in America."[2] The industries that lined the banks of the river had fouled the air and the water. New federal clean-air and clean-water regulations were adopted. Over time, some of the factories shut down; others modernized. Prodded by the chamber of commerce, the city underwent a period of intense self-study and emerged with a new vision for the future. The vision? Chattanooga would transform itself from a polluted wasteland to an ecologically sound community. Today, it is well on the way to doing so.[3]

Environmental protection policy in the United States is characterized by three features: its intergovernmental nature, its regulatory focus, and (lately) its innovative design. The federal government is extensively involved

- The Political Economy of Environmental Protection
- Clean Air, Clean Water, and Politics
- The Greening of States and Localities
- Dealing with Waste
- Two Challenges for Policymakers

495

in environmental policy, as are states and localities. These governments play different roles depending on the environmental problem and the era. The activity of government tends to be regulatory, that is, making rules and setting standards that affect the private sector, monitoring compliance, and imposing penalties. Finally, solutions to environmental problems are moving beyond the more traditional approaches and are becoming increasingly innovative and fresh. The rebirth of Chattanooga reflects all these features of environmental policy. As will be evident in the chapter, this policy area tests the capacity of states and localities to make smart choices for the future.

# THE POLITICAL ECONOMY OF ENVIRONMENTAL PROTECTION

Environmental policy choices are made especially difficult by their economic implications. Controlling pollution is a significant economic cost for many firms today. In the essentially nonregulatory era prior to the 1960s, this expense was either quite low or nonexistent. Increasing government regulatory intervention in industrial processes and outputs reflects the indisputable fact that market forces by themselves will not guarantee the protection of our health and the environment. Clean air and clean water are public goods that should be available to all of us, but polluters often have little economic incentive to stop polluting.

When left unregulated, most firms tend to maximize profits by minimizing costs—including the costs of environmental protection. Determining exactly what constitutes pollution or environmental degradation and deciding how stringently to regulate polluting activities have tremendous economic implications for firms and governments. Too much regulation could depress economic growth at national, state, and local levels; reduce employment; and even force some companies into bankruptcy. These concerns are not simply conjecture. To some degree, states that imposed costlier regulatory burdens on the private sector experienced lower rates of new capital investment.[4] Obviously, the trade-offs between economic growth and environmental protection can spawn conflict.

## Public Opinion

Research tells us that Americans generally support the goals of environmental protection. Public opinion polls indicate that most people are in favor of increased government spending for environmental protection and oppose efforts to weaken environmental standards.[5] This resounding endorsement lessens, however, when environmental protection is pitted against goals such as economic growth and adequate energy. When members of Earth First! square off against loggers in the forests of the Pacific Northwest, environmentalism becomes more than an abstraction. Environmental protection does not occur in a vacuum; achievement of its goals comes at a cost to other valued objectives.

Although support among the public for protecting the environment remains fairly strong, it has dropped since 1998. At the same time, the priority accorded economic growth has increased. Figure 18.1 shows the fluctuation in national public opinion from 1998 to 2009, as reported by the Gallup Poll. The polling question itself is called a forced choice because respondents with an opinion have to select either environmental protection or economic growth as a priority. Therefore, it requires the respondent to weigh the two options against each other. The question was worded in this manner:

> With which one of these statements about the environment and the economy do you most agree—protection of the environment should be given priority, even at the risk of curbing economic growth (or) economic growth should be given priority, even if the environment suffers to some extent?[6]

As Figure 18.1 shows, the gap between the two priorities narrowed over time and by 2009, the public accorded higher priority to economic growth. The increased importance of economic growth can be attributed in part to the downturn in the nation's economy during the period. Even so, environmental protection continues to be valued because all of us are potential or actual victims of environmental problems. Polluted air, water, and land offend us aesthetically but, more important, they threaten the health and safety of ourselves, our children, and our grandchildren. People who drink contaminated water and breathe polluted air experience the costs directly.

**Changing Priorities in Public Opinion**

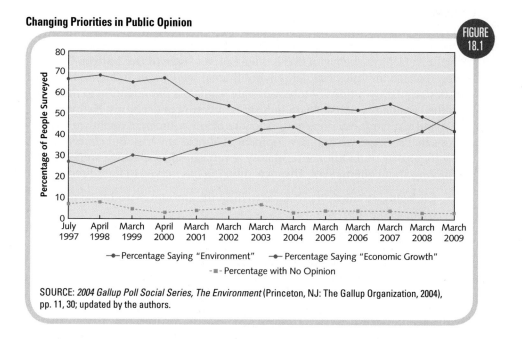

FIGURE
18.1

SOURCE: *2004 Gallup Poll Social Series, The Environment* (Princeton, NJ: The Gallup Organization, 2004), pp. 11, 30; updated by the authors.

From a different perspective, all citizens must help pay the price of a safe and clean environment. We pay for a clean environment through the portion of our taxes that goes to government pollution-control efforts and through the prices we pay for goods, which include the cost of pollution control. The costs to consumers are especially heavy where the products of chemical companies, the auto industry, and coal-burning power plants are concerned. These industries have lobbied vigorously against what they perceive to be excessive regulation. One policy that is intended to improve relations between business and regulators is the **environmental self-audit**, which allows firms to self-report violations. If the firm then corrects the problem voluntarily, the penalty levied by government is less than it would have been otherwise. Although proponents of this approach tout its promise, a recent study found that the environmental performance of firms participating in these self-monitoring programs actually lags that of firms subject to traditional regulation.[7]

**environmental self-audit**

A form of self-policing in which the regulated firm conducts its own review of its performance and voluntarily reports violations.

Because of the link between environmental protection and economic development, public policy is inevitably a compromise. Integrating environmental accounting with traditional economic assessments continues to be a goal of environmentalists. Including the degradation of natural resources in the U.S. Department of Commerce's calculations of the nation's gross domestic product (GDP) was proposed in the mid-1990s but rejected by Congress.

## New Approaches: Moving Toward Sustainability

Government's role is to balance economic growth with environmental protection by regulating polluters. The political economy of environmental protection argues strongly for national domination of policy making. Because states and local governments compete for industry (as discussed in Chapter 14), some jurisdictions might be tempted to relax environmental protection standards and thus influence a firm's decision about where to construct or expand a new manufacturing facility, a behavior that is often called a **"race to the bottom."** Indeed, new research indicates that state environmental agencies are influenced by other states' regulatory actions.[8] Moreover, state regulators pay attention to the effects of their regulatory decisions on industries' investment decisions. National policies and standards can prevent the sacrifice of environmental quality in jurisdictions that seek growth and development at almost any cost. But concern about the high costs of traditional regulatory approaches has spawned some creative thinking about alternatives. This new thinking has moved in four directions:

**race to the bottom**

Occurs when states alter their behaviors—relaxing regulations, lowering taxes, or reducing benefits—to gain an advantage over competing states.

- Changing production processes to limit the amount of pollution produced in the first place.
- Reducing exposure to pollutants rather than trying to eliminate pollution altogether.
- Exploring the trade-offs between regulatory costs and environmental benefits to determine when an unacceptable imbalance exists.
- Replacing traditional administrative procedures with economic incentives and other market strategies with the hope of achieving both environmental protection and economic efficiency.[9]

It is not clear whether these new approaches will achieve what some of their proponents intend, that is, the marrying of environmental protection and economic development. The word often used to describe this marriage is **sustainability**, that is, an approach to economic growth that prevents harm to the environment.[10] But numerous studies have shown that as a nation's economy prospers, the public's concern over environmental quality increases.[11] These intertwined goals present continued challenges for policy makers.

**sustainability**
The simultaneous achievement of economic development and environmental protection.

# CLEAN AIR, CLEAN WATER, AND POLITICS

In the early days of the United States, government involvement in environmental protection was minimal at best. Natural resources were abundant, the country was developing, and the future seemed limitless. The first government forays into the now-tangled jungle of environmental protection policy began in the early 1800s with local ordinances aimed at garbage; human and animal waste; contaminated drinking water; and other unsanitary, health-endangering conditions in American cities. Local failures to contain and control such problems were punctuated by cholera and typhoid epidemics throughout the nineteenth century and into the early twentieth century. In 1878, a yellow fever epidemic caused 5,000 deaths and the exodus of another 25,000 fearful residents from Memphis, Tennessee. Such episodes prompted the states to begin regulating conditions causing waterborne diseases, thereby redefining what had been a private problem into a problem for state government. By 1948, states had taken over responsibility for water pollution control. Their early regulatory efforts were rather weak, however.

## The Centralization of Environmental Policy

The issue of water pollution control shows the evolving centralization of federal government authority in environmental decision making. Although the federal government acted to protect natural resources by setting aside land for national parks in the late nineteenth century, it paid little attention to environmental problems until after World War II. At that point, the forces of urbanization and industrial production began to draw attention to the national dimensions of environmental dangers. The initial federal statutory step into the policy field was the Water Pollution Control Act of 1948. Under the original version of this act, the national government assumed limited enforcement authority for water pollution. Since then, seven other major federal statutes or amendments have been enacted to address the problem. Using this overall statutory framework, the federal government pre-empted existing state and local water quality standards and substituted national standards.

The reasons for this pre-emption are not difficult to understand. We have already noted that as states compete for economic development, they may be tempted to lower environmental standards to gain an edge over other states.

In addition, because pollution problems are often cross-boundary (i.e., they extend beyond a single jurisdiction), solutions can be difficult to design. Toxins dumped into a river upstream have deleterious consequences for jurisdictions located downstream. The failure of states to work together to solve shared environmental problems led to more involvement by the federal government.

Increasingly strong federal statutes also addressed the problems of air pollution, pesticides, and hazardous waste. For example, the first national legislation on air quality, the Air Pollution Control Act of 1955, made funding available for research on the health effects of bad air. It was superseded by the Clean Air Act of 1963, which encouraged the development of emissions standards. The Clean Air Act of 1970, a massive overhaul of its predecessor, set air quality standards and strictly regulated emissions from factories and motor vehicles. By the late 1970s, the federal government had extended its authority to endangered species, strip mining, coastal zones, toxic substances, and many other areas. Thus, environmental protection was redefined as a national problem requiring national solutions. The national government does not operate alone, however; state and local governments play a significant role in implementing federal legislation.

States and localities speak with an important policy voice even in environmental fields that appear to be outside their sphere of influence. For example, one group of states took on the issue of greenhouse gas emissions in a creative way, as the Engaging Environmental Policy box details. Another example is public lands. Governed by Congress and managed by eight federal agencies, including the Bureau of Land Management, Forest Service, and National Park Service, the nation's 700 million acres of public lands make up almost one-third of the continental United States and more than 60 percent of the land area of four western states: Alaska, Idaho, Nevada, and Utah. These lands contain vast timber, petroleum, coal, and mineral resources. The states have an enormous economic stake in the way these resources and their environmental implications are managed. The western states, in particular, have consistently sought a greater role in deciding how these resources are used, even insisting that much of the land be handed over to the respective states.[12]

## National Politics and the Environment

The lead agency in national environmental policy is the U.S. EPA, which was created in 1970 as an independent regulatory body for pollution control. With its director appointed by the president, the EPA is faced with the task of coordinating and enforcing the broad array of environmental protection programs established by Congress. To help with this task, the agency has decentralized much of its operation to ten regional offices located in major cities throughout the country. The scope of the EPA's responsibility can be overwhelming, involving regular interaction and conflict with other federal agencies, powerful private interests, and state and local governments. Its job is complicated by the tendency of Congress to pass environmental legislation that sets unattainable program goals and unrealistic implementation dates. Many deadlines for compliance

## Engaging Environmental Policy

### The States Take on Global Warming

Greenhouse gas emissions are a hot topic these days. These emissions contribute to global warming, but debate swirls over their long-term impact. New York did not wait for scientists to arrive at a universally agreed upon conclusion before taking action. The Empire State adopted an energy plan that aims to reduce the state's carbon emissions to 5 percent below 1990 levels by 2010 and to 10 percent below those levels by 2020. But action by one state really isn't sufficient if other nearby states don't effect similar reductions. So New York invited other states in the region to join it. The result is the Regional Greenhouse Gas Initiative (RGGI), a cooperative agreement among nine states (Connecticut, Delaware, Maine, Maryland, New Hampshire, New Jersey, New York, Rhode Island, and Vermont) to develop a plan for reducing carbon dioxide emissions from power plants by 10 percent by 2018.

The centerpiece of the plan is a cap-and-trade program that sets an allowable level of emissions (a cap) and permits power plants to buy and sell (trade) the right to pollute. Power plants with emissions below the cap can sell the rest of their pollution allowance to facilities whose emissions exceed the cap. Clearly, an economic incentive exists for power plants to pollute at a level that is below the cap.

The auctioning of permits began in September 2008 with six RGGI states participating in the sale of 12.5 million carbon permits. An estimated $38.6 million was raised in the first auction, nearly $107 million in the second. Proceeds from the quarterly auctions are used to promote energy conservation and renewable energy in the participating states. While there was some early skepticism regarding the viability of RGGI's approach, initial results suggest that the program has clearly engaged potential participants, not only energy companies and investors but environmental groups, also. And when Congress developed national climate change legislation in 2009, it borrowed a page from RGGI and included a cap and trade program.

Sources: Regional Greenhouse Gas Initiative, www.rggi.org (August 3, 2009); "With something for Everyone, Climate Bill Passed," *The New York Times*, www.nytimes.com (July 1, 2009); "*RGGI*'s Latest Carbon Auction Raises $117M" *Environmental Leader*,www.environmentalleader.com (August 3, 2009).

with federal laws have been missed by the EPA, which lends ammunition to its critics on all sides.[13] Litigation brought by regulated industries and environmental groups has further ensnarled the agency, and a shortage of money and staff has plagued the EPA since the administration of President Reagan.

An example of the scope of the EPA's responsibilities is water pollution control. Every private and public facility that discharges wastes directly into water must obtain a permit from the EPA or, in some instances, from its state counterpart. The national government, through the EPA, establishes specific discharge standards. Day-to-day oversight and implementation, however, are performed by the states. In effect, the national government makes the rules and lets the states enforce them according to their own circumstances (a process known as **partial pre-emption**). The national government also disburses grants to state and local governments for the treatment and monitoring of water resources. Billions of federal dollars have been spent for the construction of wastewater treatment plants; millions more have gone for technical assistance and research and development.

One interesting attempt to build a more cooperative relationship between the EPA and state-level environmental protection agencies is the performance partnership agreement (PPA) that was promoted by the Clinton administration.

**partial pre-emption**

An approach common to federal environmental laws that requires states to apply federal standards.

PPAs allow a state to combine its EPA funding into block grants that can be used for comprehensive statewide environmental problems.[14] Basically, PPAs give states more power to set their own spending priorities. The idea was pilot-tested in North Dakota, New Hampshire, and Massachusetts with sufficient success to warrant its extension to other interested states, and now nearly all states are engaged in PPAs.

During the presidency of George W. Bush, several states challenged the federal government, arguing that EPA should regulate greenhouse gases as pollutants under the Clean Air Act. In 2007, a U.S. Supreme Court ruling instructed the agency to study the issue and in 2009, after thorough scientific analysis, the agency declared greenhouse gases pollutants that threaten public health. Within three months, Congress began debating climate change legislation that, among other things, establishes a ceiling on the emission of greenhouse gases like carbon dioxide.[15]

## THE GREENING OF STATES AND LOCALITIES

State and local governments have taken on greater responsibility for financing and operating environmental protection programs and have become policy initiators. For example, Congress was gridlocked on acid rain legislation for years, but some states took unilateral actions to cut sulfur dioxide emissions within their borders (New Hampshire and New York were the first). Several states, including New Jersey and Ohio, passed legislation requiring firms to clean up hazardous wastes from industrial property before selling the property. Such legislation helps prevent companies from abandoning polluted sites that present health risks and leaving them for the states to clean up. California's far-reaching policies to improve the nation's worst air quality have become a model for other states and the national government. The Golden State also has led the way in its efforts to conserve water through, among other things, a statute requiring the use of water-efficient washing machines.

Today, states have ventured forth on several environmental fronts, notably climate change. One-quarter of the states require utilities to use renewable sources for at least some of their power generation; for example, the state of Washington has created a series of financial incentives to spur the use of renewable energy sources. The state gives homeowners and small businesses with solar power and wind power systems a credit on their electric bills. Consumers get an even bigger break for using systems whose components were manufactured in Washington.[16] The bottom line is that states have become central actors in environmental protection through their innovative ideas. The Breaking New Ground box below explores the prospects of alternative fuels, an idea whose time has come.

States operate many of their pollution-control programs under the auspices of federal legislation and the EPA. They must develop and implement plans and standards under a host of federal laws. The Safe Drinking Water Act, for instance, requires local water systems to meet national standards for acceptable levels of contaminants such as coliform (a type of bacteria), asbestos, copper, and lead in their water supply. The Clean Air Act mandates the creation of vehicle inspection and maintenance programs for smog-stricken jurisdictions. States and localities are closer to pollution problems and hence are best situated to address them on a day-to-day basis. The problem with this approach, according to states and localities, is that they have to pay a large portion of the costs themselves. Approximately 77 percent of the money in state environmental budgets comes from state revenues. Even the EPA acknowledged that the cost of federally imposed environmental mandates on state and local governments could bust their budgets, requiring millions of dollars of new spending. Table 18.1 shows state and local spending on environmental protection for 2008. California, Illinois, and Florida spend the most in terms

| State Environmental Budgets, 2008 | | | TABLE 18.1 |
|---|---|---|---|
| | STATE ENVIRONMENTAL SPENDING TOTAL | TOTAL PER CAPITA | PER CAPITA RANK |
| Alabama | 58,750,977 | 12.6 | 46 |
| Alaska | 75,832,900 | 110.5 | 6 |
| Arizona | 191,425,100 | 29.45 | 37 |
| Arkansas | 105,485,578 | 36.94 | 30 |
| California | 2,080,591,000 | 56.6 | 16 |
| Colorado | 57,647,863 | 11.67 | 47 |
| Connecticut | 145,583,654 | 41.58 | 22 |
| Delaware | 137,456,200 | 157.44 | 3 |
| Florida | 1,072,843,657 | 58.53 | 14 |
| Georgia | 135,600,000 | 14 | 45 |
| Hawaii | 263,891,754 | 204.85 | 1 |
| Idaho | 60,850,400 | 39.93 | 24 |
| Illinois | 1,299,243,700 | 100.7 | 8 |
| Indiana | 303,755,276 | 47.63 | 19 |
| Iowa | 118,793,356 | 39.56 | 25 |
| Kansas | 72,772,922 | 25.97 | 39 |
| Kentucky | 113,571,900 | 26.6 | 38 |
| Louisiana | 163,402,497 | 37.05 | 29 |
| Maine | 80,567,231 | 61.2 | 13 |
| Maryland | 110,245,525 | 19.57 | 43 |

(*Continued*)

**TABLE 18.1    State Environmental Budgets, 2008 (Continued)**

| | STATE GOVERNMENT SPENDING TOTAL | TOTAL PER CAPITA | PER CAPITA RANK |
|---|---|---|---|
| Massachusetts | 133,800,626 | 20.59 | 42 |
| Michigan | 370,964,400 | 37.08 | 28 |
| Minnesota | 190,729,802 | 36.54 | 31 |
| Mississippi | 138,969,055 | 47.29 | 20 |
| Missouri | 325,564,220 | 55.07 | 17 |
| Montana | 80,730,441 | 83.45 | 9 |
| Nebraska | 85,947,670 | 48.19 | 18 |
| Nevada | 177,887,759 | 68.41 | 11 |
| New Hampshire | 153,427,724 | 116.6 | 4 |
| New Jersey | 338,858,000 | 39.03 | 27 |
| New Mexico | NA | NA | NA |
| New York | NA | NA | NA |
| North Carolina | 379,750,557 | 41.18 | 23 |
| North Dakota | 23,425,243 | 36.52 | 32 |
| Ohio | 86,314,093 | 7.51 | 48 |
| Oklahoma | 56,700,966 | 15.57 | 44 |
| Oregon | 148,999,972 | 39.31 | 26 |
| Pennsylvania | 717,292,000 | 57.62 | 15 |
| Rhode Island | 86,314,093 | 82.14 | 10 |
| South Carolina | 149,387,711 | 33.35 | 34 |
| South Dakota | 85,915,799 | 106.83 | 7 |
| Tennessee | 190,946,400 | 30.72 | 36 |
| Texas | 548,898,921 | 22.56 | 41 |
| Utah | 86,167,124 | 31.49 | 35 |
| Vermont | 38,167,969 | 61.44 | 12 |
| Virginia | 189,640,074 | 24.41 | 40 |
| Washington | 235,646,000 | 35.98 | 33 |
| West Virginia | 305,989,209 | 168.64 | 2 |
| Wisconsin | 237,466,091 | 42.19 | 21 |
| Wyoming | 61,168,228 | 114.83 | 5 |

SOURCE: "State Environmental Budgets and Budget Plans, FY 2005–2008," *The Environmental Council of the States*, www.ecos.org/files/3058_file_March_2008_ECOS_Green_Report_Appendix.pdf.

## BREAKING NEW GROUND

### Driving Green: Environmentally Friendly Alternative Fuels

Did you know that each gallon of gas we burn releases up to twenty-eight pounds of carbon dioxide into the atmosphere? Or that driving a sport utility vehicle (SUV) instead of a typical passenger car for one year uses more energy than if you had your TV on for twenty-eight years? It is no wonder that emissions from our automobiles are the leading culprit in the global warming debate in the United States. So not only for the sake of protecting our environment, but also to ease our dependence on oil, alternative fuel vehicles are becoming ever more popular on the national scene.

One option available to drivers is the hybrid vehicle, such as the Toyota Prius, which combines the gas engine with an electric motor. Flex-fuel vehicles, which are designed to run on either gasoline or a blend of corn-based ethanol (E85), are gradually making their appearance as well. And electric cars, which are powered by rechargeable battery packs, can be seen on the road from time to time. Another vehicular alternative is hydrogen power, either through internal combustion or fuel cells. California has taken the lead on alternative fuel technology with ventures such as the California Fuel Cell Partnership.

In addition to these alternative fuel options, scientists experiment daily with potential fuel sources such as organic waste from chickens, hogs, and cows as well as recycled grease from deep-fryers. Entrepreneurial firms have sprung up to help consumers convert their diesel-fueled vehicles so that they can run on vegetable oil. But constraining the popularity of alternative fuel vehicles is the limited number of next-generation fuel stations across the country. To alert drivers, the U.S. Department of Energy's Alternative Fuels and Advanced Vehicles Data Center recently created an interactive map that identifies all advanced fuel stations across the country. As of its summer 2009 reporting, the fuel stations listed offer compressed natural gas (773 locations total throughout the United States), E85 (1,937), propane (2,337), electric (452), biodiesel (697), hydrogen (60), or liquefied natural gas (35). But these stations are by no means spread evenly throughout the country. California has the most stations in several categories, including 406 of the nation's 452 electric stations. (California may be rivaled by Hawaii eventually, which is constructing a network of plug-in spots for vehicle battery recharging.) However, in terms of fuel stations per capita, the top five states are South Dakota, Wyoming, North Dakota, Minnesota, and Montana.

So the next time you are stalled in traffic and detect an aroma of French fries in the air, do not assume you are near a fast-food restaurant. The car ahead of you may be alternatively powered by recycled fryer grease.

SOURCES: "Clean Cars," *The Sierra Club*, www.sierraclub.org/energy/cleancars/default.aspx (August 2, 2009); "Driving Up the Heat: SUVs and Global Warming," *The Sierra Club*, www.sierraclub.org/energy/SUVreport/ (August 2, 2009); U.S. Department of Energy. Alternative Fuels and Advanced Vehicles Data Center, www.afdc.energy.gov/afdc/fuels/stations_counts.html (July 10, 2009); "Fuel Economy Guide 2009," *U.S. Environmental Protection Agency*. DOE-EE0325. http://www.fueleconomy.gov/feg/FEG2009.pdf (August 2, 2009).

of absolute dollars; North Dakota and Vermont, the least. Per capita, smaller states such as Hawaii, West Virginia, and Delaware top the spending, whereas Colorado and Ohio spend the least.

## State Commitment to Environmental Protection

Aggregate state spending on environmental protection is approximately $12.7 billion per year and represents less than 2 percent of total state spending.[17] Table 18.2 shows how three states—Colorado, New Jersey, and West

**TABLE 18.2    Comparing State Budgets for Environmental Program Expenditures, 2008**

**COLORADO**

| EXPENDITURES BY PROGRAM | FY 2008 BUDGETED |
|---|---|
| Air Quality Control Division | 17,678,092 |
| Water Quality Control Division | 15,777,487 |
| Hazardous Materials & Waste Management Division | 20,831,382 |
| Consumer Protection Division | 2,481,867 |
| Environmental Leadership | 879,035 |
| *Total Expenditures* | 57,647,863 |

**NEW JERSEY**

| EXPENDITURES BY PROGRAM | FY 2008 BUDGETED |
|---|---|
| Natural and Historic Resources | 93,490,000 |
| Policy and Science | 7,443,000 |
| Land Use Management | 57,290,000 |
| Site Remediation | 67,336,000 |
| Environmental Regulation | 57,932,000 |
| Compliance and Enforcement | 32,677,000 |
| Department Management | 22,690,000 |
| *Total Expenditures* | 338,858,000 |

**WEST VIRGINIA**

| EXPENDITURES BY PROGRAM | FY 2008 BUDGETED |
|---|---|
| Executive/Administration | 15,781,677 |
| Mining and Reclamation | 25,821,116 |
| Air Quality | 9,770,003 |
| Land Restoration | 175,377,477 |
| Water and Waste Management | 74,003,291 |
| Environmental Enforcement | 5,235,645 |
| *Total Expenditures* | 305,989,209 |

SOURCE: "State Environmental Budgets and Budget Plans, FY 2005–2008," *The Environmental Council of the States*, www.ecos.org/files/3058_file_March_2008_ECOS_Green_Report_Appendix.pdf.

Virginia—allocated their environmental protection expenditures for 2008 across different areas. Notice that each state organizes its environmental protection function somewhat differently. Colorado and West Virginia identify specific environmental media such as air and water while New Jersey allocates its funds by activity such as remediation or regulation. Colorado has a consumer protection division within its environmental agency; New Jersey includes spending for historic and natural resources. In West Virginia, land restoration accounts for more than 57 percent of the budget, while in Colorado the hazardous materials and waste management division receives the single largest allocation. If we were to look at three other states, we would find additional variations.

States have established their own environmental protection agencies and natural resource departments, but these organizations vary in their structure and responsibilities. An example of the more comprehensive, single-agency structure is found in Delaware's Department of Natural Resources and Environmental Control, composed of five divisions: Air and Waste Management, Fish and Wildlife, Parks and Recreation, Soil and Water Conservation, and Water Resources. Arizona separates functions across a Department of Environmental Quality, a Game and Fish Department, and a Natural Resources Division within the State Land Department. Different still are states such as South Carolina, which combine environmental protection and public health in the same department.

In the mid-1990s, the leaders of state environmental protection departments met in Phoenix to discuss common concerns and to create an organization to represent their interests. The result was the Environmental Council of the States (ECOS). ECOS is a nonprofit, nonpartisan association that has as its mission environmental improvement nationwide, with states as the driving force. The organization has three goals:

- To exchange ideas, views, and experiences among members.
- To foster cooperation and coordination in environmental management.
- To articulate state positions on environmental issues to Congress and the EPA.[18]

Ultimately, ECOS seeks greater decision-making authority for states vis-à-vis environmental policy. Acknowledging that state commitment to environmental protection varies, the amount of authority would also vary. States with an established track record would enjoy more leeway to design and implement their own programs; other states would not. PPAs, mentioned earlier, are the first step in this direction.

As noted earlier, states often face pressure from economic interests to weaken environmental regulations. Despite this pressure, at least some states have exceeded the guidelines set by the EPA to ensure better air quality. A survey of states found that nearly 30 percent had ambient air standards that went beyond the requirements of federal law.[19] What causes states to adopt more stringent regulations than the EPA requires? The answer seems to lie in the strength of green interest groups, supportive public opinion, and the ability to convert this pro-environment political climate into legislative action.

States are often ranked on their environmental conditions, policies, and programs. One recent rating is based on six equally-weighted criteria: air quality, water quality, carbon footprint, hazardous waste management, environmental policy initiatives, and energy consumption.[20] In 2007, the highest scoring states were Vermont, Oregon, Washington, and Hawaii; scoring low were Alabama, Indiana, and West Virginia. Figure 18.2 categorizes the states into five groups, based on the scores. Note that the greenest states tend to be found in the coastal west or the northeastern parts of the country. In general, research has shown that support for environmental protection tends to be stronger among Democrats, liberals, the affluent, and the educated.[21]

## Green Localities

Local governments regularly take action to protect the environment and conserve natural resources. For instance, Atlanta has sponsored a tree-planting project for National Arbor Day; Kansas City, Missouri, promoted its Keep Kansas City Beautiful anti-litter campaign; the green power program in

**FIGURE 18.2**  **How Green Are the States?**

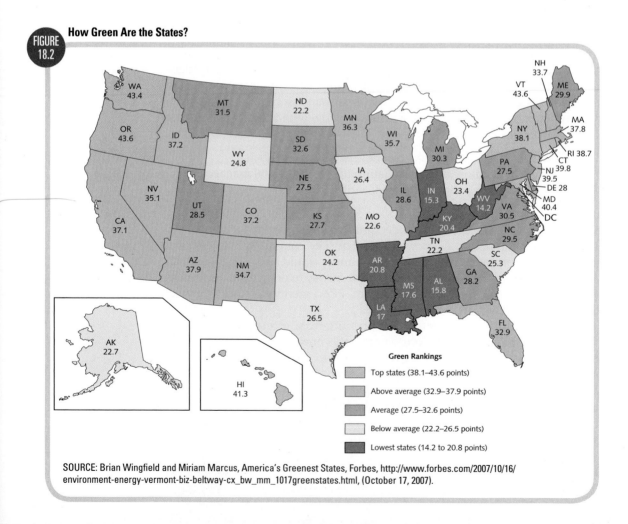

**Green Rankings**

- Top states (38.1–43.6 points)
- Above average (32.9–37.9 points)
- Average (27.5–32.6 points)
- Below average (22.2–26.5 points)
- Lowest states (14.2 to 20.8 points)

SOURCE: Brian Wingfield and Miriam Marcus, America's Greenest States, Forbes, http://www.forbes.com/2007/10/16/environment-energy-vermont-biz-beltway-cx_bw_mm_1017greenstates.html, (October 17, 2007).

Riverside, California, offered classes on recycling and composting; Spokane, Washington, adopted a special tax in support of open-space conservation. Meanwhile, New York City added 300 Toyota Prius vehicles—with a fuel efficiency rating of fifty miles per gallon—to its municipal fleet.[22] More than 900 cities joined the Cities for Climate Protection campaign to reduce the emissions of greenhouse gases. Others have adopted green building codes to spur the construction of buildings that are substantially more energy efficient and less resource intensive than regular buildings. But even as cities and counties make decisions and allocate funds to protect the environment, they take plenty of actions that contribute to environmental degradation and natural resource loss. Think about the negative environmental consequences of a city government's approval of a developer's request to construct a new shopping mall at the city's edge. Natural resources are lost as the land is cleared of trees and vegetation, and wildlife habitat is destroyed. Once the mall opens, traffic congestion leads to polluted air; storm-water runoff from parking lots results in polluted rivers. As a city grows and develops, it produces a large **ecological footprint** in terms of its impact on the earth and its resources.[23]

> **ecological footprint**
> The size of the environmental impact imposed on the earth and its resources.

Many cities have taken steps to become more green, that is, to soften the impact of their ecological footprint. Seattle is one such city, beginning with its 1994 comprehensive plan, Toward a Sustainable Seattle. In functions such as land use, transportation, and housing, among others, the city set goals and adopted policies designed to make it more environmentally friendly. City departments were required to assess the environmental impact of their operations and devise ways of lessening that impact. Political scientist Kent Portney's research compared cities' commitment to sustainability and ranked Seattle at the top of the list, followed by Scottsdale, Arizona; San Jose, California; Boulder, Colorado; Santa Monica, California; Portland, Oregon; and San Francisco, California.[24] The approach taken by San Francisco is especially interesting: The city's sustainability plan identified several areas of concern such as air quality, biodiversity, climate change, and open spaces. For these areas of concern, specific indicators were developed to gauge the progress that the city has or has not made. For instance, the number of native plant species in parks is one indicator of biodiversity, as is the number of different bird species sighted.[25] Given the city's propensity, it was not a surprise when, in 2007, it became the first jurisdiction in the country to ban the use of plastic checkout bags at supermarkets. And then in 2009, San Francisco began requiring households and businesses to compost food scraps; those who do not comply can be fined.

# DEALING WITH WASTE

One of the by-products of modern life is waste of all varieties. Households, schools, hospitals, businesses, and factories produce massive quantities of waste daily. When garbage collectors in New York City went on strike several years ago, the towers of smelly refuse that piled up on city streets reminded

New Yorkers how important this particular city service was. More threatening to public health and the environment are the toxic wastes generated by certain industrial processes and the wastes associated with nuclear power. One of the challenges for government is finding better ways to manage all this waste.

## Recycling Solid Waste

Vast quantities of household and commercial refuse are generated daily in the United States. Americans produce about 254 million tons of garbage annually, or 4.6 pounds per person per day.[26] In general, states with more commercial and industrial activity tend to generate more solid waste than those with a more agricultural economy. Of the solid waste generated in a year, nearly 13 percent is combusted in waste-to-energy plants and another 33 percent is recycled or composted, leaving about 54 percent destined for landfills. These percentages vary widely by region. In New England, waste-to-energy combustion accounts for 34 percent, recycling for 27 percent, and landfilling for 39 percent of municipal solid waste. In the Rocky Mountain region, the percentages are 1, 9, and 90, respectively.[27] Thousands of landfills were in operation in the 1980s; today there are about 1,750. Many of them are so-called super dumps, where more than 500 tons of waste is disposed daily. (And, of course, some people use the "fling it out of the car" method of disposal. One study of America's highways found an average of 950 beer and soft drink cans, plastic bags and bottles, and other items per mile.)[28]

Like nuclear and hazardous waste, solid waste often brings out the not-in-my-backyard (**NIMBY**) syndrome. Everyone generates garbage, and lots of it, but no one wants to have it smelling over the back fence or threatening the well water. (There are some exceptions, of course, which has given rise to the term **PIMBY**.) The shortage of disposal sites has naturally driven up the price of land disposal in the dumps that still operate, and disposal fees have tripled in many localities during the past few years. Many cities must ship their waste hundreds of miles and across state lines to find an open dump site. For example, household garbage from suburban New York City communities may be transported to a dump in central Illinois or rural Virginia. One-quarter of the trash dumped in Michigan's landfills comes from other states or from Canada.[29] Burning trash in waste-to-energy plants once seemed the perfect solution: disposing solid waste and creating electrical power. But the high cost of building and operating these incinerators, especially as air-quality standards increased, has lessened their promise.

Recycling is a waste management solution that makes good sense. Approximately 33 percent of municipal solid waste is paper, another 13 percent is yard trimmings, and nearly all of these waste streams could be recycled.[30] Packaging and containers, often made of plastic, make up about one-third of municipal solid waste, and at least some of this waste could be recycled. Figure 18.3 shows the types of materials that make up municipal solid waste. Many states have aggressively tackled the mounting garbage problem by adopting statewide recycling laws, and a growing number of cities and counties have begun their own

**NIMBY**

Not in my backyard; the public desire to keep an unwanted facility out of a neighborhood.

**PIMBY**

Put in my backyard; a willingness to accept what others do not want, usually because of the economic benefit.

**Materials in Municipal Solid Waste**

FIGURE 18.3

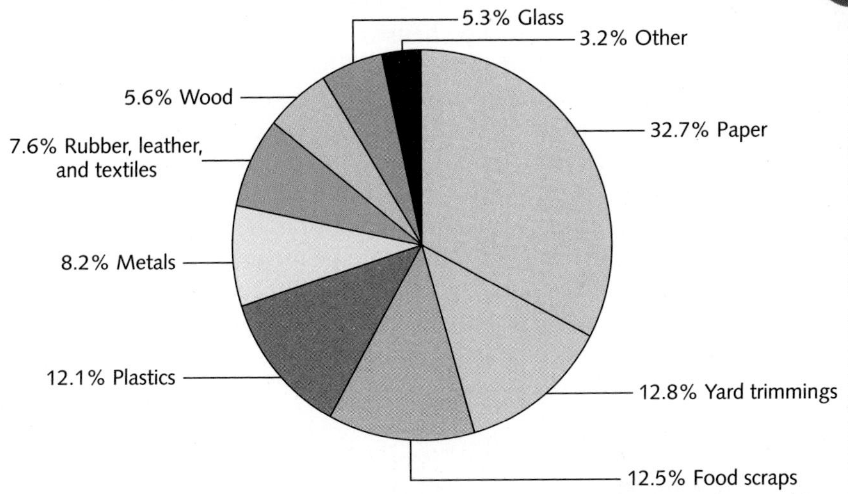
5.3% Glass
3.2% Other
5.6% Wood
32.7% Paper
7.6% Rubber, leather, and textiles
8.2% Metals
12.1% Plastics
12.8% Yard trimmings
12.5% Food scraps

SOURCE: "Municipal Solid Waste Generation, Recycling, and Disposal in the United States: Facts and Figures for 2007," U.S. Environmental Protection Agency (November 2008), p. 4.

recycling efforts. There are an estimated 8,700 curbside recycling programs in the United States. On average, we recycle or compost approximately 1.5 pounds of the waste we generate daily for a recycling rate of about 33.4 percent.[31]

Recycling is not a panacea for the solid waste problem, however. It requires citizen cooperation if it is to be affordable, and some people simply will not cooperate. Recycling rates for aluminum cans and plastic soft drink bottles peaked a few years ago at 63 percent and 41 percent, respectively. But a city cannot refuse to collect nonparticipants' garbage without creating a public health problem. Another dilemma is the shortage of markets for recycled paper, aluminum cans, plastics, and other materials.

For some states, glutted markets and low prices for recyclables make it difficult to reach their recycling goals. During the recent recession, the demand for recycled materials such as cardboard, newspaper, plastic, and metals dropped dramatically. Many states had enacted laws and adopted policies aimed at stimulating demand for recycled goods including sanctions (such as taxes on manufacturers based on their use of virgin materials), incentives (such as the provision of rebates to manufacturers using recovered materials), and exhortations (such as buy-recycled programs). And most state governments have adopted rules requiring or encouraging their agencies to purchase recycled paper products. But even with these market-priming mechanisms in place, when the economy slowed, many localities that once made money selling recyclables were forced to pay waste haulers to take the bottles, cans, and newspapers off their hands.[32]

As noted, approximately one-third of the nation's solid waste is recycled, but the figures are substantially higher in some states than in others. For instance, Virginia's recycling rate in 2007 was 38 percent; Montana's was 18 percent. The explanation for why some states recycle at a greater rate than others is fairly straightforward: access and economics. In other words, recycling rates are higher in states that offer comprehensive curbside recycling programs and impose unit charges for refuse disposal.[33] Making recycling convenient for consumers and creating an economic disincentive not to do so stimulates recycling. For instance, Michigan, which has a bottle deposit law for beverage containers, can boast that 97 percent of beverage bottles and cans are returned.[34] Managing the vast quantity of solid waste generated in our mass consumption, throwaway society is not easy. Recycling is an appealing option, but we cannot recycle everything. Some of the garbage must therefore be incinerated or deposited in a landfill. Every new waste technology has its own difficult issues, and the states and localities, with limited assistance from the federal government, are striving to deal effectively with the huge task of managing the country's garbage.

## Managing Hazardous Waste

The image of garbage mountains rising above the horizon is disconcerting, to say the least. But solid waste is just one of several contributors to environmental destruction. Another insidious public health threat comes from hazardous waste—the poisonous by-products of industrial processes. If these by-products are toxic, corrosive, flammable, or reactive, they are considered hazardous. The industries that generate 90 percent of the hazardous waste in the United States are chemical and allied products, primary metals, petroleum and coal products, fabricated metal products, and rubber and plastic products. Table 18.3 lists the five states where the largest amounts of toxic chemicals were released into the air, water, and ground in 2007. In Alaska, which leads the list, toxic releases typically end up in the ground, on-site.

Hazardous waste is more ubiquitous than most people realize. Pesticide residues, used motor oil, discarded cadmium batteries, used refrigerants, and

**TABLE 18.3    State Leaders in Toxic Releases, 2007**

| STATES LEADING IN TOTAL ON-AND-OFF SITE RELEASES (ALL INDUSTRIES, ALL CHEMICALS) | AMOUNT (IN THOUSANDS OF POUNDS) |
| --- | --- |
| Alaska | 584,447 |
| Ohio | 220,849 |
| Nevada | 219,220 |
| Texas | 192,239 |
| Utah | 166,688 |

SOURCE: TRI Explorer, "2007 National Fact Sheet. Reported Disposal or Other Releases and Other Waste Management Activities," www.epa.gov (August 8, 2009).

paint sludge are hazardous leftovers that are frequently found in households and in so-called nonpolluting industries. It is no exaggeration to say that hazardous waste is all around us.

The primary dilemma concerning hazardous waste is what to do with it. The discovery that wastes were not being properly or safely disposed of triggered government involvement; when hazardous liquids began seeping into people's basements from long-buried barrels, children playing in fields uncovered rotting drums of toxic waste, and motorists developed unusual skin rashes from pesticides sprayed along the roadway, government was called in. Some states feared that imposing tough new hazardous waste regulations would make them less attractive to industry. Others were concerned that tightening the laws for waste disposal would have the perverse effect of increasing the incidence of illegal dumping. A national policy initiative seemed preferable to state attempts at solving the problems.

The national government responded to the mounting crisis with two pieces of legislation: the Resource Conservation and Recovery Act (RCRA) of 1976 and the Comprehensive Environmental Response, Compensation, and Liability Act of 1980 (also known as Superfund). RCRA provides for cradle-to-grave tracking of waste and establishes standards for its treatment, storage, and disposal. Any firm that generates 220 pounds of hazardous waste per month (an amount that fills a fifty-five-gallon barrel about halfway) is covered by the law. RCRA is considered partially pre-emptive because states have a degree of discretion and flexibility in implementation. Once the EPA is satisfied that a state program meets its standards and possesses adequate enforcement mechanisms, the agency authorizes the state to operate its own hazardous waste management program. Under RCRA, states can impose fines and hold individuals criminally liable for violating its provisions.

Superfund was passed in recognition of the fact that no matter how comprehensive and cautious hazardous waste management will be in the future, the pollution of the past remains with us. Under Superfund, the national government can intervene to clean up a dangerous hazardous waste site and later seek reimbursement from responsible parties. Originally, the law contained a provision dubbed "polluter pays," which created a cleanup fund from fees levied on chemical manufacturers and the petroleum industry. These fees, which generated between $1 and $2 billion annually, allowed government to step in and begin the cleanup before all the complex legal issues were resolved. The cleanup fund provision expired in 1995, however, and affected industries have been successful in blocking its renewal. Thus, Superfund has become a program funded by taxpayers.[35] In fact, federal stimulus money was used in 2009 to help accelerate the cleanup of fifty Superfund sites in twenty-eight states.[36]

One of the first actions taken under Superfund was the identification of particularly troublesome sites in need of immediate cleanup, the National Priorities List (NPL). New Jersey was the state with the most sites on the list; Nevada had the fewest. One factor confounding the Superfund program is determining which parties—waste generators, waste transporters, site owners—are responsible for paying for the cleanup. Some of the firms that dumped toxic waste at these sites have gone out of business, and the hope of recovering any of the cleanup costs is remote. As time passed, frustration grew over the slow pace of remediation. Subsequent amendments to the law increased funding levels for the program (although Superfund expenditures peaked in 2001), and expanded the role for state governments in selecting cleanup remedies. In addition, the EPA launched a new initiative to clean up and redevelop contaminated industrial sites, or **brownfields**. Many states have adopted their own mini-Superfund statutes that authorize them to conduct site assessments and initiate remedial cleanup actions or force a responsible party to do so. Some states have also passed laws making it easier to redevelop brownfields, adopted community right-to-know (about hazardous wastes in the area) statutes, and conducted household hazardous waste collection drives.

An issue that has bedeviled the states is disposing of hazardous waste. Disposal sites are locally unwanted land uses (**LULUs**). When efforts to find new disposal facilities are thwarted, states look beyond their borders for solutions. Some states and tribal governments have been willing to accept other states' hazardous waste for disposal—the PIMBY phenomenon—seeing it as a way to generate revenue. But even waste-importing states have their limits. At one point, Alabama banned hazardous waste importation from twenty-two states, an action that was struck down eventually by the federal courts. Alabama lawmakers responded with a fee schedule that taxed out-of-state waste at three times the rate of in-state-generated waste. The effect was dramatic: The quantity of out-of-state waste dropped by one-half, but the business still generated $30 million for the state treasury. Unfortunately for Alabama, the U.S. Supreme Court ruled in 1992 that the surcharge on out-of-state waste violated the interstate commerce clause. Regardless, efforts to block out-of-state waste will continue until solutions to the hazardous waste disposal problem are found. One eminently plausible, if partial, solution to waste-disposal dilemmas is to reduce the amount of waste generated in the first place. Less waste produced means less waste to dispose of.

## Storing Nuclear Waste

Nuclear power is thought by some to be a solution to the nation's energy problems, but it carries a heavy price: deadly, radioactive waste. Until 2009, the federal government had planned to bury high-level nuclear waste, which retains its toxicity for hundreds of thousands of years, at Yucca Mountain, an isolated spot 100 miles northwest of Las Vegas. This plan generated a firestorm of protest from environmentalists and Nevada officials and became an issue in the 2008 presidential election. One concern was the rate of corrosion for the canisters in which the waste would be stored; another was the possibility of earthquakes in the area, and still another was the safety of shipping the waste to the site. In 2009, President Obama, making good on a campaign promise, terminated the Yucca Mountain waste disposal project and, with the support of Congress, allocated funds to convene a blue-ribbon commission to come up with an alternative plan.[37]

**brownfields**

Abandoned industrial sites with real or perceived environmental contamination.

**LULU**

Locally unwanted land use; a broad category of undesirable facilities such as landfills and prisons.

Low-level radioactive wastes (LLWs) are much less toxic in a relative sense because they break down to safe levels of radioactivity in anywhere from a few weeks or months to 300 years. LLWs are produced by commercial nuclear power installations (46 percent), nuclear-related industries (39 percent), and medical and research institutions (15 percent). The waste, much of it stored in fifty-five-gallon steel drums, includes items such as contaminated laboratory clothes, tools, equipment, and leftover bomb materials as well as bulk wastes.

The Low-Level Radioactive Waste Policy Act of 1980 made each state responsible for the disposal of the waste generated within its borders. States have the choice of managing LLWs within their own jurisdictions (i.e., developing their own disposal sites) or entering into an interstate compact for out-of-state disposal. As expected, a few states have opted to handle the problem alone, but most have joined with their neighbors to forge a regional answer to the disposal question.

The use of **interstate compacts** to address the LLW problem was particularly inventive because nuclear waste disposal has historically been considered a federal responsibility. When interstate compacts are successful, they are a shining example of what the states can accomplish when left to their own devices.[38] Potential member states have to negotiate a draft compact that must be ratified by their legislatures and by Congress. Negotiations often break down as each state tries to get the best deal for itself, precisely the goal of each of the other participating states. By 2009, ten interstate LLW compacts had been formed; six states remained unaligned, preferring to go it alone. As shown in Figure 18.4, several of the compacts are decidedly nonregional in their composition. For example, the two Dakotas joined Arizona and California to form the Southwestern Compact; Texas teamed up with Maine and Vermont to create the Texas Compact.

The case of the Midwest Compact demonstrates the hard decisions faced by all the compacts. The Midwest Compact was one of the first to win congressional consent. Seven states were members; each agreed that it would take its turn to host a disposal facility for the entire compact. Weighing three factors for each state—the volume of LLW produced, the radioactivity of that waste, and transportation modes and routes—compact members selected Michigan as the first host state. Michigan spent several years evaluating the suitability of three possible disposal locations, only to reject all of them. The compact was no closer to a regional disposal site than it had been at the outset. In reaction, the other states booted Michigan out of the Midwest Compact (Michigan is currently unaligned). Ohio, the runner-up to Michigan in the earlier state-selection process, became the host state.

With compacts in place and host states selected, the next challenge is the actual construction of new disposal facilities. This step can be difficult because of the **NIMTOO** (not in my term of office) phenomenon. But time is of the essence because existing sites have begun to restrict access. For example, the Hanford, Washington, site accepts waste only from members of the Northwest and Rocky Mountain Compacts and, beginning in 2008, the Barnwell, South Carolina, site began excluding waste from outside the Atlantic Compact. As

**interstate compacts**
Formal agreements among a subset of states, usually to solve a problem that affects each of the member states.

**NIMTOO**
Not in my term of office; the desire by elected officials to avoid accepting LULUs while they are in office.

**Low-Level Radioactive Waste Compacts**

FIGURE 18.4

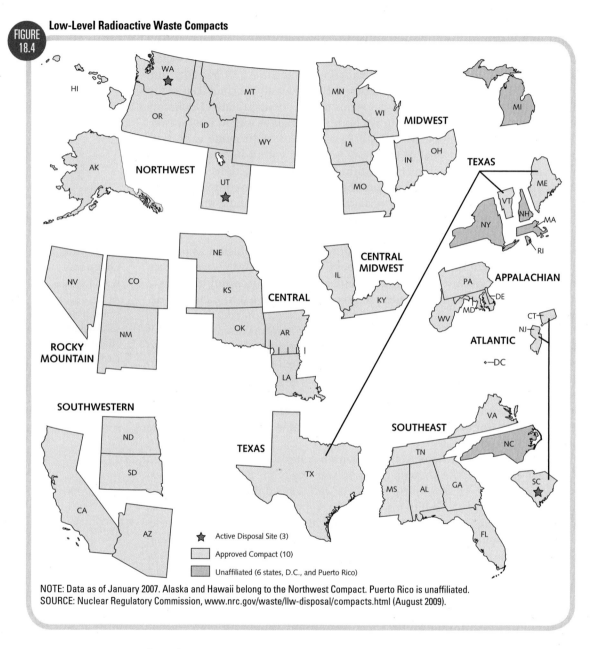

★ Active Disposal Site (3)

☐ Approved Compact (10)

▨ Unaffiliated (6 states, D.C., and Puerto Rico)

NOTE: Data as of January 2007. Alaska and Hawaii belong to the Northwest Compact. Puerto Rico is unaffiliated.
SOURCE: Nuclear Regulatory Commission, www.nrc.gov/waste/llw-disposal/compacts.html (August 2009).

for other compacts, only California and Texas are slated to begin operations at their disposal facilities in the near future. In the meantime, generators are being told to store their waste on site or contract with private vendors for safe storage.[39]

The lack of guarantees about the future consequences of nuclear waste disposal makes it a prospect both fascinating and frightening. Some observers predict that if California's power shortages of the early 2000s occur again—and spread to other states—the demand for nuclear power will grow.[40] If so, the debate over disposal issues will intensify.

# TWO CHALLENGES FOR POLICYMAKERS

Several challenges loom for those who are tangled up in the thicket of environmental protection policy making. The growing influence of economic logic on environmental decisions is one; the widespread but shifting public support for environmentalism is another. A problem that is only going to intensify is water shortages, a dilemma that already strains interstate relations in the West. The two challenges discussed below, environmental justice and ecoterrorism, will force policy makers to confront some disturbing realities of environmental policy.

## Environmental Justice

In the early 1980s, protesters who fought vigorously against the dumping of polychlorinated biphenyl (PCB)-contaminated soil in a rural North Carolina county spawned a new movement: environmental justice. In general, the argument is that poor and minority communities suffer disproportionate exposure to environmental health risks. An example of environmental injustice is the area referred to as "Cancer Alley," an eighty-five-mile strip along the Mississippi River in Louisiana that is home to over 100 chemical, petrochemical, refining, and industrial plants. The households located within harm's way of these plants are disproportionately minority and low-income.[41] Two law school professors put the matter this way:

> People of color throughout the United States are receiving more than their fair share of the poisonous fruits of industrial production. They live cheek by jowl with waste dumps, incinerators, landfills, smelters, factories, chemical plants, and oil refineries whose operations make them sick and kill them young. They are poisoned by the air they breathe, the water they drink, the fish they catch, the vegetables they grow, and in the case of children, the very ground they play on.[42]

Research has found inequities in environmental policy. For instance, one study of the relationship between race and the enforcement of environmental laws by the EPA showed that white communities received faster action and more satisfactory results than did minority communities.[43] One of the distinctive differences between areas that contain commercial hazardous waste facilities and those that do not is the proportion of minority residents.[44] Communities with these facilities tend to have double the proportion of minority residents than those without them. Another study found that single-mother families are overrepresented in environmentally hazardous areas.[45] Other research, however, takes issue with contentions of environmental inequities. Statewide studies of Superfund site locations in New Jersey and hazardous waste facilities in South

Carolina did not find statistically significant links to race or ethnicity.[46] Why are polluting facilities located where they are? The answer is multifaceted:

- scientific rationality (e.g., the geologic characteristics of the site);
- market factors (e.g., land prices, available labor pool);
- neighborhood transition (e.g., changing demographics in the area over time);
- political power (e.g., whether the residents in the area are politically active);
- intentional discrimination (e.g., targeting poor and minority neighbor-hoods).[47]

Concern over environmental justice has led more than thirty states to take some sort of policy action. For example, Arkansas passed legislation that discourages the location of high-impact solid waste management facilities within twelve miles of each other. Exemptions may be granted if specific benefits are provided to the host community in the form of jobs, fees, and improvements to infrastructure. In Louisiana, the Department of Environmental Quality was instructed to hold public hearings and make policy recommendations on environmental equity issues. Pennsylvania added an Environmental Justice Advisory Board to its environmental protection agency. The federal government and EPA took up the issue as well, establishing a National Environmental Justice Advisory Council charged with ensuring that environmental justice be addressed in the agency's policies, programs, and activities. Clearly, environmental justice will continue to be a salient topic for policy makers well into the future.[48]

## Ecoterrorism

Environmentalists have long employed tactics such as civil disobedience as a way of attracting attention to their cause. For example, some have climbed trees in old-growth forests and become tree-sitters in an effort to keep loggers from cutting down the trees and destroying wildlife habitat. Others have locked arms and stood across highways to block trucks carrying hazardous waste into their communities. But those tactics pale in comparison with the actions taken by radical environmental groups such as the Earth Liberation Front (ELF). The ELF is a shadow organization, organized into autonomous groups that operate independently, with a remarkable capacity for attracting media attention.[49] To members of this group, violence is an acceptable means of furthering their political objectives. To that end, they have vandalized new SUVs on dealership lots and set luxury homes on fire. These types of actions have been labeled ecoterrorism.

The FBI has officially labeled actions by ecoterrorists and animal rights extremists as one of the most serious domestic terrorism threats in the United States today. The reasons for this declaration are many, including the sheer volume and economic impact of the groups' crimes, estimated at more than 2,000 incidents totaling over $100 million in damage since 1979.[50] One of the first notable attacks occurred in 1998, when a new development in the Vail, Colorado, ski resort was burned to the ground. Ecoterrorists defended their actions as protecting the habitat for a threatened species, the Canadian lynx. Since then, their targets have expanded, as illustrated by the torching of a large condominium complex being built in an upscale San Diego neighborhood in 2003, and several luxury "McMansions" being developed in a Seattle suburb in 2008. At the core of the ecoterrorist agenda is opposition to the corporate sector and its profiteering. One of the ELF's goals is to "inflict economic damage on those profiting from the destruction and exploitation of the natu-

Members of radical environmental groups take actions designed to draw attention to their cause.
*SOURCE: © David McNew/Getty Images.*

ral environment."[51] Legislators in several states have responded to these incidents by sponsoring bills that increase the penalties for property damage in the name of environmental protection. In Oregon, for example, legislators debated a new category of crime, **ecosabotage**, that could be prosecuted under the state's racketeering laws. If states do not take action on this issue, Congress may. In 2003, a bill called the Stop Terrorism of Property Act was introduced in the U.S. House of Representatives. Although it has not passed, related legislation, the Animal Enterprise Terrorism Act, was signed into law at the end of 2006. It expands the number of criminal activities associated with animal rights extremism, and mandates harsher penalties for them. Caught in the middle of efforts to crack down on ecoterrorists are mainstream environmental groups that have publicly deplored the radical organizations but, by the same token, see these legislative measures as essentially anti-environmental.

**ecosabotage**
An action designed to inflict economic damage to those who profit at the expense of the natural environment; a tactic of ecoterrorists.

## CHAPTER RECAP

- Public opinion shows support for environmental protection and economic growth; however, achieving one goal often comes at the expense of the other. After many years of preferring environmental protection, public opinion recently shifted in favor of economic growth. Government's role is to balance the two objectives.

- The national government has been an important force in environmental protection. Performance partnership agreements and grants give states more power to set their own spending priorities.

- Environmental conditions and state programs vary from one state to another.

A recent study found Oregon and Vermont to be the greenest states, and West Virginia to be the least green.

- Many cities, such as Seattle, Washington, have embraced sustainability and have adopted green policies.

- A tremendous amount of solid waste is generated daily in the United States. Although most of it is disposed of in landfills, recycling continues to be a promising approach.

- Two major federal programs, RCRA and Superfund, have set the hazardous waste management agenda. States play a major part in implementing RCRA, and they partner with the federal government in Superfund cleanups.

- Interstate compacts (there are ten) are used for the disposal of low-level radioactive waste.

- Two challenges facing contemporary policy makers are environmental justice and ecoterrorism. Although states have made strides in dealing with the former, they have just begun to confront the latter issue.

## Key Terms

environmental self-audit (p. 498)

race to the bottom (p. 498)

sustainability (p. 499)

partial pre-emption (p. 501)

ecological footprint (p. 509)

NIMBY (p. 510)

PIMBY (p. 510)

brownfields (p. 514)

LULU (p.514)

interstate compacts (p. 515)

NIMTOO (p. 515)

ecosabotage (p. 519)

## Internet Resources

The official website of the Environmental Protection Agency (EPA) is **www.epa.gov**. It is packed with information about the EPA's programs and initiatives.

The official website of the Department of the Interior is **www.doi.gov**. It contains a wealth of information about the various activities of the agency.

All states have agencies devoted to environmental protection and natural resource conservation. See, for example, Oregon at **www.oregon.gov/DEQ/** and Ohio at **www.dnr.state.oh.us**.

A good place to track environmental protection policies, laws, and regulations is at **www.enviro.blr.com**. This site is maintained by Business and Legal Reports, a firm that advertises itself as "making state environmental compliance easier."

If you want to find out where alternative and advanced fueling stations are located, then check **www.afdc.energy.gov/afdc/locator/stations/**.

For more information about environmental issues, contact the Sierra Club at **www.sierraclub.org**, the National Wildlife Federation at **www.nwf.org**, the Nature Conservancy at **www.nature.org**, and the Grassroots Recycling Network at **www.grrn.org**.

To learn about the impact of pollution on the public, explore the website of the Environmental Justice Foundation at **www.ejfoundation.org**.

"No Compromise in Defense of Mother Earth" is the organizing principle of Earth First!—a group whose online journal is found at **www.earthfirstjournal.org**.

# References

## Chapter 1 New Directions for State and Local Governments

1. Governor Steven L. Beshear, "State of the Commonwealth Address," www.stateline.org/live/details/speech?contentId=374697 (February 4, 2009).

2. Bruce Wallin, "State and Local Governments Are American, Too," *Political Science Teacher* 1 (Fall 1988): 1–3.

3. Mike Sullivan, quoted in "Wyoming's Governor Signs Law to Restructure State Government," *Denver Post* (March 5, 1989), p. 8B.

4. "Harvard Kennedy School's Ash Institute Announces Top 50 Innovations in Government," http://ashinstitute.harvard.edu/ash/03.31.09_Top50.pdf (March 31, 2009).

5. Beth Walter Honadle, "Defining and Doing Capacity Building: Perspective and Experiences," in Beth Walter Honadle and Arnold M. Howitt, eds., *Perspectives on Management Capacity Building* (Albany, NY: SUNY Press, 1986), pp. 9–23.

6. Katherine Barrett and Richard Greene, "Grading the States '08," *Governing* 21 (March 2008): 24–95.

7. Julie Bund and Gene M. Lutz, "Connecting State Government Reform with Public Priorities: The Iowa Test Case," *State and Local Government Review* 31 (Spring 1999): 73–90.

8. David M. Hedge, *Governance and the Changing American States* (Boulder, CO: Westview Press, 1998).

9. National Education Association, "No Child Left Behind/ESEA: It's Time for a Change," www.nea.org/home/18138.htm (June 5, 2009).

10. Terry Sanford, *The Storm Over the States* (New York: McGraw-Hill, 1967), p. 21.

11. Quoted in Sanford, *The Storm Over the States*.

12. John Herbers, "The New Federalism: Unplanned, Innovative, and Here to Stay," *Governing* 1 (October 1987): 28.

13. Sheryl Gay Stolberg, "As Congress Stalls, States Pursue Cloning Debate," *The New York Times*, www.nytimes.com (May 26, 2002).

14. Ann O'M. Bowman and Richard C. Kearney, *The Resurgence of the States* (Englewood Cliffs, NJ: Prentice-Hall, 1986).

15. Sanford, *The Storm Over the States*.

16. Ann O'M. Bowman and Richard C. Kearney, "Dimensions of State Government Capability," *Western Political Quarterly* 41 (June 1988): 341–62; David R. Morgan and Kenneth Kickham, "Modernization Among the U.S. States: Change and Continuity from 1960 to 1990," *Publius* 27 (Summer 1997): 23–39.

17. Donald P. Haider-Markel, "Policy Diffusion as a Geographical Expansion of the Scope of Political Conflict: Same Sex Marriage Bans in the 1990s," *State Politics and Policy Quarterly* 1 (Winter 2001): 5–26.

18. Craig Savoye, "States Spare Residents from Telemarketers," *Christian Science Monitor* (December 22, 2000), p. 8.

19. Chris Hamby, " 'Fire-Safe' Cigarette Laws Spread Quickly," www.stateline.org (August 7, 2007).

20. U.S. Conference of Mayors Climate Protection Center, "Mayors Leading the Way on Climate Protection," www.usmayors.org/climateprotection/revised/ (June 12, 2009).

21. Lawrence J. Grossbeck, Sean Nicholson-Crotty, and David A. M. Peterson, "Ideology and Learning in Policy Diffusion," *American Politics Research* 32 (September 2004): 521–45.

22. David W. Winder and James T. LaPlant, "State Lawsuits Against Big Tobacco: A Test of Diffusion Theory," *State and Local Government Review* 32 (Spring 2000): 132–41.

23. Brad Knickerbocker, "States Take Clean Air Measures into Their Own Hands," *Christian Science Monitor* (April 19, 2005), p. 3.

24. Ann O'M. Bowman, "Horizontal Federalism: Exploring Interstate Interactions," *Journal of Public Administration Research and Theory* 14 (October 2004): 535–46.

25. Governor George Voinovich, quoted in "Reassessing Mandates," *State Policy Reports* 11 (October 1993): 16.

26. Knickerbocker, "States Take Clean Air Measures into Their Own Hands," pp. 1, 3.

27. John Holahan et al., *State Responses to the 2004 Budget Crisis: A Look at Ten States* (Washington, D.C.: The Urban Institute, 2004).

28. As quoted in "It's Scary: State of the States 2009," *State News* 52 (May 2009): 9.

29. National Association of State Budget Officers, "The Fiscal Survey of States," www.nasbo.org/Publications/PDFs/FSSpring2009.pdf (June 15, 2009).

30. Pamela M. Prah, "Reports: State Income Levels Plunge," www.stateline.org (June 19, 2009).

31. Rudolph Bush, "Dallas City Council Knows 'Brutal' Budget Cuts Coming," *Dallas Morning News*, www.dallasnews.com (June 18, 2009).

32. Ralph Vartebedian, "The Race to Steal Bases Heats Up," *Los Angeles Times*, www.latimes.com (November 29, 2004).

33. Michael Johnston, "Right and Wrong in American Politics: Popular Conceptions of Corruption," in Arnold J. Heidenheimer and Michael Johnston, eds., *Political Corruption: Concepts and Contexts*

(New Brunswick, NJ: Transaction, 2002), pp. 173–91; see also, Richard T. Boylan and Cheryl X. Long, "Measuring Public Corruption in the American States," *State Politics and Policy Quarterly* (Winter 2003): 420–38.

34. Steven P. Lanza, *The Economics of Ethics: The Cost of Political Corruption* (Storrs, CT.: Connecticut Center for Economic Analysis, 2004).

35. Jeff Whelan and Mark Mueller, "Statewide Sting Catches 11 Officials," *Newark Star-Ledger*, www.nj.com/news/ledger (September 7, 2007).

36. Boylan and Long, "Measuring Public Corruption in the American States."

37. U.S. Census Bureau, "2008 Population Estimates," http://factfinder.census.gov (May 25, 2009).

38. U.S. Census Bureau, "Foreign-Born Population Tops 34 Million," www.census.gov/Press-Release (February 22, 2005).

39. Thomas Frank, "Illegal Immigrant Population Declines," *USA Today* www.usatoday.com/news/nation/2009-02-23-immigration_N.htm (February 24, 2009).

40. N. C. Aizenman, "Illegal Immigrants' Legal Kids Snarl Policy," *Washington Post*, www.washingtonpost.com (April 15, 2009).

41. Rodney E. Hero and Caroline J. Tolbert, "A Racial/Ethnic Diversity Interpretation of Politics and Policy in the States of the U.S.," *American Journal of Political Science* 40 (August 1996): 851–71; Rodney E. Hero, *Faces of Inequality: Social Diversity in American Politics* (New York: Oxford University Press, 2000).

42. Genaro C. Armas, "Minority Groups to Swell by 2050," *The State* (March 18, 2004): A4.

43. U.S. Census Bureau, "Cumulative Estimates of Population Change for the United States, Regions, States, and Puerto Rico, April 1, 2000 to July 1, 2008," http://www.census.gov/popest/states/NST-pop-chg.html (May 1, 2009).

44. U.S. Census Bureau, "Cumulative Estimates of Population Change for Incorporated Places over 100,000, Ranked by Percent Change: April 1, 2000 to July 1, 2007," http://www.census.gov/popest/cities/SUB-EST2007.html (May 19, 2009).

45. Michael Barone, "The 2012 Seating Plan," *National Journal*, July 21, 2007, 34–38.

46. Daniel J. Elazar, *American Federalism: A View from the States*, 3rd ed. (New York: Harper & Row, 1984).

47. Jody L. Fitzpatrick and Rodney E. Hero, "Political Culture and Political Characteristics of the American States: A Consideration of Some Old and New Questions," *Western Political Quarterly* 41 (March 1988): 145–53.

48. Keith Boeckelman, "Political Culture and State Development Policy," *Publius* 21 (Spring 1991): 49–92; Russell L. Hanson, "Political Culture Variations in State Economic Development Policy," *Publius* 21 (Spring 1991): 63–81.

49. James P. Lester, "A New Federalism: Environmental Policy in the States," in Norman Vig and Michael Kraft, eds., *Environmental Policy in the 1990s* (Washington, D.C.: Congressional Quarterly Press, 1994), pp. 51–68; Steven A. Peterson and James N.

Schubert, "Predicting State AIDS Policy Spending," Paper presented at the annual meeting of the American Political Science Association, New York City, September 1994.

50. Joel Lieske, "Regional Subcultures of the United States," *Journal of Politics* 55 (November 1993): 888–913.

51. Mark Preston, "The 'Most' Representative State: Wisconsin," *CNN*, www.cnn.com/2006/POLITICS/07/27/mg.thu/index.html (July 27, 2006).

52. Elaine B. Sharp, "Introduction," in Elaine B. Sharp, ed., *Culture Wars and Local Politics* (Lawrence, KS: University Press of Kansas, 1999), pp. 1–20.

53. National Conference of State Legislatures, "Same Sex Marriage, Civil Unions, and Domestic Partnerships," http://www.ncsl.org/default.aspx?tabid=16430 (June 8, 2009).

54. Sara Karush, "Hamtramck Voters Back Islamic Call to Prayers," *Lansing State Journal*, www.lsj.com (July 21, 2004).

55. John Shannon, "The Return to Fend-for-Yourself Federalism: The Reagan Mark," *Intergovernmental Perspective* 13 (Summer/Fall 1987): 34–37.

56. Alan Ehrenhalt, "The Increasing Irrelevance of Congress," *Governing* 11 (January 1998): 6–7.

## Chapter 2 Federalism and the States

1. *Gonzalez v. Oregon*, No. 04-623.

2. Carmine P. F. Scavo, Richard C. Kearney, and Richard J. Kilroy, Jr., "Challenges to Federalism: Homeland Security and Disaster Response," *Publius: The Journal of Federalism* 38(1) (2008): 81–110.

3. Quoted in Richard Hofstadter, *The American Political Tradition* (New York: Vintage Books, 1948), p. 5.

4. Ibid., pp. 9–10.

5. Richard H. Leach, *American Federalism* (New York: W. W. Norton, 1970), p. 1.

6. David C. Hendrickson, *Peace Pact: The Lost World of the American Founding* (Lawrence, KS: University Press of Kansas, 2003).

7. Charles S. McCoy, "Federalism: The Lost Tradition?" *Publius* 31 (Spring 2001): 1–14.

8. Walter Berns, "The Meaning of the Tenth Amendment," in Robert A. Goldwin, ed., *A Nation of States* (Chicago, IL: Rand McNally, 1961), p. 130.

9. Forrest McDonald, *States' Rights and the Union: Imperium in Imperio* (Lawrence, KS: University Press of Kansas, 2000); David B. Walker, *The Rebirth of Federalism*, 2nd ed. (New York: Chatham House, 2000), Chapter 2.

10. Hofstadter, *The American Political Tradition*, p. 72.

11. *McCulloch v. Maryland*, 4 Wheaton 316 (1819).

12. *Gibbons v. Ogden*, 9 Wheaton 316 (1819).

13. Eric Kelderman, "Real ID Showdown Averted," *stateline.org* (April 4, 2008).

14. Jonathan Walters, "Real ID and Reality," *Governing.com* (July 1, 2008).

15. William Yardley, "Bids to Push States' Rights Falter in Face of Stimulus," *nytimes.com* (May 8, 2009).

16. *United States v. Darby*, 312 U.S. 100 (1941) at 124.

17. *National League of Cities v. Usery*, 426 U.S. 833 (1976).

18. *Garcia v. San Antonio Metropolitan Transit Authority*, 105 S.Ct. 1007, 1011 (1985).

19. Ibid. (O'Connor, dissenting).

20. John C. Pittenger, "*Garcia* and the Political Safeguards of Federalism: Is There a Better Solution to the Conundrum of the Tenth Amendment?" *Publius* 22 (Winter 1992).

21. *U.S. v. Lopez*, 115 S.Ct. 1424 (1995). See Kenneth T. Palmer and Edward B. Laverty, "The Impact of *U.S. v. Lopez* on Intergovernmental Relations," *Publius* 26 (Summer 1996): 109–26.

22. *Kansas v. Hendricks*, 117 S.Ct. 2072 (1997).

23. *Printz v. U.S.*, 521 S.Ct. 98 (1997).

24. *Kelo v. New London* (2005). 545 U.S. 469 (2005).

25. *Cuno v. Daimler-Chrysler.* 547 U.S. 332 (2006).

26. *Nevada Department of Human Resources v. Hibbs*, S.Ct. 01-1368 (2003).

27. *Seminole Tribe of Florida v. Florida*, 116 S.Ct. 1114 (1996).

28. *College Savings Bank v. Florida Prepaid Postsecondary Education Expense Board* et al., 98 S.Ct. 149 (1999); *Kimel v. Florida Board of Regents*, 120 S.Ct. 631 (2000).

29. *Federal Maritime Commission v. South Carolina Ports Authority*, No. 01-46 (2002).

30. *Tennessee v. Lane*, 124 S. Ct. 1978 (2004).

31. *Lorillard Tobacco v. Reilly*, No. 00-596 (2000).

32. *Bush v. Gore* et al., 531 U.S. 98 (2000).

33. *Rowe v. New Hampshire Motor Transport Assn.*, (No. 06-457) 448 F. 3d 66, 2008.

34. Martha Derthick, "American Federalism: Half-Full or Half-Empty?" *Brookings Review* (Winter 2000): 24.

35. William H. Stewart, "Metaphors, Models and the Development of Federal Theory," *Publius* 12 (Spring 1982): 5–24.

36. Deil S. Wright, *Understanding Intergovernmental Relations*, 3rd ed. (Pacific Grove, CA: Brooks/Cole 1988), pp. 40–42.

37. Walker, *The Rebirth of Federalism*, Chapter 4.

38. Timothy J. Conlan, "Federalism and Competing Values in the Reagan Administration," *Publius* 16 (Winter 1986): 29–47.

39. Ann O'M. Bowman and Michael A. Pagano, "The State of American Federalism 1989–1990," *Publius* 20 (Summer 1990): 1–25.

40. John Kincaid and Richard L. Cole, "Public Opinion on Issues of Federalism in 2007: A Bush Plus?" *Publius: The Journal of Federalism Publius* 38 (2008): 469–87.

41. John Kincaid and Richard L. Cole, "Changing Public Attitudes on Power and Taxation in the American Federal System," *Publius* 31 (Summer 2001): 205–14.

42. Alan Greenblatt, "The Washington Offensive," *Governing* (January 2005): 26–29.

43. Peter Harkness, " 'Shift-and-Shaft' Federalism," *Governing.com* (March 9, 2008).

44. W. Dale Mason, *Indian Gaming: Tribal Sovereignty and American Politics* (Norman, OK: University of Oklahoma Press, 2000).

45. Erich Steinman, "American Federalism and Intergovernmental Innovation in State-Tribal Relations," *Publius* 34 (Spring 2004): 95–115.

46. Mason, *Indian Gaming*.

47. Joseph F. Zimmerman, "Interstate Relation Trends," *Book of the States*, vol. 37 (Lexington, KY: Council of State Governments, 2005), pp. 36–37.

48. Jeremy W. Peters, "New York to Back Same-Sex Unions from Elsewhere," *NYTimes.com* (May 29, 2008).

49. Ann O'M. Bowman and Neal D. Woods, "Strength in Numbers: Why States Join Interstate Compacts," *State Politics and Policy Quarterly* 7 (Winter 2007): 347–68.

50. Brian H. Kehri, "States Abstain from Federal Sex Ed Money," www.stateline.org (November 9, 2005): 1–3.

51. J. Santelli, M. Ott, M. Lyon, J. Rogers, D. Summers, R. Schleifer, "Abstinence and Abstinence-only Education: A Review of U.S. Policies and Programs," *Journal of Adolescent Health* 38(1) (2006): 72–81.

52. National Conference of State Legislatures, "Mandate Monitor," (2009); http://www.ncsl.org/standcomm/ scbudg/manmon.htm; Jon Kincaid, "State-Federal Relations: Defense, Demography, Debt, and Deconstruction as Destiny," *Book of the States*, vol. 37 (Lexington, KY: Council of State Governments), pp. 25–30, 48. Pamela M. Prah, "States Stuck with Federal $29 Billion Tab, NCSL Says," www.stateline .org (March 10, 2004): 2–4.

53. U.S.G.A.O., "Unfunded Mandates: Views Vary About Reform Act's Strengths, Weaknesses, and Options for Improvement," GAO-05-454 (March 31, 2005).

54. Christopher A. Mooney, "The Decline of Federalism and the Rise of Morality—Policy Conflict in the United States," *Publius: The Journal of Federalism* 30 (Winter 2000): 171–88.

55. Derthick, "American Federalism," p. 27.

56. See David B. Walker, "The Advent of Ambiguous Federalism and the Emergence of New Federalism III," *Public Administration Review* 56 (May/June 1996): 271–80.

57. Marcia L. Godwin, "Innovations Across American States," Paper presented at the 2001 annual meeting of the American Political Science Association, San Francisco, August 30–September 2, 2002.

58. Samuel H. Beer, "The Future of the States in the Federal System," in Peter Woll, ed., *American Government: Readings and Cases* (Boston, MA: Little, Brown, 1981), p. 92.

59. Alan Greenblatt, "Recipe for Respect," *Governing* (February 2008): 22–26.

60. Richard P. Nathan, "Updating Theories of American Federalism," Paper presented at the annual meeting of the American Political Science Association, September 2, 2006.

# Chapter 3 State Constitutions

1. G. Alan Tarr, *Understanding State Constitutions* (Princeton, NJ: Princeton University Press, 1999).
2. U.S. Advisory Commission on Intergovernmental Relations (ACIR), *State Constitutions in the Federal System*, A-113 (Washington, D.C.: ACIR, 1989), p. 2.
3. Donald S. Lutz, "The United States Constitution as an Incomplete Text," *Annals of the American Academy of Political and Social Science* 496 (March 1989): 23–32.
4. G. Alan Tarr and Mary Cornelia Porter, "Introduction: State Constitutionalism and State constitutional Law," *Publius* 17 (Winter 1987): 5.
5. Donald S. Lutz, "Toward a Theory of Constitutional Amendment," *American Political Science Review* 88 (June 1994): 356; G. Alan Tarr, ed., *Constitutional Politics in the States* (Westport, CT: Greenwood Press, 1996), p. xv.
6. Donald S. Lutz, "The Iroquois Confederation Constitution: An Analysis," *Publius* 22 (Spring 1998): 99–127.
7. Daniel J. Elazar, "The Principles and Traditions Underlying State Constitutions," *Publius* 12 (Winter 1982): 11.
8. Quoted in Perry Gilbert Miller, "Thomas Hooker and the Democracy of Early Connecticut," *New England Quarterly* 4 (1931): 695.
9. Bruce Fraser, *The Land of Steady Habits: A Brief History of Connecticut* (Hartford, CT: Connecticut Historical Commission, 1986), p. 10.
10. Willi Paul Adams, *The First American Constitutions* (Lanham, MD: Madison House, 2000), p. 61.
11. John Estill Reeves, *Kentucky Government* (Lexington, KY: University of Kentucky, 1966), p. 7. As quoted in Penny M. Miller, *Kentucky Government and Politics* (Lincoln: University of Nebraska Press, 1994), p. 82.
12. Albert L. Sturm, "The Development of American State Constitutions," *Publius* 12 (Winter 1982): 61.
13. Ibid., pp. 62–63.
14. Paul G. Reardon, "The Massachusetts Constitution Makes a Milestone," *Publius* 12 (Winter 1982): 45–55.
15. David McCullough, *John Adams* (New York: Touchstone Books, 2001).
16. Quoted in James Bryce, "Nature of the American State," in Bruce Stinebrickner, ed., *State and Local Government*, 3rd ed. (Guilford, CT: Dushkin, 1987), pp. 20–23.
17. Quoted in Thomas Parrish, "Kentucky's Fourth Constitution Is a Product of Its 1980 Times," in Thad L. Beyle, ed., *State Government: CQ's Guide to Current Issues and Activities 1991–92* (Washington, D.C.: Congressional Quarterly Press, 1991), p. 46.
18. U.S. Advisory Commission on Intergovernmental Relations (ACIR), *The Question of State Government Capability* (Washington, D.C.: ACIR, 1985), p. 36.
19. Council of State Governments, *The Book of the States*, Vol. 33 (Lexington, KY: Council of State Governments, 2000), Table 1.1, footnote (a).
20. David Fellman, "What Should a State Constitution Contain?" in W. Brooke Graves, ed., *Major Problems in State Constitutional Revision* (Chicago, IL: Public Administration Service, 1960), p. 146.
21. Sturm, "The Development of American State Constitutions," p. 64; see Christopher W. Hammons, "Was James Madison Wrong? Rethinking the American Preference for Short, Framework-Oriented Constitutions," *American Political Science Review* 93 (December 1999): 837–49.
22. Josh Goodman, "Seizing the Initiative," *Governing* (October 2008), p. 32.
23. David C. Nice, "Interest Groups and State Constitutions: Another Look," *State and Local Government Review* 20 (Winter 1988): 22.
24. Donald S. Lutz, "Patterns in the Amending of American State Constitutions," in G. Alan Tarr, ed., *Constitutional Politics in the States* (Westport, CT: Greenwood Press, 1996), pp. 24–27.
25. U.S. Advisory Commission on Intergovernmental Relations (ACIR), *A Report to the President for Transmittal to the Congress* (Washington, D.C.: U.S. Government Printing Office, 1955).
26. National Municipal League, *Model State Constitution*, 6th ed., rev. (New York: National Municipal League, 1968).
27. John J. Carroll and Arthur English, "Traditions of State Constitution Making," *State and Local Government Review* 23 (Fall 1991): 103–9.
28. *Gitlow v. New York* 268 U.S. 652 (1925).
29. Thomas C. Marks, Jr., and John F. Cooper, *State Constitutional Law* (St. Paul, MN: West, 1988), p. 38.
30. Ibid., pp. 38–42.
31. Michael Besso, "Constitutional Amendment Procedures and the Informal Political Construction of Constitutions," *The Journal of Politics* 67 (February 2005): 6987.
32. Marks and Cooper, *State Constitutional Law*, p. 47.
33. Tarr and Porter, "Introduction," p. 9.
34. Stanley H. Friedelbaum, "The Complementary Role of Federal and State Courts," *Publius* 17 (Winter 1987): 48.
35. Goodman, "Seizing the Initiative," 2008.
36. Janice C. May, "State Constitutions and Constitutional Revision: 1988–89 and the 1980s," *The Book of the States 1990–91* (Washington, D.C.: Council of State Governments, 1991), p. 25.
37. Quoted in U.S. Advisory Commission on Intergovernmental Relations, *State Constitutions in the Federal System* (Washington, D.C.: ACIR, 1989), p. 37.
38. W. Brooke Graves, "State Constitutional Law: A Twenty-five Year Summary," *William and Mary Law Review* 8 (Fall 1966): 12.
39. ACIR, *The Question of State Government Capability*, p. 60.
40. Richard H. Leach, "A Quiet Revolution: 1933–1976," in *The Book of the States 1975–76* (Lexington, KY: Council of State Governments, 1976), p. 25.
41. Terry Sanford, *Storm Over the States* (New York: McGraw-Hill, 1967), p. 1983.

# Chapter 4 Citizen Participation and Elections

1. Randal C. Archibold, "Arizona Ballot Could Become Lottery Ticket," *The New York Times*, www.nytimes.com (July 17, 2006).
2. Robert D. Putnam, *Bowling Alone: The Collapse and Revival of American Community* (New York: Simon & Schuster, 2000); see also Nojin Kwak, Dhavan V. Shah, and R. Lance Holbrook, "Connecting, Trusting, and Participating: The Direct and Interactive Effects of Social Associations," *Political Research Quarterly* 57 (December 2004): 643–52.
3. John D. Griffin and Brian Newman, "Are Voters Better Represented?" *Journal of Politics* 67 (November 2005): 1206–27.
4. William E. Lyons, David Lowery, and Ruth Hoogland De Hoog, *The Politics of Dissatisfaction* (Armonk, NY: M. E. Sharpe, 1992); Albert O. Hirschman, *Exit, Voice and Loyalty: Responses to Decline in Firms, Organizations, and States* (Cambridge, MA: Harvard University Press, 1972).
5. Henry E. Brady, Sidney Verba, and Kay Lehman Schlozman, "Beyond SES: A Resource Model of Political Participation," *American Political Science Review* 89 (June 1995): 271–94; see also Jennifer Jerit, Jason Barabas, and Toby Bolsen, "Citizens, Knowledge, and the Information Environment," *American Journal of Political Science* 50 (April 2006): 266–82.
6. Richard Murray and Arnold Vedlitz, "Race, Socioeconomic Status, and Voting Participation in Large Southern Cities," *Journal of Politics* 39 (November 1977): 1064–72; Fredrick C. Harris, Valeria Sinclair-Chapman, and Brian D. McKenzie, "Macrodynamics of Black Political Participation in the Post-Civil Rights Era," *Journal of Politics* 67 (November 2005): 1143–63.
7. Virginia Sapiro, *The Political Integration of Women* (Urbana, IL: University of Illinois Press, 1983).
8. Amy Linimon and Mark R. Joslyn, "Trickle Up Political Socialization: The Impact of Kids Voting USA on Voter Turnout in Kansas," *State Politics and Policy Quarterly* 2 (Spring 2002): 24–36.
9. J. Eric Oliver, "City Size and Civic Involvement in Metropolitan America," *American Political Science Review* 94 (June 2000): 361–73.
10. Anthony Downs, *An Economic Theory of Democracy* (New York: Harper & Row, 1957). See also Moshe Haspel and H. Gibbs Knotts, "Location, Location, Location: Precinct Placement and the Costs of Voting," *Journal of Politics* 67 (May 2005): 560–73.
11. Jan E. Leighley and Arnold Vedlitz, "Race, Ethnicity, and Political Participation," *Journal of Politics* 61 (November 1999): 1092–14; Debra Horner, "Critiquing Measures of Political Interest," Paper presented at the annual meeting of the Midwest Political Science Association, Chicago, IL, 2000.
12. Kim Quaile Hill and Jan E. Leighley, "Party Ideology, Organization, and Competitiveness as Mobilizing Forces in Gubernatorial Elections," *American Journal of Political Science* 37 (November 1993): 1158–78.
13. The United States Elections Project, "2008 General Election Turnout Rates," elections.gmu.edu/voter_turnout.html (June 22, 2009).
14. "Voter Registration Information," in *The Book of the States 2008* (Lexington, KY: Council of State Governments, 2008), pp. 316–317.
15. "Absentee and Early Voting Laws," Early Voting Information Center at Reed College, http://earlyvoting.net/states/abslaws.php (June 26, 2009).
16. Priscilla Southwell and Justin Burchett, "The Effect of All-Mail Elections on Voter Turnout," *American Politics Quarterly* 29 (February 2000): 72–80. See also Cynthia Rugeley and Robert A. Jackson, "Getting on the Rolls: Analyzing the Effects of Lowered Barriers on Voter Registration," *State Politics and Policy Quarterly* 9 (Spring 2009): 56–78.
17. Michael McDonald, "(Nearly) Final 2008 Voting Statistics," http://elections.gmu.edu/Early_Voting_2008_Final.html (June 17, 2009).
18. "Methods of Nominating Candidates for State Offices," in *The Book of the States 2008* (Lexington, KY: Council of State Governments, 2008), pp. 307–8.
19. Thomas M. Holbrook and Ray Lajara, "Parties and Elections," in Virginia Gray and Russell L. Hanson, eds., *Politics in the American States,* 9th ed. (Washington, D.C.: Congressional Quarterly Press, 2007).
20. Alexandra Marks, "New York Wrestles with Its 'Party Machine' in Historic Vote," *Christian Science Monitor* (October 31, 2003), p. 2.
21. Charles S. Bullock, III, Ronald Keith Gaddie, and Anders Ferrington, "System Structure, Campaign Stimuli, and Voter Falloff in Runoff Primaries," *Journal of Politics* 64 (November 2002): 1210–24.
22. Kentucky Legislative Research Commission, "Election Filing Dates and Runoff Primary," www.lrc.ky.gov/record/08RS/SB3/SCS1LM.doc (July 1, 2009).
23. Peter L. Francia and Paul S. Herrnson, "The Synergistic Effect of Campaign Effort and Election Reform on Voter Turnout in State Legislative Elections," *State Politics and Policy Quarterly* 4 (Spring 2004): 74–93.
24. Randall W. Partin, "Economic Conditions and Gubernatorial Elections," *American Politics Quarterly* 23 (January 1995): 81–95.
25. Kimberly L. Nelson, *Elected Municipal Councils: Special Data Issue* (Washington, D.C.: International City/County Management Association, 2002).
26. Brian F. Schaffner, Gerald Wright, and Matthew Streb, "Teams Without Uniforms: The Nonpartisan Ballot in State and Local Elections," *Political Research Quarterly* 54 (March 2001): 7–30.
27. Zoltan Hajnal and Jessica Trounstine, "Where Turnout Matters: The Consequences of Uneven Turnout in City Elections," *Journal of Politics* 67 (May 2005): 515–36.

28. Arnold Fleischmann and Lana Stein, "Campaign Contributions in Local Elections," *Political Research Quarterly* 51 (September 1998): 673–89.

29. Luis Ricardo Fraga, "Domination Through Democratic Means: Nonpartisan Slating Groups in City Electoral Politics," *Urban Affairs Quarterly* 23 (June 1988): 528–55; Christopher A. Cooper and Anthony J. Nownes, "Citizen Groups in Big City Politics," *State and Local Government Review* 35 (Spring 2003): 102–11.

30. David B. Magleby, "Taking the Initiative: Direct Legislation and Direct Democracy in the 1980s," *PS: Political Science and Politics* 21 (Summer 1988): 600.

31. Elizabeth R. Gerber, ed., *Stealing the Initiative* (Upper Saddle River, NJ: Prentice-Hall, 2001).

32. M. Dane Waters, "2002 Initiatives and Referenda," in *The Book of the States 2003* (Lexington, KY: Council of State Governments), pp. 281–85.

33. "Election 2008 Mixed Results," www.iandrinstitute .org (December 10, 2008).

34. Mark A Smith, "The Contingent Effects of Ballot Initiatives and Candidate Races on Turnout," *American Journal of Political Science* 45 (July 2001): 700–706; Caroline J. Tolbert, Ramona S. McNeal, and Daniel A. Smith, "Enhancing Civic Engagement: The Effect of Direct Democracy on Political Participation and Knowledge," *State Politics and Policy Quarterly* 3 (Spring 2003): 23–41; John A. Grummel, "Morality Politics, Direct Democracy, and Turnout," *State Politics and Policy Quarterly* 8 (Fall 2008): 282–92.

35. Joshua J. Dyck, "Initiated Distrust: Direct Democracy and Trust in Government," *American Politics Research* 37 (July 2009): 539–68. See also Justin H. Phillips, "Does the Citizen Initiative Weaken Party Government in the U.S. States?" *State Politics and Policy Quarterly* 8 (Summer 2008): 127–149.

36. Alana S. Jeydel and Brent S. Steel, "Public Attitudes Toward the Initiative Process in Oregon," *State and Local Government Review* 34 (Fall 2002): 173–82.

37. Elisabeth R. Gerber, Arthur Lupia, and Mathew D. McCubbins, "When Does Government Limit the Impact of Voter Initiatives? The Politics of Implementation and Enforcement," *Journal of Politics* 66 (February 2004): 43–68.

38. Valentina A. Bali, "Implementing Popular Initiatives: What Matters for Compliance?" *Journal of Politics* 65 (November 2003): 1130–46.

39. Thad Kousser, "The California Governor's Recall," *Spectrum: The Journal of State Government* 77 (Winter 2004): 32–36.

40. Thomas E. Cronin, "Public Opinion and Direct Democracy," *PS: Political Science and Politics* 21 (Summer 1988): 612–19.

41. Melissa Maynard, "Open Government: A Little Sunshine," *Governing* http://www.governing.com/archive/archive/2007/jul/open.txt (June 24, 2009).

42. Jonathan Walters, "Polling the Populace," *Governing* 20 (April 2007): 66–68.

43. Neal D. Woods, "Promoting Participation: An Examination of Rulemaking Notification and Access Procedures," *Public Administration Review* 69 (May/June 2009): 518–30.

44. Christopher Swope, "E-Gov's New Gear," *Governing* 17 (March 2004): 40–42.

45. Minnesota Department of Transportation, "Don't Waste Our State: Adopt a Highway," www.dot.state.mn.us/adopt (June 30, 2006).

46. Stephen Knack, "Social Capital and the Quality of Government: Evidence from the States," *American Journal of Political Science* 46 (October 2002): 772–85.

47. Ericka Harney, "State of Volunteers," *State News* 52 (Mary 2009): 16–18.

48. Markus Prior, "News vs. Entertainment: How Increasing Media Choice Widens Gap in Political Knowledge and Turnout," *American Journal of Political Science* 49 (July 2005): 577–92.

49. Evan J. Ringquist et al., "Lower-Class Mobilization and Policy Linkage in the U.S. States: A Correction," *American Journal of Political Science* 41 (January 1997): 339–44.

50. Rob Gurwitt, "A Government That Runs on Citizen Power," *Governing* 6 (December 1992): 48.

51. Jonathan Walters, "O Citizen, Where Art Thou?" *Governing* (April 2009): 60–62.

52. Robert M. Stein and Greg Vonnahme, "Engaging the Unengaged Voter: Vote Centers and Voter Turnout," *Journal of Politics* 70 (April 2008): 487–97.

## Chapter 5 Political Parties, Interest Groups, and Campaigns

1. Alan Ehrenhalt, "Rivals on the Right," *Governing* 19 (July 2006): 11–12.

2. "GOP Party Identification Slips Nationwide and in Pennsylvania," *Pew Research Center for People and the Press*, pewresearch.org/pubs/1207/republican-party-identification-slips-nationwide-pennsylvania-specter-switch (April 29, 2009).

3. Sarah M. Morehouse and Malcolm E. Jewell, "State Parties: Independent Partners in the Money Relationship," in John C. Green and Rick Farmer, eds., *The State of the Parties*, 4th ed. (Lanham, MD: Rowman & Littlefield, 2003), pp. 151–68.

4. "Marjorie Randon Hershey," *Party Politics in America*, 11th ed. (New York: Pearson Longman, 2005).

5. Jeffrey M. Jones, "State of the States: Political Party Affiliation," www.gallup.com/poll/114016/state-states-political-party-affiliation.aspx (January 28, 2009).

6. David Von Drehle, "Culture Clash: Geography, Technology, and Strategy Have Nurtured a Political Split," *Washington Post National Weekly Edition* (May 24–30, 2004), pp. 6–7.

7. James G. Gimpel and Jason E. Schuknecht, "Reconsidering Political Regionalism in the American States," *State Politics and Policy Quarterly* 2 (Winter 2002): 325–52.

8. Hershey, *Party Politics in America.*

9. Malcolm E. Jewell and Sarah M. Morehouse, *Political Parties and Elections in American States*, 4th ed.

(Washington, D.C.: Congressional Quarterly Press, 2001).

10. John H. Aldrich, "Southern Parties in State and Nation," *Journal of Politics* 62 (August 2000): 643–70.

11. Ibid.

12. Robert E. Hogan, "Candidate Perceptions of Political Party Campaign Activity in State Legislative Elections," *State Politics and Policy Quarterly* 2 (Spring 2002): 66–85.

13. Ibid.

14. Shanna Pearson-Merkowitz and John Michael McTigue, "Partisan Mountains and Molehills: The Geography of U.S. State Intraparty Factionalism," *State Politics and Policy Quarterly* 8 (Spring 2008): 7–31.

15. James Dao, "Churches in Ohio Flex Political Muscle," *The New York Times* (March 27, 2005), p. 12.

16. Richard L. Berke, "U.S. Voters Focus on Selves, Poll Says," *The New York Times* (September 21, 1994), p. A12; Todd Donovan, Janine A. Parry, and Shaun Bowler, "O Other, Where Art Thou? Support for Multiparty Politics in the United States," *Social Science Quarterly* 86 (March 2005): 147–59.

17. Thomas M. Holbrook and Emily Van Dunk, "Electoral Competition in the American States," *American Political Science Review* 87 (December 1993): 955–62.

18. Gary F. Moncrief, Peverill Squire, and Malcolm E. Jewell, *Who Runs for the Legislature?* (Upper Saddle River, NJ: Prentice-Hall, 2001).

19. Charles Barrilleaux, "A Test of the Independent Influence of Electoral Competition and Party Strength in a Model of State Policymaking," *American Journal of Political Science* 41 (October 1997): 1462–66.

20. Thomas M. Holbrook and Raymond J. LaRaja, "Parties and Elections," in Virginia Gray and Russell L. Hanson, eds., *Politics in the American States: A Comparative Analysis*, 9th ed. (Washington, D.C.: Congressional Quarterly Press, 2008), pp. 61–97.

21. Everett Ehrlich, "Virtual Political Reality," *Washington Post National Weekly Edition* (December 22, 2003–January 4, 2004), p. 22.

22. Michael Slackman, "Voters Choosing None of the Above, and Parties Scramble," *The New York Times*, www.nytimes.com (April 13, 2004).

23. Ibid.

24. Justin H. Phillips, "Does the Citizen Initiative Weaken Party Government in the U.S. States?" *State Politics and Policy Quarterly* 8 (Summer 2008): 127–149.

25. J. P. Monroe, *The Political Party Matrix: The Persistence of Organization* (Albany, NY: SUNY Press, 2001).

26. Pew Research Center for the People and the Press, "Independents Take Center Stage in the Obama Era," people-press.org/report/517/political-values-and-core-attitudes (July 15, 2009).

27. Charles W. Wiggins, Keith E. Hamm, and Charles G. Bell, "Interest Group and Party Influence Agents in the Legislative Process: A Comparative State Analysis," *Journal of Politics* 54 (February 1992): 82–100.

28. Anthony J. Nownes, Clive S. Thomas, and Ronald J. Hrebenar, "Interest Groups in the States," in Virginia Gray and Russell L. Hanson, eds., *Politics in the American States: A Comparative Approach* (Washington, D.C.: Congressional Quarterly Press, 2008), p. 121.

29. Sarah M. Morehouse, "Interest Groups, Parties, and Policies in the American States," Paper presented at the annual meeting of the American Political Science Association, Washington, D.C., 1997.

30. Virginia Gray and David Lowery, *The Population Ecology of Interest Representation: Lobbying Communities in the American States* (Ann Arbor, MI: University of Michigan Press, 1996).

31. David H. Folz and P. Edward French, *Managing America's Small Communities* (Lanham, MD: Rowman & Littlefield, 2005).

32. Christopher A. Cooper and Anthony J. Nownes, "Perceptions of Power: Interest Groups in Local Politics," *State and Local Government Review* 37 (2005): 206–16.

33. Brian E. Adams, *Citizen Lobbyists: Local Efforts to Influence Public Policy* (Philadelphia, PA: Temple University Press, 2007).

34. Juliet Musso, Christopher Weare, and Kyu-Nahm Jun, "Democracy by Design: The Institutionalization of Community Participation Networks in Los Angeles," Paper presented at the Tenth National Public Management Research Conference, Columbus, OH, 2009.

35. Christopher A. Cooper and Anthony J. Nownes, "Citizen Groups in Big City Politics," *State and Local Government Review* 35 (Spring 2003): 102–11.

36. Virginia Gray and David Lowery, "A Niche Theory of Interest Representation," *Journal of Politics* 58 (February 1996): 91–111; Michael T. Heaney, "Issue Networks, Information, and Interest Group Alliances, The Case of Wisconsin Welfare Politics, 1993–99," *State Politics and Policy Quarterly* 4 (Fall 2004): 237–70.

37. Donald P. Haider-Markel, "Interest Group Survival: Shared Interests versus Competition for Resources," *Journal of Politics* 59 (August 1997): 903–12.

38. Clive S. Thomas, Ronald J. Hrebenar, and Anthony J. Nownes, "Interest Group Politics in the States," in *The Book of the States 2008* (Lexington, KY: Council of State Governments, 2008), p. 327.

39. Center for Public Integrity, "Ratio of Lobbyists to Legislators, 2006," projects.publicintegrity.org/hiredguns/chart.aspx?act=lobtoleg (June 30, 2009).

40. Jim Snyder and Jeffrey Young, "Like Congress, State Legislatures Wrestle with Lobbying Reforms," *The Hill*, www.startribune.com (May 17, 2006).

41. Virginia Gray and David Lowery, "Trends in Lobbying in the States," in *The Book of the States 2003* (Lexington, KY: Council of State Governments, 2003), pp. 257–62.

42. Alan Rosenthal, *The Third House* (Washington, D.C. Congressional Quarterly Press, 1993).

43. Anthony J. Nownes and Patricia Freeman, "Interest Group Activity in the States," *Journal of Politics* 60 (February 1998): 86–112.

44. Daniel E. Bergan, "Does Grassroots Lobbying Work?" *American Politics Research* 37 (March 2009): 327–52.

45. William P. Browne and Delbert J. Ringquist, "Michigan Interests: The Politics of Diversification," Paper presented at the annual meeting of the Midwest Political Science Association, Chicago, IL, 1987, p. 24.

46. Fred Monardi and Stanton A. Glantz, "Tobacco Industry Campaign Contributions and Legislative Behavior at the State Level," Paper presented at the annual meeting of the American Political Science Association, San Francisco, CA, 1996, p. 8.

47. Louay M. Constant, "When Money Matters: Campaign Contributions, Roll Call Votes, and School Choice in Florida," *State Politics and Policy Quarterly* 6 (Summer 2006): 195–219.

48. National Conference of State Legislatures, "State Limits on Contributions to Candidates," http://www.ncsl.org/Portals/1/documents/legismgt/limits_candidates.pdf (April 30, 2009).

49. Daniel M. Shea and Michael John Burton, *Campaign Craft: The Strategies, Tactics, and Art of Political Campaign Management* (Westport, CT: Praeger, 2001), pp. 75–98.

50. J. Cherie Strachan, *High-Tech Grass Roots* (Lanham, MD: Rowman & Littlefield, 2003).

51. Jerry Hagstrom and Robert Guskind, "Selling the Candidate," *National Journal* 18 (November 1, 1986): 2619–26.

52. Christine B. Williams and Jeff Gulati, "Checking the Data," *Politics*, http://politicsmagazine.com/magazine-issues/july-2009/learning-from-youtube/checking-the-data/ (July 10, 2009).

53. Laurent Belsie, "The Surfing Majority? Candidates Expand Presence Online," *Christian Science Monitor* (March 4, 2003), p. 4.

54. Michael Hurta, "Houston Mayoral Candidates Rake in the Cash," *Burnt Orange Report*, http://www.burntorangereport.com/diary/8996/houston-mayoral-candidates-rake-in-the-cash (July 15, 2009).

55. L. Marvin Overby and Jay Barth, "Radio Advertising in American Political Campaigns," *American Politics Research* 34 (July 2006): 451–78.

56. Owen G. Abbe and Paul S. Herrnson, "Campaign Professionalism in State Legislative Elections," *State Politics and Policy Quarterly* (Fall 2003): 223–45.

57. Cleveland Ferguson, III, "The Politics of Ethics and Elections," *Florida State University Law Review* 25 (Fall 1997): 463–503.

58. Ted Braden, "Striking a Responsive Chord: How Political Ads Motivate and Persuade Voters by Appealing to Emotions," *American Journal of Political Science* 49 (April 2005): 388–405.

59. Thad Beyle, "Gubernatorial Elections, Campaign Costs, and Powers," in *The Book of the States 2008* (Lexington, KY: Council of State Governments, 2008), pp. 165–73.

60. Ibid, p. 170.

61. "Election Summary," *National Institute of Money in State Politics*, www.followthemoney.org/database/state_overview.phtml?y=2008&s=IL (July 19, 2009).

62. Sarah M. Morehouse, "Money versus Party Effort: Nominating for Governor," Paper presented at the annual meeting of the American Political Science Association, Chicago, IL, 1987.

63. Donald A. Gross and Robert K. Goidel, "The Impact of State Campaign Finance Laws," *State Politics and Policy Quarterly* 1 (Summer 2001): 180–95.

64. Robert E. Hogan, "Campaign and Contextual Influences on Voter Participation in State Legislative Elections," *American Politics Quarterly* 27 (October 1999): 403–33.

65. Eric Kelderman, "Report Ranks Campaign Disclosure Laws," www.stateline.org (October 17, 2007).

66. Eric Kelderman, "Small Donors Equal Big Bucks for State Party Coffers," www.stateline.org (July 3, 2004).

67. National Conference of State Legislatures, "State Limits on Contributions to Candidates," http://www.ncsl.org/Portals/1/documents/legismgt/limits_candidates.pdf (April 30, 2009).

68. National Conference of State Legislatures, "Public Financing of Campaigns: An Overview," www.ncsl.org/default.aspx?tabid=16591 (July 14, 2009).

69. Neil Malhotra, "The Impact of Public Financing on Electoral Competition: Evidence from Arizona and Maine," *State Politics and Policy Quarterly* 8 (Fall 2008): 263–81.

70. Kedron Bardwell, "Campaign Finance Laws and the Competition for Spending in Gubernatorial Elections," *Social Science Quarterly* 84 (December 2003): 811–25.

71. General Assembly of North Carolina, ssl.csg.org/dockets/29cycle/29B/2009bdocketbills/1629b01nc.pdf (July 16, 2009).

## Chapter 6 State Legislatures

1. Daniel Petty, "When Sessions End, Gavels and Hankies Fall," www.stateline.org (June 23, 2008).

2. Karl T. Kurtz et al., "Full-Time, Part-Time, and Real Time: Explaining State Legislators' Perceptions of Time on the Job," *State Politics and Policy Quarterly* 6 (Fall 2006): 322–38.

3. Ellen Perlman, "The 'Gold-plated' Legislature," *Governing* 11 (February 1998): 36–40.

4. National Conference of State Legislatures, *Legislators' Occupations*, www.ncsl.org/?tabid=17922 (July 21, 2009).

5. Lilliard E. Richardson, Jr., Brian E. Russell, and Christopher A. Cooper, "Legislative Representation in Single-Member versus Multiple-Member District System: The Arizona State Legislature," *Political Research Quarterly* 57 (June 2004): 337–44.

6. *Reynolds v. Sims*, 84 S.Ct. 1362 (1964).

7. Michael P. McDonald, "A Comparative Analysis of Redistricting Institutions in the U.S.," *State Politics and Policy Quarterly* 4 (Winter 2004): 371–95.

8. Andrew Karch, Corrine M. McConnaughy, and Sean M. Theriault, "The Legislative Politics of Congressional Redistricting Commission Proposals," *American Politics Research* 35 (November 2007): 808–25.

9. Michael C. Herron and Alan E. Wiseman, "Gerrymanders and Theories of Law Making: A Study of Legislative Redistricting in Illinois," *Journal of Politics* 70 (January 2008): 151–67.

10. William March, "Black Voters Win, Lose with Districting," *Tampa Tribune* (April 6, 1998), pp. B-1, B-5.

11. Ronald E. Weber, "Emerging Trends in State Legislative Redistricting," *Spectrum* 75 (Winter 2002): 13.

12. Michael A. Smith, "One Piece at a Time: The Role of Timing and Sequencing in Pivotal Politics," *Perspectives on Politics* 2 (March 2004): 85–89.

13. "2009 Legislator Compensation," National Conference of State Legislatures, www.ncsl.org/default.aspx?tabid=14785.

14. Peverill Squire, "Member Career Opportunities and the Internal Organization of Legislatures," *Journal of Politics* 50 (August 1988): 726–44.

15. "Women in State Legislatures 2009," Center for American Women and Politics, www.cawp.rutgers.edu/fast_facts/levels_of_office/documents/stleg.pdf (July 16, 2009).

16. Henry A. Kim and Justin H. Phillips, "Dividing the Spoils of Power: How Are the Benefits of Majority Party Status Distributed in U.S. State Legislatures?" *State Politics and Policy Quarterly* 9 (Summer 2009): 125–50.

17. Keith E. Hamm, Ronald D. Hedlund, and Stephanie S. Post, "Committee Specialization in State Legislatures During the Twentieth Century," Paper presented at the annual meeting of the American Political Science Association, Washington, D.C., 1997.

18. Ralph G. Wright, *Inside the Statehouse: Lessons from the Speaker* (Washington, D.C.: Congressional Quarterly Press, 2005).

19. L. Marvin Overby, Thomas A. Kazee, and David W. Prince, "Committee Outliers in State Legislatures," *Legislative Studies Quarterly* 29 (February 2004): 81–107; David W. Prince and L. Marvin Overby, "Legislative Organization Theory and Committee Preference Outliers in State Senates," *State Politics and Policy Quarterly* 5 (Spring 2005): 68–87.

20. Allen Ehrenhalt, "Putting Practice into Theory," *Governing* 14 (November 2000): 6, 8.

21. Roy Brasfield Herron, "Diary of a Legislator," *Southern Magazine* 2 (May 1988).

22. Christopher A. Cooper and Lilliard E. Richardson, Jr., "Institutions and Representational Roles in American State Legislatures," *State Politics and Policy Quarterly* 6 (Summer 2006): 174–94. See also Shannon Jenkins, "The Impact of Party and Ideology on Roll-Call Voting in State Legislatures," *Legislative Studies Quarterly* 31 (May 2006): 205–34.

23. Eric M. Uslaner and Ronald E. Weber, "U.S. State Legislators' Opinions and Perceptions of Constituency Attitudes," *Legislative Studies Quarterly* 4 (November 1979): 582.

24. "Bill and Resolution Introductions and Enactments, 2008 Regular Sessions," *The Book of the States 2009* (Lexington, KY: Council of State Governments, 2009), pp. 132–33.

25. Smith, "One Piece at a Time."

26. Alan Rosenthal, "The Legislature as Sausage Factory," *State Legislatures* 27 (September 2001): 12–15.

27. Tom Loftus, *The Art of Legislative Politics* (Washington, D.C.: Congressional Quarterly Press, 1994), p. 76.

28. Ibid., p. 77.

29. David C. Saffell, "School Funding in Ohio: Courts, Politicians, and Newspapers," *Comparative State Politics* 18 (October 1997): 9–25.

30. "Getting from No to a Little Yes," *State Legislatures* 24 (January 1998): 18.

31. Citizens' Conference on State Legislatures, *The Sometimes Governments: A Critical Study of the 50 American Legislatures,* 2nd ed. (Kansas City, MO: CCSL, 1973), pp. 41–42.

32. Alan Rosenthal, "The New Legislature: Better or Worse and for Whom?" *State Legislatures* 12 (July 1986): 5.

33. Charles Mahtesian, "The Sick Legislature Syndrome," *Governing* 10 (February 1997): 16–20.

34. Charles W. Wiggins, as quoted in Andrea Patterson, "Is the Citizen Legislator Becoming Extinct?" *State Legislatures* 12 (July 1986): 24.

35. Representative Vic Krouse, as quoted in Patterson, "Is the Citizen Legislator Becoming Extinct?" p. 24.

36. Alan Rosenthal, "The State Legislature," Paper presented at the Vanderbilt Institute for Public Policy Studies, November 1987; James D. King, "Changes in Professionalism in U.S. State Legislatures," *Legislative Studies Quarterly* 25 (May 2000): 327–43.

37. Richard Nathan, as cited in Kathe Callahan and Marc Holzer, "Rethinking Governmental Change," *Public Productivity Management & Review* 17 (Spring 1994): 202.

38. Stuart Rothenberg, "How Term Limits Became a National Phenomenon," *State Legislatures* 18 (January 1992): 35–39.

40. Joel A. Thompson and Gary F. Moncrief, "The Implications of Term Limits for Women and Minorities: Some Evidence from the States," *Social Science Quarterly* 74 (June 1993): 300–9.

41. Karen Hansen, "The Third Revolution," *State Legislatures* 23 (September 1997): 20–26; Thad Kousser, "The Limited Impact of Term Limits Contingent Effects on the Complexity and Breadth of Laws," *State Politics and Policy Quarterly* 6 (Winter 2006): 10–29.

42. Robert A. Bernstein and Anita Chadha, "The Effects of Term Limits on Representation: Why So Few Women?" in Rick Farmer, John David Rausch, Jr., and John C. Green, eds., *The Test of Time: Coping with Legislative Term Limits* (Lanham, MD: Lexington Books, 2003), pp. 147–58; Stanley M. Caress et al.,

"Effect of Term Limits on the Election of Minority State Legislators," *State and Local Government Review* 35 (Fall 2003): 183–95.

43. Gary Moncrief and Joel A. Thompson, "On the Outside Looking In: Lobbyists Perspectives on the Effects of State Legislative Term Limits," *State and Local Government Review* 1 (Winter 2001): 394–411; Joel Thompson and Gary Moncrief, "Lobbying Under Limits: Interest Group Perspectives on the Effects of Term Limits in State Legislatures," in Farmer, Rausch, and Green, eds., *The Test of Time: Coping with Legislative Term Limits*, pp. 211–24; Thad Kousser, *Term Limits and the Dismantling of State Legislative Professionalism* (New York: Cambridge University Press, 2005).

44. John M. Carey, Richard G. Niemi, Lynda W. Powell, and Gary F. Moncrief, "The Effects of Term Limits on State Legislatures: A New Survey of the 50 States," *Legislative Studies Quarterly* 31 (February 2006): 105–34.

45. Carol S. Weissert and Karen Halperin, "The Paradox of Term Limit Support: To Know Them is Not to Love Them," *Political Research Quarterly* 60 (September 2007): 516–30.

46. Daniel A. Smith, "Overturning Term Limits: The Legislature's Own Private Idaho?" *PS: Political Science and Politics* 36 (April 2003): 215–20.

47. Governor Haley Barbour, State of the State Address, January 26, 2004.

48. Thomas M. Carsey and Geoffrey C. Layman, "Policy Balancing and Preferences for Party Control of Government," *Political Research Quarterly* 57 (December 2004): 541–50.

49. Alan Ehrenhalt, "Butch's Battle," *Governing* (June 2009), pp.11–12.

50. Madeleine Kunin, as quoted in Sharon Randall, "From Big Shot to Boss," *State Legislatures* 14 (June 1988): 348.

51. Brian J. Gerber, Cherie Maestas, and Nelson C. Dometrius, "State Legislative Influence over Agency Rulemaking," *State Politics and Policy Quarterly* 5 (Spring 2005): 24–46.

52. Jerry Brekke, "Supreme Court of Missouri Rules Legislative Veto Unconstitutional," *Comparative State Politics* 19 (February 1997): 32–34.

53. As quoted in Dave McNeely, "Is the Sun Setting on the Texas Sunset Law?" *State Legislatures* 20 (May 1994): 17–20.

54. Ibid.; see also "Summary of Sunset Legislation," *The Book of the States 2006* (Lexington, KY: Council of State Governments, 2006), pp. 132–34.

55. William M. Pearson and Van A. Wigginton, "Effectiveness of Administrative Controls: Some Perceptions of State Legislators," *Public Administration Review* 46 (July/August 1986): 328–31.

56. Alan Rosenthal, *Heavy Lifting: The Job of the American Legislature* (Washington, D.C.: Congressional Quarterly Press, 2004), p. 85.

57. Ibid.; see also Alan Ehrenhalt, "An Embattled Institution," *Governing* 5 (January 1992): 28–33; Alan Rosenthal, *Engines of Democracy: Politics and Policymaking in State Legislatures* (Washington, D.C.: Congressional Quarterly Press, 2009).

58. Dianna Gordon, "Theme for a Day," *State Legislatures* 30 (January 2004): 29.

59. Ibid.

## Chapter 7 Governors

1. James Dao, "After Storm, She Tries to Mend State, and Career," *The New York Times* (December 29, 2005), pp. 1–4.

2. Thad Beyle, "The Governors," in Virginia Gray and Russell L. Hanson, eds., *Politics in the American States: A Comparative Analysis*, 8th ed. (Washington, D.C.: Congressional Quarterly Press, 2004), pp. 194–231.

3. Larry Sabato, *Goodbye to Goodtime Charles: The American Governorship Transformed* (Lexington, MA: Lexington Books, 1978), p. 13.

4. www.jonathanforgovernor.us (accessed May 15, 2006; no longer active in October 2006).

5. Dylan Otto Krider, "Georgia Candidate for Governor Says Sex with Mules, Watermelon Behind Him," http://www.examiner.com/ (April 28, 2009).

6. Quoted in Jonathan D. Austin, www.cnn.com2000allpolitics (November 7, 2000).

7. Thad L. Beyle, "The Governors: Election, Campaign Costs, Profiles, Forced Exits, and Powers," in *The Book of the States 2004* (Lexington, KY: Council of State Governments, 2004), p. 150.

8. Thad L. Beyle, "Gubernatorial Elections, Campaign Costs and Powers," *Book of the States*, vol. 40 (Lexington, KY: Council of State Governments, 2008), p. 170.

9. Randall W. Partin, "Assessing the Impact of Campaign Spending in Governors' Races," *Political Research Quarterly* 55 (March, 2002): 213–24.

10. Thad L. Beyle, "The Governors," *Book of the States 2005* (Lexington, KY: Council of State Governments), p. 180.

11. Ibid., p. 180.

12. Peveril Squire, "Challenger Profile and Gubernatorial Elections," *Western Politics Quarterly* 45 (1992): 125–42.

13. Charles Johnston, "Montana's New Gov Takes Fresh Approach," www.stateline.org (November 17, 2004).

14. Thad L. Beyle, "Being Governor," in Carl E. Van Horn, ed., *The State of the States*, 3rd ed. (Washington, D.C.: Congressional Quarterly Press, 1996), p. 88.

15. Josh Goodman, "Against the Grain," *Governing* (October 2006): 32–38; Louis Jacobson, "Partisan Mix in R.I., Conn. Poses Challenges," *stateline.org* (April 10, 2008).

16. Sandor M. Polster, "Maine's King Makes Independence a Virtue," www.stateline.org (November 17, 2004).

17. *New York Daily News* as reported by www.governing.com (September 11, 2008).

18. Josh Goodman, "A Government Adrift," *Governing* (August, 2008), pp 36–40; wistv.com/global/story.asp?s=1895905 (accessed May 21, 2009).

19. Michael Dukakis, as quoted in Thad L. Beyle and Lynn Muchmore, *Reflections on Being Governor* (Washington, D.C.: National Governors association, 1978), p. 45

20. www.nga.org/Files/pdf/GOVSPEAK0904.PDF (accessed May 15, 2009).

21. *Book of the States*, vol. 40, pp. 183.

22. Thad L. Beyle and Lynn R. Muchmore, "The Governor and the Public," in Beyle and Muchmore, eds., *Being Governor*, p. 24.

23. Josh Goodman, "Guest Column: For Governors, Era of Good Feelings Is Over," *CQ Today Online News*, www.cqpolitics.com (February 25, 2009).

24. Alan Greenblatt, "States of Frustration," *Governing* (January 2004): 28.

25. Jonathan Walters, "Full Speed Ahead: Remaking a State Through Ideology and Determination," *Governing* (November 2001): 44–51.

26. Jeffrey Cohen and James King, "Relative Unemployment and Gubernatorial Popularity," *The Journal of Politics* 66 (November 2004): 1267–82.

27. This exchange is cited in Rosenthal, *Governors and Legislators*, p. 18.

28. Thad L. Beyle and Lynn R. Muchmore, "The Governor as Party Leader," in Beyle and Muchmore, eds., *Being Governor*, pp. 44–51; Morehouse, *Governor as Party Leader*, pp. 45–51.

29 Alfred E. Smith, as quoted in George Weeks, "Statehouse Hall of Fame, Ten Outstanding Governors of the 20th Century," Paper presented at the annual meeting of the Southern Political Science Association, Memphis, Tennessee, November 1981.

30. John Wagner, "Hunt," *The News and Observer* (April 1, 2001): 1A, 18A.

31. Tom McCall, as quoted in Samuel R. Soloman, "Governors: 1960–1970," *National Civic Review* (March 1971): 126–46.

32. Diane Kincaid Blair, "The Gubernatorial Appointment Power: Too Much of a Good Thing?" in Beyle and Muchmore, eds., *Being Governor* p. 117.

33. *Rutan et al. v. Republican Party of Illinois*, 1110 S.Ct. 2229, 1990.

34. Thad Beyle, "The Governors," in Virginia Gray and Russell Hanson, eds., *Politics in the American States* (Washington, D.C.: Congressional Quarterly Press, 2004), p. 216.

35. Alan Ehrenhalt, "The Veto Gambit," *Governing* (August 2006): 11–12.

36. Mike Kaszuba, "With 34 Vetoes, Pawlenty Is New Godfather of 'No,' *Minneapolis Star Tribune* (May 29, 2008).

37. Matthew Yi, "Governor Sets Record for Vetoing Bills," *San Francisco Chronicle*, www.sfgate.com (October 2, 2008).

38. Daniel C. Vock, "Govs Enjoy Quirky Veto Power," *stateline.org* (April 24, 2007): 1–3 (accessed at www.stateline.org).

39. Charles Barrilleaux and Michael Berkman, "Do Governor's Matter? Budgeting Rules and the Politics of State Policymaking," *Political Research Quarterly* 56 (December 2003): 409–17.

40. Margaret F. Ferguson and Cynthia J. Bowling, "Executive Orders and Administrative Control," *Public Administration Review* (December 2008): 520–528.

41. James Conant, "Executive Branch Reorganization: Can It Be an Antidote for Fiscal Stress in the States?" *State and Local Government Review* 24 (Winter 1992): 3–11.

42. James K. Conant, "State Reorganization: A New Model?" *State Government* 58 (April 1985): 130–38.

43. Robert F. Bennett, as quoted in H. Edward Flentje, "The Political Nature of the Governor as Manager," p. 70 in Beyle and Muchmore, 1983. For a description of failure in reorganization in Florida, see also Less Garner, "Managing Change through Organization Structure," *State Government* 60 (July/August 1987): 191–95.

44. Garrett, Reorganizing State Government, pp. 124–25; Michael Berkman and Christopher Reenock, "Incremental Consolidation and Comprehensive Reorganization of American State Executive Branches," *American Journal of Political Science* 48 (October 2004): 796–812.

45. Norma Riccucci and Judith Saidel, "The Demographics of Gubernatorial Appointees: Toward an Explanation of Variation," *Policy Studies Journal* 29, no. 1 (2000): 1–22; Thad L. Beyle, "The Governors: Elections, Campaign Costs, Profiles, Forced Exits, and Powers," in *The Book of the States 2004*, vol. 36 (Lexington, KY: Council of State Governments, 2004), p. 215.

46. *Book of the States*, vol. 40, p. 183.

47. Barry L. Van Lare, "The Many Roles of the Governors' Chiefs of Staff," *Book of the States*, vol. 40, 174–179.

48. Thomas M. Holbrook, "Institutional Strength and Gubernatorial Elections: An Exploratory Analysis," *American Politics Quarterly* 21 (July): 261–71.

49. Brendan Buhler, "How Did the Ferret Weasel into This Mess?" *Las Vegas Sun*, lasvegassun.com/news/2009/apr/09 (accessed May 21, 2009).

50. Beyle, "The Governors," p. 206.

51. Rob Gurwitt, "The Ordeal of David Paterson," *Governing* (March 2009): 26–33.

52. Kathleen Murphy, "Lame Duck Govs Offer Tips to Rookies," www.stateline.org (November 13, 2002), pp. 1–3.

53. See Thad L. Beyle, "Enhancing Executive Leadership in the States," *State and Local Government Review* 27 (Winter 1995): 18–35.

54. Louis Jacobson, "Keystone State's Gov Looms Large," *stateline.org* (September 13, 2007) (accessed at www.stateline.org).

55. Jonathan Walters, "Negotiator-in-Chief," *Governing* (November 2007), 37.

56. Beyle, "Enhancing Executive Leadership."

57. See Paul West, "They're Everywhere! For Today's Governors, Life is a Never-Ending Campaign," *Governing* 3 (March 1990): 51–55.

58. Beyle, "Governors, Elections, Campaign Costs and Powers," in *Book of the States 2005* (Lexington, KY: Council of State Governments, 2005), 215.

59.  Alan Greenblatt, Private Investigator," www
     .governing.com/articles/1daniels.htm (January
     2008); Josh Goodman, "Major Mover," *Governing.
     com*, www.governing.com/poy/2008/daniels.htm
     (November 2008).
60.  Eric Kelderman, "Spitzer, 22nd Disgraced Gov to
     Leave Office," *stateline.org* (March 13, 2008); Daniel
     C. Vock, "Blagojevich is at Least 14th Impeached
     Gov," *stateline.org* (January 9, 2009).
61.  Josh Goodman, "The Second Best Job in the State,"
     *Governing* (April 2009).
62.  Julia Nienaber Hurst, "Pathways and Powers: The
     Office of Lieutenant Governor," *Book of the States*,
     vol. 40 (2008), p. 209.
63.  Kay Stimson, "Secretaries of State: Focused on
     Redacting Social Security Numbers from Public
     Records in the Digital Age," *Book of the States*, vol. 40
     (2008), pp. 218–22.

## Chapter 8 Public Administration: Budgeting and Service Delivery

1.   H. George Frederickson, "Can Bureaucracy Be
     Beautiful?" *Public Administration Review* 60 (January/
     February 2000): 47–53.
2.   Richard W. Stackman, Patrick E. Connor, and Boris
     W. Becker, "Sectoral Ethos: An Investigation of
     the Personal Values Systems of Female and Male
     Managers in the Public and Private Sectors," *Journal
     of Public Administration Research and Theory* 16
     (October 2006): 577–97.
3.   See, for example, Theodore H. Poister and Gary
     T. Henry, "Citizen Ratings of Public and Private
     Service Quality: A Comparative Perspective," *Public
     Administration Review* 54 (March/April 1994): 155–59.
4.   Erwin C. Hargrove and John C. Glidewell, *Impossible
     Jobs in Public Management* (Lawrence, KS: University
     Press of Kansas, 2000).
5.   Mary E. Guy, Meredity A. Newman, and Sharon
     H. Mastracci, *Emotional Labor: Putting the Service in
     Public Service* (Armonk, NY: M. E. Sharpe, 2008).
6.   Steven Maynard-Moody and Michael Musheno, *Cops,
     Teachers, Counselors: Stories from the Front Lines of
     Public Service* (Ann Arbor, MI: University of Michigan
     Press, 2003).
7.   Harold D. Laswell, *Politics: Who Gets What, When,
     Where, How?* (Cleveland, OH: World, 1958).
8.   Kurt M. Thurmaier and Katherine G. Willoughby,
     *Policy and Politics in State Budgeting* (Armonk, NY:
     M. E. Sharpe, 2000); Dall W. Forsythe, *Memos to the
     Governor*, 2nd ed. (Washington, D.C.: Georgetown
     University Press, 2004).
9.   Josh Goodman, "Mischief after Midnight," *Governing*
     (June 2009): 40–44.
10.  Council of State Governments, *The Book of the
     States*, Vol. 36 (Lexington, KY: Council of State
     Governments, 2004), pp. 260–61.
11.  Ellen Perlman, "Stat Fever," *Governing* (January
     2007): 48–49.
12.  Zach Patton, "Culture Change," *Governing* (January
     2008): 68–69.
13.  Aaron Wildavsky, "Toward a Radical
     Incrementalism," in Alfred De Grazia, ed., *Congress:
     The First Branch of Government* (Washington, D.C.:
     American Enterprise Institute, 1966).
14.  Thurmaier and Willoughby, *Policy and Politics in State
     Budgeting*, 2000; Glenn Abney and Thomas P. Lauth,
     *The Politics of State and City Administration* (Albany,
     NY: SUNY Press, 1986), pp. 110–11, 115, 142–43;
     Rubin, *Class, Tax, and Power*, Chapter 6.
15.  Jonathan Walters, "O Citizen, Where Art Thou?"
     *Governing* (April 2009): 58–62.
16.  Ellen Perlman, "See Thru Government," *Governing*
     (May 2009): 34–37.
17.  Charles E. Lindblom, "The Science of Muddling
     Through," *Public Administrative Review* 19 (Spring
     1959): 79–88.
18.  Janet M. Kelly and William C. Rivenbark, *Performance
     Budgeting for State and Local Government* (Armonk,
     NY: M. E. Sharpe, 2003); Jonathan Walters,
     "Performance-Driven Government: Using Measures
     to Manage," *Governing* (January 2000): 69–73;
     Jonathan Walters, "Deeds, Data, and Dollars,"
     *Governing* (November 2000): 98–102.
19.  Laurie Cohen, "City Hiring to Remain under Court
     Scrutiny," www.chicagotribune.com (March 21, 2009).
20.  David K. Hamilton, "The Staffing Function in Illinois
     State Government after Rutan," *Public Administration
     Review* 53 (July/August 1993): 381–86.
21.  H. George Frederickson, "The Airport That Reforms
     Forgot," *PA Times* (January 2000): 11.
22.  J. Edward Kellough and Sally Coleman Selden, "The
     Reinvention of Public Personnel Administration: An
     Analysis of the Diffusion of Personnel Management
     Reforms in the States," *Public Administration* Review
     63 (November/December 2003): 165–76; Steven W.
     Hays and Richard C. Kearney, "Anticipated Changes
     in Human Resource Management: Surveying the
     Field," *Public Administration Review* 61 (September/
     October 2001).
23.  Jerrell D. Coggburn, "Deregulating the Public
     Personnel Function," in Steven W. Hays and Richard
     C. Kearney, eds., *Public Personnel Administration:
     Problems and Prospects*, 4th ed. (Upper Saddle River,
     NJ: Prentice-Hall, 2003), pp. 75–79.
24.  Lael R. Keiser, et al., "Lipstick and Logarithms:
     Gender, Institutional Context, and Representative
     Bureaucracy," *American Political Science Review* 96(3)
     (2002): 553–64; Vicky M. Wilkins and Lael R. Keiser,
     "Linking Passive and Active Representation by Gender:
     The Case of Child Support Agencies," *Journal of Public
     Administration Research and Theory* 16 (Winter 2005):
     87–102; Vicky M. Wilkins "Exploring the Causal
     Story: Gender, Active Representation, and Bureaucratic
     Priorities," *Journal of Public Administration Research and
     Theory* 17 (Winter 2006): 77–94.
25.  See, for example, Kenneth J. Meier, "Representative
     Bureaucracy: An Empirical Analysis," *American
     Political Science Review* 69 (June 1975): 526–42;

But see also Kenneth J. Meier, "Latinos and Representative Bureaucracy: Testing the Thompson and Henderson Hypotheses," *Journal of Public Administration Research and Theory* 3 (October 1993): 393–414; Judith Saidel and Karyn Loscocco, "Agency Leaders, Gendered Institutions, and Representative Bureaucracy," *Public Administration Review* 65 (March/April 2005): 158–70; and Shelton Goode and Norman Baldwin, "Predictors of African American Representation in Municipal Government," *Review of Public Personnel Administration* 25 (March 2005): 29–55.

26. Nick A. Theobald and Donald P. Haider-Markel, "Race, Bureaucracy, and Symbolic Representation: Interactions between Citizens and Police," *Journal of Public Administration Research and Theory* 19(2) (2008): 409–26.

27. Melissa J. Marschall and Anirudh V.S. Ruhil, "Substantive Symbols: The Attitudinal Dimension of Black Political Incorporation in Local Government," *American Journal of Political Science* 51(1) (2007): 17–36.

28. See *Ricci v. DeStefano* (No. 07-1428 (2009); J. Edward Kellough, "Affirmative Action and Diversity in the Public Sector," in Steven W. Hays, Richard C. Kearney, and Jerrell D. Coggburn, *Public Human Resource Management: Problems and Prospects, 5th ed.* (New York: Pearson Education (2009), pp. 219–35.

29. *Hopwood v. Texas*, 78 F.3d 932 (5th Cir; 1990) cert denied, 1996 WL 227009.

30. *Gretz v. Bollinger*, No. 02-516 (June 23, 2003); *Grutter v. Bollinger*, No. 02–241 F.3d732 (June 23, 2003).

31. Jared J. Llorens, Jeffrey B. Wenger, and J. Edward Kellough, "Choosing Public Sector Employment: The Impact of Wages on the Representation of Women and Minorities in State Bureaucracies," *Journal of Public Administration Research and Theory* 18(3) (2008): 397–413.

32. Mary E. Guy, "The Difference That Gender Makes," in Hays and Kearney (2003), pp. 256–70; Norma M. Riccucci, *Managing Diversity in Public Sector Workforces* (Boulder, CO: Westview Press, 2002).

33. Mary E. Guy, "Three Steps Forward, Two Steps Backward: The Status of Women's Integration into Public Management," *Public Administration Review* 53 (July/August 1993): 285–91.

34. Cynthia J. Bowling, et al., "Cracked Ceilings, Firmer Floors, and Weakening Walls: Trends and Patterns in Gender Representation among Executives Leading American State Agencies, 1970–2000," *Public Administration Review* 66 (November/December 2006): 823–36.

35. Daniel N. Lipson, "Where's the Justice? Affirmative Action's Severed Roots in the Age of Diversity," *Perspectives on Politics* 6 (December 2008): 691–705.

36. Sonia Ospina and James F. O'Sullivan, "Working Together: Meeting the Challenge of Workplace Diversity," in Hays and Kearney (2003), pp. 238–55; Riccucci, *Managing Diversity in Public Sector Workforces*, 2002.

37. *Meritor Savings Bank v. Vinson*, 1986, 477 U.S. 57; *Teresa Haris v. Forklift Systems, Inc., U.S. Supreme Court*, 92–1168 (November 9, 1993).

38. Sally Coleman Selden, "Sexual Harassment in the Workplace," pp. 225–237 in Steven W. Hays and Richard C. Kearney, *Public Personnel Administration: Problems and Prospects* (Englewood Cliffs, NJ: Prentice Hall, 2003.

39. www.bls.gov/news.release/pdf/union2.pdf (accessed June 27, 2009).

40. Richard C. Kearney, *Labor Relations in the Public Sector*, 4th ed. (New York: CRC Press, 2009): 180–92.

41. Jeffrey S. Banks and Barry R. Weingast, "The Political Control of Bureaucracies Under Asymmetric Information," *American Journal of Political Science* 36 (May 1992): 509–24.

42. Gerald T. Gabris and Douglas M. Ihrke, "Unanticipated Failures of Well-Intentioned Reforms: Some Lessons Learned from Federal and Local Sectors," *International Journal of Public Organization and Behavior* 6 (February 2003): 195–225.

43. Donald Moynihan, "Managing for Results in State Government: Evaluating a Decade of Reform," *Public Administration Review* 66 (January/February 2006): 77–89.

44. David Osborne and Ted Gaebler, *Reinventing Government* (New York: Penguin Books, 1993).

45. E. S. Savas. *Privatization in the City: Successes, Failures, Lesson* (Washington, D.C.: Congressional Quarterly Press, 2005); Keon S. Chi, Kelley A. Arnold, and Heather M. Perkins, "Privatization in State Government: Trends and Issues," *Spectrum: The Journal of State Government* (Fall 2003): 1.

46. Alan Greenblatt, "Sweetheart Deals…." *Governing* (December 2004): 20–25; Elliot Sclar, *You Don't Always Get What You Pay For: The Economics of Privatization* (Ithaca, NY: Cornell University Press, 2000).

47. Alan Greenblatt, "Private Instigator," *Governing* (January, 2008): 39–44.

48. Stephen C. Fehr, "Study: Why Pa. Turnpike Plan Failed," www.stateline.org (March 24, 2009); Gerald T. Gabris and Douglas M. Ihrke, "Unanticipated Failures of Well-Intentional Reforms: Some Lessons Learned from Federal and Local Governments," *International Journal of Organization Theory and Behavior* 6 (February 2003): 195–225; George A. Boyne, "Bureaucratic Theory Meets Reality: Public Choice and Service Contracting in U.S. Local Government," *Public Administration Review* 58 (November/December 1998): 474–84.

49. Steven Rathgeb Smith, "The Challenge of Strengthening Nonprofits and Civil Society," *Public Administration Review* 68 (December 2008): S132–S145.

50. Lawrence L. Martin, "Public–Private Competition: A Public Employee Alternative to Privatization," *Review of Public Personnel Administration* 19 (Winter 1999): 59–70.

51. See Eliot D. Sclar, *You Don't Always Get What You Pay For: The Economics of Privatization* (Ithaca, NY: Cornell University Press, 2000); Katherine Barrett and Ricgard Greene, "A Balancing Act," *Governing* (March 2005): 59.

52. Ellen Perlman, "311 Potholes," *Governing* (August, 2007): 67.

53. John Buntin, "Alert! Alert!" *Governing* (October 2008): 68.

54. Christopher Swope, "Working without a Wire," *Governing* (June 2002): 32–34; Ellen Perlman, "Inside Information," *Governing* (October 2008): 47–48.

55. Sharon S. Dawes, "The Evolution and Continuing Challenges of E-Governance," *Public Administration Review* 68 (December 2008): S86–S102; Donald Norris and Jae Moon, "Advancing E-Government at the Grassroots: Tortoise or Hare?" *Public Administration Review* 65 (January/February 2005): 64–75.

56. Theo Emery, "In Tennessee, Goats Eat the 'Vine That Ate the South,'" *nytimes.com* (June 5, 2007).

## Chapter 9 The Judiciary

1. Aaron Marshall, "Ohio House Makes 'Don't Touch' the Rule in Strip Clubs," www.Cleveland.com (accessed September 22, 2007).

2. W. John Moore, "In Whose Court?" *National Journal* (October 15, 1991): 2396.

3. Melinda Gann Hall, "State Judicial Politics: Rules, Structures, and the Political Game," in Ronald E. Weber and Paul Brace, eds., *American State and Local Politics: Directions for the 21st Century* (New York: Chatham House, 1999), pp. 114–38.

4. Henry Robert Glick and Kenneth N. Vines, *State Court Systems* (Englewood Cliffs, NJ: Prentice-Hall, 1973), p. 19.

5. Ibid., p. 21.

6. Kevin Sack, "Where the Bench Orders Some Southern Comfort," *The New York Times*, www.nytimes.com (January 29, 2002).

7. John Gramlich, "New Courts Tailored to War Veterans," www.stateline.org (June 18, 2009).

8. *Goodridge v. Department of Public Health et al.*, 440 Mass 309 (2003).

9. American Bar Association, *Standards Relating to Court Organization* (New York: ABA, 1974), pp. 43–44.

10. Charles H. Sheldon and Linda S. Maule, *Choosing Justices: The Recruitment of State and Federal Judges* (Pullman: Washington State University Press, 1997).

11. Council of State Governments, *Book of the States*, vol. 40 (Lexington, KY: Council of State Governments, 2008), p. 268.

12. Lawrence Baum, "State Courts in Their Political Environments," in Carol E. Van Horn, ed., *The State of the States*, 4th ed. (Washington, D.C.: Congressional Quarterly Press, 2006), pp. 91–92.

13. Adam Liptak and Janet Roberts, "Campaign Cash Mirrors a High Courts' Rulings," *The New York Times* (October 1, 2006): 1–10.

14. Paul Brace and Brent D. Boyea, "State Public Opinion, the Death Penalty, and the Practice of Electing Judges," *American Journal of Political Science* 52(2) (April 2008): 360–72.15. *Republican Party of Minnesota v. White*, No. 01–521 (2000).

16. Adam Liptak and Janet Roberts, "Campaign Cash Mirrors a High Court's Rulings," *The New York Times* (October 1, 2006): 1–10.

17. Stephen Ware, "Money, Politics, and Judicial Decisions: A Case Study of Arbitration Law in Alabama," *Journal of Law and Politics* 15 (Fall 1999): 645–86; Madhavi McCall, "The Politics of Judicial Elections: The Influence of Campaign Contributions on the Voting Patterns of Texas Supreme Court Justices," *Politics and Policy* 31 (June 2003): 314–33.

18. Chris W. Bonneau, "Campaign Fundraising in State Supreme Court Elections," *Social Science Quarterly* 88 (March 2007): 68–85.

19. "The Best Judges Business Can Buy," *The New York Times* editorial, www.nyt.com (accessed June 18, 2007).

20. See David B. Rottman and Roy A. Schotland, "2004 Judicial Elections," in *The Book of the States 2005* (Lexington, KY: Council of State Governments, 2005), pp. 305–8.

21. Kathleen Hunter, "Money Mattering More in Judicial Elections," www.lawforum.net (May 12, 2004): 1–3.

22. Adam Liptak, "Justices Tell Judges Not to Rule on Major Backers," ww.nyt.com (June 9, 2009); Len Boselovic, "W. Va. Chief Justice Accused of Bias," www.post-gazette.com (January 15, 2008).

23. Stacy Forster and Patrick Marley, "Gableman Victorious," http://www.jsonline.com (April 3, 2008).

24. Damon M. Cann, "Justice for Sale? Campaign Contributions and Judicial Decisionmaking," *State Politics and Policy Quarterly* 7 (Fall 2007): 281–97; Chris W. Bonneau, "Campaign Fundraising in State Supreme Court Elections."

25. As quoted in Sheila Kaplan, "Justice for Sale," *State Government: CQ's Guide to Current Issues and Activities, 1986–87* (Washington, D.C.: Congressional Quarterly Press, 1987), pp. 51–57.

26. William Glaberson, "States Take Steps to Rein in Excesses of Judicial Politicking," *The New York Times* (June 15, 2001): 1–4.

27. *Caperton v. A.T. Massey Coal Co.*, No. 08–22, U.S. Supreme Court, 2009.

28. See, for example, Henry R. Glick and Craig Emmert, "Selection Systems and Judicial Characteristics: The Recruitment of State Supreme Court Justices," *Judicature* 70 (December/January 1987): 228–35.

29. Melinda Gann Hall, "State Supreme Courts in American Democracy: Probing the Myths of Judicial Reform," *American Political Science Review* 95 (June 2001): 315–30.

30. John Culver, "California Supreme Court Election: 'Rose Bird and the Supremes,'" *Comparative State Politics Newsletter* (February 1987): 13.

31. Steven D. Williams, "The 1996 Retention Election of Justice White," *Comparative State Politics* 17 (October 1996): 28–30.

32. John Paul Ryan et al., *American Trial Judges* (New York: Free Press, 1980), pp. 125–30.

33. Melinda Gann Hall, "Electoral Politics and Strategic Voting in State Supreme Courts," *Journal of Politics* 54 (1992): 427–46.

34. Hall, "State Supreme Courts in American Democracy," p. 319.

35. Kathleen Bratton and Rorie Spill, "Existing Diversity and Judicial Selection: The Role of Appointment Method in Establishing Gender Diversity in State Supreme Courts," *Social Science Quarterly* 83 (June 2002): 504–18.

36. American Bar Association, *National Database on Judicial Diversity in State Courts* www.abanet.org (accessed July 1, 2009).

37. Melinda Gann Hall, "Electoral Politics and Strategic Voting in State Supreme Courts," *Journal of Politics* 54 (1992): 427–46; Melinda Gann Hall, "Toward an Integrated Model of Judicial Voting Behavior," *American Politics Quarterly* 20 (1992): 147–68.

38. Hall, "State Judicial Politics," p. 136.

39. James P. Wenzel, Shaun Bowler, and David J. Lanoue, "Legislating from the State Bench: A Comparative Analysis of Judicial Activism," *American Politics Quarterly* 25 (July 1997): 363–79.

40. David Rottman and Roy Schotland, "2004 Judicial Elections," in *The Book of the States 2005* (Lexington, Ky.: Council of State Governments, 2005), p. 307.

41. Ian Urbina and Sean D. Hamill, "Judges Plead Guilty in Scheme to Jail Youths for Profit," www.nyt.com (February 13, 2009).

42. "New Questions about Rhode Island Chief Justice," *The New York Times* (October 3, 1993), section 1, p. 22; "Ex-Top Judge Ends Rhode Island Appeal with a Guilty Plea," *The New York Times* (April 30, 1994), section 1, p. 12; "Justice in Impeachment Inquiry Quits in Rhode Island," *The New York Times* (May 29, 1986), p. A14.

43. David Rottman, "Trends in State Courts: Rising Caseloads and Vanishing Trials," in *The Book of the States 2005* (Lexington, Ky.: Council of State Governments, 2005), p. 301.

44. Susan Carol Losh, et.al., "What Summons Responses Reveal about Jury Duty Attitudes," *Judicature* 83 (May/June 2000): 304–09; National Center for State Courts www.nsconline.org/wc/courtopics/Resource Guide.asp?topic=JurInn (accessed July 6, 2009).

45. Walter Schaefer, "Precedent and Policy: Judicial Opinions and Decision Making," in David M. O'Brien, ed., *Judges on Judging: Views from the Bench* (Washington, D.C.: Congressional Quarterly Press, 2004), p. 108.

46. Hall, "Electoral Politics and Strategic Voting."

47. Melinda Gann Hall, "Justices as Representatives: Elections and Judicial Politics in the American States," *American Politics Quarterly* 23 (October 1995).

48. Jake Dear and Edward W. Jessen, "Followed Rates and Leading State Cases, 1940–2005," *Davis Law Review* 41 (2007): 683.

49. Gregory A. Caldeira, "Legal Precedent: Structures of Communication Between State Supreme Courts," *Social Network* 10 (1988): 29–55.

50. Darrell Steffensmeier and Chester L. Britt, "Judges' Race and Judicial Decision Making: Do Black Judges Sentence Differently?" *Social Science Quarterly* 82 (December 2001): 749–64.

51. S. Fernando Rodriguez, Theodore R. Curry, and Gand Lee, "Gender Differences in Criminal Sentencing: Do Effects Vary across Violent, Property, and Drug Offenses?" *Social Science Quarterly* 87 (June 2006): 318–39.

52. Gerald S. Gryski, Eleanor C. Main, and William J. Dixon, "Models of State High Court Decision Making in Sex Discrimination Cases," *Journal of Politics* 48 (February 1986): 143–55; Donald R. Songer and Kelley A. Crews-Meyer, "Does Judge Gender Matter? Decision Making in State Supreme Courts," *Social Science Quarterly* 81 (September 2000): 750–62.

53. S. Fernando Rodriguez, Theodore R. Curry, and Gand Lee, "Gender Differences in Criminal Sentencing: Do Effects Vary across Violent, Property, and Drug Offenses?" *Social Science Quarterly* 87 (June 2006): 318–39.

54. John J. Scheb, III, Terry Bowen, and Gary Anderson, "Ideology, Role Orientations, and Behavior in the State Courts of Last Resort," *American Politics Quarterly* 19 (July 1991): 324–35.

55. Ibid.

56. Bradley Cannon, "Defining the Dimensions of Judicial Activism," *Judicature* 66 (1983): 236–46.

57. See John Patrick Hagan, "Patterns of Activism on State Supreme Courts," *Publius* 18 (Winter 1988): 97–115.

58. Laura Langer and Paul Brace, "The Preemptive Power of State Supreme Courts: Adoption of Abortion and Death Penalty Legislation," *Policy Studies Journal* 33 (2005): 317–39.

59. Brenda Goodman, "Georgia Murder Case's Cost Saps Public Defense System," www.nyt.com (March 22, 2007).

60. John Gramlich, "Court Cuts Trigger Blunt Warnings," www.stateline.org (February 18, 2009).

61. James Douglas and Roger Hartley, "The Politics of Court Budgeting in the States: Is Judicial Independence Threatened by the Budgetary Process?" *Public Administration* 63 (July–August 2003): 449.

62. National Center for State Courts, *State Court Caseload Statistics 2007*, ncsonline.org (accessed July 2, 2009).

63. www.nesi.dni.us. Researchtcps-web (November 3, 2000).

64. National Center for State Courts, *Survey of Judicial Salaries,* nsconline.org (accessed July 2, 2009).

65. George F. Cole, "Performance Measures for the Trial Courts, Prosecution, and Public Defense," in U.S. Department of Justice, *Performance Measures for the Criminal Justice System* (October 1993), pp. 87–108.

66. Sharon Paynter and Richard C. Kearney, "Who Watches the Watchmen? Evaluating Judicial Performance in the States," *Administration and Society* (forthcoming 2009).

# Chapter 10 The Structure of Local Government

1. Jim Schutze, quoted in Rob Gurwitt, "Can Dallas Govern Itself?" *Governing* 19 (August 2006): 42.

2. John Kincaid, "Municipal Perspectives on Federalism," unpublished manuscript, 1987.

3. Dennis Hale, "The City as Polity and Economy," *Polity* 17 (Winter 1984): 205–24.

4. Kincaid, "Municipal Perspectives," p. 56.

5. "Local Governments and Public School Systems by Type and State: 2007," *2007 Census of Governments*, www.census.gov/govs/cog/GovOrgTab03ss.html (August 9, 2009).

6. Council for Excellence in Government 2000, www.excelgov.org (July 9, 2003).

7. Christopher Hoene, Mark Baldassare, and Michael Shires, "The Development of Counties as Municipal Governments," *Urban Affairs Review* 37 (March 2002): 575–91.

8. Dale Krane, Platon N. Rigos, and Melvin B. Hill Jr., *Home Rule in America: A Fifty State Handbook* (Washington, D.C.: Congressional Quarterly Press, 2001).

9. Tanis J. Salant, "Trends in County Government Structure," *The Municipal Year Book 2004* (Washington, D.C.: International City/County Management Association, 2004).

10. Alan Greenblatt, "New Clout in a Big County," *Governing* 20 (May 2007): 22–23.

11. J. Edwin Benton, "The Impact of Structural Reform on County Government Service Provision," *Social Science Quarterly* 84 (December 2003): 858–74.

12. "Counties Out of Date," *State Legislatures* 17 (March 1991): 17.

13. Jonathan Walters, "The Disappearing County," www.governing.com (July 5. 2000).

14. Jerome Sherman. "6 Elected Row Officers Become 3 Appointed." *Pittsburgh Post–Gazette*, www.post-gazette.com (May 18. 2005).

15. Joel Miller, "Boundary Changes 1990–1995," *The Municipal Year Book 1997* (Washington, D.C.: International City/County Management Association, 1997). See also Olesva Tkacheva, "New Cities, Local Officials, and Municipal Incorporation Laws: A Supply-Side Model of City Formation," *Journal of Urban Affairs*. 30 (2008): 155–174.

16. David R. Morgan, *Managing Urban America*, 6th ed. (Washington, D.C.: Congressional Quarterly Press, 2007).

17. James H. Svara, *Official Leadership in the City* (New York: Oxford University Press, 1990).

18. Victor S. DeSantis and Tari Renner, "City Government Structures: An Attempt at Clarification," *State and Local Government Review* 34 (Spring 2002): 95–104; H. George Frederickson. Gary A. Johnson, and Curtis H. Wood, *The Adapted City: Institutional Dynamics and Structural Change* (Armonk. N.Y.: M.E. Sharpe, 2004); Megan Mullin, Gillian Peele, and Bruce E. Cain, "City Caesars? Institutional Structure and Mayoral Success in Three California Cities," *Urban Affairs Review* 40 (September 2004): 19–43.

19. Jered Carr and Shanthi Karuppusamy, "Beyond Ideal Types of Municipal Structure," *American Review of Public Administration*, 39 (2009): 304–321.

20. Brian M. Green and Yda Schreuder, "Growth, Zoning and Neighborhood Organizations," *Journal of Urban Affairs* 13, no. 1 (1991): 97–110.

21. Arnold Fleischmann and Carol A. Pierannunzi, "Citizens, Development Interests, and Local Land-Use Regulation," *Journal of Politics* 52 (August 1990): 838–53.

22. Mary Edwards, "Annexation: A Winner-Take-All Process?" *State and Local Government Review* 31 (Fall 1999): 221–31.

23. Rex L. Facer II, "Annexation Activity and State Law in the United States," *Urban Affairs Review* 41 (May 2006): 697–709. See also David Rusk, "Annexation and the Fiscal Fate of Cities," *Brookings Institution Survey Series* (August 2006).

24. Rob Gurwitt, "Not-So-Smart Growth," *Governing* 14 (October 2000): 34–38.

25. "Cities with 100,000 or More Population in 2000 Ranked by Land Area," *County and City Data Book 2000*, www.census.gov/statab/ccdb/cityrank.htm (January 17, 2006).

26. Christopher W. Hoene and Michael A. Pagano. *City Fiscal Conditions in 2009* (Washington, D.C.: National League of Cities, 2009).

27. Susan Welch and Timothy Bledsoe, *Urban Reform and Its Consequences: A Study in Representation* (Chicago: University of Chicago Press, 1988).

28. Chandler Davidson and Bernard Grofman, "The Effect of Municipal Election Structure on Black Representation in Eight Southern States," in Davidson and Grofman, eds., *Quiet Revolution in the South* (Princeton, N.J.: Princeton University Press, 1994), pp. 301–21.

29. Curtis Wood, "Voter Turnout in City Elections," *Urban Affairs Review* 39 (November 2002): 209–31.

30. Welch and Bledsoe, *Urban Reform and Its Consequences*; Jeffrey D. Greene, "Reformism and Public Policies in American Cities Revisited," paper presented at the annual meeting of the Southern Political Science Association, Atlanta, Ga., 2000.

31. Kenneth J. Meier et al., "Structural Choices and Representational Biases: The Post-Election Color of Representation," *American Journal of Political Science* 49 (October 2005): 758–68.

32. Richard L. Cole and Delbert A. Taebel, "Cumulative Voting in Local Elections: Lessons from the

Alamogordo Experience," *Social Science Quarterly* 73 (March 1992): 194–201.

33. Shaun Bowler et al., "Candidate Activities, Strategies, and Organization in U.S. Cumulative-Voting Elections," paper presented at the annual meeting of the American Political Science Association, San Francisco, Calif., 1996.

34. Victor S. DeSantis and David Hill, "Citizen Participation in Local Politics: Evidence from New England Town Meetings," *State and Local Government Review* 36 (Fall 2004): 172.

35. Melissa Conradi, "But Definitely Not St. Ventura," *Governing* 14 (January 2001): 16.

36. Dave Drury, "Town Meetings: An Enduring Image Changes," *Hartford Courant* (September 22, 1991), pp. A1, A10–A11: See also David K. Hamilton. "Township Government A Tale of One State," *National Civic Review.* (2008): 37–49.

37. Kathryn A. Foster, *The Political Economy of Special Purpose Government* (Washington, D.C.: Georgetown University Press, 1997).

38. U.S. Bureau of the Census, "Individual State Descriptions," *2007 Census of Governments.* www.census.gov (August 7, 2009).

39. John C. Bollens, *Special District Governments in the United States* (Berkeley: University of California Press, 1957).

40. Barbara Coyle McCabe, "Special District Formation Among the States," *State and Local Government Review* 32 (Spring 2000): 121–31.

41. Michael A. Molloy, "Local Special Districts and Public Accountability," paper presented at the annual meeting of the Midwest Political Science Association, Chicago, Ill., 2000. See also Nicholas Bauroth, "The Effect of Limiting Participation in Special District Elections to Property Owners: A Research Note," *Public Budgeting & Finance* 27 (2007): 71–88.

42. Nancy Burns, *The Formation of American Local Governments* (New York: Oxford University Press, 1994).

43. Foster, *The Political Economy of Special Purpose Government.*

44. Alan Ehrenhalt, "The Consolidation Divide," *Governing* 16 (March 2003): 6.

45. Michael Dobbs, "At the Heart of Reform," *Washington Post National Weekly Edition* (January 12–18, 2004), p. 31. See also David M. Dunaway and Ausband. "An Analysis of the Organizational Patterns of North Carolina School Districts." *Academic Leadership.* 6 (2008).

46. Clarence N. Stone, Jeffrey R. Henig, Bryan D. Jones, and Carol Pierannunzi, *Building Civic Capacity: The Politics of Reforming Urban Schools* (Lawrence: University Press of Kansas, 2001); Michael B. Berkman and Eric Plutzer, *Ten Thousand Democracies: Politics and Public Opinion in America's School Districts* (Washington, D.C.: Georgetown University Press, 2005).

47. "2009 All-America City Award Winners Announced." National Civic League. www.ncl.org (June 19, 2009).

48. Katherine Barrett and Richard Greene, "Grading the Cities," *Governing* 13 (February 2000): 22–91.

## Chapter 11 Local Leadership and Governance

1. "LA Mayor Villaraigosa Sworn in to 2nd Term," *Mercury News,* www.mercurynews.com/breakingnews/ (July 1, 2009).

2. Susan E. Howell and William P. McLean, "Performance and Race in Evaluating Minority Mayors," *Public Opinion Quarterly* 65 (2001): 321–43.

3. Mark Schneider, "Public Entrepreneurs as Agents of Change in American Government," *Urban News* 9 (Spring 1995): 1.

4. Rob Gurwitt, "Welcome Mat," *Governing* 22 (December 2008): 32–37.

5. Martin Saiz, "Do Political Parties Matter in U.S. Cities?" in Martin Saiz and Haus Geser, eds., *Local Parties in Political and Organizational Perspective* (Boulder, CO: Westview, 1999).

6. Gaetano Mosca, *The Ruling Class* (New York: McGraw-Hill, 1939).

7. Robert S. Lynd and Helen M. Lynd, *Middletown* (New York: Harcourt Brace and World, 1929); Robert S. Lynd and Helen M. Lynd, *Middletown in Transition* (New York: Harcourt Brace and World, 1937).

8. Floyd Hunter, *Community Power Structure* (Chapel Hill, NC: University of North Carolina Press, 1953); Floyd Hunter, *Community Power Succession* (Chapel Hill, NC: University of North Carolina Press, 1980).

9. Harvey Molotch, "Strategies and Constraints of Growth Elites," in Scott Cummings, ed., *Business Elites and Urban Development* (Albany, NY: SUNY Press, 1988), pp. 25–47.

10. Robert Dahl, *Who Governs?* (New Haven, CT: Yale University Press, 1961).

11. Charles M. Bonjean and David M. Olson, "Community Leadership: Directions of Research," *Administrative Science Quarterly* 9 (December 1964): 278–300.

12. Christopher A. Cooper and Anthony J. Nownes, "Citizen Groups in Big City Politics," *State and Local Government Review* 35 (Spring 2003): 102–11.

13. G. William Domhoff, *Who Really Rules?* (Santa Monica, CA: Goodyear, 1978).

14. Robert Agger, Daniel Goldrich, and Bert Swanson, *The Rulers and the Ruled,* rev. ed. (Belmont, CA: Wadsworth, 1972).

15. Juliet Gainsborough, "A Tale of Two Cities: Civic Culture and Public Policy in Miami." *Journal of Urban Affairs* 30 (2008): 431.

16. Monica Davey, "Recession Shadowing Chicago Bid for Games," *The New York Times,* nytimes.com (July 26, 2009).

17. Clarence N. Stone, *Regime Politics: Governing Atlanta, 1948–1988* (Lawrence: University Press of Kansas, 1989), p. 3.

18. Clarence N. Stone, "Systemic Power in Community Decision Making," *American Political Science Review* 74 (December 1980): 978–90.

19. Ibid., p. 989.

20. Peter Burns and Matthew O. Thomas, "The Failure of the Nonregime: How Katrina Exposed New Orleans as a Regimeless City," *Urban Affairs Review* 41 (March 2006): 517–27.

21. J. M. Ferris, "The Role of the Nonprofit Sector in a Self-Governing Society," *Voluntas* 9 (1998): 137–51.

22. Richard C. Hula and Cynthia Jackson-Elmoore, "Governing Nonprofits and Local Political Processes," *Urban Affairs Review* 36 (January 2001): 324–58.

23. Ibid., p. 326. See also Kelly LeRoux, "Nonprofits as Civic Intermediaries," *Urban Affairs Review* 42 (January 2007): 410–22.

24. Christopher A. Cooper, Anthony J. Nownes, and Steven Roberts, "Perceptions of Power: Interest Groups in Local Politics," *State and Local Government Review* 37, no. 3 (2005): 206–16.

25. William Yardley, "After Eminent Domain Victory, Dispute Project Goes Nowhere," *The New York Times*, www.nytimes.com (November 21, 2005).

26. Sandra Day O'Connor, dissenting, *Kelo et al. v. City of New London et al.*, No. 04-108, www.laws.findlaw .com/us/000/04-108.html (June 23, 2005).

27. Elizabeth Kolbert, "The Un-Communicator," *The New Yorker* (March 1, 2004): 38–42.

28. Jessica Garrison and Patrick McGreevy, "Parks to File for Mayoral Race," *Los Angeles Times*, www.latimes .com (April 7, 2004).

29. Victor S. DeSantis and Tari Renner, "City Government Structures: An Attempt at Clarification," *State and Local Government Review* 34 (Spring 2002): 95–104.

30. Rob Gurwitt, "The Lure of the Strong Mayor," *Governing* 6 (July 1993): 36–41; Terrell Blodgett, "Beware the Lure of the 'Strong' Mayor," *Public Management* 76 (January 1994): 6–11.

31. David R. Morgan and Sheilah S. Watson, "The Effects of Mayoral Power on Urban Fiscal Policy," Paper presented at the annual meeting of the American Political Science Association, New York City, 1994.

32. W. John Moore, "From Dreamers to Doers," *National Journal* (February 13, 1988): 372–77.

33. Cory Booker, "Fighting for Newark's Future," (audio) www.corybooker.com/main/cfm (July 5, 2006).

34. Huey L. Perry, "Deracialization as an Analytical Construct in American Urban Politics," *Urban Affairs Quarterly* 27 (December 1991): 181–91; Nicholas O. Alonzie, "The Promise of Urban Democracy: Big City Black Mayoral Service in the Early 1990s," *Urban Affairs Review* 35 (January 2000): 422–34.

35. Mary E. Summers and Philip A. Klinkner, "The Daniels Election in New Haven and the Failure of the Deracialization Hypothesis," *Urban Affairs Quarterly* 27 (December 1991): 202–15.

36. Robert M. Stein, Stacy G. Ulbig, and Stephanie Shirley Post, "Voting for Minority Candidates in Multiracial/Multiethnic Communities," *Urban Affairs Review* 41 (November 2005): 157–81.

37. Philip J. LaVelle, "S.D. Political Hounds Catch First Scent of Recall Bid," *San Diego Union-Tribune*, www.signonsandiego.com (January 4, 2005).

38. Several of these studies are summarized in Susan A. MacManus and Charles S. Bullock III, "Women and Racial/Ethnic Minorities in Mayoral and Council Positions," *The Municipal Year Book 1993* (Washington, D.C.: ICMA, 1993), pp. 70–84.

39. "What Makes a Great Mayor?" *Talk of the Nation*, www.npr.org (December 10, 2003).

40. "From Vision to Reality: How City Administrations Succeed in the Long Haul," www.civic-strategies.com (September 30, 2003).

41. Clifford J. Wirth and Michael L. Vasu, "Ideology and Decision Making for American City Managers," *Urban Affairs Quarterly* 22 (March 1987): 454–74.

42. Martin Vanacour, "Promoting the Community's Future," in Charldean Newell, ed., *The Effective Local Government Manager*, 3rd ed. (Washington, D.C.: International City/County Management Association, 2004), pp. 84–85.

43. James H. Svara, "Conflict and Cooperation in Elected-Administrative Relations in Large Council-Manager Cities," *State and Local Government Review* 31 (Fall 1999): 173–89.

44. Douglas J. Watson and Wendy L. Hassett, "Career Paths of City Managers in America's Largest Council-Manager Cities," *Public Administration Review* 64 (March 2004): 192–99.

45. Mark M. Levin, "How to Work with Elected Officials," *Public Management* (December 2008): 4–5.

46. H. George Frederickson, Gary A. Johnson, and Curtis H. Wood, *The Adapted City: Institutional Dynamics and Structural Change* (Armonk, NY: M. E. Sharpe, 2004). See also Alan Ehrenhalt, "The Mayor-Manager Merger," *Governing* 20 (October 2006): 9–10.

47. Larry Azevedo, as quoted in Alan Ehrenhalt, "How a Liberal Government Came to Power in a Conservative Suburb," *Governing* 1 (March 1988): 51–56.

48. Kenneth Prewitt, *The Recruitment of Political Leaders: A Study of Citizen-Politicians* (Indianapolis, IN: Bobbs-Merrill, 1970).

49. "State and Local Officials of Color," *Gender and Multicultural Leadership Project*, www.gmcl.org/maps/ national/state.htm (August 10, 2009).

50. MacManus and Bullock, "Women and Racial/Ethnic Minorities in Mayoral and Council Positions," pp. 70–84; Joshua G. Behr, *Race, Ethnicity and the Politics of Redistricting* (Albany, NY: SUNY Press, 2004).

51. Bari Anhalt, "Minority Representation and the Substantive Representation of Interests," Paper presented at the annual meeting of the American Political Science Association, San Francisco, California, 1996.

52. Manning Marable, "Building Coalitions Among Communities of Color," in James Jennings, ed., *Blacks, Latinos, and Asians in Urban America* (Westport, CT: Praeger, 1994), pp. 29–43.

53. Paula D. McClain and Steven C. Tauber, "Racial Minority Group Relations in a Multiracial Society," in Michael Jones-Correa, ed., *Governing American Cities: Immigrants and Inter-Ethnic Coalitions, Competition, and Conflict* (New York: Russell Sage Foundation, 2001).

54. Christian Collett, "Bloc Voting, Polarization, and the Panethnic Hypothesis: The Case of Little Saigon," *Political Research Quarterly* 67 (August 2005): 907–33.

55. "Openly LGBT Appointed and Elected Officials," *Gay and Lesbian Partnership Institute*, www.glli.org/out_officials/officials_map (August 13, 2009).

56. James W. Button, Kenneth D. Wald, and Barbara A. Rienzo, "The Election of Openly Gay Public Officials in American Communities," *Urban Affairs Review* 35 (November 1999): 188–209.

57. James Svara, "Council Profile: More Diversity, Demands, Frustration," *Nation's Cities Weekly* 14 (November 18, 1991): 4.

58. James B. Kaatz, P. Edward French, and Hazel Prentiss-Cooper, "City Council Conflict as a Cause of Psychological Burnout and Voluntary Turnover Among City Managers," *State and Local Government Review* 31 (Fall 1999): 162–72.

59. William J. Pammer, Jr., et al., "Managing Conflict and Building Cooperation in Council-Manager Cities," *State and Local Government Review* 31 (Fall 1999): 202–13.

60. Rob Gurwitt, "Are City Councils a Relic of the Past?" *Governing* 16 (April 2003): 20–24.

61. Charles Mahtesian, "Mayor Deadlock," *Governing* 13 (February 2000): 10.

62. Alan Ehrenhalt, "Boldness Without Bluster," *Governing* 14 (December 2000): 8.

63. Ibid., p. 6.

64. Susan A. MacManus and Charles S. Bullock, III, "Women on Southern City Councils: A Decade of Change," *Journal of Political Science* 17 (Spring 1989): 32–49.

65. Svara, "Council Profile," p. 4.

66. Susan Adams Beck, "Rethinking Municipal Governance: Gender Distinctions on Local Councils," in Debra L. Dodson, ed., *Gender and Policymaking: Studies of Women in Office* (New Brunswick, NJ: Center for the American Woman and Politics, 1991), p. 103.

67. Rita Mae Kelly, Michelle A. Saint-Germain, and Jody D. Horn, "Female Public Officials: A Different Voice?" *Annals of the American Academy of Political and Social Science* 515 (May 1991): 77–87.

68. Jack E. White, "Bright City Lights," *Time* (November 1, 1993): 30–32; "Hell Is a Dying City," *The Economist* (November 6, 1993): 13–14.

69. White, "Bright City Lights," p. 32.

70. Michael Bloomberg, as quoted in "Observer," *Governing* 19 (July 2006), p. 18.

71. Robert J. Chaskin, "Building Community Capacity," *Urban Affairs Review* 36 (January 2001): 291–323.

## Chapter 12 State–Local Relations

1. Amy Sherman, "Brakes Put on Stoplight Cameras," *Miami Herald*, www.miami.com (July 18, 2005); Breanne Gilpatrick, "Florida Could Green Light Red-Light Cameras on State Roads," *Miami Herald*, www.miamiherald.com/news/legislature/story/1000231.html (April 15, 2009).

2. Steven D. Gold, "NCSL State-Local Task Force: The First Year," *Intergovernmental Perspective* 13 (Winter 1987): 11.

3. *Merriam v. Moody's Executors*, 25 Iowa 163, 170 (1868). Dillon's rule was first written in the case of *City of Clinton v. Cedar Rapids and Missouri Railroad Co.* (1868).

4. Jeffrey I. Chapman, "Local Government Autonomy and Fiscal Stress: The Case of California Counties," *State and Local Government Review* 35 (Winter 2003): 15–25.

5. U.S. Advisory Commission on Intergovernmental Relations, *The Organization of Local Public Economies* (Washington, D.C.: ACIR, December 1987), p. 54.

6. Peter J. May, "Policy Design and Discretion: State Oversight of Local Building Regulation," Paper presented at the annual meeting of the American Political Science Association, San Francisco, California, 1996.

7. David R. Berman and Lawrence L. Martin, "State-Local Relations: An Examination of Local Discretion," *Public Administration Review* 48 (March/April 1988): 637–41.

8. Dale Krane, Platon N. Rigos, and Melvin B. Hill, Jr., *Home Rule in America: A Fifty State Handbook* (Washington, D.C.: Congressional Quarterly Press, 2001).

9. As quoted in Laura Vozzella and David Nitkin, "City Rejects State Plan, Offers Own School Loan," *Baltimore Sun* (March 9, 2004): 1.

10. Wendy Culverwell, "Restaurant Chains Brace for New Menu Labeling Law," *Portland Business Journal*, portland.bizjournals.com/portland/stories/2009/08/17/focus3.html (August 14, 2009).

11. "Wild West Budgeting," *Governing* 22 (April 2009): 13.

12. Alicia Caldwell, "High Court Pulls Reins on Eminent Domain," *Denver Post*, www.denverpost.com/cda/article (March 2, 2004).

13. Christopher Swope, "States Go for the Biotech Gold," *Governing* 17 (March 2004): 46.

14. David K. Hamilton, David Y. Miller, and Jerry Paytas, "Exploring Horizontal and Vertical Dimensions of the Governing of Metropolitan Regions," *Urban Affairs Review* 40 (November 2004): 147–82.

15. David Kocieniewski and Eric Lipton, "Two States Get High Marks for Five-Day Antiterrorism Exercise," *The New York Times*, www.nytimes.com (April 9, 2005).

16. Renu Khator, "Coping with Coercion: Florida Counties and the State's Recycling Law," *State and Local Government Review* 26 (Fall 1994): 181–91.

17. Lawrence J. Grossback, "The Problem of State-Imposed Mandates: Lessons from Minnesota's Local

Governments," *State and Local Government Review* 34 (Fall 2002): 183–97.

18. Ibid., p. 191.

19. "Indiana Advisory Commission on Intergovernmental Relations," iacir.spea.iupui.edu/

20. Bruce Katz, *Smart Growth: The Future of the American Metropolis?* (Washington, D.C.: The Brookings Institution, 2002), p. 2.

21. William Fulton and Paul Shigley, "Operation Desert Sprawl," *Governing* 12 (August 1999): 16.

22. Christina McCarroll, "Measuring the Cost of Growth," *Christian Science Monitor* (February 6, 2002): 13.

23. Moon-Gi Jeong, "Local Choices for Development Impact Fees," *Urban Affairs Review* 41 (2006): 338–57.

24. Joseph Giordono, "California Sprawl Spawns Competing Ballot Initiatives," www.stateline.org (October 31, 2000).

25. Land Trust Alliance, "State Funding for Land Conservation," www.landtrustalliance.org (August 22, 2009).

26. Jayson T. Blair, "Maryland Draws Line Against Sprawl," *Boston Globe* (December 7, 1997): A26.

27. Christopher Swope, "McGreevey's Magic Map," *Governing* 16 (May 2003): 45–48.

28. Iver Peterson, "War on Sprawl in New Jersey Hits a Wall," *The New York Times* (October 21, 2003): A15.

29. Christopher R. Conte, "The Boys of Sprawl," *Governing* 13 (May 2000): 28–33.

30. Alan Ehrenhalt, "Breaking the Density Deadlock," *Governing* 20 (March 2007): 11–12.

31. Robert Jay Dilger, "Residential Community Associations: Issues, Impacts, and Relevance for Local Government," *State and Local Government Review* 23 (Winter 1991): 17–23.

32. Evan McKenzie, *Privatopia: Homeowners' Associations and the Rise of Residential Private Government* (New Haven, CT: Yale University Press, 1996).

33. Jered B. Carr and Richard C. Feiock, "Who Becomes Involved in City-County Consolidation?" *State and Local Government Review* 34 (Spring 2002): 78–94.

34. H. V. Savitch and Ronald K. Vogel, "Suburbs Without a City: Power and City-County Consolidation," *Urban Affairs Review* 39 (July 2004): 758–90.

35. Alan Greenblatt, "Anatomy of a Merger," *Governing* 16 (December 2002): 20–25.

36. Ronald J. Oakerson, *Governing Local Political Economies: Creating the Civic Metropolis* (Oakland, CA: Institute for Contemporary Studies, 1999).

37. David Rusk, *Cities Without Suburbs* (Washington, D.C.: Woodrow Wilson Center Press, 1993), p. 5.

38. Daniel Kemmis, as quoted in Neal R. Peirce, "Missoula's 'Citistate' Claim Marks a New Way to Define Regions," *The News & Observer* (July 1, 1993): 14A

39. Randolph P. Smith, "Region Idea Works, Oregon City Says," *Richmond Times-Dispatch* (October 30, 1994): A1, A18.

40. Myron Orfield, *American Metropolitics: The New Suburban Reality* (Washington, D.C.: The Brookings Institution, 2002).

41. Margaret Weir, Harold Wolman, and Todd Swanstrom, "The Calculus of Coalitions: Cities, Suburbs, and the Metropolitan Agenda," *Urban Affairs Review* 40 (July 2005): 730–60.

42. James F. Wolf and Tara Kolar Bryan, "Identifying the Capacities of Regional Councils of Government," *State and Local Government Review* 41 (2009): 61–68.

43. James F. Wolf and Margaret Fenwick, "How Metropolitan Planning Organizations Incorporate Land Use Issues in Regional Transportation Planning," *State and Local Government Review* 35 (Spring 2003): 123–31. See also Alan Ehrenhalt, "Ready-To-Go Regionalism," *Governing* 22 (May 2009): 11–12.

44. David S. T. Matkin and George Frederickson, "Metropolitan Governance: Institutional Roles and Interjurisdictional Cooperation," *Journal of Urban Affairs* 31 (2009): 45–66.

45. Richard Feiock, "Metropolitan Governance and Institutional Collective Action," *Urban Affairs Review* 44 (2009): 338–57.

46. Mara S. Sidney, *Unfair Housing: How National Policy Shapes Community Action* (Lawrence: University Press of Kansas, 2003).

47. *Beyond Shelter: Building Communities of Opportunity* (Washington, D.C.: U.S. Department of Housing and Urban Development, 1996).

48. Christopher Swope, "Little House in the Suburbs," *Governing* 13 (April 2000): 18–22.

49. Tom Arrandale, "Cities Take the Sewer Plunge," *Governing* 15 (August 2002): 24–25.

50. Tom Arrandale, "Atlanta to Spend Billions to Clean Water," *Governing* 16 (January 2003): 56.

51. Josh Goodman, "Minneapolis Speedway," *Governing* 22 (March 2009): 36–40.

52. Hugh Bartling, "Private Governance and Public Opinion in a Company Town: The Case of Celebration, Florida," Paper presented at the annual meeting of the Midwest Political Science Association, Chicago, Illinois, 2000.

53. Peter T. Kilborn, "Boom in Economy Skips Towns on the Plains," *The New York Times* (July 2, 2000): A12.

54. "The Great Plains Drain," *The Economist* (January 19, 2007): 35.

55. Jim Seroka, "Community Growth and Administrative Capacity," *National Civic Review* 77 (January/February 1988): 45.

56. Steve Piper, Marquette Development Company, Inc., interview (August 14, 2009).

57. Patrik Jonsson, "North Carolina's Gambit to Bring Internet Age to Rural Areas," *Christian Science Monitor* (July 1, 2004).

58. Beryl A. Radin et al., *New Governance for Rural America* (Lawrence: University Press of Kansas, 1996).

59. Arthur Holst, "Review of Local Government and the States: Autonomy, Politics, and Policy," *Publius* 35 (Fall 2005): 644–45.

60. Christopher Conte, "Dry Spell," *Governing* 16 (March 2003): 20–24.

61. George Pataki, "Governor Pataki Offers $1 Billion Plan to Help Local Governments," Press Release, January 10, 1997.
62. Patrick McGreevy, "Cities Counties Pay Price for Capital Clout," *Los Angeles Times*, www.latimes.com/news/local (September 12, 2007).

## Chapter 13 Taxing and Spending

1. Brendan Schlauch, "On the Verge of Collapse," *Governing* (July, 2008): 57; Carolyn Jones, "Vallejo One of Few Cities to Use Chapter 9," *SFGate.com* (May 11, 2008).
2. U.S. Bureau of the Census, www.census.gov (July 2009).
3. Ibid.
4. Mark Schneider, "Local Budgets and the Maximization of Local Property Wealth in the System of Suburban Government," *Journal of Politics* 49 (November 1987): 1114.
5. Thomas R. Dye and Richard C. Feiock, "State Income Tax Adoption and Economic Growth," *Social Science Quarterly* 76 (September 1995): 648–54.
6. *The Book of the States* (Lexington, KY: Council of State Governments, 2008), p. 405.
7. Neal R. Peirce, "Service Tax May Rise Again," *Public Administration Times* 11 (August 12, 1996): 2.
8. *Quill v. North Dakota* 504 U.S. 298 (1992).
9. Laura Wilbert, "Taxing Times in Cyberspace," *New England Financial Journal* 3 (Summer 2000): 14–16; David C. Powell, "Internet Taxation and U.S. Intergovernmental Relations: From Quill to the Present," *Publius* 30 (Winter 2000): 39–51.
10. Steven Walters, "State to Start Charging Sales Tax on Online Digital Purchases Oct. 1," *Journal Sentinel Interactive* (February 20, 2009).
11. Stephen C. Fehr, "Stimulus Tax Breaks Threaten State Revenues," *stateline.org* (April 9, 2009).
12. Tony Romm, "Recession Ushers in More Tobacco Taxes," *stateline.org* (June 17, 2009). Stateline.
13. http://sourcebook.governing.com/ (accessed July 14, 2009).
14. The Book of the States Table 7.21 2008.
15. Alaska Permanent Fund, www.apfc.org (July 14, 2009).
16. Lucy Dadayan and Robert B. Ward, "For the First Time, a Smaller Jackpot," www.Rockinst.org (September 21, 2009); Rockefeller Institute, *Ten-Year Trends in Gambling Revenue to the States*, www.rockinst.org (accessed July 12, 2009).
17. See Donald E. Miller and Patrick A. Pierce, "Lotteries for Education: Windfall or Hoax?" *State and Local Government Review* 29 (Winter 1997): 34–42.
18. See, for example, Mary Herring and Timothy Bledsoe, "A Model of Lottery Participation: Demographics, Context, and Attitudes," *Policy Studies Journal* 22, no. 2 (1994): 245–57.
19. Elizabeth A. Freund and Irwin L. Morris, "The Lottery and Income Inequality in the States," *Social Science Quarterly* 86 (2005): 996–1012; Patrick A. Pierce and Donald E. Miller, *Gambling Politics* (Washington, D.C.: Congressional Quarterly Press, 2004).
20. Center on Budget and Policy Priorities, www.cbpp.org (accessed July 15, 2009).
21. Timothy Egan, "They Give, But They Also Take: Voters Muddle States' Finances," *The New York Times* (March 2, 2002): 1–4.
22. Kendra A. Hovey and Harold A Hovey, *State Fact Finder 2005* (Washington D.C., CQ Press, 2006).
23. Christine R. Martell and Paul Teske, "Fiscal Management Implications of the TABOR Bind," *Public Administration Review* (July/August, 2007): 673–86.
24. Daniel R. Mullins and Bruce A. Wallin, "Tax and Expenditure Limitations: Introduction and Overview," *Public Budgeting and Finance* 24 (Winter 2004): 2–15.
25. Daniel R. Mullins and Bruce A. Wallin, "Tax and Expenditure Limitations: Introduction and Overview," *Public Budgeting and Finance* 24 (Winter 2004): 2–15.
26. Thad Kousser, Matthew D. McCubbins, and Ellen Moule, "For Whom the TEL Tolls: Can State Tax and Expenditure Limits Effectively Reduce Spending?" *State Politics and Policy Quarterly* 8 (Winter 2008): 331–61.
27. James W. Endersby and Michael J. Towle, "Effects of Constitutional and Political Controls on State Expenditures," *Publius* 27 (Winter 1997): 83–98; Daniel E. O'Toole and Brian Stipak, "State Tax and Expenditure Limitations: The Oregon Experience," *State and Local Government Review* 30 (Winter 1998): 9–16; Irene S. Rubin, *Class, Tax, and Power* (Chatham, NJ: Chatham House, 1998).
28. Josh Goodman, "Minneapolis Speedway," *Governing* (March 2009): 35–40.
29. Alan Greenblatt, "Paradise Insolvement," *Governing* (November 2005): 41–46.
30. "Losing Control," *The New York Times* (November 13, 2001): 1–2.
31. David W. Chen, "Mayor Bloomberg and Council Agree on Budget," www.nytimes.com (June 16, 2009).
32. David Brunori, *State Tax Policy: A Political Perspective* (Washington, D.C.: The Urban Institute, 2001); Fiscal Survey of the States, 2008.
33. Neal R. Peirce, "State Budget Disaster: Any Way Out?" *National Journal* (April 27, 1991): 1008.
34. Michael A. Pagano and Jocelyn M. Johnston, "Life at the Bottom of the Fiscal Food Chain: Examining City and Council Revenue Decisions," *Publius* 30 (Winter 2000): 159–70.
35. Brendan Schlauch, "The Pension Pinch," *Governing* (September 2008): 59. 08
36. Richard. C. Kearney, Robert Clark, and Jerrell Coggburn, *At a Crossroads: The Financing and Future of Health Benefits for State and Local Government Retirees* (Washington, D.C. Center for State and Local Government Excellence, 2009): Table 2.6.
37. Girard Miller, "Passing on Our Debts," *Governing* (June 2009): 54.
38. Christopher G. Reddick, "Assessing Local Government Revenue Forecasting Techniques,"

*International Journal of Public Administration* 27, no. 8–9 (2004): 597–615.

39. Sallie Hofmeister, "Fund Head Resigns in California" and "Too Many Questions, But Too Late," *The New York Times* (December 6, 1994): D1, D2.

40. Mark Balddassare, *When Government Fails: The Orange County Bankruptcy* (Berkeley, CA: University of California Press, 1998).

41. Center on Budget Priorities.

42. Jeffrey I. Chapman, "State and Local Fiscal Sustainability: The Challenges," http://www.cbpp.org/ *Public Administration Review* special issue (December 2008): S115–S130.

43. Emily Kimball, "Bills Would Boost Spending Transparency," *stateline.org* (March 10, 2009).

## Chapter 14 Economic Development

1. Jack Lyne, "Virginia Readies for Rolls," *Site Selection,* www.siteselection.com/ssinsider/bbdeal/bd071206 .htm (December 3, 2007).

2. Christine Todd Whitman, as quoted in Tom Redburn, "2 Governors Split on Tax Strategies," *The New York Times* (January 20, 1994): A20.

3. W. Mark Crain, *Volatile States: Institutions, Policy, and the Performance of American State Economies* (Ann Arbor, MI: University of Michigan Press, 2003).

4. Bureau of Labor Statistics, "Metropolitan Area Employment and Unemployment Summary," http:// www.bls.gov/news.release/metro.nr0.htm (July 29, 2009).

5. "State Economic Momentum," *Governing Sourcebook 2008*, sourcebook.governing.com/subtopicresults.jsp ?yr=34&cha=n&sort=n&mrtype=2&ctype=1&ind=60 6&x=43&y=13 (June 18, 2009).

6. Michael Janofsky, "Among 4 States, a Great Divide in Fortunes," *The New York Times*, www.nytimes .com/2003/01/23/national (January 23, 2003).

7. "America's Top States for Business," *CNBC,* www.cnbc.com/id/31765926 (July 20, 2009).

8. Maryann P. Feldman and Johanna L. Francis, "Homegrown Solutions: Fostering Cluster Formation," *Economic Development Quarterly* 18 (May 2004): 127–37.

9. Mary Jo Waits, "Building an Economic Future," *State Government News* 38 (September 1995): 6–10.

10. Susan E. Clarke and Gary L. Gaile, *The Work of Cities* (Minneapolis, MN: University of Minnesota Press, 1998).

11. J. Mac Holladay, "Trends That Strengthen Economies," *State Government News* 40 (August 1997): 6–7.

12. Robert D. Atkinson and Scott Andes, "The 2008 State New Economy Index." *The Information and Technology Innovation Foundation,* http://www.kauffman.org/ uploadedfiles/2008_state_new_economy_index_ 120908.pdf (July 23, 2009), p. 3.

13. Governor's Office of Economic Development, www.goed.utah.gov (July 5, 2006).

14. As quoted in Richard Reeves, *American Journey* (New York: Simon & Schuster, 1982), p. 46.

15. Committee for Economic Development, *Leadership for Dynamic State Economies* (Washington, D.C.: Committee for Economic Development, 1986), pp. 73–77.

16. As quoted in Laurie Clewett, "State of the States," *State Government News* (March 2004): 20.

17. National Association of State Development Agencies, *The NASDA Newsletter* (January 21, 1987), p. 5.

18. "Accelerating/Growth: Indiana's Strategic Economic Development Plan," www.in.gov/iedc/files/Strategic_ Plan.pdf (August 1, 2009).

19. Mary Branham, "Traveling On: States Alter Message to Keep Tourism Strong," *State News* (June/July 2009): 17–21.

20. Heather Kleba, "Wisconsin Will Certify Green Tourist Sites," *Governing* 19 (December 2005): 70; Ellen Perlman, "That's Agritainment," *Governing* 19 (December 2005): 44–45.

21. David Reynolds, as quoted in Charles Mahtesian, "How States Get People to (Love) Them," *Governing* 7 (January 1994): 47.

22. "Beaches and Coastlines," www.visitmaine.com/ home.php (July 25, 2006).

23. "So Watcha Wanna Do Is," www.visitpa.com/visitpa/ home.pa (July 25, 2006).

24. J. Allen Whitt, "The Arts Coalition in Strategies of Urban Development," in Clarence N. Stone and Heywood T. Sanders, eds., *The Politics of Urban Development* (Lawrence: University Press of Kansas, 1987), pp. 144–56.

25. "If You Build It," *Governing* 19 (January 2006): 18.

26. Michael Janofsky, "Providence Is Reviving, Using Arts as the Fuel," *The New York Times* (February 18, 1997): A8.

27. William Fulton, "Planet Downtown," *Governing* 10 (April 1997): 23–26.

28. Richard Sandomir, "A Texas-Size Stadium," *The New York Times,* www.nytimes.com/2009/07/17/ sports/football/17cowboys.html?scp=1&sq=a+texas+ size+stadium&st=nyt (July 17, 2009).

29. Ibid.

30. Conrad Defiebre and Jay Weiner, "Pawlenty Unveils Plans for Stadiums," *Minneapolis Star Tribune,* www .startribune.com/viewers/story (March 16, 2004).

31. Rodd Zolkos, "Cities Blast Stadium Study," *City & State* 4 (April 1987): 3, 53. See also Kevin G. Quinn, Christopher P. Borick, and Paul B. Bursick, "The Stadium Game: An Empirical Analysis," Paper presented at the annual meeting of the Midwest Political Science Association, Chicago, Illinois, 2000.

32. Gary Enos and Rodd Zolkos, "Stadiums Ding Home Runs," *City & State* 8 (September 23–October 6, 1991): 1, 24.

33. Matthew J. Burbank, Charles H. Heying, and Greg Andranovich, "Antigrowth Politics or Piecemeal Resistance?" *Urban Affairs Review* 35 (January 2000): 334–57.

34. John Larkin, "States Spark Foreign Relations of Their Own," *PA Times* (June 1, 1992): 1, 20. See also Jeffrey A. Finkle, "State Economic Development Strategies: Trends and Issues," in *The Book of*

the States 2006 (Lexington, KY: Council of State Governments, 2006), pp. 511–14.

35. "Trade Statistics," *Statemaster.com*, www.statemaster.com/graph/tra_exp_tot_per_sha_of_us_tot-totals-percent-share-us-total (July 2, 2009).

36. U.S. Census Bureau, "Foreign Direct Investment in the United States," *Statistical Abstract of the United States: 2009* (Washington, D.C.: U.S. Census Bureau, 2009), Table 1253.

37. Conrad Weiler, "Free Trade Agreements: A New Federal Partner," *Publius* 24 (Summer 1994): 113–33.

38. Mark K. Matthews, "States Chart Their Own Foreign Policy," *stateline.org*, http://www.stateline.org/live/ViewPage.action?siteNodeId=136&languageId=1&contentId=103597 (April 12, 2006).

39. Richard S. Krannich and Craig R. Humphrey, "Local Mobilization and Community Growth: Toward an Assessment of the 'Growth Machine' Hypothesis," *Rural Sociology* 48 (Spring 1983): 60–81; John M. Levy, *Urban and Metropolitan Economics* (New York: McGraw-Hill, 1985).

40. Roger Schmenner, "Location Decisions of Large Firms: Implications for Public Policy," *Commentary* 5 (January 1981): 307.

41. Paul Brace, *State Government and Economic Performance* (Baltimore, MD: Johns Hopkins University Press, 1993).

42. Margery Marzahn Ambrosius, "Are Political Benefits the Only Benefits of State Economic Development Policies?" Paper presented at the annual meeting of the American Political Science Association, San Francisco, California, 1990; Paul Brace, "The Changing Context of State Political Economy," *Journal of Politics* 53 (May 1991): 297–316.

43. Michael A. Pagano and Ann O'M. Bowman, *Cityscapes and Capital* (Baltimore, MD: Johns Hopkins University Press, 1995).

44. Ben Delman, "A Beef Plant Goes Bust," *Governing* 18 (September 2005): 76.

45. Parris Glendening, "Smart Growth Tops Governors' Agenda," *Washington Post* (July 12, 2000): A14.

46. Craig Jenkins, Kevin T. Leicht, and Arthur Jaynes, "Creating High-Technology Growth: High-Tech Employment Growth in U.S. Metropolitan Areas, 1988–1998." *Social Science Quarterly* 89, no. 2 (2009): 456–81.

47. Sujit M. CanagaRetna, "The Drive to Move South: The Growing Role of the Automobile Industry in the Southern States," *Spectrum: The Journal of State Government* 77 (Winter 2004): 22–24.

48. Mac R. Holmes, as quoted in Peter Applebome, "States Raise Stakes in Fight for Jobs," *The New York Times* (October 4, 1993): A10.

49. Charles Mahtesian, "Romancing the Smokestack," *Governing* 8 (November 1994): 36–40.

50. Greg LeRoy, "Trends in State Business Incentives: More Money and More Accountability," *Spectrum: The Journal of State Government* 77 (Winter 2004): 15–18.

51. William Fulton, "The Clawback Clause," *Governing* 16 (October 2002): 72.

52. Ann O'M. Bowman, *The Visible Hand: Major Issues in City Economic Policy* (Washington, D.C.: National League of Cities, 1987).

53. David Osborne, *Laboratories of Democracy* (Boston, MA: Harvard Business School Press, 1988).

54. Darrene Hackler and Heike Mayer, "Diversity, Entrepreneurship, and the Urban Environment," *Journal of Urban Affairs* 30 (2008): 273–307.

55. Peter Waldman, "Cities Are Pressured to Make Developers Share Their Wealth," *The Wall Street Journal* (March 10, 1987): 1.

56. Carol Steinbach, "Tapping Private Resources," *National Journal* (April 26, 1986): 993.

57. "Taking Care of Business," *The Economist* (February 18, 1989): 28.

58. Neal Peirce, "Cities Must Learn When to Say No," *Houston Chronicle* (February 13, 1989): A12.

59. "The Best Places for Business and Careers," *Forbes.com*, www.forbes.com/2009/03/25/best-cities-careers-bizplaces09-business-places_lander.html (March 25, 2009).

60. Charles J. Spindler, "Winners and Losers in Industrial Recruitment: Mercedes-Benz and Alabama," *State and Local Government Review* 26 (Fall 1994): 192–204.

61. Joel Rast and Virginia Carlson, "When Boeing Landed in Chicago: Lessons for Regional Economic Development," *State and Local Government Review* 38 (Winter 2006): 1–11.

62. Daniel C. Vock, "Court Allows Smokestack Chasing—For Now," www.stateline.org (May 16, 2006).

63. Charles Mahtesian, "A Non-Poaching Peace Pact Is Under Fire in Florida," *Governing* 13 (May 2000): 88.

## Chapter 15 Education Policy

1. National Commission on Excellence in Education, *A Nation at Risk: The Imperative for Educational Reform* (Washington, D.C.: U.S. Government Printing Office, 1983), p. 1

2. National Center for Education Statistics, *Digest of Education Statistics: 2008* Table 403 (March 2009), www.nces.org.

3. Ibid, Table 29.

4. Ibid, various tables.

5. National Center for Education Statistics, *Digest of Education Statistics*.

6. National Governors Association, *Building the Foundation for Bright Futures* (Washington, D.C.: National Governors Association, January 2005).

7. College Board, www.collegeboard.com (July 21, 2009).

8. Kevin Peterson, "Fewer Choosing Teaching Jobs," *stateline.org* (March 28, 2006): 1–2.

9. Tiffany Danitz, "More Respect Please, Teachers Say," www.stateline.org (May 31, 2000).

10. John Bohte, "School Bureaucracy and Student Performance at the Local Level," *Public Administration Review* 61 (January/February 2001): 92–99; John E. Chubb and Terry Moe, *Politics, Markets, and*

*America's Schools* (Washington, D.C.: The Brookings Institution, 1990).

11. Kevin B. Smith and Kenneth J. Meier, *The Case Against School Choice: Politics, Markets, and Fools* (Armonk, NY: M. E. Sharpe, 1995); Kevin B. Smith and Christopher W. Larimer, "A Mixed Relationship: Bureaucracy and School Performance," *Public Administration Review* 64 (November/December 2004): 728–36; Also see Robert Maranto, Scott Milliman, and Scott Stevens, "Does Private School Competition Harm Public Schools?" *Political Research Quarterly* 53 (March 2000): 177–92.

12. Patrick McGuinn, "The National Schoolmarm: No Child Left Behind and the New Educational Federalism," *Publius* 35 (Winter 2005): 41–69.

13. William J. Mathis, "No Child Left Behind: Costs and Benefits," *Phi Delta Kappan* (May 2003): 68

14. Sam Dillon, "Education Standards Likely to See Toughening," *nytimes.com* (April 15, 2009).

15. Allison Armour-Garb, "Three Sticking Points Could Stunt Stimulus Education Reform,"*stateline.org* (May 4, 2009).

16. *Serrano v. Priest,* 5 Cal.3d 584 (1971).

17. *San Antonio Independent School District v. Rodriguez,* 411 U.S. 1 (1973).

18. Kenneth K. Wong, "The Politics of Education," in Virginia Gray and Russell L. Hanson, eds., *Politics in the American States,* 9th ed. (Washington, D.C.: CQ Press, 2008): Table 12.3.

19. B. Dan Wood and Nick A Theobald, "Political Responsiveness and Equity in Public Education Finance," *The Journal of Politics* 65 (August 2003): 718–38; Bill Swingford, "A Predictive Model of Decision Making in State Supreme Courts: The School Financing Cases," *American Politics Quarterly* 19 (July 1991): 336–52.

20. Kristen Alloway and Jeanette Rundquist, "Court Shifts on School Aid," *The Star-Ledger* www.nj.com (May 29, 2009).

21. Wong, "The Politics of Education."

22. William Celis, III, "Michigan Debates What Tax Is Best to Pay for Education," *The New York Times* (March 14, 1994): A12.

23. Michele Moser and Ross Rubenstein, "The Equality of Public School District Funding in the United States: A National Status Report," *Public Administration Review* 62 (January/February 2002): 63–72.

24. Douglas S. Reed, *On Equal Terms: The Constitutional Politics of Educational Opportunity* (Princeton, NJ: Princeton University Press, 2001).

25 James S. Coleman, *Equality of Educational Opportunity* (Washington, D.C.: U.S. Government Printing Office, 1966).

26 Eric A. Hanushek, John F. Kain, Jacob M. Markman, and Steven G. Rivkin, "Does Peer Ability Affect Student Achievement?" *Journal of Applied Econometrics* 18 (September/October 2003): 527–44; available at http://www.edpro.stanford.edueahpaperspeersaug01.pdf/.

27. Eric A. Hanushek, "The Economics of Schooling: Production and Efficiency in Public Schools," *Journal of Economic Literature* 24 (September 1986): 1141–77.

28 Nathan Glazer, *We Are All Multiculturalists Now* (Cambridge, MA: Harvard University Press, 1997).

29. R. L. Linn and K. G. Welner, eds., *Race-conscious Policies for Assigning Students to Schools: Social Science Research and the Court Cases* (Washington, D.C.: National Academy of Education, 2007).

30. Eric A. Hanushek and Steven G. Rivkin, "Harming the Best: How Schools Affect the Black-White Achievement Gap," *Journal of Policy Analysis and Management* 28, no. 3 (2009): 366–93.

31. *Meredith v. Jefferson County Board of Education* U.S. Sup Ct No. 05-915 (2007).

32. Hanuschek and Rifkin, "Harming the Best."

33. Karl L. Alexander, Doris R. Entwisle, and Linda Steffel Olson, "Lasting Consequences of the Summer Learning Gap," *American Sociological Review* 72 (April 2007): 167–80.

34. See, for example, Fryer G. Roland, " 'Acting White': The Social Price Paid by the Best and Brightest Minority Students," *Education Next* 6 (1) 2006: 52–59.

35. Clive S. Thomas and Ronald J. Hrebenar, "Interest Groups in the States," in Virginia Gray and Herbert Jacob, eds., *Politics in the American States: A Comparative Analysis,* 6th ed. (Glenview, IL: Scott, Foresman/Little, Brown, 1996). See Tom Loveless, ed., *Conflicting Missions? Teachers Unions and Educational Reform* (Washington, D.C.: The Brookings Institution, 2000).

36. Rob Gurwitt, "Battered School Boards," *Governing* (May 2006): 38–45; William G. Howell, ed., *Beseiged: School Boards and the Future of Education Politics* (Washington, D.C.: The Brookings Institution, 2005).

37. Michael B. Berkman and Eric Plutzner, *Ten Thousand Democracies: Politics and Public Opinion in America's School Districts* (Washington, D.C.: Georgetown University Press, 2005).

38. Ibid.

39. Wong, "The Politics of Education," p. 355.

40. Kevin Kiley, "Atkinson Wins Right to Run Public Schools," www.newsobserver.com (July 17, 2009).

41. *Brown v. Board of Education of Topeka,* 347 I.S. 483 (1954).

42. *Swann v. Charlotte-Mecklenberg County Schools,* 402 U.S. 1 (1971).

43. Wong, "The Politics of Education," p. 362.

44. Reed, *On Equal Terms.*

45. Charles T. Clotfelter, "Public School Segregation in Metropolitan Areas," *Land Economics* 75 (December 1999): 487–504.

46. Digest of Educational Statistics 2008, www.ncssm.edu (July 21, 2009).

47. Sam Dillon, "Federal Researchers Find Lower Standards in Schools," *nytimes.com* (October 30, 2009).

48. "Ed Issues A–Z: Year-Round Schooling," www.edweek.org (January 27, 2004).

49. David L. Kirp, *The Sandbox Investment: The Preschool Movement and Kids-First Politics* (Cambridge, MA: Harvard University Press, 2007).

50. Eric Kelderman, "Three States Lead in Preschool Programs," www.stateline.org (February 19, 2004): 1–2.

51. Center for Effective Discipline, www.stophitting.com (accessed July 23, 2009); Jodi Wilgoren, "Lawsuits Touch Off Debate Over Paddling in the Schools," *The New York Times* (May 3, 2001): 1–4; U.S. General Accounting Office, *School Safety: Promising Initiatives for Addressing School Violence* (Washington, D.C.: U.S. Government Printing Office, 1995).

52. Elissa Gootman, "Mixed Results on Paying City Students to Pass Tests," *nytimes.com* (August 20, 2008).

53. National Commission on Teaching and America's Future, "Learning Teams: Creating What's Next," www.nctaf.org (accessed July 23, 2009).

54. Diana Jean Schemo, "Study of Test Scores Finds Charter Schools Lagging," *The New York Times* (August 2 3, 2006): 1–3 (citing a federal study); Chubb and Moe, *Politics, Markets, and America's Schools.*

55. Center for Policy Alternatives, *Education: School Vouchers* (Washington, D.C.: Policy Alternatives, 2005), p. 85.

56. *Zelman et al. v. Simmons-Harris et al.* (No. 001751, June 27, 2002).

57. Ibid.

58. Sam Dillon, "Florida Court Strikes Down School Voucher Program," *The New York Times* (January 5, 2006).

59. Alan J. Borsuk, "Voucher Study Finds Parity," www.jsonline.com (February, 25, 2008).

60. See Paul E. Peterson, *The Education Gap: Vouchers and Urban Schools* (Cambridge, MA: Harvard University Press, 2002); Terry Moe, *Schools, Vouchers, and the American Public* (Washington, D.C.: The Brookings Institution, 2001).

61. Borsh and Wolf; "Study Finds Academic Gains Not Superior Among Students Enrolled in Privately-Run Schools," www.rand.org (February 1, 2007); John F. Witte, *The Market Approach to Education: An Analysis of America's First Voucher Program* (Princeton, NJ: Princeton University Press, 2000); Richard Rothstein, "Failed Schools? The Meaning Is Unclear," *The New York Times* (July 3, 2002): 1–2; Christopher Conte, "The Boundaries of Choice," *Governing* (December 2002): 40–44; Kim Metcalf et al., *Evaluations of the Cleveland Scholarship and Tutoring Program, Summary Report, 1998–2001* (Bloomington, IN: Indiana University Press, 2003).

62. Jacques Steinberg, "At 42 Newly Privatized Philadelphia Schools, Uncertainty Abounds," *The New York Times* (April 19, 2002): 1–3.

63. Kristen A. Graham, "Philadelphia Taking Back 6 Privatized Schools," www.philly.com (June 19, 2008).

64. Brian Gill, Michael Timpane, and Dominic Brewer, *Rhetoric versus Reality: What We Know and What We Need to Know About School Vouchers and Charter Schools* (Santa Monica, CA: Rand Corporation, 2001).

65. "1.5 Million Homeschooled Students in the U.S. in 2007," nces.ed.gov (December 2008).

66. Brian D. Ray and Bruce K. Eagleson. "State Regulation of Homeschooling and Homeschoolers' SAT Scores," *Academic Leadership*, www.academicleadership.org (August, 2008).

67. Kevin B. Smith and Kenneth J. Meier, "Public Choice in Education: Markets and the Demand for Quality Education," *Political Research Quarterly* 48 (June 1995): 461–78.

68. Mark Schneider et al., "Heuristics, Low Information Rationality, and Choosing Public Goods: Broken Windows as Shortcuts to Information About School Performance," *Urban Affairs Review* 34 (May 1999): 728–41.

69. Clarence N. Stone, Jeffery R. Henig, Bryan D. Jones, and Carol Pierannunzi, *Building Civic Capacity: The Politics of Reforming Schools* (Lawrence, KS: University Press of Kansas, 2001).

## Chapter 16 Criminal Justice

1. William J. Wilem, *When Work Disappears: The World of the New Urban Poor* (New York: Alfred A. Knopf, 1996); Alex Piquero, John MacDonald, and Karen F. Parker, "Race, Local Life Circumstances, and Criminal Activity," *Social Science Quarterly* 83 (September 2002): 654–70.

2. Bruce Western, *Punishment and Inequality in America* (New York: Russell Sage Press, 2006).

3. Federal Bureau of Investigation, *Crime in the United States*, www.fbi.govucrcivs (2008): Section III. http://www.fbi.gov/ucr/cius2007/offenses/clearances/index.html (accessed August 10, 2009).

4. James Q. Wilson and George L. Kelling, "Broken Windows: The Police and Neighborhood Safety," *Atlantic Monthly* (March 1982): 29–38. See also Rob Gurwitt, "Not By Cops Alone," *Governing* 8 (May 1995): 16–26.

5. John Buntin, "Gundemic," *Governing* (June 2008). http://www.governing.com/node/840/.

6. *Terry V. Ohio*, 392 U.S. 1 (1968).

7. Ellen Perlman, "Bait and Switch Off," *Governing* (February 2003): 16.

8. John Buntin, "Long Lens of the Law," *Governing* (May 2009): 24–30.

9. Ellen Perlman, "Policing by the Odds," *Governing* (December 2008).

10. Ellen Perlman, "To Catch a Thief," *Governing* (April 2008): 52.

11. Jonathan Walters, "Data on the Beat," *Governing.com*, http://www.governing.com/article/data-beat (August 1, 2007).

12. "Crime and the Tech Effect," special issue, *Government Technology*, http://www.ojp.usdoj.gov/bjs/glance/exptyp.htm (April 2000).

13. Federal Bureau of Investigation, *Crime in the United States* (Washington, D.C.: U.S. Department of Justice, 2008).

14. David A. Harriss, "The Stories, the Statistics, and the Law," *Minnesota Law Review* 84 (December 1999): 1–42; David Kocieniewski, "U.S. Wrote Outline for

Race Profiling, New Jersey Argues," *The New York Times* (November 29, 2000).

15. Timothy Eagan, "Police Forces, Their Ranks Thin, Offer Bonuses, Bounties, and More," *The New York Times* (December 28, 2005): 1–3.

16. *Gideon v. Wainwright*, 372 U.S. 335 (1963).

17. *Escobedo v. Illinois*, 478 U.S. (1964).

18. *Miranda v. Arizona*, 384 U.S. 486 (1966).

19. *Mapp v. Ohio*, 307 U.S. 643 (1961).

20. "Free at Last, Free at Last," *Time* (November 2, 1987): 55.

21. Christopher Swope, "Kentucky Goes Statewide with Automated Victim Notification," *Governing* 11 (March 1998): 58.

22. http://klaaskids.org/pg-legmeg2.htm.

23. C. Peter Rydell and Susan S. Everingham, *Controlling Cocaine: Supply versus Demand Programs* (Santa Monica, CA: RAND Corporation, 1994).

24. *Furman v. Georgia*, 408 U.S. 239 (1972).

25. *Roper v. Simmons* (2005).

26. *Singleton v. Norris*, 02–10605 (2003).

27. *Kennedy v. Louisiana* (2008) U.S. Sup Ct. No. 07–343.

28. *Baze v. Rees* (2008) U.S. Sup. Ct No. 07–5439.

29. Death Penalty Information Center, www.deathpenaltyinfo.com (August 12, 2009).

30. John Gramlich, "No End in Sight to Death Penalty Wrangling," *Stateline.org* (July 31, 2008).

31. Death Penalty Information Center, http://www.deathpenaltyinfo.org/race-death-row-inmates-executed-1976#inmaterace (2009).

32. Melinda Gann Hall and Paul Brace, "The Vicissitudes of Death by Decree: Forces Influencing Capital Punishment Decision Making in State Supreme Courts," *Social Science Quarterly* 75 (March 1999): 1368.

33. Ibid., pp. 1136–51.

34. Adam Liptak, "Judges Set Hurdles for Lethal Injection," *The New York Times* (April 12, 2006), pp. 1–3.

35. Gramlich, "No End in Sight to Death Penalty Wrangling."

36. Jeff Yates and Richard Fording, "Politics and State Punitiveness in Black and White," *Journal of Politics* 67 (November 2005): 1118.

37. Jon Hurwitz and Mark Peffley, "Explaining the Great Racial Divide: Perceptions of Fairness in the U.S. Criminal Justice System," *Journal of Politics* 67 (August 2005): 762–83.

38. Stephen Demuth and Darrell Steffensmeier, "Ethnicity Effects on Sentence Outcomes in Large Urban Courts: Comparisons Among White, Black, and Hispanic Defendants," *Social Science Quarterly* 85 (December 2004): 994–1011.

39. Ibid.

40. Marie Gottschalk, *The Prison and the Gallows: The Politics of Mass Incarceration in America* (New York: Cambridge University Press, 2006).

41. D. Walsh, "Judges Order California to Cut Prison Population By 40,591," *Sacramento Bee* (August 5, 2009).

42. National Association of State Budget Officers, www.nasbo.org (accessed August 6, 2009).

43. John Buntin, "Mean Streets Revisited," *Governing* (April 2003): 30–33.

44. Pew Center on the States, *One in 31: The Long Reach of American Corrections* (Washington, D.C.: Pew Center on the States, 2009), p. 12.

45. Ibid, p. 13

46. Keith B. Richburg, "States Seek Less Costly Substitutes for Prison," *The Washington Post* (July 13, 2009).

47. Pew Center on the States, *One in 31*, p. 80.

48. Greg Lucas, "Chemical Castration Bill Passes," *San Francisco Chronicle* (September 31, 1996): A1, A8.

49. Judy Farah, " 'Ratlord' Sent to Live in Own Dump," *The State* (July 14, 1987): 1.

50. Christine Vestal, "States Adopt Missouri Youth Justice Model," *Stateline.org* (March 7, 2008); Peters, D. Thompson and C. Zamberlan, *Boot Camps for Juvenile Offender Programs* (Washington, D.C.: Office of Juvenile Justice and Delinquency, 1997).

51. Fox Butterfield, "Study Tracks Boom in Prisons and Notes Impact on Counties," *The New York Times* (April 30, 2004); Peter T. Kilborn, "Rural Towns Turn to Prisons to Reignite Their Economies," *The New York Times* (August 1, 2001); Sarah Lawrence and Jeremy Travis, *The New Landscape of Imprisonment* (Washington, D.C.: The Urban Institute, 2004).

52. *Prison and Jail Inmates at Midyear 2005*; James Austin and Garry Coventry, "Emerging Issues in Privatized Prisons," *U.S. Bureau of Justice Statistics* (February 2001).

53. B. E. Price, *Merchandizing Prisoners: Who Really Pays for Prison Privatization* (Westport, CT: Praeger, 2006).

54. Anne Morrison Piehl and John J. DiIulio, Jr., "Does Prison Pay?" *The Brookings Review* (Winter 1995): 21–25.

55. Lawrence and Travis.

## Chapter 17 Social Welfare and Health Care Policy

1. Larry Bartels, "Inequalities," *nytimes* (April 27, 2008).

2. Timothy M. Smeedling, "Public Policy, Economic Inequality, and Poverty: The United States in Comparative Perspective," *Social Science Quarterly* 86 (2005): 955–83.

3. www.aspe.hhs.gov/poverty/09poverty.shtml (accessed August 15, 2009).

4. Fred Block, Richard A. Cloward, Barbara Ehrenreich, and Francis Fox Piven, *The Mean Season: The Attack on the Welfare State* (New York: Pantheon Books, 1987), p. 4.

5. Martin Gilens, *Why Americans Hate Welfare: Race, Media, and the Politics of Antipoverty Policy* (Chicago, IL: University of Chicago Press, 1999).

6. Governing Sourcebook, www.sourcebook.governing.com (accessed August 18, 2009).
7. Matthew C. Fellowes and Gretchen Rowe, "Politics and the New American Welfare States," *American Journal of Political Science* 48 (April 2004): 362–73.
8. Christine Vestal, "States Cope with Rising Homelessness," *Stateline.org* (March 18, 2009).
9. Fellowes and Rowe, "Politics and the New American Welfare States"; Marcia K. Meyers, Janet C. Gornick, and Laura R. Peck, "More, Less, or More of the Same? Trends in State Social Welfare Policy in the 1990s," *Publius* 32 (Fall 2002): 91–108.
10. Center for Disease Control and Prevention, *NCHS Data Brief*, No. 18 (May 2009).
11. Francesca Jaroz, et al., "Rollout of Indiana Welfare Changes Halted," *INDYSTAR.com*, www.indystar.com (July 31, 2008).
12. Jonathan Walters, "Is Welfare Working?" *Governing* (February 2008): 28–34.
13. U.S. General Accounting Office, *Welfare Reform: More Coordinated Federal Effort Could Help States and Localities Move TANF Recipients with Impairments Toward Employment*, GAO-02-286SP (Washington, D.C.: U.S. GAO, 2001).
14. Gregory Acs, Katherine Ross Phillips, and Sandi Nelson, "The Road Not Taken? Change in Welfare Entry During the 1990s," *Social Science Quarterly* 86 (2005): 1060–79.
15. Richard M. Francis, "Prediction, Patterns, and Policymaking: A Regional Study of Devolution," *Publius* 28 (Summer 1998): 143–60; Jack Tweedie, "From D.C. to Little Rock: Welfare Reform at Mid-Term," *Publius* 30 (Winter 2001): 66–97.
16. National Coalition on Health Care, www.nchc.org (accessed August 20, 2009).
17. Penelope Lemov, "Medicaid's New Math," *Governing* (December 2008): 18.
18. Marilyn Werber Serafini, "Medicare Crooks," *National Journal* 29 (July 19, 1997): 1458–60; Malcolm Sparran, *License to Steal: Why Fraud Plagues America's Health Care System* (Boulder, CO: Westview Press, 1996).
19. Gary Enos, "Universal Appeal," *Governing* (June 2006): SA2–SA6.
20. United Health Foundation, *America's Health Rankings: A Call to Action for Individuals and their Communities* (United Health Foundation, 2008).
21. American Medical Association, www.ama-assn.org (accessed August 20, 2009).
22. "Medicaid Spending Projected to Rise Much Faster than the Economy," U.S. Department of Health and Human Services, www.hhs.gov/news/press (October 18, 2008).
23. Craig Volden, "States as Policy Laboratories: Emulating Success in the Children's Health Insurance Program," *American Journal of Political Science* 50 (April 2006): 294–312; Marian Lief Palley, "Intergovernmentalization of Health Care Reform: The Limits of the Devolution Revolution," *Journal of Politics* 59 (August 1997): 657–79.
24. www.statehealthfacts.org (accessed August 21, 2009).
25. See www.dirigohealth.maine.gov (accessed August 20, 2009).
26. For detailed information on Tenncare, see www.state.tn.us/tenncare.
27. Ibid.
28. Abby Goodnough, "Massachusetts Takes a Step Back From Health Care for All," www.nytimes.com (July 15, 2009).
29. Josh Goodman, "The Coverage Connection," *Governing* (December 2008): 18–22; Greg Vadala, "Studies Analyze Impact of Massachusetts Health Care Law," www.cqpolitics.com (October 30, 2008).

# Chapter 18 Environmental Policy

1. As quoted in "Chattanooga on a Roll," *E Magazine* 9 (March/April 1998): 15.
2. As quoted in ibid., p. 14.
3. Kent E. Portney, *Taking Sustainable Cities Seriously* (Cambridge, MA: MIT Press, 2003), pp. 185–93.
4. Richard C. Feiock and Christopher Stream, "Environmental Protection versus Economic Development: A False Trade-Off?" *Public Administration Review* 61 (May/June 2001): 313–21.
5. Deborah Lynn Guber, *The Grassroots of a Green Revolution* (Cambridge, MA: MIT Press, 2003).
6. *2003 Gallup Poll Social Series, The Environment* (Princeton, NJ: The Gallup Organization, 2003); Steven E. Barkan, "Explaining Public Support for the Environmental Movement: A Civic Voluntarism Model," *Social Science Quarterly* 85 (December 2004): 913–37.
7. Nicole Darnall and Stephen Sides, "Assessing the Performance of Voluntary Environmental Programs: Does Certification Matter?" *Policy Studies Journal* 36 (2008): 95–117.
8. David M. Konisky, "Regulator Attitudes and the Environmental Race to the Bottom Argument," *Journal of Public Administration Research and Theory* 18 (2008): 321–44.
9. Walter A. Rosenbaum, *Environmental Politics and Policy*, 5th ed. (Washington, D.C.: Congressional Quarterly Press, 2002), pp. 12–13.
10. Portney, *Taking Sustainable Cities Seriously*, p. 9.
11. Lawrence S. Rothenberg, *Environmental Choices: Policy Responses to Green Demands* (Washington, D.C.: Congressional Quarterly Press, 2002).
12. Rosenbaum, *Environmental Politics and Policy*.
13. See U.S. General Accounting Office, *Hazardous Waste: Much Work Remains to Accelerate Facility Clean-Ups* (Washington, D.C.: U.S. GAO, January 1993).
14. "Performance Partnership Agreements," www.epa.gov/ocir/nepps/pp_agreements.htm (July 24, 2006).
15. John M. Broder, "With Something for Everyone, Climate Bill Passed," *The New York Times*, www.nytimes.com (July 1, 2009).
16. "National Model for Renewable Energy," *State Legislatures* (February 2006), p. 9.

17. "Spending," *Environmental Council of the States,* www
.ecos.org/section/states/spending (March 12, 2008).

18. Environmental Council of the States, www.ecos.org
(October 15, 2000).

19. Matthew Potoski, "Clean Air Federalism: Do States
Race to the Bottom?" *Public Administration Review* 61
(May/June 2001): 335–42.

20. Brian Wingfield and Miriam Marcus, "America's
Greenest States," *Forbes,* http://www.forbes.com/
2007/10/16/environment-energy-vermont-
biz-beltway-cx_bw_mm_1017greenstates.html
(October 17, 2007).

21. Travis Coan and Mirya R. Holman, "Voting Green,"
*Social Science Quarterly* 89 (2008): 1121–35;
David M. Konisky, Jeffrey Milyo, and Lilliard E.
Richardson, "Environmental Policy Attitudes: Issues,
Geographical Scale, and Political Trust," *Social
Science Quarterly* 89 (2008): 1066–85.

22. Ann O'M. Bowman, "Environmental Issues in Big-
City Politics," Paper presented at the annual meeting
of the American Political Science Association,
Philadelphia, PA, 2006.

23. See the discussion in Portney, *Taking Sustainable
Cities Seriously,* pp. 18–21.

24. Ibid., pp. 70–71.

25. Ibid., pp. 210–11.

26. "Municipal Solid Waste Generation, Recycling, and
Disposal in the United States: Facts and Figures
for 2007," U.S. Environmental Protection Agency
(November 2008).

27. Scott M. Kaufman et al., "The State of Garbage in
America," *BioCycle* 45 (January 2004): 32.

28. Kierstan Gordan, "The Can Man," *Governing* 14
(November 2000): 17.

29. Hugh McDiarmid, Jr., "Michigan's Trash Heap Grows
Larger," *Detroit Free Press,* www.freep.com (February 3,
2004).

30. "Municipal Solid Waste Generation, Recycling, and
Disposal in the United States," p. 4.

31. Ibid., p. 1.

32. Christopher Swope and Brendan Schlauch,
"Recycling Recession," *Governing* (June 2009): 20.

33. Christopher Borick, "Assessing the Impact of Solid
Waste Management Initiatives in the American
States," Paper presented at the annual meeting of the
American Political Science Association, Washington,
D.C., 1997.

34. "Recycling: For Economy and Environment, We Must
Improve Dismal Rate," *Lansing State Journal,* www.lsj
.com (April 23, 2006).

35. Katherine N. Probst and David M. Konisky,
*Superfund's Future: What Will It Cost?* (Washington,
D.C.: Resources for the Future, 2001).

36. John M. Broder, "Without Superfund Tax, Stimulus
Aids Cleanups," *The New York Times,* www.nytimes
.com (April 26, 2009).

37. "Yucca Mountain Nuclear Waste Dump Dead,"
*Environment News Service,* www.ens-newswire.com/
ens/jul2009/2009-07-30-01.asp (July 30, 2009).

38. Anthony L. Dodson, "Interstate Compacts to Bury
Radioactive Waste: A Useful Tool for Environmental
Policy?" *State and Local Government Review* 30 (Spring
1998): 118–28.

39. Dianna Gordon, "Low-Level Waste Controversy,"
*State Legislatures* 20 (September 1994): 30–31.

40. Josh Goodman, "The Nuclear Option," *Governing* 20
(November 2006): 43–45.

41. Abigail D. Blodgett, "An Analysis of Pollution and
Community Advocacy in 'Cancer Alley': Setting an
Example for the Environmental Justice Movement
in St James Parish, Louisiana," *Local Environment* 11
(2006): 647–61.

42. Regina Austin and Michael Schill, "Black, Brown,
Red, and Poisoned," in Robert D. Bullard, ed.,
*Unequal Protection* (San Francisco, CA: Sierra Club
Books, 1994), p. 53.

43. Deb Starkey, "Environmental Justice: Win, Lose, or
Draw?" *State Legislatures* 20 (March 1994): 28.

44. United Church of Christ Commission for Racial
Justice, *Toxic Waste and Race* (New York: United
Church of Christ, 1987).

45. Liam Downey and Brian Hawkins, "Single-Mother
Families and Air Pollution: A National Study," *Social
Science Quarterly* 89 (2008): 523–36.

46. Susan Cutter, "Race, Class, and Environmental
Justice," *Progress in Human Geography* 19 (March
1995): 111–22.

47. Evan J. Ringquist, "Environmental Justice:
Normative Concerns, Empirical Evidence, and
Government Action," in Norman J. Vig and Michael
E. Kraft, eds., *Environmental Policy: New Directions
for the Twenty-First Century* (Washington, D.C.:
Congressional Quarterly Press, 2006).

48. Evan J. Ringquist and David H. Clark, "Issue
Definition and the Politics of State Environmental
Justice Policy Adoption," *International Journal of
Public Administration* 25 (February/March 2002):
351–89.

49. Robert J. Duffy, *The Green Agenda in American
Politics* (Lawrence, KS: University Press of Kansas,
2002).

50. Federal Bureau of Investigation, "Putting Intel to
Work Against ELF and ALF Terrorists," www.fbi.gov/
page2/june08/ecoterror_063008.html (June 30,
2008).

51. Brad Knickerbocker, "Firebrands of 'Ecoterrorism' Set
Sights on Urban Sprawl," *Christian Science Monitor*
(August 6, 2003): 2–3.

# Index

| STATE | CAPITAL | OFFICIAL NICKNAME | YEAR ENTERED UNION |
|-------|---------|-------------------|--------------------|
| Alabama | Montgomery | Yellowhammer State | 1819 |
| Alaska | Juneau | The Last Frontier | 1959 |
| Arizona | Phoenix | Grand Canyon State | 1912 |
| Arkansas | Little Rock | Natural State | 1836 |
| California | Sacramento | Golden State | 1850 |
| Colorado | Denver | Centennial State | 1876 |
| Connecticut | Hartford | Constitution State | 1788 |
| Delaware | Dover | First State | 1787 |
| Florida | Tallahassee | Sunshine State | 1845 |
| Georgia | Atlanta | Peach State | 1788 |
| Hawaii | Honolulu | Aloha State | 1959 |
| Idaho | Boise | Gem State | 1890 |
| Illinois | Springfield | Prairie State | 1818 |
| Indiana | Indianapolis | Hoosier State | 1816 |
| Iowa | Des Moines | Hawkeye State | 1846 |
| Kansas | Topeka | Sunflower State | 1861 |
| Kentucky | Frankfort | Bluegrass State | 1792 |
| Louisiana | Baton Rouge | Pelican State | 1812 |
| Maine | Augusta | Pine Tree State | 1820 |
| Maryland | Annapolis | Old Line State | 1788 |
| Massachusetts | Boston | Bay State | 1788 |
| Michigan | Lansing | Great Lakes State | 1837 |
| Minnesota | St. Paul | North Star State | 1858 |
| Mississippi | Jackson | Magnolia State | 1817 |
| Missouri | Jefferson City | Show Me State | 1821 |